OXFORD EARLY CHRISTIAN STUDIES

General Editors

Henry Chadwick   Andrew Louth

THE OXFORD EARLY CHRISTIAN STUDIES series includes scholarly volumes on the thought and history of the early Christian centuries. Covering a wide range of Greek, Latin, and Oriental sources, the books are of interest to theologians, ancient historians, and specialists in the classical and Jewish worlds.

Titles in the series include:

Arnobius of Sicca

Religious Conflict and Competition in
the Age of Diocletian

by
The Revd Dr Michael Bland Simmons

CLARENDON PRESS · OXFORD
1995

Oxford University Press, Walton Street, Oxford OX2 6DP
Oxford New York
Athens Auckland Bangkok Bombay
Calcutta Cape Town Dar es Salaam Delhi
Florence Hong Kong Istanbul Karachi
Kuala Lumpur Madras Madrid Melbourne
Mexico City Nairobi Paris Singapore
Taipei Tokyo Toronto
and associated companies in
Berlin Ibadan

Oxford is a trade mark of Oxford University Press

Published in the United States
by Oxford University Press Inc., New York

British Library Cataloguing in Publication Data
Data available

Library of Congress Cataloging in Publication Data
Arnobius of Sicca : religious conflict and competition in the age
of Diocletian / Michael Bland Simmons.
(Oxford early Christian studies)
Includes bibliographical references.
1. Arnobius, of Sicca. 2. Persecution—History—Early church, ca.
30-600. 3. Christianity and other religions—Roman. 4. Rome—
Religion 5. Neoplatonism. I. Title. II. Series.
BR65.A413S55 1995 270.1'092—dc20 94-46412
ISBN 0-19-814913-1

1 3 5 7 9 10 8 6 4 2

Typeset by Selwood Systems, Midsomer Norton
Printed in Great Britain on acid-free paper by
Biddles Ltd., Guildford and King's Lynn

In memoriam

Levi Heniford Simmons

6 February 1918–26 December 1983

Ἔχομεν δὲ τὸν θησαυρὸν τοῦτον
ἐν ὀστρακίνοις σκεύεσιν,
ἵνα ἡ ὑπερβολὴ τῆς δυνάμεως
ᾖ τοῦ θεοῦ καὶ μὴ ἐξ ἡμῶν †

In honorem

Ruth Kathryn Bland Simmons

mulierem fortem quis inveniet procul et de
ultimis finibus pretium eius
confidit in ea cor viri sui
et spoliis non indigebit
reddet ei bonum et non malum
omnibus diebus vitae suae

PREFACE

The present study is the first comprehensive work on Arnobius of Sicca to appear in English. This is significant for several reasons. First, although the *Adversus nationes* is the last Christian 'apology' written before the peace of Constantine in AD 311, and therefore merits the careful attention of patristic scholars, classicists, and historians, it nevertheless still remains one of the least understood and most controversial works of Ante-Nicene Christianity. I have attempted to show that Arnobius is important for an understanding of the great religious changes which were occurring in the late third and early fourth centuries of the Christian era within the Roman Empire generally and, specifically, within Roman North Africa where Arnobius taught rhetoric. Two main religious conflicts occurred in this period: the greatest state persecution of Christians that Rome had ever initiated; and the tremendous conflict and competition between the Saturn cult of Roman North Africa and Christianity. Arnobius sheds some historically important light on both events.

To clarify more specifically how the first of these (the Great Persecution) relates to the *Adversus nationes*, I have argued that the successful anti-Christian writings of Porphyry of Tyre have received the main brunt of Arnobius' attack *throughout* his work. Until now scholars have restricted his rebuttal of Porphyry to the first two books, but the present work is significant for revealing an anti-Porphyrian argumentation which permeates the *Adv. nat.* as a whole and has given Arnobius the framework according to which he developed the basic premises of his frontal assault upon religious paganism. The remark of Jerome that Arnobius always used to attack Christianity, and for this reason the bishop at Sicca refused to admit him into membership in the church, makes perfect sense in light of this association with the anti-Christian propaganda of Porphyry. Because he is much more adept in his attack upon paganism than he is in his 'defence' of Christianity, scholars have failed to understand Arnobius simply because they have tried to make him something that he himself never intended to be, and that was a Christian *apologist*. I have therefore further argued that Arnobius was using this Porphyrian propaganda before he became a Christian, and Jerome's statement that the bishop demanded a pledge of faith resulted in the writing of the *Adversus nationes*, which was never intended to be an apology, but rather a retraction of previously held Porphyrian concepts that posed a great threat to the Church throughout the Roman Empire before and during Diocletian's persecution. This study is unique in applying the *Adv. nat.* as a whole, and not just a few sections, to the anti-Christian works of Porphyry.

The other important event mentioned above has never been adequately investigated, and therefore I have attempted to show that Arnobius is sensitive to the religious conflict and competition taking place between the Saturn cult and Christianity—one of the greatest religious upheavals in the history of the Roman Empire. The *Adv. nat.* is an important historical document partly because it provides invaluable insight into the cultural transformation arising from the conflict between paganism and Christianity.

Arnobius' African background is another theme analysed in conjunction with Jerome's statement that he taught rhetoric at Sicca; I have concluded that there is every good reason to believe this testimony. A unique discovery is the relationship between Arnobius' remarks about Peter and the important cult of this early Apostle which was practised in North Africa, even in Sicca! I was enabled to make this discovery by adopting the new comprehensive method of scholarship that uses all available data—archaeological, numismatic, and literary—to arrive at an objective portrayal of Arnobius and his work which has hitherto been inaccessible owing to the narrow and often esoteric methodologies implemented in all-too-recondite aspects of Arnobiana. The main significance of the study is hopefully that it reveals Arnobius as a man of his age, and that his age can now be better understood as a result.

One final observation needs to be made. Many scholars have concluded that Arnobius was an Epicurean. I have argued that he was not a follower of Epicurus because of his doctrine of divine providence, the belief in personally experiencing the deity in acts of worship, and a number of other ideas clearly expressed in the *Adv. nat.* which either oppose or contradict the basic doctrines of Epicureanism. There is therefore no sound reason for labelling Arnobius an Epicurean, and hopefully we can now and forever lay to rest this groundless argument which has for many years prevented the progressive development of scholarship in Arnobiana.

I should like to acknowledge those who have been instrumental in making this work a success. First, I have had two mentors in my academic career. Dr Orval Wintermute, Professor of Old Testament,

Duke University, taught me the indispensable value of linguistic studies in Ancient History. Also, the Revd Dr Rowan A. Greer, III, Professor of Anglican Studies, Yale Divinity School, Yale University, has contributed immensely to my understanding of Patristic theology and its relationship to Graeco-Roman culture. Any success attained in my academic career will always, to some degree, be indebted to the very positive influence that these two scholars have had on my understanding of Antiquity.

There have been others who helped along the way. Professor Frank Young of Duke University was the one responsible for 'converting' me from Comparative Semitics to Patristics during a seminar in the Greek Apologists. Professor W. H. C. Frend kindly provided answers to questions concerning Roman North Africa during several visits when he was at the University of Glasgow. Professor Marcel Leglay of La Faculté de Lettres et Sciences Humaines de Lyon provided illuminating information about the Saturn Cult while I was still a doctoral student at the University of Edinburgh (1982–5). Mr David Wright, the former Dean of New College, the University of Edinburgh, who served as my thesis supervisor, offered invaluable guidance for the original project. The Revd Dr Rowan A. Greer, III, and the Revd Gail Freeman were exceptionally kind for arranging accommodations at the Berkeley Divinity School at Yale which enabled me to do research in the summer of 1992 at Yale University. The staffs at the following libraries were very helpful: Sterling Memorial Library at Yale; Auburn University Library, Auburn, Alabama; and Auburn University at Montgomery, Montgomery, Alabama. At the latter, Mrs Carolyn Johnson was very helpful in acquiring badly needed Inter-Library Loans. Dr Michael Daniel, Chairman of the Social Sciences Division of Lurleen Burns Wallace State Junior College, Andalusia, Alabama, provided the necessary electronic equipment to finish the final stages of the project. I am also grateful to my Bishop, the Revd Dr W. S. 'Bill' Hamon, and the Board of Directors of the Christian International School of Theology, Santa Rosa Beach, Florida, for conferring upon me the Doctor of Theology (Th.D.) degree upon the publication of this book.

I owe a great debt of gratitude to the editors at Oxford University Press, without whose superb assistance and sound advice this project would not have been accomplished. Miss Hilary O'Shea and Professor Andrew Louth saved me from a good number of pitfalls. Finally, Professor Henry Chadwick, whose magisterial knowledge of Patristics served as a guiding light through every phase of the work, gave me the high honour of being my external examiner at Edinburgh, as well as serving as a general editor, along with Professor Andrew Louth, of the Oxford Early Christian Studies series. I will always be grateful to Professor Chadwick for his kind encouragement and judicious advice.

To my wife, Maria Antonieta, and to my daughters, Tania Luisa and Alexandra Maria, I am grateful, for their understanding of the sacrifices that this work demanded of our family. Also, to a very dear friend who has left an immeasurable influence upon my life since childhood, Mr Augustus Crum Schambeau of Bayou La Batre, Alabama, I owe a great debt of gratitude. Dr John Fair, Head of the History Department, Auburn University at Montgomery, was very kind to me by offering the administrative assistance of the department during the final stages of manuscript preparation. Finally, I have dedicated this book in honour of my beloved mother, Ruth Kathryn Bland Simmons; and in memory of my father, and my best friend, Levi Heniford Simmons.

M. B. S.

December 7 1994
'The Miracle Room'
Bayou La Batre, Alabama

CONTENTS

Contents   xiii

ABBREVIATIONS

AASF	Annales Academiae Scientiarum Fennicae
AAR	Papers and Monographs of the American Academy in Rome
AB	*Analecta Bollandiana*
AChr	*Antike und Christentum*
ACM	*Acts of the Christian Martyrs* (Musurillo)
ACUSD	*Acta Classica Universitatis Scientiarum Debreceniensis*
ACW	Ancient Christian Writers
AFFB	*Annuario de Filología. Facultad de Filología de Barcelona*
AfR	*Archiv für Religionswissenschaft*
AH	*Ancient History*
AIRA	Acta Instituti Romani Finlandiae
AJA	*American Journal of Archaeology*
AJPh	*American Journal of Philology*
AJT	*American Journal of Theology*
AKPAW	*Abhandlungen der Königlich Preussischen Akademie der Wissenschaften. Philosophisch-Historische Klasse*
Altaner–Stuiber	*Patrology*
ANCL	Ante-Nicene Christian Library
ANF	Ante-Nicene Fathers
AnGreg	*Analecta Gregoriana*
ANRW	*Aufstieg und Niedergang der Römischen Welt*
AntAfr	*Antiquités Africains*
APC	Antiquité Païenne et Chrétienne
AR	*Archiv Religionswissenschaft*
ARIV	*Atti del Regio Instituto Veneto di Scienze Lettere ed Arti*
BACTH	*Bulletin Archéologique du Comité des Travaux Historiques*
BAGB	*Bulletin de l'Association Guillaume Budé*
BCG	Biblioteca Clásica Gredos
BIEH	*Boletín del Instituto de Estudios Helénicos*
BPELS	Bibliotheca Patrum Ecclesiasticorum Latinorum Selecta
BPW	*Berliner Philologische Wochenschrift*
Bryce–Campbell	*The Seven Books of Arnobius Adversus Gentes*, tr. H. Bryce and H. Campbell (ANCL 19; Edinburgh, 1871 (= ANF 6; Buffalo, 1886))
BSR	Biblioteca di Scienze Religiose
BUAM	Biographie Universelle Ancienne et Moderne
Budé	L'Association Guillaume Budé

Caes	*Caesarodum.* Tours, Inst. d'Études Latines de l'Université, Centre de Recherches A. Piganiol
CAH	*Cambridge Ancient History*
CahEA	*Cahiers des Études Anciennes*
CahTun	*Cahiers de Tunisie*
CARB	*Corsi di Cultura sull'Arte Ravennate e Bizantina*
CBM	Chester Beatty Monographs
CCC	*Civiltà Classica e Cristiana*
CH	Church History
CChr	Corpus Christianorum
CDO	*Cahiers D'Orientalisme*
CHA	*Cambridge History of Africa*
CIL	*Corpus Inscriptionum Latinarum* (vol. 8 unless otherwise indicated)
CMS	*Classical Mediterranean Spirituality*
CNRS	Éditions du Centre National de la Recherche Scientifique
CNS	Cristianesimo nella Storia
CollLat	Collection Latomus
CoTh	*Chaldaean Oracles and Theurgy* (Lewy)
CP	*Classical Philology*
CPER	*Cultes païens de l'empire romain.* J. Toutain
CQ	*Classical Quarterly*
CR	*Classical Review*
CRAI	*Comptes Rendues de l'Académie des Inscriptions et Belles-Lettres*
CRTP	*Cahiers de la Revue de Théologie et de Philosophie*
CSEL	Corpus Scriptorum Ecclesiasticorum Latinorum
CSHB	Corpus Scriptorum Historiae Byzantinae (Bonn, 1828–78)
CSLP	Corpus Scriptorum Latinorum Paravianum
CUAPS	The Catholic University of America Patristic Studies
CUASCA	The Catholic University of America Studies in Christian Antiquity
CUNC	*Crescita dell'Uomo nella Catechesi* (Eta Postnicena)
CW	*The Classical World*
DA	*Dialogue and Alliance*
DACL	*Dictionnaire d'archéologie chrétienne et de liturgie*
DAGR	*Dictionnaire des antiquités greques et romaines*
DCB	*A Dictionary of Christian Biography*
DHGE	*Dictionnaire d'histoire et de géographie ecclésiastique*
Didask	*Didaskaleion*
Dion	*Dionysius*
DLFAC	*Dictionnaire Latin–Française des Auteurs Chrétiens*
DPAC	*Dizionario Patristico e di Antichità Cristiane*
DPCR	*Dictionnaire Pratique des Connaissances Religieuses*

DR	*The Downside Review*
DTC	*Dictionnaire de Théologie Catholique*
EA	*Études Augustiniennes*
EEC	*Encyclopedia of Early Christianity* (Ferguson)
EECh	Encyclopedia of the Early Church (Di Berardino)
EMA	Europe in the Middle Ages. Selected Studies
EncBrit	*Encyclopaedia Britannica*
EncItal	*Enciclopedia Italiana*
EP	*The Encyclopedia of Philosophy* (ed. Paul Edwards)
EphLit	*Ephemerides Liturgicae*
EPRO	Études Préliminaires aux Religions Orientales dans L'Empire Romain (Vermaseren)
EQ	*The Evangelical Quarterly*
FC	The Fathers of the Church
FGH	*Die Fragmente der Griechischen Historiker* (Jacoby)
FIRA	*Fontes Iuris Romani Antejustiniani* (Riccobono)
FLA	Publications de la Faculté des Lettres et Sciences Humaines d'Alger
FRIC	*Rivista di Filologia e di Istruzione Classica*
GRBS	*Greek, Roman, and Byzantine Studies*
Greg	*Gregorianum*
GRRS	Graeco-Roman Religion Series
Gymn	*Gymnasium.* Zeitschrift für Kultur der Antike und Humanistische Bildung (Heidelberg)
H	*Hermes*
HAAN	*Histoire ancienne de l'Afrique du nord* (Gsell)
HC	Humanitas et Christianitas
Hel	*Helikon*
Hesp	*Hesperia*
His	*Historia*
Hist	*History*
HJ	*The Hibbert Journal*
HSCP	*Harvard Studies in Classical Philology*
HTR	*Harvard Theological Review*
IAMLat	*Inscriptions Antiques du Maroc,* II: *Inscriptions Latines*
IEJ	*Israel Exploration Journal*
ILAfr	*Inscriptions Latines d'Afrique* (Tripolitaine, Tunisie, Maroc)
ILAlg I	*Inscriptions Latines de l'Algérie* I (Gsell)
ILAlg II	*Inscriptions Latines de l'Algérie* II (Pflaum)
ILT	*Inscriptions Latines de la Tunisie*
IRT	*The Inscriptions of Roman Tripolitania*
JAOS	*The Journal of the American Oriental Society*
JBT	*A Journal of Bible and Theology*

JEH	*Journal of Ecclesiastical History*
JfLW	*Jahrbuch für Liturgiewissenschaft*
JHP	*Journal of the History of Philosophy*
JHS	*Journal of Hellenic Studies*
JRLM	*Bulletin of the John Rylands University Library of Manchester*
JR	*The Journal of Religion*
JRH	*Journal of Religious History*
JRS	*Journal of Roman Studies*
JS	*Journal des Savants*
JTS	*Journal of Theological Studies*
Kar	*Karthago*
Ker	*Kernos*. Revue internationale et pluridisciplinaire de religion greque antique
Lab	*Labeo*
Lat	*Latomus*
LCL	Loeb Classical Library
LeB	H. Le Bonniec, *Arnobe: Contre les Gentils*
Lib	*Libyca*
LPSL	*Proceedings of the Literary and Philosophical Society of Liverpool*
LS	Lewis and Short, *A Latin Dictionary*
LTK	*Lexikon für Theologie und Kirche*
Maia	*Maia*. Rivista di letterature classiche
MCC	*Mondo Classico e Cristianesimo*
McCr	George E. McCracken, *Arnobius of Sicca: The Case Against the Pagans*
MEFR	*Mélanges d'Archéologie et d'Histoire de l'École Française de Rome.*
MEFRA	*Mélanges d'Archéologie et d'Histoire de l'École Française de Rome. Antiquité*
MelCarth	*Mélanges de Carthage Offerts à Charles Saumage, Louis Poinssot, Maurice Pinard*
MGH	Monumenta Germaniae Historica
MH	*Museum Helveticum*
MHTP	Les Monuments Historiques de la Tunisie. Première Partie. Les Monuments Antiques. Les Temples Païens
ML	*Memorial Lagrange*
Mnem	*Mnemosyne*
MusAfr	*Museum Africum*
NAM	*Nouvelles Archives des Missions Scientifiques et Littéraires*
NASS	*The North African Stones Speak* (Mackendrick)
NCE	*The New Catholic Encyclopedia*
ND	*Nuovo Didaskaleion*

NHL	The Nag Hammadi Library
NPNF	The Nicene and Post Nicene Fathers
NSH	*The New Schaff-Herzog Encyclopedia of Religious Knowledge*
NTA	The New Testament Apocrypha
NTT	Nederlands Theologisch Tijdschrift
OC	*Oracles Chaldaïques* (Des Places)
OCA	Orientalia Christiana Analecta
OCD	*Oxford Classical Dictionary*
OCT	Oxford Classical Texts
ODCC	*Oxford Dictionary of the Christian Church*
OECT	Oxford Early Christian Texts
OG	Opuscula Graecolatina
OL	*L'Onomastique latin* (Duvaland Pflaum)
OLD	*Oxford Latin Dictionary*
Orph	*Orpheus*
P	*Codex Parisinus* no. 1661 of the *Adversus nationes*
P. Beatty Pan.	*Papyri From Panopolis in the Chester Beatty Library Dublin* (Skeat)
PCEAfr 1	*Prosopographie Chrétienne du Bas-Empire. Afrique 303–533* (Mandouze)
PECS	*Princeton Encyclopedia of Classical Sites*
Peg	*Pegaso. Rassegna di Lettere e Arti*
PG	*Patrologia Graeca* (Migne)
PhAnt	Philosophia Antigua. A Series of Monographs on Ancient Philosophy
Philol	*Philologus*
Phnx	*Phoenix*
PL	*Patrologia Latina* (Migne)
PLRE	*Prosopography of the Later Roman Empire*
POxy	Oxyrhynchus Papyri (Grenfell and Hunt)
PUT	*Publications de l'Université de Tunis, Faculté de Lettres*
PW	A. Pauly and G. Wissowa (eds.), *Realencyklopädie der classischen Altertumswissenschaft* vii (Stuttgart, 1951)
RAC	*Reallexikon für Antike und Christentum*
RB	*Revue Biblique*
RC	*Romanitas et Christianitas*
RCA	*Realencyclopädie der Classischen Altertumswissenschaft*
RCS	*Roman Civilization Sourcebook I & II* (Lewis and Reinhold)
REA	*Revue des Études Anciennes*
RFIC	*Rivista Filologia e Istruzione Classica*
REAug	*Revue des Études Augustiniennes*
RecConst	*Recueil des Notices et Mémoires de la Société Archéologique de Constantine*

REG	*Revue des Études Greques*
Reiff.	A. Reifferscheid's edition of the *Adversus nationes*
REL	*Revue des Études Latines*
RGG	*Die Religion in Geschichte und Gegenwart*
RHCM	*Revue de l'Histoire et Civilisation du Maghreb*
RHE	*Revue d'Histoire Ecclésiastique*
RHPR	*Revue d'Histoire et de Philosophie Religieuse*
RHR	*Revue d'Histoire des Religions*
RIC	*Roman Imperial Coinage* (Mattingly and Sydenham)
RIL	*Rendiconti dell'Instituto Lombardo* (Milan)
RM	*Rheinisches Museum*
RPTK	*Realencyclopädie fur Protestantische Theologie und Kirche*
RR	Ricerche Religiose
RSA	*Rivista di Storia Antica*
RSC	*Rivista de Studi Classici*
RSCI	*Rivista di Storia della Chiesa in Italia*
RSF	*Rassegna di Scienze Filosofiche*
RSM	*Religion, Science, and Magic*
RSPT	*Revue des Sciences Philosophiques et Théologiques*
RTSS	*Revue Tunisienne du Centre d'Études et de Recherches des Sciences Sociales*
RUO	*Revue de l'Université d'Ottowa*
Saec	*Saeculum*
SAH	*Saturne Africain Histoire* (Leglay)
SAM 1 and 2	*Saturne Africain Monuments*, vols. 1 and 2 (Leglay)
San	*Sandalion*
SAP	*Société d'Anthropologie de Paris*
SAS	*Studies in Ancient Society* (Finley)
SBAW	*Sitzungsberichte der Bayerischen Akademie der Wissenschaften*
SBL	Society of Biblical Literature
SC	Sources Chrétiennes
SCent	*The Second Century: A Journal of Early Christian Studies*
SCH	*Studies in Church History*
SDHI	*Studia et Documenta Historiae et Iuris*
SEA	Studia Ephemerides Augustinianum
SF	*Studi Filosofici*
SGLG	Studia Graeca et Latina Gothoburgensia
SGRR	Studies in Greek and Roman Religion
SHHA	*Studia Historica. Historia Antiqua* (Salamanca)
SIFC	*Studi Italiani di Filologia Classica*
SII	Studi Pubblicati dall'Istituto Italiano per la Storia Antica
SNAF	*Bulletin de la Société Nationale des Antiquaires de France*
SNP	Studies in Neoplatonism

SO	Symbolae Osloensis
SSFCHL	*Societas Scientiarum Fennica. Commentationes Humanarum Litterarum*
ST	Studi e Testi
StudPatr	*Studia Patristica*
TDAA	*Tunisia. Direction des Antiquités et Arts. Notes et Documents Publiés par la Direction des Antiquités*
TheolHist	Théologie Historique
Theoph	*Theophaneia*
TLL	*Thesaurus Linguae Latinae*
TPAPA	*Transactions and Proceedings of the American Philological Association*
TS	*Theological Studies*
TU	Texte und Untersuchungen
UALG	Untersuchungen zur Antiken Literatur und Geschichte
VC	*Vigiliae Christianae*
VDI	*Vestnik Drevnej Istorii*
Vic	Vichiana
WKP	*Wochenschrift für Klassische Philologie*
WS	*Wiener Studien*
WSEH	World Spirituality: An Encyclopedic History of the Religious Quest
YSR	Yale Studies in Religion
ZfK	*Zeitschrift für Kirchengeschichte*
ZKPP	*Zeitschrift für Klassische Philologie und Patristik*
ZMKA	Zetemata. Monographien zur Klassischen Altertumswissenschaft
ZNTW	*Zeitschrift für die Neutestamentliche Wissenschaft*
ZPE	*Zeitschrift für die Papyrologie und Epigraphie*
ZSSR	*Zeitschrift der Savigny-Stiftung für Rechtsgeschichte*

I

Arnobius and the Age of Diocletian

Introductory Observations: An Overview to
Rationale and Format

It cannot be said that Arnobius needs no introduction.[1] Even if
this book had been written primarily for Church historians, or classicists, or specialists in the area of ancient religion and philosophy, this
would still be the case. He certainly needs an introduction to the
general reader, not just because this is the first work ever written
in English exclusively devoted to Arnobius and the *Adversus nationes*,
but also because he has been misinterpreted,[2] described as 'perhaps
the most bizarre of the Fathers of the Church',[3] or simply ignored[4]
by many modern scholars. Indeed too many have concluded that
he was an insignificant personage who had a very minor part, if any,
to play in the Diocletianic drama of the late third and early fourth
centuries of the imperial period (AD 284–305). Derived mainly from
an unclear perception of who he was before and after his conversion
to Christianity and why he wrote the *Adv. nat.*, scholars have called

[1] See the excellent introductions to Arnobius in P. Monceaux, *Histoire littéraire de
l'Afrique chrétienne depuis les origines jusqu'à l'invasion arabe* (Paris, 1901–23), 3. 241–86;
McCr 3–57; LeB 7–108; G. Gierlich, *Arnobius von Sicca: Kommentar zu den ersten beiden
Büchern seines Werkes Adversus nationes* (Diss., Mainz, 1985); cf. also R. Laurenti, 'Spunte
di teologia arnobiana', *Orph* 6 (1985), 270–303; and Paolo Siniscalco, 'Arnobius of Sicca',
in Angelo Di Berardino (ed.), EECh (Oxford, 1992), tr. Adrian Walford, I. 82.
[2] Monceaux, 3. 241–86: because Arnobius denies providence he is Epicurean; cf.
Baynes, *CAH* 12. 652; A clear affirmation of this concept is found in *Adv. nat.* 3. 24.
[3] J. D. Madden, 'Jesus as Epicurus: Arnobius of Sicca's Borrowings from Lucretius',
CCC2 (1981), 215.
[4] No references to Arnobius are found in such works as T. D. Barnes, *Constantine and
Eusebius* (Cambridge, Mass., 1981): pp. 3–27 deal with Diocletian and the persecutions;
R. MacMullen, *Paganism in the Roman Empire* (New Haven, Conn. 1981); id., *Christianizing
the Roman Empire* (ibid., 1984); S. Williams, *Diocletian and the Roman Recovery* (New
York, 1985); F. Millar, *The Emperor in the Roman World (31 BC–AD 337)* (Ithaca, NY,
1977), 573, says that Lactantius 'is the only witness to the intellectual background of the
persecutions' (?); and R. L. Fox, *Pagans and Christians* (New York, 1987).

Arnobius 'everything in the book' from a Platonist,[5] to an Epicurean,[6] a Marcionite,[7] a Gnostic,[8] a Hermetist,[9] an orthodox Christian(!),[10] a 'pessimist',[11] and even a pagan who simply desired to write a rhetorical exercise.[12] And we may add that modern works that have studied Arnobius meticulously have sometimes made gross errors as well.[13] Harsh and very often negative judgements, beginning with Jerome[14] and continuing to the present,[15] have frequently been made about this ancient writer who 'in modern times has suffered much from undeserved neglect'.[16] And though some have recently paid him a greater tribute by recognizing the *Adv. nat.* as rather significant for the Diocletianic period,[17] it is a main premiss of this study that modern scholarship can no longer afford to divorce Arnobius from the critical period in which he lived: the generation between Gallienus in 260 and the outbreak of the Persecution in 303. A thorough appraisal of this Christian writer whose contemporaries included such divines as Lactantius, Eusebius, Paul of Samosata, Methodius of Olympus, and Plotinus and Porphyry, is therefore necessary.

But first we may rightfully ask why has he been so neglected and misinterpreted. Four main reasons might be given. First, antiquity has bequeathed to us very meagre information about Arnobius. In addition to the brief description of the *Adv. nat.* as 'opuscula Arnobii, apocrypha'

---

[5] C. Burger, *Die theologische Position des älteren Arnobius* (Diss., Heidelberg, 1970).
[6] E. Klussmann, 'Arnobius und Lucrez, oder ein Durchgang durch den Epicuräismus zum Christentum', *Philol* 26 (1867), 363–6; cf. J. Quasten, *Patrology*, 2. 388 f.
[7] F. Scheidweiler, 'Arnobius und der Marcionitismus', *ZNTW* 45 (1955), 42–67; F. G. Sirna, 'Arnobio e l'eresia marcionita di Patrizio', *VC* 18 (1964), 37–50; cf. LeB 80.
[8] See McCr 27 f., 41; A. W. Newton, 'The *Adversus Gentes* of Arnobius. A Study in Christian Apologetics', *LPSL* 52 (1897–8), 155 f.; A. J. Festugière, *Hermetisme et mystique païenne* (Paris, 1967), 261–312; The latter two refute the view that Arnobius was a Gnostic.
[9] J. Carcopino, *Aspects mystiques de la Rome païenne* (Paris, 1941), 293–301.
[10] E. Rapisarda, *Arnobio* (Catania, 1945).
[11] Baynes, *CAH* 12. 653; C. Marchesi, 'Il pessimismo di un apologeta cristiano', *Peg* 2 (1930), 536–50.
[12] S. Colombo, 'Arnobio Afro e i suoi libri *Adversus Nationes*', *Didask* 9 (1930), 1–124.
[13] McCr 13, who says that Arnobius mentions no Christian predecessor by name; but in *Adv. nat.* 2. 12 he gives the story of the apostle Peter and Simon Magus, with no acknowledgement by McCr 313 n. 85.
[14] Jerome, *Ep.* 58. 10, 62. 2; McCr 2.
[15] See McCr 3.
[16] Ibid. 4; cf. A. Wlosok, 'Zur lateinischen Apologetik der Constantinischen Zeit', *Gymn* 96 (1989), 133–48.
[17] See R. L. Wilken, *The Christians as the Romans Saw Them* (New Haven, Conn., 1984), 153 ff.; J. H. W. G. Liebeschuetz, *Continuity and Change in Roman Religion* (Oxford, 1979); and W. H. C. Frend, 'Prelude to the Great Persecution: the Propaganda War', *JEH* 38 (1987), 1–18.

in the *Decretum Gelasianum de libris recipiendis et non recipiendis* of the early sixth century,[18] the only other data we have on Arnobius until the time of Trithemius,[19] come from six passages found in five works of Jerome (*c.*AD 342–420).[20] Of these, two concern the literary style and contents of the work,[21] and the remainder provide exiguous biographical and chronological data,[22] which are generally surveyed in the following section.[23]

Second, although Arnobius was an intellectual writing to the intelligentsia of his day,[24] modern scholarship has not successfully explained how he is related to the intellectual developments antecedent to the Great Persecution,[25] the time during which Arnobius wrote.[26] A 'specialist' or 'vested interest' approach to the *Adv. nat.* has often blurred the greater vision and purpose of its author. The classicist or the Church historian has many times 'strained at a gnat and swallowed a camel' by devising a too narrow interpretive method of analysing Arnobius' work. We therefore fail to see the greater picture, how Arnobius fits into it, and the way in which his work represents a part of the larger intellectual development, and the pagan–Christian debate related to it, which occurred during the Diocletianic period. That period was characterized by the break-up of the old pagan *Weltanschauung*, based upon the great religious, social, political, and philosophical traditions of Graeco-Roman culture, and the beginning of a new world order established upon the values of the Christian Church. It is the view of the present writer that 'the broader way' will not in this case 'lead to destruction', but it will

---

[18] For the date see E. von Döbschütz, *Das Decretum Gelasianum de libris recipiendis et non recipiendis* (Leipzig, 1912; TU 38).

[19] The abbot of Sponheim who mentions Arnobius in his *De scriptoribus ecclesiasticis* (Basle, 1494), 53; for Arnobius in other works see F. J. Closa, 'Lectura critica de los autores latinos por los humanistas del siglo de oro', *AFFB* 11 (1985), 7–17; and G. M. Pintus, 'Arnobio e il pari di Pascal', *San* 10–11 (1987–8), 145–51.

[20] Jerome, *De vir. ill.* 79; *Chron.* s.a. (AD) 326–7; *Ep.* 70. 5 (Ad Magnum); *De vir. ill.* 80; *Ep.* 58. 10 (Ad Paulinum), 62. 2 (Ad Tranquillinum).

[21] Ep. 58. 10, 62. 2; See *PLRE* 1. 108.

[22] *De vir. ill.* 79; *Chron.* s.a. 326–7; *Ep.* 70. 5; *De vir. ill.* 80.

[23] A critical study of the chronological and biographical data about Arnobius is found in Chs. 2 and 3 below.

[24] Arnobius was a very learned rhetor. On his Greek and Latin sources see McCr 34–40; LeB 34–54; Jerome, *Chron.* s.a. 326–7, says he was a very successful rhetor.

[25] See Chs. 9, 10, and 11 below for works that have laid a good foundation for the argument that I develop, esp. in relation to the Porphyrian connection.

[26] Jerome, *Chron.* s.a. 326–7, which dates should be changed: see McCr 7 f.; LeB 7 f.; the correct, though general period occurs in *De vir. ill.* 79: during the reign of Diocletian (AD 284–305).

enable modern scholarship to get a better understanding of the relationship between the *Adv. nat.* and the intellectual background to the Great
Persecution. And this broad portrait can be painted without sacrificing
a thorough investigation of *all possible data* (e.g. archaeological, literary,
epigraphical, numismatic) and sources (Christian and pagan).

A third reason for the neglect and misunderstanding is perhaps
because too much emphasis has been placed upon the weak foundation
of Arnobius' 'Christianity'. Even considering the fact that he is the last
of the ante-Nicene 'apologists' writing before 'orthodoxy' was beginning
to be defined by the great Church councils, nevertheless it would be
extremely difficult, if not impossible, to describe Arnobius as 'orthodox'.
That he certainly was not. But neither would it be accurate to label him
a heretic as some have done. Like nervous mice moving back and forth
in a maze, scholars historically have vacillated between one extreme or
the other in their attempt to identify an enigmatic personality espousing
a hybrid pagan–Christian religion.[27] What has been the cause of this
confused state of affairs? The answer just might be found in the fact
that neither in Jerome nor in the *Adv. nat.* itself is there any evidence
to support either view; and we may find a clear path out of the jungle
by suggesting that Arnobius—and Jerome implies this as we shall see
below—never intended to be something into which modern scholars
have transformed him, and that is a Christian 'apologist', at least in the
traditional meaning of the word. So if we can establish that Jerome's
testimony is reliable and identify other motives for writing the *Adv.
nat.*, perhaps Arnobius can be better understood as an ancient 'Christian'
writer.

The fourth reason is due to the 'historical isolationist' approach to
the study of Arnobiana. By this term we refer to the erroneous
presupposition made by many scholars that Arnobius neither affected,
nor was affected by, the Age of Diocletian, regardless of the fact that it
was a critical moment in the history of the Roman Empire and the
Church. This method of interpretation has caused many who have
studied the period (AD 284–305) either to ignore Arnobius totally,[28] or
to make weak generalizations that often betray an ignorance of the
subject.[29] From the perspective of historical relevance, Arnobius has too
frequently been viewed almost as a potentially dangerous micro-organism

---

[27] Cf. McCr 3 f., 27 ff., 40 ff.; Leb 60–7, for good discussions.
[28] See n. 4 above.
[29] See e.g. nn. 6 and 7 above.

requiring analysis in an isolated laboratory under the microscope of the classicist, the historical theologian, or the student of ancient religions. This is, of course, not to say that specialist studies have no part to play in helping us understand the historical significance of the *Adv. nat.*, but rather that the work has never been allowed to stand on its own feet as an historical document. Even McCracken argues that Arnobius was a person who 'though living at a critical moment in history, nevertheless seems to have been relatively unaffected by his times'.[30] Suffice it to say that we shall take the opposite side of the argument in the present study: the *Adversus nationes* is an ancient document that possesses a great deal of historical significance for the age of Diocletian.

There were three fundamental institutions in the Diocletian period which were about to come together and form an unprecedented political and religious synthesis in the Roman world: the Church, Graeco-Roman culture, and the State. The ancient world was in the process of passing away, and in its place, beginning with Constantine the Great, a new order, the Middle Ages, was about to be born: it was the product of a long development comprising the doctrines of Christianity, the philosophy of Hellenism, and the political traditions of the Roman Empire. And from the time of Jesus to that of Constantine, intermittently the relationship between the Church and the other two components can be described as being in bitter conflict and in fierce competition with each other. The age we are about to explore, using the *Adv. nat.* as our compass, can be defined in exactly those terms: religious conflict and competition.

The following sections of this chapter will correspond to these three categories, the Church, Graeco-Roman culture, and the State. In the first we shall examine to what extent, based upon Jerome's testimony and the *Adv. nat.* itself, Arnobius can be described as a representative of the Church. In the second section the reader will be given a panoramic view of the pagan intellectual background to the Great Persecution. Porphyry of Tyre and Hierocles will be surveyed as the main leaders of the pagan intelligentsia. Some of the important questions here are: Did the anti-Christian propaganda published before the outbreak of persecution have a causal effect upon the State's official decision to mount its greatest attack upon the Church in its history? What were the main themes in the pagan attack upon Christianity? What specific role, if any, did such Hellenists as Porphyry and Hierocles play? The final section will deal with the Great Persecution under Diocletian

---

[30] McCr 3.

during the period AD 302–5. (I shall not go beyond 305, the year of the
emperor's abdication, because there is no evidence to suggest that
Arnobius wrote after this date.) Some important lines of investigation
here are: Why did Diocletian wait nearly two decades before deciding
to go against the Christians? Who was the main instigator, Diocletian
or Galerius? Can we discover the real motives? Were they religious?
Did they mainly come from the military? After reading the chapter it
is hoped that the reader will have a better understanding of Arnobius
and his work, the main issues of the age in which he lived, and therefore
a good foundation for the technical analysis found in the following
chapters.

I. *The Church: Was Arnobius a Christian Apologist?*

The purpose of this section is to give a general survey of Jerome's
testimony concerning Arnobius, investigate the identity of his opponents,
and then analyse most of the important aspects of his thought related
to Christian doctrine.

Jerome's longest and most revealing biographical passage on Arnobius
occurs in the *Chronicon*, s.a. 326–7:

Arnobius enjoys great repute as a rhetorician in Africa. While he was giving
instruction in oratory to the youth of Sicca and was yet a pagan, he was drawn
as a result of dreams to belief in Christianity. Failing, however, to obtain from
the bishop acceptance into the faith which he had hitherto always attacked, he
gave all his efforts to the composition of most splendid books against his former
religion; and with these as so many pledges of his loyalty, he at last obtained
the desired affiliation.[31]

Although we shall investigate this testimony in greater detail in Chapter
3, we may here make the following general comments. First, six main
points may be deduced from this: (1) Arnobius was a famous rhetor. (2)
He taught at Sicca in Africa. (3) Dreams caused his conversion from
Paganism. (4) The bishop refused to admit him to the Church because
he had consistently attacked the faith. (5) Arnobius therefore wrote

---

[31] McCr 2 for the English text. The Latin is: 'Arnobius rhetor in Africa clarus habetur.
Qui cum Siccae ad declamandum iuvenes erudiret et adhuc ethnicus ad credulitatem
somniis compelleretur neque ab episcopo impetraret fidem, quam semper impugnaverat,
elucubravit adversus pristinam religionem luculentissimos libros et tandem velut quibusdam obsidibus pietatis foedus impetravit.'

books against his former religious views. (6) He was admitted to the Church due to this 'pledge of loyalty'.

Jerome's dates (326–7) are certainly erroneous,[32] and we may now give 302–5 for the period when the *Adversus nationes* was written.[33] Concerning the first statement, no one has doubted that Arnobius was a rhetor.[34] Between books 4 and 5 of the Parisinus (P) text of the *Adv. nat.*[35] are found the words ARNOVII ORATORIS LIB IIII EXP. INCP. LIB V.[36] And his literary style,[37] vocabulary,[38] his method of argumentation,[39] and his use of sources[40] confirm the veracity of Jerome's assertion. The second point also coheres well with the contents of the work. In *Vir. ill.* 79–80 we are told that Arnobius taught rhetoric during the reign of Diocletian (AD 284–305), which makes sense in light of the rather frequent allusions to the persecutions of Christians found throughout the *Adv. nat.* (1. 26; 1. 31; 1. 35; 1. 65; 2. 5; 2. 76; 2. 77; 2. 78; 3. 36; 4. 36; 5. 29; 6. 27), and one passage which refers to Diocletian's First Edict of 23 February 303 ordering the destruction of churches and the burning of scriptures (4. 36).

Jerome's second statement also locates Arnobius in Sicca, due southwest of Carthage in Africa Proconsularis,[41] a provincial city of some

---

[32] See Ch. 2 below for a technical study of the problems related to dating the work.

[33] See Ch. 2 §XI.

[34] Ch. 3 §IV. Cf. also Y. M. Duval, 'Sur la biographie et les manuscrits d'Arnobe de Sicca', *Lat* 45 (1986), 69–99.

[35] McCr 6; LeB 8.

[36] Cf. LeB 8.

[37] Cf. LeB 86 ff.; Le Bonniec, 'L'exploitation apologétique par Arnobe de *De natura deorum* de Cicéron', *Caes* 19 (1984), 89–101; D. R. Shackleton Bailey, 'Arnobiana', *RFIC* 116 (1988), 198–202; P. Santorelli, 'Parodia virgiliana in Arnobio', *Maia* 41 (1989), 241–50.

[38] See McCr 22 ff.; and LeB 86–92.

[39] He uses such literary devices as the *digressio*, *suasoria*, etc. See Ch. 3 §IV.

[40] See McCr 34–40; LeB 34–59; see also K. Gaiser, *Il paragone della caverna* (Naples, 1985); C. Santini, 'Il lessico della spartizione nel sacrificio romano', *L'Uomo* 9. 1–2 (1985), 63–73; P. Mastandrea, *Lettori cristiani di Seneca filosofo* (Brescia, 1988); G. Valditara, 'A proposito di un presunto ottavo re di Roma', *SDHI* 54 (1988), 276–84.

[41] For the historical background see: T. R. S. Broughton, *The Romanization of Africa Proconsularis* (Westport, Conn., 1972); L. Teutsch, *Das Städtewesen in Nordafrica in der Zeit von C. Gracchus bis zum Tode des Kaisers Augustus* (Berlin, 1962); P. Romanelli, *Storia delle province romane dell'Africa* (Rome, 1959), SII 14; M. A. Beschaouch, 'Le territoire de Sicca Veneria (El-Kef), Nouvelle Cirta, en Numidia Proconsulaire (Tunisie)', *CRAI* (1981), 105–22; B. H. Warmington, *The North African Provinces from Diocletian to the Vandal Conquest* (Cambridge, 1954); A. Ennabli, 'Sicca Veneria (Le Kef)', *PECS* 834; C. Lepelley, *Les cités de l'Afrique romaine au bas-empire* (Paris, 1979–81), 2 vols. N. Duval, F. Baratte, and J. C. Golvin, 'Les églises d'Haidra VI: La basilique des martyrs de la persécution de Dioclétien', *CRAI* (1989), 129–73.

prominence that had become an Augustan colony shortly after the annexation of Africa Nova.[42] Several passages in Arnobius clearly reveal an African background.[43] For example, he mentions local deities worshipped by the Moors,[44] a remark resembling passages found in his fellow Africans Tertullian,[45] Cyprian,[46] and Lactantius, who was his pupil (Jerome, *Vir. ill.* 80; *Ep.* 70. 5).[47] The Psylli, the Garamentes, the Gaetuli, and the Zeugitani, which were other African ethnic groups, are also named,[48] sometimes along with a comment about local customs.[49] The main agrarian deity of Roman North Africa, Saturn, is mentioned frequently.[50] Proconsular marble quarries like those found at Simitthu (Chemtou) may be alluded to in one passage.[51] African patriotism may have motivated his praise of the martial skills of Hannibal.[52] And in the conversion passage the author describes various pagan religious practices which point to an African background.[53]

Jerome's third point is that dreams were instrumental in Arnobius' conversion to Christianity. There was a very strong belief permeating Antiquity that the supernatural world could communicate with human beings through dreams.[54] And although Arnobius refers to *vana somnia* (1. 46) and the description of his conversion does not mention dreams (1. 39), this does not mean, as Le Bonniec has rightly argued, 'que *tous* les songes sont vains'.[55]

Some scholars have rejected as spurious Jerome's fourth point that the bishop refused to admit Arnobius to the Church. The entire 'story'

---

[42] *CIL* 8. 15858; 8. 27568.

[43] S. Fasce, 'Paganesimo Africano in Arnobio', *Vic* 9 (1980), 173–80, offers stimulating information on the subject.

[44] *Adv. nat.* 1. 36.

[45] *Ap.* 24.

[46] *Quod idola dii non sint* 2 (*PL* 4. 568).

[47] *Div. inst.* 1. 15.

[48] Psylli: *Adv. nat.* 2. 32; Garamentes: 6. 5; Gaetuli and Zeugitani: 1. 16.

[49] *Adv. nat.* 2. 32.

[50] Ibid. 1. 36; 2. 68, 70, 71; 3. 6–29; 4. 9 (protecting sowing); 4. 14, 20, 22, 24, 26 (called the *senex*); 5. 3; 6. 12 (with a crooked sickle), 25 (the sickle casts fear upon people).

[51] Ibid. 2. 40.

[52] Ibid. 1. 14.

[53] Ibid. 1. 39; see pp. 109–111 below.

[54] See pp. 117–120 below and, in general, P. C. Miller, 'A Dubious Twilight: Reflections on Dreams in Patristic Literature', *CH* 55 (1986), 153–64; McCr 16; LeB 9; and Liebeschuetz (1979), 258, accept the dream story; Bryce–Campbell, ANF 6. 406, reject it.

[55] LeB 9.

has been called 'aitiological',⁵⁶ and this interpretation portrays Jerome
to be saying that the bishop required the famous rhetor to 'explain his
faith'.⁵⁷ (We recall that Arnobius had *always* attacked the Christian
faith.)⁵⁸ Another objection has been that it is not credible that a pledge
of loyalty would be demanded of anyone desiring to cast his lot in with
a persecuted Church.⁵⁹ Yet nowhere does Jerome say that Arnobius was
required to explain his faith, but only that the bishop was hesitant to
admit a famous rhetor, who had been consistently assailing Christianity,
into his church. It is therefore the reluctance of the bishop to accept a
known enemy of the faith which Jerome accentuates.⁶⁰ Also, the *Adv.
nat.* was written when the revival of Hellenism had produced anti-
Christian writers like Porphyry and Hierocles who vehemently attacked
the beliefs of the Church in the period *c.*AD 270–302.⁶¹ And the greatest
state persecution of the Christians began in February 303.⁶² Any bishop
would have found just cause to refuse him without a pledge of loyalty.
But this does not necessarily compel us to conclude that the *Adv. nat.*
was written as 'proof' of Arnobius' conversion.⁶³

If we read Jerome's last three points together (4, 5, 6), then perhaps
we get a clearer picture of the bishop's demand and the motives for
writing. Because Arnobius had always attacked Christianity, the bishop
did not admit him to the Church (4), whereupon he wrote books against
his former religion (5), and was finally admitted (6). Jerome clearly did
not understand the *Adv. nat.* to be a 'Christian apology', but rather a
revocation of the views Arnobius held as an anti-Christian intellectual!
We may now turn to the question about motives for writing.

As the reader will discover in the chapters that follow, Arnobius was
familiar with Porphyrian anti-Christian propaganda published before
the Great Persecution. He had furthermore been using the criticisms of
Christianity contained in Porphyry's works, and it was due to this
association with the great Neoplatonist that the bishop got cold feet.
Arnobius took the initiative to write seven books, as Jerome states,

---

⁵⁶ Madden (1981), 217; cf. Bryce–Campbell, ANF 6. 406; and A. D. Nock, *Conversion*
(Oxford, 1933), 258 reject the conversion story (*Adv. nat.* 1. 39).
⁵⁷ Madden (1981), 216 f.
⁵⁸ *Chron.* s.a. 326–7.
⁵⁹ Bryce–Campbell, ANF 6. 406; cf. also E. G. Sihler, *From Augustus to Augustine*
(Cambridge, 1923), 167.
⁶⁰ See pp. 122–125 below.
⁶¹ See §II.
⁶² See §III.
⁶³ e.g. Y. Duval (1986), 97–8.

'against his former religion'. Books 1 and 2 appear to be a revocation of the (predominantly) Porphyrian criticism of Christianity which Arnobius used himself in attacking it before his conversion, and derived from (e.g.) the *Philosophia ex oraculis* and the *Contra Christianos*. In books 4–7 he goes entirely on the attack by using the same method of argumentation, literary retortion, against the pagans as Porphyry had used against the Christians in the *Contra Christianos* (*CC*). He might have even named the work *Adversus nationes* in reply to the latter. When he had proved to the bishop that (1) he had revoked his (mainly Porphyrian) criticisms of the faith (bks. 1–2) and (2) used Porphyry's method (literary retortion) against his 'former religion',[64] he then had his retraction in writing and was admitted.

We may conclude that (1) Jerome is a reliable witness, and (2) Arnobius never had any intentions of being a 'Christian apologist'. This does not mean, however, that Arnobius was not a Christian; nor would it imply that it is unnecessary to ask *why* he responded to the pagan attacks upon Christianity as he did. We shall analyse these two matters in the following sections.

Turning first to the identification of his opponents, *Adv. nat.* 1. 1 is significant. Reference is made to those who believe in their own wisdom and 'speak in oracular fashion' as if they were the mouthpiece of a god, that many ills have come to the earth since the beginning of the Christian religion.[65] Although years earlier Cyprian had responded to a similar charge,[66] and Maximin Daia years later revived this criticism,[67] the opponent here appears to be Porphyry of Tyre, who in *Phil. or.* argued that human bliss had been impaired by the entrance of Christianity into the world.[68] Arnobius asks his opponents from what science have they

---

[64] Note Bryce–Campbell, ANF 6. 409: 'Christianity is indeed defended, but it is by attacking heathenism.' M. Smith, 'A Hidden Use of Porphyry's History of Philosophy in Eusebius' Preparatio Evangelica', *JTS* 39 (1988), 503, notes if Porphyry had done his homework in scripture, so must Eusebius exhibit equal or superior knowledge of pagan sources. So also with Arnobius.

[65] *Adv. nat.* 1. 1. 1–6: 'Quoniam comperi nonnullos, qui se plurimum sapere suis persuasionibus credunt, insanire, bacchari et velut quiddam promptum ex oraculo dicere: postquam esse in mundo Christiana gens coepit, terrarum orbem perisse, multiformibus malis affectum esse genus humanum . . .'.

[66] Cyprian, *Ad Demetrianum* 2–5 (CChr, Simonetti); cf. Tertullian, *Ap.* 40. 1–2; Arnobius, *Adv. nat.* 1. 9; 1. 13; 1. 16; 1. 26.

[67] Eusebius, *HE* 9. 7. 8–9, blaming the evils occurring in the world upon the Christians.

[68] In *De cons. evang.* 1. 15. 23 Augustine names Porphyry as one who used the oracles to 'exalt' Christ. He refers to 'false applauders' of Christ in 1. 33. 50; the oracle mentioned occurs in 1. 33. 51; see also *Civ. Dei* 19. 23. Porphyry was still revered in Africa in Augustine's day; *Civ. dei* 10. 29.

been able to drink in so much power of prophecy?[69] This mention of science (Philosophy) in the context of references to oracles used by an opponent who 'velut quiddam promptum ex oraculo dicere'[70] would indeed seem to be an allusion to Porphry's *Philosophia ex oraculis*, an anti-Christian work published before the Great Persecution.

The use of *viri novi*[71] to describe his opponents supports this interpretation which several studies have analysed since the last century.[72] Beatrice has argued that Arnobius' 'new men' (*Adv. nat.* 2. 15) correspond to the Porphyrian group attacked in *PE* 3. 6. 7 by Eusebius, who was living in the eastern part of the Empire, and who also calls his enemies νέοι![73] If Arnobius is attacking Porphyry and followers in books 1–2, and he 'remains the best witness for the Christian reply'[74] to the pagan charges against Christianity c.270–302, it must be emphasized that the *Adv. nat.* is significant for an understanding of the intellectual background to the Great Persecution.[75] Conceptual parallels between Arnobius' opponents and Porphyry are numerous: the souls are immortal;[76] they are very near in rank to God;[77] they are divine and wise;[78] they are to have no contact with the body;[79] they live blamelessly and practise all virtues;[80] and they all know God.[81] This resembles the

---

[69] *Adv. nat.* 2. 6.

[70] Ibid. 1. 1.

[71] Ibid. 2. 15.

[72] The *viri novi* have been associated with a Porphyrian group by: W. Kroll, 'Die Zeit des Cornelius Labeo', *RM* 71 (1916), 356; J. Bidez, *Vie de Porphyre* (Gand, 1913), 160; P. Courcelle, 'Les sages de Porphyre et les "uiri noui" d'Arnobe', *REL* 31 (1953), 257–71; P. Hadot, *Marius Victorinus* (Paris, 1971), 2. 999; E. L. Fortin, 'The *Viri Novi* of Arnobius and the Conflict Between Faith and Reason in the Early Christian Centuries', in Neiman and Schatkin (Rome, 1973), 197–226; J. O'Meara, *Porphyry's Philosophy From Oracles in Augustine* (Paris, 1959), 145 f.; R. L. Wilken, 'Pagan Criticism of Christianity: Greek Religion and Christian Faith', in Schoedel and Wilken (Paris, 1979), 123; Frend, *JEH* 38 (1987), 1–18; and P. F. Beatrice, 'Un oracle antichrétien chez Arnobe', in *de Andia* (1988), 107–29; the latter being one of the most important works on Arnobius in the last 50 years.

[73] Beatrice (1988), 120–3.

[74] Frend (1987), 16.

[75] Ibid. 14–7. Frend shows how passages in books 1–2 of the *Adv. nat.* echo Porphyry's charges against Christianity. Beatrice (1988), 114, claims that Arnobius had read the *Phil. or.*; contrast B. Croke, 'The Era of Porphyry's Anti-Christian Polemic', *JRH* 13 (1984), 1–14, p. 7: 'Arnobius saw no occasion to use Porphyry' (!)

[76] *Civ. Dei* 10. 1; *Adv. nat.* 2. 15.

[77] *Civ. Dei* 22. 25; 19. 23; *Adv. nat.* 2. 15.

[78] *Civ. Dei* 10. 27, 29; *Adv. nat.* 2. 15.

[79] *Civ. Dei* 22. 26; cf. 10. 29; *Adv. nat.* 2. 15.

[80] *Civ. Dei* 19. 23; 10. 27; *Adv. nat.* 2. 15.

[81] *Civ. Dei* 10. 29.

Neoplatonist spirituality for which Porphyry's soteriological investigations were famous throughout the Roman Empire. And his extended
visit to Carthage (*Abst.* 3. 4. 7) sometime between 268 and 71, might
have given Arnobius an opportunity to come in contact with his anti-
Christian and other views.[82]

Oracles played an influential role during the period in the anti-
Christian movement.[83] Echoes of this reverberate through the pages of
the *Adversus nationes*. Christianity is called wicked and polluting, which
is similar to an oracle of Apollo given by Porphyry.[84] Diocletian consulted
the oracle of Apollo at Didyma (§ III below) before deciding to persecute
the Christians in 303:[85] Arnobius may allude to this when he asks
whether it is the judgement of the gods to be offended by Christians
who believe that Christ is God.[86] Also, before the persecution the
haruspices could not discover the necessary omens because certain
Christians had crossed themselves.[87] Arnobius may be referring to this
in 1. 46 when he says that a contemporary miracle of Christ is the
imposition of silence upon the soothsayers.[88] In remarking about the
persecutions of the Christians Arnobius says that Jupiter calls Christians
wicked, an allusion perhaps to Diocletian who was Jovius under the
Tetrarchy.[89] Finally, he addresses his opponent as someone of divine
intelligence, or named most wise by the oracles of the gods.[90]

There is little doubt that this is Porphyry. We must also give an
oracle from the Porphyrian dossier which accused Peter of using magic
to ensure that the name of Christ should be worshipped for 365 years
and then come to an immediate end.[91] Though he had no sound
knowledge of Christianity, it is again remarkable that the only Christian
predecessor mentioned by Arnobius in the *Adv. nat.* is Simon Peter.

---

[82] On the date see Bouffartigue and Patillon (1977), i. xviii.

[83] See O'Meara's work listed in n. 72 above, as well as Beatrice's; and Henry Chadwick,
'Oracles of the End in the Conflict of Paganism and Christianity in the Fourth Century',
in Lucchesi and Saffrey (1985), 125–9 (includes bibliographical data); P. F. Beatrice,
'Quosdam Platonicorum Libros', *VC* 43 (1989), 248–81; L. Brisson, 'L'oracle d'Apollon
dans la vie de Plotin par Porphyre', *Ker* 3 (1990), 77–88; M. J. Edwards, 'A Late use of
Empedocles: the Oracle on Plotinus', *Mnem* 43 (1990), 151–5.

[84] *Adv. nat.* 1. 25; *Civ. Dei* 19. 23.

[85] Lact. *Mort. pers.* 11; Eus. *VC* 50.

[86] *Adv. nat.* 1. 36.

[87] Lact. *Mort. pers.* 10.

[88] *Adv. nat.* 1. 46. 32 f.: 'inponit silentium vatibus, haruspices inconsultos reddit.'

[89] Ibid. 1. 26.

[90] Ibid. 2. 21.

[91] *Civ. Dei* 18. 53.

And in light of the Porphyrian oracle his comments about him are noteworthy: Peter caused the great *magician* Simon Magus to vanish simply by mentioning Christ's *name*.[92] The apostle is not praised as a great martyr, but as a wonder-worker whose work alone conquered magic. Such attacks upon Peter, published before the persecution by Porphyry and Hierocles, may explain why Arnobius names this leader of Christianity in 2. 12. This is placed in the context of an argument which offers Christ as the *via universalis animae liberandae* identical to what Porphyry was researching in the *De regressu animae*.[93] Finally, Chaldaean/Neoplatonic theurgy,[94] the Pythagorean concept of silence,[95] and the belief that divine power abrogates the law of fate[96] are further examples of the numerous parallels between Arnobius and Porphyry that we shall investigate in the following chapters. Suffice it to say that it would appear certain that Porphyry and his followers (*viri novi*) are the main opponents of Arnobius in the *Adversus nationes*.

It is now necessary to survey the salient features of Arnobius' thought related to Christian doctrine (bks. 1 and 2). First, in speaking of the divine nature he rejects the pagan notions of the anthropomorphic and

---

[92] *Adv. nat.* 2. 12. See Ch. 3 § 3 for critical analyses.

[93] *Civ. Dei* 10. 32.

[94] *Adv. nat.* 2. 13 addresses the followers of Mercury, Plato, and Pythagoras and their esoteric rituals enabling them to return to their 'ancestral homes'; cf. *Civ. Dei* 22. 26; 10. 27; 10. 1; in *Adv. nat.* 1. 46, Christ is said to appear to men in pure simplicity, not in vain dreams; cf. *Civ. Dei* 10. 10: theurgical rites enable men to have visions of the gods or angels; *Adv. nat.* 2. 35 gives demons, angels, gods; cf. *Civ. Dei* 10. 9; Julian the great Chaldaean theologian is named in *Adv. nat.* 1. 52; *Adv. nat.* 1. 23 says demons concern themselves with the coarser things of the earth; cf. the Ep. to Anebo in *Civ. Dei* 10. 9 and 11; see Chadwick (1985), 125; On theurgy/Chaldaean oracles in Arnobius see I. P. Culianu, 'Le vol magique dans l'antiquité tardive (quelques considérations)', *RHR* 198 (1981), 57–66; and Beatrice (1988), esp. 127 ff.

[95] On Pythagorean silence before the deity see *Adv. nat.* 1. 31; cf. Aug., *Ep.* 102. 32; *De Trin.* 8. 12; 12. 13; O'Meara (1959), 160; *Adv. nat.* 2. 16; Porphyry, *Abst.* 2. 34. 1; Firmicus Maternus, *Math.* 7. 1. 1: 'Pythagoras etiam et noster Porphyrius religioso putant animum nostrum silentio consecrari.' cf. *De antro nymph.* 27; Eus. *Cont. Hier.* 12: the pagan belief that Apollonius kept silent for five years proved his divinity; *Adv. nat.* 1. 31: to understand God we must be silent. See also G. Luck, 'Theurgy and Forms of Worship in Neoplatonism', in Neusner, *RSM* (Oxford, 1989), 185–225, esp. pp. 192 and 202.

[96] On Porphyry and the Chaldaean concept of Heimarmene see: *Civ. Dei* 19. 23 (Christians are fated not to receive *dona deorum*); *COTh* 266: Heimarmene was regarded as the primary source of all evils; Proclus, *Tim.* 3. 266. 18; Lydus, *Mens.* 2. 10. 16; Porph. *Phil. or.* in *PE* 6. 1 (an oracle of Apollo concerning fate); *COTh* 213 (the neophyte initiated into the mystery is exempt from the laws of fate); and *Adv. nat.* 1. 40 (common law of fate); 1. 42, 47 (Christ overcame the fates); 1. 49 (Christ helped those wronged by fate); 1. 62 (the plan of fate); 1. 62 speaks of philosophers (= theurgists) who overcome fate.

anthropopathic gods of the myths. These form the main premiss of his
argument of books 4–7 that the gods are mortal. The motive is polemical
and the method of argumentation is literary retortion: in *Adv. nat.* 1.
36–47 the main pagan charge is that Christians worship a human being.[97]
Since Porphyry gave an oracle of Hecate in *Phil. or.* which recognized
Christ only as a man whose disciples were mistaken to proclaim him as
God,[98] it is logical to conclude that this source both lay behind the
pagan attack (1. 36–47) and motivated his response (bks 3–7). And
although the anthropomorphic nature of the gods is caricatured *ad
nauseam*,[99] Arnobius gives special attention to their anthropopathic
behaviour to prove their mortality.

The anthropopathic motif is used to turn Porphyry's argument against
him by showing that these notions are the fabrications of pagan writers.
It was the same method, using the scripture against the Christians,
that Porphyry employed in the *CC*.[100] And though the divine *ira* is
accentuated,[101] it is only one amongst many human emotions treated in
books 4–7 to prove the mortality of the gods.[102] And we shall see that
he reinforces his argument by placing six résumés at strategic locations
in the work (1. 18; 3. 12–13; 4. 28; 6. 2; 7. 4–5; 7. 35–6).[103] To sum up,
he is saying: (1) All emotional agitation is foreign to a deity. (2)
Otherwise it is mortal. (3) The gods are emotionally agitated. (4) They
are therefore mortal. Cicero's Stoic list of emotions may be the source

[97] *Adv. nat.* 1. 42: 'Natum hominem colitis.' cf. esp. 1. 45–7; on Arnobius' use of
myth in his attack see J. P. Sorensen, 'The Myth of Attis: Structure and Mysteriosophy',
in Sorensen (Copenhagen, 1989), OP 30. 23–30.

[98] *Civ. Dei* 19. 23; cf. Eus. *PE* 4. 7.

[99] *Adv. nat.* 3. 6 (gods divided into sexes); 3. 8, 9, 10 (gods do not procreate); 3. 11
(rejects human forms); 3. 15 (gods do not have hair); 3. 20 (skilled in arts); 3. 25 (gods
are immoral); 3. 29–32 (their human-ness ridiculed); 4. 22, 27 (sex affairs); 4. 28 (behave
like humans); 4. 29 (pagan myths are to be blamed); 4. 32 (the poets made this up); 4. 35
(dramatists' lies); book 5 (myths are false); book 6 (temple worship is ludicrous); book 7
(sacrifice is rejected).

[100] See M. V. Anastos, 'Porphyry's Attack on the Bible', in Wallach (Ithaca, NY, 1966),
421–50; V. den Boer, 'A Pagan Historian and His Enemies: Porphyry Against the
Christians', *CP* 69 (1974), 198–208; M. Casey, 'Porphyry and Syrian Exegesis of the
Book of Daniel', *ZNTW* 81 (1990), 139–42; B. Croke, *JRH* 13 (1984), 1–14; C.
Evangeliou, 'Porphyry's Criticism of Christianity and the Problem of Augustine's Pla-
tonism', *Dion* 13 (1989), 51–70; and a very fine article by A. Meredith, 'Porphyry and
Julian Against the Christians', *ANRW* II. 23. 2, 1119–49.

[101] See E. R. Micka, *The Problem of Divine Anger in Arnobius and Lactantius* (Washington,
DC, 1943; CUASCA 4), who fails to see that the divine *ira* in Arnobius is used in a
larger argument which includes all anthropopathic behaviour.

[102] For a list see p. 247 below; for an analysis of the motif see Ch. 9 §11.

[103] See Ch. 9 §11.

here, as it was for Augustine,[104] and might have served a double purpose. For Porphyry also attributed to the celestial deities the capability of emotional agitations.[105] Porphyry had nothing to complain about, although he *appeared* to praise Jesus the human while certainly rejecting Christ the God.[106] Arnobius posits that the gods were not only mortal; they also possessed reprehensible characters.

Saturn was the main god of Roman North Africa, and there was religious conflict and competition between his cult and Christianity during the age of Diocletian.[107] Of more than 3,000 Saturnian monuments that survive, a majority comes from Africa Proconsularis.[108] Worshipped as the *Deus frugifer par excellence*,[109] his symbols included the sickle, pine cone, grapes, and the cornucopia.[110] He was the great *dominus* of the land: he blessed the earth,[111] controlled the weather,[112] made the crops grow,[113] and provided bountiful harvests.[114] His cult was still alive in Arnobius' day as an inscription dated 8 November 323 at Béja (Vaga), located not far from Sicca, proves. An hierarchical priesthood is shown supervising the sacrifices offered to the god of the land.[115] And there were at least five ways that Saturn challenged Christianity in North Africa: (1) his regal position in the pantheon; (2) his Semitic nature portraying him to be very jealous and potentially vindictive; (3) his fierce nature that historically demanded child sacrifice from his devotees; (4) the fear he evoked from his worshippers; (5) his Lordship over the land and harvests in an area significant for agriculture.

During the Tetrarchy the cult was strongly competing with the Church. In Siliana, about 48 km. south-east of Le Kef (Sicca), Tunisia, the famous Boglio stele depicts an active harvest scene with Saturn the *dominus* of the land situated on the top register.[116] Epigraphical evidence

---

[104] Cicero, *De fin.* 3. 10. 35; *Civ. Dei* 10 *passim*.
[105] Ibid. 10. 27.
[106] Ibid. 19. 23.
[107] The main works are those of M. Leglay (*SAH* and *SAM*) and others found in Ch. 7 below.
[108] See Fasce, *Vic* (1980), 179 f.; *SAH* 7 ff.
[109] See *SAH* 120–4.
[110] *SAH* 153–214.
[111] See e.g. *SAM* 1. 141 no. 44 (Ain Tounga); 147 no. 64 (Ain Tounga) = *CIL* 15147; *SAM* 1. 153 no. 96 = *CIL* 15157; *SAM* 1. 188 no. 234 = *CIL* 15140.
[112] *SAH* 226 f.
[113] *SAH* 120–4.
[114] *SAH* 187–207.
[115] A. Beschaouch, 'Une stèle consacrée à Saturne le 8 Novembre 323', *BACTH* NS 4 (1968), 253–68.
[116] See p. 193 below.

confirms that he was being worshipped in the Le Kef area.[117] And when Arnobius was writing the *Adv. nat.* there had already been a resurgence of the rural economy;[118] an interesting fact in light of the possibility that it seems to have been written during a period of crop failures and drought.[119]

Saturnian theology may have influenced his understanding of the Christian God. For example, Arnobius says that God gives the produce of the land.[120] He is acknowledged as the Lord of Heaven.[121] Saturnian epithets are attributed to him: *genitor*,[122] *pater*,[123] *dominus*,[124] and the agrarian term *frugifer*.[125] Clearly indicating a fiercely contested conflict between Saturn and the Christian God, Arnobius consistently attacks the agrarian aspects of Saturn's lordship. He makes fun of the 'protector of sowing'.[126] Saturn is mockingly referred to as 'the Old Man'.[127] He is scorned as the 'guardian of the countryside' with his crooked sickle,[128] which casts fear upon people and is therefore purported to make them live virtuously![129] As we shall see below in greater detail (Ch. 7), this religious conflict focused upon four main issues in the *Adversus nationes*. First, there was an intense working of the land since Probus which revived the rural economy. Second, the agrarian situation in the early fourth century was characterized by drought. Third, there was sharp competition between Saturn and the Christian God as to who is the true *dominus* of the land. Fourth, as we have noted, Saturnian religious terminology influenced Arnobius' concept of God.

It is mainly due to his recent conversion[130] that 'Arnobius had a very poor grasp of the doctrine of Christianity'.[131] There are therefore unorthodox concepts in this thought,[132] and we may begin our survey with his under-

---

[117] See e.g. *SAM* 1. 291 f. nos. 1–2, 5–6; *SAH* 192 n. 1; 194; 195 n. 1.
[118] See J. Peyras, 'Le fundus aufidianus: étude d'un grand domaine romain de la région de Mateur', *AntAfr* 9 (1985), 181–222.
[119] *Adv. nat.* 1. 9, 19, 21; 2. 40; 3. 11; 6. 2, 16; see also Liebeschuetz (1979), 254.
[120] *Adv. nat.* 1. 29; see Ch. 6 n. 77.
[121] *Adv. nat.* 1. 29.
[122] Ibid.; see *SAH* 114.
[123] *Adv. nat.* 1. 29; *SAH* 114.
[124] *Adv. nat.* 1. 30.
[125] Ibid.
[126] Ibid. 4. 9, 26; *SAH* 120–4.
[127] *Adv. nat.* 4. 26; see *SAH* 118 ff.
[128] *Adv. nat.* 6. 12.
[129] Ibid. 6. 25.
[130] Ibid. 1. 39.
[131] Micka (1943), 158.
[132] Liebeschuetz (1979), 257, says his departure from standard doctrine makes his work important historically because it (1) views Christianity from the outside and (2) displays

standing of man and creation. According to Arnobius, it is natural weakness
that makes man a sinner, not free will or choice.[133] Human nature is weak
and absolutely powerless.[134] Man is wretched and unhappy,[135] a creature
of countless vices and an ignoble lineage.[136] Being deceitful, lustful, and
fickle,[137] man possesses an innate perverseness.[138] There is only a very
small number of good men in the world.[139] Man lives in this 'husk of petty
flesh'[140] which is nothing more than a shadow and a form.[141] Finally, man
is totally blind and ignorant, not knowing where he is going.[142] This
anthropological assessment is placed, of course, in contradistinction with
that of his pagan opponents who believe that man should be assigned,
immortal and supreme, to the *ordinibus primis*[143] alongside God. And
though this view of man may accurately be called pessimistic and even
quite unorthodox, it would be incorrect to say that man is almost an animal
according to Arnobian anthropology.[144]

If man is depreciated, the Arnobian 'High God' is transcendent and
highly exalted. One unorthodox feature here is his insistence upon God
not being responsible for the creation of man.[145] For how could God,
who is perfect and begets only that which is perfect, create such a fickle
creature as man?[146] And even though Arnobius is ignorant of the source
of evil, he is certain that it cannot be God.[147] And when he attempts to
identify the creator of human beings we are met with a barrage of
conflicting answers. Once he says that Christ taught that some other
creature far removed from the Supreme God created man.[148] Elsewhere
we find him saying the creator cannot be specified;[149] or some 'unfor-

---

features that attracted an educated pagan. For a general survey of Arnobius' thought see
B. Amata, *Problemi di antropologia arnobiana* (Rome, 1984), BSR 64.

[133] *Adv. nat.* 1. 49; cf. 1. 63.
[134] Ibid. 2. 33; 3. 24.
[135] Ibid. 2. 46 f.
[136] Ibid. 2. 48.
[137] Ibid.
[138] Ibid. 2. 50.
[139] Ibid. 2. 49.
[140] Ibid. 2. 76.
[141] Ibid. 2. 77.
[142] Ibid. 2. 60.
[143] Ibid. 1. 29.
[144] Micka (1943), 167.
[145] *Adv. nat.* 2. 7.
[146] Ibid. 2. 45 f.
[147] Ibid. 2. 55–8.
[148] Ibid. 2. 36.
[149] Ibid. 2. 47.

tunate something' brought forth man;[150] or the causes from which souls
derive their existence are unknown;[151] or finally, we simply do not know
who the creator is.[152] Criticizing a view held by Porphyry, he is certain
that God did not send the souls to earth to learn evil![153] Even the
human soul itself, according to Arnobian psychology, is not immortal.[154]
Possessing an intermediate character (*media qualitas*),[155] it can be immor-
talized only after it receives knowledge from the 'High God' which
saves it not from sin, but from ignorance.[156] Otherwise it will simply
disintegrate after an indefinite period in a place of punishment.[157]

To sum up, Arnobius' concept of God is, at points, unorthodox. God
did not create man. The soul is not immortal. Also, his soteriology is
not in line with standard Christian doctrine: man is saved from ignorance,
not from sin, when he is graciously granted knowledge of the High
God. He also rejects the doctrine of an eternal hell. And although the
Arnobian God is transcendent and exalted, even apophatically conceived
in some passages (e.g. 1. 31), it would still be totally inaccurate to deny
him the quality of providence.[158] It is obvious that Arnobius is not
orthodox in his Christian thought, but he was probably unaware of such
distinctions due to his newly acquired religious world-view. Based on
the evidence of books 1–2 where a vast majority of his 'Christian'
concepts are found, we must also conclude that he was not undergoing
catechetical instruction. In Arnobius we simply see the thought of a
recent convert in transition: contradictory elements have not been
worked out.

Polemics have informed Arnobius' understanding of Christ, so we
cannot speak of a Christology in the work. He is silent about the
incarnation, the Trinity, the sacraments, the Old Testament and a great

---

[150] *Adv. nat.* 2. 7.
[151] Ibid. 2. 51.
[152] Ibid. 2. 58.
[153] Ibid. 2. 39; the Porphyrian passage is *Civ. Dei* 10. 30.
[154] *Adv. nat.* 2. 31 f.
[155] Ibid. 2. 14, 31 f., 35 f., 53.
[156] Ibid. 2. 32. God also granted immortality to the gods, a concept he derived from *Tim.*, which supports his view of the *media qualitas animae* in *Adv. nat.* 2. 36; cf. *Civ. Dei* 22. 26.
[157] *Adv. nat.* 2. 61; see also 2. 30 and 2. 53.
[158] As Baynes, *CAH* 12. 652, does; cf. Micka (1943), 159; Disproved by *Adv. nat.* 3. 24 (mainly) and 1. 9, 13, 29, 30 (physical and material needs); cf. 1. 55; 2. 5, 8, 64 (spiritual needs); 1. 31 (a forgiving God); 1. 25 (a sense of safety from worship); cf. 1. 26, 27; 2. 55.

majority of the New,[159] the theological meaning of the crucifixion, and much that is related to worship and liturgy. With the exception of allusions to his miracles, there is very little said about the earthly life of Christ.[160] The name *Jesus* never appears in the work, and Arnobius does not have (as noted) even a basic knowledge of Christian scripture.[161] His remarks about Christ seem to have been motivated by the desire to revoke the charges he brought against him while still a pagan.

Four main themes are discernible. First, Arnobius is emphatic that Christ is God and not a mortal being.[162] This appears to be a response to Porphyry's Hecatean Oracle in *Phil. or.* which denied the divinity of Christ and called him a mere man.[163] The first great blessing of Christ is his withdrawing his followers from errors by introducing the truth to them.[164] According to Porphyry, Hecate proclaimed that the disciples were entangled in error and estranged from the truth.[165] Arnobius contends that Christians worship one born a man but who is absolutely God as well: 'He was God sublime, God from the innermost roots, God from realms unknown, and was sent by God the Ruler of all as a Saviour.'[166] Porphyry despised the teaching of Christ's divinity.[167] Perhaps this is why Arnobius minimizes the physical body of Christ,[168] and the reason for the remark about the crucifixion of a man who died ignominiously.[169] This also sounds Porphyrian.[170] The pagans charge that Christians worship a man who died a disgraceful death for the lowest of men (1. 36). Porphyry's oracle praised the judgement ordering

[159] The OT prophecies would have served him well, as they did many of his predecessors, if he had had knowledge of them.

[160] See McCr 25–8, and LeB 68–80, for the critical interpretations.

[161] See McCr 25–7; LeB 68–71, for the question of scriptural knowledge in the *Adv. nat.*

[162] *Adv. nat.* 1. 32–53; F. Gabarrou, *Arnobe* (Paris, 1921), 61, says that Arnobius does not positively affirm Christ's divinity; cf. Micka (1943), 52 f.; Arianizing tendencies are suspected by C. T. Cruttwell, *A Literary History of Early Christianity* (London, 1893), 2. 633; cf. McCr 26 f.; A. C. McGiffert, *A History of Christian Thought* (London, 1933), 2. 43 f.; Arnobius has a subordinationist understanding according to H. D. McDonald, 'The Doctrine of God in Arnobius, Adversus Gentes', *StudPatr* 9, part 3 (Berlin, 1966; TU 94), 75–81; Scheidweiler (1954) and Sirna (1964) argue that he was a Marcionite; finally, in general see M. Jufresa, 'La divinidad y lo divino en Arnobio', *BIEJ* 7 (1973), 61–4.

[163] *Civ. Dei* 19. 23; Eus. *PE* 4. 7.

[164] *Adv. nat.* 1. 38.

[165] *Civ. Dei* 19. 23; cf. *PE* 4. 7.

[166] *Adv. nat.* 1. 53; cf. also 1. 37 f.; 1. 40; 1. 42; 1. 65.

[167] *Civ. Dei* 10. 28.

[168] *Adv. nat.* 1. 53.

[169] Ibid. 1. 40 f.

[170] *Civ. Dei* 19. 23.

Christ to suffer the worst of deaths.[171] Arnobius is well aware in the first two books that the belief that Christ is God is attacked by the pagans.[172]

Second, Christ has power over the fates.[173] By his miraculous power Christ broke and dissolved 'all those ordinances of fate'.[174] His healing miracles prove that he 'overcame the laws of the fates'.[175] Christ's power is superior to philosophy (2. 11) and magic (2. 12). This seems to be a critique of the Neoplatonist's use of theurgy to liberate the common lot subject to fate.[176] Allusions to such theurgical practices are found throughout the *Adversus nationes*.[177] Also, Porphyry in *Phil. or.* decreed through Hecate that Christians were fated not to receive blessings from the gods.[178]

Third, the miracles of Christ are used to prove: (1) their unusual quality (1. 42); (2) they were not caused by magic (1. 43–4); (3) man has benefited spiritually from them (1. 44); (4) the divinity of Christ (1. 45; 1. 53); (5) their occurrence in the past and the present (1. 46); (6) the nature of a *verus Deus* (1. 47); (7) Christ's superiority to the pagan gods (1. 49); and (8) they are based upon reliable witnesses (1. 54). Finally, in response to Porphyry who 'praised' Christ's wisdom while condemning his disciples' ignorance,[179] Arnobius emphasizes that the disciples did the same miracles as their master 'with like right and power'.[180]

Arnobius' fourth feature about Christ is that he has given to his followers the great *dona dei* of the Father. As noted, Porphyry prophesied through Hecate that Christians were fated not to receive *dona deorum*.[181] It is because of this that Arnobius rather frequently refers to the many gifts given by Christ for mankind's welfare.[182] Even scientific knowledge

[171] *Civ. Dei* 19. 23.
[172] *Adv. nat.* 2. 60; cf. 1. 32–47.
[173] Ibid. 1. 47–53.
[174] Ibid. 1. 42; cf. 2. 11 f.: Christ is more powerful than philosophy and magic.
[175] Ibid. 1. 47.
[176] See Luck (1989), 189; the concept of fate is attacked in Eus. *Cont. Hier.* 41.
[177] *Adv. nat.* 2. 13 and 2. 62.
[178] *Civ. Dei* 19. 23.
[179] Ibid.
[180] *Adv. nat.* 1. 56; in 1. 50 he says Christ delegated this power to his disciples; compare 1. 54 with *Civ. Dei* 19. 23; 1. 55 (people saw miracles performed by Christ and his disciples); 1. 56; Eusebius has a similar argument: see *DE* 3. 4; 3. 5; 3. 6.
[181] Porphy, *Phil. or.* in Aug. *Civ. Dei* 19. 23.
[182] *Adv. nat.* 1. 39.

like cosmology and physiology came from him.[183] Responding to the pagan charge that Christians worship a mortal, he retorts 'on account of the many gifts which have come from Him to us, He ought to be called and addressed as God.'[184] Christ's heralds also gave God's gifts to 'souls and bodies'.[185] One gift accentuated is salvation from ignorance of God, another response to Porphyry who said Christians were uninstructed and ungodly natures fated not to know immortal Jupiter (*Civ. Dei* 19. 23). Ignorance could not be purified by theurgy, but only by the mind of the Father according to Porphyry (*Civ. Dei* 10. 28). Arnobius claims that Christ did not teach iniquity but delivered men from ignorance.[186] He has removed the great peril of ignorance,[187] and came to earth to give knowledge of the true God.[188] He alone has revealed who God truly is.[189] Superhuman knowledge has now been given to mankind.[190] By clearing up ignorance Christ has given believers immunity from corruption.[191] Knowledge of the Head of the universe revealed by Christ is the 'true and greatest knowledge'.[192] And the supreme gift is the immortality of the soul which Christ alone can bestow.[193] Finally, the insistence of Christ being the *via universalis salutis animae liberandae*, expressed eloquently in *Adv. nat.* 2. 65, should be compared with Porphyry's research to find this universal way for the soul's salvation in his studies, especially the *De regressu animae*.[194] We should therefore reject the interpretation that claims to find a Gnostic soteriology in Arnobius' 'Christology', but rather view his concept of salvific knowledge being given by Christ as a response to the Porphyrian diatribe against the deity of Christ current in Roman North Africa during the Age of Diocletian.

Before turning to Section II we may offer the following conclusions. (1) Arnobius was certainly not 'orthodox' in respect of a good number of standard Christian doctrines. (2) He was evidently a sincere, albeit newly converted, Christian from the pagan intelligentsia. (3) He should

[183] Ibid. 1. 38.
[184] Ibid. 1. 42.
[185] Ibid. 1. 55.
[186] Ibid. 2. 4.
[187] Ibid. 2. 2.
[188] Ibid. 1. 47.
[189] Ibid. 1. 38.
[190] Ibid.
[191] Ibid. 2. 53; cf. 2. 65.
[192] Ibid. 2. 61.
[193] Ibid. 2. 65.
[194] *Civ. Dei* 10. 32; *Adv. nat.* 2. 65; cf. 1. 55 and 2. 5.

not be called a 'heretic', even though it is understandable why Jerome found some things in the *Adv. nat.* unacceptable.[195] He did not have a sound knowledge of standard doctrine, and it would require a stretch of the imagination to say that he was a catechumen at the time of writing. And this is why he has been associated by scholars with such a wide diversity of philosophical and religious sects. (4) He is apparently revoking mainly Porphyrian charges against Christianity which he himself used while he was a pagan adversary of the religion. (5) The reversal of his views put in writing in *Adv. nat.* 1–2, reassured the bishop that he had left the Porphyrian camp for a change of colours. (6) The frontal assault in books 4–7 entirely on the offensive might have been inspired by Porphyry's method of attacking Christianity in the *Contra Christianos*, where he exclusively used scripture against the Christians. (7) The *Adv. nat.* should not be classified as a 'Christian Apology' in the traditional meaning; and for those who would still insist that Arnobius should be called a 'Christian Apologist', all would undoubtedly agree that he is much more successful in his attack upon paganism than he is in his 'defence' of Christianity. (8) The *Adv. nat.* is therefore—and the following chapters will demonstrate this—of much greater historical significance for the intellectual background to the Great Persecution of Diocletian than has been assumed hitherto.

II. *Graeco-Roman Culture: The Pagan Intellectual Attack upon Christianity in the Diocletianic Age*

Between the Peace of Gallienus (*c.*260) and the outbreak of the Great Persecution under Diocletian (303), the pagan intelligentsia of the Roman world, led by Porphyry of Tyre and Sossianus Hierocles, developed the most formidable assault upon Christianity in its brief history. Storm clouds were gradually gathering over the Church during this generation, and we may agree with Millar that 'it would be rash to discount too readily the possible influence of intellectual factors on the great persecution.'[196] Porphyry was the greatest anti-Christian writer in Antiquity. Being both despised and respected (if not feared) by his

[195] Jerome, *Ep.* 62.2 (Ad Tranquillinum).
[196] Millar (1977), 573. Cf. p. 9: Moving the capital to a Greek city under the Tetrarchy exposed the imperial court to pagan Greek intellectuals; cf. Liebeschuetz (1979), 252; Williams (1985), 173–85; J. Geffcken, *The Last Days of Greco-Roman Paganism* (Amsterdam, 1978), tr. S. MacCormack, EMA 8. 56–74.

enemies, he was described by them as exceptionally talented,[197] especially in regard to his historical criticism,[198] and well known for his Neoplatonic spirituality which offered a *via salutis* to the common masses.[199] A century after Arnobius he was still the most highly esteemed of the Greek philosophers in Roman North Africa.[200] Greatly influenced by Chaldaean theology, as we shall see below,[201] he nevertheless appeared to compliment Christ in one of his works.[202] He was quite renowned for his erudition,[203] and Eusebius quotes extensively from his writings.[204] He may indeed have had an 'encyclopedic knowledge of the Bible',[205] which he used against the Christians, and pagan admirers attributed an almost divine status to him.[206] Overall he was highly revered for his philosophical pursuits and exhaustive research in religious subjects, mockingly called 'magic arts' (theurgy) by Augustine.[207] Finally, Porphyry had a threefold purpose in his anti-Christian works:

(1) To show that Christianity was absolutely devoid of a rational basis (e.g. *CC*, *Phil. or.*).

(2) To offer a *via universalis liberandae animae* for the common man (e.g. *De reg. an.*, *Phil. or.*).

(3) To offer the way of philosophic wisdom and the purification and the liberation of the soul from the body for the philosopher (*De reg. an.*, *Phil. or.*, *Abst.*, etc.).[208]

[197] *Civ. Dei* 10. 32; see the biography below, pp. 218–222.

[198] See M. Smith, *JTS* 39 (1988), 494–504.

[199] See P. Hadot, 'Neoplatonist Spirituality: Plotinus and Porphyry', in A. Armstrong (ed.), *CMS* (New York, 1986), 230–49; L. Jerphagnon, 'Les sous-entendus anti-chrétiens de la Vita Plotini ou l'évangile de Plotin selon Porphyre', *MH* 47 (1990), 41–52; R. M. Grant, 'Porphyry Among the Early Christians', in W. den Boer *et al.* (eds.) *RC* (Amsterdam, 1973), 181–7.

[200] *Civ. Dei* 8. 12.

[201] Ibid. 10. 9.

[202] *De cons. evang.* 1. 15. 25; 1. 31. 47; *Phil. or.* in *PE* 4. 7; *Civ. Dei* 19. 23.

[203] Aug. *Civ. Dei* 7. 25.

[204] According to Smith (1988), Eusebius quotes from the *Phil. or. c.*40 times. See also the articles by M. J. Hollerich, 'Myth and History in Eusebius' *De Vita Constantini*', *HTR* 82 (1989), 421–45; and 'Religion and Politics in the Writings of Eusebius: Reassessing the First Court Theologian', *CH* 59 (1990), 309–25.

[205] See Anastos (1966), 449.

[206] Eunapius, *Vit. Soph.* 457. Libanius, *Or.* 18. 178, calls him the old sage from Tyre.

[207] *Civ. Dei* 10. 29. His active involvement in spreading philosophical and religious ideas endeared him to the masses. See A. Smith, *Porphyry's Place in the Neoplatonic Tradition* (The Hague, 1974), 21 f.

[208] Porphyry is identified as the pagan opponent of M. Magnes in the *Apocriticus* by R. Goulet, *Makarios Magnès: Monogénès (Apocriticus)* (Thesis, University of Paris, 1974), 2 vols.

Porphyry was born at Tyre *c*.234, studied under Longinus at Athens, and became a disciple of Plotinus in Rome.[209] He died *c*.305. At least two anti-Christian writings are known to have been written by him, the *Philosophia ex oraculis* and the *Contra Christianos*. How far he was associated with the imperial court has not been established,[210] but the remark by Lactantius that a 'priest of philosophy' dined in the emperor's palace may be an allusion to him.[211] For it is Porphyry in the *De abstinentia* who calls the philosopher 'priest of the Supreme God',[212] and Lactantius interestingly in the next sentence of the *Div. inst.* calls his philosopher a 'teacher of abstinence'![213] He also informs us that he wrote three books against the Christians, an apparent reference to the *Phil. or.* Finally, Lactantius says a main purpose of the work was to recall people from errors,[214] bringing to mind the oracle of Hecate which condemned Christians for being entangled in error;[215] and Porphyry's pronouncement in the preface to *Phil. or.* that 'steadfast is he who draws his hopes of salvation from this as from the only sure source.'[216] Two other factors may also shed some light on the problem. First, in the *Ad Marcellam* Porphyry defined the greatest expression of piety as honouring the gods according to 'ancestral traditions'.[217] This will have cohered well with Diocletian's religious programme based upon the traditional paganism of the Roman Empire (see §III). Second, in the same epistle the Neoplatonist tells his wife that he was away in the East because of a need of the Greeks. This occurred just before the outbreak of the persecution in 303, and it has been suggested by Chadwick and (later) Wilken that Porphyry attended the imperial conference whose purpose it was to decide what to do with the Christians (late 302).[218]

The close association between the pagan intellectuals and imperial

---

[209] See E. R. Dodds, 'Porphyry', *OCD* 865; I follow the dating of Bouffartigue–Patillon (1977), p. xi; see also J. Bidez (1913); and A. C. Lloyd, 'Porphyry', *EP* 5. 411 f.

[210] See Wilken (1984), 134 ff.

[211] Lactantius, *Div. inst.* 5. 2. 12; T. D. Barnes, 'Porphyry Against the Christians: Date and Atrribution of Fragments', *JTS* NS 24 (1973), 438 f., argues against this interpretation with unconvincing results; see Wilken (1984), 135 ff.

[212] Porph. *Abst.* 2. 49. 1; cf. Wilken (1984), 135.

[213] *Div. inst.* 5. 2. 12.

[214] Ibid.

[215] *Civ. Dei* 19. 23.

[216] Eus. *PE* 4. 7.

[217] *Ad Marc.* 18.

[218] Wilken (1984), 136, says that *Phil. or.* was possibly written at the request of the emperor; cf. also id. in Schoedel and Wilken (1979), 118–23; H. Chadwick, *The Sentences of Sextus* (Cambridge, 1959; TS 5), 66, was the first to make the connection; the conference is described in Lact. *Mort. pers.* 11.

policies that brought about the persecution is confirmed in the case of Hierocles,[219] who is said to have been an 'instigator and adviser' of the persecution.[220] He probably attended the imperial conference (late 302) which resulted in Diocletian's serious consideration to move against the Christians.[221] Eusebius makes note of his political influence in the 'supreme courts' throughout the province.[222] At the beginning of the persecution he was governor of Bithynia in the East[223] and wrote the *Lover of Truth* to (not against) the Christians.[224] In this he compares the second-century wonder-worker Apollonius of Tyana with Jesus who, he claims, has been given divine status by his followers on account of a few miracles.[225] It is clear that Hierocles did not deny the occurrence of Christ's miracles, but rather attributed the working of magical powers to them.[226] Christ was therefore simply a magician.[227] He condemned the disciples as ignorant fishermen, and especially attacked Peter and Paul who were 'liars, devoid of education, and wizards.'[228] These illiterate men were responsible for writing the 'tales' of Jesus.[229] Christian scripture was the product therefore of simpletons and deceivers. The main purpose of this diatribe was to convince the Christians that a greater religious teacher (Apollonius) had come years before Jesus, the tradition about him was scientifically reliable and written for the love of mankind,[230] and Graeco-Roman pagan culture was superior to

---

[219] See *PLRE* 1. 432; and T. D. Barnes, 'Sossianus Hierocles and the Antecedents of the Great Persecution', *HSCP* 80 (1976), 239–52.

[220] Lact. *Div. inst.* 15.

[221] See now Barnes (1981), 22.

[222] Eus. *Cont. Hier.* 4.

[223] See *Mort pers.* 16. 4; *Div. inst.* 5. 2. 12; Barnes, *HSCP* 80 (1976), 243.

[224] Composed shortly before 303 according to Barnes (1981), 165.

[225] *Cont. Hier.* 2. For the text with introduction and commentary see M. Forrat and E. des Places, *Contre Hiéroclès* (Paris, 1987; SC no. 333); also F. C. Conybeare, *Philostratus, The Life of Apollonius of Tyana and the Treatise of Eusebius against Hierocles* (Cambridge, Mass., 1912; LCL, 2 vols.), 2. 483–605.

[226] Lact. *Div. inst.* 5. 3 confirms this; Arnobius responds to the charge that Christ worked by magic in *Adv. nat.* 1. 43.

[227] *Cont. Hier.* 1–2.

[228] Ibid. 2.

[229] Ibid.

[230] Cf. ibid. Hierocles says the history of Apollonius, unlike the unreliable tales of Jesus, was written by trustworthy witnesses (Maximus, Damis, and Philostratus) who lived with him constantly. They were well educated, unlike the disciples, and highly respected the truth. They also loved mankind. For possible Christian influences upon pagan concepts like faith, truth, and love see *Ad Marc.* 24; and R. Baine Harris, 'Faith and Reason in the Early Neoplatonists', *DA* 1 (1987), 6–17.

Christian teaching because it alone possessed the truth.[231] It too will
have cohered well with the Empire's decision to persecute the Christians.

It was the two works of Porphyry, however, the *Philosophia ex oraculis*
and the *Contra Christianos*, that posed a greater threat than the second-
century writer Celsus[232] and Porphyry's contemporary Hierocles. For in
addition to demonstrating the falsity of his enemies' beliefs, Porphyry
went farther than any anti-Christian writer before him by offering a
more acceptable way of salvation to the philosopher and the man in the
street.[233] Though a pre-Plotinian date has been given for the *Phil. or.*,[234]
both the intense research and the philological editorial work that it
necessitated[235] presuppose that a mature scholar was responsible for its
creation.[236] Thus the date for the work and its immediate influence
would be *c.*270–300, the period just before the persecution.

Designed as a religious manual upholding traditional Graeco-Roman
piety and deriving its authority from the divine revelation of the oracles,
the *Phil. or.* had six main objectives. First, Jesus Christ was only a 'wise
man' and certainly not divine.[237] Also, neither Christ nor Christianity can
give the blessings of the gods to humans.[238] Third, Porphyry demonstrated

---

[231] See Baynes, *CAH* 12. 646–77; W. H. C. Frend, *Martyrdom and Persecution in the
Early Church* (Grand Rapids (1981), repr.), 477–535; Barnes (1981), 15–27; and for
Hierocles esp. 164–7.

[232] A significant anti-Christian writer of the 2nd cent. who wrote *The True Discourse*;
Origen wrote the *Contra Celsum* (3rd cent.) in response to his accusations; see H.
Chadwick, *Origen: Contra Celsum* (Cambridge, 1953).

[233] See esp. Ch. 10 below; and Fox (1987), 197.

[234] F. E. Peters, *The Harvest of Hellenism* (New York, 1970), 672, believes it was
composed in Syria; Geffcken (1978), 57, says Athens; see also G. Wolff, *De Philosophia
ex Oraculis Haurienda Librorum Reliquiae* (Berlin, 1856), 38; Bidez (1913), 15; Lewy,
COTh 449; and Barnes (1981), 174 ff.

[235] The intense research in other religious traditions for the *via salutis universalis*,
explored in the *De reg. an.* in *Civ. Dei* 10 (*passim*) seems to have laid the foundation for
Porphyry's claim in the pref. of *Phil. or.* (noted above) of having at last found it for all
who would desire salvation as the only 'sure source' (*PE* 4. 7). For the meticulous
editorial work see also *PE* 4. 7.

[236] For the title see Aug. *Civ. Dei* 19. 23; See also O'Meara (1959), 35 ff.; Chadwick
(1959), 142; also id. (1985), 125 and esp. n. 1; Wilken (1979), 131; Fox (1987), 191 and
196 f., believes the *Phil. or.* was compiled *c.*270–300; Finally, Beatrice, *VC* 43 (1989),
248–81, argues that the work should be identified with the lost work written against the
Christians. Scholarship still desperately awaits a very thorough study of Porphyry and his
work.

[237] Aug. *Civ. Dei* 19. 23; 10. 29. For the format of *Phil. or.* see Wolff (1962), 42 f.; book
1 dealt with (e.g.) the gods, piety, cultic worship, idols; book 2: demons, theosophia,
astrology, fate, etc.; book 3: heroes, Christ, and the falsity of the apostles' doctrines.

[238] Cf. again Wolff (1962), 42 f.; *Civ. Dei* 19. 23; *PE* 4. 7.

to his readers the excellence of the gods.[239] Next, he encouraged the common man to practise theurgy for soteriological purposes.[240] Fifth, a *via salutis universalis animae liberandae*, though not discovered when the *De reg. an.* was being written, has now been extended to mankind.[241] Finally, revelation of the truth by the oracles, described as the only sure source, can now be apprehended by all who wish to receive salvation.[242] Although it may go too far to say that it 'sets forth his most important criticism of the Christian movement',[243] modern scholarship has on the whole overlooked the importance of the *Phil. or.* for the intellectual background to the Great Persecution.

Porphyry's *Contra Christianos* ('Against the Christians') in fifteen books[244] has survived only in quotations from Christian adversaries. In it he restricted his argument to an attack upon Christian scripture.[245] The contradictions and poor literary quality of the Bible were analysed to prove its falsity,[246] and faith was considered inferior to Hellenic wisdom.[247] Although a date has not been agreed upon for

[239] *PE* 4. 6 f.

[240] On the striking parallels between Porphyry's view of theurgy and the Chaldaean Oracles see R. Berchman, '*Arcana Mundi* between Balaam and Hecate: Prophecy, Divination, and Magic in Later Platonism', in Lull (ed.) (Atlanta, 1989), 107–85, with refs. to Arnobius.

[241] *Phil. or.* dealt with philosophical matters: see *Civ. Dei* 19. 23; see M. J. Edwards, 'Porphyry and the Intelligible Triad', *JHS* 110 (1990), 14–25, for Porphyry's use (e.g.) of the Platonic Triad in the *Phil. or.*; the main purpose for writing seems to have been to offer salvation for the soul (*PE* 4. 6–8); divination was also dealt with for the common man (*PE* 4. 7); for the *via universalis* in the *De reg. an.* see Bidez (1913), 94 ff.

[242] Augustine says he borrowed heavily from the Chaldaean Oracles and refers to them frequently in his works (*Civ. Dei* 10. 32); cf. Chadwick (1985), 125 f.; Smith (1974), 127 ff.; Porphyry explicitly declared that his collection revealed divine truth to people who acknowledge the gods (*PE* 4. 7); for the Chaldaean Oracles see E. des Places, 'Les oracles chaldaïques dans la tradition patristique africaine', in F. L. Cross (ed.) (*StudPatr* 2, pt. 2 (1972), (= TU 108), 27–41; id., 'Les oracles chaldaïques', *ANRW* II. 17. 4, 2299–335; id., *Oracles Chaldaïques* (Paris, 1971; Budé), esp. 7–24, incl. a good analysis of Porphyry; and R. Majercik, *The Chaldaean Oracles: Text, Translation, and Commentary* (Leiden, 1989; SGRR 5). The latter includes a very good bibliography for the interested scholar.

[243] Wilken (1984), 160 f. For the background to the oracles in general see H. W. Parke, *The Oracles of Zeus: Dodona–Olympia–Ammon* (Oxford, 1967); and id., *The Oracles of Apollo in Asia Minor* (London, 1985).

[244] See A. Harnack, 'Porphyrius, "Gegen die Christen", 15 Bücher: Zeugnisse, Fragmente und Referate', *AKPAW* (1916), Nr. 1 (Berlin, 1916), for a list of fragments, incl. passages from M. Magnes' *Apocriticus* concerning which scholars have not reached an agreement.

[245] See A. Meredith, *ANRW* (1980), 1119–49.

[246] See Anastos (1966), 421–7; and Casey (1990), 139 ff.

[247] See den Boer (1974), 198–205; R. Baine Harris (1987), 6–17; and Barnes (1981), 21 f.

the CC,[248] it was certainly contributing to the growing pagan intellectual hostility towards Christianity by the late third century, and may have even influenced the imperial court to persecute the Christians.[249]

There were four primary charges brought against Christianity by these pagan intellectuals. First, the nature and character of Jesus Christ was assailed. We have already seen that Arnobius was familiar with Porphyry's prophetic revelation which rejected the deity of Christ. The objective was to convince the Christians they were mistaken to worship a man. And although Eusebius could turn the argument around and say that Apollonius was a 'magician',[250] pagans believed that he was divine,[251] possessed of supreme knowledge,[252] and performed many miracles.[253] He could also understand all languages,[254] even those of animals,[255] cure diseases,[256] perceive silent thoughts,[257] and accurately predict the future.[258] So who needed Jesus? Traditional Graeco-Roman piety offered the way of salvation. Basing his argument upon the Platonic psychology which placed a greater value upon the soul while denigrating the body,[259] Porphyry found the doctrine of the incarnation deplorable.[260] And even though Hierocles said he was a magician,[261] Porphyry seems to have pretentiously praised Jesus as a wise man whose disciples were deceived to think he was a god.[262]

Second, an unprecedented attack was mounted against Christian

---

[248] The traditional date is *c*.270 in Sicily, on which see Peters (1970), 675; B. Croke, *JRH* (1984), 13; C. Evangeliou, *Dion* (1989), 67 f.; Fox (1987), 586; the late 3rd cent. according to P. Pirioni, 'Il soggiorno siciliano di Porfirio e la composizione del Κατὰ Χριστιανῶν', *RSCI* 39 (1985), 502–8; Barnes, *JTS* (1973), 442, argues for the later date of *c*. early 4th cent.

[249] See Barnes (1981), 22.

[250] Cf. *Cont. Hier.* (e.g.) 26, 33, 35, 36, 37, 38, 39, 40.

[251] Ibid. 11, 38.

[252] Ibid. 21, 26.

[253] Ibid. e.g. 8, 12, 23, 26, 28, 35, 38.

[254] Ibid. 8.

[255] Ibid. 10.

[256] Ibid. 12.

[257] Ibid. 8.

[258] Ibid.

[259] Cf. *Civ. Dei* 10. 28 f.; one must abandon everything material and mortal, *Abst.* 1. 30. 5; flee all that make us strangers to our race, *Abst.* 1. 30. 3; mortality is abandoned, 1. 30. 4; in *Civ. Dei* 10. 29, Porphyry says 'omne corpus esse fugiendum'; a good reason for his despising Christ in the flesh according to Aug. *Civ. Dei* 10. 24; see also Eus. *DE* 3. 6 f.

[260] *Civ. Dei* 10. 29.

[261] *Cont. Hier.* 1–2.

[262] Cf. *De cons. evang.* 1. 15. 23; *Civ. Dei* 19. 23; *PE* 4. 7; *DE* 3. 6 f.

scripture. By attacking the Bible the pagans hoped to destroy the basis of the Christian faith.[263] Literary and historical criticism of scripture therefore played a significant role in the pagan–Christian conflict in the age of Diocletian.[264] Compared with the elegant language of the oracles described as finely adorned poetry, Christian scripture was thought to be inferior in its style, full of bad grammar, and written by uneducated fishermen.[265] The authors were simply liars who invented stories about Christ.[266] Porphyry charged the evangelists with falsity.[267] Responding to a common enemy, Arnobius and Eusebius insist the Apostles were eyewitnesses of the events they narrated.[268] Stories like Jesus walking on the water were ridiculed.[269] Another facet of the conflict was the question as to whose prophetic tradition contained authentic divine revelation. Focusing especially upon the book of Daniel,[270] Porphyry's historical criticism of the OT prophetic books attempted to prove their falsity because they concerned 'worldly matters',[271] they were restricted to the present life, and their predictions were given by unreliable men.[272] The main objective here appears to have been to dismantle the *Heilsgeschichte* argument, developed by the Christian apologists since Justin Martyr, that (1) the Christians possessed a divine revelation older than that of the pagans in the form of OT prophecies; and (2) Christ was the fulfilment of OT prophecy.[273] Therefore the divine revelation transmitted through the oracles of the gods offered the true way of salvation (*PE* 4. 7). Arnobius sums up the pagan view: they will never be happy that Christ's identity can be proved on the basis of written testimony.[274]

---

[263] See Evangeliou (1989), 56.

[264] See e.g. Wilken (1984), 147; W. H. C. Frend, *The Rise of Christianity* (Philadelphia, 1984), 440–4; id. (1987), 14–17.

[265] On the fine style of literature offered by paganism see *PE* 4. 1, 4. 7; on the attack upon the illiterate apostles see *DE* 3. 5, 3. 7; and Arnob. *Adv. nat.* 1. 50, 2. 72; cf. 1. 58, revealing parallels with Eusebius.

[266] *De cons. evang.* 1. 20. 28.

[267] Jerome, *Ep.* 57. 9.

[268] *DE* 3. 6; *Adv. nat.* 1. 54; 1. 55.

[269] See *CC* frag. no. 55 in Harnack (1916).

[270] See Wilken (1984), 137–43.

[271] Chadwick (1985), 125, notes: 'Porphyry allowed that the divine powers responsible for oracles and divination are of a lowly and earthly level or milieu (Philoponus, *De opif. mundi* iv, 20).'

[272] *Civ. Dei* 10. 32: All three reasons are found in this passage.

[273] See ibid. Augustine appears to have Porphyry's criticism in mind when he says that he can prove the truth of prophecy by (1) noting the text from scripture; (2) reciting the predictions; and (3) demonstrating that the event historically occurred.

[274] *Adv. nat.* 1. 56.

Third, the disciples were deceived persons whose teachings differed greatly from those of their master. They did not teach the same doctrines as he. Exaggerations based upon a few miracles caused the disciples to proclaim Christ to be a divine person.[275] His followers fabricated stories of his deity and resurrection,[276] and performed miracles[277] and predicted the future by means of magic.[278] Though their master might have been wise,[279] the disciples were contaminated by the error of worshipping a man,[280] and are hated by the gods.[281] They are doomed for disaster.[282] Even though Christ did not teach the abandonment of traditional pagan piety, his disciples nevertheless deviated from his doctrine.[283] The pagans tried to discredit Christianity by driving a wedge between Christ and his followers: truth could not be found in this religion due to the numerous contradictions existing between Christ and his disciples. The Christians retorted not only by affirming the unity of the Christian tradition,[284] but also by demonstrating how (e.g.) Porphyry himself had been a 'Platonist departing from Plato'.[285]

A fourth accusation was that Christian 'faith' was not rational. This religion should be rejected, so they argued, because it cannot provide certain proof of its doctrines.[286] It would be easier to fly than to recall a Christian woman to her senses: 'Let her go as she pleases, persisting in her vain delusions, singing in lamentation for a god who died in delusion, who was condemned by right-thinking judges, and killed in

---

[275] *Cont. Hier.* 1–2.

[276] Cf. *De cons. evang.* 1. 31. 48.

[277] Jerome, *Tract. de Psalmo* 81 (Harnack *CC* frag. no. 4).

[278] *Civ. Dei* 22. 25.

[279] Wilken (1984), 148, says that in *Phil. or.* Porphyry 'sought to make a place within this scheme for the new religion founded by Jesus of Nazareth'. The 'scheme' = the traditional Graeco-Roman religions. Cf. Barnes (1981), 175: 'Porphyry saw no difficulty in integrating Jesus into this scheme.' Yet the fine points of Porphyry's Hecatean Oracle in *Civ. Dei* 19. 23 do not support this interpretation, on which see Ch. 8 below. Arnobius, Eusebius, and Augustine saw through this smoke screen. Cf. *De cons. evang.* 1. 31. 47, where Augustine calls the Porphyrian oracle-mongers those 'evil applauders of Christ'. The incorporation of Jesus into his 'scheme' was far from Porphyry's overall purpose in his anti-Christian propaganda.

[280] *Civ. Dei* 19. 23.

[281] Ibid.

[282] Ibid.

[283] *De cons. evang.* 1. 31. 47; cf. 1. 15. 24.

[284] Cf. *Adv. nat.* 1. 50; Eus. *DE* 3. 4–8; Aug. *De cons. evang.* 1. 32. 50; the main point in all of these being that the disciples taught exactly what Christ had taught; cf. also *De cons. evang.* 1. 15. 24; 1. 26. 40; Eus. *Cont. Hier.* 4.

[285] *Civ. Dei* 10. 30; cf. also 13. 19; 22. 27.

[286] Eus. *PE* 1. 2 (Harnack *CC* frag. no. 1).

hideous fashion by the worst of deaths, a death bound with iron.'[287] This came from the pen of the erudite Syrian. He also argued that the Apostles did not have faith because they were unable to remove mountains.[288] More incredible than the notion of an 'almighty God' was the teaching, quite ludicrous to educated pagans, that all things are possible to the 'believer'.[289] Hierocles also made a point to condemn the Christians for their 'excessive credulity'.[290] On the other hand, evidence derived from educated men like Damis and Philostratus prove that the claims found in the *Lover of Truth* about Apollonius are truthful.[291] The 'easy credulity' of the Christians is contrasted with the accurate judgement of Hierocles' sources.[292] Christians are therefore 'foolish and deluded mortals'.[293] Yet particularly in the case of Porphyrian soteriology, the Christians found a weak link in this chain. For man's need of divine aid in the salvific process is much more pro-nounced in Porphyry's soteriology than that of his master Plotinus.[294] It would come as no surprise therefore that the Christians responded by saying: (1) Greek philosophy is the product of human conjectures;[295] (2) the pagan argument based on miracles cannot be proved;[296] (3) the authors of scripture have offered proof based upon reliable witnesses;[297] and (4) an objective examination of pagan religious literature will clearly demonstrate it is based upon falsehoods.[298]

In light of this it is noteworthy that Arnobius frequently throughout the *Adv. nat.* refutes this pagan accusation;[299] and *Adv. nat.* 2. 8–9 and *PE* 1. 5 contain so many parallels that there is little doubt Porphyry is their common enemy.[300]

---

[287] *Civ. Dei* 19. 23.

[288] Jerome, *Comm. in Matt.* 21. 21 (Harnack *CC* frag. no. 3).

[289] Did. the Blind's *Comm. in Iob.*, on Job 10: 13; see D. Hagedorn and R. Merkelbach, 'Ein neues Fragment aus Porphyrios "Gegen die Christian" ', *VC* 20 (1966), 86–90.

[290] *Cont. Hier.* 19.

[291] Ibid. 16. In 39 Eusebius says they contradict themselves and are liars who are devoid of education, and charletans.

[292] *Cont. Hier.* 4.

[293] Ibid. 4.

[294] Admirably brought out in the fine work on Porphyry by A. Smith (1974), 104. In *Ad Marc.* he continues to speak of what God gives to man = δῶρον θεοῦ, interpreted by Augustine as 'grace' in *Civ. Dei* 10. 29.

[295] Eus. *PE* 14. 9. Cf. Porphyry's attack in *PE* 1. 2.

[296] Eus. *Cont. Hier.* 26. The miracles of Apollonius need not be refuted since they demonstrate Hierocles' 'easy credulity'.

[297] *De cons. evang.* 1. 1. 1; *DE* 4. 15.

[298] Cf. *Cont. Hier.* 4.

[299] So many indeed that it warranted a separate enumeration (see Appendix IV).

[300] It is known that Eusebius is responding to Porphyry's vituperation of the Christians' 'faith'; Arnobius is responding to the same attack. Examples of the pagans' need for faith

Before proceeding to §III, we may offer the following conclusions. First, it seems highly possible that the pagan oracles, viewed as a significant source of divine authority and revelation of the truth, were used to justify the persecution of the Christians. Second, there was an attempt on both sides of the pagan–Christian debate to offer clear proof of their respective positions and disprove the beliefs of their opponents. Third, taken as a whole the anti-Christian propaganda of the late third century provided for the pagans what will have been a sound intellectual justification for a renewed state persecution. Fourth, Hierocles certainly, and Porphyry most probably, were personally involved in influencing the imperial court to persecute. Finally, the Porphyrian corpus posed a double threat to the existence of the Christian religion by (1) attacking it exclusively from within its own tradition by the use of historical and literary criticism of scripture; and (2) offering a better way of salvation based on the authority of divine revelation (oracles) to all humanity which served the purpose of reinforcing traditional pagan piety. It was again the kind of apology for paganism that will have admirably served the official programme of Diocletian.

III. *The State: The Roman Empire's Persecution of the Christians under Diocletian* (AD 298–305)

In November 284 Diocletian, a military man of humble Dalmatian origins,[301] was chosen by the army 'on account of his wisdom' to be emperor of the Roman Empire.[302] After taking the purple he became puffed up, and began to pattern his court in the fashion of an oriental despot.[303] By 293 his organizational skills had transformed the government into a Tetrarchy led by two Augusti and two Caesars.[304] Throughout the 290s intermittent rebellions erupted in various parts of the

in Arnobius (*Adv. nat.* 2. 8) and Eusebius (*PE* 1. 5) include trips, voyages, sowing, marriage, raising children, physicians (cf. *Adv. nat.* 1. 65), wars, and (*Adv. nat.* 2. 9) doctrines accepted from teachers.

[301] See Lact. *Mort. pers.* 9; Aur. Vict. *Epitome* 39. 1; cf. Eutr. 9. 22; Williams (1985), 15–23; W. Seston, *Dioclétien et la Tetrarchie* (Paris, 1946), 1. 38–40; Barnes (1981), 4 f.

[302] Aur. Vict. *Caes.* 39. 1: 'ob sapientiam deligitur'.

[303] Cf. Theophanes, *Chron.* 5793. 1–15; Aur. Vict. *Caes.* 39. 1; see also A. H. M. Jones, *The Later Roman Empire 284–602* (Oxford, 1964), 3 vols., 1. 40. In many ways still the best work in English on the Age of Diocletian.

[304] Oros. *Adv. pag.* 7. 25. 4; Eutr. 9. 22. 1; Jerome, *Chron.* s.a. 289–90; Aur. Vict. *Caes.* 39. 18–24.

empire, causing the members of the newly formed imperial college to
remove these threats to their security.[305] A 'New Imperial Theology',
clearly revealing anti-Christian sentiments (see Ch. 2 below), designated
Diocletian as 'Jovius', son of Jupiter, and the other Augustus Maximian
as 'Herculius', son of Hercules. One scholar has concluded that at no
other time in their respective histories did the Church and the religious
programme of the Empire look so much alike.[306] For at least fourteen
years Diocletian had tolerated Christianity, the rulers being, according
to a contemporary, friendly and peaceable toward the Church. But he
continues to say that 'suddenly they changed their peaceable attitude
toward us, and began an implacable war'.[307] Was it all a matter of storm
clouds suddenly gathering on a clear day?

Not quite, if we consider the fact that Christianity had been growing
numerically, expanding geographically, and causing religious conflict
and competition with paganism since the peace of Gallienus (260).[308]
The social status of Christians had also immensely improved.[309] Pagans
of noble birth, honourable social and political positions, and great
erudition were beginning to join the ranks of the faithful.[310] Rulers even
showed favour to Christians,[311] who sometimes were found governing a
province and exempt from sacrificing to the gods before the transaction
of imperial business.[312] A late third-century eye-witness attests the rapid
growth of the Church in the provinces.[313] Contrast this vivacious picture

---

[305] Diocletian led such campaigns as those against the Allemanni (288); the Sarmatians (289); the Saracens (290); the Carpi (296); and the revolts in Egypt (297–8). See T. D. Barnes, 'Imperial Campaigns, A.D. 295–311', *Phnx* 30 (1976), 174–93; and id., *The New Empire of Diocletian and Constantine* (Cambridge, Mass.), 49–56.
[306] Liebeschuetz (1979), 243: 'The pagan state religion and Christianity were never closer in theology than at the time of the Great Persecution.'
[307] Eus. *HE* 8. 13. 9. For the date of the *HE* see now A. Louth, 'The Date of Eusebius' *Historia Ecclesiastica*', *JTS* NS 41. 1 (1990), 111–23; see also Jones (1964), 1. 71; and W. H. C. Frend, 'The Failure of the Persecutions in the Roman Empire', *SAS* 263–87.
[308] See the excellent article by Frend, *JEH* 38 (1987), 1–18. Frend is one of the few English-speaking scholars who have recognized the importance of Arnobius for the intellectual background to the Great Persecution; for example see also id. (1984), 443, 450 f.; for a different view see Fox (1987), 588, who does not believe the Church was 'a great and growing presence' during this period. He has a tendency to depreciate the witness of Lactantius and Eusebius, and he totally ignores Arnobius.
[309] For the background see the various works by Frend and Barnes listed throughout this chapter and those found in the bibliography.
[310] Eus. *HE* 8. 9. 6–7.
[311] Ibid. 1. 1–5.
[312] Ibid.
[313] *Adv. nat.* 1. 55; cf. 2. 5.

with the sombre neglect of the rites of the gods[314] and it is clear that religious paganism was in decline by the beginning of the fourth century.[315]

The upper classes were abandoning ship as well. Theodotus, the bishop of Laodicea, and Zenobius, a presbyter at Sidon, were both Christian physicians.[316] Prominent Christian philosophers were amongst the 'ablest men' of the period.[317] Peter the bishop of Alexandria was a great teacher.[318] Anatolius of the same city was a man renowned for his great erudition, being skilled in Greek philosophy, mathematics, geometry, astronomy, physics, and rhetoric.[319] Pierius the presbyter and Meletius were also known for their learning.[320] Christians even served in the sacred bodyguard of the emperors.[321] We also hear of first-generation Christians coming from wealthy pagan families.[322]

Alphaeus, a reader and an exorcist in the church of Caesarea, came from such a noble family.[323] Two sisters martyred in Antioch were also from an illustrious social background.[324] And all kinds of intellectuals were being converted: men endowed with great ability, orators, grammarians, rhetors, lawyers, physicians, and philosophers.[325] The very learned bishop of Lower Egypt, Phileas;[326] Lactantius, who was summoned to teach at Diocletian's court;[327] and Arnobius are other examples. Finally, there were Christians in governmental positions. Dorotheus, a presbyter of the church in Antioch, was placed by Diocletian over the purple dye-works at Tyre.[328] Adauctus, an Italian nobleman, advanced to the position of finance minister.[329] Philoromus held a high position

---

[314] *Adv. nat.* 1. 24; 2. 2.
[315] Cf. Fox (1987), 585: 'In the later third century, therefore, the ceremonies of the pagan gods were undergoing a relative lull.'
[316] Cf. Eus. *HE* 7. 32. 23; 8. 13. 4.
[317] Ibid. 7. 32. 6 f.
[318] Ibid. 8. 13. 7.
[319] Ibid. 7. 32. 6 f.
[320] Ibid. 7. 32. 26 f.
[321] Musurillo, *ACM* no. 17, *Acta Maximiliani*, 244–9: The proconsul Dion at Tebessa declares, 'In the sacred bodyguard of our lords Diocletian and Maximian . . . there are soldiers who are Christians, and they serve.'
[322] e.g., Eus. *Mart. Pal.* 4. 2 f., proving that Apphianus did not come from a Christian background; cf. id. *HE* 8. 12. 3; Arnob. *Adv. nat.* 1. 16.
[323] Eus. *Mart. Pal.* 1. 5.
[324] Eus. *HE* 8. 12. 5.
[325] Arnobius, *Adv. nat.* 2. 5.
[326] Jerome, *De vir. ill.* 78; Eus. *HE* 8. 9. 7.
[327] *PLRE* 1. 338; Jerome, *Chron.* s.a. 318; *De vir. ill.* 80; see also Frend, *SAS* 275 ff.
[328] Eus. *HE* 8. 32. 2.
[329] *PLRE* 1. 12 f.; *HE* 8. 11. 2.

in the imperial government at Alexandria.[330] Many Christians served in
the royal household.[331] Prisca and Valeria, the wife and daughter of
Diocletian, might even themselves have been Christians (*HE* 8. 1; *De
mort. Pers.* 15). We may add that the entire government of a city in
Phrygia was in the control of Christians.[332] When the opportunity availed
itself, the combined forces of the pagan intellectuals and the imperial
government were alerted to strike against a strong and growing Church
increasingly seen as a threat to the traditional piety that was thought to
have made Rome a great and enduring world power.

But why then did Diocletian wait so long before persecuting the
Christians? Various answers have been given.[333] Meticulous attention to
organizational details driven by a perfectionist personality may indicate
a possible answer. This assumes that Diocletian did not act on impulse;
but, indeed, everything we know about his character suggests a pre-
meditating mind which systematically planned the details of every
programme of government. Possessing a mind that acutely believed in
thoroughness, he masterminded in the late 290s 'the most thorough
overhaul of the tax system ever undertaken' in the Empire.[334] Ancient
sources praised his administrative *foresight* which caused the methodical
execution of premeditated plans.[335] One example is the well-planned
fortification of frontier defences like those at Circesium.[336] We are told
that he was possessed of such a perfectionist mentality that he would
order the destruction of recently built buildings and have them immediately rebuilt.[337] During the imperial campaign in Egypt in 298 we find
him concerned about the details of transporting columns from the

[330] *HE* 8. 9. 7; cf. *PLRE* 1. 698.
[331] *HE* 8. 1. 4 and 6. 5.
[332] Ibid. 8. 11. 1.
[333] e.g., Williams (1985), 174; P. S. Davies, 'The Origin and Purpose of the Persecution
of A.D. 303', *JTS* 40 (1989), 66–94; Frend (repr. 1981), 477, says we may never know
why Diocletian promulgated the Edict of 303.
[334] See Williams (1985), 105.
[335] Zos. *Hist. nova* 2. 34; Amm. 23. 5. 2; cf. Procopius, *De bello Persico*, 2. 5. 2 f.;
Diocletian was always making 'deep plans' according to *SHA*, Carus, 12. 1–2.
[336] Amm. 23. 5. 2; Cf. also Israel Roll, 'A Latin Inscription From the Time of Diocletian
Found at Yotvata', *IEJ* 39 (1989), 239–260, esp. 253 f., and 254, fig. no. 2, showing the
Diocletianic *limes* (military system of fortifications) along the eastern frontier of the
Empire. For a good analysis of the Diocletianic fortifications in the East see F. Millar,
The Roman Near East 31 BC–AD 337 (Cambridge, Mass., 1993), 180–9.
[337] Lact. *Mort. pers.* 7. 8–10; see Roll (1989), 245–9; G. Waldherr, *Kaiserliche Baupolitik
in Nordafrika* (Frankfurt, 1989); and a wealth of primary source material found in M. H.
Dodgeon and Samuel N. C. Lieu (eds.), *The Roman Eastern Frontier and the Persian Wars
A.D. 226–363* (London, 1991).

quarries at Assuan to Alexandria.[338] As the revolt in Alexandria shows, he could be quite stubbornly dedicated to executing a well-planned siege.[339] And long-range planning is evidenced in the vast reduction of the provinces,[340] the reorganization of the imperial bureaucracy, and the military.[341] A recent description is worth quoting:

Masterful, able, ambitious, of course. But a naturally shrewd, calculating nature, keeping his own counsel, trying to see more moves ahead than others. A man who would accomplish the most difficult tasks through tireless attention to planning, seeking always to compute all the contingencies and build up sufficient resources before launching into action: the kind of commander who would not forgive sloppy staff work, even if an operation was successful.[342]

There is every indication, based upon a composite portrait of the ancient sources, that he was cautious, methodical, and very thorough in his preparations for any programme he was about to undertake. And everything we know of his religious policies points to a strong anti-Christian sentiment. There is good reason to suggest, therefore, that such a mind had been thinking about what to do with the Christian problem *once and for all* after the governmental and military matters had been securely put in order.

Another factor to consider is Diocletian's superstitious nature.[343] From what is known about him according to more reliable sources, there might be a modicum of truth behind the statement in the *Historia Augusta*, that Diocletian received 'many omens of future rule' before coming to the purple.[344] A Druidess prophesied that one day he would be the emperor.[345] The truth behind all of this might be that Diocletian constantly consulted the oracles even before he became emperor, and

---

[338] *P. Beatty Pan.* II. 43–50; and Lact. *Mort. pers.* 7. 30.

[339] See Seston (1946), 1. 137–83; Eutr. 9. 24; Oros. *Adv. pag.* 7. 25.

[340] *Mort. pers.* 7. 4; see also Roll (1989), 249 ff.

[341] *Mort. pers.* 7. 1–2; Roll (1989), 252–60, esp. 260, referring to the 'unprecedented military build-up during the Tetrarchy'; see fig. no. 2, 254. See also Millar (1993), 189.

[342] Williams (1985), 26; see also P. S. Davies, *JTS* 40 (1989), 92 ff.

[343] In general see R. M. Grant, 'Eusebius and Imperial Propaganda', in Attridge and Hata (Detroit, 1992), 658–83; and G. Haertel, 'Die Religionspolitik der Römischen Kaiser von Diokletian bis Justinian', *ACUSD* 22 (1986), 69–86; and T. D. Barnes, 'The Constantinian Settlement', in Attridge and Hata (1992), 635–57.

[344] *SHA*, Carus, 12. 1.

[345] Ibid. 14. 2–3; For the *SHA* and Diocletian see I. M. Ferrero, 'La figura de Diocleciano en la *Historia Augusta*', *SHHA* 2–3 (1984–5), 225–37; See also S. Xeres, 'La riabilitazione di Valeriano e la politica anticristiana nell'epoca diocleziana', *RIL* 118 (1984), 69–76. On Diocletian and the cult at Didyma see A. Rehm, 'Kaiser Diokletian und das Heiligtum von Didyma', *Philol* 93 (1938), 74–84.

the tradition has been reinterpreted with pro-imperial features.[346] He was obviously *always* religiously superstitious, and after he became emperor two facts are quite clear: he continued to be devoted to the oracles of the gods, and he firmly believed in the traditional religion of the Roman Empire.[347] A good example of these very superstitious proclivities can be found in the two letters dated 23 September 298, from the Strategus of the Panopolite nome in Egypt to a certain Theodotus and a Miccalus who had been appointed 'overseers of animals' responsible for the meticulous planning of sacrificial sites situated along the imperial itinerary.[348] Evidently his reputation as 'a searcher into futurity'[349] was widely known throughout the provinces.

Diocletian's religious views were very traditional and therefore highly supportive of the conservative piety (*mos maiorum*) of the Roman cults which were thought to have caused the initial success and subsequent continuation of the Empire. Any religious system that did not acknowledge the gods of the Roman order was seen as a serious threat to the welfare of the newly created Tetrarchy. We may give examples of this religious conservatism. The preface to the Edict Against the Manichees, dated 31 March 302[350] and addressed to Julianus the Proconsul of Africa, clearly illustrates three important concerns for the present study. First, it reveals Diocletian's unremitting commitment to the traditional religious paganism of the Roman Empire. Second, his philosophy concerning any religion viewed as a threat to the order established by the gods is concisely delineated. Finally, the contents may indeed give the reader an example of the kind of language found the following year in the Edict Against the Christians. Expressing ideas reminiscent of the imperial conservative attitude towards Roman morality and religion found in the earlier Edict Against Incest (*c*.295), and after mentioning the 'scandalous kinds of superstitious doctrine' of the Manichees, the emperor continues:[351]

But the immortal gods, in their providence, have thought fit to ordain that the

---

[346] See *Mort. pers.* 10 for Diocletian's superstitious practices.

[347] Zos. 2. 7, 10; *Mort. pers.* 10. 1.

[348] *P. Beatty Pan.* I. 14, 380–4. Note well Skeat's remark, p. 128: 'The evidence of the present papyrus leaves no room for doubt that, as here, they were intended to provide victims for sacrifices.' There is only one other mention of these 'overseers of animals' in the papyri (Skeat, 128), and that is *P. Oxy.* 1626.

[349] Cf. *Mort. pers.* 10. 1.

[350] On this see Barnes, *HSCP* 80 (1976), 247; and id., (1981), 20.

[351] On the subject of Manichaeism and the Tetrarchy see Seston (1946), 156 ff.; for the cult in N. Africa see F. Decret, *L'Afrique Manichéenne. (IV*ᵉ*–V*ᵉ *Siècles)* (Paris, 1978).

principles of virtue and truth should, by the counsel and deliberations of many good, great and wise men, be approved and established in their integrity. These principles it is not right to oppose or resist, nor ought the ancient religion to be subjected to the censure of a new creed. It is indeed highly criminal to discuss doctrines once and for all settled and defined by our forefathers, and which have their recognized place and course in our system.[352]

Condemning primarily the opposition of the Manichees to the established Roman creeds, and their new and unheard-of sects,[353] Diocletian ordered that the leaders of the cult, along with unrepentant followers and their scriptures, be burnt, and their goods be forfeited to the imperial treasury. The law also ordered the loss of offices or social status where applicable, the estates owned by any Manichee to be confiscated, and their owners to be sent to the mines at Phaeno or Proconnesus.[354] Anullinus the Proconsul of Africa Proconsularis, on 5 December 304, expresses an identical attitude toward the young Christian Crispina, on trial during the Great Persecution: 'Revere the religion of Rome,' he says, 'which is observed by our lords and unconquerable Caesars as well as ourselves.'[355] According to the governor all that is required of the Christians is that they go to the temples and give their humble and reverent acknowledgement of the gods of Rome.[356] Crispina, obstinate in her refusal to sacrifice to the gods, was immediately escorted from the tribunal and decapitated. As many have already suggested, there is every indication that religious concerns were strong motivations for the State persecution of the Christians during the age of Diocletian.[357]

The military also had a significant role to play. A contemporary text of the period abounds with passages which reveal a constantly delicate

---

[352] See Williams (1985), 128–31; see also Appendix to T. Frank, *An Economic Survey of Ancient Rome* (Baltimore, 1933–40), 6 vols.; the text is found in *FIRA* 3; cf. also E. Sironen, 'The Edict of Diocletian and a Theodosian Regulation at Corinth (Plate 52)', *Hesp* 61 (1992), 223–6; Diocletian's taste for traditional Roman paganism is obvious in the ornamentation of his temple at Split, on which see J. J. Wilkes, *Diocletian's Palace, Split* (Sheffield, 1986), 45–8.

[353] *Collatio mosaicarum* 15. 4, *FIRA* 3.

[354] Ibid. 6–7.

[355] Musurillo, *ACM* no. 24. 304 f.: 'Cole religionem Romanam, quam et domini nostri invictissimi Caesares et nos ipsi observamus.'

[356] Ibid. 305. For Diocletian's support of traditional Roman paganism see K. Stade, *Der Politiker Diocletian und die letzte große Christenverfolgung* (Diss. Frankfurt, 1936), 10 f.

[357] Cf. e.g. Jones (1964), 1. 73; J. L. Creed, *Lactantius De Mortibus Persecutorum* (Oxford, 1984), OECT, xxii; G. E. M. de Ste Croix, 'Why Were the Early Christians Persecuted', *SAS* 243; Fox (1987), 592; Williams (1985), 174; and M. J. Hollerich, *HTR* (1989), 443.

situation in the armies of the Tetrarchy.[358] Ancient sources also agree that the persecution began with the military.[359] One scholar has gone so far as to conclude that the Great Persecution was not born out of the Empire's fear of the Christians, but rather because of its recent military success, particularly over the Persians.[360] Diocletian therefore began the campaign against the Christians from a position of strength, not of weakness. This interpretation coheres with our observation noted above (pp. 35–36) that the senior Augustus was a meticulous and methodical planner of everything he did. Be that as it may, it is known that trouble started brewing in the army in North Africa.[361] For it was in March 295 that Maximilian refused to be recruited in the Legio III Augusta by the Proconsul Dion at Tébessa in Numidia.[362] After being informed that there were Christians in the imperial bodyguard of Diocletian, the young man persisted in his obstinacy and was later executed.[363]

Of greater significance perhaps is the martyrdom of the centurion Marcellus, who served in the Legio II Traiana, in October 298 in Mauretania Tingitana. During a celebration of the emperors' birthdays (July 298) he threw down his military belt in front of the legionary standards, and was taken before the prefect Fortunatus. Before sending him to Agricolanus at Tingis, the latter questioned Marcellus as to the reasons for which he violated military discipline. He responded that he had declared publicly he was a Christian and could not therefore serve

---

[358] Lact. *Mort. pers.* 7 (unprecedented military build-up); 10 (purge of armies); 17 (fear of a military takeover); 18 (Galerius augments his army); 24 (possible military uprising); 25 (fear of Constantine's forces); 26 (Maxentius' military support); 27 (conflicts); 28 (the emperor gets aid); 29 (donations to soldiers); 32 (Daia selected by the army); cf. also 36, 37, 43, 44. Roll (1989), 241 ff., who shows that the desire to have a perpetual peace is a theme frequently found expressed on the military inscriptions during the Age of Diocletian. See Millar (1993), 180–9.

[359] Eus. *HE* 8. 1. 7 f.; 8. 4. 2 ff.; Lact. *Div. inst.* 4. 27. 4 f.; *Mort. pers.* 10. 1–5; Jerome, *Chron.* s.a. 301.

[360] Fox (1987), 592 ff.; note his remark at 594: 'Victory gave a new force to the ideals of Roman discipline and Roman god-given glory.' Cf. Liebeschuetz (1979), 249.

[361] See Seston (1946), 1. 116–20; M. A. Tilley, 'Scripture as an Element of Social Control: two Martyr Stories of Christian North Africa', *HTR* 83 (1990), 383–97; Frend (1981, repr.), 487 ff.; A. R. Birley, 'A Persecuting Praeses of Numidia under Valerian', *JTS* NS 42, pt. 2 (1991), 598–610. Diocletian's organizational skills have been questioned by Ingemar Koenig, 'Lactanz und das System der Tetrarchie', *Lab* 32 (1986), 180–93.

[362] Musurillo, *ACM* no. 17, *Acta Maximiliani*, 244–9.

[363] Ibid. 246 f.: 'In sacro comitatu dominorum nostrorum Diocletiani et Maximiani … milites Christiani sunt et militant.' For the military Martyr Tipasius see Seston (1946), 1. 122 f.; and D. Woods, 'Two Notes on the Great Persecution', *JTS* NS 43, pt. 1 (1992), 131.

under the military oath, 'but only for Christ Jesus, the Son of God'.[364]
Fortunatus promised to report this at once to the emperors, specifically
mentioning Diocletian and Maximian by name.[365] (We recall that Diocletian was not very far away on campaign in Egypt at this time.)
Unaffected by these threats, Marcellus stubbornly stood by his convictions, and was later that year tried and executed by Agricolanus. And
we must emphasize that though this is an example of an army officer
tried for breaking military law, and not therefore an incidence of an
official State persecution of the Christians,[366] neither can we simply call
it an isolated event[367] that had no bearing upon Diocletian's decision to
persecute. For we know that during the summer and autumn of 298
the emperor was restoring peace to restive areas of Egypt,[368] and
Fortunatus' report despatched to him at this time might have strongly
influenced his decision, made shortly thereafter, to start persecuting the
Christians in the army.[369]

This brings us now to 299.[370] Galerius, the eastern Caesar, had
returned from his Persian victory of 298, and he and the senior Augustus
were in Antioch in 299. Christians present at the sacrifices attended by
Diocletian and his entourage sometime during this period made the sign
of the Cross, and the omens were interrupted.[371] The story continues
that after many attempts to procure the desired marks on the livers of
the animals, Tagis the Chief Soothsayer attributed the failure to 'profane
persons here, who obstruct the rites'.[372] Concluding that this referred
to the Christians, Diocletian then ordered that all soldiers must sacrifice

---

[364] *Acta Maximiliani* 250 f.; according to M. P. Speidel and M. F. Pavkovic, 'Legio II
Flavia Constantia at Luxor', *AJPh* 110 (1989), 152, military dedications of the Diocletianic
period follow 'a pattern in which army units pronounce themselves lucky so long as the
Emperors are safe'. See Millar (1993), 187 ff.

[365] *Acta Maximiliani* 250 f.: 'et ideo referam hoc imperatoribus et Caesari.'

[366] Cf. Baynes, *CAH* 12, 663.

[367] As Seston (1946), 1. 122 says.

[368] See T. D. Barnes (1981), 17 f.

[369] For the background see Williams (1985), 173–85; Frend (1981, repr.), 477–505; cf.
also Woods, *JTS* 43 (1992), 130 f.

[370] Scholarly opinion varies as to the date for the persecution of Christians in the
military: 297 according to Woods, *JTS* (1992), 129 (cf. *PLRE* 1. 955); 298: Jones (1964),
1. 71: 298/9: Williams (1985), 171; 299: Barnes (1981), 18 f., Creed (1984), Fox (1987),
594, and P. S. Davies, *JTS* (1989), 91–3; 301: Frend (1981, repr.), 489; 298–301: Baynes,
CAH 12. 664.

[371] *Mort. pers.* 10; referred to apparently by Arnobius, *Adv. nat.* 1. 46: 'haruspices
inconsultos reddit'; cf. J. Moreau, *Lactance De la Mort des Persécuteurs* (Paris, 1954), 2
vols., SC 39, 2. 264; for the place and chronology see now Barnes, *Phnx* 30 (1976), 174–
93, 186 f.; cf. P. S. Davies, *JTS* 40 (1989), 90 f.

[372] *Mort. pers.* 10. For the practice of divination see Cicero, *De div.* 1. 1; 2. 3; 16. 28.

to the gods or be discharged from the army.[373] The military commander
Veturius carried out the imperial order.[374] But at this juncture the official
persecution was still restricted to Christians in the army.

During the winter of 302 Diocletian and Galerius held council
together.[375] Advisers of all sorts, including civil magistrates and army
commanders, were called in for their advice concerning whether there
should be launched a State persecution of the Christians.[376] We recall
that Porphyry (probably) and Hierocles, 'the author and adviser of the
persecution', were at this conference.[377] If indeed Porphyry was at the
meeting, he might have used his knowledge of the oracles to convince
Diocletian that the blessings of the gods had now vanished from the
world since Jesus began to be worshipped.[378] In any event, Diocletian
decided to consult the oracle of Apollo at Didyma which gave an hostile
condemnation of the Christians and justified Diocletian's decision to
begin the persecution.[379] For Apollo had proclaimed that the 'just upon
the earth' had prevented the conveyance of the oracle.[380] 'Apollo' that
year might very well have been a priest-philosopher who had been
reading Porphyry.[381]

Before completing our survey in this section, we must investigate the

---

[373] Eus. *HE* 8. 4. 2–5; *Mort. pers.* 10. 2–4; *Div. inst.* 4. 27. 4 f., alluding to the presence
of Diocletian and Galerius. For the use of the sign of the Cross by Christians during this
general period see G. A. Lordkipanidze, N. S. Kiguradze, and T. T. Todua, 'An Early
Christian Stele From Picunda', *VDI* 194 (1990), 63–7.

[374] Jerome, *Chron.* s.a. 301: 'Veturius magister militiae Christianos milites persequitur,
paulatim ex illo iam tempore persecutione adversum nos incipiente.' Eusebius simply
gives his title but not his name in *HE* 8. 4. 3: ὁ στρατοπεδάρχης. For Veturius see *PLRE*
1. 955.

[375] *Mort. Pers.* 11.

[376] Ibid.; *Div. inst.* 5. 2. 13; cf. *Mort. pers.* 16. 4.

[377] See T. D. Barnes, *HSCP* 80 (1976), 246.

[378] *PE* 5. 1. 10; see Hollerich, *HTR* (1989), 443: 'Porphyry's explanation for religious
decline thus agreed with the imperial rationale for persecution.' Note Chadwick (1985),
126.

[379] Constantine in Eus. *VC* 2. 50; *Mort. pers.* 2. 7 f.; cf. Arnob. *Adv. nat.* 1. 26, which
appears to be another possible allusion.

[380] *VC* 2. 50. The oracle of Daphne might also have been consulted according to
Barnes, *HSCP* (1976), 252, referring to *Oratio ad coetum sanctorum*, *VC* 4. 32; on the
importance Diocletian placed upon the oracles see Zos. *Hist. nova* 2. 12; 2. 36 f.; Frend,
JEH (1987), 9; and in general an old but still interesting work by L. Robert, *Les fouilles
de Claros* (Limoges, 1954), 27 ff.

[381] Suggested by Fox (1987), 595. See Eus. *HE* book 9 for later emperors' dependence
upon the oracles in making imperial decisions. For Eusebius' 'political theology' see S.
Calderone, 'Il pensiero politico di Eusebio di Cesarea', in Bonamente and Nestori
(Macerata, 1988), 45–54; and in general see C. Tibiletti, 'Politica e religione nelle
persecuzioni cristiane', in ibid. 195–204.

question of who was the main instigator of the persecution, Diocletian or Galerius? Several scholars have argued for the 'Galerian Hypothesis',[382] maintaining that Galerius was the author of the persecution, and Diocletian was simply making decisions under his intimidating influence. It must be admitted, however, that this interpretation is based upon meagre evidence.[383] For example, a recent work states that after the Persian Campaign of 298, which was led by Galerius, supposedly 'Diocletian now feared him'[384] (Galerius). Yet taken as a whole the ancient sources overwhelmingly refute this explanation. For it was Diocletian who flew into a rage resulting in the purge of the army in 299.[385] Also, there is no convincing evidence to support the contention that Galerius *in any way* intimidated Diocletian either before or after the Persian victory.[386] Nor can we find any evidence which would suggest 'that Galerius was more "fanatical" than Diocletian, or that he had been the driving force behind the persecution'.[387] Not only is there no strong case for the theory that Galerius influenced an intimidated Diocletian to persecute the Christians, but also the ancient sources indicate that it was the Senior Augustus who was the driving force behind the decisions to move against them. On this interpretation which we have called the 'Galerian Hypothesis' Millar's judicious appraisal is certainly worthy of our serious consideration: 'This view was not shared by a witness of even better credentials, namely Constantine, who was now at Nicomedia, and whose later references attribute the blame to Diocletian.'[388] According to Constantine in *VC* 2. 50–1, it was Diocletian who enthusiastically persecuted the Christians and justified his actions on the response from Apollo's oracle.[389]

---

[382] See esp. Davies *JTS* 40 (1989), 66 n. 2, who gives a lengthy list, a good number of whom is found in the following: Baynes, *CAH* 12. 665; Frend, *JEH* (1987), 5; Williams (1985), 173; Barnes (1981), 19; id., in Attridge and Hata (1992), 639; G. E. M. de Ste Croix, 'Aspects of the "Great Persecution"', *HTR* 47 (1954), 109; id., *SAS* 243 n. 148; Creed (1984), p. xxii; and Grant, in Attridge and Hata (1992), 664.

[383] Lact. *Mort. pers.* 9. 5–10, on which testimony see Jones (1964), 1. 37: 'The work is a highly polemical tract, and Lactantius' judgements must be treated with reserve.' Jones (p. 71) does, however, accept the probability.

[384] Barnes (1981), 19.

[385] See P. S. Davies, *JTS* (1989), 84 f.; and the fine work by F. Kolb, *Diocletian und die Erste Tetrarchie* (Berlin, 1987; UALG Band 27), 134 f.

[386] Cf. Williams (1985), 173: 'It is preposterous to suppose that the Senior Augustus . . . should have been intimidated by him.'

[387] Davies, *JTS* (1989), 75; a good overview to the historical background is M. Pavan, 'Cristianesimo e impero romano nel IV secolo d. C.', in Bonamente and Nestori (1988), 1–16, who admittedly goes well beyond the period we are covering.

[388] Millar (1977), 574; cf. P. S. Davies, *JTS* (1989), 77.

[389] Observed by Davies, ibid.

After stating that he was an eyewitness of the events he describes, Constantine informs us that Diocletian 'without the slightest provocation' planned the destruction of a multitude of Christians.[390] He also saw Diocletian receive 'like some honeyed draught' the interpretation of Apollo's oracle about the 'righteous on the earth' referring to the Christians.[391] Galerius is not even mentioned. It was Diocletian who forced a humiliated Galerius to walk by his chariot after his army was defeated by the Persians (296).[392] After Galerius' victory over the Persians in the campaign of 298, there is still no strong evidence to support the view that the Senior Augustus was fearful of him.[393] Indeed, Aurelius Victor says that Diocletian, 'whose will ruled all' ('cuius nutu omnia gerebantur'), restrained Galerius from transforming his newly acquired territory into a province of the Empire.[394] The ancient sources relate other qualities of Diocletian like wisdom,[395] great courage,[396] and exceeding firmness with his subordinates;[397] but nothing about being intimidated by or fearful of *anyone*. Even years after his death his name was still evoking fear from the residents of Antioch.[398]

We now turn to the actual outbreak of the Great Persecution, dated 23 February 303 and corresponding to the pagan feast of the Terminalia.[399] The First Edict was universally promulgated and ordered the destruction of the Christian churches and the burning of the scriptures. Christians holding places of honour were to be degraded, and they lost their judicial rights. Those who were household servants were deprived of their freedom.[400] The church at Nicomedia, in view

---

[390] Constantine, *Or. ad coetum sanc.* 25. NB F. Kolb, 'L'ideologia tetrarchica e la politica religiosa di Diocleziano', in Bonamente and Nestori (1988), 17–44, esp. p. 31: 'L'imperatore Constantino considera Diocleziano stesso come autore della persecuzione.'

[391] Eus. *VC* 2. 51.

[392] Amm. 14. 11. 10; Festus, *Brev.* 25; Eutr. 9. 24–5. 1; Oros. *Adv. pag.* 7. 25. 9 ff.; Theophanes, *Chron. a.m.* 5793.

[393] Julian, *Or.* 1. 18 A–B; Festus, *Brev.* 25; Eutr. 9. 24–5. 1; Jerome, *Chron.* s.a. 302; Oros. *Adv. pag.* 7. 25. 9 ff.; Theophanes, *Chron. a.m.* 5793.

[394] Aur. Vic. *Caes.* 39. 36.

[395] Ibid. 39. 1.

[396] *Pan. Lat.* 9. 1–2; Syncellus in *CSHB* 724. 16–725. 5 (English text in Dodgeon and Lieu (1991), 119); Zonaras, 12. 30.

[397] *SHA*, Carus, 12. 1–2.

[398] Lib. *Or.* 19. 45.

[399] *Mort. pers.* 13; *HE* 8. 2. 4; *Mart. Pal. Praef.* 1. For a general description of Eusebius' position see A. Nestori, 'Eusebio e il luogo di culto cristiano', in Bonamente and Nestori (1988), 55–62.

[400] *HE* 8. 2. 4; *Mort. pers.* 13. 1, 15. 5; *Mart. Pal. Praef.* 1, 2. 1; *HE* 9. 10. 8; Optatus, App. 1 (Ziwsa, 186 ff.); see also Frend (1981, repr.), 490 ff.; Barnes (1981), 22 f.; and the very fine article by de Ste Croix, *HTR* 47 (1954), 75 f.

of the imperial palace, was destroyed and its valuables were confiscated.[401] Whether by human[402] or natural[403] causes, a fire broke out in the palace shortly after the edict was issued. Apostates appear to have been numerous, indicating that the persecuting officials took their responsibilities seriously.[404] We hear of Christians willingly flocking to pagan temples in Antioch to honour the gods.[405] The Patriarch of Alexandria fled to his secret headquarters outside the city to conduct his church's business there.[406] Christians were brought before Diocletian to be tortured, and he was known for his cruelty.[407] Not long after the First Edict, a second one ordered the imprisonment of all leaders. Shortly thereafter the Third Edict offered a general amnesty to all leaders in the prisons of the Empire on the condition that they first sacrifice to the gods.[408] Eusebius says that bishops, presbyters, deacons, readers, and exorcists filled the prisons throughout the provinces.[409] We may never know how many of these became apostates under pressure, thereby winning their freedom, and how many persevered either to martyrdom or the Edict of Toleration issued by Galerius in 311.[410] Finally, the Fourth Edict was issued in the spring of 304, ordering all the inhabitants of the Empire to sacrifice to the gods.[411] The trial of Crispina, a laywoman in North Africa, and her subsequent execution on 4 December 304, indicates that it was promulgated in the West,[412] for Anullinus the governor states during her trial that all Africa had sacrificed, so why should not she?[413]

Diocletian left Nicomedia after a second fire broke out in the palace.[414] He journeyed to Rome to celebrate the *vicennalia* of both Augusti

---

[401] *Mort. pers.* 12.

[402] Ibid. 14, says it was started by Galerius.

[403] Constantine in Eus. *Or. ad coetum sanc.* 25, says that lightning destroyed the palace and Diocletian's private chamber.

[404] *Mart. Pal.* 2. 1.

[405] Ibid.

[406] See generally J. Barnes and H. Chadwick, 'A Letter Ascribed to Peter of Alexandria', *JTS* NS 24 (1973), 443–55; and O. Nicholson, 'Flight from Persecution as Imitation of Christ: Lactantius' *Divine Institutes* IV, 18, 1–2', *JTS* NS 40. 1 (1989) 48–65.

[407] *HE* 8. 6.

[408] *HE* 8. 2. 5; *Mart. Pal. Praef.*

[409] *HE* 8. 6. 8. f.

[410] *HE* 8. 6. 10.

[411] *Mart. Pal.* 3. 1.

[412] Cf. Frend (1981, repr.), 502 f. See also Ch. 2 below, pp. 85–87.

[413] Musurillo, *ACM* no. 24, *Acta Crispinae*, 1. 2–3; cf. Millar (1977), 574 n. 49.

[414] *Mort. pers.* 14. 6.

(November 303).[415] On his return trip he contracted an illness that left him comatose by December 304.[416] Rumours about his death and burial spread through the capital.[417] By 1 March 305 he was hardly recognizable at his first public appearance since his illness.[418] According to Lactantius, Galerius forced the declining emperor to retire.[419] But the analysis of a recent study is worth quoting here: 'If Galerius did exert pressure, it was only to hasten the implementation of a step that had already been carefully planned.'[420] On 1 May 305 Diocletian finally abdicated. He assembled his imperial entourage outside Nicomedia, and the scene is described by Lactantius:

An assembly of the soldiers was called. Diocletian, with tears, harangued them, and said that he was become infirm, that he needed repose after his fatigues, and that he would resign the empire into hands more vigorous and able, and at the same time appoint new Caesars. . . . Diocletian took off his purple robe, put it on Daia, and resumed his own original name of Diocles. He descended from the tribunal, and passed through Nicomedia in a chariot; and then this old Emperor, like a veteran soldier freed from military service, was dismissed into his own country.[421]

He died after a lengthy illness at his palace at Split on the Adriatic coast c.312.[422]

We may offer the following conclusions. The military trials of Christians who refused to serve in the army which occurred during a critical period (the late 290s) of the Tetrarchy, probably had a significant influence upon Diocletian to begin the persecution with the military. If Fortunatus in 298, at the very time when Diocletian was pacifying Egypt, did report Marcellus' insubordination to the emperor—and there is not any reason for us to believe he did not—the news might have influenced him to begin the military purge the following year. Second, the superstitious nature of Diocletian and his strict adherence to the traditional piety of the Roman Empire should not be discounted in attempting to discover the motives for persecution. These are clearly revealed in the imperial edicts, the Tetrarchy's 'theology', and such data

[415] Ibid. 17. 1.
[416] Ibid. 2 ff.
[417] Ibid.
[418] Ibid.
[419] Ibid.
[420] Williams (1985), 190.
[421] *Mort. pers.* 19; cf. Eus. *HE* 8. 13. 11.
[422] Cf. *HE* 8, App. 3; Williams (1985), 200.

as the Panopolite sacrifices. Christianity posed a threat to the sacred traditions that made Rome a great empire, and which would also ensure the success of Diocletian's new order. Third, we should also not overlook the systematic administrative skills of the emperor which were driven by a perfectionist mind. His was the kind of personality that used foresight and caution, accompanied by an acute attention to detail, in every programme. He would normally wait until the opportune moment and, when all things were in proper order, methodically execute his plan. It is the view of the present writer that he had been planning what to do with the Christians after the political and military institutions of the Tetrarchy were organized and the recurrent rebellions/wars of the 290s were finished. Fourth, the anti-Christian propaganda written by such authors as Porphyry and Hierocles undoubtedly had a direct influence upon Diocletian's decision to go against the Christians. And in the case of at least one work, the *Phil. or.*, there might have been a closer association between the two than has hitherto been thought. We shall investigate this question, and others that we have posed in the three sections of this chapter, in the remaining chapters of this book. The final conclusion is that there is little doubt that Diocletian, not Galerius, was the chief instigator of the Great Persecution which began 23 February 303.

The general themes that we have surveyed in this chapter will be analysed in greater detail in the following chapters. Before turning to these technical studies, however, a final observation is necessary. How does Arnobius of Sicca fit into this picture that we have sketched? It is quite simple. We are not arguing that he should be promoted to centre-stage in the great Diocletianic drama about to unfold before the reader: we simply desire to give him his rightful part in it.

2

The Date of the *Adversus Nationes*

I. *External Evidence: Jerome, Oral Tradition(s), and Lactantius*

Beginning with Conrad Orelli's *Arnobii afri disputationum adversus gentes libri vii* in 1816 and continuing to the present, modern scholars have not reached a consensus concerning the date in which Arnobius of Sicca Veneria wrote his *Adversus nationes* in seven books. The suggested dates of the work have ranged from AD 295 to 320. Most historians and classicists who have studied the work in any detail are usually content with the general chronological designation of either before, during, or after the Diocletianic Persecution.

The external evidence outside the *Adv. nat.* is meagre. With the exception of the brief reference to the 'Opuscula Arnobii, apocrypha' found in the sixth-century *Decretum Gelasianum*,[1] the only ancient writer who provides information about Arnobius, from the time in which he lived to Trithemius (1462–1516),[2] is Jerome (AD 342–420).[3] In the *Chronicon*, the earliest[4] of the five writings in which Arnobius is named, Jerome gives a rather lengthy biographical sketch:

Arnobius in Africa rhetor clarus habetur, qui cum in civitate Siccae ad declamandum iuvenes erudiret, et adhuc ethnicus ad credulitatem somniis compelletur, neque ab episcopo impetraret fidem, quam semper impugnaverat: elucubravit adversus pristinam religionem luculentissimos libros, et tamen velut quibusdam obsidibus pietatis foedus impetravit.[5]

---

[1] The Latin text is found in *PL* 59. 157–64. For a critical edn. with comm. see E. von Döbschütz, *Das Decretum Gelasianum de libris recipiendis et non recipiendis* (Leipzig, 1912). The *Notitia librorum apocryphorum qui non recipiuntur* (Part V) lists the *Adv. nat.* as apocryphal. Cf. E. Schwartz, *ZNTW* 29 (1930), 161–8; and Yves-Marie Duval, 'Sur la biographie et les manuscrits d'Arnobe de Sicca', *Lat* 45 (1986), 69–99.

[2] Abbot of Sponheim, who mentions Arnobius in his *De scriptoribus ecclesiasticis* (Basel, 1494), 53.

[3] Six times: 4 passages are biographical (*De vir. ill.* 79, 80; *Chron.* s.a. 327; *Ep.* 70); 2 concern his writing style (*Epp.* 58 and 62).

[4] Written *c.*AD 380 according to J. N. D. Kelly, *Jerome* (London, 1975), 33.

[5] *PL* 27. 675 f.

Jerome places this information *ad annum* 327, the year of the *Vicennalia* of Constantine. He explicitly makes his reader aware that this section constitutes the beginning of his own chronological data, Eusebius having written everything up to this date.[6] However, in the *De vir. ill.*, written *c.*392–3,[7] in chapters 79 (Arnobius) and 80 (Lactantius), Arnobius is now placed in the reign of Diocletian (20 November 284[8]–1 May 305). In addition to this problem of conflicting dates is the fact that Lactantius never mentions Arnobius in any of his extant works, even though Jerome maintains that the former was a student of the latter.[9] In order to date Arnobius and his work with the help of Jerome, therefore, it is necessary to explain the conflicting dates found in the *Chronicon* and the *De vir. ill.*, and identify Jerome's sources.

Some scholars have attempted to explain the conflict of dates in the two works of Jerome as being due to mistaking the *Vicennalia* of Constantine for those of Diocletian.[10] Jerome simply intended to place Arnobius *ad annum* AD 303, under the *Vicennalia* of Diocletian, but because of an editorial error placed him under 327, the *Vicennalia* of Constantine. The argument would have much to commend it. First, in the introduction of the *Chronicon*[11] Jerome states that Eusebius had not included a sufficient amount of information about Roman personalities and events to suit his Latin readers. He therefore found it necessary to add this information and inserted it in the section of Eusebius' *Chronicle* covering the period between the fall of Troy and Constantine's *Vicennalia*.[12] He then notes that all information from Constantine to the sixth

---

[6] *Chron.* s.a. 327: 'Huc usque historiam scribit Eusebius Pamphili martyris contubernalis. Cui nos ista subiecimus.'

[7] Kelly (1975) 174.

[8] See Eutr. *Brev. con.* 20. 1. On the date of the proclamation see now T. D. Barnes, *The New Empire of Diocletian and Constantine* (London, 1982), 49: *P. Beatty Pan* 2. 162 confirms the date of Lact. *Mort. pers.* 17. 1. Jerome's other date occurs in *De vir. ill.* 79: 'Arnobius sub Diocletiano principe Siccae apud Africam florentissime rhetoricam docuit, scripsit adversus gentes, quae vulgo exstant, volumina.' Cf. also, ibid. 80: 'Firmianus, qui et Lactantius, Arnobii discipulus, sub Diocletiano principe . . .'.

[9] M. Perrin, *REAug* 30. 1–2 (1984), 36–41, argues that Lactantius may have read Arnobius owing to phrases common to both; cf. Barnes (1981), 291 n. 96: Lactantius probably completed the *Div. inst.* in Africa in 308/9.

[10] F. Oehler, *Arnobii oratoris Adversus Nationes Libri Septem* (Leipzig, 1846), 9 n. 2; Bryce–Campbell, ANF 6. 406.

[11] Not noted by Oehler or Bryce–Campbell. The text of the *Chronicon* is found in R. Helm, *Eusebius Werke* (Berlin, 1956; vol. 7, GCS 47), 4–10.

[12] Ibid. 6: 'A Troia usque ad vicesimum Constantini annum nunc addita, nunc admixta sunt plurima.'

consulship of Valentinian and Valens (AD 378), 'totum meum est'.[13] As McCracken observed, the date of Arnobius where it appears in the *Chronicon* (AD 327) seems impossible because there is no reference in the *Adv. nat.* to the Edict of Toleration of 30 April 311, issued by the eastern Augustus, Galerius.[14] For the time being, 311 may be taken as a *terminus ante quem* for the date of the *Adv. nat.*

Jerome's introduction to the *Chronicon* provides more evidence for the theory of editorial error. He admits that a secretary interpolated the additions to the text of Eusebius and wrote hurriedly as he dictated them.[15] The whole process was undoubtedly an onerous task: Eusebius' chronological tables were transcribed as faithfully as possible by alternating in red and black ink so that the 'regnorum tramites' could be separated from each other.[16] Mosshammer suggests that Jerome dictated the Latin version of the work hastily to his secretary, who had first transcribed the numerals of the chronological framework. He must have required the secretary to prepare for dictation of the text by first copying the columns of numbers converted from the Greek alphabet to Roman numerals. 'Thus the scribe had to preserve with great care the format and relative spacing of the original tables.'[17] A painful eye malady that Jerome was experiencing during this period and careless working habits are two other facts that might have created the conditions for the scribal error that perhaps placed Arnobius during the reign of Constantine rather than Diocletian.[18]

The year AD 327 might have signified something other than the date of the work. Some scholars argue that it is the date of Arnobius' death.[19] However, Jerome is usually careful about giving the date of an individual's death in the *Chronicon*, if he knows it, sometimes separate

---

[13] Ibid. 7.

[14] McCr 8.

[15] Helm (1956), 2: '. . . obsecro, ut, quidquid hoc tumultuarii operis est, amicorum, non iudicum animo relegatis, praesertim cum et notario, ut scitis, velocissime dictauerim . . .'.

[16] Ibid. 5 f.; cf. A. Mosshammer, *The Chronicle of Eusebius and the Greek Chronographic Tradition* (London, 1979), 37. For the separation of the 'regnorum tramites' in red and black ink see Helm (1956), 5.

[17] Mosshammer (1979), 52, 68.

[18] Already at Constantinople (*c*.AD 381), in *Ep.* 18 A. 16 (CSEL 54: Hilberg), Jerome complained that his painful eyes caused his inability to make corrections to dictated material; cf. *Ep.* 21. 42 (*c*.383–4): eye disease ('dolentibus oculis') required the dictation to a scribe of a letter to Pope Damasus. See also Kelly (1975) 79, 84, and 87: 'he always worked in a hurry and could be extremely careless.'

[19] McCr 243 n. 51, with refs.; cf. R. K. Poetzel, *NCE* 1. 843; M. Niccoli, EncItal (1929), 4. 551.

from the details listed in a previous section.[20] Such a proposed solution is too simple for a difficult problem.[21] The date of Arnobius' death, as in the case of his birth, will undoubtedly remain a mystery forever. Based upon information found in the introduction to the *Chronicon*, the scribal error theory regarding Arnobius' date would therefore seem to be highly probable.

The identification of the sources about Arnobius to which Jerome had access may provide a better solution to the problem of dating the *Adv. nat.* and a more plausible elucidation for the conflicting dates in Jerome. Since Arnobius is not mentioned in any of the works of Eusebius, the first historian of the Church cannot help to solve the problem.[22] It is also regrettable that Lactantius is absolutely silent about his former professor. However, in *De vir. ill.* 80 Jerome names several works and letters of Lactantius which are now lost. *The Banquet* was written when Lactantius was young.[23] This suggests an African context, and a reference in the work to his professor, who Jerome states taught the youth at Sicca Veneria, might have been a source for his chronicle. *The Itinerary* was written during Lactantius' trip from Africa to Nicomedia. A work entitled *Grammaticus* is also mentioned. The lost letters enumerated in the same passage were known to Pope Damasus, who lamented that they dealt mainly with profane subjects.[24]

Exactly when Lactantius made the trip from Africa to Nicomedia is not known. Some have suggested that he was already teaching Latin Literature in Bithynia by *c.*295.[25] It is not clear why and how he was selected to fill this position. One scholar suggests that Maximian's triumphal entry into Carthage during the spring of 298, after quelling the Quinquegentani, was celebrated by speeches in his honour. Perhaps Lactantius (along with Arnobius?) was one of the rhetors who gave a speech. Two facts indirectly support this theory: Eumenius' appointment as professor of Latin Literature, backed by the imperial government, at

---

[20] e.g., biographical information on Hilarius given s.a. 356 and 359; date of death given s.a. 367.

[21] As found in McCr 8; O. Bardenhewer, *Patrology* (Freiburg, 1908), 2. 518.

[22] T. D. Barnes, *Tertullian* (Oxford, 1971), 5: 'For the years before 300, the genuine evidence outside Eusebius was almost as exiguous then as it is now.'

[23] *De vir. ill.* 80: 'Habemus eius Symposium, quod adolescentulus scripsit.'

[24] Letter names in *De vir. ill.* 80 are: four books of epistles to Probus; two to Severus; and two to Demetrianus. On the uncertainty of the dates see J. Moreau, *De la mort des persecuteurs* (Paris, 1954; SC 39), 15.

[25] H. Kraft and A. Wlosok, *Lactantius De Ira Dei* (Darmstadt, 1957), p. x, give the departure date between 285 and 295; M. F. McDonald, *Lactantius: Divine Institutes* (Washington, DC, 1965; FC 49), p. xii, suggests *c.*290.

the rebuilt college at Autun in Gaul for 600,000 sesterces annually;[26] and the *Mort. pers.* lacks the story of Galerius' humiliation,[27] which would have suited Lactantius' purposes very well.[28] Thus the latter's appointment might have been part of the imperial policy whose goal was the revival of Latin Literature. It would be reasonable to suggest that the trip to Nicomedia took place very late in the third century.

No one argues that Arnobius was a Christian by 290, and few would give 295. If he was converted *c.*297, as some suggest, and if the above date is accurate for Lactantius' departure from Africa, the latter's silence about his professor is difficult to explain. If he had known about Arnobius' conversion, he probably would have mentioned him in one of his extant works.[29] Because he is silent about Arnobius, he probably never heard of his conversion to Christianity.[30] Since the *De vir. ill.* was written *c.*392–3, one assumes that any statement about Arnobius which Jerome might have found in the works or epistles of Lactantius must undoubtedly have related to Arnobius' pre-Christian period. And it is significant in light of this interpretation that Jerome's letter to Pope Damasus,[31] dated 384 according to Kelly,[32] provides evidence that after the *Chronicon* was written but before the *De vir. ill.* was begun, Jerome had access to Lactantius' letters.

Three clauses found in the *Chronicon* might shed light on the problem of identifying the information which Jerome possibly received about Arnobius from the lost works or epistles of Lactantius: 'Arnobius rhetor in Africa clarus habetur, qui cum in civitate Siccae ad declamandum iuvenes erudiret . . . quam semper impugnaverat . . .'.[33] Concerning the last clause, it is reasonable to assume that if Arnobius was the hostile opponent of the Church as noted, Lactantius might very well have mentioned this in that profane corpus of writings to which Damasus referred in his letter to Jerome. The remaining information concerns Arnobius' Christian experience which cannot have come from Lactantius.

---

[26] *Pan. lat.* 5(9); 9(4).

[27] Eutr. *Brev. con.* 9. 24.

[28] O. P. Nicholson, *Lactantius: Prophecy and Politics in the Age of Constantine the Great* (D.Phil. thesis, Oxford, 1981), 14–15.

[29] He might have made known his theological disagreement with such topics as divine passibility, providence, etc.

[30] If this occurred at all, I suggest a late date in agreement with Barnes's (1981) suggestion that Lactantius completed the *Div. inst.* in Africa *c.*308/9; cf. Perrin (1984), 3 f., 9.

[31] CSEL 54: Hilberg.

[32] Kelly (1975), 83 n. 19.

[33] Helm (1956), 231; *PL* 27. 675 f.: s.a. 327.

It is also possible that oral tradition provided all the information about Arnobius found in the *Chronicon*.[34] One indeed wonders whether Jerome had even read the *Adv. nat.* at all by this time (*c*.380), since he describes the seven books as *luculentissimos*, a statement which does not cohere with more balanced assessments of the work given in later statements in his letters. On the other hand, the apologetic purpose of the *Chronicon* must not be overlooked.[35]

One can go further. In the *Chronicon* Jerome does not mention the *Adv. nat.* by name. Suffice it to say that if the source about Arnobius which Jerome used there did not derive from information gathered at a later date, after he had read the now lost works of Lactantius, a source of this kind might have given him the inaccurate date of AD 327.[36] For in the next work written after the *Chronicon* in which Arnobius is named by Jerome (*c*.392–3), his date is now changed to 'sub Diocletiano principe' (284–305). In chapter 80 he repeats this, the same chapter in which he refers to the works and letters of Lactantius now lost.

One may conclude that the only new information about Arnobius in *De vir. ill.* 79 that can have come from the lost writings of Lactantius found in *De vir. ill.* 80, is the date, i.e. 'sub Diocletiano principe'. This appears very likely because Jerome has already stated that Arnobius taught rhetoric at Sicca in Africa, and the mention of the *Adversus gentes* cannot have come from Lactantius because his information will have concerned only the pagan Arnobius. Jerome probably discovered the accurate date in one or more of the lost works of Lactantius mentioned in *De vir. ill.* 80, and the *Chronicon* source was mistaken. This source has been described as oral tradition, but it is possible that some, if not

---

[34] Cf. McCr 12: '. . . he may even have derived his knowledge of Arnobius from oral tradition.' Neither McCr nor LeB mentions the lost works as possible sources for Jerome.

[35] The same can be said about *De vir. ill.*, in which Jerome is silent about the contents of the work, although in ch. 79, *Adversus gentes* is given for the name, commonly available ('quae vulgo exstant'). MS evidence (cf. McCr 241 n. 25) gives the title used herein. If Jerome had read the work by the time he had written *De vir. ill.* (*c*.392–3), the reason he makes no negative comment about it, as he does in his later letters, can be found in the impressive list of pagan authors found in the preface. His desire to set before Dexter all those who have written on Holy Scripture suggests that he had not read Arnobius in detail, if at all: the latter betrays very little knowledge of the NT and none of the OT, on which see M. Strachy, *The Fathers Without Theology* (London, 1957), 227.

[36] Superseding the 'scribal error' theory. On Jerome's apologetic purpose in *De vir. ill.*, see Barnes (1971), 4; and 'Appendix A', 235–41. He is partly incorrect to suggest that ch. 80 supplied facts about Arnobius found in ch. 79, since Jerome names the work which cannot have come from Lact. Jerome's later, more sober statements about the work appear in *Ep.* 58. 10 (*PL* 22. 585: *c*.395), Ad Paulinum; and in *Ep.* 62. 2 (*PL* 22. 606: *c*.397–8), Ad Tranquillinum.

all, of the information that Jerome received about Arnobius' Christian experiences came from a North African source. Damasus wrote to Jerome in 384, which was four years after the completion of the *Chronicon* and about eight years before the *De vir. ill.* was begun. And the Pope is explicit about the profane nature of these writings.[37]

It is not known how long Jerome had possession of these writings, but they probably did not give him any information about Arnobius' Christian period. It is fairly clear that he got possession of them only after the *Chronicon* was completed, and the accurate date of Arnobius was provided by Lactantius. Jerome was not actually conscious of the erroneous date given in the *Chronicon* when he discovered the accurate one before he wrote *De vir. ill.* Oral tradition perhaps initially supplied some facts about Arnobius' Christian experiences, which might have led Jerome to ascertain their accuracy by writing to a North African ecclesiastical figure. The problem here is that his earliest North African correspondence, to Aurelius and contained in the letters to Augustine discovered by Divjak, dated *c.*392–3,[38] acknowledges that Tertullian, Cyprian, and Lactantius came from Aurelius' province. Arnobius' name is absent. Yet Aurelius initiated the correspondence, and this suggests that Jerome's North African epistles antedate 392. How far they go back is uncertain. Thus the facts of Arnobius' life found in the *Chronicon* probably derive from oral tradition, with the possibility that a North African ecclesiastical source contributed some of the information. Lactantius' only correction was the date, 'sub Diocletiano principe'. Therefore, the date of Arnobius and the writing of the *Adv. nat.* derived from external sources alone is to be placed during the reign of Diocletian: 20 November AD 284–1 May 305.

II. *Internal Evidence: Historical References*

Two passages describing historical events found in the *Adv. nat.* rehearse common pagan–Christian diatribes of the two centuries preceding Arnobius. First, he refutes the pagan accusation that since Christianity began, the world has deteriorated, and, subsequently, the gods have withdrawn their providential blessings from mankind (1. 1). Pestilences,

[37] Jerome, *Ep.* 35. 2 (CSEL 54: Hilberg).
[38] See W. H. C. Frend, *JEH* 34 (1983), 497–512; CSEL 87: Divjak, Aug. *Ep.* 27, pp. lxvi–lxvii.

wars, famines, and such calamities are symptomatic of the gods' wrath now punishing men for neglecting their cults (1. 3). Germanic and Scythian invasions in the Roman Empire occurred for the same reason, according to the pagan view, ardently attacked by the African rhetor (1. 4). Courcelle therefore argues that book 1 was written *c*.296–7.[39] Arnobius refers to the frequent wars of the Empire, possibly meaning any one of the campaigns of C. Gothicus (268–70), Aurelian (270–5), Probus (276–82), Maximian (286–7), or even Diocletian himself, who was proclaimed *Germanicus Maximus* in 285, 287 (twice), 288, 293, and 300/1.[40] A general remark like this cannot provide a precise date. Another problem in dating book 1 in 296–7 is the allusion in *Adv. nat.* 4. 36. 22–3 to Diocletian's First Edict of 23 February 303. With respect to dating the first book, Courcelle's suggestion thus parallels the double composition theory originally developed by Monceaux and later, Moricca.[41]

These scholars have held that books 1 and 2 are to be dated *c*.297, and 3–7 not until 303. This is unsupportable because Arnobius explicitly states at the beginning of book 3, that book 2 was a planned digression from his theme. Le Bonniec suggested a quite different date for, and sequence of, the books: 'en effet le livre 1 est peut-être postérieur à 300; mais le livre 2 est sûrement soit de 297, soit un peu antérieur a cette date.'[42] Certainly book 2 was published alone because it constitutes 'une démonstration autonome et l'auteur lui-même le présent comme une sort de corps étranger dans l'économie générale de son œuvre'.[43] This is weak because it ignores the internal evidence which McCracken noticed concerning 2. 1 and 3. 2.[44] Also, it completely overlooks, as McCracken himself did, the external evidence which the Latin rhetorical tradition reveals from the Late Republic/Early Empire. Cicero shows the importance of a planned *digressio* (*De orat.* 3. 3. 202), and Arnobius uses the same word in 3. 2. 2. Quintilian quotes and comments upon Cicero in *Inst. orat.* 9. 1. 28. *Digressio* added beauty to a speech (4. 2. 19); it provided embellishments for

---

[39] P. Courcelle, 'Anti Christian Arguments and Christian Platonism: From Arnobius to St. Ambrose', in A. Momigliano (ed.), *The Conflict between Paganism and Christianity in the Fourth Century* (Oxford, 1963), 152. Arnobius was influenced by his times. For different views see: McCr 3; L. Berkowitz, *Index Arnobianus* (Hildesheim, 1967), p. vii.

[40] See Table 5 in Barnes (1982), 255.

[41] P. Monceaux, *Histoire littéraire de l'Afrique chrétienne* 7 vols. (Paris, 1901–23), 3. 248; U. Moricca, *Storia della letteratura latina cristiana*, 2 vols. (Turin, 1923), 1. 610.

[42] LeB 32.

[43] LeB 27 f. I maintain that the seven books form an organic whole and represent a finished product.

[44] McCr 10; cf. LeB 27.

oratorical style (9. 1. 35 f.; cf. 9. 2. 55; 10. 1. 33); and it was a technical rhetorical device that the authority of Latin education esteemed highly (4. 3. 14). According to Jerome, it will be remembered that Arnobius was a rhetor. Neither *Adv. nat.* 1. 4 nor any passage in book 1 provides evidence that the book was written *c.*296–7.

The second historical reference occurs in 1. 5, where Arnobius, using *Timaeus* 23 E as his text, asks whether Christians were also responsible for the war in Atlantis ten thousand years ago. Solon is told by Egyptian priests that the invasion of the inhabitants occurred nine thousand years before his time. Since he lived *c.*638–558 BC, Arnobius is inexact wherever he is placed in Diocletian's reign, the aim of the passage is purely apologetical, and it cannot provide any specific information for the date of the work.

Two passages concern how long Christianity has existed. In 1. 13 Arnobius states: 'trecenti sunt anni ferme, minus vel plus aliquid, ex quo coepimus esse Christiani et terrarum in orbe censeri.' Other Christian writers compute the origin of Christianity to the birth of Christ.[45] Arnobius probably concurs, since by placing the date at the beginning of Christ's ministry, the crucifixion, or as Augustine does, at Pentecost,[46] would all give a date beyond our tentative *terminus ante quem* of AD 311. However, the 'minus vel plus aliquid' betrays his inexactness, and we do not know the chronological system, if any, which he used. Also, a pagan in 2. 71. 9 asserts: 'Ante trecentos annos religio, inquit, vestra non fuit.' Although the manuscript (P) gives 'quadringentos', Marchesi's suggestion of 'trecentos' makes better sense.[47] Even though a pagan speaks, we again find the same chronological obscurity which will allow only the very general designation of the reign of Diocletian (284–305).

III. Adversus Nationes 2. 71: *A Varronian Chronology?*

The most controversial passage related to the dating of the text is 2. 71: 'Aetatis urbs Roma cuius esse in annalibus indicatur? Annos ducit

---

[45] Tertullian, *Apol.* 7. 3; McCr 244 n. 58, giving also Lact. *Mort. pers.* 2; Eus. *HE* 1. 5. 1.

[46] *Civ. Dei* 18. 54.

[47] This passage may represent Arnobius' own chronological computations rather than those of a real pagan opponent, although in many instances the reverse is true. The figure 300 in 2. 71 coheres with that given in 1. 13.

quinquaginta et mille aut non multum ab his minus.' Emperor Philip
the Arab celebrated the millennium of Rome in AD 247, calculated
according to the Varronian chronology which dated Rome's foundation
in 753 BC. If Arnobius used Varro's system here, that would place the
writing of the work to this passage sometime before 21 April AD 297,
depending upon the meaning of 'aut non multum ab his minus'.
Bryce–Campbell,[48] McCracken,[49] and Mulvey[50] argue for the Varronian
chronology. The system is used in 5. 8. 30–6, causing Le Bonniec to
conclude it was used also in 2. 71.[51] Nicholson expresses doubts based
on the usage in Roman North Africa of consular dates and the years of
the emperors.[52] Apologetics were the purpose of 5. 8, however, and the
method of attacking the writings of religious paganism is developed by
using literary retortion: Arnobius turns his opponents' arguments back
upon themselves by admirably demonstrating the contradictions of their
beliefs. Christianity to the pagan was new and, consequently, lacked the
authority of antiquity. Responding to this well-worn criticism—Celsus
had used it more than a century before—Arnobius offers his reprisal by
using the Varronian chronology: from the deluge to the consulship of
Hirtius and Pansa there are not quite 2,000 years. Since Deucalion and
Pyrrha, the survivors of the flood, threw down the stones from which
the Great Mother was born, she is not even 2,000 years old, only a
baby, and her religion is therefore quite new (5. 8. 41).

Remaining concealed from scholarly observations has been the general
outline of a distinct chronology, in 2. 71. 11–34, possibly deriving from
early republican annalistic traditions, and covering a majority of the
chapter. Proving that the pagan deities are new to human history forms
the basis of the apologetics. In 5. 8 and 2. 71 the same numerical limits
are placed upon the divinities: 2,000 years. Roman paganism cannot
claim authority on the grounds of antiquity. Evidently Arnobius was
ignorant of the Old Testament, causing him to attack his opponents
with their own weapons, simply because the Heilsgeschichte argument
based on the writings of the prophets was unknown to him. 'Annalibus'
(2. 71. 32) suggests the use of an early annalistic tradition separate from

[48] Bryce–Campbell 407.
[49] McCr 10; cf. p. 9 for other foundation dates: 728 BC (L. Cincius Alimentus); 747
BC (Q. Fabius Pictor); 750 BC (Polybius); 752 BC (M. Porcius Cato).
[50] T. J. Mulvey, *The Seven Books of Arnobius Adversus Nationes* (Ph.D. thesis, New
York University, 1908), 7. Until now this work was unknown to scholars.
[51] LeB 32.
[52] O. P. Nicholson, *StudPatr* 15, part 1 (1984), 100–7, 101.

the antiquarian history that Varro wrote.[53] Frier has shown that the
Latin writers made a distinction between *historia*, or descriptive narrative,
and *annalis*, which is a year-by-year account of past events.[54] Macrobius
associates *annales* with the chronicle written by the *pontifices maximi* of
Rome entitled *Annales Maximi*.[55] Arnobius appears to have had knowledge of the early annals of Rome written in Greek: in 1. 3. 43 the
pagans are informed that the maladies occurring in the world for which
the Christians are blamed, are recorded in the annals of various
languages.[56] Q. Fabius Pictor's *Graeci annales* is a possible source here:
Cicero reveals that it contained the story of the dancer who made Jupiter
angry, found also in *Adv. nat.* 7. 39 with an acknowledgement that it is
found in the annalists' works.[57]

In our passage (2. 71. 11–34) Arnobius begins with Saturn, the father
of Jupiter. There are three generations from Jupiter and Picus down to
Latinus. Faunus, Latinus, and Picus each lived 120 years, an age which
no one can live beyond. Aeneas and Ascanius follow, the latter having
founded Alba Longa. Alba's kingdom existed *c.*420 years, and the
annalistic age of Rome is given as around 1,050 years. Arnobius then
deduces from this chronology that from the time of Jupiter to the
present, there are nearly 2,000 years, and the Roman gods are therefore
recent introductions to history.

Attempting to identify Arnobius' source reveals two problems: Varro's
work on the antiquities of the Roman people is lost; and the lack of a
consensus about the genealogies of the pre-regal and regal periods in
the early annalists and the historians. For example, Arnobius gives
Latinus as the father-in-law of Aeneas. Timaeus says the exact opposite.
Surviving fragments of Pictor do not cover this subject.[58] Cato's version
of Latinus and Aeneas agrees with our passage. Virgil follows Cato;
Livy does not. Appian combines the two as Latinus Faunus.[59] Saturn

[53] See B. W. Frier, *Libri Annales Pontificum Maximorum: The Origins of the Annalistic Tradition* (Rome, 1979; AAR 27), 27–37.
[54] Ibid.
[55] Ibid.
[56] *Adv. nat.* 1. 3. 43 f.: 'Annalium scripta percurrite linguarum diversitatibus scripta', strongly implying personal familiarity.
[57] See McCr 615 n. 130, for other possibilities. Cf. *Adv. nat.* 7. 44. 7 f.: 'Non imus infitias in annalium scriptis contineri haec omnia quae sunt a vobis in oppositione prolata.' This is identical to 7. 39. 8–10, rejected as spurious by most eds., but see Marchesi ad loc.
[58] Frier (1979), 322, lists the fragments.
[59] Appian, *De reg.* 1. 1 in Photius.

is absent from the list of the Chronographer of AD 354.[60] As Mommsen suggested,[61] since he was a Christian, the god-kings of paganism were unacceptable. And his calculations for Alba's kingdom are 500 years. Both Jerome's addition to Eusebius' *Chronicle, ad annum* 1178 a. Chr., and the *Bedae chronica*, concur in respect of sequence of persons and years ruled.[62]

Recent scholarship has not reached a consensus on the date of Saturn's reign in Italy. Because of the mythological character of the literature which covers the passage, the attempt to ascertain the exact period for this god-king is problematical and dependent upon more reliable historical events contemporaneous with him. Thus Tertullian gives Thallus' rendition that Belus the Assyrian king and Saturn were contemporaries,[63] which agrees with, and may derive from, Theophilus.[64] Chronological sources are again unknown, but Belus preceded the fall of Troy by 322 years, placing Saturn somewhere in the sixteenth century BC.[65] Troy's fall occurred *c.*1200 BC,[66] and if Arnobius followed the same chronological computation by making Saturn and Belus contemporaries, his reasoning 'anni ad haec tempora prope milia duo sunt aut pleni' (2. 71. 36 f.), from Jupiter to the time of writing the *Adv. nat.* would be, 1,824 Fabian or 1,819 Varronian. But the Belus/Saturn connection is not found in Arnobius.[67]

Familiarity with the *Graeci annales* is very possible in *Adv. nat.* 6. 7. 9. McCracken tries to make a strong case of Arnobius' use of Varro— fifteen direct citations—to support the Varronian chronology theory of 2. 71. Referring to the early regal period, however, he places Piso, Aelius, and Granius in contradistinction with Varro, who, he emphasizes, was mistaken: 'qui rebus in (sub)stantia constitutis inanissimas subdit

[60] 'Item origo gentis Romanorum, ex quo primum in Italia regnare coeperunt . . . Picus Saturni filius regnavit agro Laurentino usque ad eum locum ubi nunc Roma est, ann. XXXVIII . . . Faunus Pici filius eisdem locis regnavit annis XLIII . . . Latinus eisdem locis regnavit . . .' (lacuna).

[61] T. Mommsen, *Gesammelte Schriften*, 7 vols. (Berlin, 1909), 7. 566.

[62] 'Ante Aeneam Ianus Saturnus Picus Faunus Latinus in Italia regnarunt ann. circiter CL.' Helm (1956), 62b; *PL* 27. 271 f.; the *Bedae chronica* is found in Mommsen's *MGH* vol. 3, (Berlin, 1898).

[63] Tert. *Apol.* 19. 2 (CChr: Dekkers).

[64] Theophilus, *Ad Autol.* 3. 27.

[65] So Leglay, *SAH* 455: 'Si le règne de Saturnus fut, comme le text semble le dire, contemporain de celui de Belus, la ruine de Troie étant fixée vers 1183 . . . le règne de Saturne correspondrait bien au XVIᵉ siècle av. J.-C.'

[66] Cf. N. G. L. Hammond, *A History of Greece to 322 B.C.* (Oxford, 1967), Appendix 2, p. 653.

[67] Cf. *Div. inst.* 1. 23. 5.

et res cassas' (3. 39. 9 f.). 'Inanissimas' are evidently replacements of
'rebus in (sub)stantia constitutis', which can only directly relate to the
persons named at the beginning of the passage. Hercules, Romulus, and
Aeneas—the latter appears in 2. 71. 29—are personages from the
historical period covered by the genealogy of 2. 71. But what is
the relationship between Varro, 'inanissimas', and these mythological
persons? Augustine reveals that Eusebius and Jerome did not follow
Varro's chronology for the pre-regal and early-regal periods.[68] According
to Varro, some men believed falsely that they were descended from the
gods, a remark which does not cohere well with Arnobius' genealogy,
but makes sense when compared with his statement about men being
made gods in 3. 39. Also, in the section of the *Civ. Dei.* covering the
period of Picus, Faunus, and Latinus (18. 15 f.), the name of Varro is
absent, and Augustine seems to be following another ancient source.

Censorinus further elucidates the rejection of Varro in respect of the
pre-regal age: according to the Latin polymath, from man's beginnings
to the first deluge of Ogyges, one cannot comprehend the exact number
of years because the period is too obscure.[69] Eusebius gives 1757 BC for
the latter,[70] 579 years before Ianus *et al.*,[71] whose date begins in 1178
BC. Varro's dating of Ogyges cannot have been far from this, if indeed
it was different. Censorinus states that Varro's second period, from the
deluge to the first Olympiad (776 BC), was called 'mythical'.[72] Note that
we are now later than the period covered by *Adv. nat.* 2. 71. His third
period, from the first Olympiad to the present, was the only one worthy
of being called 'historical'.[73] Varro's second period, the 'mythical', thus
corresponds chronologically to the period which most of *Adv. nat.* 2. 71
covers. One doubts whether Varro both dealt with the same persons
and used the chronological exactness found in Arnobius. He probably
did not even name Aeneas.[74] Of equal importance is that Varro, in *Ant.
rer. div.* (book 16) used the Stoic allegorization of Liber (male sexual
principle), Hercules, and Aesculapius, who are also named in *Adv. nat.*
3. 39. 2 f. Varro's substitution of 'inanissimas' for 'established reality'

[68] *Civ. Dei* 18. 8.
[69] *Die nat.* 21. 1 f. (Jahn).
[70] Helm (1956), 31b.
[71] Jerome's addition: Helm (1956), 62b.
[72] *Die nat.* 21. 1 f. (Jahn).
[73] Ibid.
[74] H. D. Jocelyn, *JRLM* 65 (1982), 148–205, esp. 170: 'The way that Augustine refers to Varro leaves it a little uncertain whether the latter even mentioned Aeneas.' Cf. *Civ. Dei* 18. 15 f.

(McCracken: 3. 39) probably refers to this kind of allegorization of the Graeco-Roman gods, to refute which Arnobius devotes fourteen chapters (5. 32–45).

In light of these data, one must prove that the Varronian chronology is used in *Adv. nat.* 2. 71, independent of its use elsewhere in the work. To say that Varro was used in 2. 71 because he was in 5. 8 simply is not supportable. A recent study of Graeco-Roman chronologies has revealed that the year 752 BC, corresponding to Varro's 753, was also frequently given for the date of Rome's foundation,[75] evidence derived from the practice of chronographers of the early Empire and deduced from later sources. Eusebius is invaluable: the *Chronicon* places the foundation date in a. Abr. 1264 = ol.6,4 = 752 BC. The Armenian text concurs. He acknowledges that 'nonnulli Romanorum scriptores Romam conditam ferunt' for the preceding year (753 BC).[76] The year 752 BC was used as frequently as the Varronian epoch.[77] Roman scholarship seems never to have reached agreement on the precise date.[78] Samuel's conclusion is important for our investigation: 'This so-called Varronian era can only be used for an ancient author if the base date 753 can be established for that author.'[79]

Can this base date be established for Arnobius? First we turn to the statement that Alba lasted 420 years, and we find a plethora of dates: Dionysius of Halicarnassus gives 487 years,[80] Livy has 400,[81] while Virgil produces 300.[82] Justinus' *Epitome* of Pompeius Trogus agrees with Livy. Florus follows Livy's description of events under Tullus Hostilius, but does not note the length of Alba's kingdom.[83] And Arnobius himself later changes the 420 to 400 years exactly (7. 26. 17 f.), perhaps denoting the use of two chronologies which gave different periods for Alba. Added to this problem is the fact that Dionysius, Livy, and Virgil do not name their sources that gave them Alba's dates.[84]

---

[75] A. E. Samuel, *Greek and Roman Chronology: Calendars and Years in Classical Antiquity* (Munich, 1972), 252.

[76] Ibid.

[77] Ibid.

[78] e.g., Censor. *Die nat.* 21. 4 ff.; Plut. *Rom.* 12; Macr. *Sat.* 1. 13. 20; V. Paterculus, *Hist. rom.* 1. 8; Tac. *Ann.* 11. 10; Eutr. *Brev. con.* 1. 2; Eus. *Chron. a. Abr.* 1264; Oros. *Hist. adv. pag.* 5. 3.

[79] Samuel (1972), 251.

[80] *Ant. rom.* 3. 31. 4.

[81] 1. 28.

[82] *Aen.* 1. 270–4.

[83] *Epit. bell. omn. ann.* 1. 3. 8 f. (LCL: Forster).

[84] Theophilus of Antioch does not give specific dates for the pre-regal period in Roman

Other evidence to be used against the Varronian chronology is the
limit of 120 years for the earthly lives of Faunus, Latinus, and Picus
(*Adv. nat.* 2. 71. 25 f.), which should be compared with Lactantius, *Div.
inst.* 2. 14. There the Erythraean Sibyl is quoted to demonstrate the
serpent's deception of man, who then took up death beyond what had
been fated. Man's life was now temporary, though long, for it lasted
1,000 years. Lactantius states that although Varro was not unaware of
this information, he nevertheless explained why the ancients lived
according to the Egyptian computation of one year being equal to one
month. Lactantius believes this is false and adds that 'certain authors'
believe that 'some were accustomed to attain to the age of 120 years.'
He now puts Varro in contradistinction to this theory: 'But because
Varro did not know why or when the life of man was shortened, he
himself shortened it, although he knew that a man could live 1,400
months.'[85] So who are the 'certain authors' to whom Lactantius refers?
Surviving fragments of Fabius and Cincius do not cover this subject.
According to Cicero's *De senectute*, however, Cato, who dated Rome's
foundation in 752 BC, gives the 'utmost limit of life' as 120 years.[86]
Although this evidence speaks against the use of the Varronian chronology in 2. 71, the possibility that Arnobius followed either Fabius or
Cincius, both of whom Cato used as sources for his historical writing,
cannot be rejected. Plutarch held the latter in high esteem, mentioning
Varro solely in passing.[87] Now Censorinus' remark about Varro's description of the early periods of human history as incalculable in the exact
number of years is more clearly understood. Since the chronology of 2.
71 begins with Jupiter continuing to the present, totalling *c.*2,000 years,
it is difficult, if not impossible, to prove that Varro is used. Yet although
the *Graeci annales* was probably available in Africa during Arnobius'
time,[88]—and we shall observe in the next chapter that he knew Greek—

history. See Ad Autol. 3. 27 in R. M. Grant, *Theophilus of Antioch* (Oxford, 1970), p.
141. On Alba Longa see D. H. Müller, PW, 1, cols. 1301–2.

[85] R. M. Ogilvie, *The Library of Lactantius* (Oxford, 1978), 51, includes Varro in the
group. Arguing that Varro was not used directly by Lactantius, he then notes on the same
page that Varro discussed the expectation of life in the *Libri fatales* as 84 years, and
elsewhere as not more than 100. The source is *Die nat.* 14. 6: 84: the Etruscans; and 17.
4: no more than 100: the Alexandrian embalmers.

[86] *De sen.* 19. 69 (LCL: Falconer): 'Quamquam, o di boni, quid est in hominis natura
diu? Da enim supremum tempus; expectemus Tartessiorum regis aetatem . . . qui octoginta
regnaverat annos, centum viginti vixerat . . .'; cf. *Die nat.* 17. 4: 'alii ad centum viginti
annos produci posse'. He seems not to include Varro in the 'alii'.

[87] *In Rom.* 12. 3 f. (LCL: Perrin).

[88] The writer of the *Origo gentis romanae* used Q. Fabius Pictor as a source. It is dated

it is equally difficult to prove that Fabius or any other of the early annalists were followed.

Tertullian's remark in *De idol.* 10 about professors of literature who publicly make known the gods' genealogies divulges more evidence against Varro's chronology. The most interesting fact about the list in 2. 71 is that he deviates from naming the mother of Saturn normally found in Latin writers, since Terra is usually given and not Hectate; this bewildered Kroll, forcing him to confess his inability to identify the underlying source, although his guess was the Chaldaean Oracles.[89] Tertullian discloses that Varro listed Coelus and Terra as the parents of Saturn,[90] and Varro himself confirms this.[91] Certainly we can conclude this much: Arnobius did not use Varro in 2. 71; the reference to 120 years parallels Cato; and the remark about recorded calamities in the annals of various languages, compared with 6. 7. 9, where there is a specific reference to a passage in Fabius covering the Roman regal period (Tarquinius Superbus), implies the use of a chronology derived from the early annals of Rome. The work was not begun in AD 297.

IV. Adversus Nationes 2. 71: A Porphyrian Connection?

One final observation about *Adv. nat.* 2. 71 is necessary. It is possible that the genealogy was used purely for apologetical motives and cannot, therefore, serve as a guide for dating the text. Polemics more than chronological purposes may have determined the selection of the list. The best explanation is found in the *Contra Christianos* of Porphyry.[92] Augustine's epistle to Deogratias[93] responds to a pagan's questions about a number of Christian beliefs. One is among 'the more weighty arguments of Porphyry against the Christians'[94] which criticized the doctrine that

*c.*AD 360 by A. Momigliano, *JRS* 48 (1955), 56–73, esp. 59; indicating Fabius' work was used during the second half of the 4th cent. Cf. F. Pichlmayr, *Sexti Aurelii Victoris Liber De Caesaribus* (Leipzig, 1966), p. ix.

[89] W. Kroll, *RM* 71 (1916) 348: '. . . die eigentliche Ursache davon kann ich nicht angeben, vermute sie aber in Arn. Bekanntschaft mit späterer mystischer Literatur wie den Chaldäischen Orakeln.'

[90] *Adv. nat.* 2. 12; cf. Lact. *Epit. div. inst.* 14.

[91] *De ling. lat.* 5. 57.

[92] Many more parallels between Porphyry and Arnobius are analysed in chs. 4, 6, and 7 below.

[93] CSEL 34. 2. 551; NPNF 1. 416; Harnack, *CC* fr. no. 81.

[94] *Ep.* 102. 8.

Christ is the only way to salvation because he had so recently arrived in human history. Courcelle has already convincingly shown that Porphyry and Arnobius reveal striking parallels: there is a similarity between Augustine, *Ep.* 108. 8 and Arnobius 2. 63. 1–4, 64. 1–3, 65. 18 f., 66. 8–10, 71. 9, 74. 1–3, 75. 1 f.[95] These deal with the fate of souls before Christ came (2. 63); Christ the one way of salvation (2. 64–5); the newness of Christianity (2. 66); and the accusation that Christ has recently appeared (2. 71, 74, 75). We may add to these the accusation in 2. 67. 1–4, that Christians have abandoned ancestral religious customs, corresponding to a criticism of Porphyry found in Eusebius.[96] The challenge to the pagans to examine[97] the reason of such abandonment may also indicate a response to Porphyry's criticism of Christians who assent to faith without examination.[98] Porphyry also considered it a crime punishable by death for those who disrespect ancestral customs, and Arnobius responds to a similar charge in 2. 67. 4 ff. Also, in 2. 77, pagans speak of persecution as just punishment for the Christians.[99]

Augustine's quotation from Porphyry's famous work against the Christians clearly shows his chronological expertise used to prove that Christianity, a very new religion, cannot claim authority as the one way of salvation compared with the religious practices which antedate even the foundation of Rome itself. Passing over the time which preceded the founding of Latium, he begins with the latter as if it were the beginning of humanity. Gods were worshipped in Latium before Alba was built. In Alba's temples religious rites were practised. Porphyry then turns to Rome: for many centuries Rome was unacquainted with the Christian religion, so what has happened to those who lived during these periods? The gist is that the ancient religion is to be authoritative for man's salvation. Arnobius begins in the very period passed over by Porphyry because it would have defeated his purpose. Arnobius believes the divinity worshipped, not the length of time his cult has existed, gives a religion its authority. Pagans should not examine the day they began to worship but what: 'nec colere qua die sed quid coeperis,

[95] Cf. *Tract. in Ioh.* 31. 5; *PL* 35. 1638; P. Courcelle, *REL* 31 (1953), 265–6. I agree with Courcelle (271 n. 1) that Arnobius had read Porphyry without an intermediary.
[96] *PE* 4. 1; cf. 14. 2.
[97] *Adv. nat.* 2. 67. 2.
[98] *PE* 1. 1 = Harnack, *CC* fr. no. 1.
[99] For Porphyry's views see *PE* 4. 1. Cf. *Adv. nat.* 2. 67. 4 ff.: 'Nam si mutare sententiam culpa est ulla vel crimen et a veteribus institutis . . . migrare'; and 2. 77. 1–3: 'ista quam dicitis persecutionis asperitas liberatio nostra est, non persecutio, nec poenam vexatio inferet'.

convenit intueri' (2. 71. 8). From Jupiter to Latinus, the hero of Latium, there are exactly three generations (2. 71. 22–4). From Picus, Faunus, and Latinus there have been 360 years (2. 71. 27 f.). After Ascanius, Alba existed *c.*420 years (2. 71. 30–2). The annalistic age of Rome is then given (2. 71. 32–4: *c.*1,050 years). His conclusion is that the religion of the pagans, like the gods themselves, has recently arisen (2. 71. 34–42). He elsewhere proves that all kinds of novelties have been introduced since the pre-regal period. We recall that Porphyry began with Latium and focused upon Alba and Rome.[100] Arnobius begins 2. 68 by referring to the senate's decision to change sacrificial practices at Alba. Tullus' disregard for ancient religious custom (2. 68. 4–8) is mentioned. And the reference to sacrificing human heads to Saturn before Hercules came to Italy points to one geographical region only: Latium.[101] Although Porphyry probably is the adversary who inspired Arnobius' polemical argument in 2. 71, we cannot ascertain whether both used the same chronology.

V. *References to the Persecutions of Christians*

Primarily because of the kinds of statements about the persecutions of Christians found in the *Adv. nat.*, a majority of scholars date the work during the Great Persecution under Diocletian (303–11).[102] None of these has done a thorough analysis of each passage wherein a reference to the persecutions is found, to ascertain whether all statements about the persecutions of Christians can be dated after 23 February 303, the date of the promulgation of Diocletian's First Edict.[103]

Arnobius first mentions the persecution of Christians in *Adv. nat.* 1. 26. 1–7:

---

[100] Aug. *Ep.* 102. 8.

[101] Cf. Lact. *Div. inst.*, 1. 21. Courcelle (1953), 266 n. 1, noticed the mention of Alba made by both. Jerome gives a similar account of Porphyry's rejection of Christianity which should be compared to Aug. *Ep.* 102. 8; 133. 9 (NPNF 6) = Harnack, *CC* fr. no. 82. M. Magnes' opponent also asks what happened to our ancestors diseased with sin (*Apoc.* 4. 10) and ridicules the persecution of Paul and Peter (4. 4). On the abandonment of marriage customs in *Adv. nat.* 2. 67, see H. Le Bonniec, 'Le témoignage d'Arnobe sur deux rites archaïques du mariage romain', *REL* 54 (1976), 110–29.

[102] For a complete list see M. B. Simmons, 'Concepts of Deity In Arnobius Of Sicca In The Context Of The Contemporary Pagan–Christian Debate' (unpub. Ph.D. thesis, University of Edinburgh, 1985), 24 n. 84, and 57 f. n. 210.

[103] Nicholson (1984), 106, concludes that the *Adv. nat.* is not datable.

Hoccine est quaeso audax illud facinus et inmane, propter quod maximi caelites aculeos in nos intendunt irarum atque indignationum suarum, propter quod vos ipsi, cum libido incesserit saeva, exuitis nos bonis, exterminatis patriis sedibus, inrogatis supplicia capitalia, torquetis dilaceratis exuritis et ad extremum nos feris et beluarum laniatibus obiectatis?

The First Edict was promulgated in Nicomedia on 23 February 303, ordering the destruction of Christian churches, the burning of scriptures, and the confiscation of all church property. Christians lost their legal rights in the courts and were forbidden to worship. Those in imperial service were reduced to slavery.[104] Dioocletian's persecution was unprecedented in the focus upon annihilating places of worship and holy scriptures. It was a frontal assault, a forceful strike at the jugular vein with a very sharp knife. By April the First Edict arrived in Africa, and the governmental officials carried out its provisions immediately.[105]

In the passage above (1. 26. 1–7), the mention of 'exuitis nos bonis' could be an allusion to the First Edict. On 19 May 303, in the vicinity of Cirta, the capital of Numidia, the mayor of the city, Munatius Felix,[106] confiscated the church plate, scriptures, and all movable wealth of the church house where Christians met.[107] He then moved from house to house in the city, demanding at each entry, 'proferte scripturas quas habetis'.[108] Christians in Africa Proconsularis met the same fate.[109] The phrase, 'exterminatis patriis sedibus', may be associated with the Edict if 'sedibus' denotes 'governmental seats' or 'positions', referring to the loss of dignities held by Christians in the imperial government. It is more likely, however, that the statement is connected with the widespread imprisonment of clergymen proscribed by the Second Edict.[110]

Words like 'inrogatis supplicia capitalia' might be a general statement

---

[104] Eus. *HE* 8. 2. 4; Lact. *Mort. pers.* 13; see also G. E. M. de Ste Croix, 'Aspects of the "Great" Persecution', *HTR* 47 (1954), 75.

[105] See W. H. C. Frend, *Martyrdom and Persecution in the Early Church* (Grand Rapids, 1981; repr. of Oxford, 1965), 500; cf. Barnes (1981), 22 f.

[106] His Latin title was *curator*; he was also *flamen perpetuus*; see *PCEAfr* 1. 407; *Gesta apud Zenophilum*, CSEL 26 (Ziwsa), 186–8. On the date: *Gesta ap. Zenoph.* (Ziwsa, p. 186): 'Diocletiano VIII et Maximiano VII consulibus XIIII kal. Iunias . . .'.

[107] *Gesta ap. Zenoph.* (Ziwsa, p. 187).

[108] Ibid. *passim*.

[109] *Act. purg. Fel.* (CSEL 26: Ziwsa, p. 198): 'nam cum persecutio esset indicta christianis . . . ut sacrificarent aut quascumque scripturas haberent, incendio traderent . . . erat tunc temporis magistratus Alfius Caecilianus . . .'. The latter was *duumvir* at Abthugni (Hr. es Souar) in Africa Proconsularis during the Diocletianic persecution. See *PCEAfr* 1. 175 f.

[110] See LS 1659, I. A.; cf. *OLD* 1725. 7 ff. I am aware of the debate as to whether Edicts 1–2 were promulgated in the West.

about the persecution specified in the list that follows. *Torqueo* can mean, 'to torture', 'to mangle', or even 'to put to the rack', all suiting well the tortures described by Eusebius in book 8 of his *Ecclesiastical History*. For example, Peter, a member of the imperial household, within weeks after the First Edict's promulgation, was scourged so badly that his bones protruded through the mangled parts of his body. This happened in Nicomedia,[111] and Eusebius uses the story to demonstrate what happened to 'the others'.[112] North Africa had its martyrs: thirty-four were executed at Ammaedara (Haidra);[113] some were tortured on the 'horse' (*eculeus*) or rack, on 12 February 304, before the proconsul Anullinus in Carthage;[114] and the executions of the martyrs of Milev (Mila, Algeria);[115] Maxima, Donatilla, and Secunda at Thuburbo Maius or Minus (Hr. Kasbat or Tebourba) in July 304;[116] and Crispina at Theveste (Tébessa) on 5 December 304.[117] Anullinus appears to have had his savage moments,[118] as for example, when he shouted at Hilarianus[119] on 12 February 304 at the tribunal in Carthage: ' "Amputabo" inquit "et comam tibi et nasum et auriculas, et sic te dimittam".'[120] Finally, 'dilaceratis' fits well the persecutions that immediately broke out in Nicomedia and continued through the provinces. For a little more than two weeks after the First Edict was proclaimed, the palace in Nicomedia was set on fire for the second time since the persecution began. Diocletian became enraged, assuming the Christians were the culprits. Many lost their lives: Eusebius informs us that whole families in heaps were butchered with the sword.[121]

---

[111] Eus. *HE* 8. 6. 3.

[112] Ibid. 8. 6. 1.

[113] *ILT* 470b–d. See also Y. Duval, *Loca Sanctorum Africae*, 2 vols. (Rome, 1982), 1. 110, no. 52, fig. 75.

[114] *Pass. SS. Dat. Sat.* in P. Franchi de'Cavalieri, *Note Agiografiche* (Rome, 1935; ST 65), 5. 2: Dativus (cf. *PCEAfr* 1. 267 f.) on the rack; 5. 4: tortured with the hooks ('ungulis'); 8. 4: Victoria on the same: 'membra rumpantur, divellantur viscera'; the same verb found in *Adv. nat.* 1. 26. 6 occurs in *Pass. SS. Dat. Sat.* 8. 5; cf. 9. 2: 'clarissimus martyr etiam pro Christo torqueri'; also 9. 4: 'at martyr inter vulnerum cruciatus gravissimos'; 15. 4: Anullinus to Saturninus (*PCEAfr* 1. 1038) on the *eculeus*: ' "Quid" inquit, Saturnine, profiteris? Vide ubi positus sis. habes scripturas aliquas?'

[115] *CIL* 8. 6700: 2nd half of 303 according to Barnes (1981), 22.

[116] *PCEAfr* 1. 715 f., 288 f., 1047; Duval (1982), 1. 33, fig. 24, no. 15, Testour (Tichilla) = *CIL* 8. 1392 (*mensa marturum?*).

[117] P. F. de'Cavalieri, *Nuove note agiografiche* (Rome, 1902; ST 9).

[118] See on Anullinus, *PCEAfr* 1., 78–80.

[119] Ibid. 556 f.

[120] *Pass. SS. Dat. Sat.* 18. 6 (de'Cavaelieri, ST 65).

[121] *HE* 8. 6. 6.

Arnobius mentions Christians being burned to death ('exuritis'). Lactantius and Eusebius tell the story that a prominent Christian tore down the First Edict after it was put up in Nicomedia, crying out that victories of the Goths and Sarmatians were proposed in it. He was immediately taken away and, Lactantius reveals, cooked according to the directions of a particular recipe. Diocletian himself witnessed some of his Christian domestics 'roasted at the fire'.[122] Eusebius relates that whole families were 'perfected' by fire.[123] Arnobius' student claims that it was the priests and deacons of the palace, with their families irrespective of sex and age, who were seized and herded into the flames.[124] And both Eusebius and Lactantius mention the burning to death of every man, woman, and child in a certain Phrygian town,[125] probably Eumeneia because inscriptions cease there *c*.AD 300.[126] The phrase, 'beluarum laniatibus obiectatis' fits the description of the persecution in Egypt with which Eusebius explicitly compares that of North Africa.[127]

An allusion to the oracles preceding the persecution may be found in 1. 26. 12–24, in relation to the god named and how he is attacked. Jupiter calls Christians wicked and impious and has invented a charge of impiety against them:[128] 'Profanos[129] nos impios Dodonaeus aut Iuppiter nominat, et ipse dicetur deus atque in ordine conputabitur numinum, qui aut summo servientibus regi crimen impietatis adfingit aut sibi torquetur maiestatem eius cultumque praeponi?' (1. 26. 12–16). While Diocletian and Galerius were in the East (*c*.299) sacrificing to the gods,[130] some Christians in attendance made the sign of the cross. After the haruspices repeatedly failed to ascertain the customary signs, Tagis, the 'magister haruspicum', said that profane men at the rites were the cause: 'quod rebus divinis profani homines interessent'.[131] Diocletian

---

[122] Ibid. On the cooked man see *Mort. pers.* 13; *HE* 8. 5. 1.

[123] *HE* 8. 6. 6.

[124] *Mort. pers.* 15.

[125] *HE* 8. 11. 1; *Div. inst.* 5. 11. 10.

[126] Baynes, *CAH* 12. 674.

[127] *HE* 8. 6. 10.

[128] Cf. Liebeschuetz (1979), 254 n. 2; Nicholson (1984), 106 n. 51. See also P. F. Beatrice, 'Un oracle antichrétien chez Arnobius,' in Y. de Andia *et al.* (eds.), *Memorial Dom Jean Gribomont* (Rome, 1988) 107–29.

[129] There is a lacuna in the text. Pithoeus emended the MS reading (*P*) *profan-us* (see McCr 279 n. 106) to *Trophonius*, followed by Marchesi and McCracken. I follow (as also LeB 152, 253 f.) Ursinus' *profanos*, followed by Reifferscheid.

[130] Lact. *Mort. pers.* 10; see Jones (1964), 1. 71, who dates the incident in AD 298.

[131] Lact. *Mort pers.* 10.

ordered all present to sacrifice or face punishment. Noteworthy also is Arnobius' testimony that Christ's contemporary miracles include the nullifying of the haruspices: '. . . qui [sc. Christus] iustissimis viris etiamnunc inpollutis ac diligentibus sese non per vana insomnia sed per purae speciem simplicitatis apparet . . . haruspices inconsultos reddit . . .'.[132] And after comparing the Christian God with Jupiter (1. 34), he comments: '. . . ecquid ergo iniustis persequimini nos odiis? Quid ut ominis pessimi nostri nominis inhorrescitis mentionem, si quem deum colitis, eum et nos? Aut quid in eadem causa vobis esse contenditis familiares deos, inimicos atque infestissimos nobis?' (1. 35. 2–7).

Diocletian consecrated the Tetrarchy under the protection of Jupiter and Hercules: as the Augustus of the East, he became Jovius, the son of Jupiter; Maximian, the Augustus of the West, was Herculius, the son of Hercules.[133] Jupiter and Hercules dominate the numismatic evidence of the Tetrarchy, the former exalted as 'conservator', 'tutator', and 'fulminator'; and the latter is addressed, 'Herculi pacifero invicto' and 'victori'.[134] Praise is given for the emperors' 'salus', 'victoria', and 'virtus'.[135] The Lugdunum mint accentuates their 'providentia' who stands holding cornucopiae.[136] Diocletian is depicted receiving Victory on a globe from Jupiter.[137] Eumenius expressed the same idea at Autun in the spring of 298: the best youths will learn at the newly rebuilt college of rhetoric how to celebrate the exploits of their illustrious princes.[138] Coins from the mint at Cyzicus show Maximian receiving the globe from Diocletian.[139] Mamertinus proclaims that all blessings come from Jupiter and Hercules: Diocletian initiates and Maximian realizes.[140] From the mint at Antioch comes a scene in which Jupiter stands, holding the globe and sceptre, and faces Hercules who holds Victory, a club, and a lion's skin.[141] Sometimes the emperors are seated and each holds a globe, thereby magnifying the 'concordia Augustorum'.[142]

[132] *Adv. nat.* 1. 46. 29–33; cf. Lact. *Div. inst.* 4. 27.
[133] Cf. Liebeschuetz (1979), 240; Mattingly, *CAH* 12. 330.
[134] *RIC* 5. 2. 225 ff.
[135] Ibid. 229.
[136] Ibid. 228 no. 77.
[137] Ibid. 295 no. 626: AD 285–90.
[138] *Pan. Lat.* 9(4). 8. 2; 10. 2 (Mynors).
[139] *RIC* 288 no. 583.
[140] *Pan. Lat.* 10(2). 11. 6. For Mamertinus, see *PLRE* 1. 539.
[141] *RIC* 256 no. 323.
[142] Ibid. 250 and 254, nos. 290 and 313.

The concord existing between the human and divine realms is a theme found in the panegyrics. When Maximian needed fair weather to build a fleet to conquer Carausius, it did not rain.[143] But when the ships were launched, the river which had long been unable to bear ships, now filled up because Jupiter sent rain.[144] The Augusti are extolled for bringing *salus* to the Roman Empire: before their advent there were poor harvests, famine, and disease, but now the natural world is blessed.[145]

Maximian's *numen* illuminates Italy.[146] When he approaches his realm, villagers burn incense and sacrifice to the gods. A real and visible Jupiter is invoked, not a legendary figure. Maximian is a real Hercules.[147] The emperors' blessings outnumber those of the gods,[148] and today men understand the power of the gods when they see the Augusti.[149] The address, 'Sancte Iuppiter et Hercules'[150] was not restricted to professional rhetors: a fragment of an epic poem addresses Diocletian as Zeus and Galerius as Apollo[151] and derives from the autumn of 296.[152]

The main emphases of the new imperial theology under the Tetrarchy derived from these data are clear. Diocletian is the son of Jupiter who preserves the Roman Empire. A new age has dawned: the great heavenly emperor manifests his will through his son, the great king of earth. Herculius pacifies the realm and realizes what his brother—the augusti called each other *frater*—has initiated. Jovius and Herculius have established a blessed and glorious age permeated by *salus* for all citizens of the Empire freely to enjoy. As Liebeschuetz maintains, at no other time than during the Tetrarchy were Christianity and the Imperial Religion so similar.[153] Indeed, for this study it is important to observe that 'Jupiter' or 'Zeus' often designated 'Diocletian'. It is rather highly likely that such an association is made in *Adv. nat.* 2. 26. 12–16, referring to

---

[143] *Pan. Lat.* 10(2). 12. 4.

[144] Ibid. 12. 6.

[145] Ibid. 11(3). 15. 4.

[146] Ibid. 10. 4: 'tota Italia clarior lux diffusa'.

[147] Ibid. 10. 5.

[148] *Pan. Lat.* 8(5). 4. 3.

[149] Ibid. 11(3). 6. 2.

[150] Ibid. 16. 2.

[151] In T. D. Barnes, 'Imperial Campaigns, A.D. 285–311', *Phnx* 30 (1976), 183: 1 verso 1–11.

[152] Ibid. 183.

[153] Liebeschuetz (1979) 243; on Diocletian see e.g. Eutr. *Brev. con.* 9. 26; Aur. Vict. *Caes.* 39. 2 ff.; Amm. 15. 5. 18; W. Ensslin, *CAH* 12. 383–8. See also Frend (1987), 1–18.

the event preceding the outbreak of persecution in 303 described in *Mort. pers.* 10.[154]

Now Arnobius mentions Apollo: 'Delius Apollo vel Clarius, Didymaeus Philesius Pythius et hic habendus divinus est, qui aut summum imperatorem nescit aut ignorat a nobis cotidianis ei precibus supplicari?' (1. 26. 16–20). The persecution began probably in 302 when Diocletian and various governmental and military leaders held secret meetings during the winter to decide what should be done about the Christians. Judges and military officers of superior rank advised that they be exterminated. Diocletian, who was evidently a religious—if not superstitious—person, decided to consult the oracle of Apollo at Didyma. Apollo proclaimed the Christian God to be the enemy of the divine religion.[155] Sol Invictus was the patron deity of Galerius, a god associated with Apollo, and the Eastern Caesar was with Diocletian when the oracle was consulted.[156] Apollo replaces the name of Galerius in the poem (1 verso 6) written after the first Persian campaign.[157] Arnobius mentions the Didymaean Apollo and other epithets, but by whatever name he is called, he does not know the Most High Ruler of the Christians. There may also be a connection between the event at Didyma and *Adv. nat.* 1. 35. 2–7, where the rhetor relates that the name 'Christian' is a terrible omen and the gods are most inimical to the faithful.

VI. *Allusions to Diocletian's Moral Reforms*

Diocletian was acutely concerned about improving the morality of his subjects. A law dated either 15 March 291 (Hermogenianus) or 13 June 287 (Gregorianus) stipulated that those who entered into incestuous marriages 'per errorem' were not subject to penalties if they annul their relationship.[158] Other proscriptions concerned polygamy[159] and sexual incontinence.[160] Adultery was a primary focus: laws of varying speci-

---

[154] Nicholson (Thesis, 1981), 55, makes a similar observation about Lactantius: 'It is often possible to find under Lactantius' denunciation of each god an allusion to the emperor he protected.'

[155] Lact. *Mort. pers.* 11.

[156] On the Galerius/Sol Invictus/Apollo association see Barnes (1981), 12.

[157] Id. (1976), 183.

[158] *Mos. et rom. leg. coll.* 6. 5. 1 in *FIRA* 2. 560 f.

[159] *CJ* 5. 5. 2: 11 Dec. 285.

[160] *CJ* 9. 9. 24: 15 Mar. 291; 9. 9. 20: 5 Oct. 290.

fications were sent to many parts of the Empire in the years 287,[161] 290,[162] 293,[163] 294,[164] and 295, for example.[165] Valerius Concordius, *praeses* ,of Numidia in Cuicul (Djemila, Algeria) from 293 to 305, was the recipient of the latter on 1 June 295.[166]

Incestuous marriages insulted Diocletian's traditional morality. An Edict Against Incest preserved fully in the *Mosaicarum et Romanarum Legum Collatio*, 6. 1,[167] was issued at Damascus on 1 May 295.[168] Referring first to the Roman laws that have been established chastely and with holy awe (6. 4. 1: 'caste sancteque sunt constituta'), the emperors confess that some unchaste acts have been committed (6. 4. 1: 'nefarie incesteque commissa sunt'). The gods will show favour to all in their rule who live a pious, religious, peaceful, and chaste life (6. 4. 1). Clemency will be given to those who have contracted unlawful marriages if they repent (6. 4. 2). Incestuous marriages ('inlicta conubia') disregard decency and piety ('sine ullo respectu pudoris ac pietatis'), and those who practise them are compared to cattle and wild beasts[169] ('pecudum ac ferarum') who are ignorant of morality (6. 4. 2). Instincts of detestable lust motivate such persons (6. 4. 2: 'instinctu execrandae libidinis'), and they should depart from an abominable and criminal life (6. 4. 3: 'ut post tam nefaria facinora vitam quidem sibi gratulentur esse concessam'). Children of such unions are illegitimate (6. 4. 3). No one should ever obey unbridled lust (6. 4. 3: 'infrenatis cupiditatibus'). All citizens will henceforth preserve the sanctity of marriage (6. 4. 4: 'sanctitatemque in conubiis') and know which marriages are permitted under Roman law (6. 4. 4: 'sciant nuptias licitas, quae sunt Romano iure permissae'). Specifically defined illegal are the following marriages:

Cum quibus autem personis tam cognatorum quam ex adfinium numero contrahi non liceat matrimonium, hoc edicto nostro conplexi sumus: cum filia nepte pronepte itemque matre avia proavia et ex latere amita ac matertera sorore

---

[161] *CJ* 9. 9. 19: 5 Dec. 287 (Egypt).
[162] Three: *CJ* 9. 9. 21–3: 18 and 21 Oct.; 1 Nov.
[163] *CJ* 9. 9. 25: 28 Aug.
[164] *CJ* 9. 9. 26: 15 Dec.
[165] *CJ* 9. 9. 27.
[166] *PLRE* 1. 219; Barnes (1982), 172.
[167] *FIRA* 2. 558–60. A condensed version appears in *CJ* 5. 4. 17.
[168] *Mos. et rom. leg. coll.* 6. 4. 8: 'Dat. kal. Mai. Damasco Tusco et Anullino cons.'
[169] Cf. Eus. *PE* 2. 4; Ael. *De nat. anim.* (LCL: Scholfield), 3. 47: animals know they should not commit incest; humans do not (cf. 4. 7).

sororis filia et ex ea nepte. Itemque ex adfinibus privigna noverca socru nuru ceterisque quae antiguo iure prohibentur, a quibus cunctos volumus abstinere.[170]

A skilled and very successful rhetor,[171] knowledgeable in civil law and the religious literature of Roman paganism, could find plenty of material here to incorporate into his attack upon the immoralities of the gods. And the god which Arnobius most frequently attacks is Jupiter. Although, as Chadwick has ingeniously shown,[172] this edict looks 'like part of Diocletian's general justification of his eastern campaigns', the fundamental concern is Arnobius' polemical use of it. First, in relation to marriage and adultery laws, the slander that destroys the 'deorum principis auctoritatem' (4. 22. 16) is Jupiter's heart hot with lust for women. One wife was not enough for him (4. 22. 20, 24). He is a criminal (4. 22. 31). In 4. 23. 1–9, he affirms that although man has a propensity for lust (1. 1: 'libidinem'), there are laws stipulating capital punishment for adultery (11. 2–5).[173] Yet the 'regnorum maximus' did not know the shame of adultery (11. 5 ff.)? He not only committed adultery with goddesses, but also humans (11. 10–22). It is not the Christians who have written that the 'rex mundi' (4. 26. 15) changed himself into a satyr, snake, or a bull to lust after women (4. 26. 19–26). And now follows an apparent parody of the panegyrics noted above: 'Et sane adiungitis beneficia non parva, siquidem vobis deus Hercules natus est, qui in rebus huiusmodi patris sui transiret exuperaretque virtutes' (4. 26. 26–9). Jupiter preferred mistresses and concubines to his wife (4. 34. 1–6). Why prevent the Senate from issuing a decree against such irreverence (4. 34. 12–18)? And he adds: 'nec a vobis saltem istum meruerunt honorem, ut quibus expellitis a vobis eisdem ab his legibus propulsaretis iniurias?' (11. 18–20).

He appears to have a special axe to grind for Jupiter's incestuous affairs. In 4. 24. 22 f., he asks: 'numquid incestas nuptias cum sorore

---

[170] *Mos. et rom. leg. coll.* 6. 4. 5: *FIRA* 2. 560.

[171] Jerome, *Chron.* s.a. 327; *De vir. ill.* 79.

[172] H. Chadwick. 'The Relativity of Moral Codes: Rome And Persia in Late Antiquity', 152, in W. R. Schoedel and R. L. Wilken (eds.), *Early Christian Literature and the Classical Intellectual Tradition* (Paris, 1979; TheolHist 53). Chadwick makes the same observation regarding the Edict Against the Manichees. The incest edict is the latest dated law appearing in the *Codex Gregorianus*, which was compiled in the last decade of Diocletian's reign by the eastern lawyer Gregorius (p. 136). For the rhetor knowledgeable in civil law see Quint. *Inst.* 12. 3. 1, 7 f.

[173] McCr 555 n. 150 refers to Dölger, who cites this passage for evidence of capital punishment for this offence before Constantine without reference to the Edict Against Incest.

Iovem ipsum dicimus fecisse nos . . .?' He charges the god with criminal behaviour in 5. 9. 6–15, using expressions reminiscent of those found in *Mos. et rom. leg. coll.* 6. 4. 2:

Post innumeras virgines et spoliatas castitate matronas etiamne in matrem cupiditatis infandae spem Iuppiter cepit, nec ab illius adpetitionis ardore horror eum quivit avertere, quem non hominibus solis sed animalibus quoque nonnullis natura ipsa subiecit, et ingeneratus ille conmuniter sensus? An respectus pietatis et honesti Capitoliorum defuit praesidi, nec quid sceleris cuperet conturbatis per insaniam mentibus aut retractare poterat aut providere? (*Adv. nat.* 5. 9. 6–15)

Id enim pietati nostrae maxime placuit, ut sancta necessitudinum nomina optineant apud affectus suos piam ac religiosam consanguinitati debitam car-itatem. Nefas enim credere est ea, quae in praeteritum a conpluribus constat esse conmissa, cum pecudum ac ferarum promiscuo ritu ad inlicita conubia instinctu execrandae libidinis sine ullo respectu pudoris ac pietatis inruerint. (*Mos. et rom. leg. coll.* 6. 4. 2 (*FIRA* 2. 559))

This attack upon Jupiter is not so much directly aimed at Diocletian as it is the idea, found in *Mos. et rom. leg. coll.*, 6. 4. 1, that the gods will favour all who live a pious, religious, and chaste life and worship them purely.[174] He uses an argument apparently indebted to Porphyry's *De abstinentia*[175] that animals and humans both possessed reason and an understanding of morality. The edict simply compares those who commit incest to beasts who have no aptitude for morality. Arnobius' 'An respectu pietatis et honesti' should be compared with the 'sine ullo respectu pudoris ac pietatis' of the edict. He also charges Jupiter for the crime of having incest with his mother. Compare Arnobius' 'cupiditatis infandae' with the edict's (6. 4. 3) 'infrenatis cupiditatibus'.

At the beginning of 5. 10 he states: 'Nisi forte dicitis, conventionis huiusmodi coetum genus vitat atque execratur humanum, apud deos incesta sunt nulla.' His next question is significant: 'Cur ab illius amplexibus tamquam inlicitos vitans refugiebat adtactus?' This makes explicit that incest is illegal. In 5. 13. 16, he refers to the illicit love of a grandmother, Cybele, for her grandson, Attis. He would have passed over the Phrygian mysteries had not the name of Jupiter been found therein. Jupiter had evil passions and illicit lusts for his own mother:

[174] '. . . ipsos inmortales deos Romano nomini, ut semper fuerunt, faventes atque placatos futuros esse non dubium est, si cunctos sub imperio nostro agentes piam religiosam et quietam et castam in omnibus mere colere perspexerimus vitam.'

[175] Porphyry was dependent upon the early Academics, Theophrastus, Pythagorean thought, and Plutarch's *De sollertia animalium, et al.*

'cum in Cererem suam matrem libidinibus improbis atque inconcessis cupiditatibus aestuaret' (5. 20. 9 ff.). He elucidates an unfamiliar story to his readers: the Phrygians' claim that Ceres is Jupiter's mother, which suggests that incest was his primary interest. In 5. 20. 16–20, he ridicules Jupiter's transformation into a bull in order to rape his mother. From the union Proserpina is born. When Jupiter sees his daughter, he changes himself into a dragon because he knows it is impious for a father to have sex with his daughter: 'et quia nefarium videbatur satis patrem cum filia comminus uxoria coniugatione misceri, in draconis terribilem formam migrat' (5. 21. 19 ff.). He continues in 5. 22: Jupiter burned for his mother Ceres. Indeed, many mothers lost their honour and chastity because of him: 'pudoris spoliatus est honestate' (5. 22. 19).

Jupiter is vividly described as an animal in 5. 23. 1–6. His question, 'Et eos qui haec tractant existimari se velle pios, sanctos religionumque custodes?' (5. 23. 20 f.), should be compared with a number of phrases in the edict:

Quoniam piis religiosisque mentibus nostris ea, quae Romanis legibus caste sancteque sunt constituta   (*Mos. et rom. leg. coll.*, 6. 4. 1).

Id enim pietati nostrae maxime placuit, ut sancta necessitudinum nomina optineant apud affectus suos piam ac religiosam consanguinitati debitam caritatem.   (6. 4. 2)

Nihil enim nisi sanctum ac venerabile nostra iura custodiunt et ita ad tantam magnitudinem Romana maiestas cunctorum numinum favore pervenit   (6. 4. 6)

The *coup de grâce* occurs in 5. 29: he enquires whether pagans are attempting to force Christians to worship these gods, 'the like of which you would not wish yourselves to be, nor anyone related to you by blood or ties of friendship'? In the section of the Edict preceding the definition of illegal marriages, we find a possible parallel: 'cum quibus autem personis tam cognatorum quam ex adfinium numero contrahi non liceat matrimonium, hoc edicto nostro conplexi sumus' (6. 4. 5). It is possible that the following questions posed by the African rhetor were intended to disparage this section (6. 4. 5) of the Edict:

Potestisne impubibus et praetextatis vestris quas Liber induxerit pactiones suis cum amatoribus indicare? Potestis vestras nurus, quinimmo vobis matrimonio coniugatas ad verecundiam Baubonis impellere atque ad pudicas Cereris voluptates? Vultis vestri iuvenes sciant audiant discant, Iuppiter ipse qualis in unam extiterit atque alteram matrem? vultis adultae virgines robustique adhuc patres, idem iste in filiam qua luserit arte, cognoscant? vultis germani iam fervidi atque ex isdem seminibus fratres eundem rursus accipiant concubitus, lectulos non esse aspernatum sororis?   (5. 29. 18–29)

The condemnation of Jupiter's incest with his sister would appear significant: the main innovation of the Edict was forbidding the marriages of siblings.[176] The remainder of the chapter is important and possible parallels with the Edict are bracketed.

Ita ergo non protinus ab huiusmodi fugiendum diis longe ac ne inrepat in animum tam inpurae religionis obscenitas, audientia tota claudenda est? Quis est enim mortalium tam pudicis moribus institutis [a possible retortion of *Mos. et rom. leg. coll.* 6. 4. 2 above], quem non ad huiusmodi furias deorum documenta proritent? aut quis suas comprimere cupiditates a cognatis valeat reverendisque personis [6. 4. 5: 'personis tam cognatorum'; 6. 4. 3.: 'nemo audeat infrenatis cupiditatibus oboedire'], cum apud superos sanctum nihil in libidinum videat confusione servatum? [6. 4. 2: 'execrandae libidinis'; 6. 4. 4: 'Sed posthac religionem sanctitatemque in conubiis copulandis volumus ab unoquoque servari.'] Ubi enim primam perfectamque naturam inter fines constiterit iustos cupidinem suam non valuisse frenare [6. 4. 3], cur non in promiscuos adpetitus effundat se homo [6. 4. 2: 'cum pecudum ac ferarum promiscuo ritu ad inlicita conubia'] et ingenita fragilitate praeceps datus et magisterio sanctae divinitatis adiutus? [See n. 173 above].   *Adv. nat.* 5. 29. 29–42

Finally, the criticisms of Jupiter's committing incest with his daughter (5. 35. 19 ff.: 'quid exsecti arietis proles, quid satisfactio his facta, quid quae rursus gesta sunt libidine obsceniore cum filia') and mother (5. 37. 16 f., 44. 3–10) end book 5. It is highly possible that the references to Jupiter's incest are allusions to Diocletian's Edict Against Incest.[177]

VII. *References to Persecutions in* Adversus Nationes *1. 26*

We cannot date *Adv. nat.* 1. 26 after 23 February 303 solely because the persecutions of Christians are mentioned. All methods of torture

---

[176] Barnes (1981), 19 f., 295 n. 50.

[177] As a rhetor, Arnobius will have studied the contents of the edict. It cannot be argued that Clem. Alex. supplied Arnobius with his ideas: see A. Röhricht, *De Clemente Alexandrino Arnobii in irridendo gentilium cultu deorum auctore.* (Dissertatio Kiel, Hamburg, 1892), 6 f.; F. Tullius, *Die Quellen des Arnobius im 4., 5. und 6. Buch seiner Schrift Adversus Nationes.* (Diss. Berlin, Bottrop, 1934); and E. Rapisarda, *Clemente fonte di Arnobio* (Turin, 1939); McCr 42 ff.; LeB 58 f., and M. Marcovich, 'Demeter, Baubo, Iacchus, and a Redactor', *VC* 40 (1986), 294–301.

enumerated can easily describe those used under either Decius or Valerian. And in the case of being thrown to beasts (1. 26. 7: 'beluarum laniatibus'), there is explicit evidence for these third-century persecutions, but none for 303–5 in North Africa.[178] Also, his reference in 1. 26. 4 f., 'exuitis nos bonis', could apply to any of the three. Eusebius informs us that under Decius, Christians suffered the spoiling of their goods;[179] and the confiscation of church property was the centrepiece of Valerian's persecution.[180] Cyprian evidently gives a paraphrase of the latter's Second Edict promulgated in 258 and addressed to the senate. It directed that all clergy be punished. Senators, men of rank, and knights were to lose their dignity and be deprived of their property.[181] Anyone persisting in the faith would be executed. 'Matronae' were to forfeit their property or be banished.[182] Arnobius' phrase, 'exterminatis patriis sedibus' could refer either to the banishments or to the loss of dignities described by Cyprian.[183] Thus all the methods named by Arnobius can apply to the reign of either Decius or Valerian. Every form of capital punishment listed can be found either in Eusebius or in the epistles of Cyprian which date from these two persecutions.[184] And a strong case can be made for Tertullian's time. He is also silent about the burning of scriptures and destruction of Christian churches, the two features unique to Diocletian's persecution. Consequently, the reference to persecutions in *Adv. nat.* 1. 26 does not provide evidence for dating the work after 23 February 303.

---

[178] *Adv. nat.* 1. 26. 7.

[179] Eus. *HE* 7. 11. 18.

[180] Cf. Kidd (1922) 476 f.

[181] Cypr. *Ep.* 82 (*PL* 4. 429–31).

[182] Ibid. cf. Tert. *Apol.* 12. 5; Eus. *HE* 7. 11. 24 f. (banishments under Decius).

[183] Cypr. *Ep.* 82 (*PL* 4. 429–31).

[184] For 'torquetis dilaceratis' in *Adv. nat.* 1. 26. 6, cf. Eus. *HE* 7. 11. 20, 24 f.; Cypr. mentions in *Ep.* 26 (*PL* 4. 290–7), the 'excruciato et excarnificato corpore'; cf. also *Ep.* 31. 4 (*PL* 4. 307–15) and *Ep. 53* (*PL* 4. 346–8). Cypr. was himself beheaded on 14 Sept. 258 (*Acta Proconsularia*: *PL* 3. 1557–66). On 'exuritis' of 1. 26. 6, cf. Cypr. *Ep.* 35 (*PL* 4. 325), who mentions Numidicus and a host of martyrs who 'lapidibus et flammis nacatam'; cf. Tert. *Apol.* 12; one should not ignore the military martyrs who died in the 290s in Arnobius' homeland: Maximilian at Theveste (Tébessa, Tunisia), 12 Mar. 295; the centurion Marcellus of Tingi (Tanger, Mar.), on 30 Oct. 298; and Fabius at Caesarea in Mauretania Caesariensis, *c*.299, on which see D. L. Jones, 'Christianity and the Roman Imperial Cult', *ANRW* II. 23. 2, 1023–54, p. 1048; on banishment see Cypr. *Ep.* 19 (*PL* 4. 273 f.); *Ep.* 21 (*PL* 4. 279–82).

VIII. *The Neoplatonic Proselytizers*

n his invocation to the High God,[185] Arnobius petitions the deity (1. 31)
o pardon the persecutors of his servants and forgive those who flee from
vorshipping his name.[186] 'Persequentibus' (1. 31. 17) appears not to rep-
esent the officials of the government, but rather advocates of the new
ntellectual movement who included Neoplatonists. As we noted in
Chapter 1, the latter had developed an increasingly political posture after
he death of Plotinus. Their argument, although not a new one (Celsus
iad said the same in the second century, and Cyprian refuted similar views
ield by Demetrianus), was that Christianity was intellectually dis-
eputable. Porphyry published a work in fifteen books entitled *Against the
Christians*, which ridiculed both Christ and Christians and maintained that
oractising Christianity should be a capital offence. His method of attack
vas very similar to the manner in which Eusebius and Arnobius criticized
eligious and philosophical paganism; all use the authorities of their
opponents to prove their unreliability as sacred truth.

Sossianus Hierocles, the governor of Bithynia,[187] wrote his *Lover of
Truth* before the persecution began, addressing it to the Christians. He
ipheld the laws against the Christians in Nicomedia enthusiastically
fter the promulgation of the First Edict. Eusebius wrote a refutation
f his work. Also, Lactantius speaks of a philosopher, perhaps a
Neoplatonist, who wrote a tract in three books against the Christians
nd used to dine in the imperial palace at Nicomedia.[188] We do not
now his name, but the suggestion of Chadwick[189] and Wilken[190] that it
iay be Porphyry is reasonable.[191] Equally important is *Ad Marc.* 4:

---

[185] Not noted by McCr 243 n. 46; cf. LeB 30–4.

[186] *Adv. nat.* 1. 31. 16–19: 'da veniam, rex summe, tuos persequentibus famulos, et
uod tuae benignitatis est proprium, fugientibus ignosce tui nominis et religionis cultum.'

[187] Lact. *Mort. pers.* 16. 4; *Div. inst.* 5. 2; *PLRE* 1. 432.

[188] *Div. inst.* 5. 2. 3 ff.

[189] H. Chadwick, *The Sentences of Sextus* (Cambridge, 1959), 141, 143 n. 1.

[190] R. L. Wilken in Schoedel and Wilken (1979: TheolHist 53), 130 f., argues that the
iree books mentioned by Lactantius refer to the *Phil. Or.* and not to the *CC*.

[191] T. D. Barnes, 'Porphyry Against the Christians: Date and Attribution of Fragments',
TS NS 24 (1973) 438, argues that Lactantius cannot be describing Porphyry: the easiest
o disallow is his style of life and moral character, traits irreconcilable with the 'known
icts' about Porphyry. This is weak. Eus. (*PE* 4. 10) notes the contradictions of Porphyry
n animal sacrifice in *Phil. Or.* (accepted) and *Abst.* (rejected). And Chadwick (1959), 143,
efers to the *Ad Marc.* as being an 'Apologia pro Nuptiis Suis', which defended against
ie criticisms that he had deviated from his master's celibacy. Hence the 'known facts'
oout Porphyry's life suggest a degree of moral/philosophical vacillation: the *Ad Marc.*
as written *c.*300/1, a few years before he died.

Porphyry informs his new wife Marcella that he has been called away because of business with the Greeks. Chadwick has interpreted this to mean 'that he had been invited to attend the confidential deliberations which preceded the launching of the persecution of the Church under Diocletian in 303'.[192] The Neoplatonic influence would appear to have been significant: 'Porphyry desired to encourage the imperial authorities in a policy of bloody repression.'[193]

These evangelists of the Great Persecution understood that the New Age of the Augusti could materialize only upon the eradication of the Christian religion. They provided the intellectual justification for, and might indeed have been one of the principal causes of, the militant anti-Christian wing of the new imperial theology of the Tetrarchy. The same kind of condemnation of Christianity is found in the first two books of the *Adversus nationes*. The prayer to the High God for the persecutors in 1. 31 is indicative of the conflict between the pagan intelligentsia and the leaders of the Church. And in 1. 65. 17–22, he refers to the hostilities directed against Christ: 'Quaenam est ista crudelitas, inhumanitas quae tanta, quinimmo, ut verius eloquar, fastidium, supercilium, nuntiatorem muneris et portitorem tanti non tantum verborum maledictionibus scindere, verum etiam bello gravi atque omnibus persequi telorum effusionibus et ruinis?'[194] Although Cyprian's letters abound with military terms to describe the state persecutions of his day,[195] Arnobius' warfare appears to refer to the mounting persecution of pagan intellectuals.[196]

Arnobius concentrates upon the intermittent persecutions of the past in 2. 5. 22–7: 'quod cum genera poenarum tanta sint a vobis proposita religionis huius sequentibus leges, augeatur res magis et contra omnes minas atque interdicta formidinum animosius populus obnitatur et ad credendi studium prohibitionis ipsius stimulis excitetur?' At the begin-

---

[192] Chadwick (1959), 141.

[193] Barnes (1981), 22.

[194] Hierocles is named on an inscription (*CIL* 3. 133) from Palmyra, *c.* the end of the 3rd cent.; cf. Lact. *Div. inst.* 5. 2; A. Meredith, 'Porphyry and Julian Against the Christians', ANRW, II. 23. 2, 1119–49, for the anti-Christian propaganda of the Neoplatonists; A. Cameron, 'The Date of the Kata Christianon', *CQ* NS 17 (1967), 382–4; and Barnes (1973), 424–42, who gives late 3rd/early 4th cent. for the date of the *Kata Christianon*, which suggests a connection with the Great Persecution.

[195] Cf. *Ep.* 15. 1 (*PL* 4. 264): Celerinus described as a soldier of God in glorious conflicts; *Ep.* 25. 2 (*PL* 4. 288): the victorious warfare of the martyrs ('militiae victricis') praised; *Ep.* 53 (*PL* 4. 346 ff.): the fortitude of Ninus' (*et al.*) warfare ('militiae suae fortitudine'); *Ep.* 78 (*PL* 4. 420): martyrs called the 'Dei milites' furnished with 'coelestibus armis'.

[196] Cf. *Adv. nat.* 1. 64. 25–43: Christ 'solum' (1. 25), not the Christian, is persecuted.

ning of the chapter he mentions those who find the Christian religion
ludicrous. Obstinately they reject the credibility of the faith revealed by
Christ. To prove its veracity, he refers to the enormous growth of
Christianity throughout the world in a brief period. Resembling Tertullian, he argues that now barbaric nations have been ameliorated
because of Christ's love and the acceptance of his doctrines. These
premises are only stepping stones to his main point: only Christ offers
the one way of the soul's salvation. Eusebius develops the same argument
in *PE*, and it appears that he and the African professor had a common
enemy. Arnobius continues by accentuating that persecutions in the past
have failed to stop the spread of Christianity. He apparently thought
that he could turn what appeared to the pagans as the weakness of his
religion—i.e. it is persecuted it must therefore be 'bad'—into one of its
greatest strengths by using the execution of the faithful to prove the
sacredness of their creed (*Adv. nat.* 2. 25. 27–35). The statement about
the executioner's hooks recalls Cyprian's remark that the martyrs who
vanquished the grappling-hooks that mangled them were stronger than
their torturers.[197] And Anullinus the proconsul is found frequently
ordering the mangling of Christians stretched out upon the 'horse'
('eculeus') with these same instruments of torture.[198] Arnobius was
raised in the second half of the third century, when Christians enjoyed
the peace which existed in the Church since Gallienus, when the Church
continued to grow throughout the Roman Empire, but nevertheless
when the horrors of former persecutions were still very much alive in
the minds of the faithful. Cyprian explicitly urged the presbyters and
deacons to mark down the dates of all martyrs' deaths and celebrate
their memories.[199] Calendars of the North African Church surviving
from the period indicate that they followed his advice. It is certain that
'the terror of those days was long remembered in Africa and the west.'[200]

All of 2. 77 refutes the pagan view that the persecution is just
punishment. The passage provides evidence for the growing movement
within the pagan intelligentsia which preceded the Great Persecution
and argued for the total annihilation of the Christian religion. Augustine
and Eusebius inform us that Porphyry had an identical intention.[201]

---

[197] *Ep.* 8. 1 (*PL* 4. 246); the same kinds of torture occurred under Diocletian: *Mort.
pers.* 16; cf. Tert., *Ap.* 12. 4.
[198] *Pass. SS. Dat. Sat.* (de' Cavalieri: ST 65): e.g. 9. 3; 10. 1.
[199] *Ep.* 37. 2 (*PL* 4. 328).
[200] Frend (repr. 1981), 427.
[201] *Civ. Dei* 10. 31; *PE* 1. 2. 2 ff.; 4. 1. 3.

Compare *Adv. nat.* 2. 77. 1 ff.: 'Itaque ista quam dicitis persecutionis asperitas liberatio nostra est, non persecutio, nec poenam vexatio inferet sed ad lucem libertatis educet.' He has just before (2. 76. 1–5) responded to a pagan's—most probably Porphyry's—question as to why God allows the Christians to suffer persecution if they trust him for their safety. Then in 2. 77. 11 f. he mentions the execution of Christians by flames, tortures, and beasts. Such a death, he concludes, is a liberation for the believer, a deliverance from corporeal bonds. Martyrdom will only bless the Christians. He is assuredly communicating in language that Neoplatonists understood.

The end of book 2 does not refer to the persecution of Christians because Arnobius includes his opponents in the passage. Pagans should stop their senseless investigations and accept the tenets of the Christian religion (2. 78. 1–4). He adds: 'Urgent tempora periculis plena et exitiabiles imminent poenae' (2. 78. 4 f.). Since the pagans are included, this probably refers to 1. 3, which indicates that a famine was occurring during the writing of book I. Arnobius in 2. 78 simply acknowledges that natural calamities have occurred, but denounces the pagan attempt to blame the Christians and consequently offers them a better hope through the 'rei augustae' of Christ.

The obvious conclusion concerning all references to the persecution of Christians from *Adv. nat.* 1. 1–2. 78, is their derivation from information possibly received about the persecutions which preceded Diocletian's First Edict of 23 February 303. The use of the imperfect subjunctive in *Adv. nat.* 3. 36. 1–6, denoting a present contrary-to-fact, conditional sentence, further corroborates this conclusion: 'Si totidem nos modis totidemque sententiis deorum vestrorum subrueremus fidem, nulli esset dubium, quin ira et rabie concitati ignes, feras et gladios atque alia postularetis suppliciorum in nos genera, quibus sitim soletis vestram nostri sanguinis adpetitione proluere.'

It cannot be deduced from this passage that Arnobius was writing during a time when the Roman Empire was persecuting Christians. We can say the same for 3. 7: some intellectuals were presumably advising the senate to destroy Cicero's works in order to preserve the *mos maiorum*. The passage does not imply that Christian scriptures were already being burnt.[202] Although storm clouds were gathering over the Church, we must conclude that all references to persecutions found

---

[202] As the ch. heading in McCr 197 indicates: 'Some Would Burn Not Only Christian Books But Also Cicero's.'

between *Adv. nat.* 1. 26 and 4. 16 concern those which preceded the promulgation of Diocletian's First Edict in Roman North Africa *c.* April 303.

Allusions to Jupiter and Apollo in 1. 26. 12–24 appear to relate to two events, as we have seen,[203] which occurred during the winter of 302.

IX. *An Allusion to Diocletian's First Edict*

An explicit reference to Diocletian's First Edict occurs in 4. 36. 17–18: 'Nam nostra quidem scripta cur ignibus meruerunt dari? cur immaniter conventicula dirui?' Immediately preceding this is a vituperation of Hercules and Jupiter, and one logically wonders whether it is a veiled criticism of the policies of the Augusti; especially if—and there is no reason to expect otherwise—the First Edict was pregnant with the same kind of religious language that appears in the edicts Against Incest, On Maximum Prices, and Against the Manichees. The orders to burn scripture and destroy churches were unique to the Great Persecution. Alfius Caecilianus, the duumvir of Abthugni, informed Christians who asked him whether the edict had come to him that it had not, but he had already seen its provisions enforced at Zama Regia (Seba Biar, Tunisia: *c.* 56 km. SE of Sicca Veneria (henceforth = 'SV')) and Furnos Maius (Aïn Fourna: *c.* 120 km. NE of SV). Their churches had been destroyed and scriptures burnt.[204] In Abitina, Africa Proconsularis (Chouhoud el Batin: *c.* 80 km. NE of SV), Bishop Fundanus[205] delivered his scriptures to the authorities and they were burnt at the forum.[206] Arnobius does not mention the execution of Christians in 4. 36, and is

---

[203] See §v above.

[204] Cf. e.g. Frend (1952), 4; C. Lepelley, 'Chrétiens et païens au temps de la persécution de Dioclétien: le cas d'Abtugni', *Stud Patr* 15, part 1 (1984), 231 (TU 128); *Act. purg. Fel.* (CSEL 26: Ziwsa, p. 199). For the general background in N. Africa see P. Friedriksen, 'Apocalypse and Redemption in Early Christianity', *VC* 45 (1991), 105–22.

[205] See *PCEAfr* 1. 514.

[206] *Pass. SS. Dat. Sat.* 3 (ST 65). *Mos. et rom. leg. coll.* 15 (FIRA 2. 580 f.) gives the Law Against the Manichees, proving that the burning of religious literature was not unprecedented in N. Africa: see F. Decret, *L'Afrique Manichéenne*, 2 vols. (Paris, 1978), 1. 162–6; Barnes (1982), 55 n. 41. An English translation is found in N. Lewis and M. Reinhold (eds.), *Roman Civilization*, 2 vols. 2: *Sourcebook II: The Empire* (New York, 1966), 580 f.

silent about it until 5. 29. Bishop Felix of Thibiuca(?)[207] (Hr. Zouitina: *c.*108 km. NE of SV) was executed 15 July 303. Had this event already occurred by the time he wrote 4. 36, his silence is perhaps best explained because of the major themes—the immoralities of pagan theatrical performances and literature—that he addresses.

State officials were forcing Christians to worship the gods by torturing their bodies, according to 4. 17. 7–10, and this fits well the evidence from North Africa under Anullinus. A statement in *Act. purg. Fel.* leaves little doubt whether Christians were forced to sacrifice to the gods during the persecution in Roman Africa.[208] Also, Anullinus remarked to Crispina on 5 December 304, that all Africa had sacrificed to the gods.[209] We have already seen that believers were tortured in Carthage on 12 February 304. We conclude that 4. 17. 7–10 most probably relates to the incipient phases of the persecution in North Africa; and 4. 34–36. 23 includes a possible veiled criticism of the anti-Christian policies of the Augusti (4. 34; 4. 35. 22–32) and an explicit reference to the First Edict (4. 36. 22 f.).

Arnobius addressed the nations in 5. 29. 10–14: 'Quid dicitis o gentes, quid occupatae, quid deditae templorum venerationibus nationes? Ad haecine nos sacra flammis exiliis caedibus atque alio genere suppliciorum compellitis et crudelitatis metu?' Executions by incineration have been noted above.[210] The exiling of Christians came late in the persecution when Maximin modified the death penalty. It is possible that 'exiliis . . . compellitis' refers to the overcrowding of the prisons in the eastern half of the Empire owing to the Second Edict, which ordered the imprisonment of all clergymen. This would explain the reason for promulgating the Third Edict before Diocletian's *Vicennalia* on 20 November 303, offering amnesty to imprisoned clergymen if they first sacrifice to the gods.[211] We can safely date the passage after 23 February 303.

---

[207] See *PCEAfr* 1. 407 f., for the problems inherent in the attempt to identify the location of the city referred to in Felix's *passio* as '. . . episcopus . . . in civitate T(. . .) . . .'.

[208] 'nam cum persecutio esset indicta christionis, id est, ut sacrificarent aut quascumque scripturas haberent, incendio traderent . . . et erat tunc temporis magistratus Alfius Caecilianus' (CSEL 26: Ziwsa, p. 198).

[209] In disagreement with de Ste Croix (1954), 91, who explains Anullinus' statement as a rhetorical exaggeration.

[210] See Ch. 2 §III.

[211] Eus. *HE* 8. 2. 5, 8 f.

X. *The Meaning of 'New Penalties'*

The historical significance of *Adv. nat.* 6. 11. 22 ff. has apparently been completely overlooked by scholars. Arnobius devotes book 6 to a refutation of pagan temples (6. 1–8) and images (6. 9–27). Almost in the middle of the book is found the following: 'Sed studiis facere quid pervicacibus possumus, quid intentantibus gladios novasque excogitantibus poenas?' (6. 11. 22 ff.). What does he mean by 'novasque ... poenas?' There are three possibilities of interpretation. First, he may simply be referring to the new punishments contained in Diocletian's First Edict compared with those of earlier persecutions. This would relate directly to 4. 36. 22 f., which enumerates specifically the two provisions that distinguished the Great Persecution from its predecessors. Second, he may be focusing upon unprecedented methods of bodily torture devised by the North African officials particularly for the enforcement of the Edict(s) in their provinces. Lactantius acknowledges the excesses of cruelty during the persecution,[212] agreeing with Eusebius' account of events in the East.[213] Third, 'new punishments' may refer to the proscriptions which any edicts issued after the First Edict contained. In this case 'penalties' may be a better term. The first interpretation is unacceptable for the simple reason that there is no evidence to establish that Edicts Two, Three, and Four were actually promulgated and enforced in the western provinces, although, as we saw (Ch. 1 §III), the evidence from the *Acta Crispinae*, as well as other data, would lend credence to the high possibility that the Fourth Edict was promulgated in the West. It becomes problematical when we consider the fact that 'penalties' are mentioned in 5. 29. 13 f. without this qualification, and 6. 11 appears in the same book at the end of which Arnobius acknowledges that the refusal to sacrifice to the gods is a capital offence. The second interpretation is based upon sources which are not directly related to the persecution in Roman North Africa. The third and most plausible concerns the reference to the First Edict in 4. 36. 17 f., focusing upon the destruction of churches and scriptures, which were new proscriptions in themselves. Furthermore, he mentions in 5. 29. 13 f., 'alio genere suppliciorum' in addition to flames, exiles, etc., perhaps implying penalties contained in a new edict. 'New punishments' of 6. 11. 24 may allude to any of the edicts issued after the First Edict.

[212] *Mort. pers.* 14.
[213] e.g. *HE* 8. 6. 10: compared with the persecution in Africa.

Finally, the statement precedes by only fifteen brief chapters the remark in 6. 27. 1–10, that Christians are executed for refusing to offer sacrifice.

XI. *Sacrifices: The Fourth Edict?*

The last chapter of Book Six contains the final reference to the persecution of Christians (6. 27. 1–9). It introduces the longest attack upon a pagan religious practice, animal sacrifice, found in the work. Thirty-two chapters of book 7 (7. 1–32) are devoted to refuting it, and we shall observe in Chapter 7 that the *De abstinentia* appears to have been a main source for the development of Arnobius' argument. With respect to sacrificing and other cultic practices related to it, Christians are given capital punishment:

Quoniam satis, ut res tulit, quam inaniter fiant simulacra monstratum est, de sacrificiis deinceps, de caedibus atque immolationibus hostiarum, de mero, de thure deque aliis omnibus quae in parte ista confiunt poscit ordo quam paucis et sine ullis circumlocutionibus dicere. In hac enim consuestis parte invidias nobis tumultuosissimas concitare, appellare nos atheos, et quod minime (muni)a tribuamus diis, poenas etiam capitis beluarum crudelitatibus inrogare.

The Fourth Edict ordered men, women, and children living in every city to assemble for worship, sacrifice to the gods, and pour libations.[214] It was during the first half of 304. Scholars are not agreed as to whether the Edict was enforced in the West,[215] and Arnobius cannot solve the problem, mainly because it was after the promulgation of the First Edict in Africa Proconsularis and Numidia that Christians were compelled to sacrifice to pagan deities. There is no indication in the passage above whether the victims were clergymen or laypeople.

There are other problems. It is impossible to determine whether the statement about Christians being executed by using beasts describes events which occurred in North Africa or in other provinces about which Arnobius had been informed. If the Fourth Edict was promulgated

[214] Eus. *Mart. Pal.* 3. 1.
[215] Frend (repr. 1981); 502, argues that the Fourth Edict was both promulgated and enforced in the West. Cf. Mandouze, *PCEAfr* 1. 716. The fact that the Numidian martyrs were laypeople, and the evidence from the *Acta Crispinae*, are in his favour. A. H. M. Jones (1964), 1. 72; Baynes, *CAH*, 12. 665; and de Ste Croix (1954), 88 f., agree that only the First Edict was enforced in the West. Barnes (1981), 23, believes that Anullinus added forced sacrifice to the First Edict.

in North Africa, it did not arrive until *c*.April/May.[216] At least thirty-four laypersons were executed at Ammaedara in 304,[217] but the method of execution is unknown. Authentic North African martyrologies surviving from the period do not provide evidence that Christians were executed by being thrown to wild animals. But we do not know how *most* martyrs were executed. Maxima,[218] Donatilla,[219] and Secunda[220] were possibly executed in this manner at Thuburbo Maius (Hr. Kasbat, Tunisia: *c*.112 km. E of SV) on 30 July 304.[221] They were all young girls, and this supports the argument that the Fourth Edict was enforced in Arnobius' homeland. The story of Marciana, who was fed to a leopard, seems to be based upon fact, but her illegality was turning over a cult statue.[222]

Crispina[223] was brought before the tribunal at Theveste (Tébessa, Algeria: *c*.105 km. SW of SV) before Anullinus the proconsul on 5 December 304.[224] Augustine and the Calendar of Carthage confirm, in addition to her *passio*, that she was a real martyr.[225] Her crime was expressly defined by the proconsul: 'Ut omnibus diis nostris pro salute principum sacrifices, secundum legem datam a dominis nostris Diocletiano et Maximiano piis Augustis et Constantio et Maximo nobilissimis Caesaribus . . . Amputa superstitionem et subiuga caput tuum ad sacra deorum Romanorum.'[226] It was at the end of the year 304, and Crispina, a laywoman, was brought to the tribunal for neglecting to sacrifice to the gods for the health of the Roman emperors. According to the text, the law was used by all four rulers. With an obstinate spirit

---

[216] It reached Palestine around the same time: *Mart. Pal.* 3. 1.

[217] See n. 113 above.

[218] Cf. *PCEAfr* 1. 715 f.

[219] Ibid. 288 f.

[220] Ibid. 1047.

[221] *PCEAfr* 1. 716: their *passio* gives, 'civitas Tu(bu)rbitana'. Thus Thuburbo Minus (Tebourba, Tunisia, *c*.72 km. NE of Sicca) is also possible. On the Numidians see: Monceaux (1905), 3. 148 ff.; Frend (repr. 1981), 502; C. de Smedt, 'Passiones Tres Martyrum Africorum SS. Maximae, Donatillae, Et Secundae,' *AB* 9 (1890), 107–10; H. Delehaye, 'Contributions récents à l'hagiographie de Rome et d'Afrique', *AB* 54 (1935), 265–315; and W. H. C. Frend, 'A Note on the Great Persecution in the West', *SCH* 2 (London, 1965), 141–8.

[222] Cf. Monceaux (1905), 158.

[223] Cf. *PCEAfr* 1. 251 f.; *Passio Sanctae Crispinae* is found in de' Cavalieri (1902).

[224] *Pass. Crisp.* 1: 'Diocletiano novies et Maximiano (octies) Augustis consulibus die nonarum Decembrium aput coloniam Thebestinam in secretario pro tribunali adsidente Anulino proconsule . . .'.

[225] See *PCEAfr* 1. 251 f.

[226] *Pass. Crisp.* 1. Barnes (1981), 20–4, does not mention Crispina; he only refers (1982), 177 and n. 11, to 'some interpolations' found in the *acta*.

recalling the tradition of the North African martyrs, Crispina responded: 'Cotidie adoro deum meum omnipotentum: praeter eum nullum alium deum novi.'[227] Anullinus' attempts to force her to worship the 'sacra numina'[228] recalls *Adv. nat.* 5. 29. 10–14, where Arnobius responds to Christians who are forced under torture to worship the gods. The proconsul's threat to decapitate Crispina if she did not burn incense to the gods in the temples[229] should be compared with Arnobius' 'quid deditae templorum venerationibus nationes? Ad haecine nos sacra . . . caedibus atque alio genere suppliciorum compellitis . . .?' (5. 29. 11–14); and the 'de thure' of the above passage (6. 27. 4). Another comparison is Arnobius' comment that it is in respect of the refusal to sacrifice, pour libations, and burn incense that Christians are called 'atheos' (6. 27. 7); and Anullinus' utter frustration communicated by the question, 'Quid pluribus sufferimus impiam Christianam?'[230] The proconsul threatened Crispina with the sword,[231] with which we should compare a similar statement in *Adv. nat.* 6. 11. 22 ff.

Yet the most significant passage describing Crispina's tribunal is the following: 'Caput tibi amputari praecipio, si non obtemperaveris praeceptis imperatorum dominorum nostrorum, quibus deservire cogeris subiugata: quod et omnis Africa sacrificia fecit, nec tibi dubium est.'[232] Here Anullinus' sole interest is that a Christian laywoman sacrifice to the Roman gods. We find no mention of surrendering scriptures in this *passio*. Yet early in the same year, on 12 February 304, he is found repeatedly demanding from the tortured Christians stretched out upon the *eculeus* any scriptures that they might have.[233] How can we account for the proconsul's change of emphasis? Why is nothing mentioned about giving up scriptures? At an official tribunal we should expect to hear the governor clearly define the charges that have been brought against the accused. Crispina was beheaded[234] on 5 December 304, at Theveste, Africa Proconsularis, for refusing to sacrifice to the gods. The Numidian martyrs, executed at Milev (Mila, Algeria: *c.*250 km. W of SV) in the summer of 303 under the governorship of Valerius Florus,

---

[227] *Pass. Crisp.* 1.

[228] Ibid.

[229] Ibid.: 'ut in templis sacris flexo capite diis Romanorum tura immoles . . . Caput tibi amputari praecipiam, si venerabiles deos adorare contempseris.'

[230] Ibid. 2.

[231] Ibid.: 'gladio eam animadverti iussi.'

[232] Ibid. 1.

[233] See n. 114 above.

[234] *Pass. Crisp.* 2: 'extendens cervicem suam decollata est'.

'in diebus turificationis'[235] undoubtedly relate to the First Edict. Yet it is clear from Optatus, writing a little more than sixty years after the events that he describes, that under Anullinus and Florus, those who could not come to the sacrifices were forced to burn incense.[236] According to the *Acta purgationis Felicis*, it would appear indisputable that Christians were forced to sacrifice to the gods during the enforcement of the First Edict in North Africa.[237] We recall also Arnobius' remark 'de thure' in 6. 27. 4, specifically revealing the state's imposition of capital punishment upon Christians who refuse to sacrifice to the gods, and introducing his lengthiest and most detailed attack upon a pagan religious practice (*Adv. nat.* 7. 1–32) found in the work. These data are understandable historically in light of: (1) the enforcement of the First Edict in North Africa also required Christians to offer sacrifices; (2) Optatus' remark about the burning of incense and offering sacrifices; and (3) Anullinus' attempts to force Crispina to burn incense and sacrifice as well, which supports the argument that the Fourth Edict was both promulgated and enforced in Roman North Africa sometime after April/May 304.

The statement made by Anullinus at Crispina's tribunal on 5 December 304, 'quod et omnis Africa sacrificia fecit, nec tibi dubium est', is not a 'rhetorical exaggeration',[238] but a description of actual events which occurred during the period *c.*April 303 to 5 December 304. Arnobius informs his readers that Christians were thrown to the lions for refusing to sacrifice (6. 27. 8 f.). Christians were executed by this method in Palestine and Phoenicia, according to Eusebius, who unfortunately does not organize the events of the persecution in a systematic chronological order.[239] He nevertheless compares the large number of martyrs in Egypt with those of Africa, but once again the manner of their death is not mentioned.[240] However, it would be erroneous to conclude from this frequent silence in the sources that Arnobius' information is not factual.

The persecution in North Africa lasted about two years. A possible

---

[235] *CIL* 8. 6700. For V. Florus' date see now Barnes (1981), 23 n. 77.

[236] *De schism. Donat.* 3. 8.

[237] See n. 208 above. Frend (1981), 500, gives an early date (April 303) for the events; Lepelley (1984), 230 n. 30, disagrees: forced sacrifice came in 304 after Caecilianus had left office; and the proconsul's *iussio* did not apply in Byzacena. Both are weak: the former overlooks provincial interpretations added to Edict I (See Barnes (1981), 23); the latter assumes that Abthungi was not governed by the proconsul (against the text).

[238] The opinion of the de Ste Croix (1954), 91.

[239] e.g. *HE* 8. 7. 1 ff.

[240] *HE* 8. 6. 10. See Simmons (1985), 57 f.

terminus ante quem for *Adv. nat.* 6. 27 may be 5 December 304, when
Anullinus told Crispina that all Africa had sacrificed. In light of
Crispina's trial, this passage and the lengthy refutation of animal sacrifice
in book 7 suggest that the Fourth Edict was enforced in North Africa.
The fact that the Roman Empire attempted legally to force all Christians
to sacrifice in the period between mid-April 303 and 5 December 304
in Africa Proconsularis, can assist the historian to explain (1) the
statement that Christians are executed for refusing to sacrifice to the
gods (6. 27. 1–9: burning incense and pouring libations are also
mentioned; on the latter, Eusebius, *Mart. Pal.* 3. 1 reveals that it was a
requirement of the Fourth Edict); and (2) the lengthiest attack upon a
pagan religious practice, animal sacrifice, found in the work (7. 1–32)
which follows. The crucial question is: would Arnobius have devoted
thirty-two chapters to attacking sacrifice, including incense in 7. 26–8
and wine libations in 7. 29–31, all of which he himself defines as being
directly related to sacrifice in 6. 27. 1–9, and have begun his diatribe
with such a preface (6. 27. 1–9), if forcing Christians to sacrifice had
not been a contemporary issue in North Africa when he was writing
this section of his work? We may rather safely give a date sometime
before the termination of the persecution in North Africa for these
passages.

XII. *Allusions to Other Imperial Reforms*

In *Adv. nat.* 1. 14. 6 f., Arnobius states: 'abundantias rerum tantas ut
commercia stuperent universa pretiorum auctoritate prostrata.' Monceaux believed that this was an allusion to Diocletian's *De pretiis rerum*.[241]
Le Bonniec agreed, adding that it was made under favourable economic
circumstances and from the consumer's point of view.[242] If the Edict
was neither promulgated nor enforced in any of the western provinces,
this would not pose a serious problem.[243] First, as a professional rhetor,
Arnobius will have certainly been both informed about and interested
in any new law of the Empire.[244] Second, the title of his work indicates
that he was not addressing a select group of geographically restricted

---

[241] Monceaux, 3. 247.
[242] LeB 232 f.
[243] See Ch. 3, and Barnes (1981), 10 f., for the date.
[244] See n. 172 above.

people.[245] Third, the allusions to the policies of the Tetrarchy noted above should not be ignored.[246] The passage (1. 14. 6 f.), therefore, appears to be an allusion to Diocletian's Edict On Prices issued November/December 301. Note that the Edict stipulates that no one can exceed the prices now fixed by the emperors, 'but that the blessing of low prices has in no way been impaired in those places where supplies actually abound'.[247] Compare *Adv. nat.* 1. 14. 6 f., revealing a striking parallel.

Arnobius apparently responds to a Porphyrian concept in 2. 40.[248] His opponents believe that God sent souls into the world to learn evil and return to him. His remark about souls being most greedy[249] for possessions agrees both with the tone and the language found in the preface to *The Edict On Maximum Prices*: 'Thus, when the pressure of high prices appears anywhere—may the gods avert such a calamity!— avarice . . . will be checked by the limits fixed in our statute and by the restraining curbs of the law.'[250] Another probable allusion to the Edict may be found in the comment about seeking to obtain high and cheap prices for goods,[251] with which we should compare the passage just quoted. His condemnation of those who count money coming from the blood of the poor (2. 40. 23 f.) may have been inspired by the statement found in the Edict that profiteers charge an indescribably high price for their goods in villages and on every road: 'human speech cannot find words to characterize their profit and their practices. Indeed, sometimes in a single retail sale a soldier is stripped of his donative and pay.'[252]

In the same chapter occurs another possible allusion to a Diocletianic reform. Arnobius refers to the reduction of the provinces of the Roman Empire to the size of one country estate: 'quamvis provincias totas rus facerent unum' (2. 40. 26 f.). For the division of the North African provinces under Diocletian, a manuscript from the seventh century

---

[245] See p. 10f. above.

[246] See e.g. §VI above. A partial English translation of *The Edict On Maximum Prices* is readily available in Lewis and Reinhold (1955), 2. 464–72.

[247] Lewis and Reinhold (1955), 2. 466.

[248] See Ch. 4.

[249] *Adv. nat.* 2. 40. 17: 'avarissimae'.

[250] Lewis and Reinhold (1955), 2. 465. The statement in *Adv. nat.* 2. 40. 19 ff. about excavations may be an allusion to the marble quarries which existed at Simitthu (Chemtou, Tunisia: *c.*40 km. N. of Sicca; see Ch. 3).

[251] *Adv. nat.* 2. 40. 22: 'caritatem'; 2. 40. 23: 'vilitatemque'.

[252] Lewis and Reinhold (1955), 2. 465.

preserved in the library of Verona's cathedral and known as the *laterculus Veronensis*, provides invaluable information:

16 Diocensis africae habet prouincias numero. VII.
17 proconsularis; bizacina. zeugitana. numidia cirtensis
18 numidia miliciana; mauritania caesariensis.
19 mauritania tabia; insidiana. felix saeculum;   (fo. 256, recto, 16–19).[253]

Dates of the divisions pertinent to the present enquiry are: Byzacena: before 305; the two Numidias: between June and November of 303; Caesariensis: 293.[254] Divisions of other provinces were also made,[255] causing Lactantius to report that Diocletian 'cut up the provinces into tiny pieces'.[256] Arnobius is not that explicit, and although his remark will not allow a precise calculation, 'totas' in 2. 40. 26, following 'provincias', may help to argue for a date between June and November of 303 when the division of the Numidias occurred. Similar divisions had been made throughout the Empire between 293 and 302 in such provinces as e.g. Aegyptus, Arabia, Asia, Britannia, Creta et Cyrene, Hispania Tarraconensis, Italia, and Moesia Inferior.[257] It is reasonable to suggest that *Adv. nat.* 2. 40. 26 f., considered in light of all the internal evidence found in the work which provides chronological data, may be an allusion to Diocletian's reduction of the Roman Empire's provinces, and a possible *terminus post quem* is between June and November of 303, when Numidia was divided into Numidia Cirtensis and Numidia Militana.[258]

XIII. *Conclusions*

Concerning the date (AD 327) given by Jerome in the *Chronicon*, which conflicts with that found in the *De vir. ill.* 79, we have concluded that the theory of an editorial error, though impressive, is not as convincing as the suggestion that Jerome probably discovered the correct date in one of the lost works/letters of Lactantius. The other information found

---

[253] The text with critical analysis can be found in Barnes (1981), 201–25. He dates (203 ff.) the division of the western provinces depicted in the list between 303 and 314.
[254] See Barnes (1982), 212, 220, 222.
[255] Ibid. 209–24.
[256] *Mort. pers.* 7.
[257] Barnes (1982), 211–22.
[258] Ibid. 222: 'Aurelius Quintianus is attested as *praeses* on 20 November 303 at Macomades Minores, i.e. as governor of Numidia Cirtensis.' For the evidence see p. 172.

in the *Chronicon* derives either from oral tradition or a North African ecclesiastical source, perhaps even a combination of the two. Jerome provided the general date of the Tetrarchy for Arnobius and the writing of the *Adversus nationes.*

General allusions to foreign invasions (1. 4) do not allow a precise date for book 1. One should not automatically assume that the Varronian Chronology is used in *Adv. nat.* 2. 71 simply because it is used in 5. 8. 30–6. It must be established that Varro is used in 2. 71, independent of any passage which reveals a direct influence from him. Porphyry's *Contra Christianos* explains why Arnobius develops his argument and makes the specific chronological points found in 2. 71. An early chronology from the Republican period may have supplied him with the genealogical material beginning with Saturn, and Cato or Fabius are possible sources. We have shown that Arnobius in 2. 71. 24 ff. and Varro are not in agreement about 120 years being the length of human life. Finally, Varro and Arnobius do not give the same mother of Saturn: the former gives Hecate and the latter gives Terra.

We saw that most scholars date the *Adversus nationes* during the persecution begun by Diocletian owing to the allusions to the persecution of Christians which occur in the work. This method is not sound. It was necessary, therefore, to analyse each reference to persecutions in comparison with those preceding the Tetrarchy. We concluded that all such allusions found in 1. 26, 1. 31, 1. 65, 2. 5, 2. 76, 2. 77, and 2. 78, cannot establish that Arnobius was writing during the Great Persecution. And 3. 36. 1–6, by referring to the persecutions in contrary-to-fact sentences using verbs in the imperfect subjunctive, establish that *Adv. nat.* 1. 1–3. 36. 1–6 can be given 23 February 303 as a *terminus ante quem.* It is highly probable that we can say the same about all references to persecutions found between 1.26 and 4.16; and the vituperations of Jupiter and Apollo in 1. 26 could very well be allusions to the events which occurred late in 302 before the persecution began. There is evidence found elsewhere in the *Adv. nat.* that Arnobius uses the Jupiter/Diocletian association: attacks upon Jupiter's committing incest appear often to include allusions to Diocletian's law *De incestis nuptiis*; 1. 14. 6 f., 2. 40. 17, 22, 23 f., probably refer to his edict *De pretiis rerum*; 2. 40. 26 f., to his reduction of the provinces; 4. 34–6, to the *Edict Against The Christians.* External evidence from pagan sources reveals that this was not an uncommon association.

Statements about the persecutions which occur between 4. 17 and 6. 27 were given a date after 23 February 303 because of the explicit reference to the First Edict in 4. 36. 22 f. The section 6. 27–7. 32 is explicable in light of prima-facie evidence derived from proconsular legal proceedings under Anullinus, the latest dated 5 December 304, which establish that Christians[259] were being executed for their refusal to sacrifice to, and burn incense in honour of, the gods in North Africa. We may illustrate the historical data analysed above by giving the following chronological outline:

Adversus nationes	*Historical Reference*	*Date*
1. 14. 6 f.; 2. 40. 17, 22, 23 f.	*Edictum de pretiis rerum venalium*	Nov./Dec. 301.
1. 26. 12–16	Syrian haruspices nullified: Diocletian and Galerius present.	299 (Spring)
1. 26. 16–20	Apollo at Didyma consulted by the Augusti.	Winter of 302, Nicomedia.
2. 40. 26 f.	Diocletian's reduction of the provinces: probably the division of the Numidias is meant.	Between June and Nov. 303.
4. 22. 16–31, 23. 1–9, 24. 23 f., 26. 15–29, 34. 1–6, 12–20; 5. 9. 6–15, 10. 1–5, 13. 16, 20. 9 ff., 16–20, 21. 15–17, 19 ff., 22. 8 f., 19 f., 29–33, 23. 1–6, 20 f., 29. 14–17, 18–29, 29–42, 35. 19 f., 37. 16 f., 44. 3–10.	*Edictum de incestis nuptiis.*	1 May 295, Damascus.
4. 36. 12–18 (cf. 4. 34 f., 4. 17. 7–10)	*Edictum de Christianis.*	23 Feb. 303, Nicomedia; *c.*April: Africa.
5. 29. 10–14	*Secundum edictum de Christianis.*	Spring/Summer 303.
6. 11. 22 f. esp. 'novasque . . . poenas'; 6. 27. 1–9;	*Edictum de Christianis:* Christians forced to	Apr.[260]

[259] Duval (1982), 2. 693–5, gives an inscription dated 22 Dec. 304, in the central apse of a chapel annexed to the basilica at Tébessa, in honour of seven martyrs, six of whom are associated with the name of Crispina in various MSS commemorating 5 Dec. 304.

[260] This does not mean that 6. 11. 2 ff. refer to Edict I, but that Christians were forced to sacrifice beginning with its enforcement in N. Africa.

7. 1–32: refusing to sacrifice is a capital offence; followed by the lengthiest attack upon a pagan religious practice (sacrifice) found in the *Adv. nat.*	sacrifice in North Africa. *Quartum Edictum de Christianis*: At Crispina's trial in Theveste, Annullinus says, 'quod et omnis Africa sacrificia fecit'.	Apr./May 304.
	The Persecution ends in North Africa.	*c.* 1st half of 305.

We conclude that Arnobius began to write the *Adversus nationes* no earlier than the last quarter of AD 302, and finished book 7[261] before the persecution had ended, and thus sacrifice was a contemporary issue, probably sometime during the first half of 305.[262]

[261] There is no hard evidence to establish that the books were not written in the sequence in which they appear.

[262] According to the chronology of Cato, Rome's foundation (= FR) occurred in 752 BC. This would place *Adv. nat.* 1. 1–2. 71 sometime before AD 298. The chronological outline above would appear to rule this out. According to Cincius, FR was in 728 BC, which would place *Adv. nat.* 1. 26 (allusions to events before the persecution) sometime before 322. This is impossible (see n. 14 above). Polybius places FR in 750 BC, and this would place *Adv. nat.* 1. 26 shortly before AD 300. The only chronological system that coheres with the interpretation of the passages given above, assigning to *Adv. nat.* 1. 26 a date as late as the winter of 302, is the Fabian, which gave 747 BC for FR. This would place *Adv. nat.* 2. 71 as late as the end of 302 or, more likely, the beginning of 303. Yet there is a good possibility that the chronology used in 2. 71, as we know in the case of the Varronian in 5. 8. 30–6 (see § III, above), was selected for purely apologetical purposes.

3

A Biographical Evaluation: Jerome[1]

Jerome is the only ancient author who provides any biographical information about Arnobius, and the following two passages will form the basis of this chapter:

Arnobius sub Dioclctiano principe Siccae apud Africam florentissime rhetoricam docuit scripsitque Adversus Gentes quae vulgo exstant volumina.[2]

Arnobius in Africa rhetor clarus habetur, qui cum in civitate Siccae ad declamandum iuvenes erudiret . . .[3]

I. 'Arnobius': An Onomastic Analysis

The author of the *Adversus nationes* is known only by the apparent *cognomen* of *Arnobius*. It is mis-spelled several times in the MS *codex Parisinus* (1661) as 'Arnovius', a mistake, as McCracken has correctly noticed,[4] understandable when one considers the confusion which arose in late Latin between the *b* and the *v*. Jerome's source(s) provided only the one name as well. The title page is absent in *P*, however, and it is here that the *tria nomina* would have been found, if indeed Arnobius possessed both the *praenomen* and *nomen*. Although some scholars have argued that *Arnobius* is a Greek name, either for etymological[5] or onomastic[6] reasons, a fresh appraisal is necessary.

The following pagan epitaph from Tébessa (Theveste, Africa Proconsularis) does not support the theory of the Greek origin for the

---

[1] On the data concerning biographical evaluations of Arnobius, see my Ph.D. thesis (Edinburgh, 1985).

[2] Jerome, *De vir. ill.* 79.

[3] Id. *Chron. s.a.* AD 327.

[4] McCr 5.

[5] Cf. U. Moricca, *Storia della letteratura latina cristiana*, 2 vols. (Rome, 1923), 1. 607; C. T. Cruttwell, *A Literary History of Early Christianity*, 2 vols. (London, 1893), 2. 630–42; M. Montaut, '3° Inscriptions du Kef', *BACTH* (1934–5), 34–6.

[6] Moricca (1923), 607; cf. McCr 5; LeB 7.

name: 'C. IVL. VICTORINVS V. A. LX H. S. E. IVLII VITALIS ET
ARNOBIVS. PATR. KARISS. TRITURRI.'[7] This is easily interpreted:
'G(aius) Iul(ius) Victorinus v(ixit) a(nnis) LX. H(ic) s(itus) e(st). Iulii
Vitalis et Arnobius patr(i) kariss(imo) Triturri.' The father's full name
was obviously Gaius Iulius Victorinus Triturrius, the latter being a
nickname and forming a detached signum.[8] No exact date can be given
this inscription, but a possible *terminus post quem* about the early third
century AD is logical, because this period provides the earliest dated
example of a *cognomen* in the suffix ius/ia in Latin epigraphy.[9] The
names *Triturrius* and *Arnobius* are such *cognomina*.[10] A possible *terminus
ante quem* may be about the early fourth century, when the *praenomen*
and *nomen*, here attested by *Gaius Iulius*, were already in decline, with
the exception of the aristocracy, in Latin nomenclature.[11] Since C. Iulius
was apparently not an aristocrat, a date about the late second/early third
century may be affixed to this epitaph.[12] This proposed *terminus ante
quem* takes into account the survival of the first two traditional names
to the end of the fourth century among the upper classes, and also the
African inscriptions derived from a later period than those of Rome
which are more difficult to date.[13]

The Iulius Arnobius in the inscription has customarily taken his
father's *nomen*,[14] *Arnobius* thus being a *cognomen*.[15] All the other names
in the epitaph are common Latin names which ostensibly denote a
Roman descent. This inscription establishes that a North African,
undoubtedly a pagan,[16] possessed the name *Arnobius* as a *cognomen*, was
of paternal Roman descent, and probably retained the traditional *tria
nomina* as well. By the beginning of the fourth century AD, the use of

---

[7] *ILAlg* 1. 3284 = *CIL* 8. 1951.

[8] I. Kajanto, *Onomastic Studies in the Early Christian Inscriptions of Rome and Carthage*
(AIRF 2. 1; Helsinki, 1963), 35–43.

[9] Ibid. 72: *CIL* 6. 1056: 'T. Iuni(us) Laurenti(us).'

[10] Id. 'The Latin Cognomina', *SSFCHL* 36. 2 (Helsinki, 1965), 1–418, shows that
new *cognomina* in ius/ia began to be significant in Latin nomenclature in the 4th cent.

[11] For a good introduction to the problem see Arthur E. Gordon, *Illustrated Introduction
to Latin Epigraphy* (London, 1983), 17–30; cf. Kajanto (1963), 3.

[12] Kajanto (1963), 2.

[13] Ibid.

[14] Cf. other epitaphs from Tébessa following the same pattern: *ILAlg* 1. 3105, 3156,
3187, 3212, 3271, and 3282.

[15] I. Kajanto, 'The Emergence of the Late Single Name System', in N. Duval and
H.-G. Pflaum (eds.), *L'Onomastique Latine. Paris 13–15 Octobre 1975* (CNRS 564; Paris,
1977), 421–30, reveals that the *gentilicium* went rapidly out of use during the 4th cent.
AD, supporting the proposed *terminus ante quem*.

[16] There is no evidence to conclude that he was a Christian.

the *praenomen* and *nomen* were in acute decline.[17] Also, Christian inscriptions from both Rome and Carthage reveal that most persons had only a *cognomen*.[18] Roman Christian inscriptions from *c.*200 to 410 disclose that 82.5 per cent of the men and 80.5 per cent of the women had only a single or double *cognomen*.[19] Carthaginian epigraphy of the second century AD gives a higher percentage: 98 per cent for men and 99 per cent for women.[20] One cannot argue that Arnobius of Sicca was a Greek only because he bore one name. One may give another example from the fourth century, Optatus of Milev: the title page of his work simply gives *Sancti Optati Mileuitani Libri VII.*[21]

The onomastic works of Kajanto do not analyse *Arnobius*. He does conclude, however, that the *cognomen Arnensis*, which incidentally was popular in Roman North Africa, is derived from *Arnus*, a river in Etruria.[22] It was also found frequently in northern Italy.[23] There were even inhabitants of Sicca Veneria who possessed it, a fact which led Lassère[24] and Ferchiou[25] to suggest that this indicates a reinforcement of people by colonies derived from the provincial capital. An original Latin derivation of the tribe appears to be indisputable.[26] *Arnobius* may even be a geographical *cognomen*, having derived its form from Arna, a Latin city in Umbria.[27]

There are on record three persons who possessed the name *Arnobius*, and all were apparently from North Africa.[28] All three were Latin-speaking, and an unquestionable Roman descent can be established for one, the Iulius Arnobius in the inscription, who is probably the earliest of the three.[29] *Arnobius* is not attested in Greek nomenclature, and the

---

[17] Kajanto (1963), 122.

[18] Ibid. 14 f.

[19] Ibid. 9, table 3.

[20] Ibid. 10 f.

[21] CSEL 26 (Ziwsa), 1.

[22] Kajanto (1965), 190, with reference to *ILAlg* 1. 2640.

[23] Cf. e.g. *CIL* 8. 854, 1035; *IAMLat* 2 no. 94; and the indices of *cognomina* in *CIL* 8. For the geographical extension in Italy and N. Africa see *TLL* 2. 624 f.

[24] J.-M. Lassère, *VBIQUE POPVLVS* (Paris, 1977), 216.

[25] N. Ferchiou, 'Remarques sur la colonisation en Proconsulaire, au cours du premier siècle après J. C.', *CahTun* 28 (1980), 49.

[26] F. Bechtel, *Die Historischen Personennamen des Griechischen bis zur Kaiserzeit* (Halle, 1917), 75 f.; Cf. J. K. Davies, 'Lexicon of Greek Proper Names: A Progress Report', in Duval–Pflaum (CNRS 564; Paris, 1977), 465–71, esp. p. 468.

[27] See *TLL* 2. 624, s.v. 'Arna' or 'Arne'; *CIL* 6. 8790.

[28] Namely the Iulius Arnobius from Theveste; Arnobius of Sicca; and Arnobius 'the younger', but some suggest Africa: cf. Altaner–Stuiber, 459.

[29] The *praenomen* and *nomen* had almost disappeared by the end of the 2nd cent. AD.

suffixes ius/ia appeared quite late in Latin nomenclature.[30] Evidence
which associates the name with a Greek background is absent, and a
safe conclusion is that the author of the *Adversus nationes* was probably
of Latin/Roman descent. We may conjecture a derivation along geographical lines of *Arnus/Arnensis/Arnobius*.

II. *Sicca Veneria in Roman North Africa*

Jerome informs us that it was in Sicca Veneria (henceforth, 'SV'),
Africa Proconsularis, the modern Le Kef, Tunisia, that Arnobius very
successfully taught rhetoric. Both his birthplace and where he grew up
are unknown. It has been suggested that SV was his birthplace,[31] and
a recent work on Graeco-Roman authors gives the date '*c*.235' for his
birth.[32] Some argue that SV was undoubtedly his birthplace because
the city would not have attracted an orator from a non-African province
of the empire.[33] Recent studies have shown that such an assumption is
fallacious, as we shall see. It is possible that he immigrated to SV from
another North African city. An African provenance is likely in view of
the passages in the *Adv. nat.* which betray an African context or cultural
affinity. One example is 1. 39, where Arnobius enumerates several
curious religious practices indigenous to Roman (and earlier) North
Africa, of which some are still practised in modern Tunisia.[34]

Dated either under Elagabalus (AD 218–22) or Alexander Severus
(222–35), an inscription reveals the official Roman name for the city:
Colonia Iulia Veneria Cirta Sicca Nova. Probably a few years after the
annexation of Africa Nova, Sicca Veneria became an Augustan colony.[35]
Pliny informs us that it was one of the early Numidian colonies.[36]

---

[30] AD 205 (*CIL* 6. 1056) is the earliest dated inscription.

[31] e.g., M. Freppel, *Commodien, Arnobe, Lactance et autres fragments inédits* (Paris, 1893),
31; P. Godet, 'Arnobe l'Ancien', *DTC* 1. 1985 f.; B. H. Warmington, 'Sicca Veneria',
OCD 984.

[32] M. Grant, *Greek and Latin Authors* (New York, 1980), 52.

[33] McCr 242 f. n. 40; LeB 8.

[34] Analysed in this section.

[35] *CIL* 8. 15858: 'C(oloni) C(oloniae) I(uliae) V(eneriae) C(irtae) S(iccae) N(ovae)'; cf.
8. 1632; 16258; 1634; 1648; 16367; 18868; *ILAlg* 1. 1347 f.; on the Augustan connection,
CIL 8. 27568: 'Divo Augusto conditori Siccenses'; T. R. S. Broughton, *The Romanization
of Africa Proconsularis* (Westport, Conn., 1972, 2nd repr.), 49, 76.

[36] *HN* 5. 2. 22.

Solinus' statement that SV was founded by Sicilians may be wrong[37] since there is no archaeological, epigraphical, or literary evidence to support him.[38] And scholars have not reached a consensus concerning the meaning of *Cirta nova*. It has been variously explained that it denotes a geographical similarity between Cirta (Constantine) and SV;[39] or SV was a *castellum* of Cirta;[40] that the ancient Cirta of Sallust was actually located at Le Kef;[41] a double community existed in SV comprising of *Cirtenses* and *Siccenses*, the former representing for a lengthy period a *municipium*;[42] or finally, that the name represents a moral rather than an administrative substitution.[43] Salama's study of a milestone found at Lorbeus[44] designating SV as the point of departure on the way to Carthage, suggesting the administrative independence of the cities, caused him to theorize that SV was the provincial capital of Africa Nova.[45] Also, based on an onomastic study of inscriptions from SV, Lassère has concluded that the names bear the mark of a romanization of the Numidian population which occurred after the promotion of the city to colonial status by Augustus. Secondly, only forty-one of the 163 gentilic names found at SV are not found at Cirta, intimating a movement of people from Cirta to Sicca and its *castella*, Nebeur and Ucubi.[46] Augustus' reinforcement of the colony of Cirta and its *pagi* in 26 BC, makes perfect sense in light of this.[47] Although noting that the problem is not solved, Desanges posits that the term 'doit être mis en parallèle avec l'expression *Noumidia néa* employée par Ptolémée par opposition à l'*ager* Cirtensis.'[48] A new Numidia was thus gradually organized around a New Cirta.[49] Finally, Beschaouch's

---

[37] *Coll. rer. mem.* 27. 5, accepted by R. Charlier, 'La nouvelle série de stèles puniques de Constantine et la question des sacrifices dits 'Molchomor' en relation avec l'expression BSRM BTM', *Kar* 4 (1953), 1–48; G. Charles-Picard, *Les religions de l'Afrique antique* (Paris, 1954), 116.

[38] Cf. L. Teutsch, *Das Städtewesen in Nordafrica in der Zeit von C. Gracchus bis zum Tode des Kaisers Augustus* (Berlin, 1962), 173 ff.

[39] P. Salama, 'Le miliaire archaïque de Lorbeus', *MelCarth* (1964–5), 112 n. 9.

[40] Dessau, PW 2. A2, cols. 2187 f.; Broughton (1972), 76; Teutsch (1962), 174.

[41] A. Berthier, J. Juillet, and R. Charlier, 'Le "Bellum Jurjurthinum" de Salluste et le problème de Cirta', *RecConst* 64 (1950), 1–104.

[42] A. Berthier, 'Note sur l'épigraphie du Kef', *RecConst* 68 (1953), 177–98.

[43] P. Romanelli, *Storia delle province romane dell'Africa* (Rome, 1959), 198.

[44] *Lares*: *ILTun* 1636.

[45] Salama (1964–5), 97–115. It is dated *c.*44–27 BC.

[46] Lassère (1977), 151.

[47] Ibid. 216 f.

[48] J. Desanges, *Pline L'Ancien: Histoire Naturelle. Livre V* (Paris, 1980, Budé), 199.

[49] Ibid., and adding: 'Toutefois on ne saurait, en l'absence de preuves, considérer le problème comme résolu.'

epigraphical study has revealed that the *ager Cirtensis*, to which Desanges referred, and an *ager Siccensis* existed under the empire, and *pagi*[50] were subdivisions of their territories. The coexistence of Roman tribes[51] and the similar territorial organization of these two Julian colonies account for the 'Cirta Nova' title.[52]

Beschaouch derived his interpretation from a new inscription found in the summer of 1980 at Henchir Mest[53] which describes the town as being an enclave between two territories. Its eastern gate was the western limit of the *pertica* of Carthage constructed under Gordian III in AD 239. The western gate was the eastern limit of the territory of SV, covering an area of *c.*47 km². and called the *pertica Siccensium*.[54] *Pagi* included in the latter territory were e.g. Aubuzza,[55] Ucubi,[56] Nebeur,[57] and Pagus Veneriensis.[58] Of the studies mentioned, those of Salama, Lassère, and Beschaouch appear to be the most convincing and technically do not exclude each other. Sicca Veneria seems to have had a much more prominent provincial status than has hitherto been thought.

Salama's map reveals that the city was located at the intersection of three roads in Roman North Africa: the main road leading from Carthage to Thagaste (Souk-Ahras, Algeria); another going from Ammaedara (Haïdra, Tunisia) to Bulla Regia (Hammam Daradji, Tun.) to Thabraca (Tabarca, Tun.); and one from Althiburos (Médeïna, Tun.) to Simitthu (Chemtou, Tun.), also ending at the port of Thabraca.[59] Sicca was located at the south-west tip of the Djebel Dyr (1,050 m.), which was 8 km. to the north-east,[60] and *c.*168 km. south-west of Carthage. An exact figure for the population of SV has never been calculated and an

---

[50] On the *pagus* see G. Charles-Picard, 'Le pagus dans l'Afrique romaine', *Kar* 15 (1969–70), 3–12.

[51] e.g., the *Quirina*.

[52] M. A. Beschaouch, 'Le territoire de Sicca Veneria (El-Kef), Nouvelle Cirta, en Numidia Proconsulaire (Tunisie)', *CRAI* (1981), 105.

[53] Le Krib = Mustis: *c.*48 km. NE of Sicca.

[54] Beschaouch, 115, map, fig. 7.

[55] Henchir Zezza: *c.*25 km. S of Sicca: cf. *CIL* 8. 16367.

[56] Henchir Kaoussat: *c.*29 km. E of Sicca: *CIL* 8. 15669.

[57] *c.*16 km. NE of Sicca.

[58] Koudiat es Souda: *c.*18 km. SE of Sicca. Cf. L. Poinssot, 'Note sur une inscription de Koudiet-es-Souda (Tunisie)', *CRAI* (1913), 424–28.

[59] P. Salama, *Les voies romaines de l'Afrique du Nord* (Algiers, 1951). The latter was the marble route (p. 61) connecting the port of Thabraca with the Numidian quarries at Simitthu, AD 129, under Hadrian: *CIL* 8. 2119 f.; cf. P. Toussaint, 'Note sur la région econnue en 1897 par la 2ᵉ brigade topographique de Tunisie', *BACTH* (1898), 199.

[60] K. Mason, *Tunisia* (Oxford, 1945), 215. BR 523 of the Naval Intelligence Division.

attempt to do so may prove an impossible task,[61] a main reason being that apparently a considerable number of its citizens lived outside the city limits.[62]

The inhabitants lived off the land. St Jean studied the agricultural establishments dating from the Roman period located to the north and east of the city.[63] Some of the buildings measured *c*.50–60 m. long and 30–40 m. wide, they were fortified on the rocky plateaux around the Djebel Dyr and the right bank of the oued Smida,[64] and the size of the farms often measured *c*.200 acres (*c*.80 hectares).[65] Buildings found on these sites included the owner's residence, often containing a private bath, and barns, stables, and oil mills.[66] Residences were often found exquisitely ornamented. Numerous fragments of fine statues, columns, and mosaics in marble were discovered,[67] suggesting the existence of a rather wealthy farming community in and around the city.[68] Epigraphical evidence confirms this: P. Licinius Papirianus bequeathed 1,300,000 sesterces to the city during the reign of Marcus Aurelius (AD 161–80) to sustain 600 children annually.[69] Arnobius himself refers to Christians and pagans who make up both aristocratic[70] and working classes[71] and live off the land.

On the slopes of the hills located on these farms notched steps in

[61] But cf. R. P. Duncan-Jones's study of Siagu (Ksar ez Zit, Tunisia): *c*.4,000 citizens; *c*.10,000 in total area, and *c*.3,000 slaves = 17,000 total, in 'City Population in Roman Africa', *JRS* 53 (1963), 85–90; and A. Lézine, 'Sur la population des villes africaines', *AntAfr* 3 (1969), 69–82.

[62] *CIL* 8. 641 distinguishes between residents who live within and outside the city, but exact figures are lacking. See A. Mahjoubi, *Les cités romaines de la Tunisie* (Tunis, 1969), 7.

[63] R. Lantier and L. Poinssot, 'Note sur les établissements agricoles d'époque romaine dans Le Kef', *SNAF* (May 1928), 211–16.

[64] Ibid. 213 f. Cf. C. Denis, 'Fouilles d'une nécropole romaine au Kef (Tunisie)', *BACTH* (1894), 374–78. As far as I know, there have not been any recent excavations at Le Kef.

[65] Lantier and Poinssot (1928), 214.

[66] Ibid. 215.

[67] Ibid. 214.

[68] Lassère (1977), 155.

[69] *CIL* 8. 641. See A. R. Hands, *Charities and Social Aid in Greece and Rome* (London, 1968), no. 20, p. 185; and pp. 89–115 for the historical background for these philanthropical acts.

[70] *Adv. nat.* 1. 16. 19 f.: 'Christianos ditiores et locupletissimos', the context being a discussion of crop production.

[71] Ibid. 1. 21. 2–8: 'Opportunis imbribus vestra inrigent rura, pluviarum quicumque sunt rores nostris ab agellulis abigant. Lanitia curent vestra numerosis fetibus multiplicari, sterilitatem infaustam nostris pecuariis inferant. Ex olivis vestris atque vinetis plenam faciant autumnitatem fundi, at ex nostris exprimi unum prohibeant palmitis rorem.'

successive gradations were discovered which had been made to ensure
the stability of the soil against torrential rains. Arnobius responds to the
unjust pagan accusation that the Christians were to blame for the hard
rains that kill their crops.[72] Finally, on the north side of the city, St Jean
found the remains of ancient olive orchards and vineyards.[73] A number
of passages in the *Adv. nat.* can be understood against this geographical
background: a reference to olive vineyards (1. 21. 6 ff.); Saturn plants
the vine and bears the pruning-hook (3. 29. 32 ff.); Minerva discovered
the olive (3. 31. 9 f.); Saturn protects sowing (4. 9. 16 f.) and is called
the guardian of the countryside (6. 12. 5 ff.: 'custos ruris') and a pruner
of branches (6. 12. 6 f.).

Early literary sources reveal that the strip of land stretching from
Sicca to Sitifis (Sétif), and from   Calama (Guelma) to Madauros
(Mdaourouch), was very fertile for the cultivation of cereals, especially
wheat.[74] For example, Sallust's description of the first campaign of
Metellus in 109 BC includes a remark about Marius being detached
from the marching column with a few cohorts to obtain maize at Sicca.[75]
The connection between religion and the agrarian life which the *Adversus
nationes* betrays, especially in light of crop production, is certainly
suitable for a North African[76] environment. Finally, it might have been
for the purpose of acquiring a sufficient amount of grain that Carthaginian mercenaries rebelled in 241 BC and went to Sicca.[77]

Little can be said about the topography of Sicca. Excavations led by
d'Aubigny, curator of La société archéologique du Kef, late in the
nineteenth century, resulted in the discovery of an amphitheatre outside
the city.[78] Elliptic in form, its great axis measured *c.*100 m., the smaller

---

[72] 1. 3. 39 f.: 'Difficiles pluviae sata faciunt emori et sterilitatem indicunt terris.'
[73] St Jean in Lantier and Poinssot (1928), 215. Ancient oil vats were discovered on
some of the farms.
[74] See B. H. Warmington, *The North African Provinces from Diocletian to the Vandal
Conquest* (Cambridge, 1954), 55; Lassère (1977), 155; for the Djebel Zaghouan area note
J. Heurgon, 'Inscriptions Étrusques de Tunisie', *CRAI* (1960), 528 n. 1; and the classic
introduction to N. African agriculture during the Punic and Carthaginian eras, *HAAN*
4. 1–52.
[75] *Bell. Jug.* 56. For possible grain storage barns at Sicca see *NASS* 321; and N. and
Y. Duval, 'Fausses basiliques (et faux martyrs): quelques "bâtiments à auges" d'Afrique',
MEFRA 84 (1972), 708.
[76] The following contain invaluable information: 1. 2, 3, 9, 13, 14, 15, 16, 19, 20, 21,
29, 30, 33, 38; 2. 8, 37, 40, 65, 74; 3. 6, 11, 23, 24, 29, 31, 32, 33, 34, 36; 4. 7, 8, 9, 11;
5. 32, 35, 37, 39, 40; 6. 2, 12, 16, 25; 7. 32, 34, 38.
[77] Polybius, *Hist.* 1. 66. 6. Note that Augustine refers to Sicca in passing in *Ep.* 229.
[78] É. Espérandieu, *Étude sur Le Kef* (Paris, 1889), 141.

being *c.*80 m.[79] Ruins of rowed seats were poorly preserved.[80] Depicting chase scenes in this amphitheatre, a mosaic found at Le Kef in May 1932 vividly portrays life-size ostriches and deer. Owing to its finesse, realism, and attention given to detail, it is one of the best mosaics preserved from Roman North Africa.[81] Near the Turkish kasbah (1679) outside the city there was a theatre.[82] There Arnobius probably saw the plays of Euripides when he was a pagan which he later derided zealously as a Christian.[83] A huge fountain connected to a great subterranean canal has also been preserved.[84] As in the case of most Roman cities in North Africa, Sicca had its baths, on the west side of the city, a part of which was enclosed in a large hexagonal hall preceded by a double portico.[85] It was probably the eleven large cisterns (28×7 m.)[86] located north of the kasbah that provided most of the water for the baths and met the other needs of the townspeople as well.[87] A small aqueduct passed close to the theatre.[88] Concerning churches, Espérandieu discovered that a vast majority of Christian inscriptions were found in the environs of the Bab-El-Cherfline mosque, and suggested that one should look there for the ancient Christian necropolis of Le Kef.[89] He conjectured that the earliest of the Christian places of worship might have been in the vicinity as well. Two Christian basilicas have survived: Ksar-el-Ghoul (33×16 m.)[90] and Dar-el-Kous, a grand Byzantine basilica whose apse of 6 m. in width was still standing in 1976.[91]

The picture drawn from the primary data is not much clearer. Punic

---

[79] É. Espérandieu (1889), 141.

[80] Ibid.

[81] L. Poinssot and P. Quoniam, 'Bêtes d'amphithéatre sur trois mosaïques du Bardo', *Kar* 3 (1952), 157–65.

[82] A. Ennabli, 'Sicca Venereia (Le Kef)', *PECS* 834.

[83] e.g. 7. 33. 21; Sophocles: *Adv. nat.* 4. 35. 22–6; 7. 33. 20. He did not have to go to Carthage to see the plays, assumed by Warmington (1954), 104. Thugga (Dougga, Tunisia) had a theatre also: see P. A. Février, 'Urbanisation et urbanisme de l'Afrique romaine', *ANRW* II. 10. 2, 387, fig. A10.

[84] J. Toutain, *Les cités romaines de la Tunisie* (Paris, 1896), 61.

[85] Ennabli, *PECS* 834.

[86] É. Espérandieu, 'Note sur des fouilles exécutées aux citernes du Kef (Tunisie)', *BACTH* (1885), 569.

[87] Ennabli, *PECS* 834, observes their remarkably preserved condition (1976) and that they were served by springs flowing from the southern flank of the Djebel Dyr.

[88] Toutain (1896), 71.

[89] Espérandieu (1889), 42 no. 80.

[90] Ibid. 139; see id., 'Note sur quelques basiliques chrétiennes de Tunisie', *BACTH*, (1884), 158, theorizing that Ksar-el-Ghoul might have been a pagan edifice because its form resembled Roman judicial basilicas.

[91] Ennabli, *PECS* 834.

steles bearing diamond-shaped objects and a man entering a (temple?) door overlaid with palm leaves reveal striking resemblances to those of Leglay's dossier on the Saturn cult.[92] Turning to the imperial period, neither an unusual number of standard Roman gods nor any particularly indigenous North African deities are revealed in the epigraphical evidence of Sicca. A priest of the Great Mother honours the goddess on his epitaph.[93] Dedications are found to the *Cereres*,[94] *Fortuna Redux*,[95] *Hercules*,[96] *Juppiter*,[97] *Honos* and *Virtus*,[98] *deis Parentibus*,[99] *Sol*,[100] and the *di superi* and *inferi*.[101] Archaeological discoveries have confirmed the veneration in Sicca of Mercury,[102] and possibly of Roma[103] and Neptune[104] as well. Finally, according to Cagnet and Gaulkler, there were temples existing in the city dedicated to *Pietas Augusta*,[105] *Venus*,[106] and *Virtus Augusta*.[107] Many fragments formerly belonging to pagan temples dedicated to unidentified deities were found embedded in the walls of the Christian basilica Dar-el-Kous.[108]

---

[92] Espérandieu (1889), 147 pl. I; 149 pl. II; cf. (e.g.) *SAM* 1. 406 no. 6; 405 no. 1 and pl. XV, fig. 1, all derived from Aïn-Nechma (Thabarbusis).

[93] *CIL* 8. 1649: 'DMS Q. Valerivs Severvs Platienses sacerdos Matris Magnae pivs vixit ann. LV HSE'; cf. ibid. 15848: 'Matri devm Magnae sacrvm.' See Toutain (1896), 212 n. 5, for the *criobolium* and *taurobolium* practised at Mactar (Mactaris) under Probus (AD 276–82).

[94] *CIL* 8. 1623.

[95] Ibid. 1624.

[96] Ibid. 1625.

[97] Ibid. 1627 f.

[98] Ibid. 1626: from the reign of Carus (AD 282–3); cf. *CIL* 8. 15565: the same divinities are found venerated at Ucubi, a castellum of Sicca, and cf. *Adv. nat.* 4. 1. 3.

[99] *ILTun* 1609.

[100] L. Poinssot, 'Quelques inscriptions de Tunisie', *BACTH* (1911), 307: cf. *Adv. nat.* 1. 29. 23.

[101] See É. Espérandieu, 'Inscriptions inédits recueillies en Tunisie par M. Denis et communiquées par M. Espérandieu', *BACTH* (1892), 169 no. 52 (= *CIL* 8. 17516), a pagan epitaph: 'Qui hoc sepulcrum violarit, deos superos inferosq(ue) iratos habeat!' Cf. *IRT* 274.

[102] See R. Cagnat, '13 Novembre 1923. Séance de la Commission de l'Afrique du Nord', *BACTH* (1923), 189 f. = 'II. Le Kef', by M. St Jean, describing a statue of Mercury standing with a cock at his feet perched upon a turtle. Cf. *ILTun* 1610.

[103] H. Saladin, 'Rapport sur la mission accomplie en Tunisie (Le Kef)', *NAM* 2 (1892), 559 fig. 167.

[104] Mahjoubi (1969), 111: several temples have been found close to springs at e.g. Carthage, Sicca, Hammam Daradji (Bulla Regia), and the principal deities were Neptune and the nymphs.

[105] *MHTP* 75 (*CIL* 8. 15849).

[106] Ibid. 96 (*CIL* 8. 15881).

[107] Ibid. 100 (*CIL* 8. 15850).

[108] Ibid. 126.

The deity that made Sicca famous as a leading centre of cultic prostitution in North Africa was Venus: 'Siccae enim fanum est Veneris, in quod se matronae conferebant, atque inde procedentes ad quas tum, dotis corporis iniuria contrahebant, honesta nimirum tam in honesto vinculo coniugia iuncturae.'[109] It is obvious from the preceding passage,[110] and the imperfect tense of *conferre*,[111] that Valerius Maximus is describing a moribund cultic practice.[112] Although it is based upon inferences recognizing common sociohistorical characteristics of the ancient and modern periods that may be too subjective, Teutsch claims to have noticed the possible continuation of a similar practice in the Ouled Nail in S. Algeria among some of the women there.[113] Solinus maintains that the practice was introduced at Sicca by immigrants who came from Eryx,[114] but Teutsch rightly observes that onomastic and archaeological evidence is lacking to support this.[115] Arnobius may be referring to a possible continuation of the practice in *Adv. nat.* 3. 27. 6 ff.: 'Ergone dea cogente in vilissimi nominis scorta suam saepius produnt etiam nobiles dignitatem . . .'.

In respect of the cult of Venus at Sicca, the following inscription of possibly the early fourth century AD reveals that the *curator* of the *res publica* was also the *curator Veneris*:

Mirae bonitatis adque integritatis viro, Valerio Romano v[iro] c[larissimo], curator reip[ublicae] col[oniae] Siccensium et Veneris, ob restauratum deae simulacrum quod iamdudum a latronibus fuerat, interrupta templi munitione, sublatum, statuam Venerii ad propagandam saeculis omnibus memoriam, patrono fido amore posuerunt.[116]

The 'iamdudum' may be directly related to *Adv. nat.* 6. 20. 1–10 and 6. 21, but especially 6. 22. 1–5 which precedes a scathing attack upon the image of Venus that continues for two chapters (6. 22–3). Robberies

---

[109] Val. Max., *Fact. et dict. mem.*, 2. 6. 15 (Kempf). See McCr 242 n. 37, for palaeographical evidence against Halm's reading *Cirtae* in place of *Sicca* in the passage cited.

[110] 'Cui gloriae Punicarum feminarum, ut et comparatione turpius appareat, dedecus subnectam.'

[111] Noted years ago by the great Africanist J. Toutain, *CPER* 3.

[112] Cf. Warmington, *OCD* 984; R. C. C. Law, 'North Africa in the Period of Phoenician and Greek Colonization, *c*.800 to 323 BC', *CHA* 2. 130: immigrants from Eryx introduced the practice.

[113] Teutsch (1962) 173 n. 333.

[114] *Coll. rer. mem.*, 27. 7.

[115] Op cit. 173.

[116] *CIL* 8. 15881.

of the statues of the gods is the main theme. His remark about the *Caracheni* (6. 23. 29 f.) who 'lift bars by devices unknown' to strip bare the pagan temples, may indicate a reliance upon personal and even local experiences of the robberies of idols. It is possible that the statue of Venus mentioned in the inscription, which had for a long time been in need of restoration, might have inspired Arnobius' statement that robbers take the images from temples unprotected by the gods (6. 20–3). The date assigned to the *Adv. nat.* compared with the suggested date of the inscription makes it an acceptable hypothesis. According to *PLRE* 1,[117] Valerius Romanus may have been the father of F. Valerius Theopompus Romanus,[118] who was unknown before the fourth century. Lepelley seems to be right to suggest the late third/early fourth century AD for the inscription.[119]

A few references to various aspects of North African culture appear in the *Adversus nationes*. In 2. 32. 12–8 the Psylli are mentioned. Famous for possessing an antidote for snake bites in their bodies,[120] they lived around the Greater Syrtes.[121] Pregnant with the names of Graeco-Roman, Syrian, Egyptian, and Ethiopian gods is 1. 36, wherein the 'Titanes et Bocchores Mauri' alludes to the local gods of the Moors. Note well Cyprian's comment: 'Mauri vero manifeste reges colunt, nec ullo velamento hoc nomen obtexunt.'[122] Similar statements appear in Tertullian[123] and Lactantius.[124] The Mauri comprised the indigenous masses living in eastern Mauretania Tingitana who eventually expanded by immigrating into N. Morocco.[125] Although Arnobius may be referring to Mauretanian chieftain-worship, a specification of divinities venerated by the *gens Maura* is perhaps a better interpretation. In 1947 M. A. Merlin discovered an inscription at Béja (Vaga) containing the names of

---

[117] *PLRE* 1. 770.

[118] *CIL* 6. 6993.

[119] C. Lepelley, *Les cités de l'Afrique romaine au bas-empire*, 2 vols. (Paris, 1979–81) 2. 157.

[120] Pliny, *HN* 7. 2. 14. The tribe was named after king Psyllus whose tomb was located in the area of the Greater Syrtes.

[121] See Desanges (1980), 252 f. on *HN* 5. 4. 27; and id., *Catalogue des tribus Africaines de l'antiquité classique à l'ouest du Nil* (Dakar, 1962), 155 f.

[122] *Quod idola dii non sint*, 2 (*PL* 4. 568).

[123] *Ap.* 24.

[124] *Div. inst.* 1. 15.

[125] *CPER* 3. 39; Strabo, 17. 3. 2. Desanges (1980), 144 f., on *HN* 5. 17; *HAAN* 5. 107; and the following are related to the *Mauri*: *CIL* 8. 2637–41; 8435; 9195; 9327; 14644; 20251 f.; 21486; 21665; and 21720.

seven Moorish gods,[126] two of which resemble deities mentioned in the works of Tertullian and Arnobius. The former's *Varsutina Maurorum*[127] is similar to the *Varissima* of the inscription and another found close to Béja (Vaga): 'Diis Mauris Fudina Vacurtum Varsis.'[128] A closer resemblance exists between Arnobius' *Bocchores* and Merlin's *Bonchor*.[129] Béja was *c.*72 km. north-east of Sicca, and both cities were in the same province. Arnobius' knowledge of these local African gods was evidently not derived from literary sources, but rather indicates a familiarity with the cultic practices of the *gens Maura*. Their gods were worshipped in such African cities as Theveste (Tébessa), Madauros (Mdaourouch), and Thubursicu Numidarum (Khamissa).[130] Note also the plural of Arnobius' *Bocchores*, the fact that no one *deus Maurus* was apparently ever worshipped alone, and the appearance of *Macurtam* and *Macurgum*, two very similar names, in the same inscription.[131] In 6. 5. 6 f. the *Garamentes* are named, an ethnic group which occupied the long valley of the Wadi el-Agial due south of the Hamada el-Hamra in Libya.[132] *Frugiferius* designates Saturn the national deity of Roman North Africa in 6. 10. 24,[133] and the epithet *frugifer* was very popularly used to underscore the deity's lordship over the fecundity of crops.[134]

Finally, in 1. 16. 12–6, Arnobius asserts that the Gaetuli and Zeugitani[135] experienced a drought in the same year that the Mauri and the nomads reaped 'messes amplissimas' (1. 14). According to the *Peutinger Table*,[136] the geographical extension of the Gaetuli proceeds from Theveste (Tébessa) and Thelepte (Medinet el Kdima) to Capsa (Gafsa)

---

[126] G. Camps, 'L'inscription de Béja el le probléme des Dii Mauri', *RAfr* 98 (1954), 233–60.

[127] *Adv. nat.* 2. 8. 5: CChr (Borlieffs).

[128] *CIL* 8. 14444: Hr. Ramdan, *c.*24 km. NE of Béja (Vaga); cf. Camps (1954), 235.

[129] Camps (1954), 235.

[130] Ibid., twenty-one inscriptions mention the *Dii Mauri*, but only the one noted above provides specific names.

[131] Ibid. 234; cf. the *Vacurtum* of *CIL* 8. 14444.

[132] See Desanges (1980), 249 f., on *HN* 5. 26; also, 376 ff.; and map no. 7 in the back of the book.

[133] See Ch. 7.

[134] e.g. *CIL* 8. 2666 (Lambèse = Lambaese); 4581 (Aïn Zana = Diana Veteranorum); *CPER* 3. 19; *SAH* 120–4.

[135] P = *cumaquitanos*; Brakman and Marchesi = *Zeugitanos*; Sabaeus = *tum Aquitanos*; Ursinus = *et Tingitanos*; Reifferscheid and Partsch = *Quinquegentanos*; Meiser = *Garamantas*; McCr 276 n. 77 = *Zeugitanos*; and LeB 236 f. = *Tinquitanos*. Those who accept P have the problem of explaining *cum*. I accept *Zeugitanos* because Arnobius compares four African ethnic groups; he appears to be relying upon local, personal, and non-literary knowledge; and the *Regio Zeugitana* was (originally) due N of Sicca.

[136] *Peut. Tab.* 4. 5–5. 1; see Desanges (1980), 342–6, on *HN* 5. 30.

in the south-western part of Africa Proconsularis. Gascou's onomastic study reveals that their territory extended into Numidia up to Gadiaufala (Ksar Sbahi),[137] to due south of Cirta (Constantine) and due north of Madauros (Mdaourouch).[138] And the *Peutinger Table* (7. 2) gives the farthest extension southward of Gaetulia as south of Sabratha in Tripolitana in the area of the Djebel Nefoussa. Zeugitana by the beginning of the fourth century appears to have been synonymous with Africa Proconsularis.[139] The Mauri were indigenous to eastern Mauretania Tingitana, the oued Moulouya (*Mulcha sive Malva*) forming the limit of their kingdom.[140] *Nomades* probably designates the wandering Numidians who lived in transportable *mapalia*.[141]

In *Adv. nat.* 2. 40. 15, 19 ff., in response to the question why God has sent souls to the earth, Arnobius asks the pagan philosophers: 'Idcirco animas misit, ut . . . effoderent altos montes et viscera ignota terrarum in materias verterent alieni nominis atque usus . . .'. This could be an allusion to the marble quarries located at various places in North Africa. At Simitthu (Chemtou) the *giallo antico* or yellow-orange marble was quarried and still in use when Arnobius was writing the *Adv. nat.* (Diocl. *Ed. de pret.* 32. 6).[142] Ancient quarries were also located at Sicca's *pagus*, *Pagus Veneriensis* (Koudiat es Souda), on the Djebel Bou Rbîa, *c.*16 km. south-east of Sicca.[143]

African patriotism is often expressed by anti-Roman sentiment in the work. For example, Roman imperialistic expansion is condemned as insanity in one passage[144] and praised in another.[145] Attacking the belief

[137] Ibid. 4. 2.
[138] J. Gascou, 'Le cognomen Gaetulus, Gaetulicus en Afrique romaine', *MEFR* 82 (1970), 724–8; see map no. 2 in Desanges's comm. on *HN*; *HAAN* 5. 110 f.; Dessau, 'Gaetuli', PW 7, cols. 461–5; Barnes (1971), 86; and id. (1982), 212 n. 15.
[139] W. Seston, *Dioclétien et la tétrarchie*, 2 vols. (Paris, 1946), 1. 327 f.; cf. Desanges (1980), 210, on *HN* 5. 23 f.; and K. Ziegler, 'Zeugitana regio', PW 10, col. 251.
[140] See *HAAN* 5. 93; Desanges (1980), 145, observes that *Mauri* eventually came to be associated with the eastern peoples of N. Africa and became synonymous with both of the *Mauretaniae*. If Arnobius is accurately describing the geographical extension of Christianity in Roman North Africa, not only was it spreading throughout the provinces, but also it was penetrating all social strata related to the rural economy (cf. 1. 16. 19 f.); and *Adv. nat.* 2. 5. 15–18 proves it was making converts amongst the upper classes and intelligentsia.
[141] Pliny, *HN* 5. 22.
[142] Cf. Toutain (1896), 46; *NASS* 36; A. Ennabli, 'Simithu (Chemtou)', *PECS* 841; Desanges (1980), 292, on *HN* 5. 29.
[143] See Poinssot, *CRAI* (1913), 424 n. 2.
[144] *Adv. nat.* 1. 5. 16–19; On his views of war in relation to his critique of Roman religion see D. F. Wright, 'War in a Church-Historical Perspective', *EQ* 57, (1985), 141.
[145] *Adv. nat.* 1. 14. 1–4.

that attributed Roman imperialism to the *pax deorum*, Arnobius asks
where was Pellonia when the Romans were defeated at the Caudine
Forks in the Second Samnite War,[146] or when Hannibal defeated their
army at the Trasimene Lake.[147] The latter may reveal anti-Roman
sentiment equated with African patriotism, as well as the observation
that the Punic Hannibal plundered Italy's wealth (near Cannae) and
claimed world domination.[148] Also, Venus is referred to as the source of
Roman supremacy,[149] which is an insult when one considers the vituperation of her cult throughout the work. His argument that Pellonia
has failed to uphold Roman national honour probably emphasizes the
vanity of worshipping the goddess rather than any ill-will towards the
Empire.[150] Of greater significance is his ending of book 7 by stating that
the Great Mother has subjugated the innocent world so that the Roman
Empire might become pre-eminent and its rise to power prove the
perdition of mankind.[151]

We may conclude that *Adv. nat.* 1. 16. 12–16, 1. 36. 25, 6. 5. 6, and
6. 10. 24 lend support for locating Arnobius in a North African
environment, and often anti-Roman sentiment appears to enfold African
patriotism in the *Adversus nationes*. There are historical parallels in the
religious development of North Africa. Manichaeism's success in this
part of the Roman Empire can be at least partly explained as being due
to its anti-Roman outlook.[152] And it was the same attitude towards Rome
that might have played a significant social and economic role in initiating
Donatism,[153] although this would not permit one to 'find in Arnobius
... a hatred of Rome unknown to the early Africans, and one which
will very soon give strong support to the Donatist schism'.[154] Yet
acknowledging that anti-Roman statements almost invariably appear in
passages that attack the gods, we may best explain them as being due

---

[146] *Adv. nat.* 4. 4. 19 ff.; Livy, 9. 2. 6.

[147] Under C. Flaminius, *Adv. nat.* 1. 14. 21 f.; Livy, 22. 4–7.

[148] *Adv. nat.* 2. 73. 6–9; Livy, 22. 44–50.

[149] *Adv. nat.* 4. 27. 8 f.

[150] Ibid. 4. 4. 19–26.

[151] Ibid. 7. 51. 16–21.

[152] See F. Decret, *L'Afrique Manichéenne*, 2 vols. (Paris, 1978), 1. 188, giving examples
from *Adv. nat.* 1. 5; 2. 73; 4. 4; 7. 50 f.

[153] The thesis of W. H. C. Frend, *The Donatist Church* (Oxford, 1952); cf. also id.,
'The Christian Period in Mediterranean Africa, *c.*AD 200 to 700', *CHA* 2. 455.

[154] J. Lebreton and J. Zeiller, *The History of the Primitive Church*, 4 vols. (London,
1947), 4. 925; cf. E. Buonaiuti, *Il cristianesimo nell'Africa Romana* (Bari, 1928), 281 n. 3;
and Monceaux, 3. 242, on *Adv. nat.* 1. 3, 16, 21, 36; 2. 73; 4. 4, 27; 5. 1–4, 18; 7. 40,
50 f.

to the zeal of a convert for his new religion in the midst of official state persecution. There are only a few glimpses of the attitude that had an effect upon such religious movements as Manichaeism and Donatism in North Africa, to be found in the pages of the *Adversus nationes*.

In order to evaluate Jerome's locating Arnobius in Sicca, an analysis of *Adv. nat.* 1. 39. 1–11 is necessary, which is a passage enumerating specific pagan beliefs and practices of Arnobius derived from his pre-Christian period:

Venerabar, o caecitas, nuper simulacra modo ex fornacibus prompta, in incudibus deos et ex malleis fabricatos, elephantorum ossa, picturas, veternosis in arboribus taenias; si quando conspexeram lubricatum lapidem et ex olivi unguine sordidatum, tamquam inesset vis praesens, adulabar, adfabar et beneficia poscebam nihil sentiente de trunco, et eos ipsos divos, quos esse mihi persuaseram, adficiebam contumeliis gravibus, cum eos esse credebam ligna lapides atque ossa aut in huius (modi) rerum habitare materia.

Although Nock seriously doubted the authenticity of this statement as a genuine autobiographical account of Arnobius' former religious beliefs and practices,[155] there is a greater possibility that the opposite is true. Nock failed to consider that 1. 39 might represent an assurance that Arnobius' desire to join the faithful (see below) was genuine; and he did not take into account North African religious practices very similar to some listed in the passage. For example, the 'veternosis in arboribus taenias' may imply a conceptual antecedent of modern Tunisian animistic beliefs (not to be confused with dendrolatry): 'Aux branches de l'arbre, on attachait des chiffons, des rubans, des vêtements; c'était sans doute à l'occasion d'un voeu, d'une prière.'[156] The deity (was and) is thought to reside in the tree. At Fernana in the region of Aïn-Drahem, the practice continues: there is a giant tree whose sacred character is recognized by the whole population of the village.[157]

The belief that a divine power resides in a stone, not to be confused with litholatry, is the centrepiece of Arnobius' testimony and may well have been one of the predominant religious practices before his conversion. Constituting a part of ancient Berber religious culture, it

---

[155] A. D. Nock, *Conversion* (Oxford, 1933), 258, suggests 'that his account of his former attitude agrees almost verbally with the common ancient description of the type of the superstitious man.'

[156] F. Decret and M. Fantar, *L'Afrique du nord dans l'antiquité* (Paris, 1981), 251; cf. W. H. C. Frend, 'Arnobius', OCD 122.

[157] Ibid.

goes back to prehistoric North Africa.[158] Basically the passage expresses
a form of animism, which is the belief in and veneration of spirits which
reside in inanimate objects.[159] The description of the manner of his
devotion to the deity, by prayer and verbal address, denotes a kind of
fetishism, or the attributing of a protective power to an impersonal
force.[160] Philo of Byblos describes the practice among the Pheonicians
by the use of *baetuli*.[161] Apuleius of Madauros (Mdaourouch: *c*.72 km.
south-west of Sicca) mentions it in several of his works, and it seems
to have taken an active part in his religiosity.[162] Cyprian condemned
the practice,[163] as did M. Felix,[164] Lactantius,[165] and Augustine.[166]
Epigraphical data from such places as Thala,[167] Henchir-es-Srira,[168] and
Djebel-bou-Kourneïn[169] attest its use in the Saturn cult. It has apparently
survived in modern Tunisia, especially among the Bedouins in the
southern part of the country.[170] At the *Mzara* (consecrated place)
two kilometres from Sidi Asker, animistic practices associated with
dendrolatry and litholatry occur.[171] Adoration of spirits believed to reside
in stones is practised in the same way described by Arnobius, by
anointing with oil, at the *Msara* of Sidi bel Mabrouk.[172] Another modern
parallel is that *koura* cult objects ('boulets de pierre') in Tunisia are
similarly venerated: worshippers confide in them, speak to them, and

[158] *SAH* 157; Decret and Fantar (1981), 252 f.
[159] *HAAN* 4. 243.
[160] Ibid. 244.
[161] *FHG* 3. 568; Damascius, *Vit. Is.* 94, 203; cf. *HAAN* 4. 372 f.; *SAH* 279 f.
[162] *Flor.* 1. 3 (Budé: Vallette): 'Neque enim iustus religiosam moram viatori obiecerit
... vel lapis unguine delibutus. Parva haec quippe et quamquam paucis percontantibus
adorata, tamen ignorantibus transcursa.' Cf. *Apol.* 56. 6; *De deo Soc.*: 'Iurabo per Iovem
lapidem, romano vetustissimo ritu.'
[163] *Ad. Dem.* 12 (*CChr*: Simonetti): 'Crocodili et cynocephali et lapides coluntur . . .'.
On the sacred stones with Punic inscriptions found at the Tophet in Carthage, see *SAH*
157; Charles-Picard (1954), 5; and *HAAN* 4. 374–7.
[164] *Oct.* 3. 1.
[165] *Div. inst.* 1. 20 (Terminus, on which see also Ovid, *Fast.* 2. 641–4).
[166] *Civ. Dei* 16. 38; *Ep.* 17. 2; and the reference to the *Abaddiri Sancto* of the Numidians
in *CIL* 8. 21481.
[167] *CIL* 8. 23283: 'baetilum cum columna'; a sacred stone was placed in the temple
also (*SAM* 1. 301 no. 2); Thala was *c*.64 km. S. of Sicca.
[168] Ibid. 23156: 'dealbavit petra(m or s S)aturni.'
[169] *CPER* 3. 86.
[170] E. G. Gobert, 'Essai sur la litholatrie', *RAfr* 92 (1948), 26 f.; cf. *SAH* 157 f.;
HAAN 4. 374 n. 1.
[171] Cf. Gobert (1948), 24–30.
[172] Ibid. 29 ff.; cf. A. Mahjoubi, 'Découvertes archéologiques dans la région de Béja',
RTSS 12 (1975), 29.

ask blessings from them.[173] It seems that *Adv. nat.* 1. 39 is a genuine autobiographical statement which describes authentic pre-Christian practices of Arnobius and support the argument for his African provenance.

III. *The Cult of St Peter*

It is necessary to observe a final fact about Sicca and another possible connection with Arnobius. In the vaulting of a Byzantine basilica (Dar-el-Kous) at Le Kef, on a Greek cross the letters s PTRS have survived. There is little doubt that these stand for SANCTUS PETRUS.[174] Another Greek cross found at the site had the letters scs on the top vertical beam in the centre, a P on the left horizontal beam, and an R on the right horizontal beam. At the bottom of the vertical beam there was an s.[175] Again, this strongly suggests SANCTUS PETRUS. If this is correct, Sicca is not unique as a site in North Africa where Christians dedicated a place of worship to the apostle.[176] Raynal has observed that the names of Peter and Paul were inscribed upon the beams of the cross in a mosaic in the church at Uppena (Chigarnia, Tunisia).[177] This exactly resembles the crosses from Sicca. Veneration of these apostles appears to have had a rich history in North African Christianity,[178] but scholars are not in agreement concerning the sociohistorical development of the cult. Frend has argued for the existence of a Donatist cult of these saints,[179] and this has been criticized by Février,[180] who has interpreted

---

[173] Gobert (1948), 30, with a discussion about anointing stones with olive oil; cf. *Adv. nat.* 1. 39.6 f.

[174] H. Leclercq, 'Kef (El)', *DACL* 8. 1, cols. 689–701; Monceaux, 3. 170–5, lists the martyrs: Sicca is on p. 171 no. 14; cf. M. Gauckler, 'Rapport épigraphique sur les découvertes faites en Tunisie par le service des antiquités dans le cours des cinq dernières années', *BACTH* (1897), 413; *CIL* 8. 27691; Y. Duval, *Loca Sanctorum Africae*, 2 vols. (Rome, 1982), 1. 97 no. 45, fig. 67; *ILTun* 1606. For Dar-el-Kous see N. Duval, F. Barratte, and J.-C. Golvin, 'Les églises d'Haidra, VI: la basilique des martyrs de la persécution de Dioclétien. Bilan de campagne 1983', *CRAI* (1989), 129–73, and esp. 152 fig. 16.

[175] Leclercq, *DACL* 8. 1, col. 697 and fig. 6456, col. 699; cf. Y. Duval (1982), 1. 96 f. no. 44, fig. 65; *CIL* 8. 27690 = *ILTun* 1605; and 2. 638.

[176] D. Raynal, 'Culte des martyrs et propagande Donatiste à Uppena', *CahTun* 81–2 (1973), 54 n. 59.

[177] Ibid.

[178] Cf. P. Mesnage, *Le christianisme en Afrique* (Paris, 1912), 74 f. n. 2; Monceaux, 3. 179.

[179] W. H. C. Frend, 'The *Memoriae Apostolorum* in Roman North Africa', *JRS* 30 (1940), 32–49.

[180] P. A. Février, 'Martyrs, polémique et politique en Afrique (IVᵉ–Vᵉ siècles)', *RHCM* 1 (1966), 15.

certain Numidian inscriptions to identify the cult as Catholic.[181] Yet the evidence, as Raynal has also observed,[182] appears to suggest that both groups participated. Donatism did not flourish at Sicca, and the inscribed crosses there will not allow a Donatist interpretation. One can deduce from the evidence that a cult of St Peter existed at Sicca at least as early as the Byzantine period. It would be going beyond the evidence to identify it as either Catholic or Donatist. An early date for the origin of the tradition at Sicca is probable, but how far it goes back is presently not—and may never be—ascertainable.[183]

Focusing upon Arnobius, it is perhaps significant that the *only* Christian predecessor named in the *Adv. nat.* is St Peter:[184] 'Viderant [sc. Romani] enim currum Simonis magi et quadrigas igneas Petri ore difflatas et nominato Christo evanuisse.' Contextual comparisons of the passage with similar stories about the apostle Peter absolutely justify Marchesi's emendation of P's *paetri* to *Petri* (2. 12. 22). Appearing at the end of a discussion about the universal appeal of Christianity, the fantastic encounter between Peter and Simon is given. Some of Arnobius' details are not found in any other literary source. Whether there is any relation between the passage and the legends claiming that Peter brought the Christian faith to Africa is unclear.[185] Information from Tertullian's works cannot identify Arnobius' sources.[186] And too many differences exist between the *Acta Petri* and Arnobius to suggest a literary dependence. In the former,[187] written *c*.AD 180–90, Simon is carried into the air while all Rome observes.[188] Peter asks Christ to let Simon fall down and break his legs in three places. He falls, is stoned, and is then carried to Africa where he dies. The differences in *Adv. nat.* are: Simon flies in a chariot, his legs are not broken in three places, and he is carried to Brundisium where he commits suicide. We may compare *The Apostolic Constitutions*: Simon flies over Rome carried by demons; Peter asks Christ to throw Simon down and bruise him; he commands the demons

[181] Février (1966), 15.

[182] D. Raynal (1973), 43.

[183] Leclercq, *DACL* 8. 1, col. 698; Frend (1940), 32 f.; and Février (1966), 9–14, give the epigraphical evidence.

[184] McCr is totally inaccurate to state that 'Arnobius nowhere names a single Christian predecessor' (p. 41; cf. p. 34); the most recent introduction to Arnobius' Christianity, LeB 68–80, does not mention the following significant passage.

[185] See Monceaux, 1. 5.

[186] Cf. *De an.* 34; *Adv. omn. haer.* 1. 2; *De idol.* 9; *Ap.* 13. 9. The latter confuses the statue inscribed *Sancti deo* with the Sabine god *Semo Sancus*.

[187] *NTA* 2: Schneemelcher.

[188] *Acta Petri* 2. 9. 32.

to let him fall down headlong (cf. *Adv. nat.* 2. 12. 26: *praecipitatum*), and his hip and ankle bones are broken.[189] A three-day dispute between Simon and Peter is given, after which the former departs for Tyre, in *The Pseudo-Clementine Homilies*.[190] The unique characteristics of the Arnobian source are: Simon is in a chariot, after his fall he is carried to Brundisium, and there he commits suicide.

Arnobius portrays Peter as a great wonder-worker rather than a holy martyr. He may have selected this story and placed it at the climax of an argument concerning the universal appeal of Christianity, to counter-attack Porphyry's scathing criticism of this famous saint. Hierocles also compared the miracles of Apollonius of Tyana with those of Christ, arguing that they were of inferior quality. Later, the opponent of Macarius Magnes followed these examples.[191] Thus published vit-uperations of Peter in the period immediately preceding the Diocletianic Persecution may explain why Arnobius used the legend in 2. 12–29, but not the source(s) that supplied him with it. A reasonable hypothesis is that a local Petrine myth associated with the cult of the apostle in North Africa, possibly deriving from Sicca, might have been Arnobius' immediate source. It is the kind of Christian myth with which a pagan, fresh from the opposite camp, would have been confronted. It is very likely that he would have also used it, especially if he wanted to impress the bishop of the church where the saint was venerated.[192]

IV. *Arnobius the Rhetor*

In both passages Jerome acknowledges Arnobius' fame and success as a rhetor,[193] and no one has disputed his word.[194] Internal evidence found in P supports Jerome: 'ARNOVII ORATORIS LIB IIII EXP. INCP. LIB

[189] *Apost. const.* 6. 7 ff. (ANCL: Peterson).

[190] Ps.-Clem., *Hom.* 3. 29–58 (*NTA* 2: Irmschen and Ogg, 549–52).

[191] I am not convinced that in some passages of the *Apocr.* Porphyry is not the opponent of M. Magnes. Contra: Barnes (1973), 424–42.

[192] Archaeological excavations at Le Kef may shed some light on the problem.

[193] *De vir. ill.* 79: 'florentissime rhetoricam docuit'; *Chron. s.a.* AD 327: 'rhetor clarus habetur'.

[194] e.g. B. B. Warfield, 'Africa and the Beginnings of Christian Latin Literature', *AJT* 11 (1907), 107; C. A. Contreras, 'Christian Views of Paganism', ANRW II. 23. 2, 1019; Quasten, 2. 385; G. L. Ellspermann, *The Attitude of the Early Christian Latin Writers Toward Pagan Literature and Learning* (CUAPS 82; Washington, DC, 1949), 63–5; L. J. Swift, 'Arnobius and Lactantius. Two Views of the Pagan Poets', *TPAPA* 96 (1965), 439 f.; Mulvey, (1908), 14–25.

v.'[195] Arnobius thus stands in the North African rhetorical tradition which includes such men as Fronto, Tertullian, Cyprian, Lactantius, Victorinus, and Augustine. The teaching of rhetoric may have consistently improved both in respect of the quality of teachers and the requirements of the syllabi given in classes after the promulgation of an edict of Gordian III (AD 238–44), which ordered the dismissal of any incompetent *grammatici* and *oratores* from their positions.[196] Yet by the sixth century, Greek literary culture had disappeared from Africa probably because the *grammaticus* and the *rhetor* were thought to be insufficient disseminators of literary culture.[197] This may help to explain Arnobius' knowledge of Greek sources; and the epitaphs—there are similar inscriptions from Roman North Africa—of the two sons of Q. Vetidius Juvenalis that boasted 'utraq(ue) lingua eruditus', both having studied at Carthage.[198] It is unknown whether the enforcement of Gordian III's edict entailed a more regimented educational system requiring a standard syllabus for all teachers.[199] Equally unclear is the specific content of rhetorical education in North Africa at the beginning of the fourth century (AD). A passage in Apuleius[200] (2nd cent.) refers to the feast of the muses wherein the first cup is poured by the *litterator* who teaches one how to read. The *grammaticus* then adorns with different kinds of knowledge, followed by the *rhetor* who furnishes one with the weapons of eloquence. Based upon the Greek educational system, this general structure had not changed in Augustine's day,[201] it could provide a lucrative income,[202] and its close affiliation with pagan religious culture was unavoidable.[203] Indeed, Tertullian explicitly states that pagan

---

[195] See McCr 566; LeB 8.

[196] *CJ* 10. 53. 2 (Krüger): 'Imp. Gordianus A. Heracliano. Grammaticos seu oratores decreto ordinis probatos, si non se utiles studentibus praebeant, denuo ab eodem ordine reprobari posse incognitum non est.'

[197] P. Courcelle, *Late Latin Writers and their Greek Sources* (Cambridge, Mass., 1969), 2–8.

[198] *c.* late 2nd./early 3rd. cent. AD; See T. Kotula, '*Utraque lingua eruditi.* Une page relative à l'histoire de l'éducation dans l'Afrique romaine', *CollLat* 102 (1969), 386–92, esp. pl. xx, figs. 1 f.; *ILAlg* 1. 1363 f.

[199] If such details were known, one might get a better picture as to the sources Arnobius used.

[200] *Flor.* 20; cf. D. L. Clark, *Rhetoric in Greco-Roman Education* (New York, 1957), 65; S. F. Bonner, *Education in Ancient Rome* (London, 1977), 34–89.

[201] e.g. *Conf.* 1. 9, 13, 14, 16, etc.; see J. O'Meara, *The Young Augustine* (Dublin, 1954), 40 f.; for general background see M. L. W. Laistner, *Christianity and Pagan Culture in the Later Roman Empire* (New York, 1951), 8–17.

[202] Aug. *Conf.* 4. 2.

[203] Ibid. 1. 19; Tert. *De idol.* 10. 1, reveals that the first payment received by the *ludimagister* is consecrated to Minerva.

literature was the basis for training 'ad prudentiam et liberalia officia'.[204]

The goal of rhetorical instruction was to enable the student to become eloquent, to speak and write persuasively, to present a declamation comprised of examples from history, to argue one's point of view commandingly, and to prove one's case at the bar.[205] The student then could go to a career in the imperial civil service. Quintilian envisaged a programme that was both varied and flexible. The rhetor in the Early Empire developed exercises in composition and declamation; selected prose works for critical exegetical analysis; and lectured on formal theories of rhetoric.[206] Works selected were undoubtedly determined by the professor's formal educational background, extra-curricular readings, and personal literary tastes. For example,[207] Augustine could boast of understanding all that he read on rhetoric, logic, geometry, music, and the maths without the aid of a teacher. From this it would be difficult to ascertain which texts Arnobius might have used in his classes, and the frequency with which an author's name appears in the work cannot be illuminating. Lucretius, for example, is named only once (*Adv. nat.* 2. 10. 19 = *De rer. nat.* 4. 1168), yet there are no less than fifty passages which betray a literary dependence upon him.[208] Also, it is possible that the polemical argument has determined the selection of sources. An example is 1. 38, where Arnobius' praise is indebted in form and content to Quintilian's delineation of the *laus deorum* of *Inst.* 3. 4–9, and also resembles Lucretius' eulogy of Epicurus in *De rer. nat.* 5.[209] Finally, his fondness for a polemical method of literary retortion may indicate that he is using his opponents' sources against them, and a possible example is the chronological details of 2. 71 which correspond to a passage in the *Contra Christianos* of Porphyry. Such interests evidently took Arnobius beyond the familiar works of the syllabus and his own library.

[204] *Ap.* 14. 2.
[205] W. M. Smail, *Quintilian on Education* (Oxford, 1938), pp. xxxii–xxxv, but note p. xxxv: 'There is no indication of a serious and methodical study of history in the Roman schools.' Later in N. Africa this had changed: Aug. (*Conf.* 1. 13) had to memorize the lessons of Aeneas, Dido, *et al.*; and Tert., M. Felix, Arnobius, and Lactantius demonstrate a knowledge of Roman history.
[206] Ibid. 64. The tradition showed little change throughout the imperial period.
[207] P. Brown, *Augustine of Hippo* (Los Angeles, 1967), 36, suggests Virgil, Cicero, Sallust, and Terence; O'Meara (1954), 41, adds Horace, Lucan, Persius, Ovid, and Catullus.
[208] Cf. H. Hagendahl, *Latin Fathers and the Classics* (SGLG 6; Göteborg, 1958), 12–47.
[209] The purpose of the *laus deorum* (aretalogy) was to praise the gods' majesty, special powers, and the discoveries whereby they benefit the human race (Quint. *Inst.* 3. 7. 7); cf. the praise of Christ in *Adv. nat.* 1. 38.

It is significant that the two main rhetorical devices used in the orator's educational discipline are indicated in the work. The *controversia* involved a debate concerning the correct course of action to take in legal cases. Focusing upon a real law, it necessitated the fabrication of fictitious court cases.[210] In order to assign his students these exercises, the rhetor had to have ample legal knowledge, and Arnobius provides familiarity with forensic science.[211] The goal of the *suasoria* was declamation, to persuade one's audience to accept a certain point of view.[212] It was presented in the form of a speech written by the rhetor or student himself, but put into the mouth of a well-known historical figure. Hannibal was a favourite subject in Roman education.[213] *Suasoriae* would often attempt to establish whether an action was safe (*tutum*), legally permissible (*ius*), etc., and Seneca offers many examples.[214] Compare key words appearing in Arnobius' conclusion to a series of *suasoriae* in 4. 16. 58–65, such as *iusta* and *tutius*. He is the first Christian writer to use this device in a critique of a pagan religious idea. In this passage he plays off the five Minervas against each other in the form of short speeches put into the mouth of each goddess which contradict each other. Another example occurs in 7. 9, where an innocent ox gives a speech against animal sacrifice. Although technically each speech is representative of an exercise known as a *prosopopoeia*,[215] the general tone of the argument fits well the designation of *suasoria*.[216] The former was an actual impersonation of an historical personage (cf. *Adv. nat.* 4. 16) through whom the rhetor could skilfully develop a major premiss of his argument. Quintilian stated that Cicero's characters spoke in his speeches better than they did in real life.[217] It was the most difficult to master of all skills related to the delivery of the *suasoriae*.[218]

During the Great Persecution orators apparently formed only one segment of the upper classes who were joining the ranks of the faithful.

---

[210] Quint. *Inst.* 2. 1. 9; see also H. I. Marrou, *Saint Augustin et la fin de la culture antique* (Paris, 1938), 53; O'Meara (1954), 43; Smail (1938), p. xxxvi.

[211] e.g. *Adv. nat.* 1. 59; 2. 6, 19, 67; 4. 34. The only studies in any detail of Arnobius' legal knowledge are C. Ferrini, 'Die juristischen Kenntnisse des Arnobius und Lactantius', *ZSSR* 15 (1894), 343–6; and the hitherto unknown work of Mulvey (1908).

[212] H. I. Marrou, *Histoire de l'éducation dans l'antiquité* (Paris, 1948), 279 f., 383; Quint. *Inst.* 3. 8.

[213] Bonner (1977), 279.

[214] *Suas.* 2. 11; 6. 18, 26; Quint. *Inst.* 3. 8. 26; Bonner (1977), 279–87.

[215] Quint. *Inst.* 3. 8. 49.

[216] Ibid. 3. 8. 49 f.

[217] Ibid. 3. 8. 50; Seneca, *Suas.* 6. 18.

[218] Quint. *Inst.* 3. 8. 49.

Arnobius himself discloses that 'oratores grammatici rhetores consulti iuris ac medici, philosophiae etiam secreta rimantes' (2. 5. 15 ff.) now seek instruction in the Church. Liebeschuetz has observed that the *Adv. nat.* is significant for the evolving attitudes of the Roman classes.[219] We should not interpret the passage (2. 5. 15 ff.) as rhetorical exaggeration because a contemporary of Arnobius, Victor of Cirta (Constantine, Algeria), a *grammaticus latinus*, was a Christian.[220]

Finally, although Diocletian's *Edictum de pretiis* fixes the rhetor's monthly salary at 250 *denarii* per student, many factors such as class size, his popularity, how many students actually paid fees at the end of the term (professors then did not have the blessings of advance term fees as they do now), whether he possessed a municipal chair, etc., make it impossible to estimate Arnobius' social position and wealth. Furthermore, the edict was probably not promulgated in the west.[221] Considerations of the provincial status of Sicca, Jerome's testimony, and Nicholson's suggestion that Eumenius' appointment as Professor of Latin Literature at Autun for 600,000 sesterces annually (and the restoration of its college) may have been part of official governmental policy to revive Latin letters, all strongly suggest that Arnobius enjoyed a prominent status as a rhetor in Roman North Africa at the beginning of the fourth century. Jerome's assertion that Arnobius was a successful professor of rhetoric in Sicca is therefore absolutely credible.

V. *The Means and Motives of the Conversion: Dreams*

et adhuc ethnicus ad credulitatem somniis compelletur

Most scholars have accepted Jerome's account that dreams led Arnobius to embrace Christianity. For example, Waszink suggests that *Adv. nat.* 2. 46. 29 ff. and Jerome's testimony do not conflict with each other—an argument used by some who reject the story's authenticity—'for in the second and third centuries of our era there was a general interest in dreams and their classification . . . in which unreliable dreams had their

---

[219] Liebeschuetz (1979), 253; cf. G. Boissier, *La fin du paganisme*, 2 vols. (Paris, 1891), I. 236.

[220] *Gesta apud Zenophilum* (CSEL 26; Ziwsa, p. 185).

[221] R. Goodchild, 'Diocletian's Price-Edict at Ptolemais (Cyrenaica)', *JRS* 45 (1955), 106–15.

place no less than prophetic ones.'[222] Yet doubters remain.[223] In 2. 39 the motive of the conversion is not mentioned. Cyprian's account of his conversion stresses deliverance from sin and vice through the holy water of baptism.[224] Arnobius emphasizes the abandonment of former superstitious practices in favour of the true religion. Christ has simply led him to the truth. One should perhaps not expect Arnobius to conceal the fact that he had been recently converted. *Adversus nationes* 3. 24 provides no occasion to speak of dreams.[225]

An argument from silence to disprove Jerome is quite weak. A statement about the conversion being recent may have served well a double purpose. First, it may have assured the bishop of the church at Sicca of his sincerity to join his flock. Second, it may have prevented any hasty conclusions being made concerning the authenticity of his faith or the orthodoxy of his religious ideas. On the latter, note the sensitivity to his scriptural apology in 1. 47: he twice states cautiously that he is only giving a summary, which may imply that his opponents were more familiar with the contents of Christian scripture[226] than he.

One looks in vain, however, for an explanation as to how the conversion occurred. McCracken refers to the story about Jupiter's revelation to T. Latinius in a dream[227] in *Adv. nat.* 7. 39 as if it invalidated Jerome's account.[228] Le Bonniec has observed, however, that the pagan was punished in the story for not positively responding to the message communicated by the dream. Also, 7. 39 coheres well with 1. 46. 29 ff., since the former highlights the ridiculous nature of Jupiter's revelation, namely to a dancer in the secular games. Both passages are restricted to *vain* dreams, and one should not deduce therefrom that Arnobius interpreted all dreams in this manner.

A very common religious belief in antiquity was the ability of the divine world to communicate with humans in dreams. Experienced by philosophers such as Plato[229] and the Stoic Marcus Aure-

---

[222] J. H. Waszink, *VC* 4 (1950), 117 ff.

[223] e.g. Cruttwell (1893), 2. 631; Neander (1872), 449; Freppel (1893), 32; Moule (1877), *DCB* 50; Oehler (1846), p. x; Bryce–Campbell p. x; and Mulvey (1908), 10, who thinks that Jerome is reporting a legend.

[224] *Ad. Don.* 3 (CChr: Simonetti).

[225] Against McCr 15.

[226] *Adv. nat.* 1. 54–9.

[227] McCr 615 n. 130, argues that Arnobius used Cicero, *De div.* 1. 26. 55. Q. Fabius Pictor is another possibility.

[228] McCr 15.

[229] *Charm.* 173 A; *Rep.* 9. 572 A; *Tim.* 71 D; important also are Iamblichus, *De myst.* 3. 3; Diog. Laer. 8. 32; Cic. *De div.* 1. 57. 129 f.

lius,[230] it was common among both pagans[231] and Christians.[232] The historian Dio Cassius believed that a demon instructed him in a dream to write his history.[233] Oneirocritical studies reached an apex in Artemidorus of Ephesus (2nd century AD), who wrote a book of dream-interpretations. Aelius Aristides (AD 118–80), the greatest hypochondriac of antiquity—or at least the greatest on record, since *Adv. nat.* 1. 49. 1–16 informs us there were many thousands more—from 145–7 remained *incubated* in the temple complex at Pergamum and received prescriptions in dreams from Asclepius.[234] The religious experiences of Roman North Africa were no exception: Saturn frequently communicated with his devotees through or *ex visu*.[235] The latter, though not related to the national deity, is attested in epigraphical evidence at Sicca.[236] Such notable North African Christians as Tertullian[237] and Cyprian[238] firmly believed in experiencing the divine world *per visionem*. One can also recall the visions of the North African martyrs,[239] and there is the memorable dream of Monica.[240] By the end of antiquity, Macrobius, who was probably a North African,[241] developed a sophisticated classification of dreams.[242] And it is worth noting in conjunction with Jerome's assertion about the importance of dreams in the conversion of Arnobius, that Augustine highly respected a dream sent to a potential catechumen by God.[243] Revelations of this nature indicated God's willingness to

---

[230] *Med.* 1. 17; 9. 27.

[231] e.g., Hom., *Il.* 23. 65; *Od.* 24. 12; Philos. *Vit. Apoll.* 8. 12; Virg. *Aen.* 5. 719–39.

[232] Tert. *De an.* 47; Lact. *De opif. dei* 18. 9; Aug. *Civ. Dei* 18. 18. 2.

[233] *Hist. rom.* 72. 23.

[234] e.g. *Or.* 48. 3; 42–5; 48. 9; 49. 2; 49. 34 (Keil, 1898). Ample bibliography appears in *SAH* 342.

[235] e.g. *CIL* 8. 8201; 8826: *somnio monitus*; 9650 = *SAH* 313, 336, 339, and esp. 341 f.; Frend (1952), 79 n. 7. The god could order his servant to sacrifice *ex visu, ex visu capite, ex visu monitus, somnio iussus*, etc. (*SAH* 341); or build a temple, e.g. at Thala (*SAM* 1. 300 no. 1); or an altar erected at Aïn-Tounga (Thignica) 'ex praecepto domini Saturni' (*SAM* 1. 417 no. 2); *SAM* 1. 211 no. 1.

[236] *CIL* 8. 1629: 'Portae novae sacrum ex visu Q. Iunius Terminianus fecit.'

[237] *De idol.* 15. 7.

[238] *Ep.* 7. 5 (*PL* 4. 243): warned about laxity in prayer; *Ep.* 9. 4 (*PL* 4. 253): visions about the lapsed; *Ep.* 33. 1 (*PL* 4. 321): a night vision; *Epp.* 34 and 45. 1 (*PL* 4. 325; 349 f.); *Ep.* 53.5 (*PL* 3. 887 f.); and *De mortal.* 25 (*PL* 4. 600: CChr: Simonetti).

[239] e.g. *Pass. Perpet. et Fel.*

[240] Aug. *Conf.* 3. 11 (LCL: Watts).

[241] Cf. T. D. Barnes, 'Aspects of the Background of the City of God', *RUO* 52 (1982), 79 with bibliography.

[242] *Comm. somn. Scip.* 3. 2, in H. Stahl, *Macrobius. Commentary on the Dream of Scipio* (New York, 1952).

[243] *De cat. rud.* 6. 10 (CChr: Bauer).

admonish the new convert to join the faithful.[244] The fact that Augustine mentions this to Deogratias, who is seeking advice on catechetical exercises, suggests that this was a common experience among new converts to North African Christianity.

The most common North African experience seems to have been that which occurred *ex visu* or the simple *visio* for which Cyprian has a remarkable fondness.[245] Arnobius enumerates the *contemporary* miracles of Christ in 1. 46, acknowledging that he 'iustissimis viris etiamnunc inpollutis ac diligentibus sese non per vana insomnia sed per purae speciem simplicitatis apparet'. This sounds like a definite affirmation of the belief in some kind of theophany. Possible noun parallels, to be compared with the soteriological *aura* of 2. 60. 25 found in a discussion of a personal act of meditation, might be *ex visu*, *visio*, and *apparentia*. Number five of Macrobius' Neoplatonic classification of dreams equates *visum* with apparition. These considerations may indeed indicate that Arnobius believed in the ability of Christ to reveal himself to persons in his day and may imply that an original personal experience of *ex visu compelletur* might have undergone a trans-mediterranean name change to *somniis compelletur*.[246]

Jerome states how, but not why Arnobius became a Christian. The content of the dreams/visions and the specific message that they revealed is unknown. The faith of the martyrs probably played a part in the conversion.[247] Some suggest the decision was influenced by a desire for a personalized immortality.[248] Other factors undoubtedly were Arnobius' strong fear of death,[249] a dissatisfaction with religious paganism,[250] the revolting character of the cult of Venus,[251] the moral superiority of Christ,[252] and a concomitant disdain for the immoralities of the gods.[253]

---

[244] *De cat. rud.* 6. 10 (CChr: Bauer).

[245] See n. 238 above.

[246] Jerome's personal experience might account for a change. We recall the divine admonition, 'Ciceronianus es non Christianus' (*Ep.* 22. 30: LCL (Wright)).

[247] Cf. e.g. Freppel (1893), 32; Moule (1877), *DCB* 50; Monceaux, 3. 244; Moricca (1923), 1. 608; LeB 11.

[248] e.g. Quasten, 2. 391; and F. Cumont, *Les religions orientales dans le paganisme romain* (Paris, 1929), 220 n. 55, add the fear of death; Altaner–Stuiber, 184; LeB 11; Monceaux, 3. 244, says that it was mainly an 'intellectual' conversion.

[249] A non-Epicurean idea analysed in the following chapter.

[250] Cruttwell (1893), 2. 631; Neander (1872), 449; Frend (1970), OCD 122.

[251] A. W. Newton, 'The *Adversus Gentes* of Arnobius. A Study in Christian Apologetics', *LPSL* 52 (1897–8), 156; Mulvey, 12.

[252] Monceaux, 3. 244; McGiffert (1933), 2. 41.

[253] Moricca (1923), 1. 608 f.; McGiffert (1933), 2. 41; Liebeschuetz (1979), 39–54.

An ambiguous relationship always existed between religion and morality in Roman paganism, and Arnobius takes full advantage of this in books 3–7.[254] His attack reaches a climax in 6. 25 (cf. 4. 36), where he criticizes the building of temples.[255] Note especially 6. 3. 15–18: 'Templa igitur, quaerimus, in deorum quos usus aut in rei cuius necessitatem aut dicitis esse constructa aut esse rursus aedificanda censetis?' This may allude to contemporary construction or renovation of temples. It is known that Africa Proconsularis experienced twenty-one constructions or repairs between 284 and 306.[256] This is significant because every religious revival from Augustus to Diocletian included both moral reforms and the erection of temples.[257] During the Tetrarchy moral reforms were applicable to all provinces, but the most active programme of temple building or renovation appears to have been restricted to North Africa. It would appear that Arnobius was writing during an attempted pagan religious revival in his homeland. This would help to explain the sustained diatribe of the immoralities of the gods in books 3–7, and one reason why he became a Christian.

Arnobius' soteriology may reveal the motives of his conversion. There are two principal reasons for this. First, the main work of Christ in the work is redemptive.[258] He grants immortality to the human soul.[259] The immortalization of the soul is the centrepiece of his defence of Christianity.[260] Although his soteriology is predominantly coloured by an eschatological application, an unquestionably clear concept of temporal experiences of salvation occurs as well.[261] This eschatological accentuation may reveal what appealed to him about Christianity and what perhaps his former religious beliefs either lacked totally or did not clarify precisely.[262] By this period the Christian doctrine of personalized

[254] Liebeschuetz (1979), 39–54.

[255] See ibid. 236 f.

[256] Warmington, 33.

[257] Liebeschuetz (1979), 236–8.

[258] See Ch. 7.

[259] i.e. by transforming the *media qualitas animae* into an essential condition of immortality (*Adv. nat.* 2. 65).

[260] In bk. 2, the overriding concern is how the soul can become incorrupt. McCr 301, gives a different interpretation.

[261] I mean a divinely initiated experience which ameliorates some aspect of earthly existence: cf. *Adv. nat.* 1. 3; 1. 6 (wars are reduced by Christ: cf. Eus *PE* 1. 4); 1. 22, 27, 38 f., 42, 44–54, 63, 65; 2. 2, 12, 34, 60, 63, 65.

[262] A principal cause of the religious success of Christianity in the Graeco-Roman world appears to have been its explicit eschatology compared with ambiguous ideas about the end of the world found in Isisism and other pagan cults. The fact that the Saturn cult did not have a well-defined eschatology might have led to its demise. See my 'A

immortality had found a receptive audience throughout the Graeco-Roman religious world. Second, the clearly defined and unambiguous relationship between religion and morality which characterized Christianity appears to have made an indelible impression upon him.[263]

VI. *The Enemy of the Faith and the Hesitant Bishop*

> neque ab episcopo impetraret fidem quam semper impugnaverat,
> elucubravit adversum pristinam religionem luculentissimos libros,
> et tandem veluti quibusdam obsidibus pietatis, foedus impetravit.

Jerome associates the bishop's hesitation to admit Arnobius into the Church—taking here *fidem* to designate specifically catechetical training which culminates in baptism and communicating membership in the local church at Sicca—with the fact that he always (*semper*) used to attack the faith. In the first two books it is interesting to observe that Arnobius does betray a good amount of familiarity with contemporary pagan attacks upon Christianity, principally a number of Porphyrian anti-Christian comments,[264] all of which may imply that he is himself now using against his opponents some of the weapons formerly used against the Church. It would consequently be logical to view books 1 and 2 as retractations of the anti-Christian propaganda which Arnobius himself incorporated in his attack upon the faith.

There are historical precedents for such recantations. Two examples are: Porphyry's acknowledgement that his ideas that the object of thought exists outside the *nous* were not correct, having recanted in writing on his third response to Amelius' criticisms;[265] and Augustine's *Retractationes* written in 426/7, although technically he was giving revisions rather than retracting former statements. Therefore Porphyry offers a better parallel with Arnobius. After reading his recantation at the Neoplatonic School in Rome, Porphyry says that he believed in Plotinus' writings.[266] His recantation was thus a pledge of faith in Plotinus' teachings. He was converted, i.e., he began to use these new doctrines as the authoritative norms for his philosophical worldview.

Study of Graeco-Roman Pagan and Christian Soteriologies of the Second Century A.D.' (STM thesis catalogued in the Yale Divinity School Library, New Haven, Conn., 1982).

[263] See Ch. 7.
[264] See Ch. 6.
[265] *Vit. Plot.* 18 (LCL: Armstrong).
[266] Ibid.

The same procedure may be applied to Arnobius, and it is quite possible that the purpose for writing books 1 and 2 is best understood as a recanting of former beliefs rather than as a Christian apology in a strict sense. If Arnobius was as ruthless in his attacks upon Christianity as he displays (books 3–7) in his attack upon paganism, the bishop would have had good reasons to question the sincerity of his desire to become a member of his church. Most scholars accept Jerome's story without critical analysis,[267] some reject it,[268] or assert that it is improbable,[269] and others have been unable to come to a definite decision.[270] Mulvey thought it was spurious because Arnobius claims to be a Christian in 1. 39, noting the *nunc* of 1. 11, but this fails to distinguish between personal experience and official ecclesiastical recognition.

Evidence from the North African ecclesiastical tradition reveals that the only bishop known by name from Sicca who precedes Arnobius is Castus. He attended the Seventh Council of Carthage on 1 September 256.[271] It is improbable that he was still bishop of Sicca in 302–5. The Decian (AD 250–1) and Valerian (257–8) persecutions had not yet occurred, and we know that bishops in particular were executed during this time. Also, judging from extant cemetery inscriptions from Sicca, one undoubtedly considered himself fortunate to have lived beyond the age of 50.[272] So if Castus was (e.g.) in his mid-20s at the council in 256, this would place him over 70 by the year 302. An analysis of the city's epitaphs has revealed that of 109 inscriptions, six males (5.5 per cent) and three females (2.8 per cent) had lived past 100; and the average life span was 47.5 to 59.2 years.[273] Yet it is certain that Arnobius presented himself to a bishop in order to be admitted into the Church. Cyprian had once stated that 'no one can come to communion unless the hands

[267] e.g. A. G. Amatucci, *Storia della letteratura latina cristiana* (Turin, 1955), 99; L. Salvatorelli, *Storia della letteratura latina cristiana dalle origini alla metàdel VI secolo* (Milan, 1946), 105; Le Nourry, *PL* 5. 391; Hanslik, *RGG* 631; H. Jordan, *Geschichte der altchristlichen Literatur* (Leipzig, 1911), 229; Martin, *LTK* 1. 891; Krüger, *RPTK* 1. 116; LeB 12.
[268] e.g. Altaner–Stuiber, 183; Buonaiuti (1928), 279; Burger (1970), 6; F. A. Wright, *Fathers of the Church* (London, 1928), 140.
[269] E. G. Sihler, *From Augustus to Augustine* (Cambridge, 1923), 167.
[270] e.g. E. J. Goodspeed, *A History of Early Christian Literature* (Chicago, 1942), 282; McCr 17; compare LeB 11 f., with bibliography; I find no evidence that Arnobius was a presbyter, as Trithemius asserts (*De script. eccles.* 53); cf. LeB 13 n. 2.
[271] *De sent. epis.* (CSEL 3: Hartel).
[272] *CIL* 8. 1650 (75 yrs.); 1655 (79 and 83); 1662 (81).
[273] G. I. Ikurite, 'Notes on Mortality in Roman Africa', *MusAfr* (1973) 67 table 5; cf. *NASS* 231.

of the bishop and clergy be first imposed upon him.'[274] By the Council
of Carthage in 411 the African bishops were 'the masters of their small
worlds and so virtually irremovable'.[275] Cyprian wrote mainly concerning
the unity of the Church in relation to schismatics and the lapsed seeking
re-entry into its fellowship, so it should not be surprising that he
nowhere cautions against the acceptance of a pagan. His advice to
Euchratius about a *histrio* assumes that the latter was a communicating
member of a Church who needed spiritual reindoctrination.[276] Such
silence on the subject does not necessarily mean that there was not an
episcopal policy related to accepting pagans who might be potentially
dangerous to the unity and peace of the Church, and rhetors were not
particularly popular in the eyes of the faithful: 'fideles magis discere
quam docere litteras capit.'[277] It has been suggested that Cyprian wrote
his *Quod idola dii non sint* to demonstrate the sincerity of his desire to
become a member of the Church;[278] and that M. Victorinus might have
completed Hymns 1–2 for the same reason.[279] We must analyse the
ecclesiastical evidence from Roman North Africa. None of the councils
sheds any light on the problem. The Synod of Elvira allows a period of
two years for a catechumen, provided that he has a good name, but this
was Spanish and took place *c*.306. Augustine may at least indirectly
help to solve the problem.

In the *De catechizandis rudibus*, written *c*.400, Augustine advises
Deogratias about how to develop an acceptable catechetical method.[280]
If there is suspicion that the candidate falsely desires the faith, it is
necessary to acquire information about his character and motives for
seeking entrance into the Church.[281] If this cannot be ascertained, the
man is to be interrogated. Deogratias is then advised to reprove him if
his views conflict with those normally expected of a catechumen. He is
to acquaint him with Christian doctrine, but not to set a date for the

[274] *Ep.* 11. 2 (*PL* 4. 257).

[275] P. R. L. Brown, 'Religious Dissent in the Later Roman Empire: The Case of North
Africa', *Hist* 46 (1961), 95.

[276] *Ep.* 61 (*PL* 4. 362 ff.): 'nec alios extra ecclesiam mortalia docere, sed et ipse salutaria
in ecclesia discere.'

[277] *De idol.* 10. 5.

[278] H. Koch, *Cyprianische Untersuchungen* (Bonn, 1926), 53; Quasten, 2. 364, rightly
asks whether the work was ever intended for publication.

[279] P. Hadot, *Marius Victorinus* (Paris, 1971), 259; cf. F. J. Dölger, 'Das Garantiewerk
der Bekehrung als Bedingung und Sicherung bei der Annahme zur Taufe', *AChr* 3 (1932),
260–72.

[280] *De cat. rud.* 1 (CChr: Bauer).

[281] Ibid. 5. 9.

first catechetical instruction.[282] Educated persons are to be asked about the motives for desiring the faith.[283] The fact that Deogratias was writing to Augustine only five years after being consecrated a bishop might suggest that the latter was relying upon an established episcopal tradition for his advice. Although there is no hard evidence to prove that the bishop of Sicca was able to use such a tradition, the most prudent conclusion would appear to be that both Augustine and Arnobius' bishop were probably acting in accordance with established tradition. It is therefore reasonable to accept Jerome's account as accurate.

VII. *Accepted by the Church*

foedus impetravit

Jerome's final statement has not been sufficiently investigated by modern scholarship. The main problem is whether Arnobius was actually accepted into the Church. Dölger has interpreted *fidem* and *foedus* in the passage as being synonymous with Christian baptism and the *obsidibus pietatis* as a 'Garantiewerk der Frömmigkeit'.[284] According to this hypothesis, full communicating membership did not occur until after the bishop had the *Adv. nat.* in his hands as a pledge of the former antagonist's sincerity. The bishop then had tangible proof that Arnobius desired to go the *via Christi* (books 1–2) and forsake the errors of the *nationes* (books 3–7). But does Jerome's statement allow this interpretation? There are two possible meanings. First, the bishop initially had serious reservations about the rhetor's intentions and suggested (or required) that he write some kind of recantation both of his anti-Christian comments and of his former pagan religion. Second, the bishop immediately rejected Arnobius without any further explanation because his fame had preceded him. It was Arnobius himself who decided, independent of the bishop and perhaps without his knowledge, to write the *Adv. nat.* as a demonstration of his sincerity. The first interpretation seems to be the best for the following reasons.

First, the bishop undoubtedly was able to conclude that his church would benefit from the conversion of a prominent rhetor who had been

[282] Ibid.
[283] Ibid. 8. 12.
[284] Dölger (1932), 262 f.

causing problems for the Christian churches in his area. Second, there is some evidence in the *Adv. nat.* to suggest that Arnobius was personally involved in the Christian Church while writing the work. It appears fairly clear that he was being exposed to worship services in a local church, although it is extremely doubtful that he had been baptized. If he had received this sacrament at all, and Jerome's *foedus impetravit* implies that this happened, it took place after the work was completed.[285] Third, on the objection that a bishop would never have accepted such a mixture of heterodox beliefs as one finds in books 1–2, it must be emphasized that the theological position of the bishop is unknown; and the latter might have suggested that Arnobius write his best profession of faith and recantation of attacks upon Christianity and pagan religious beliefs and practices, without receiving catechetical instruction, but concentrate upon renouncing paganism. The remaining five books would have compensated for any doctrinal deficiencies of the first two.

How can books 1–2 be called an apology when Arnobius betrays very little knowledge of that which modern historians impose upon him to defend? One hears nothing about the organization, liturgy, sacraments, or polity of the North African Church. He is apparently ignorant of the Old Testament, and there are only two possible allusions to the New Testament (1. 6. 6 f.; 2. 6. 24 f.: although 1. 45–8, and 50 suggest a fair knowledge of Christ's miracles).[286] There is not a reference made to the Virgin Birth, the Holy Spirit, and only one Christian predecessor is named. Also, he twice mentions his recent conversion (1. 39; 3. 24), and the logical conclusion to make is that Arnobius was an uninstructed neophyte while he was writing the work. Finally, the bishop undoubtedly interpreted a possible *testimonium* written by a prominent rhetor and a former enemy of the Church as an invaluable asset during the crucial conflict between hostile forces: the cult of Saturn and the Great Persecution.[287]

It seems clear that Arnobius had attended, and therefore had personal experiential knowledge of, some kind of Christian worship service. Undoubtedly this took place in one of the many *conventicula* scattered throughout the Roman Empire which Diocletian's First Edict aimed at destroying. The *Gesta apud Zenophilum* describes how Felix the *curator*

---

[285] F. Cayré, *Manual of Patrology* (1935), 270 f., believes that he had been baptized by this time.
[286] See LeB 330–7, 345–9.
[287] See Chs. 1 and 7.

of Cirta[288] moved from house to house and confiscated the scriptures which the subdeacons and lectors possessed. A similar situation probably existed at Sicca, and it might have been in one of these house-churches that Arnobius met on a regular basis—he says daily, and Crispina also![289]—to learn about Jesus, his miracles (which he is probably recalling from memory in 1. 45–8, 50), his divinity, how he immortalizes the human soul (1. 65), hell's torments (2. 14; 2. 54), other basic teachings, and to pray. This does not mean that he was undergoing catechetical instruction, although a number of scholars have suggested otherwise.[290] Burger goes too far to conclude that Arnobius knew the Church only as an outsider. It would appear safe to accept Le Bonniec's suggestion that 4. 36. 22–30 displays personal experience of a Christian community:[291]

cur immaniter conventicula dirui? in quibus summus oratur deus, pax cunctis et venia postulatur magistratibus exercitibus regibus familiaribus inimicis, adhuc vitam degentibus et resolutis corporum vinctione; in quibus aliud auditur nihil nisi quod humanos faciat, nisi quod mites verecundos pudicos castos, familiaris communicatores rei et cum omnibus quos solidet germanitatis necessitudine copulatos.

It is significant that Cyprian[292] and Lactantius[293] use *conventiculum* to describe Christian places of worship. Blaise also gives examples of its use, and all are derived from African sources.[294] The phrase, 'in quibus summus oratur deus', may suggest a personal experience of public worship.[295] Indeed, it is prayer offered to the Christian God which reveals the most conspicuous of Arnobius' Christian experiences. He twice refers to the daily prayers of the Christians.[296] Christians prostrate

[288] CSEL 26: Ziwsa, 186 ff.
[289] *Pass. Crisp.* 1 (ST 9: de'Cavalieri): 'Cotidie adoro deum meum omnipotentem: praeter eum nullum alium deum novi.'
[290] Micka (1943), 75: his NT knowledge was derived from catechetical instruction; cf. Hagendahl (1958), 32; Neander (1872), 449 f., 'a man already mature in his convictions'; McCr 249 n. 136.
[291] Burger (1970), 6 and 58; LeB 72.
[292] *De unit. eccl.* 12 (CChr: Bénevot; *PL* 4. 509); most often *ecclesia*, sometimes *templa dei*, are used: e.g. *De hab. virg.* (*PL* 4. 442).
[293] *Div. inst.* 5. 11. 10.
[294] *DLFAC* 219.
[295] Cf. McCr 565 n. 237.
[296] *Adv. nat.* 1. 26. 16–20: 'Delius Apollo vel Clarius, Didymaeus . . . hic habendus divinus est, qui aut summum imperatorem nescit aut ignorat a nobis cotidianis ei precibus supplicari?' 1. 36. 1–6: 'Sed non, inquit, idcirco dii vobis infesti sunt, quod omnipotentem colatis deum, sed quod hominem natum et . . . deum fuisse contenditis et . . . cotidianis supplicationibus adoratis.'

themselves before God's name.[297] Tertullian gives a similar description
of worship in his day.[298] Christ receives the same veneration: Christians
fall down before his name and majesty and worship him.[299] Hands are
raised in supplication.[300] Tertullian says the same, addressing Christians.[301] Arnobius claims that it is according to custom that Christians
fall down, worship, and pray in common supplications.[302] All nature
should bend its knee to the *rex summus*.[303] Christ himself has taught his
disciples how to pray to the *rerum dominus*,[304] an allusion perhaps to the
oratio dominica. Personal experience seems to lie behind his statement
about the sounds of the Christians' voices during prayer: 'Qui (sc.
Apollo) si pectorum secreta nesciret nec quid in intimis sensibus
contineamus agnosceret, summum tamen invocare nos deum et ab eo
quod postulamus orare vel auribus potuit scire vel ipsius vocis sono qua
utimur in precibus noscitare' (1. 26. 20–4). This may be referring to
the vocal intonations of the liturgy. Also note 1. 31. 16 f.: 'Da veniam,
rex summe, tuos persequentibus famulos', a petition attached to a
philosophically pregnant passage, and it looks badly out of place.[305] A
request of *venia* for his enemies, compared with the 'venia postulatur
... inimicis'[306] of 4. 36. 24 f., strongly indicates that Arnobius is drawing
from personal experience of Christian worship. The phrase, 'pax cunctis
et venia postulatur magistratibus exercitibus regibus' (4. 36. 24 f.) is
similar to Tertullian's description of worship in his day: 'Oramus etiam
pro imperatoribus, pro ministris eorum et potestatibus, pro statu saeculi,
pro rerum quiete'.[307] Compare also his remark about praying for *familiaribus* and *inimicis*, with Tertullian's, 'ut et huic praecepto pareamus
orando pro omnibus, etiam pro inimicis nostris.'[308]

   The reference to prayers for the dead (*resolutis corporum vinctione*)
coheres well with North African ecclesiastical practices. In was Perpetua

[297] Cf. *Adv. nat.* 1. 27; 2. 34. 16 ff. (Christ).
[298] Cf. *De or.* 23 (CChr: Dekkers).
[299] *Adv. nat.* 2. 34. 14–20.
[300] Ibid. 3. 6. 3 f.: 'Devotas etenim mentes et manus protendimus supplices.'
[301] Cf. *De spec.* 25. 5 (CChr: Dekkers): 'Illas manus quas ad Deum extuleris'; *De or.*
14 and 17.
[302] *Adv. nat.* 1. 27. 6–12.
[303] Ibid. 1. 31. 6 f.
[304] Ibid. 1. 38. 44 ff.
[305] Cf. LeB, 274–85.
[306] Cf. B. Amata, 'Testimonianze di Arnobio Afro sulle assemblee liturgiche agli inizi
del secolo IV', *EphLit* 98 (1984), 513–25.
[307] *Ap.* 39. 2.
[308] *De or.* 3. 4.

who prayed in prison for her deceased brother, Dinocrates.[309] Compare Cyprian: 'Apud inferos confessio non est, nec exomologesis illis fieri potest.'[310] Yet Tertullian and Cyprian are familiar with the custom of praying for the dead,[311] and commemorative prayers for the martyrs were also quite common.[312] The tradition may lie behind *Adv. nat.* 2. 63. Responding to the question what has happened to those who died before the advent of Christ, his answer again seems to reveal personal involvement in Christian worship: 'Miseratio et illis impert ita est regia et aequaliter per omnes divina beneficia concurrerunt: conservatae sunt, liberatae sunt et mortalitatis sortem condicionemque posuerunt.'[313]

Similar parallels occur in the last half of the passage. Note that *auditur* (4. 36. 27) followed by a short list of Christian virtues may imply admonitions heard in homilies. His use of *verecundos* in 4. 36. 28 resembles Tertullian's remark that the pagans celebrate holidays of the Caesars without *verecundia* (*Ap.* 35. 5). He next affirms that Christian worship makes men *pudicos*, and with this we should compare the *pudicitia* of Tertullian, found in the context of a discussion about worship.[314] His use of *castos* (4. 36. 28) recalls Tertullian's *casti* (*Ap.* 35. 4).[315] Finally, we should compare the 'familiaris communicatores rei' of *Adv. nat.* 4. 36. 29, with the 'itaque qui animo animaque miscemur, nihil de rei communicatione dubitamus' of *Ap.* 39. 11. Offerings taken up in the churches for Christian benevolence are probably indicated here and in the following, 'et cum omnibus quos solidet germanitatis necessitudine copulatos' (*Adv. nat.* 4. 36. 29 f.). This is a North African ecclesiastical tradition found in the works of Tertullian[316] and Cyprian.[317] If the *Adv. nat.* was written during a drought and subsequent crop failure[318] and food shortage,[319] such humanitarian programmes might have had a profound effect upon Arnobius.

[309] *Pass. Perpet. et Fel.* 2. 3 f. (ANF 3).

[310] *Ep.* 52.

[311] Tert. *De monog.* 10. 4 (CChr: Dekkers); *De or.* 29. 2; Cyprian, *Ep.* 66.

[312] e.g. Cyprian, *Ep.* 33. 3 (*PL* 4. 322 f.); *Ep.* 36. 2 (*PL* 4. 328 f.).

[313] Cf. *Apost. Const.* 8. 41.

[314] Cf. *Ap.* 39. 19; Cyprian, *De hab. virg.* (*PL* 4. 458).

[315] Cf. *Ap.* 39. 19; 39. 21: 'Cum probi, cum boni coeunt, cum pii, cum casti congregantur'.

[316] *De idol.* 22; *Ap.* 39. 6: offerings to feed the poor or bury them; for orphans, old slaves, shipwrecked mariners, those in the mines, islands, prisons; *Ap.* 39. 10.

[317] *De unit. eccl.* 24. (*PL* 4. 518); *De hab. virg.* (*PL* 4. 449); *De op. et eleem.* (CChr: Simonetti); *De unit. eccl.* 27 (*PL* 4. 520); Pont., *Vit. et pass. Cypr.* 2 (*PL* 3. 1542 f.); Cypr. *Ep.* 6; *Ep.* 35.

[318] As noted in Ch. 2.

[319] e.g. 1. 3, 13, 19; 3. 11, 24; 6. 2, 16; 7. 38; and cf. Liebeschuetz (1979), 254: 'It might be concluded that in Africa the Great Persecution took place against a background of food shortage.'

The question must be asked, however, whether the similarities between Arnobius and Tertullian are due solely to a literary dependence. We can answer in the negative for the following reasons. First, a number of passages reveal that Arnobius describes Christian worship from the perspective of a participant recently converted who betrays only a superficial knowledge of the things he relates. These are: the remark about daily prayers, confirmed by Crispina at her trial; the comment about the sound of Christian voices during prayer; two references to praying for one's enemies, implying a knowledge of the *oratio dominica*; a statement about praying for the dead; and that it is in the churches where Christians *hear* (4. 36. 27: *auditur*) how to live virtuous lives. Second, literary influences do not exclude the possibility that Arnobius is basing his information upon personal experience. He could be describing Christian worship in the language of those whose ranks he has recently joined.[320] Also, some of the parallels noted above are marginal, and differences existing between the two authors support the present argument. And, if we rigorously adhere to the *literary dependence* theory, we must explain the elements in Arnobius which do not occur in Tertullian. Third, Jerome's text does not allow an interpretation of immediate and total rejection by the bishop and implies that the opposite was true.

A reasonable theory would be that the bishop himself required Arnobius to write a recantation of his former religious beliefs and anti-Christian views. Arnobius' *straw man* was Arnobius, who was furnished with a significant amount, as Chapters 4, 8, and 9 will reveal, of very powerful Porphyrian artillery.[321] It is possible that each book was submitted to the bishop after it had been written, and Jerome's *foedus impetravit* describes the beginning of a rather lengthy process, which is explicitly confirmed by his statement that the *Adversus nationes* was not Arnobius' only pledge of sincerity.[322]

[320] On Tertullian's influence upon Arnobius, see McCr 45–7; LeB 57 f.

[321] McCr 45, uses the term 'straw man' to describe the adversaries of Tertullian and Arnobius.

[322] In light of the little we know of Arnobius, it is regrettable that Jerome does not explain in detail the meaning of *obsidibus*.

4

God and the World

Arnobius' understanding of God takes into account the relationship between the deity and the world, including humanity, man's
natural environment, and the great cosmos beyond him. Two main subdivisions are discernible. First, a significant number of passages
focuses upon a divine concern for mankind's temporal and non-
temporal (eschatological) welfare. Arnobius believed in a God who
initiates a beneficial association with mankind which sometimes has
spiritual applications, and at others, material. God is depicted as being
immanent and approachable in some passages and, indeed, as he who
makes the initial step forward to man. This understanding of the
divine nature is frequently found in a description about worshipping
the Christian God. Second, another set of passages portrays an exalted,
quite transcendent deity. His nature and being are mysterious, almost
totally unknown and unknowable, and often Arnobius' only recourse is
to describe God in apophatic terms. Organically related to this is his
affirmation that the High God is not the immediate creator of human
souls. The following analysis of the concept of God in the *Adv. nat.*
possesses three general classifications: God and the world, God and
Christ, and God and the gods. In this and the next two chapters we
will focus upon each of these classifications.

I. *The Epicurean Debate*

In the post-World War II era, there have been several works published
which analyse the concepts of God in the *Adversus nationes*. Micka
developed what appeared to be a strong case for an Epicurean understanding of God. The great weakness of this thesis is that so much
attention is given to the bad things that the God of Arnobius does not
do to man, that the good things he does do for him are almost totally
ignored. One must recall that the basic conception of deity according
to Epicurean doctrine was that of divine indifference to human affairs,

whether good or bad.[1] The gods did not have anything to do with
humans: they neither cursed nor blessed them. McDonald's article does
not attempt to identify the pre-Christian religious and philosophical
components of Arnobius' understanding of deity.[2] Although Burger's
study has not been published, it is significant for offering a convincing
demonstration of the Platonic character of the African's conception of
God.[3] Also, Jufresa concluded that his perception of God is better
understood in light of the heterodox religious beliefs current in Roman
North Africa at the end of the third century, rather than by giving it
an Epicurean origin.[4] Finally, an excellent general survey appears in an
appendix of Amata's work.[5]

Many scholars have argued that the God of Arnobius is indisput-
ably Epicurean. The conclusion of Contreras is representative of this
school of thought: 'His god is more the god of Epicurus than the God
of the Bible: indifferent and impassible.'[6] The same interpretation can
be found in e.g. Micka,[7] de Labriolle,[8] Mulvey,[9] Quasten,[10] Rapisarda,[11]
Bardy,[12] Liebeschuetz,[13] and Hallman.[14] None of these, however, has
thoroughly analysed all the passages in the *Adv. nat.* related to
Arnobius' understanding of God to establish unequivocally that it
is Epicurean.

One must be forewarned about the dangers of making gross generalizations. For example, if by 'indifferent' Contreras refers to the
Epicurean belief that the gods, existing in the *intermundia*, are not
concerned about the welfare of mankind and therefore do not intervene

[1] E. F. Micka, *The Problem of Divine Anger in Arnobius and Lactantius* (Washington,
DC, 1943; CUSCA 4); cf. K. Meiser, *Studien zu Arnobius* (Munich, 1908), 11.
[2] H. D. McDonald, 'The Doctrine of God in Arnobius, *Adversus Gentes*', StudPatr 9
(= TU 94; 1966), 3. 75–81.
[3] C. Burger, *Die theologische Position des Älteren Arnobius* (Diss., Heidelberg, 1970).
[4] M. Jufresa, 'La divinidad y lo divino en Arnobio', *BIEH* 7 (1973), 61–4.
[5] B. Amata, *Problemi di Antropologia Arnobiana* (Rome, 1984; BSR 64), 137–44.
[6] C. A. Contreras, 'Christian Views of Paganism', *ANRW* 11. 23. 2, 974–1022.
[7] Micka (1943), 11 ff.
[8] P. de Labriolle, 'Arnobe', *DHGE* 4. 544.
[9] T. J. Mulvey, 'The Seven Books of Arnobius Adversus Nationes' (Ph.D. thesis, NY
University, 1908), 67–74.
[10] *Patrology*, 2. 388.
[11] E. Rapisarda, *Arnobio* (Cantania, 1945), 126 n. 1, who believes the Epicurean influence
upon his idea of God did not endanger his orthodoxy!
[12] 'Arnobius', *RACh*, 1. 710.
[13] J. H. W. G. Liebeschuetz, *Continuity and Change in Roman Religion* (Oxford, 1979),
260.
[14] J. R. Hallman, 'The Mutability of God: Tertullian to Lactantius', *TS* 42 no. 3
(1981), 388.

to ameliorate human existence in any way, then it is not difficult to
demonstrate that there is ample evidence in Arnobius' thought to the
contrary. Also, the concept of divine impassibility was not restricted to
Epicureanism, and we may give the statement of Balbus the Stoic as an
example: 'Nam et perturbatis animis inducuntur [sc. dii]: accepimus
enim deorum cupiditates aegritudines iracundias.' The doctrine of Stoic
ἀπάθεια[15] forms the basis of his argument. A more significant example
for the present study perhaps is a statement which appeared in the
Contra Christianos of Porphyry of Tyre, a contemporary of Arnobius,
cited by Methodius of Olympus:

τί ὠφέλησεν ἡμᾶς ὁ υἱὸς τοῦ θεοῦ σαρκωθεὶς ἐπὶ γῆ καὶ γενόμενος ἄνθρωπος;
καὶ διὰ τί τῷ τοῦ σταυροῦ σχήματι ἠνέσχετο παθεῖν καὶ οὐκ ἄλλῃ τινὶ τιμωρίᾳ;
καὶ τί τὸ χρήσιμον τοῦ σταυροῦ; πῶς ὁ τοῦ θεοῦ υἱός, ὁ Χριστος, ἐν βραχεῖ τε
καὶ περιωρισμένῳ χρόνῳ διαστολαῖς σώματι ἐκεχώρητο; καὶ πῶς ἀπαθὴ ὢν
ἐγένετο ὑπὸ πάθους;[16]

Porphyry rejected the Christian doctrine of the incarnation on the
grounds that a deity cannot suffer. Christ was not impassible; he
therefore was not God. A passage cannot therefore be identified as
Epicurean in the *Adv. nat.* simply because it contains the doctrine of
divine impassibility.

Some scholars have concluded that Arnobius was an Epicurean
philosopher before his conversion to Christianity. For example,
Klussman's study of the Lucretian influence upon Arnobius caused him
to make this assumption.[17] He believed that a long interval occurred
between Arnobius' involvement in idolatry and his conversion, the main
text of his argument being *Adv. nat.* 1. 39. One main weakness of this
is that Klussman incorrectly asserts that all Epicureans abstained from
worshipping images. The academic Cotta knew otherwise: 'novi ego
Epicureos omnia sigilla venerantes.'[18] We may go further. An overwhelming majority of scholars who have studied the extent of Lucretian
influence in the *Adv. nat.*[19] would not agree with Klussman's belief that

---

[15] See J. M. Rist, *Stoic Philosophy* (Cambridge, 1969), 22–36.
[16] Methodius Κατὰ Πορφυρίου (= Harnack *CC* fragment no. 84) ap. GCS 27. 503:
Bonwetsch.
[17] E. Klussman, 'Arnobius und Lucrez', *Philol* 26 (1867), 362–6.
[18] *De nat. deor.* 1. 85. 30.
[19] It is commonly believed that any Epicurean influence upon Arnobius comes from
Lucretius. Epicurus' name appears in 2. 9. 16 and 2. 30. 32.

Arnobius was an Epicurean, and these would include Jessen,[20] Röhricht,[21] Spindler,[22] Tschiersch,[23] Dalpane,[24] Gabarrou,[25] Rapisarda,[26] Marchesi,[27] and Hagendahl.[28] The latter has concluded that there are three main areas of Lucretian influence upon Arnobius: the belief that the world was not created for man; the mortality of the soul; and the inability of a deity to become angry. In taking up Klussman's text and using it against him (*Adv. nat.* 1. 39), Hagendahl asserts: 'If Arnobius had ever been an Epicurean, he would surely have shown some reminiscence of Lucretius' contempt for such acts of worship.'[29] Having done the most thorough analysis of the influence of Lucretius upon Arnobius, the cutting edge of Hagendahl's argument is that any positive Epicurean influence upon the *Adv. nat.* is to be derived solely from Lucretius' poem. It appears that Lucretius had predominately a literary, and not a conceptual, influence upon the African rhetor. Also, Hagendahl observed that *nuper* in 1.39.10 opposes *nunc* in l. 18 of the same passage, which is inconsistent with Klussman's contention that there was a lengthy interval between the practice of idol worship and the conversion to Christianity.

The only other passage in the *Adv. nat.* which reveals his pre-Christian religious beliefs and practices and has been the focus of scholarly debate, is 3. 24. 6 ff.: 'Atquin ego rebar paulo ante, spontaneas esse numinum benignitates ultroque ab his fluere inexpectata beni-volentiae munera.' Note that the *paulo ante* invalidates Klussman's 'interval theory'. One may go further. Epicureans would not have found acceptable the belief that kindnesses (*benignitates*) and gifts of benevolence (*benivolentiae munera*) spontaneously flowed (*fluere*) from the gods. The theme of 3. 24 is divine providence, and it is clear that humans are understood as the objects of divine blessings (rain, wind,

[20] J. Jessen, *Ueber Lucrez und sein Verhältnis zu Catull und Späteren* (Kiel, 1872), 17–20.

[21] A. Röhricht, *Die Seelenlehre des Arnobius nach ihren Quellen und ihren Entstehung untersucht* (Hamburg, 1893), 2–21.

[22] P. Spindler, *De Arnobii genere dicendi* (Diss. Strasbourg, 1901), 3–11.

[23] W. Tschiersch, *De Arnobii studiis Latinis* (Diss. Jena, 1905), 8–11.

[24] F. Dalpane, 'Se Arnobio sia stato un Epicureo', *RSA* 10 (1906), 403–35.

[25] F. Gabbarou, *Arnobe* (Paris, 1921), 27–37.

[26] Op. cit. (1945), 162–79.

[27] C. Marchesi, 'Questioni Arnobiane', *ARVS* 88 (1929), 1024.

[28] H. Hagendahl, *Latin Fathers and the Classics* (Göteborg, 1958; SGLG 6), 12–47.

[29] Ibid. 17 n. 2. Compare J. D. Madden, 'Jesus as Epicurus. Arnobius of Sicca's Borrowings from Lucretius', *CCC* 2 (1981), 215–22.

good harvests) flowing from heaven. Arnobius therefore believed in divine providence, a concept repugnant to Epicureans, before and after his conversion to Christianity. Also, in 6. 2. 21 f., he states that the gods should show impartial benevolence to all ('et individuas cunctis benivolentias exhibere'). Yet according to Epicurean thought, any kind of contact with human beings initiated by the gods in the *intermundia* and whether for the purposes of cursing or blessing, was the indisputable mark of weakness (*De nat. deor.* 1. 124. 44). The concept of deity central to Epicureanism is that the gods were aloof from and totally unconcerned about intervening into the affairs of humans *for any reason*. They reposed in their own ἀταραξία. Divine providence was rejected by Epicureans, and this chapter will reveal that it was accepted by Arnobius.[30]

Another cardinal Epicurean theological doctrine was the quasi-anthropomorphic form of the gods. This apparently means that the bodies of the gods are similar to those of humans. Philodemus thought that the gods both ate and drank.[31] And Sextus Empiricus, following Epicurus himself, refers to the gods who possess lungs, tongues, and other parts.[32] Lucretius also refers to the gods' bodies.[33] Note a statement of Velleius: 'Nam a natura habemus omnes omnium gentium speciem nullam aliam nisi humanam deorum.'[34] Yet the main attack of Arnobius upon the gods is found in their anthropomorphic nature: 'Nam quid in homine pulcrum est, quid, quaeso, admirabile vel decorum, nisi quid et clurino cum pecore nescio quis auctor voluit esse commune?' (3. 16. 30 ff.). Compare 7. 15. 12 ff.: '[Primum] ut neque illos credas quicquam hominis habere consimile.' In his comparison of pagan and Christian concepts of divinity in 7. 35. 24–8, he similarly argues that he may not know the form of God, but he is certain that it is not human.[35]

Another preliminary observation is necessary. In a majority of the passages in which he discusses the Christian God, Arnobius invariably uses an epithet to describe the particular aspect of the divine nature he desires to accentuate. According to the number of occurrences found

[30] Cf. A. J. Festugière, 'Arnobiana', *VC* 6 (1952), 210.
[31] H. Diels, 'Philodemus über die Götter', *AKPAW* (1916), Nr. 4, 1–69, fr. 77, p. 67; cf. J. M. Rist, *Epicurus* (Cambridge, 1972), 146–56.
[32] *Adv. Math.* 9. 178; see Rist (1972), 152.
[33] *De rer. nat.* 5. 151–4.
[34] *De nat. deor.* 1. 18. 46.
[35] *Adv. nat.* 3. 19. 19 ff.

for each epithet, it is important to note that there are twenty-eight for *princeps*[36] and seven for the similar *principalis*,[37] totalling thirty-five and representing his preferred terms; twenty-six for *rex*;[38] fifteen for *pater*;[39] fourteen for *dominus*;[40] eleven for *omnipotens*;[41] ten for *caput*;[42] seven for *primus*;[43] five for *auctor*;[44] five for *fons rerum*;[45] four for *imperator*;[46] three each for *moderator*,[47] *sumus deus*,[48] and *conditor*;[49] two each for *columen*,[50] *constitutor*,[51] *procreator*,[52] *sator*,[53] and *deus superior*;[54] and one each for *causa prima* (1. 31. 7), *conservator* (2. 65. 1),[55] *liberator* (2. 32. 11 f.), *maximus* (2. 52. 27 f.), *unus* (4. 13. 11), *verus* (7. 2. 12),[56] *divinitas* (3. 2.

---

[36] 1. 25. 16; 1. 27. 1; 1. 28. 36; 1. 32. 8; 1. 33. 2; 1. 53. 11; 1. 65. 33; 2. 2. 13, 14; 2. 15. 4; 2. 16. 7; 2. 19. 10; 2. 25. 4; 2. 32. 4; 2. 35. 14; 2. 36. 12; 2. 48. 2, 8; 2. 53. 6; 2. 55. 6, 26 f.; 2. 60. 12; 2. 61. 14; 2. 65. 4; 2. 74. 1; 3. 3. 12; 3. 6. 7; 4. 19. 20. Cf. J. M. P. B. van der Putten, *Arnobii Adversus Nationes, 3, 1–19* (Thesis, Leiden, 1970), 43, who gives 32 including *principalia*, followed by LeB 250; McCr 279 n. 101 gives 18.

[37] 2. 6. 7; 2. 22. 10; 2. 36. 20; 2. 37. 2; 2. 48. 21; 2. 64. 4; 3. 3. 7.

[38] Actually the *miseratio regia* should make the total 27; cf. 1. 26. 14 f.; 1. 27. 7 (with *princeps*); 1. 31. 16; 1. 33. 5; 1. 42. 11; 1. 60. 16; 1. 61. 1; 1. 64. 1; 1. 64. 33; 2. 6. 7 (with *princeps*); 2. 35. 6; 2. 36. 11, 24; 2. 39. 1; 2. 44. 1; 2. 47. 13; 2. 51. 13; 2. 55. 6 (with *princeps*); 2. 58. 4; 2. 65. 35; 2. 74. 1 (with *princeps*); 2. 75. 22; 3. 3. 10, 12 (the latter with *princeps*); 3. 6. 7 (with *princeps*); 3. 24. 8 f.; 6. 3. 6 (with *dominus* and *caput*). LeB 254 (on *Adv. nat.* 1. 26. 3) gives 16 occurrences for *rex*; on 2. 63. 18 f.: P gives *miserationet*; Marchesi has *miseratio*.

[39] 1. 28. 4, 25, 40; 1. 55. 11; 2. 2. 15; 2. 13. 12; 2. 15. 5; 2. 16. 11; 2. 28. 25; 2. 35. 21; 2. 36. 2; 2. 44. 2; 2. 65. 22; 2. 74. 23; 3. 2. 10. *Pater* in 1. 38. 20 is a demiurgic creator.

[40] 1. 25. 17; 1. 33. 5, 12; 1. 38. 45; 2. 13. 12; 2. 15. 4; 2. 33. 20; 2. 60. 21; 2. 62. 26; 2. 74. 24; 3. 2. 10; 4. 19. 20; 6. 3. 5; 7. 32. 10.

[41] 1. 34. 7 f.; 1. 36. 2; 2. 37. 12; 2. 45. 2; 2. 53. 9 f.; 2. 55. 3; 2. 62. 14; 2. 72. 8; 2. 75. 18 f.; 2. 76. 1; 7. 2. 10 f.

[42] 1. 29. 4; 2. 2. 15; 2. 45. 19; 2. 46. 3; 2. 48. 22; 2. 60. 32; 2. 72. 14; 3. 2. 14; 3. 3. 7; 6. 3. 5.

[43] 2. 6. 25; 2. 29. 25; 2. 43. 1; 2. 52. 24; 2. 72. 8; 3. 2. 9 (*bis*).

[44] 1. 30. 17; 1. 63. 25; 2. 32. 2; 2. 46. 13; 7. 35. 23.

[45] 1. 28. 36; 1. 34. 12; 2. 2. 15; 2. 45. 18; 2. 72. 14.

[46] 1. 26. 18; 2. 3. 2; 2. 36. 28; 2. 65. 36 f.

[47] 1. 33. 6; 2. 74. 23 f.; 3. 2. 10.

[48] 1. 26. 21 f.; 4. 36. 24; 7. 35. 15 f.

[49] 1. 29. 23; 2. 2. 16; 2. 45. 2.

[50] 1. 29. 5; 2. 46. 4.

[51] 2. 44. 7; 3. 2. 10.

[52] 1. 31. 2; 2. 45. 3.

[53] 1. 34. 12; 2. 45. 3.

[54] 2. 47. 16; cf. the similar *potentiae superioris* of 2. 20. 3; and J. C. Plumpe, 'Some Critical Annotations to Arnobius', *VC* 3 (1949), 230–6.

[55] The reasons it enters the Arnobian list of epithets are: (1) it describes Christ in a soteriological passage; and (2) the redemptive power and mission of Christ have been made possible by the command and direction of the High God.

[56] For its use in Tertullian see R. Braun, *Deus Christianorum* (Paris, 1962; FLA 41), 74 ff.

8), *fabricator* (1. 29. 25), *fundamentum* (1. 31. 8), *fundator* (2. 2. 15), *genitor* (1. 29. 25), *locus rerum ac spatium* (1. 31. 8), *opifex* (1. 29. 24), *salus rerum deus* (2. 46. 3), *salutaris deus* (2. 78. 6), *sapientissimus* and *iustus* (2. 46. 5). At first sight, some of these (e.g. *fons rerum, salutaris deus, fabricator*) count against an Epicurean identification. Others (e.g. *primus, causa prima, fons rerum*) may betray either a Platonic or Chaldaean influence. Throughout this chapter and those that follow, we shall attempt to isolate and identify the underlying philosophical and religious traditions belonging to many of these epithets.[57]

II. *Experiencing God in Acts of Worship*

Human dependence upon God in acts of worship, mainly prayer,[58] and a concomitant divine concern to respond positively to human needs and satisfy them, characterize a majority of passages in the first subdivision. Thus in common prayers Christians ask God the *princeps* and *rex*[59] to give them just and honourable things.[60] These will enable the recipient to overcome his proneness to faults (*culpa*), wantonness (*libido*), and passion (*adpetitus*). During prayer God allows himself to be comprehended in the thoughts of his worshippers, and this results in receiving divine *munera* (1. 27. 20) which further produces an innocent will (1. 27. 20 f.) to cleanse themselves (*purgare*) from sin (*delictum*). The human propensity to commit transgressions, therefore, is overcome because of the individual's communion with a God who takes an active part in improving his spiritual condition.[61]

Through prayer the petitioner asks for the divine intervention to

---

[57] Religious polyonymy had a rich and varied history. For Isis see R. E. Witt, *Isis in the Graeco-Roman World* (London, 1971), 121; on Apuleius see my Yale thesis (1982) with bibliography, 3 ff.; and J. G. Griffiths, *The Isis-Book* (Leiden, 1975), 142–45; Y. Grandjean, *Une nouvelle arètalogie d'Isis à Maronée* (Leiden, 1975), 17; *POxy* no. 1380, ll. 43–64 (Grenfell–Hunt, ll. 202); Plutarch, *De is. et os.* 377 D; A. D. Nock, *HTR* 27 (1934), 53–104; and generally, R. MacMullen, *Paganism in the Roman Empire* (New Haven, Conn., 1981), 90; W. H. C. Frend, *Martyrdom and Persecution* (Grand Rapids, 1981), 456 and n. 122.

[58] 1. 31 is the principal passage.

[59] See 1. 26. 14 f.

[60] *Adv. nat.* 1. 27. 6 f., and 9–13: 'nihil sumus aliud Christiani nisi magistro Christo summi regis ac principis veneratores . . . Haec totius summa est actionis . . . huic omnes nos] ex more prosternimus, hunc conlatis precibus adoramus, ab hoc iusta et honesta et auditui eius condigna deposcimus . . .'.

[61] 1. 27. 16–22.

occur which produces only beneficial results: God does nothing 'except that which is for the well-being of all, which is agreeable, which is very full of love and joy and gladness, which has unbounded and imperishable pleasures, which every one may ask in all his prayers to befall him, and think that otherwise life is pernicious and fatal.'[62] Arnobius is making three clear affirmations about the divine nature: God is concerned to help man in his earthly life; he initiates this help; and he only does good things to man. The third point does not cohere with the second clause of the first of Epicurus' Κύριαι Δόξαι.[63] Porphyry, however, holds similar views: God does not do anything unless it is good, and anger is foreign to his nature.[64] The difference between this and the Epicurean idea of deity is that it allows a positive relationship to be initiated by the gods from which humans can benefit; whereas Epicureans believed that the gods were absolutely indifferent towards man and did not have any intercourse with him, whether good or bad.

In turning to the concept that good things come from God, in *Adv. nat.* 2. 2. 12–15 Arnobius refers to the *princeps* to whom Christians pray, 'qui bonorum solus caput et fons est'. In a Chaldaean oracle designed to proclaim the monarchical rule of the Supreme God, Porphyry gives the similar Ἀρχὴ πηγή τε Ζωῆς.[65] The African M. Victorinus' epithets are the same, 'caput fontemque dicemus, principium' (*Adv. Ar.* 4. 12. 6–9),[66] and Hadot,[67] concurring with Courcelle,[68] has concluded that they are indebted to Porphyry. And both agree that *Adv. nat.* 2. 2 owes much to Porphyry.[69] According to Chaldaean theology, one specialized use of πηγή accentuated

---

[62] 2. 55. 27–34: 'Hoc tenemus, hoc novimus, in hac una consistimus cognitionis et scientiae veritate, nihil ab eo fieri nisi quod sit omnibus salutare, quod dulce, quod amoris et gaudii laetitiaeque plenissimum, quod infinitas habeat atque incorruptibiles voluptates, quod sibi quisque contingere votis omnibus expetat, forisque ab his esse exitabile ac mortiferum ducat.'

[63] Diogenes Laertius, *Vit. phil.*, 10. 139.

[64] *Ad Marc.* 12. Porphyry emphasizes more than Plotinus divine aid in the redemptive process: see A. Smith, *Porphyry's Place in the Neoplatonic Tradition* (The Hague, 1974), 103; cf. *Civ. Dei*, 10. 29, and a similar idea in Sev. Gabal, *De mun. creat. or.* 6. 3 (*PG* 56. 487 = Harnack, *CC* Fr. 42).

[65] *COTh* 26: *Theos.* 35; cf. Fr. no. 49 (= Proclus, *In Tim.* 3. 14. 3–10) in E. Des Places, *Oracles Chaldaïques* (Paris, 1971; Budé), 79.

[66] SC 68 I: Hadot.

[67] M. Vict. *Adv. Ar.* 4. 10. 45–11. 13 (SC 68 I), indebted to Porphyry, provides parallels with *Adv. nat.* 2. 2, according to Hadot, *Porphyre et Victorinus* (Paris, 1968), 406; therefore the *De reg. an.* has influenced the terminology in *Adv. nat.* 2. 2.

[68] P. Courcelle, 'Les sages de Porphyre et les *uiri noui* d'Arnobe', *REL* 31 (1953), 257–71.

[69] Throughout this chapter possible Porphyrian Neoplatonic influences are noted.

the paternal intellect as the preeminent source from whom all cosmic powers emanated. He is πάντων πηγή, πάντων δὲ καὶ ἀρχή.[70] A closer conceptual parallel exists between Arnobius and Porphyry in respect of a deity capable of doing good[71] and who does not cause the bad. An example of this similarity is *Adv. nat.* 2. 55. 27–34 and *Ad. Marc.* 24: κακῶν ἀνθρώπῳ οὐδεὶς θεὸς αἴτιος ἀλλὰ νοῦς ἑαυτῷ ὁ ἑλόμενος.

What did the Epicureans teach about a display of divine kindness toward mankind? The first of Epicurus' Κύριαι Δόξαι is illuminating: Τὸ μακάριον καὶ ἄφθαρτον οὔτε αὐτὸ πράγματα ἔκει οὔτε ἄλλῳ παρέχει, ὥστε οὔτε ὀργαῖς οὔτε χάρισι συνέχεται, ἐν ἀσθενεῖ γὰρ πᾶν τὸ τοιοῦτον.[72] Epicurus taught that an expression of divine kindness towards man was a sign of weakness. Velleius,[73] Philodemus,[74] Lucretius,[75] and Diogenes of Oenoanda[76] followed their master. Again compare a statement of Porphyry, καὶ πάντων ὧν πράττομεν ἀγαθῶν τὸν θεὸν αἴτιον ἡγώμεθα. τῶν δὲ κακῶν αἴτιοι ἡμεῖς ἐσμεν οἱ ἑλόμενοι, θεὸς δὲ ἀναίτιος,[77] with *Adv. nat.* 2. 55. 29–34: 'nihil ab eo [sc. Deo] fieri nisi quod sit omnibus salutare, quod dulce, quod amoris et gaudii laetitiaeque plenissimum, quod infinitas habeat atque incorruptibiles voluptates, quod sibi quisque contingere votis omnibus expetat, forisque ab his esse exitiabile ac mortiferum ducat.' The God of Arnobius is therefore neither absolutely transcendent[78] nor isolated from man.[79] It is noteworthy that this passage received no critical analysis from McCracken, who interprets the first part as being Epicurean.[80]

---

[70] Aion and Hecate were thought to be noetic entities forming a reservoir of the transcendent Father's powers. See *COTh* 82 n. 58: Procl. *Crat.* 59. 3: Aion = πασῶν συνοχεὺς τῶν πηγῶν; 82 n. 59; 83 nn. 61–3; for Arnobius' use of *fons* and its association with Porphyry, see E. Des Places, 'Les Oracles Chaldaïques', *ANRW* II. 17. 4, 2313 f.

[71] *Ad Marc.* 17.

[72] Diog. Laer. 10. 139.

[73] *De nat. deor.* 1. 45. 17; 1. 51. 19 f.

[74] *De dis* 3, fr. 85, 5 ff., p. 17 (Diels); discussion in Rist (1972), 154; cf. *De dis* 1, col. 7, 1 ff., p. 14 (Diels).

[75] *De rer. nat.* (LCL: Rouse-Smith), 1. 44–9; 2. 646–51, 1090–104; 4. 12–39; 5. 76–90, 110–234; 6. 379–422.

[76] Diog. Oen., fr. 29, speaks of the fear of the gods which is a πάθη that disturbs the soul in M. F. Smith, 'New Fragments of Diogenes of Oenoanda', *AJA* 75 (1971), 376; cf. id., 'Seven New Fragments of Diogenes of Oenoanda', *Hermathena*, 118 (1974), 114 f.: *NF* 32 cols. 1 f. probably continued with a discussion about the indifference of the gods towards humans.

[77] *Ad Marc.* 12.

[78] K. B. Francke, *Die Psychologie und Erkenntnislehre des Arnobius* (Diss., Leipzig, 1878), 73.

[79] LeB 76.

[80] McCr 333 n. 312.

Another passage that reveals his belief that God gives assistance to worshippers is 1. 28. 2–5: 'Meliorisne sunt causae, qui Grundulios adorant Lares . . . quam sumus nos omnes, qui deum colimus rerum patrem atque ab eo deposcimus rebus fessis lanquentibusque tutamina?' God is expected to give protection to the faint and weary. The exact meaning of the Virgilian *rebus fessis*[81] is derived from other passages where it occurs. In 1. 25. 16–20 it denotes the absence of that sense of safety (*salus*) which only the worship of *deus dominus* provides.[82] It is also defined as the frailty and weakness of humans whom the *rex poli* providentially blesses with sunshine, rain, and good harvests.[83] The *caput rerum* has caused man to exist on the earth.[84] Man is able to enjoy good health because of him. He has given man the right to keep the earth's produce and established the sunshine to make it grow.[85] Humans can ask the *deus summus* to give them what they need.[86] Finally, accentuating God's lordship over man's natural environment, his ability to regulate and control its processes, and the close relationship between the agrarian life and religion often found in Roman North Africa, *Adv. nat.* 1. 30. 1–8 reveals God's providential concern for man.[87]

How do these data compare with Epicurean theology? First, the explanations of Epicurus in Diogenes Laertius[88] about such celestial phenomena as the sun's heat, night-time, the winds, and the rains are clearly incompatible with *Adv. nat.* 3. 24. 11–12.[89] The divine nature has absolutely nothing to do with the physical world.[90] This seems to have been a cardinal doctrine of the Epicureans, for it is revealed in

[81] Cf. *Aen.* 11. 335 (LCL: Fairclough).

[82] The 'rerum cunctorum quaecumque sunt dominum' of *Adv. nat.* 1. 25. 17 has a number of N. African theological parallels: Saturn was believed to be the great Lord of heaven and earth; cf. Isis' sovereignty in *Met.* 11. 5: 'elementorum omnium domina'; 11. 7: 'orbisque totius dominam', emphasizes her power over cosmic fatalism; cf. the Kyme aretalogy in Grandjean (1975), 123; and *De Is. et Os.*, 359 D, F.

[83] *Adv. nat.* 3. 24. 11 f.

[84] Ibid. 1. 29. 3–6.

[85] Important if we keep in mind that the *Adv. nat.* appears to have been written during difficult agricultural conditions in N. Africa.

[86] *Adv. nat.* 1. 26. 21–4.

[87] 'Nonne cogitatio vos subit considerare, disquirere, in cuia possessione versemini, cuia in re sitis, cuius ista sit quam fatigatis terra, cuius aer iste quem vitali reciprocatis spiritu, cuius abutamini fontibus, cuius liquore, quis ventorum disposuerit flamina, quis undosas excogitaverit nubes, quis seminum frugiferas potestates rationum proprietate distinxerit?'

[88] *Vit. phil.* 10. 139.

[89] Ibid. 10. 90–5.

[90] Ibid. 10. 97: καὶ ἡ θεία φύσις πρὸς ταῦτα μηδαμῇ προσαγέσθω, ἀλλ᾽ ἀλειτούργητος διατηρείσθω καὶ ἐν τῇ πάσῃ μακαριότητι.

Lucretius' praise of his master's discoveries;[91] Velleius' attack upon the Platonic and Stoic teachings on providence;[92] and similar views are found in Philodemus[93] and Diogenes of Oenoanda.[94] It is certain that Epicureans separated the regulation of celestial phenomena and the laws of the natural world from any kind of divine control or supervision. According to Arnobius, however, all terrestrial and celestial beings depend upon God for their life and substance.[95]

Two passages concern the practice of prayer during worship. Both focus upon the belief in a deity who forgives the misdeeds of humans and therefore relate to their moral and spiritual needs. The first occurs at the end of a prayer to the *summus rex* which is pregnant with philosophical language: 'Da veniam, rex summe, tuos persequentibus famulos, et quod tuae benignitatis est proprium, fugientibus ignosce tui nominis et religionis cultum.'[96] An indication that the pagan Arnobius may have held similar views to those found in this statement may be derived from 7. 8. 15–20,[97] where he argues against a sacrificial theory that offered pardon (*venia*) in exchange for animal life. The availability of divine favour (*venia*) directly from God to man proves that the God of Arnobius is not far removed from the affairs of man, which is what one would expect if he were conceiving the nature of divinity in Epicurean terms. But beyond this one can add another important conclusion: a concept basic to Arnobius' understanding of God is that the latter takes an active part in actually ameliorating man's spiritual condition during his earthly life, and this results from an act of worship called prayer. Specifically the text portrays a God willing to forgive the present persecutors of the Church (*famulos*), and the Christian precept lying behind this is probably Jesus' injunction to pray for one's enemies.

---

[91] *De rer. nat.* 5 (*passim*).

[92] *De nat. deor.* 1. 19–24. 8–9; 52–4. 20.

[93] *De Dis* 1, col. 7, 1 ff., p. 14 (Diels); cf. also 3. 8, 20 ff., p. 26.

[94] Cf. Smith (1974), 114 f.: *NF* 32, cols. I–II, who suggests that Diog. Oen. argued that celestial phenomena are not governed by the gods; see also id. (1971), 360.

[95] *Adv. nat.* 2. 2. 16–19: 'a quo omnia terrena cunctaque caelestia animantur motu nriganturque vitali, et qui si non esset, nulla profecto res esset quae aliquod nomen substantiamque portaret.'

[96] Ibid. 1. 31. 16–19.

[97] 'Atquin ego rebar deos, si modo rectum est credere quod motibus exagitentur irarum, sine ullis praemiis nullisque mercedibus iras atque animos ponere et peccatoribus delicta donare. Hoc est enim proprium numinum, liberales venias et concessiones habere gratuitas.' give this interpretation as a result of comparing this with 1. 39 and 3. 24. Cf. the venerabar of 1. 39. 1 and (better) the *Atquin ego rebar* of 3. 24. 6: both describe religious ideas or practices of his pre-Christian period.

142 God and the World

The dissimilarities between the Arnobian understanding of divine providence (*venia*) and the fundamental Epicurean doctrine that a god does not show favour (χάρις), are obvious.[98]

Although some passages in the *Adv. nat.* concerning worship suggest an indebtedness to Platonism,[99] the second text provides more evidence for the Epicurean debate. It is in 4. 36. 23–7, a reference to the ecclesiastical practice of praying for the dead,[100] a rite also implied in 2. 63. 18 f., where Arnobius seems to be responding to Porphyry of Tyre's question about what has happened to those who have died before the advent of Christ.[101] The fact that Arnobius answers by affirming the availability of God's mercy for the dead demonstrates two important things. First, it may point to an existential involvement in a Christian community, and 4. 36. 22–7 corroborates this interpretation. Also, it provides more *prima facie* evidence against an Epicurean identification of Arnobius' God. An Epicurean would have found ludicrous enough the idea that a deity has mercy at all, especially on the living, and much more so on the dead. At death the human being simply ceased to exist.[102]

III. *Soteriology: Temporal and Eschatological Benefits*

A significant number of passages in the *Adv. nat.* concern what the historian of ancient religions may call *salvation*, which in this context can often mean the amelioration of an individual's physical or spiritual condition directly resulting from his commitment to and dependence upon his deity. Sometimes it can mean, in the typically Roman conceptualization of *salus*, the continuous preservation of man's sense of

[98] Diog. Laer. *Vit. phil.* 10. 139; see *De rer. nat.* 5. 165 ff.; and *Adv. nat.* 1. 31. 16–19.
[99] Cf. 1. 26. 14 f. On *summus rex* cf. *Enn.* 5. 5. 3: νοῦς = βασιλεὺς ὁ μέγας; *De Is. e Os.* 355 E: Osiris = μέγας βασιλεύς; Max. Tyr. *Diss.* 11. 5; Dio. Chrys. *Or.* 2. 72 (LCL Cohoon): μέγιστος βασιλεύς; Porph. *De reg. an.* in Aug. *Civ. Dei* 19. 23; *COTh* 318 f. on the *patrem rerum ac dominum* of *Adv. nat.* 2. 13. 12, cf. Plutarch's similar κύριο ἁπάντων καὶ πατὴρ (*De def. or.* 426 A (LCL: Babbit)); Max. Tyr. *Diss.* 11. 5; and Porph *Phil. or.* in Aug. *Civ. Dei* 10. 23, 26 f., 30 (the latter from *De reg. an.*): *principia = deu pater et filius.*
[100] *Adv. nat.* 4. 36. 23–7: 'Nam nostra scriptura cur ignibus meruerunt dari? cu immaniter conventicula dirui? in quibus summus oratur deus . . . adhuc vitam degentibu et resolutis corporum vinctione . . .'.
[101] See P. Courcelle (1953), 265 f.
[102] Diog. Laer. *Vit. phil.* 10. 125; *De rer. nat.* 1. 102–11; 3. 37–93; also Diog. Oen. *N* 2, col. II in A. Laks and C. Millot, 'Réexamen de quelques fragments de Diogèn d'Oenoanda sur l'âme, la connaissance et la fortune', in Bollack and Laks (1976), 330 f.

safety or well-being in the world as the result of his religious beliefs
and practices. This soteriological world-view reveals a good number of
beliefs which are in direct conflict with Epicureanism: the belief in
divine providence; the divine intervention in man's earthly life; a
personalized view of the relationship between God and man; and God's
initiation of beneficial contact with humans. We will now turn our
attention to these components of Arnobius' understanding of God.

In respect of the physical and material needs of man, the most
important text is 3. 24. 8–17:

Numquid enim rex poli libamine aliquo exambitur aut hostia, ut omnia ista
quibus vivitur commoda mortalium gentibus largiatur? Non fervorem genitalem
solis deus, noctis et tempora, ventos pluvias fruges cunctis subministrat aequaliter
bonis malis [iustis] iniustis servis pauperibus divitibus? Hoc est enim proprium
dei potentis ac veri, inexorata beneficia praebere fessis atque invalidis rebus et
multiformi semper asperitate vallatis.

It is clear from this statement about God that the benefits which man
receives from the natural elements (sunshine, wind, rain, harvest)
are the direct results of the divine will working indiscriminately for
humankind's welfare. The regulation of the elements is conceived as
being under the supervision of God for the purposes of satisfying man's
material needs. A similar idea occurs in 1. 29. 9–25, which is again in
direct opposition to Epicurean physics.[103] Finally, in 1. 30. 1–8, God is
portrayed as the great lord of the land, air, water, winds, and clouds.
He makes seeds fruitful and sends the rains, an interesting statement in
light of his earlier references to drought (1. 9. 1 f.) and crop failure (1.
13).

It is probably Porphyry who lies behind the question in 2. 76. 1–5
why the Christian God allows his followers to suffer persecutions.[104]
Arnobius' answer gives us insight into his understanding of God: 'Sed
et nobis in huiusmodi casibus minime auxiliatur deus. Prompta et
manifesta causa est. Nihil est enim nobis promissum ad hanc vitam nec in
carunculae huius folliculo constitutis opis aliquid sponsum est auxiliique
decretum.[105] The first significant term (*casibus*) conveys the idea of
equality of suffering amongst Christians and pagans. Christians cannot

[103] *De nat. deor.* 1. 52. 20.
[104] Therefore Christ does not offer the way of salvation (cf. Ch. 8): *Civ. Dei* 10.32 (*De reg. an.*): 'Videbat ista Porphyrius et per huius modi persecutiones cito istam peritura et proterea non esse ipsam liberandae animae universalem putabat . . .'.
[105] *Adv. nat.* 2. 76. 18–21.

claim immunity from the fatal blows of fortune during persecution in the same way that pagans cannot be exempted from shipwrecks, diseases, fires, and other calamities.[106] Arnobius' theodicy precludes making God responsible for the occurrence of evil in the world.[107] The main point of his argument is that God does nothing bad to man, and only that which is good.[108] He uses the same argument to prove that Christ was *deus verus*.[109] Indeed, he is as determined to show that God is not responsible for evil as he is to demonstrate that he does only what is beneficial for humankind. The latter would have been rejected by the Epicureans. Yet in the tradition of Plato, the Porphyrian theodicy is similar, the main difference being the assigning of evil to demons.[110] Arnobius nowhere makes clear why evil exists.

Turning to spiritual needs, Arnobius stresses the universal appeal of Christianity's redemptive benefits in 1. 55. 9–12: 'Immo quia haec omnia et ab ipso cernebant geri et ab eius praeconibus, qui per orbem totum missi beneficia patris et munera dei animis hominibusque portabant ...'. Whether one accepts the *P* (and Marchesi's) reading *hominibusque*, or the emendation *corporibus*,[111] the fact is clear that God's *munera* and *beneficia* in the form of visible miracles[112] have soteriologically benefited the souls and bodies of humans.[113] God is responsible for their occurrence. They are typically described as gifts (*munera*), but compared with other passages where it is used, *munus* often means 'divine power', 'miracle', or 'a divine service done on humankind's behalf'.[114] In 2. 5. 27–35 Arnobius refers to the presence of God in the martyrs' minds, without which their inner transformations could not happen.[115] These

---

[106] *Adv. nat.* 1. 29; 2. 45.

[107] Ibid. 2. 5.

[108] Ibid. 1. 29. 9–25; 1. 30. 1–8; 3. 24. 1–17.

[109] Ibid. 1. 44; 1. 47; 1. 49.

[110] Cf. *Tim.* 42 E.

[111] McCr 295 n. 276: *homo = corpus* in *Adv. nat.* 1. 62; 1. 65; 2. 28; cf. G. Wiman, 'Ad Arnobium', *Eranos*, 45 (1947), 129–52. Christ is the *praesidem nostri corporis* in 1. 42. 7 which Le Bonniec (p. 68) translates 'le Chef de notre communauté'. I agree with Laurenti' 'Protettore del nostro corpo'.

[112] For *munus* used as an anti-Porphyrian term, see Ch. 8. See MacMullen (1981), 96 '... announcement of supernatural powers new in the world it would be quite irrationa to credit, without proof of their efficiency before one's own eyes. That was what produced converts. Nothing else is attested.'

[113] See R. MacMullen, *Christianizing The Roman Empire* (New Haven, Conn., 1984) 26; cf. H. C. Kee, *Miracle in the Early Christian World* (New Haven, Conn., 1983), 293.

[114] e.g. 1. 27. 20; 1. 28. 40; 1. 38. 4, 41; 1. 50. 8; 1. 63. 5; 1. 65. 20; 2. 32. 4; 2. 34. 14 2. 36. 2; 2. 53. 5; 2. 62. 21; 2. 64. 10, 23; 2. 65. 16.

[115] The appeal of martyrdom, well attested in North African Christianity, surfaces here

concepts related to the universal appeal of Christianity may have
contained some very potent anti-Porphyrian venom, for it was the great
opponent of the Christians who disqualified their religion as the universal
way of the soul's salvation because their God allowed his servants to
suffer persecution.[116]

The act for which man is responsible and which initiates what is
perhaps best described as the redemptive process is a commitment to
God through faith (*Adv. nat.* 2. 8–11). Faith (*fides*) is conducive to
receiving God's mercy in the present life.[117] It elsewhere seems to be
understood as a simple mental act of accepting God's gift of *salus*.[118]
Man has the freedom either to accept or to reject it, and his description
of God in this context is illuminating:

Sortem vitae eligendi nulli est, inquit Plato, deus causa, neque alterius voluntas
adscribi potest cuiquam recte, cum voluntatis libertas in ipsius sit posita potestate
qui voluit. An numquid orandus es, ut beneficium salutis ab deo digneris
accipere, et tibi aspernanti fugientique longissime infundenda in gremium est
divinae benivolentiae gratia?   (2. 64. 14–21)

Here we find a writer whose concept of God is supposedly Epicurean,
speaking of God's favour of salvation being offered directly from himself
(*ab deo*) to man as a gift, and using Plato as his basic source! It is also
important to observe that *salus* in this context, as is the case throughout
the *Adv. nat.*, denotes a sense of safety in the world experienced by the
believer who has faith in the Christian God.

The *locus classicus* of Arnobius' soteriological understanding of God
occurs in 2. 65, where *salus* specifically denotes the immortalization of
the human soul. The latter is contingent upon the acceptance of God's
promise that it will actually become reality. Temporal initiation of the
redemptive process which culminates in the soul's immortality happens
in the moment when the individual believes in the *spem salutis* (2. 65.
18 f.) provided to him only by Christ the emissary of the High God.
Arnobius begins the passage by describing God as powerful (*potens*),
merciful (*misericors*), and a preserver (*conservator*). Kindness (*gratia*) and
generosity (*liberalitas*) characterize his nature (2. 65. 1–5). Humans are
the recipients of such divine largesse, and Arnobius makes explicit that
it is God who initiates this beneficial contact with man during his

---

[116] See n. 104 above.
[117] *Adv. nat.* 2. 12. 29–39.
[118] Ibid. 2. 78. 5 ff.

earthly life.[119] God has foreordained that through Christ mankind might be rescued from corruption.[120] According to Arnobius, there was a logical plan developed in the mind of God to execute the redemption of mankind: 'Hanc omnipotens imperator esse voluit salutis viam, hanc vitae ut ita dixerim ianuam, per hanc solum est ingressus ad lucem neque alias datum est vel inrepere vel invadere ceteris omnibus clausis atque inexpugnabili arce munitis' (2. 65. 36–40). It will be remembered that Epicureans believed that the gods did not concern themselves either positively or negatively with the affairs of humans.[121]

Turning to eschatology, God is responsible for the immortalization of the soul which is midway between life and death in its present condition and possesses a *media qualitas* (2. 35. 15).[122] No details are given about the place to which human souls go in the hereafter. Arnobius can only speak of an *aulam dominicam*, yet even here he seems to be using the term of his adversaries.[123] And again we find the familiar terms used to describe temporal *salus*: the gift (*munus*) and favour (*beneficium*) of the *sumus princeps* makes the souls long-lived (*longaevus*).[124] These passages, taken together with e.g. 2. 63. 18 f. and 4. 36. 23–7, depict an all-powerful deity who transcends all restrictions of time and space: he is the lord of man's past, present, and future. Note also that 2. 36 is indebted to Plato (*Tim.* 41 A–B): all things, gods and human souls included, are dependent upon the divine will for their subsistence.[125] Because he is omnipotent and immortal, only God can make the human soul eternal.[126]

But now the main soteriological question must be asked: what is it about human life from which man must be delivered? To put it differently, how does one's acceptance of the divine gift of salvation (*munus salutis*) ameliorate one's spiritual existence in this world? In answering this, momentarily leaving aside the obvious moral aspects of the Arnobius view of redemption (e.g. 1. 63. 23–35; 1. 27. 6 f., 9–15,

---

[119] *Adv. nat.* 2. 65. 13–18.

[120] Ibid. 1. 63. 16 f.; 2. 64. 27 f.

[121] Epicurus ap. Diog. Laer. *Vit. phil.* 10. 139; Velleius ap. Cic. *De nat. deor.* 1. 56. 20; Philodemus, *De piet.* 2, col. 106, p. 124 (Gomperz); Lucretius, *De rer. nat.* 1. 44–9; Diog. Oen. fr. 29 (Chilton).

[122] Cf. *Adv. nat.* 2. 62. 26–9; 2. 53. 9 f.; on 2. 62. 14 f., cf. Burger (1970), 2.

[123] *Adv. nat.* 2. 33. 18 ff.

[124] Ibid. 2. 32. 2–5.

[125] Ibid. 2. 2. 17 ff.; 2. 35 f.; cf. 1. 28. 9–12.

[126] Ibid. 2. 62. 14–18: 'Servare animas alius nisi deus omnipotens non potest, nec praeterea quisquam est qui longaevas facere, perpetuitatis possit et spiritum subrogare nisi qui immortalis et perpetuus solus est et nullius temporis circumscriptione finitus.'

16–22), we observe that the rhetor takes it for granted that the fear of death is one universal human malady which the divine gift, if accepted, can annihilate because it bestows immunity from corruption upon the soul.[127] It is therefore necessary for man to surrender to the Christian liberator-God (*deus liberator*: 2. 32. 11 f.) so that these fears (*metus*) may be eradicated.[128] Evidently Arnobius speaks from personal experience, for he gives the equation, *mors = animarum interitus*, for which he himself expresses fear.[129] The Latin *interitus* is not used to describe the dissolution of the atomic constituents which occurs immediately at death, as Epicureans taught. Arnobius explicitly states that punishments in a burning hell, though not of an eternal duration, supervised by what appear to be monsters who cast the condemned souls there, await those who do not know God.[130]

Epicurus was thought to have come to save humanity from believing in such erroneous concepts. 'Death is nothing to us; for the body, when it has been resolved into its elements, has no feeling, and that which has no feeling is nothing to us.'[131] Also, in his *Epistle To Menoeceus*, Epicurus opines that he who fears death is foolish.[132] The wise neither deprecate life nor fear death,[133] and this is the exact opposite of the Arnobian view. According to Epicurean atomic theory, the human being simply disintegrated at the moment of death, and therefore any belief in an afterlife was defined as pure superstition. We may give Diogenes of Oenoanda's vituperation of the Empedoclean doctrine of metensomatosis as a classic example of this philosophical doctrine.[134] Even more ludicrous than this for Epicureans was the idea that the soul would suffer punishment in some type of hell (Acheron) after death, and with this we should contrast the *Adv. nat.* 2. 14, which refers to 'Plato idem vester' in *Phaed.* 112 A–114 A, and 2. 53.[135] Lucretius praises

---

[127] See e.g. *Adv. nat.* 2. 65 for his Christocentric soteriology.

[128] 2. 32. 10 ff.: 'Quid est quod a vobis tamquam bruti et stolidi iudicemur, si propter nos metus liberatori dedidimus et mancipavimus nos deo?'

[129] 2. 33. 1 f.

[130] 2. 12. 27–34.

[131] Diog. Laer. *Vit. phil.* 10. 139; cf. 10. 142.

[132] Ibid. 10. 124–6.

[133] Ibid. 10. 126.

[134] Diog. Oen. *NF* 2, col. II, p. 330 (Laks and Millot); cf. fr. 29 (Chilton); M. F. Smith, 'Fragments of Diogenes of Oenoanda Discovered and Rediscovered', *AJA* 74 (1970), 51–62: *NF* 2, p. 59; *NF* 3, p. 61; Lucretius, *De rer. nat.* 3. 670–8; 1. 202–11; 3. 7–42; 6. 1182 f.

[135] Diog. Laer. *Vit. phil.* 10. 126 f.; *De nat. deor.* 1. 45. 17; 86. 31; *De rer. nat.* 3. 37–93: a reference to Acheron.

Epicurus for his ability to deliver his disciples from such superstitious beliefs.[136]

IV. *Knowledge of God: Innate and Soteriological*

Epistemology represents another facet of Arnobius' concept of God and his relationship to the world. He distinguishes between an innate knowledge of the existence of God, which everyone possesses, and a redemptive knowledge acquired as the result of accepting the truths of Christianity. A constant tension is discernible in his thought on this subject: while he stresses that God is mysterious and, to a certain extent unknowable, yet it is only by possessing knowledge of God that one can be saved from destruction. The deity's unknowability is frequently couched in the kind of apophatic language which characterizes a good number of Christian writings from the East[137] and the West,[138] and also Gnostic[139] and pagan ones as well.[140]

His prayer of thanksgiving and adoration addressed to the *rex summus* (*Adv. nat.* I. 31) is pregnant with such apophatic designations. God is invisible and unable to be understood by nature.[141] It is doubtful whether human lips can fully pronounce his worth.[142] God, he continues, is unbegotten (1. 9: *ingenitus*).[143] He is afraid to ascribe to God adjectives like steadfast (*constantem*), virtuous (*frugi*), wise (*sapientem*), honourable (*probum*), and so forth.[144] It is a wonder he is able to say that God knows, understands, or provides anything.[145] He finally reaches an apex in 3. 19. 14–21, where man's inability to express anything about the

---

[136] e.g. *De rer. nat.* 1. 102–35; 2. 45 f.; 3. 830–1094; 6. 1208–12; cf. 5. 1–54.

[137] Arist. *Apol.* 1; Athenag. *Suppl. pro Christ.* 10; J. Martyr, 1 *Apol.* 10; Theoph. *Ad Autol.* 1. 3; Greg. Nys. *Vit. Moy.* (*passim*).

[138] Tert. *Apol.* 17. 2; 2. 3; M. Felix, *Oct.* 18. 8 f.; Cypr. *Quod idola dii non sint* 9 (*PL* 4. 576 f.); Lact. *Div. inst.* 5. 3. 2; Iren. *Adv. haer.* 3. 18. 1 (SC 210–11: Doutrejean–Rousseau).

[139] NHL: 1. 3. 1, p. 38; 1. 3. 38, p. 47; 1. 3. 40; 1. 5. 52 f., p. 56; and esp. 1. 5. 54, p. 56: 'Not one of the names which are conceived, spoken, seen, or grasped, not one of them, applies to him.'

[140] Plot. *Enn.* 5. 3. 13: cf. 3. 9. 9: τὸ πρῶτον ἐπέκεινα ὄντος who has no self-consciousness, nor can it be said that he lives or thinks. Cf. Porph. *Comm. in Parmen.* (142 A), fr. 10. 29–35, in Hadot (1968), p. 125.

[141] 1. 31. 2 f.: 'o ipse invisus et nullis umquam conprehense naturis.'

[142] Ibid. 3 f.

[143] Cf. Clem. Alex. *Protr.* 6. 59: ἀγένητον.

[144] *Adv. nat.* 3. 19. 5 f.

[145] Ibid. 6 ff.

divine nature, with the exception that it is indescribable, is admirably
accentuated.[146] Man's language is designed to describe human affairs,
but not the nature and actions of God. The whole passage clearly points
to a strong influence from the Platonic tradition, not only in Plato's
works but also in those of Plotinus, and it is with the Academy's rich
heritage of apophatic theology that we can make a certain connection
with Arnobius' prayer.[147]

Arnobius develops his argument by affirming that neither any shape
nor outline of body can represent God, a statement especially useful in
light of his attack upon the anthropomorphic Graeco-Roman deities in
books 3–5.[148] Porphyry of Tyre's description of God as a being who
possesses an incorporeal nature is similar to the Arnobian understanding
of deity.[149] Plotinus' soul went to the First God μήτε μόρφην ἰδέαν ἔχων
(*Vit. Plot.* 23). In *Enn.* 5. 5. 6 the One is ἀνείδεον and an ἄμορφον εἶδος
in 6. 7. 33.[150] Arnobius further describes God as a being unlimited in
nature and magnitude ('qualitatis expers, qualitatis': 1. 31. 11–12).
Similar remarks occur in 7. 25. 29–31: 'O deorum magnitudo mirabilis,
o nullis hominum comprehensa, nullis intellecta naturis'; 7. 33. 29: 'et
illa vis praestans neque ullis hominum comprehensa naturis'; and 2. 62.
17 f.: 'nullius temporis circumscriptione finitus.' He is 'sine situ motu
et habitu, de quo nihil dici et exprimi mortalium potis est significatione
verborum' (1. 31. 12 ff.). The comparison that has been made between
Enn. 5. 5. 9 f., 6. 9. 6, and the first clause of the latter is acceptable.[151]
We may add to this Porphyry's description of the First God as ἀκίνητος
(*De abst.* 2. 37. 1); God's unknowability and incomprehensibility in
Adv. nat. 1. 31. 19 f.;[152] the highly apophatic passage in 3. 19. 14–21;
Porphyry's remark, τὸν ἐπὶ πᾶσι δὲ θεὸν ἀμήχανον εἶναι καταλαβεῖν οὐχ

[146] 'Quicquid de deo dixeris, quicquid tacitae mentis cogitatione conceperis, in humanum
transilit et corrumpitur sensum, nec habeat propriae significationis notam quod nostris
dicitur verbis atque ad negotia humana compositis. Unus est hominis intellectus de dei
natura certissimus, si scias et sentias nihil de illo posse mortali oratione depromi.'
[147] Cf. *Parmen.* 142. 12 A; 134 D–E; and *Enn.* 5. 4. 1; 5. 5. 13; 6. 7. 38; 6. 8. 15; 6. 9. 4;
6. 9. 6; and esp. 5. 5. 6: 'Its definition in fact could be only "the indefinable" . . . we are
in agony of a true expression; we are talking of the untellable; we name, only to indicate
for our own use as best we may' (MacKenna–Page).
[148] *Adv. nat.* 1. 31. 10 ff.
[149] *De abst.* 1. 57. 3; 2. 37. 1; *Adv. nat.* 3. 12. 14–19, and 3. 17. 3–5: 'Si veram vultis
audire sententiam, aut nullam habet deus formam, aut si informatus est aliqua, ea quae
sit profecto nescimus.'
[150] As in *Adv. nat.* 1. 31 and 3. 19, Plotinus says that we must make every denial and
no absolute assertion about the Absolute Good (5. 5. 13).
[151] Kroll (1916), 325 f.
[152] 'Non est mirum, si ignoraris: maioris est admirationis, si sciaris.'

ὅτι ἐκ λόγου ἀλλ' οὐδὲ διὰ νοήσεως;[153] and an Arnobian passage that perhaps describes a mystical experience of the knowledge of God in 1. 31. 14 ff.[154]

Nature enables man to confirm the presence of his knowledge that God exists, an idea found in several passages in Arnobius[155] and in varying degrees in other ante-Nicene writers.[156] Although later Stoics such as Balbus formulated a similar doctrine,[157] the unique reference to the ἔμφυται προλήψεις of Chrysippus[158] (ap. Plutarch), which many have misconstrued, disqualifies the members of the Early Stoa as possible sources for Arnobius' thinking.[159] The main text is *Adv. nat.* 1. 33, which Copleston probably had in mind when he asserted that according to Arnobius, all ideas have an experiential origin except that of God.[160] Yet he did not observe the distinction between innate knowledge of God's existence and the redemptive knowledge which culminates in the soul's immortalization. It is a theological concept that had already been penned by a number of Arnobius' North African Christian predecessors.[161]

Is Arnobius describing the Epicurean concept of πρόληψις in 1. 33? A comparison of a statement of Velleius with *Adv. nat.* 1. 33. 1–6 may be illuminating:

Solus enim vidit [sc. Epicurus] primum esse deos, quod in omnium animus eorum notionem inpressisset ipsa natura. Quae est enim gens aut quod genus hominum, quod non habeat sine doctrina anticipationem quandam deorum? quam appellat πρόληψις Epicurus, id est anteceptam animo rei quandam informationem, sine qua nec intellegi quicquam nec quaeri nec disputari possit.   Velleius (Cicero, *De nat. deor.* 1. 43. 16)

Quisquamne est hominum, qui non cum istius principis notione diem primae nativitatis intraverit? cui non sit ingenitum, non adfixum, immo ipsis paene in

---

[153] *Comm. in Parmen.* 10 fol. 92'X. 14–16, in Hadot (1968), 96 f.

[154] 'qui ut intellegaris tacendum est atque, ut per umbram te possit errans investigare suspicio, nihil est omnino muttiendum.'

[155] *Adv. nat.* 1. 33; 2. 3.

[156] Tert. *Ap.* 17. 4 ff.; Cypr. *Quod idola* 9 (*PL* 4. 577); Eus. *PE* 2. 6; Clem. Alex. *Protr.* 2. 21; 4. 59.

[157] *De nat. deor.* 2. 12. 4.

[158] See J. M. Rist, *Stoic Philosophy* (Cambridge, 1969), 134: 'There is no other "evidence" in the Old Stoic writers for a theory of any kind of "inborn" belief.'

[159] F. H. Sandbach, "Ἔννοια and Πρόληψις in the Stoic Theory of Knowledge", *CQ* 24 (1930), 48, argues that ἔμφυτος = 'ingrained' in Chrysippus. Cf. the knowledge *in genitalibus matris* of *Adv. nat.* 1. 33. 4.

[160] F. Copleston, *A History of Philosophy* (9 vols., New York, 1962), 2. 1. 39.

[161] Cypr. *Quod idola* 9; Tert. *Ap.* 17. 5: and the latter's *De test. an.*

genitalibus matris non inpressum, non insitum esse regem ac dominum cunctorum quaecumque sunt moderatorem? Arnobius (*Adv. nat.* 1. 33. 1–6)

There are obvious literary and conceptual parallels between the two writers.[162] Beyond these, however, the analogy begins to disintegrate. Epicurus' *Epistle To Menoeceus* enables one to disengage the polemical and apologetical aspects of Velleius' argument from the true doctrine of his master's concept of πρόληψις: θεοὶ μὲν γὰρ εἰσιν. ἐναργὴς δὲ ἐστιν αὐτῶν ἡ γνῶσις· οἵους δ' αὐτοὺς (οἱ) πολλοὶ νομίζουσιν.[163] Thus Epicurus made a sharp distinction between ἡ κοινὴ τοῦ θεοῦ νόησις and that which the πολλοὶ νομίζουσιν about God. This means that there was no universal knowledge of God's existence. Second, there is no hard evidence to suggest that the Epicurean πρόληψις τῶν θεῶν was thought to be implanted (inborn) at birth, which is exactly what Arnobius states in *Adv. nat.* 1. 33.[164] According to one scholar, the προ in πρόληψις possesses a logical, rather than chronological, meaning.[165] The definition of Diogenes Laertius[166] that a πρόληψις is a recollection of an idea previously made clear, makes sense in light of this.[167]

Neoplatonic philosophy most probably influenced Arnobius' concept of the innate knowledge of God's existence. Notwithstanding similar ideas espoused by Plotinus[168] and Iamblichus,[169] Porphyry affirms the belief in man's innate concepts of God (τὰς ἐμφύτους ἐννοίας).[170] They function as aids in one's flight to God.[171] God has imprinted his own image in the intellect: ἐμψύχῳ ἀγάλματι τῷ νῷ ἐνεικονισαμένου ἀγάλλοντα [τοῦ θεοῦ].[172] In *The Epistle To Marcella*, the intellect knows the law of God because it finds it already imprinted within itself.[173] The body of the intellect is the rational soul which causes it to recognize

---

[162] Arnobius' 'notione . . . inpressum' and 'insitum' are similar to Velleius' 'notione inpressisset' and 'insitas', etc.

[163] Diog. Laer. *Vit. phil.* 10. 123.

[164] See K. Kleve, *Gnosis Theon* (Oslo, 1963, SO suppl. 19), 29.

[165] Ibid. 28 f.

[166] *Vit. phil.* 10. 33; cf. 10. 124.

[167] See Rist (1972), 140 f.; *De nat. deor.* 1. 46–9. 18; *De rer. nat.* 5. 1196.

[168] *Enn.* 4. 7. 15, speaks of the soul that sees images of its primal state deeply impressed upon it.

[169] *De myst.* 1. 3. 714 f.: man has a γνῶσις ἔμφυτος vested in his soul by nature, on which see A. Smith (1974), 85.

[170] *Ad Marc.* 10.

[171] *Vit. Plot.* 23 (LCL: Armstrong).

[172] *Ad Marc.* 11: the divine image impressed upon the soul of the sage who honours God only through wisdom.

[173] Ibid. 26.

concepts imprinted in it by the truth of divine law.[174] It is this same
divine image impressed upon the soul of the sage who honours God
only through wisdom, about which Porphyry is probably speaking in
the *Commentary on Parmenides*,[175] when he refers to a προέννοιαν of the
One. Yet although both Arnobius and Porphyry agree on man's innate
knowledge of God, one main difference between them is that the latter
understands the concepts as being directly related to the redemptive
process.[176]

Arnobius describes God as 'unum et simplex' (1. 62. 3 f.). We
may compare with this Porphyry's epithet of ἁπλούστερος.[177] His
αὐταρκέστατος[178] may also be implied in *Adv. nat.* 1. 23. 4–7, 1. 27.
12 ff., and 2. 64. 25–8,[179] where he emphasizes God's self-sufficiency.
There are convincing similarities in a couple of other Porphyrian
phrases: θεὸς μὲν γὰρ δεῖται οὐδενός (*Ad Marc.* 11) and χρῄζει οὐδενὸς
τῶν ἔξωθεν (*De abst.* 2. 37. 1). According to Arnobius, God's true
being escapes all imagination.[180] And although his essential nature
remains thus a true mystery, one must still form an image (*aura*) of
the God who is subsumed in the unfathomable depths of exalted
divinity.[181] The Epicurean concept of the quasi-anthropomorphic
forms of the gods[182] does not cohere well with these descriptions, but
another problem arises in Arnobius' delegating the formation[183] of the
aura dei to man during what appears to be an act of personal meditation.[184]
Epicureans held the different view that the very fine compounds of
atoms which emit images of the gods could be passively received by
humans whether awake or asleep.[185] Suffice it to say that Arnobius

---

[174] *Ad Marc.* 26.

[175] *Comm. in Parmen.* 2. fol. 91ᵛ in Hadot (1968), 71 n. 2, concerns a προέννοιαν of the
One, which Hadot accepts rather than προσέννοιαν because of parallels with M. Vict. (i.e.,
praeintelligentia, praenoscentia) in *Adv. Ar.* 4. 19. 4 and 1. 33. 4.

[176] *Ad Marc.* 25. Porphyry stressed more than Plotinus man's need of divine aid in the
salvific process: see Smith (1974), 104; A. H. Armstrong, 'Salvation, Plotinian and
Christian', *DR* 75 no. 240, p. 132.

[177] *De abst.* 1. 57. 3.

[178] Ibid.

[179] 'Neque enim necessaria nostra illi salus est, ut conpendii aliquid dispendiive
patiatur . . .'.

[180] *Adv. nat.* 2. 60. 24 f.

[181] Ibid. 2. 60. 26 ff.

[182] e.g. *De nat. deor.* 1. 49. 18; Rist (1972), 146–56; and the fine treatment in D. Lemke,
Die Theologie Epikurs (Munich, 1973; ZMKA 57), 23–41.

[183] The term is *affingere*; cf. *Adv. nat.* 2. 60. 26.

[184] Cf. Rist (1972), 141.

[185] *De nat. deor.*, 1. 49. 19; Rist (1972), 141 f.

provides perhaps the best example of apophatic theology in ante-Nicene Latin Christianity.[186]

In addition to the concept of a deity who is transcendent, mysterious, and almost totally unknowable, one finds also in the *Adv. nat.* an emphasis upon the need to acquire knowledge of God in order to be delivered from death. But how can the idea of an unknowable God be compatible with—indeed, how can it logically relate to—that of soteriological knowledge? When Arnobius says that God is unknowable, he seems to be saying that this is true in respect of man's attempt to acquire knowledge of God's being and nature, and how he relates himself to mankind, *outside of the revelation of Christ* (*Adv. nat.* 2. 7. 7–12). God is, therefore, knowable to a certain extent, and that which he allows man to know about himself causes him to receive incorruption. He would apparently be saying that there are some aspects of God's nature that can be apprehended, but God's divine being will never be totally comprehended by man. A couple of passages illustrate how one acquires this knowledge. The first is found in 2. 14. 22–6:

Sunt enim mediae qualitatis, sicut Christo auctore compertum est, et interire quae possint deum si ignoraverint, vitae et ab exitio liberari, si ad eius se minas atque indulgentias adplicarint, et quod ignotum est pateat.

According to this, the doctrine of the *media qualitas* of the soul has been given by Christ. He refers to Plato in the same passage—a man not far from the truth whom his opponents follow[187]—to show the hypocrisy of ridiculing the Christian belief in the punishment of souls in the afterlife.[188] Souls are therefore neither mortal nor immortal. They simply perish if they do not know God.[189] (Arnobius does not espouse the idea of an eternal hell.) The only way that they receive their liberation from incorruption is by devoting themselves to the divine indulgence. Apparently this means that the acceptance of Christ's revelation as truth manifests what is otherwise unknown about the way in which the immortalization of the soul occurs. By receiving the eschatological promises of Christ, human ignorance of the true God and his plan for man's salvation is eradicated. Their rejection will eventually cause the soul's death.

[186] Cf. Francke (1878), 73; Burger (1970), 77 f.; Siniscalco, DPAC I, col. 377.
[187] Cf. *Adv. nat.* 1. 8; 2. 14; 2. 36; 2. 52 for other compliments to Plato.
[188] *Phaed.* 113 D–114 C.
[189] *Adv. nat.* 2. 14. 24.

The second passage is 2. 72. 18–24:

Non ergo quod sequimur novum est, sed nos sero addidicimus quidnam sequi oporteat [ac] colere aut ubinam conveniret spem salutis adfigere et salutaria subsidia conlocare. Nondum enim adfulserat qui viam monstraret errantibus et caligine in altissima constitutis cognitionis lumen inmitteret et ignorationis discuteret caecitatem.

The metaphors of light and darkness are used to distinguish between those who possess redemptive knowledge from those who do not. The equations *lumen = cognitio dei = salus animae*; and *caligo = ignoratio dei = mors animae*; appear to have been inspired by Clement of Alexandria.[190]

Both the *cognitionis lumen* and the *salutaria subsidia* of *Adv. nat.* 2. 72 refer to the earlier statement that he has learned what to follow in Christ.[191] This is made clear in 2. 11. 13–19: 'Ac nos quidem in illo secuti haec sumus: opera illi[us] magnifica potentissimasque virtutes, quas variis edidit exhibuitque miraculis, quibus quivis posset ad necessitatem credulitatis adduci et iudicare fideliter non esse quae fierent hominis sed divinae alicuius atque incognitae potestatis.' *Salvation-assistances* are the divine powers operating in the miracles of Christ. As MacMullen has recently shown, belief in these miracles was frequently a principal factor leading to Christian conversions in the pre-Constantinian period.[192] Although the African rhetor acknowledges the historicity of the recorded miracles of Christ, and thus reveals that Christ's miraculous powers motivated his conversion, he makes it very clear that these miracles still occur in Roman North Africa of the early fourth century. For example, the name of Christ scares away malignant spirits. He makes the works of soothsayers, fortune-tellers, and magicians ineffective.[193] It was apparently quite easy for Arnobius to take the historical correlation a step further by accepting the *munus inmortalitatis* as truth and the miracle *par excellence*, especially since he professes to have seen the divine powers at work in his own day. And there is no reason why we should not accept his word on the subject.[194] The same powers operating in Christ's ministry (1. 45–54) and in contemporary North Africa would

---

[190] *Protr.* 11. 88; cf. *Adv. nat.* 1. 65. 15 ff.; 2. 2. 1–6.

[191] For the historical development of this concept see Pelikan, 1 (1989), 141–5.

[192] MacMullen (1984), 17–42, esp. 40 ff.

[193] *Adv. nat.* 1. 46. 29–35.

[194] See R. MacMullen, 'Two Types of Conversion to Early Christianity', *VC* 37 no. 2 (1983), 181; S. Benko, *Pagan Rome and the Early Christians* (London, 1985), 118–22; and the elucidation in my Ph.D. thesis, p. 157 n. 201.

also immortalize his soul some day in the future. Note his only definition of *scire*: 'nam si scire est illud quod ipse tu videris aut cognoveris animo continere . . .',[195] which is applicable to the explanation surveyed: knowledge of God is the preservation in one's mind of what has been seen or learned about his miraculous powers operating in mankind.

An intellectual assent to Christian truth is the initial act which culminates in the incorruption of man.[196] This subjective belief is based upon such objective criteria as Christ's miracles and the rapid growth of the Christian religion in the Roman Empire.[197] In Chapter 9 we shall observe that Porphyry's anti-Christian propaganda, published before the outbreak of the Great Persecution and directly aimed at Christian soteriology, was the main inspiration of Arnobius' position here. For he insists that the pagans must believe in Christ or expect to receive punishment for a certain period in a burning hell, after which they will be destroyed.[198] He consistently emphasizes the importance of faith (*fides*) to his adversaries.[199] He demonstrates the superiority of Christian *credulitas* to philosophical speculation.[200] He similarly uses *spes*,[201] *spes salutis*,[202] and *percipere*[203] to describe the mental act that initiates the possession of salvific knowledge.[204] Only Christ can save human souls from death (2. 65). Books 1 and 2 end by exhorting the pagans to believe in Christ (1. 65; 2. 65).[205] Below we shall observe that Arnobius appears to be responding to the *Contra Christianos* of Porphyry, especially the Neoplatonist's criticism of Christians for their unaccountable faith.[206]

Because religious paganism is devoid of any eschatological benefits, knowledge of salvation is conferred only by Christ.[207] To provide proof of this theological assertion Arnobius again refers to the eyewitness accounts of Christ's miracles, passed down in written form and con-

---

[195] *Adv. nat.* 2. 51. 16 ff.
[196] Ibid. 2. 11. 4 ff.
[197] Ibid. 1. 55; 2. 5; 2. 12.
[198] Ibid. 2. 5. 4–7.
[199] Ibid. 2. 5. 7–10.
[200] Evidently responding to Porph. ap. Eus. *PE* 1. 1. (Harn. *CC* fr. 1).
[201] *Adv. nat.* 1. 65. 35–42; 2. 53. 1–7.
[202] Ibid. 2. 66. 21–5; cf. 1. 31. 23 f.
[203] Ibid. 2. 66. 7 f.
[204] Ibid. 2. 14.
[205] Rather than attempting 'to impress the pagans with their own guilt', as McCracken states.
[206] See esp. Ch. 10.
[207] *Adv. nat.* 1. 63. 5 f.; 2. 72. 23 f.

firmed, he says, by a sceptical humanity's acceptance of them as true.[208] Christianity is based upon witnesses (*testibus*) and paganism is derived solely from opinions (*opinionibus*).[209] He frequently uses *cognitio* to denote an objective perception of the divine knowledge that Christ has revealed.[210] The most important passage is 2. 32. 1–10, where he describes *cognitio dei* as a *glutinum* for the binding of incohesive elements, which appears to be a conflation of *Phaed.* 83 E and *Tim.* 41 A–D.[211] In addition to the metaphor of glue, one scholar has discovered that another Arnobius term, *nail*, also appears in Porphyry[212] to designate sensual bondage. These two metaphors were foreign to Plotinus, and the conclusion has already been made that Arnobius' immediate source is Porphyrian.[213] But the objective perception of the divine[214] entails a process of growth in one's subjective knowledge of God.[215] Meditation is the soteriological medium through which this individualized noetic experience of God traverses.[216] Suffice it to say that a departure from the natural world; a total flight to the deity with all one's heart and mind; and an effort to form an image of the divine through prayer and meditation, are the salient features of Arnobius' mystical quest for a subjective knowledge of what we may theologically describe as an ethereal and transcendent *High God*.[217] This is the *maxima scientia* that man is capable of possessing.[218]

A majority of book 2—the longest of the work—attempts to demonstrate the futility of his opponents' knowledge. He develops his argument around the belief that all human beings know God.[219] Knowledge is defined by Arnobius as that which man has seen, learned, and retained in his mind. According to these criteria, pagan science is not the result of thorough examination 'placed in the light of the clearest

---

[208] e.g. *Adv. nat.* 1. 53; also, 1. 38; 1. 40. 1–5; 1. 47; 1. 48. 11 ff.; 1. 65. 39 f.; 2. 9. 1–4; 2. 11; 2. 51. 16.

[209] Ibid. 1. 54. 6–17; 1. 57. 23.

[210] Ibid. 1. 63. 5; 2. 32. 6; 2. 51. 21, 24; 2. 72. 23.

[211] See E. L. Fortin, 'The *Viri Novi* of Arnobius and the Conflict Between Faith and Reason in the Early Christian Centuries', in D. Neiman and M. Schatkin, (eds.), *The Heritage of the Early Church* (Rome, 1973; OCA 195), 218 f.

[212] Ibid.

[213] Ibid. 219.

[214] *Cognitio* found in *Adv. nat.* 2. 32.

[215] *Adv. nat.* 2. 32. 5.

[216] Ibid. 1. 31. 14 f.

[217] Ibid. 2. 60. 30 ff.: 'quem [sc. Deum] satis sit scire ut nihil aliud noveris, sisque veram et maximam scientiam consecutus in dei rerum capitis [et] cognitione defixus.'

[218] Contrast this with his criticism of philosophical epistemology in *Adv. nat.* 2. 1–59.

[219] *Adv. nat.* 2. 15. 15 f.

truth'.[220] The selection of words here, the identity of his opponents in sections of the first two books, and the fact that Arnobius attempts to prove the veracity of Christian belief on the basis of historical events both seen and recorded by reliable eyewitnesses, strongly suggest that he is responding to Porphyry's rejection of the faith because it lacks evidence to support it.[221] Thus when Arnobius claims that pagans do not know *x*, he often means that they cannot prove what they are affirming about *x* on the basis of objective criteria.[222] Therefore human desire to achieve knowledge produces no certainty.[223]

To sum up Arnobius' soteriological epistemology, with the exception of a few ideas taught by Plato, his final word about religious and philosophical paganism is that it does not offer any knowledge of God.[224] Only Christ has revealed the authentic redemptive knowledge of God's nature, how he relates himself to man, and what man must do to become incorruptible. Only Christ has been able to remove the *periculum ignorationis* of God.[225] This revelatory knowledge is found in the teaching and miracles of Christ who was sent to earth by God and is himself God (*deus*).[226] It results from man's initial act of believing in the promises of God which have been revealed by Christ, and are based upon the historical events of his earthly ministry.

V. *Creation: God and a Christianized Demiurge*

A cardinal tenet of book 2, where Arnobius vehemently attacks Neoplatonic psychology,[227] is that the High God (*summus deus*) did not create man. The great God who is immaterial, perfect, and immortal cannot have created such a wretched being as man.[228] Because souls are changeable and deceitful, a *res invidia* is responsible for their origin. The philosophical background is certainly Plato's concept of the demi-

---

[220] Ibid. 2. 51. 12 ff.
[221] See Ch. 9.
[222] *Adv. nat.* 2. 51. 20–7.
[223] Ibid. 2. 57; 2. 78. 1 ff.
[224] Ibid. 1. 53. 1 ff.; 2. 19. 1–2; 2. 65.
[225] Ibid. 2. 2. 2.
[226] Ibid. 1. 42–7.
[227] The *viri novi* of 2. 15. 2 f. lend support to this interpretation: Plotinus, *Enn.* 5. 1. 8, defends against criticism that his doctrine is new; and the practice of theurgy appeared to be a new kind of Platonism: cf. *Adv. nat.* 1. 43; 1. 52 f.; 2. 13. 33–6; *Civ. Dei* 10. 9.
[228] *Adv. nat.* 2. 46. 11–21; 2. 32. 1 ff.; 2. 15. 1–7; 2. 72. 13–17.

urge.[229] In attacking his opponents' doctrines, he argues that souls are not immortal, divine, wise, learned, or perfect.[230] If the soul were immaterial, it would not be capable of uniting with a body.[231] Arnobius posits that wisdom comes only with the progression of education, and therefore he rejects the Platonic doctrine of ἀνάμνησις which maintained that souls came to the earth possessed with the memories of former experiences.[232] Also, the soul is not one and simple, and it is capable of suffering.[233] Christ taught that the soul's essential condition is of a *media qualitas*,[234] a doctrine actually derived from Plato.[235]

The *Adversus nationes* contains three principal passages related to the theological tenet that the High God did not create human beings. The first is *Adv. nat.* 2. 46. 1–11:

But, to say the same things over and over again, let this idea, so monstrous and wicked, be far from us, that He who is the Salvation of things, the Head of all virtues, and the Acme of benevolence, and—to exalt Him with human praise— the Most Wise, the Just, who makes all things perfect and retentive of the fulness of their perfection, either made anything defective or not wholly appropriate, or was to anything a cause for misfortunes or dangers or ordained, commanded, and enjoined the very acts by which human life is spent and employed, to deflect from His dispositions.

The second is 2. 48. 1–4, and 7–11:

So here also, in much the same manner, when we deny that the souls are the offspring of God Supreme, it does not forthwith follow that we must explain from what parent they have been brought forth and by what causes they have come into existence. . . . Because it is absolute truth and positive certainty that nothing, as has often been said, is done, made, or determined by the Supreme Being except what is right and becoming, except what is whole and entire and finished in the perfection of its integrity.

The third is 2. 52. 25–33, and the importance of this passage is the disclosure of the philosophical tradition which underlies its author's thought:

What reason do we think motivated that great Plato, a philosopher of goodness

---

[229] See McCr 306 n. 34, for discussion of the text.
[230] *Adv. nat.* 2. 15.
[231] Ibid. 2. 16. 6 f.
[232] Ibid. 2. 19–25.
[233] Ibid. 2. 27.
[234] Ibid. 2. 32.
[235] *Adv. nat.* 2. 36. 21–9; 2. 44.

above reproach, when he took away from the Supreme God the fashioning of man and gave it to some sort of lesser gods, and when he would not have the souls of the human race to be composed of that same pure mixture of which he had made the soul of the universe, except that he thought the making of man unworthy of God and the fashioning of something feeble as incompatible with His exalted greatness?

Syllogistically the argument can be given as follows: God creates only that which is essentially perfect; man is not perfect; therefore man was not created by God. Also, it must be emphasized that Arnobius' concept of creation is not in any way based upon either the doctrine of divine indifference or impassibility. It cannot therefore be concluded that he was an Epicurean because of his belief that a being other than the High God was responsible for creating man.

According to the *Adversus nationes*, the High God can create only that which is perfect. Arnobius therefore develops an intense attack upon what he understands to be a Neoplatonic anthropocentric soteriology and the exaltation of man which it entails.[236] He hammers a metaphysical wedge in book 2 between the exalted majesty of the High God and the ignoble creature called man.[237] It is therefore blasphemous to ascribe the creation of man to God.[238] The psychological experiment is developed in 2. 20–5, and its main objective is to disprove the Platonic doctrine of ἀνάμνησις.[239] In the context of this attack, he refers to a Chaldaean theological concept, that the soul is in fourth place after the High God and the twin intellects (2. 25. 1–6). Its identity was discovered by Bousset[240] and Kroll[241] early this century. It was Courcelle[242] and Lewy,[243] however, who established its Platonic association; and the former[244] more specifically made a connection with a Porphyrian (Neoplatonic) group existing in North Africa in the late third/early fourth centuries AD. Finally, if it is true that the opponents of book 2 who are called *viri novi* ('New Men': 2. 15. 2 f.) apply 'remarkably well not to the Platonists in general but to Plotinus, Porphyry, and their immediate disciples',[245]

---

[236] Ibid. 1. 43; 1. 52 f.; 2. 13. 33–6.
[237] Ibid. 2. 15. 4; 2. 16. 7; 2. 19. 10; 2. 25. 4.
[238] Ibid. 2. 46. 11–15.
[239] Ibid. 2. 24–7.
[240] W. Bousset, 'Zur Dämonologie des späteren Antike', *Afr* 18 (1915), 141.
[241] Kroll (1916), 354 f.
[242] Courcelle (1953), 269 f.
[243] *COTh* 324 n. 44; cf. Festugière, *ML* (1940), 108; O'Meara (1959), 146; Des Places, *ANRW* II. 17. 4, 2313.
[244] Courcelle (1953).
[245] Fortin (1973), 220; and see the documentation in my Ph.D. thesis, p. 165.

it is not surprising to find Neoplatonic passages that may have inspired the rhetor's psychological experiment.

One possibility is *Enn.* 5. 1. 1. According to Plotinus, a child taken away from its home and brought up at a distance will not remember its father or itself. Likewise, the souls fallen to earth no longer discern their own divinity. They must therefore recall (ἀναμιμνήσκων) their race (γένους) and worth (ἀξίας). The same ideas form the heart of the attack in *Adv. nat.* 2. 20–8.[246] Also, Porphyry in his *De antro nympharum*, following closely the Pythagoreans (ch. 3), Plato (ch. 3), Numenius and Cronius (ch. 10), states that the cavern (ch. 3: σπήλαιον; ch. 10: ἄντρον) was a symbol of the world in Homer (*Od.* 13). Porphyry continues by giving an allegorical interpretation of *Od.* 13. The nymphs signify souls who descend into the world of generation (ch. 4). Before this he refers to Cronius (ch. 1) who found it admirable that the cave has two entrances, one for the descent of the souls from the sublunary sphere, and the other for the ascent of the gods. He then discusses the immortality of human souls (ch. 11), a main concept that Arnobius' experiment attempts to disprove.[247] Souls lose their memory of divine concerns during their descent to the corporeal realm,[248] and with this one should compare Arnobius' adversary in 2. 26. 10: 'Ex opposito corporis amittit [sc. anima] repetentiam priorum.'

Porphyry expresses similar concepts in *De abstinentia*.[249] In order that it may return to its proper realm (τὰ οἰκεῖα), the soul must abandon that which made it a stranger to its race (ἀποτίθεσθαι πᾶν εἴ τι προέλαβεν ἀλλόφυλον). The mortal nature must be relinquished[250] because it was responsible for its descent (κατάβασις) to the natural realm in order to remember (ἀναμνησθῆναι) the eternal essence (αἰωνίου οὐσίας).[251] Comparison should also be made with *Adv. nat.* 2. 26. 10 f. and the idea attributed to Porphyry by Eusebius, that souls in the sublunar region forget the divine.[252] Finally, a very important detail is Porphyry's reference to, and extensive use of, Plato (*De ant. nymph.* 3, 13),

---

[246] The worth of man: 2. 20. 2; his divine race: 2. 21. 4 f.; the rejection of anamnesis: 2. 24–8; failure of the knowledge of one's divinity: 2. 27 f.; immortality of the soul: 2. 20. 2 f.; 2. 25. 1 ff.; 2. 26. 1 f.

[247] *Adv. nat.* 2. 14–53.

[248] *De ant. nymph.* 12.

[249] *De abst.* 1. 30. 3 (Budé: Bouffartigue).

[250] Ibid. 1. 30. 4: τῆς θνητῆς φύσεως.

[251] Ibid.

[252] *PE* 3. 11.

Pythagoras (ch. 3),[253] Numenius (chs. 4, 10, 16),[254] and Cronius (ch. 1, *bis*; ch. 10 with Numenius)[255] in the *De antro nympharum*. It is therefore significant that Arnobius identifies the *viri novi* in *Adv. nat.* 2. 11. 4 f. as the followers of Plato, Cronius, and Numenius; and in 2. 13. 8 f., Plato and Pythagoras.[256] Mercury is mentioned in the latter, and he had a rather rich tradition in the Platonic and Neoplatonic schools.[257]

Arnobius equally rejects his opponents' beliefs that either the souls descend of their own desire (*Adv. nat.* 2. 44. 1), originating from *deus rex* (2. 51. 13); or that God sent them to earth to learn evil.[258] Again there is evidence in the Neoplatonic tradition to suggest that he is attacking their doctrines.[259] The Iamblichian theological concept that God sent the souls to the earth to perfect the creation of the universe is not accepted in *Adv. nat.* 2. 37. 16 ff.,[260] and both Festugière[261] and Hadot[262] associate the adversary of this section with the Neoplatonic idea. According to Stobaeus (1. 49. 39), Iamblichus in his Περὶ Ψυχῆς referred to some Platonists who taught that souls are sent by the gods εἰς τελείωσιν τοῦ παντός. Plato also depicts the High God as addressing the θεοὶ θεῶν that if the three classes of mortal beings remaining to be created are not generated, heaven will be imperfect: τούτων δὲ μὴ γενομένων οὐρανὸς ἀτελὴς ἔσται (*Tim.* 41 B). Arnobius' 'universitatis haec summa' corresponds better to Iamblichus' τοῦ παντός than to Plato's οὐρανός.

God the *fons rerum*[263] begets only that which is good and perfect, and because man is neither, God is not his creator.[264] We must now

---

[253] *De ant. nymph.* 3. Both Porphyry and Iamblichus wrote a life of Pythagoras.

[254] Porphyry, *Vit. Plot.* 14, places Cronius and Numenius in a list of Platonists although they were Pythagoreans.

[255] Numenius and Cronius are frequently quoted in Porphyry. See N. Bidez, *Vie de Porphyre* (Ghent, 1913), 13; Eus. *PE* 14. 5, reveals that Numenius closely associated the followers of Plato and Pythagoras.

[256] See Fortin (1973), 201.

[257] Ibid.

[258] *Adv. nat.* 2. 39–43.

[259] See *Enn.* 1. 1. 12; 2. 3. 10; 4. 8. 1; 4. 8. 4 f.; and analysis in J. M. Rist, *Plotinus: The Road to Reality* (Cambridge, 1967), 112–29; Porph. *De reg. an.* ap. Aug. *Civ. Dei* 10. 30; cf. *Adv. nat.* 2. 43. 1–7 and *Civ. Dei* 12. 21; A. Smith (1974), 35 f.; Hadot (1971), 53.

[260] 'Ad consummandam molis huius integritatem partem aliquam conferunt, et nisi fuerint additi, inperfecta et clauda est universitatis haec summa?'

[261] A. J. Festugière, *La révélation d'Hermès Trismégiste* (Paris, 1953), 3. 219.

[262] Hadot (1968), 333 n. 3. E. R. Dodds, 'Theurgy and its Relationship to Neoplatonism', *JRS* 37 (1947), 67 n. 119, compares Iamblichus, *De myst.* 177. 7 ff. and *Adv. nat.* 4. 12. 10.

[263] *Adv. nat.* 2. 2. 12–19; cf. 1. 28. 36 ff.; 1. 34. 12 f.; 2. 45. 19 ff.; 2. 48. 22.

[264] Ibid. 2. 35. 12 ff.; 2. 47. 13 ff.; 2. 16. 7; 2. 44; 2. 46; 2. 56; 2. 58.

investigate the immediate source of this concept. In *Adv. nat.* 2. 52. 25–
33, he refers to *Tim.* 41 B–D, where Plato removes the creation of man
from the High God (*deus maximus*) and gives it to inferior gods. In 2.
36. 7–12 the *Timaeus* is named, and its author is called 'Plato ille
divinus'. His argument is that souls would be perfect, immortal, and
divine if they were created by God, and his source is certainly *Tim.*
41 C. God delegates to the θεοὶ θεῶν the creation of the remaining three
classes of mortal beings after he himself has created the gods of the
celestial sphere (*Tim.* 38 C–D; 39 B–C). If God had been their immediate
creator, they would have been equal to the gods and therefore immortal.[265]

We can go further. Arnobius acknowledges that all beings derive their
life from the divine volition, referring to the Christians 'qui dedidimus
nos deo, cuius nutu et arbitrio omne quod est constat et in essentiae suae
perpetuitate defixum est?' (1. 28. 10 ff.). The term *nutus* is used several
times in the work to denote the will of the High God,[266] and it similarly
appears in Greek[267] and other Latin texts.[268] The High God is indirectly
responsible for the existence of everything: he is the father of creation (2.
13. 12), which recalls the great πατήρ of *Tim.* 37 C. First Cause (*prima
causa*) is a divine epithet found in 1. 31, and it seems to be used to describe
the first cause of an emanational theory of the origin of souls. And again
we should not be surprised to find it used in a similar way in Plotinus[269]
and Porphyry.[270] It is not clear whether the *causae* flowing from God (*Adv.
nat.* 1. 29. 15 f.) which sustain and animate all earthly existence are to be
considered as individual hypostatic entities. But the primary source again
points to the *Timaeus*, especially the passage that makes a sharp distinction
between the primary and secondary causes.[271]

Found in the same passage which Hadot[272] convincingly argued is
indebted to the *De regressu animae*, the 'perpetuarum fundator rerum'
of *Adv. nat.* 2. 2. 15 appears not to be identical to the 'invisibilium
procreator' of 1. 13. 1, although the *perpetuarum* probably includes the
invisibilium. The High God of *Tim.* 36 E–37 A creates the visible and
invisible celestial phenomena, which are eternal (cf. *Tim.* 40 B–C). He
generates the inferior deities as well, and Arnobius refers to this concept

[265] *Tim.* 41 C.
[266] e.g. *Adv. nat.* 1. 28. 10 f.; 2. 54. 6 ff.; 7. 50. 36 f.; 4. 31. 3.
[267] Porphyry, *Theos.* 35, *COTh* 26.
[268] e.g. Cypr. *De bono pat.* 4 (*PL* 4. 624); Balbus ap. Cic. *De nat. deor.* 2. 4. 2.
[269] *Enn.* 2. 3. 6.
[270] *Ep. An.*
[271] *Tim.* 46 C–D.
[272] Hadot (1968), 406.

frequently.[273] Also, in *Adv. nat.* 1. 29. 24 f., he says that the supreme deity created the moon. Le Bonniec apparently takes *fabricator* to mean *demiurge*.[274] Yet every line of 1. 29 discusses the High God and his relationship to the world.[275] God is also depicted as the creator of the sun and the earth by Arnobius,[276] and again there is a conceptual parallel with *Tim.* 38 C–D. Plato calls the planets and stars created by God an οὐράνιον θεῶν γένος (*Tim.* 39 E–40 A), thereby confirming their eternity. In light of this we should compare the *perpetuarum conditor rerum* of *Adv. nat.* 2. 2. 16 with the *rerum [visibilium et][277] invisibilium procreator* of 1. 31. 1 f., and the *magnarum et invisibilium rerum sator et conditor, procreator* of 2. 45. 2 f. Although Balbus similarly uses *sator*, the formula is *mundus = sator* and not *deus*.[278] Stoic pantheism did not supply Arnobius with this doctrine.[279] And it is quite impossible to argue that he espoused a Marcionite view of creation.[280]

The concept of a demiurgic creator occurs in *Adv. nat.* 2. 36. 22–9 and characterizes one main aspect of the unorthodox views of Arnobius. Another passage in which we find mention of a lesser deity responsible for the creation of mankind is 2. 52. 25–8. Both point to the problems left unresolved in the *Timaeus* about the specific identities of the demiurge and the lesser gods.[281] It is not a surprise to find, therefore, that in *Adv. nat.* 2. 63. 12 f., we are informed that Christ taught about the *fabricator hominis*, but his exact identity is not clear. Elsewhere he simply says that it is unnecessary to explain who created man (2. 48. 1–5). The fact is that he was unable to reveal this information because of the ambiguity related to the demiurge which he inherited from the Platonic tradition.[282] Our conclusion to the analysis of Arnobius' concept of God and his relationship to the world is that it is not Epicurean but undeniably Platonic.

---

[273] *Adv. nat.* 1. 28. 24–42; 2. 35 f.; 2. 62; 3. 2 f.; 4. 19; 7. 35.

[274] LeB 272.

[275] *Fabricator* in *Adv. nat.* 2. 63. 13 (as also *auctor* in 2. 63. 11) and 2. 7. 22 denotes demiurgic creator. Cf. M. Capella, *De nupt. phil. et merc.* 7. 733: *fabricator* = demiurge.

[276] *Adv. nat.* 1. 38. 19 ff.

[277] I accept Marchesi's emendation, *visibilium et*, supported by the fact that the High God has created the sun and moon (*Adv. nat.* 1. 29. 23 ff.).

[278] i.e. in the Arnobian sense of *deus*.

[279] *De nat. deor.* 2. 86. 34.

[280] *Contra* F. Scheidweiler, 'Arnobius und der Marcionitismus', *ZNW* 45 (1954), 42–67; '. G. Sirna, 'Arnobio e l'eresia marcionita di Patrizio', *VC* 18 (1964), 37–50; cf. LeB 79.

[281] See J. Dillon, *The Middle Platonists* (Ithaca, NY, 1977), 6 f.; E. F. Schulze, *Das Uebel in der Welt nach der Lehre des Arnobius* (Diss., Jena, 1896), 33.

[282] See my Edinburgh thesis, pp. 172 f.

5

God and Christ

The relationship between God and Christ is the second main category of Arnobius' concept of deity. Because he is writing as a new convert not sufficiently educated in the doctrines of the Christian faith to provide an exposition of the ontological relationship between God and Christ, Arnobius is usually found discussing Christ's revelation of God and of his mission to the world as the High God's emissary. This is the heart of his understanding of the relationship between God and Christ.

In several passages he discusses the role of Christ as the one who has revealed the only true God to mankind. The works and ministry of Christ receive particular attention. The proof used to demonstrate Christ's divinity, the kindness of his deeds which he did on behalf of humanity,[1] is, as we have seen in the last chapter, in direct contra-distinction with the normative Epicurean doctrines about the nature of God. Indeed, the statement in *Adv. nat.* 1. 47. 9 f. concerning Christ, 'that from the kindliness of His deeds they might be taught to imagine what a true God is', is incompatible with the Epicurean belief that a deity did not have any *negotium* with human beings.[2] Yet Arnobius finds indisputable evidence of Christ's divinity in the fact that his great deeds *aided* humanity. Epicureans believed that the gods showed no favour (χάρις) whatsoever towards humans.

In *Adv. nat.* 1. 38 Arnobius employs a popular rhetorical device called the panegyric of the gods (*laus deorum*/aretalogy),[3] which was used in Roman oratorical practice beginning in the Republican period. His literary source appears to have been Quintilian[4] because the *Institutio*

---

[1] *Adv. nat.* 1. 47. 6–10: 'Quae quidem ab eo gesta sunt et factitata, non ut se vana ostentatione iactaret sed ... ex operum benignitate quid esset deus verus iam addiscerent suspicari.'

[2] Cotta, in Cic. *De nat. deor.* 1. 102. 36: ' "Nihil habet" inquit "negotii".' See Rist (1972), 151.

[3] One could equally praise men, animals, or inanimate objects. Cf. Quint. *Inst.* 3. 7. 6 (LCL: Butler).

[4] A study of the influence of the Roman rhetorical tradition upon Arnobius would admirably repay itself. Mulvey (1908), 14–25, is the only one who has noted parallels between Arnobius and Quintilian with any detail.

oratoria 3. 4–9 discusses the form of the *laus deorum*. First, the majesty of the god's nature is to be praised in general terms,[5] and *Adv. nat.* 1. 38. 1–5 follows this pattern. Second, one should praise the specific power possessed by each deity and the discoveries whereby each has benefited humanity.[6] In complying with this rule, both Quintilian and Arnobius name Minerva, Hercules, and Ceres as examples.[7] Third, the Latin rhetor suggests that the exploits of the gods should be commemorated just as antiquity has passed them down,[8] and it is not surprising to find Arnobius precisely following this rule by first accentuating the power and discoveries of Christ in 1. 38; and his great exploits in 1. 45–8. We may partly explain the embellishment of Arnobius' account of Christ's discoveries and powers with non-biblical and fictitious data[9] as being inspired by the basic motive which Quintilian gives for the *laus deorum*: 'Sed proprium laudis est res amplificare et ornare' (*Inst.* 3. 7. 6). The rhetor, educated in the traditions of Roman oratory, could apparently not only be pardoned for stretching the historical facts to make his point, but also be expected to do so if he was worthy of his profession.[10]

One of the great works of Christ for the benefit of humanity was to show what a true God is, his greatness, character, and indescribable profundity.[11] In a classic Arnobian definition of deity, the motive and method of the works of Christ are used to prove his divinity in *Adv. nat.* 1. 44:

But it is agreed that Christ did all He did without any paraphernalia, without the observance of any ritual or formula but only through the power of His name, and as was proper, becoming, and worthy of a true god, He granted with the generosity of His benevolent power nothing harmful or hurtful but only what was helpful, wholesome, and full of aids for us.

Although this passage betrays at least Arnobius' lack of a sound

---

[5] *Inst.* 3. 7. 7: 'Verum in deis generaliter primum maiestatem ipsius eorum naturae venerabimur . . .'.
[6] Ibid. 'deinde proprie vim cuiusque et inventa, quae utile aliquid hominibus attulerint.'
[7] *Adv. nat.* 1. 38. 5–11; Quint. *Inst.* 3. 7. 6 f.
[8] *Inst.* 3. 7. 8: 'Tum si ab iis acta vetustas tradidit, comemoranda.'
[9] Christ taught 'cur luna semper in motu, isdemne quis creditur an aliis causis lucem semper atque obscuritatem resumens, animalium origo quae sit, rationes quas habent semina . . .' etc. (1. 38. 24–7); cf. *Adv. nat.* 2. 73. 23–7.
[10] For Lucretian parallels in Arnobius 1. 38, see McCr 287 n. 176; Hagendahl (1958), 12–47. The anti-Porphyrian significance of the text is discussed in Ch. 8.
[11] *Adv. nat.* 1. 38. 16 ff.: 'deus monstravit quid sit, quis, quantus et qualis: qui profundas eius atque inenarrabiles altitudines . . .'.

knowledge of the New Testament,[12] it is highly revealing in that it contradicts Epicurean theology and offers some of the basic concepts upon which his understanding of God is founded: a true God does no harm to humans, but only what may help them. Therefore, it is in the concern to help humanity (*Adv. nat.* 1. 45–8) that one finds the *sine qua non* of the Arnobian view of the nature of a *deus verus*, and Christ has revealed this nature to mankind by his miracles that have enormously improved many lives.[13]

Several passages emphasize subordinationism in respect of God's relationship with Christ.[14] Christ spoke, so he affirms, in human form by the command of the High God.[15] As scholars have already suggested, Porphyry's criticism of Christ's recent advent receives a thorough response from Arnobius.[16] And the fact that he answers the great pagan polymath by professing the availability of the *regia miseratio* for those who died before the advent (*Adv. nat.* 2. 63. 18 f.) again demonstrates a doctrine basically incompatible with Epicurean conceptions of divinity.[17] The High God possesses powers both omnipotent and unchallenged, and his nature is mysterious and transcendent. The need for a mediator between this celestial emperor and man, an idea whose origin goes quite far back into Greek religious history,[18] was perhaps never so adroitly expostulated with ante-Nicene pagan critics of Christianity as it is in the first two books of the *Adversus nationes*.

[12] For a different view see E. Gareau, 'Le fondement de la vraie religion d'après Arnobe', *CahEA* 11 (1980), 12–23, esp. pp. 14–17; a more cautious view is found in J. D. Madden, 'Jesus as Epicurus: Arnobius of Sicca's Borrowings from Lucretius', *CCC* 2 (1981), 215–22.

[13] *Adv. nat.* 1. 49. 17–24: 'Atquin Christus aequaliter bonis malis subvenit nec repulsus ab hoc quisquam est (qui) rebus qui auxilium duris contra impetum postulabat iniuriasque fortunae. Hoc est enim proprium dei veri potentiaeque regalis, benignitatem suam negare nulli nec reputare quis mereatur aut minime, eum naturalis infirmitas peccatorem hominem faciat, non voluntatis et iudicationis electio.'

[14] Cf. G. Brunner, 'Arnobius ein Zeuge gegen das Weinachtsfest?' *JfLW* (1933), 175.

[15] *Adv. nat.* 2. 60. 12 f.: 'dei principis iussione loquens sub hominis forma'.

[16] In addition to Hadot, Courcelle, O'Meara, and Fortin, who have argued for an Arnobius–Porphyry connection, see also Frend (1981 repr.), 483; id. (1984), 442 f.; R. L. Wilken, *The Christians as the Romans Saw Them* (New Haven, Conn., 1984), 154; O. P. Nicholson, 'The Date of Arnobius' *Adversus gentes*', *StudPatr* 15, part 1 (= TU 128; Berlin, 1984), 105, and cf. also the works by Beatrice listed in the bibliography.

[17] Diog. Laer. 10. 139; Velleius *ap.* Cic. *De nat. deor.* 1. 45. 17: 'illa sententia est ab Epicuro, quod beatum aeternumque sit . . . neque ira neque gratia teneri'; *De rer. nat.* 1. 44–9; 2. 646–51; 2. 1090–104; 4. 1233–9; 5. 76–90; 5. 110–234; 6. 379–422.

[18] See e.g. M. Nilsson, 'The High God and the Mediator', *HTR* 56 (1963), 101–20, esp. p. 106; id., 'The New Conception of the Universe in Late Greek Paganism', *Eranos* 44 (1946), 20–7.

Discarding the name of Christ is tantamount to being bereft of the High God's mercy (*Adv. nat.* 2. 12. 29–39). Indeed, Christ is the mediator of God's *indulgentia principalis* (2. 64. 3–7; cf. 2. 65. 13–18). Responding to the argument that the *mos maiorum* of Roman religion, being millennia old, is true because it is more ancient than Christianity,[19] Arnobius argues that Christ brought the High God's salvation perhaps when men began to be weaker (*Adv. nat.* 2. 75. 22 f.).[20] The attempt to prove the divinity of Christ and the certainty that he has brought God's *munus salutis* to humanity[21] constitute the basis of Arnobius' understanding of the relationship between God and Christ. These are two sides of the same coin, inseparable theological concepts bound together undoubtedly more by personal experience and polemical motivation than by formal religious training. For example, it was God who sent Christ to the world for the greatest of purposes.[22] He has given to Christ, as a trust and a commission,[23] the office of granting immortality to human souls. Arnobius seems to understand Christ's main soteriological work during his earthly ministry to be the offering of God's eschatological deliverance to man.[24] The use of the pagan epithet *sospitator* solely to describe Christ as *saviour* in the *Adv. nat.* (1. 53. 11; 2. 74. 2, 17; 2. 75. 2), indeed provides irrefutable evidence that Christ's ability and desire to immortalize the soul was the main purpose for which he came to earth.

The centrality of the cross, the vicarious suffering of Christ as the Lamb of God, and the forgiveness of sins made possible by the shed blood of God's son, all salient doctrines of the early Church, do not lie at the heart of the Arnobian conception of soteriology. He is more Roman than Christian in this aspect of his thought because Roman religion did not concern itself with sin but primarily *salus*, that sense of safety and well-being in the world which the gods bestowed upon their worshippers. For Arnobius, the *salus* par excellence, in accordance with his conception of Christ more as a Graeco-Roman tutelary deity of *immortalitas* than the Christian Saviour who forgives sin, is the incorruption of the human soul which Christ offers to mankind. Therefore

[19] Cf. Porph. *Ad Marc.* 18.
[20] *Adv. nat.* 2. 74. 23 f.
[21] Ibid. 2. 60; 2. 65. 23–8: 'Ut enim dii certi apud vos habent tutelas licentias potestates neque eorum ab aliquo id quod eius non sit potestatis ac licentiae postulatis, ita unius pontificium Christi est dare animis salutem et spiritum perpetuitatis adponere.'
[22] Ibid. 1. 42. 8–12.
[23] Ibid. 2. 65. 20–3.
[24] Cf. Mulvey (1908), 122.

Christians worship the divine *rex* and Christ the *magister* who is fully divine.[25]

In a passage where *sospitator* is used to describe Christ, Arnobius refers to the ignorance of the *principes mundi* and the *dii magni* about the true purpose of his mission to earth. Although this may be an allusion to the imperial policies perpetrated against the Christians, it is better interpreted as a calumniation of Chaldaean astrophysical soteriology. The principal text is *Adv. nat.* 1. 53. 9–16:

> Deus ille [sc. Christus] sublimus fuit, deus radice ab intima, deus ab incognitis regnis et ab omnium principe deo sospitator est missus, quem neque sol ipse neque ulla, si sentiunt, sidera, non rectores, non principes mundi, non denique dii magni, aut qui fingentes se deos genus omne mortalium territant, unde aut qui fuerit potuerunt noscere vel suspicari: et merito.

The use of *princeps*, the epithet most frequently employed by Arnobius, who exists in the unknown realms (*incognitis regnis*), corresponds to the Chaldaean ἀρχή, who is the transcendent divine Father existing above the astral spheres.[26] Also, *Adv. nat.* 1. 38. 16–18 appears to have the principal Chaldaean deity in mind, for Christ is said to have shown God's depth (*profunditas*) to mankind. According to Chaldaean theology, the planetary gods were thought to meditate upon the *Paternal Depth*.[27] *Depth* in this religion 'is applied here to the Pleroma of the intelligible world, called "paternal", because the Supreme God is Himself and noetic All.'[28] Proclus' ὑπέρκοσμον may be the precise term which Arnobius, evidently being an outsider to the Chaldaean religion, has communicated with his phrase, *ab incognitis regnis*. Noteworthy also is the use of *deruptus* in *Adv. nat.* 1. 38. 14, found in the statement that Christ brought back man from the *precipices*; and the Chaldaean term κρημνός which designates Hades/Tartarus.[29]

His use of *sol* in the same passage (*Adv. nat.* 1. 53. 9–16) should be compared with the Chaldaean idea that the sun's rays draw the initiate's soul upwards during theurgical rites.[30] Playing an important soteriological role, the solar rays brought about the mystic illumination of those

---

[25] *Adv. nat.* 1. 27. 6 f.: 'nihil sumus aliud Christiani nisi magistro Christo summi regis ac principis veneratores'. Cf. B. Amata, 'Testimonianze di Arnobio Afro sulle assemblee liturgiche agliinizi del secolo IV', *EphLit* 98 (1984), 514 and n. 12.

[26] Des Places, *OC* no. 13, p. 69 (= Psellus, *Comm.* 1145 D); *COTh* 161.

[27] *COTh* 161; *OC* no. 18; *COTh* 159 n. 351 = Proc. *In Crat.* 57. 25.

[28] *COTh* 160.

[29] *COTh* 213 f.

[30] *COTh* 149 f.

initiated into the Chaldaean mysteries.[31] After walking toward the light, an initiate inhaled its divine substance, after which the ray was thought to draw up his soul and unite him 'with the centre of cosmic harmony'.[32] Comparison should be made between Arnobian terms like *sol, sidera, rectores*, and *principes mundi*, and the κοσμαγοί of Chaldaean theology, who were thought to be the leaders of the concentric celestial circles: the Empyrean, or outer intelligible world; the Ethereal, or zone of the stars and planets; and Hylic, or sublunar region including the earth.[33] He seems to allude to these circles in *Adv. nat.* 2. 16. 1 f.: 'Ac dum ad corpora labimur et properamus humana, ex mundanis circulis secuntur nos causae.' The term *mundi* (*Adv. nat.* 1. 53. 13) would denote *celestial sphere*, and the reason that a soteriological attack has been suggested is because the world's rulers, and here we must compare Arnobius' *principes* (*Adv. nat.* 1. 53. 13), participated in theurgical elevation in Chaldaean thought.[34] Finally, the term κοσμαγοί was used interchangeably with ἀρχαί, correlating with the *principes* of *Adv. nat.* 1. 53. 13.

Arnobius appears to be alluding to the practice of theurgy in two passages. The first is 2. 13. 33–6:

Quid illi sibi volunt secretarum artium ritus, quibus adfamini nescio quas potestates, ut sint vobis placidae neque ad sedes remeantibus patrias obstacula impeditionis opponant?

The second is 2. 62. 1–6:

Neque illud obrepat aut spe vobis aeria blandiatur, quod ab sciolis nonnullis et plurimum sibi adrogantibus dicitur, deo esse se gnatos nec fati obnoxios legibus, si vitam restrictius egerint, aulam sibi eius patere, ac post hominis functionem prohibente se nullo tamquam in sedem referri patritam . . .

He is here referring to the Chaldaean belief that the initiated were liberated from the ominous power of fate. The term *aulam* designates the place where souls go after death, and this corresponds linguistically and conceptually with Chaldaean eschatology. Another African influenced by this syncretism of Platonism and Chaldaean religion is Synesius, who speaks of the αὐλαὶ τῶν θεῶν to which disembodied souls were thought to ascend after death.[35] In *Adv. nat.* 2. 37. 5 *aulam* is similarly

---

[31] *COTh* 45.

[32] *COTh* 208; cf. 149 f.

[33] *COTh* 138 n. 271.

[34] Cf. *Adv. nat.* 1. 43 and Porph. *Ep. An.*; *Hyp.* 14, *COTh* 139.

[35] Hym. 3. 37, 709; 4. 292: *COTh* 33 n. 92; *OC* no. 75, p. 85; Dam. *Dub. et sol.* 2. 88. 8.

used. Because it was Porphyry who first brought the Chaldaean Oracles from obscurity and consequently came under their influence,[36] and in light of the immortalization and ascent of the soul, it is not surprising that his three purificatory *principia* taken from the Oracles undoubtedly had a direct influence upon the *principes* of *Adv. nat.* 1. 53. 13.[37] Finally, the *rectores* of the same passage appear to be an allusion to the Chaldaean belief that there was one ruler for each celestial concentric circle.[38] Signifying Aion, the sun, and the moon, they are reminiscent of Porphyry's three purificatory *principia* found in the *De Civitate Dei* 10. 23.[39] And it is not by coincidence that in *Adv. nat.* 1. 38, a text which betrays Chaldaean influence, one finds the remark that Christ has brought back man, who was blind and 'without any leader' (1. 14: *sine ullo rectore*), from the *precipices*.

Similarly, the *dii magni* of *Adv. nat.* 1. 53. 14, may represent the *Great Father* (*COTh* 76) who was conceived to rule over a henotheistic pantheon as an absolutely transcendent being. Reigning solely through his intellect ($\pi\alpha\tau\rho\iota\kappa\grave{o}\varsigma$ $\nuo\hat{u}\varsigma$) and his will ($\beta\text{o}\upsilon\lambda\acute{\eta}$),[40] he had no contact with external things or beings. Subordinate to him were Hecate-Psyche and Aion, the *Great Gods* that Arnobius mentions and whom he places in contradistinction with the Christian *princeps* who has sent Christ the *sospitator* from unknown realms of the celestial spheres. The *mentes geminas* of *Adv. nat.* 2. 54. 4 f. correspond to the two intermediaries of the Chaldaean High God, his intellect and will. The complete text is 2. 25. 2–6: 'Haecine est anima docta illa quam dicitis, immortalis perfecta divina, post deum principem rerum et post mentes geminas locum obtinens quartum et afluens ex crateribus vivis?' A connection has already been made between the *afluens ex crateribus vivis* and the reference of Proclus to the Chaldaean $\pi\eta\gamma\alpha\acuteιo\upsilon\varsigma$ $\kappa\rho\alpha\tau\acute{\eta}\rho\alpha\varsigma$.[41] Finally, we observe a parallel between Proclus' locating the Chaldaean deity in the $\acute{\upsilon}\pi\acute{\epsilon}\rho\kappaο\sigmaμ\text{o}\nu$ and the statement of Arnobius that Christ came *ab incognitis*

---

[36] *COTh* 7 ff. esp. 7: 'The Chaldaean Oracles were brought to the notice of the Neoplatonists (to whom we owe all the information we possess on this subject) by Porphyry.'

[37] Cf. Dam. *Dub. et sol.* 2. 217. 5 *ap. COTh*, 140 n. 275. Dam. postdates Arnobius (as do others cited). The logic of this method is similar to Fortin's (1973: 204) if *viri novi* (*Adv. nat.* 2. 15. 2 f.) represent an ascendant group, 'one would normally expect to find more numerous and more accurate parallels in the literature of the following rather than the preceding centuries.'

[38] *COTh* 137–57.

[39] *COTh* 455.

[40] *COTh* 79 ff.

[41] *OC* 31; fr. 42, p. 77 = Proclus, *In Parm.* 769. 8–12.

regnis (*Adv. nat.* 1. 53. 10 f.), having been sent by the divine *princeps* as saviour. Also, Porphyry's remark, in accordance with Chaldaean theology and originally appearing in his Περὶ Τῆς Ἐκ Λογίων Φιλοσοφίας,[42] that the Great Father (πατὴρ μέγας) exists ὑπερουρανίου κύτεος; should be compared to Arnobius' 'Deum principem . . . summitatem omnium summorum obtinentem' (*Adv. nat.* 1. 25. 16 ff.).

A final observation about the existence of Chaldaean influence in the *Adversus nationes* is necessary. It has already been shown that there is a conceptual correspondence between the ἀντίθεοι of Iamblichus in *De myst.* 177. 7 ff., and the reference to *antitheos* in *Adv. nat.* 4. 12. 10. The entire passage is illuminating:

If the magicians, brothers of the soothsayers, report how in their invocations pseudo-deities (*antitheos*) often steal in taking the place of those invoked, and in addition that some of these are spirits of grosser substance who pretend that they are gods, and delude the ignorant by their lying pretences, why should not we similarly believe that here also others substitute themselves for those they are not, so that they may both encourage your fancies and rejoice that victims are slaughtered to them under names of others?

It is significant that in the next chapter (4. 13. 8) the Chaldaeans are described as authorities respected by his opponents. Also, the author of the Chaldaean Oracles, Julian the Theurgist, a writer well known in Neoplatonic circles, is mentioned in *Adv. nat.* 1. 52. 6.[43] Demons are understood in the above text as spirits that deceivingly represent themselves as gods, and this concept corresponds with Chaldaean–Neoplatonic theology. The theurgists 'protected themselves by an ascetic life against the pernicious influence of these demons, called the "anti-gods", who were driven away by their action.'[44] Iamblichus is a classic example of a Neoplatonist influenced by this religious practice.[45] And because it is obvious that Porphyry has played an important role in the development of Arnobius' polemics, we should not ignore similar ideas found in his *De abstinentia*.[46] Indeed, one of the main texts analysed in this chapter (*Adv. nat.* 1. 53. 9–16, quoted above), appears after a

---

[42] *COTh* 18 = Theos. no. 13, Buresch, 97. Porphyry's rejection of the divinity of Christ and how it influenced Arnobius' polemics is analysed in the final two chapters below.

[43] See Ch. 9, p. 245.

[44] See *COTh* 284; on Julian the Theurgist, *Adv. nat.* 1. 52. 6 (cf. *OC* 32); cf. 1. 53. 14.

[45] Cf. *COTh* 285 n. 102 (*De myst.* 3. 31).

[46] *De abst.* 2. 37–43 (Cf. *COTh* 285 n. 100).

lengthy counter-attack of Porphyry's rejection of the divinity of Christ.[47]
It is therefore logical to conclude that the texts studied above represent
a critique of Chaldaean soteriology which has incorporated some effective
anti-Porphyrian elements.

We may now turn once again to Arnobius' subordinationist understanding of Christ. This concept is invariably expressed as a sub-
ordination of Christ to the High God in accordance with hierarchical
position rather than divine substance. Nowhere in the *Adv. nat.* does
Arnobius give his readers the impression that Christ as *deus* is regarded
as being in any way essentially different from the great *deus* who has
sent him to earth. One of the main emphases in the defence of his
christological argument is that Christ is perfectly divine. This should
not be surprising because one of the major attacks of Porphyry upon
the Christian faith was that, although Christ was a very good man, he
certainly was not God. Also, one should not conclude that Christ's
powers as a predominantly saving and healing deity in the *Adv. nat.* are
limited because his earthly mission is restricted specifically to the dual
purpose of bringing temporal and eschatological *salus* to mankind. It
was not heretical proclivities that informed his thinking here, but rather
insufficient instruction in biblical and Church doctrines and, mainly,
polemical objectives coupled with a desire to renounce formerly held
anti-Christian opinions.

Let us end our survey by observing some of the ways in which
Arnobius, an educated pagan, has attempted to make his new ideas
about Christ intelligible. In accordance with the concept of eschatological
deliverance, we find not infrequently the affirmation that the Great King
has sent Christ as a *custos animarum*.[48] Emphasizing temporal soteriology,
he asserts that Christ alone summons all human beings to God's mercy
(2. 64. 1–7). He has brought the High God's blessings to souls and
bodies (1. 55. 9–15). By revealing the true religion, Christ has brought
to humankind redemptive knowledge of God (2. 2). Christ has shown
that transformation of the *media qualitas animae* can occur because he
has performed many miracles (e.g. 1. 65; 2. 34) for which God is
ultimately responsible (e.g. 2. 35). His incarnation has preserved,
without impairment, the power and direction of the Most High God
(1. 60). All things and beings are subordinated to the sublime majesty

[47] See Ch. 8.
[48] *Adv. nat.* 1. 64. 33 f.; 2. 63; 2. 65. 35 f.

and power of the celestial emperor.[49] And Christ has the unique mission of bringing to humankind the gifts and the knowledge of this exalted God.

[49] Cf. van der Putten (1970), 35; J. C. Plumpe, 'Some Critical Annotations to Arnobius', *VC* 3 (1949), 231; Francke (1883), 25.

6

God and the Gods

One of the most controversial debates related to *Arnobiana* concerns the exact meaning of the relationship between the Supreme God and the gods of Graeco-Roman paganism. Some have suggested that Arnobius develops a hypothetical argument about the existence of the gods.[1] Others believe that their existence is affirmed only for polemical purposes.[2] One scholar more recently has argued, concluding that the God of Arnobius is Platonic, that the gods are not created by God, but simply emanate from him.[3] A good number have maintained that he believed in the existence of inferior deities.[4] Amata's recent analysis interprets the concept of absolute divine pre-eminence in a chronological rather than an ontological sense, but this does not preclude a hierarchical understanding of the supernatural world.[5] The highest deity of the divine realm exists at the summit (*Adv. nat.* 1. 25. 16 ff.) of the celestial spheres called unknown realms (1. 53. 10 f.), a concept directly borrowed from Chaldaean theology.[6] McDonald's observation about the Arnobian High God being at the apex of a 'graduated pantheon' is, therefore, an accurate and realistic description of Arnobius' understanding of the relationship between God and the gods.

With the exception of Le Bonniec, who has studied epithets which imply the existence of subordinate deities,[7] these scholars have not clarified exactly what Arnobius means by *gods* and the criteria which allow one to disengage polemics from personal views. This is important

---

[1] Van der Putten (1970).

[2] Le Nourry, *PL* 5. 399; E. Leckelt, *Über das Arnobius Schrift: Adversus Natione* (Neisse, 1884), 9; Marchesi (1929), 1016; Micka (1943), 43 n. 10; McCr 33.

[3] Burger (1970), 27.

[4] McDonald (1966); LeB 75; Siniscalco, *DPAC* 1. 378.

[5] Amata (1984), 144, on *Adv. nat.* 2. 2. 14–19; and his remark (143) about 7. 34. 3–13: 'Se questa pagina di Arnobio fosse tenuta nella dovuta considerazione, non si affermerebbe ancora che il *Deus Summus* di Arnobio implica l'esistenza di divinità subordinate.'

[6] McDonald (1966), 79.

[7] Cf. LeB 75 n. 3: 'Je croirais plûtot qu'Arnobe, encore à demi-païen, est resté impregn de notions philosophiques acquises avant sa conversion.'

because Arnobius conveys a fine distinction between the gods of pagan religious literature and the divine beings of the Platonic tradition. If there is a pre-Christian philosophical stratum discernible in the *Adv. nat.*, as Le Bonniec supposes, then it is mandatory to distinguish between criticism of the Graeco-Roman gods and an intellectual acceptance of, and philosophical belief in, the Platonic gods. This is the basic methodological procedure of the present chapter.

A number of possible obstacles to this method will have to be kept in mind. First, in any *Christian* concept found in the *Adversus nationes* it may be possible to find a pagan religious or philosophical idea informing Arnobius' thought. He certainly did not intentionally desire either to Platonize or paganize his new religion.[8] Understood psychologically or experientially, the influence which the old way of thinking had upon his new world-view is clearly revealed in the attempt of a well-educated former member of the pagan intelligentsia to make Christian monotheism intelligible in a polytheistic culture. One must also recall that it is extremely doubtful whether he was receiving catechetical instruction during the time of writing the *Adversus nationes*. He had as little conscious intention to paganize Christianity as he did to Christianize paganism, and any immoderate interpretations on either side are simply futile. The historical significance of the *Adv. nat.* lies chiefly in the fact that it gives its readers a relatively clear picture of an educated pagan of the upper classes of Roman North Africa who is making a valiant effort to understand Christian doctrine in its practical application.

Another significant fact to consider is that, when one converted from one religious world-view to another in antiquity, it was expected that common conceptual ground existing between the two would be discovered to make the transition both possible and beneficial; and something was thought to be lacking in the former which the new way could supply. Otherwise the conversion would not be either realistic or beneficial, especially during the Great Persecution. There is in the thought of Arnobius about God and the gods a discernible confluence of pagan religious and philosophical concepts with those of his new Christian outlook. Two examples will suffice before a detailed analysis is made. In *Adv. nat.* 1. 62, he compares the death of Christ's body, but

---

[8] Cf. P. Courcelle, 'Anti Christian Arguments and Christian Platonism: From Arnobius to St. Ambrose', in A. Momigliano (ed.), *The Conflict Between Paganism and Christianity in the Fourth Century* (Oxford, 1963), 157.

not his divine nature, to the sybyl filled with the power of Apollo. And in 2. 65, Christ's peculiar office of granting the *munus salutis* is comparable to Liber's ability to provide a vintage and other human necessities. By this kind of analogical thinking he is attempting to elucidate the meaning of his newly accepted Christian beliefs both to himself, who is still in many ways pagan in his thinking, and to those around him who lived in a pagan culture.

There is overwhelming evidence to support Le Bonniec's suggestion that there is a pre-Christian philosophical conceptual stratum which has informed Arnobius' thought *vis-à-vis* the relationship between God and the gods. The main text is *Adv. nat.* 2. 36. 1–12:

'But the gods are said to be immortal.' Not by nature, as became clear, but by the will and favour of God the Father. In that way, then, in which He granted the gift of immortality to the gods who were on a certain (day) brought forth, in the same manner will He deign to grant immortality to the souls, although savage death seems capable of blotting them out and of annihilating them in immutable destruction. That divine Plato, who expresses many worthy opinions about God which are not shared by the multitude, in that dialogue which bears the title Timaeus, says that the gods and the world are by nature corruptible and in no way free from disintegration, but that by the will of God, the King and Chief, they are preserved by an everlasting bond.[9]

Not only is Arnobius unequivocal about the philosopher who has influenced him here—he even uses a Neoplatonic term of endearment to describe Plato[10]—he does something unusual for his style of argumentation by naming his source: Timaeus 41 B is the text (*Adv. nat.* 2. 36. 7–12). The *dii* here correspond to the Platonic θεοὶ θεῶν whom the demiurge addresses in *Tim.* 41 a–D, and they are of course not totally immortal or indissoluble (ἀθάνατοι μὲν οὐκ ἔστὲ οὐδ' ἄλυτοι τὸ πάμπαν: *Tim.* 41 B). The same treatise furnished the underlying concepts of Arnobius' understanding of creation.[11] and has served as the basis for the idea of the *media qualitas animae*, as he explicitly acknowledges in

---

[9] *Adv. nat.* 2. 36. 1–12: 'Sed immortales perhibentur dii esse. Non ergo natura, sed voluntate dei patris ac munere. Quo igitur pacto immortalitatis largitus est donum dis [die] certa prolatis, et animas hoc pacto dignabitur immortalitate donare, quamvis eas mors saeva posse videatur extinguere et ad nihilum redactas inremeabili abolitione delere Plato ille divinus multa de deo digna nec communia sentiens multitudini in eo sermone ac libro cui nomen Timaeus scribitur deos dicit et mundum corruptibilis esse natura neque esse omnino dissolutionis expertes, sed voluntate dei regis ac principis vinctione in perpetua contineri.'

[10] See Ch. 3 §III.

[11] See Ch. 4 §VI.

Adv. nat. 2. 36. 16–29.[12] But he can also affirm a *media qualitas deorum* whose conditional immortality is dependent from *Tim.* 41 A, a passage that has influenced both linguistically and philosophically *Adv. nat.* 2. 35. 14–20:[13]

And yet, listen, you who do not believe that the souls are of neutral character and have their existence on the borderline midway between life and death: are not absolutely all whom fancy supposes to exist, gods, angels, demons—or whatever other name they have—are not they also of a neutral character, tottering in the condition of their doubtful lot?[14]

As Festugière has observed,[15] the reference to gods, angels, and demons corresponds to Porphyry's discussion in *De reg. an.* in Augustine, *De Civitate Dei* 10. 9, of those beings in relation to theurgical purifications, rather than to Cornelius Labeo in the same work (9. 19). And although Arnobius similarly alludes to the subject,[16] he sometimes vacillates between the affirmation that God created the gods, and simply remarking that they are unbegotten.[17]

Because of his rejection of the idea that there might be any truth in pagan religious literature, having himself an intimate knowledge of the myths owing to his profession, Arnobius will not allow the faintest possibility that the gods have births resulting from sexual intercourse. This is one belief which he attacks in books 3–5, where he develops a

---

[12] *Adv. nat.* 2. 36. 16–20: 'Ergo si res ita nec aliud convenit vel existimare vel credere, quid animas admiramini mediae dici qualitatis a nobis, cum numinibus ipsis dicat Plato medias esse naturas, sed continuam et innocciduam vitam principali benivolentia subrogari?' The divine *voluntas* is sometimes conceived as if it were an intermediary of the great transcendent God. A similar concept existed in Chaldaean theology (*COTh* 78–83).

[13] Cf. *Tim.* 41 A: θεοὶ θεῶν ὧν ἐγὼ δημιουργὸς πατήρ τε ἔργων (ἃ δι' ἐμοῦ γενόμενα) ἄλυτα ἐμοῦ γε μὴ ἐθέλουτος.

[14] *Adv. nat.* 2. 35. 14–20: 'Et tamen, o isti, qui mediae qualitatis animas esse non creditis et in medio limite vitae atque interitus contineri, nonne omnes omnino, quos esse opinatio suspicatur, dii angeli daemones aut nomine quocumque sunt alio, qualitatis et ipsi sunt mediae et in ambiguae sortis condicione nutabiles?'

[15] *Adv. nat.* 2. 20. 12 f.

[16] *Adv. nat.* 1. 28. 38–42: 'At enim esse creduntur immortales perpetui et nullius umquam participes finis. Ergo istud munus dei patris et donum est, ut infinita meruerint idem esse per saecula, cum sint labiles solubilesque natura.'; cf. 1. 34. 12 f.: 'Non enim ipsa per se sunt sed ex eius perpetuitate perpetua et infinita semper continuatione procedunt.'

[17] The following convey the concept of created gods: *Adv. nat.* 1. 28. 37–42; 2. 35 f.; for unbegotten gods see 2. 35. 21; both ideas appear in 2. 35. 20–30; cf. 7. 35. 11–18: 'At vero nos contra, si modo dii certi sunt habentque huius nominis auctoritatem potentiam dignitatem, aut ingenitos esse censemus—hoc enim religiosum est credere—aut si habent nativitatis exordium, dei summi est scire, quibus eos rationibus fecerit aut saecula quanta sint, ex quo eis adtribuit perpetuitatem sui numinis inchoare.'

lengthy vituperation with all the sarcasm of his African predecessor, Tertullian, of the anthropomorphic and anthropopathic depictions of the Graeco-Roman gods found in the myths; and it is these deities whose existence he rejects *in toto*. In a passage heavily indebted to Porphyry,[18] the *gods* are included in the Christian worship of the *deus summus*:

'If religion means anything to you, why do you neither worship the other gods with us nor reverence them nor join our nations in common sacrifices and a united religious ceremonial?' Tentatively we can say this: in attending to the worship of the Godhead, the First God—the First God, I repeat—the Father of things and the Lord, the Establisher and Governor of all things, is enough for us. In Him we worship everything that must be worshipped. We pray to what we ought to pray to. We serve with the acts of reverence what demands the homage of reverence.[19]

Taking this text in isolation, one is justified in concluding that Arnobius includes, at least indirectly, the *dii magni* in the worship of the High God. More evidence is found in *Adv. nat.* 3. 3. 6–10, where he explicitly states that the gods, whoever they might be, receive homage, though not by name, when Christians worship their divine king, provided that they derive their existence from him.[20] But as his argument develops, it becomes quite clear that the existence of the mythical gods is rejected:

Perhaps you could have summoned us to the worship of those 'divinities,' had you not yourselves been the first to fabricate such stories about them with the foulness of shameful fancies, as not only to smear their reputation but to demonstrate by the characters you assigned them the fact that they do not exist at all.[21]

---

[18] Cf. pp. 136 f. above.

[19] *Adv. nat.* 3. 2. 4–13: 'Subiciunt enim haec: si vobis divina res cordi est, cur alios nobiscum neque deos colitis neque adoratis nec cum vestris gentibus communia sacra miscetis et religionum coniungitis ritus? Possumus interim dicere: ad cultum divinitatis obeundum satis est nobis deus primus, deus, inquam, primus, pater rerum ac dominus, constitutor moderatorque cunctorum, in hoc omne quod colendum est colimus, quod adorari convenit adoramus, quod obsequium venerationis exposcit venerationibus promeremur.'

[20] '. . . si sunt progenies regia et principali oriuntur e capite, etiamsi nullos accipiant nominatim a nobis cultus, intellegunt se tamen honorari communiter cum suo rege atque in illius venerationibus contineri.'

[21] *Adv. nat.* 3. 6. 11–16: 'Invitare nos forsitan ad istorum numinum potuissetis cultum si non ipsi vos primi opinionum turpium foeditate talia de illis confingeretis quae non modo illorum polluerent dignitatem sed minime illos esse qualitatibus conprobaretis adiunctis.'

The sharp distinction made between the mythical gods and the Platonic deities is based upon his definition of a *deus verus*. A divine being must essentially be like the High God to be called a true god. Metaphysically a true god would have to be eternal (*Adv. nat.* 1. 28; 1. 34; 2. 36. 1–12); immortal (2. 16); unbegotten (*ingenitus*: 1. 31. 9); incorporeal (*incorporalis*: 7. 28. 39 ff.; cf. 2. 16. 6 f.; 7. 3. 29 ff.); and not therefore anthropomorphic nor anthropopathic (books 3–5). The *sine qua non* of a *deus verus* is that he should cause no harm to humans and should always be predisposed to bless them both materially and spiritually (2. 55. 27–34).[22] We have also seen[23] that Arnobius, following Plato, believes that the being created by the High God must be essentially divine like himself (*Tim.* 41 c). Although he concentrates upon the *media qualitas deorum*, this concept is implied in *Adv. nat.* 2. 35. 14–20, and here as in Plato, the fundamental immortality and divinity of the θεοὶ θεῶν are dependent upon the will of the High God. This is made explicit in 7. 2. 1–13: after his pagan opponent asks who the *dii veri* are, he answers that they must be like the 'dominus rerum est atque omnipotens ipse' (11. 10 f.). But the critical question is: does this definition mean *ipso facto* that Arnobius excludes the deities of the pagan myths?

We can answer affirmatively by summarily[24] referring to the presence of six résumés of Arnobius' argument concerning the true nature, and therefore the non-existence of, the mythical gods. He first devotes the whole of *Adv. nat.* 1. 28 to demonstrating that the anthropopathic gods of paganism do not possess any quality of *divinitas*. A being that behaves in this manner will perish. After giving one of the most ruthless vituperations of the anthropomorphic gods found in Ante-Nicene Christian literature (3. 1–11), Arnobius concludes that deities possessing such characteristics are simply mortal.[25] Returning to the anthropopathic theme in the fourth book, his third résumé (4. 27 f.) gives the same conclusion: 'Mortalia sunt enim quaecumque narratis' (4. 28. 30 f.).[26] His fourth résumé appears in 6. 2, and here his deduction is that any being given to emotion is subject to the laws of mortality.[27] Fifthly, the

[22] For the argument related to the *munera Christi*, see Ch. 4 §IV.
[23] See Ch. 4 §V.
[24] For details of this interpretation, see Ch. 9.
[25] *Adv. nat.* 3. 12. 19: 'mortales esse'.
[26] The pagan gods of the myths are therefore 'falsis opinionibus constitutos' (*Adv. nat.* 4. 9. 1).
[27] Ibid. 6. 2. 25 ff.

same point is made in 7. 4. 1–13, focusing upon *voluptas* and *tristitia*: a
being expressing either emotion only proves its mortality. The final
résumé occurs in 7. 35–36. 13, and the familiar judgement is: 'nos
huiusmodi motus alienos existimamus ab his [sc. diis] esse; sunt enim
ferocium generum et mortalitatis obeuntium functiones' (7. 36. 10–13).
The pagan gods of the myths (books 3–5), who receive veneration in
the temples (6. 1–8) where they are thought to dwell in images (6. 9–
27) and accept sacrifices (book 7), do not exist. These résumés, therefore,
form a basic literary structure with which Arnobius develops his attack
upon Graeco-Roman religious paganism (books 3–7).

A very important fact that we must acknowledge about the *Adv. nat.*
which has a great significance for the final chapters of the present study,
is the development of his argument against paganism according to a
method of literary retortion. It will be recalled that Porphyry devised
an identical method of literary retortion by attacking the Christians from
within their own sacred writings. This resulted from the rather ingenious
conclusion that the pagan method used up to that time of attacking
Christianity almost exclusively from within the religious and philosophical traditions of classical culture had not succeeded in destroying
the Christian religion. It was an attack planned on a grand scale with
one of the most brilliant pagan opponents of Christianity in history at
its helm, who formulated a campaign for the total eradication of the
Church which threatened its life for generations after the demise of its
creator. It is extensively argued below that Arnobius planned the *Adv.
nat.* as a counter-attack upon the anti-Christian propaganda published
by Porphyry in the period immediately preceding Diocletian's persecution. If this is true, then Arnobius used the same method (literary
retortion) in his attack upon paganism as Porphyry did upon Christianity.

An example of this method can be found in *Adv. nat.* 1. 57, where a
distinction is made between the veracity of Christian and pagan literature.
Reliable eyewitnesses characterize the former and mere opinions the
latter. Porphyry said the same thing about Christian literature.[28] Misconceptions of the gods derive directly from the religious literature of
the pagans (4. 18. 12–27).[29] Pagan stories about the gods have caused

---

[28] Analysed in the final two chapters of the present study.

[29] *Adv. nat.* 4. 18. 12–27: 'Et qui fieri potis est remotis magisteriis litterarum? quid es
enim quod dici de immortalibus diis possit, quod non ex hominum [di] scriptis ac
humanas pervenerit notiones? aut quicquam vos ipsi de illorum ritibus potestis caeri-
moniisque narrare, quod relatum in litteras non sit et scriptorum commentariis publi-
catum? Aut si ponderis existimatis nullius haec esse, aboleantur omnes libri quos de diis
habetis compositos theologorum pontificum, nonnullorum etiam philosophiae deditorum

their expulsion from mankind,[30] a retortion of a pagan criticism found in 1. 1. Because of their concepts of the gods, pagans can be called atheists, a retortion of charges against Christianity occurring in several passages.[31] There is no consensus about the gods in pagan literature, only uncertainty and conflicting opinions.[32] Roman abstract deities do not exist.[33] And it is the pagans themselves who deny the existence of the gods by believing in the myths.[34] Obviously he distinguishes between the mythical gods and the *di veri* because in *Adv. nat.* 3. 29–35, he argues that those divinities of the Graeco-Roman myths do not exist, and here he bases his conclusions upon an exegesis of the meaning of their names. They are false, he alleges, because they are the products of false opinions.[35] Instead of expecting Christians to worship such deities as Lateranus, Pertunda, and Mutunus, pagans should be careful to consider worshipping the deities who have the surest title of existence, provided that they do exist.[36]

An undeniable pre-Christian stratum is inherent in Arnobius' understanding of the relationship between the High God and the *gods*. This layer of his thinking constitutes a residue of concepts held while still a pagan, and it is indebted to Platonism. One may go further and observe that the discernible tension in this neophyte's thought reveals itself as a confluence of philosophical ideas with those of his new religion. He is, simply speaking, a new convert who is trying to make sense of any possible connections existing between philosophical (Platonic) polytheism and Christian monotheism, but at the same time categorically rejecting the gods of the myths. To argue that this tension did not seem contradictory to Arnobius is not to conclude, however, that he consciously attempted either to Platonize Christianity or to Christianize

quinimmo potius fingamus ab exordio mundi nullum aliquando mortalium commentum esse de diis quicquam: experiri volumus et cupimus scire, an muttire, an hiscere deorum in mentione possitis, an concipere eos mente quos in animis vestris nullius scripti informaverit notio.'

[30] *Adv. nat.* 5. 15.
[31] Ibid. 5. 30; cf. 1. 29. 1–6; 3. 28. 13 f.; 6. 27. 6–9.
[32] Ibid. 3. 42. 1–5: 'Infinitum est et inmensum species ire per singulas atque ipsis facere promptum libris, nullum esse a vobis deum neque existimatum neque creditum, de quo (non) ambiguas discrepantisque sententias opinionum mille varietatibus prompseritis.'
[33] Ibid. 4. 1 f.
[34] Ibid. 3. 36. 6–13.
[35] Ibid. 4. 7. 9–12: 'Quodsi minime vos admovent ad intellectum veritatis res ipsae, nec ex ipsis saltem potestis nominibus noscere inanissimae superstitionis figmenta haecesse et falsorum imaginationes deorum?' Cf. 4. 9. 1–4; and 4. 37.
[36] Ibid. 4. 11. 1–14.

Platonism. When he speaks with some certainty about the existence of the 'true gods', (*di veri*), we should understand him to be referring to those deities who must be like the High God who has granted to them a conditional immortality (*Adv. nat.* 2. 35 f. and *Tim.* 41 C). All mythical divinities, those worshipped in the pagan temples, commented upon by pagan 'theologians', and given adoration in the religious rituals, do not exist because their anthropomorphic and anthropopathic natures prove their mortality.[37] Because Arnobius was much more successful in his attack upon religious paganism of the Roman Empire than he was in his defence of Christianity, we may never be able to measure in what way the *Adv. nat.* helped to precipitate the demise of paganism in North Africa in the Post-Diocletianic period. And we shall observe below that this argument about the mortality of the gods was developed as a direct response to Porphyry's rejection of Christianity on the basis of his insistence that Christ was only mortal!

His Platonic ideas of deity probably had positive influence upon his conversion to Christianity. They might have helped in bridging the metaphysical gap separating the pagan deities from the High God *and* his mediator Christ. Also, we shall analyse how Arnobius' Platonic conception of deity contributed to the development of his counter-attack of Porphyry's criticism of Christian concepts of deity. Nevertheless, Arnobius may have rejected the mythical gods as an intellectual pagan, and we know that many before him had made the same decision. Platonism appears to have prevented him from totally rejecting polytheism, and an *ideal image* of the gods, inspired partly by *Tim.* 41 (i.e. the gods must essentially be like their Creator), and partly by his understanding of Christ's revelation of *Deus verus*, was thus presented to the pagans to show them that the entirety of their religious beliefs and practices originates from misconceptions of deity.

It must be emphasized, however, that this image is 'ideal' in the sense of an idea far superior to the concepts of deity espoused by the pagan religious institutions of his day and founded upon the Graeco-Roman myths. These gods absolutely do not exist. Yet the ideal image according to Arnobius' own religious concepts reveals that he did believe in the existence of lesser deities, subordinate to the High God and essentially like him both in respect of their individual natures and their relationship to humans. This is as far as one can go on the basis of objective data concerning his understanding of the relationship between God and the

---

[37] Cf. 1. 18; 3. 12. 13–22; 4. 27 f.; 6. 2; 7. 4. 1–13; 7. 35–36. 13.

gods: what is not clear is the relationship between Christ and the latter. This is to be expected owing to the developing Christologies of the period and his rather shallow understanding of Christian doctrine. Suffice it to say that, according to these features of his understanding of the relationship between God and the gods, making a complete transition from his own existential involvement in religious and philosophical paganism to Christianity undoubtedly only necessitated a name-change of the latter to 'angels'. Arnobius was in the process of the cumulative dynamics of conversion when he wrote the *Adversus nationes*, and this is perhaps the greatest significance of the work for the history of the Roman Empire and the Church.

7

The Supreme God and Saturn

I. *Religion and the Agrarian life in North Africa: Historical Background*

North African Neolithic sites dating *c.*3000 BC have disclosed that the inhabitants knew how to use a simple plough and hoe.[1] It is significant that the oldest *ex-voto* stelae excavated at Carthage and dated at the end of the sixth century BC, depict dolphins which symbolize the superior waters, humidity, and, of course, fertility.[2] At Utica's Punic level, six metres below the Roman stratum, one gigantic sarcophagus contained a gold ring portraying an enthroned deity (Baal?) who held a sceptre crowned with an ear of wheat.[3] More than forty Neopunic dedicatory monuments unearthed at Khamissa (Thubursicu Numidarum), Algeria, possessed etchings of agricultural grains and bunches of grapes.[4] Finally, Tanit's sign, drawn on a bust of the sun and flanked by two *cornucopiae* and pomegranates, appears on three *ex-voto* stelae originating about one kilometre north-east of Médeïna (Althiburos), Tunisia.[5] Let this evidence suffice to show the reader that there was a strong bond between religion and the agrarian life in prehistoric North Africa.

In turning our attention to the imperial period, the evidence increases: the cult of the grain goddesses, the Cereres, appears to have been significant for the emergence of Carthage as an administrative area which included the rich grain fields of the upper Bagradas.[6] The close relationship between religion and the agrarian life was indeed ubiquitous:

[1] *NASS* 3.

[2] A. Mahjoubi, 'Découvertes archéologiques dans la région de Béja', *RTRSS* 12 (1975), 28 n. 19.

[3] *NASS* 7 and fig. I. 2; cf. *HAAN* 4. 13 f. n. 5.

[4] *SAM* 1. 373 nos. 36 ff.; 45 f.

[5] J. Toutain, 'Note sur quelques stèles votives des environs de Médeïna (Tunisie)' *BACTH* (1919), 101–5 (nos. 4 ff.).

[6] D. Fishwick and B. Shaw, 'The Formation of Africa Proconsularis', *H* 105 (1977) n. 8: this coinage celebrated the new status of the province; cf. Sydenham, *CRR* 170 nos. 1023 f.; Fishwick–Shaw, p. 376, dates from 40–39 BC, and shows that holders of the Cereres priesthood were later drawn from the W and E sides of the *fossa regia*.

artistically painted upon the mosaic pavements of private residences;[7] reverently dedicated in the rural chapels of the proconsular province;[8] engraved upon domestic furniture;[9] symbolized in the images of the gods;[10] found at aqueducts and springs, often related to the cult of Neptune;[11] and not infrequently (and very solemnly) depicted on the mausolea of the wealthy.[12] These few examples from the thousands that could be given must suffice. The gist is, quite simply, that *salus deorum*, conceived as human experience of the divine largesse, often in North Africa presupposed a sense of safety in the world as the result of material—equatable with agrarian—well-being. It is not surprising, therefore, that one of the most highly acclaimed agricultural works of antiquity was written by the Carthaginian Mago;[13] and that the altar dedicated to the *gens Augusta*, discovered in 1916 on the Byrsa Hill, depicts what had by then become a standard religious theme: a *cornucopia*, pine cone, pomegranate, wheat, grapes, *and* Apollo, Roma, a winged victory, and the Penates.[14] These and many more symbols represent a

---

[7] V. T. Précheur-Canonge, *La vie rurale en Afrique d'après les mosaïques* (Tunis, 1962; PUT 6). Carthage: p. 8 no. 19 (Terra Mater); p. 8 no. 21 (Bacchus); El Djem (Thysdrus): p. 9 no. 23 (Venus, 4 seasons, basket with grain and fruits); Dougga (Thugga): p. 9 no. 27 (genie, *cornucopia*, sickle, grain); Lambèse (Lambaese): p. 10 no. 29 (Bacchus and 4 seasons); see also J. M. C. Toynbee, 'Mosaic', *OCD* 700 f.

[8] N. Ferchiou, 'Remarques sur la colonisation en Proconsulaire', *CahTun* (1980), 38: at *Fundus Tapp* . . . (Jenan ez Zaytouna) an inscription to Mercury by its proprietors; p. 33: temple of Caelestis dedicated by a *possessor* on the *fundus* at Hr.-bel Azeïz (1st cent. AD).

[9] M. Simon, 'Un document du syncrétisme religieuse dans l'Afrique romaine', *CRAI* (1978), 501 and fig. 1: bearded man on a lamp whose lower body is a menorah; a dove pecks at a bunch of grapes; cf. C. Bourgeois, 'Neptune et le dauphin à Mactar', *BACTH* NS 9 (1973), 19: Neptune lamp from Sousse (Hadrumetum) at the Bardo.

[10] A. Mahjoubi, 'Découvertes archéologiques dans la région de Béja', *CahTun* 7 (1959), 484, photo no. 4: statue of Mercury (patron deity of e.g. Sabratha, Lepcis Minor, Thysdrus); the Mercurial scorpion represents the fertility of the wheat granary of Rome (Africa) according to M. Deonna, 'Mercure et le Scorpion', *Lat* 17 (1958), 52–66, 249–61; P. Petit-Mengin, 'Inscriptions de la région de Milev', *MEFR* (1967), 165–205; and Bourgeois (1973).

[11] See *ILT* 293 Gafsa (Capsa): 'Neptuno et Nimphis sacrum CN Iunius . . . aquaeductum fontemque sua pecunia fecit et dedicavit . . .'. Neptune in Roman N. Africa was venerated as a god of springs, fountains, rivers, etc. For a dossier of *CIL* 8 inscriptions with translations and analysis see S. ben Baaziz, *Le culte de Neptune dans l'Afrique romaine* (Bordeaux III, 1973; unpub. Master's thesis).

[12] M. Yacoub, 'La christianisation des thèmes païens d'après des monuments tunisiens', *CARB* 19 (1972), 339: Christian sarcophagi mosaics of the four seasons; cf. M. S. Reinach, 'Monuments chrétiens de Tipasa', *BACTH* (1893), 129 and Pl. XIII.

[13] Pliny, *HN* 28. 22; *HAAN* 4. 4–8; *NASS* 21. Ten books discussed viticulture, ten horse-rearing, four beekeeping, etc.

[14] *NASS* 46 f.

widespread belief, documented by thousands of North African stelae from Tripolitana to the Mauretanias, in the gods' ability to provide agricultural stability, and therefore to make humans secure and happy in their world.

II. *The Cult of Saturn in Roman North Africa*

The agrarian deity *par excellence* in Roman North Africa was Saturn. Of the 3,000 dedicatory monuments that have been discovered pertaining to the Saturn cult, more than 60 per cent comes from Africa Proconsularis (i.e. including Byzacena),[15] a greater amount than those from Numidia and the Mauretanias combined. Many stelae depict the god standing, sometimes sitting, almost invariably appearing in the top register, and often holding a sickle.[16] A plethora of classical literary evidence also supports the latter as a Saturnian symbol.[17] Often the sickle and/or the pine cone completely replace the deity, as at Aïn-Tounga (Thignica), Tunisia, a Saturn stronghold in the proconsular province.[18] The god's lordship over agrarian life is frequently represented by such symbols as the pomegranate, bunches of grapes, and the pine cone.[19] In the temple of Apollo at Hammam-Daradji (Bulla Regia), Tunisia, there was a statue of Saturn in whose hand was sculptured a *cornucopia* full of fruits.[20] On both imperial estates and small farms throughout the North African provinces Saturn was worshipped as the *dominus* of the land who blessed the earth, was venerated as *deus frugifer*, and who caused the crops to

---

[15] *SAM* 1: 1352 monuments from *Africa Proconsularis*; *SAM* 2; 597 from Numidia; 247 from the Mauretanias.

[16] See the photographs of stelae in *SAM* 1–2; cf. the following proconsular strongholds of the cult: Aïn-Tounga (Thignica): 339 monuments (*SAM* 1, 125–202, esp. p. 159 no. 131, Pl. v, fig. 3 = *CIL* 8. 14934; 2 sickles replace Saturn: p. 164 no. 149 = *CIL* 8. 14958; Djebel bou-Kourneïn: 209 stelae (*SAM* 1. 32–73).

[17] Virg. *Georg.* 2. 406 f.; Ausonius, *Fer. rom.* 23; Macrobius, *Sat.* 1. 7. 25; 1. 8. 9; For the agrarian connection: Virg. *Aen.* 8. 319; 6. 794; 4. 6; 6. 41; 1. 569; *Georg.* 2. 173; Macr. *Sat.* 1. 10. 19; Dion. Hal. *Ant. rom.* 1. 36. 1; 1. 38. 1; cf. also *CPER* 3. 19 f.; *SAH* 142–6; cf. also Cyprian, *Quod idola* 2; Aug. *Civ. Dei* 7. 19; Arnob. *Adv. nat.* 6. 12. 5 ff.

[18] *SAM* 1. 188 no. 236 = *CIL* 8. 15039.

[19] Ibid. 135 no. 26; 151 no. 82 = *CIL* 8. 15171; 131–53 *passim* (Aïn-Tounga); and *SAH* 188–207.

[20] A. Merlin, *Le temple d'Apollon à Bulla Regia* (Paris, 1908), 12 f., and Pl. IV 1; cf. *SAM* 1. 270 no. 1.

be plentiful.[21] He was the chief agrarian deity of Roman North Africa.[22]

How do these data relate to the agrarian life contemporaneous with the *Adversus nationes?* We may begin to answer this question by observing that it was probably during the reign of Probus (AD 276–82) that an intense working of the land in viticulture occurred. For example, the conductor of the *Fundus Aufidianus*, during the second half of the third century, planted a *pomarium*, new vines, and many olive trees on this *ager deseratus*,[23] which was undoubtedly abandoned, as Peyras has suggested, because of over-taxation or drought.[24] A rather intricate system of small hydraulic works spread out like a spider's web throughout the fields to irrigate the domain.[25] A lengthy drought could have paralysed the entire process, pagans might blame the Christians for such misfortunes, and the latter might be defended by Tertullian, Cyprian, and, of course, Arnobius.[26] And it was there on that same *fundus* that a certain C. C. Verecundus went to the Saturn temple between whose columns was engraved a *falx arboraria* (or *vinitoria*), and accomplished his sacred vow to Saturn, the lord of the land.[27] It is the same kind of symbol which Arnobius recognizes as instilling fear in the devotees of the god.[28]

Further east of Africa Proconsularis, Tripolitanian milestones from the hinterland have been discovered which indicate that agricultural productivity was at its peak between the Severan Dynasty and the Tetrarchy,[29] and this was probably the situation of the proconsular province.[30] By the beginning of the fourth century, Numidian shrines

[21] *ILT* 767. g–n, Drâ-el-Gamra (Gori), Tunisia, an agricultural domain; small clans worshipped Saturn in the chapel at Bir-Derbal (*SAM* 1. 287 f.; 40 km. N W of Sicca); cf. J. Peyras, 'Le *fundus aufidianus*: étude d'un grand domaine romain de la région de Mateur', *AntAfr* 9 (1975), 181–222: the small rural village, Lalla Mabrouka, on this farm had a temple with an inscription to Saturn engraved between its columns (p. 194, fig. 4); and A. Mahjoubi, 'Stèles à Saturn d'el-Afareg', *CahTun* 15 (1967), 147: stelae found at the ancient farm Berni at el-Afareg, some of which have a ladder engraved on them which symbolizes victory over the difficulties of life and death.

[22] Cf. *SAH* 120–4.

[23] Peyras (1975), 216.

[24] Ibid. 198 and 205. The domain covered 4.5 km. SW to NE, and 3.5 km. NW to SE.

[25] Ibid. 196.

[26] Tert. *Ap.* 40. 2; *Ad. nat.* 1. 9. 2; Cyprian, *Ad Demetr.* 10; Arnob. *Adv. nat.* 1. 9.

[27] Peyras (1975), 194: 'Saturno Aug[usto] Sacr[um] C[aius] C[a]clius Verecundus votum solvit.'

[28] *Adv. nat.* 6. 25. 5 f.: 'Falx messoria scilicet, quae est attributa Saturno.'

[29] *NASS* 322.

[30] See B. H. Warmington, *The North African Provinces from Diocletian to the Vandal Conquest* (Cambridge, 1954), 66, for laws made to prevent land from going out of

where Saturn once reigned supremely in many agricultural villages appear to have been gradually replaced by Christian churches.[31] And one indeed wonders what was the significance of the church at Kh.-Bahrarous which formed a part of an agricultural complex.[32] Although the picture is by no means clear and further archaeological evidence is necessary,[33] it would appear safe to suggest that a resurgence of the rural economy and the concomitant belief that the gods had granted safety to the whole enterprise, might partly explain, at least in its early years, the description of the Diocletianic Age in North Africa as being a *saeculum felicissimum* or *florentissimum*.[34] And the Christian assimilation of pagan agrarian symbols and concepts had probably already begun before Arnobius took pen in hand late in AD 302.[35]

III. *Religion and the Agrarian Life: The* Adversus Nationes

In the first book Arnobius responds to the pagan accusations that Christians are to blame for many problems that have therefore occurred in the world and have incurred the wrath of the gods. Based upon both the intensity of the pagan charges and the seriousness with which Arnobius responds to them, it would seem logical to conclude that the *Adv. nat.* was written during a drought in North Africa. One example is 1. 3. 6–10: ' "But pestilence," they say, "and droughts, wars, famines, locusts, mice, and hailstorms, and other harmful things with which human affairs are visited, are brought upon us by the gods in their anger at your wrongs and evil-doings." '[36] Are these accusations made

cultivation in the 4th cent.; and W. H. C. Frend, 'A Note on Religion and Life in a Numidian village in the Later Roman Empire', *BACTH* NS fasc. 17B (1984), 264.

[31] Ibid. Frend (1984) found a dedication to Saturn depicted as the Sun-god at Bir Younken.

[32] Ibid. 267; cf. 264: by the 4th cent. the main edifices of Romano–Berber villages in Numidia were olive presses, granaries, and churches.

[33] Cf. P. Leveau, 'L'agricola de Biha Bilta', *CahTun* 26 (1978), 7: 'la vie rurale dans l'antiquité reste encore mal connue.'

[34] *ILAlg* 1. 441, Béja (Vaga), AD 296–300; *ILT* 461, Haïdra (Ammaedara).

[35] Yacoub (1972), 335: crater, vine, Dionysian agricultural symbols from mosaics utilized to represent Christian ideas; 339 f: depictions of the four seasons; cf. Frend (1984), 265: rosette design found above a door of the Kh.-Bahrarous church, which was close to an olive press.

[36] ' "Sed pestilentias," inquiunt, "et siccitates, bella frugum inopiam locustas mures et grandines resque alias noxias, quibus negotia incursantur humana, dii nobis inportant iniuriis vestris atque offensionibus exasperati." '

in response to real events, or should they be interpreted as rhetorical exaggerations? Also, how can the hail and hard rains (*Adv. nat.* 1. 3. 35 f.; 1. 3. 39 f.) relate to droughts (1. 3. 6)? These are not necessarily contradictory because 1. 16. 12–16 refers to the occurrence of droughts and full harvests during the same year in North Africa.[37] And although Liebeschuetz's conclusion that in Africa the Great Persecution might have taken place 'against a background of food shortage'[38]—and he bases this upon *Adv. nat.* 1—appears to be the best answer, the cause of the problem could be variously interpreted as the destruction of crops by (1) hard rains and hail; (2) mice and locusts; (3) droughts; (4) a combination of 1 and 2, or (5) 2 and 3; or (6) all represent contemporary regional hardships in North Africa.

As we read beyond 1. 3, however, it becomes obvious that the crisis to which Arnobius pays the most attention is drought. The absence of rain has caused a food shortage (1. 9). A drought that has destroyed crops is implied (1. 19). The gods may prevent the rains from falling upon the farms of Christians (1. 21). He asks whether the rain will relieve seasons of drought.[39] He wonders whether God sent humans to earth only to lose everything for which they had laboured because of drought (2. 40).[40] The gods daily inflict the lands with evil.[41] True deities should not destroy man's crops with droughts.[42] In another passage he mentions the pagan practice of praying to the images for bountiful harvests.[43] Finally, a major section of the final book (7. 1–38) develops an argument that the *ira deorum* has often in history caused droughts and crop failures.[44] It must be kept in mind that Sicca Veneria was situated in a fertile area of the Mejerda valley.[45] There was also a good number of active farming communities in the outskirts of the city.

---

[37] See Ch. 3 §11.

[38] Liebeschuetz (1979), 254 n. 5.

[39] *Adv. nat.* 2. 37. 21–4: 'ventorum flamina conticescent nec ex coactis et pendentibus nubilis ad terram decident imbres ariditatibus temperamenta laturi?' Arnobius appears to be arguing against the Porphyrian concept that God has sent human souls to earth specifically to learn evil.

[40] Ibid. 2. 40; cf. 2. 74. 7–10: 'Cur post messes arefactas atque extincta frumenta nonnumquam decidant pluviae, quas rebus oportuit incolumibus labi et temporis opportunitatibus ministrari?'

[41] Ibid. 3. 11. 9–12: 'miserarum omnium causa vos estis, vos deos impellitis, vos excitatis infestare omnibus malis terras et nova quaeque cotidie struere'.

[42] Ibid. 6. 2. 17.

[43] Ibid. 6. 16. 7 f.

[44] Ibid. 7. 38. 1–9.

[45] See Ch. 3 § 11.

The references to the human dependence upon the divine for the provision of rain (*Adv. nat.* 1. 30. 8–17); and to the ownership of flocks, vineyards, and the production of honey, olive oil, and wine;[46] are suitable for a North African context in the early fourth century.

Although many scholars have erroneously argued that Arnobius did not believe in the doctrine of divine providence because of his alleged Epicureanism, we may observe that a very clear picture of this concept appears in *Adv. nat.* 3. 24. 8–17.[47] Because this text has some theological and literary similarities with the *De bono patientiae* of Cyprian and the *De patientiae* of Tertullian, the three relevant passages are:

Nobis exercendae patientiae auctoritatem non adfectatio humana caninae aequanimitatis stupore formata sed vivae ac caelestis disciplinae divina dispositio delegat deum ipsum ostendens patientiae exemplum, iam primum qui florem *lucis huius* super *iustos* et *iniustos aequaliter* spargit, qui *temporum* officia *elementorum* servitia *totius geniturae* tributa dignis simul et indignis patitur occurrere (Tert. *De pat.* 2. 1–2; CChr: Borleffs)

Super *bonos* et *malos aequaliter* facit diem nasci et *lumen solis* oboriri, et cum imbribus terras rigat, nemo a *beneficiis* eius excluditur quominus *iustis* similiter et *iniustis* indiscretas *pluvias largiatur*! Videmus inseparabili aequalitate patientiae nocentibus et innoxiis, religiosis et impiis, gratias agentibus et ingratis Dei nutu *tempora* obsequi, elementa famulari, spirare *ventos*, fontes fluere, grandescere copias *messium*, fructus mitescere vinearum, exuberare pomis arbusta, nemora frondescere, prata florere. (Cypr. *De bono pat.* 4. 58–68; SC: Molager)

Numquid enim rex poli libamine aliquo exambitur aut hostia, ut omnia ista quibus vivitur commoda mortalium gentibus *largiatur*? Non *fervorem* genitalem *solis* deus, noctis et *tempora, ventos pluvias fruges* cunctis subministrat *aequaliter bonis malis [iustis] iniustis* servis pauperibus divitibus? Hoc est enim proprium dei potentis ac veri, inexorata *beneficia* praebere fessis atque invalidis rebus et multiformi semper asperitate vallatis. (Arnob. *Adv. nat.* 3. 24. 8–17; CSLP 62: Marchesi)

Italicized words denote general, similar, or exact parallels found in the works. Having begun book 3 with a reference to his Christian predecessors, Arnobius makes rather frequent mention of the continuing drought and famine to which anti-Christian propagandists paid acute attention in book 1. Also, there is a strong attack made upon agrarian deities in book 3, and it is not surprising to find Saturn at the head of

---

[46] *Adv. nat.* 1. 2. 38 ff.; cf. 1. 20; 4. 7. 23 f.; 7. 32. 24 f.; 7. 34. 29 ff.
[47] See Simmons (1985), 210–12.

a syncretistic list in 3. 6. Famine indeed appears to be in progress in 3. 11. 9–12,[48] and agrarian deities are described as failing the pagans in 3. 23. Then he affirms that the Christian 'King of heaven' indiscriminately blesses the harvests, sends the rains, and provides the winds.[49]

A number of agrarian deities receives special consideration: Saturn, the planter of the vine who bears the pruning hook;[50] Minerva, the discoverer of the olive;[51] the Great Mother who is the earth;[52] Ceres who is synonymous with *salutarium seminum frugem;*[53] and Proserpina who signifies the growing of crops.[54] The main underlying reason for this criticism is explicable in light of contemporary hardships. Cyprian has supplied him only with the basic theological ammunition with which to fire his guns, and something that every convert to a new ideology finds inspirational, namely the reliance upon an eminent authority in his newly accepted religion. This might have endeared him to the Bishop of Sicca as well.[55]

In turning to the three texts cited,[56] we may first note that the general theme is the divine providence of the Christian God indiscriminately given to all humans. The key term in each text is therefore *aequaliter.* Cyprian has expanded upon Tertullian's general *temporum officia,* and Arnobius has followed the bishop. Comparison should be made between Tertullian's 'iustis . . . et . . . iniustis' and Arnobius' 'iustis[57] iniustis'. Tertullian gives accusatives, while the others have datives. Also, observe that Cyprian and Arnobius have added 'bonos et malos' and 'bonis malis', respectively. They similarly do not incorporate Tertullian's 'dignis . . . et indignis'. The latter's 'Florem lucis huius spargit' may have inspired Cyprian's 'lumen solis . . . oboriri', and Arnobius' 'fervorem . . .

---

[48] Note esp. the use of *cotidie* in the passage.

[49] *Adv. nat.* 1. 30. 8–17.

[50] Ibid. 3. 29. 32 f.: 'vitisatorem falciferum.'

[51] Ibid. 3. 31. 9: 'inventrix oleae'.

[52] Ibid. 3. 32. 9 ff.

[53] Ibid. 3. 32. 11 f.

[54] Ibid. 3. 33. 4–10.

[55] See Simmons (1985), 214 f.

[56] Other possible literary and religious influences upon Arnobius derived from the same Cyprianic work are: his allusion to 1 Cor. 3: 19 a in *Adv. nat.* 2. 6. 24 f., 'sapientiam hominis stultitiam esse apud deum primum?', might have come from *De bono pat.* 2. 29 f. (SC: Molager): 'Sapientia enim mundi huius stultitia est apud Deum'; cf. *Adv. nat.* 1. 53. 19 f.: 'universa mundi sunt elementa turbata, tellus mota contremuit'; and *De bono pat.* 7. 169: 'elementa turbentur, contremescat terra'; *Adv. nat.* 1. 62. 6: 'Homo quem induerat'; and *De bono pat.* 6. 125: 'carnem hominis induere'. The latter example exemplifies the Arnobian equation *homo = corpus.*

[57] For the emendation see McCr 360 n. 121.

solis'. And although the third person singular, present tense of *largior* does not appear in any work of Tertullian,[58] Cyprian's *largiatur* has been taken unchanged and incorporated into *Adv. nat.* 3. 24. 11. Also, Cyprian has amplified Tertullian's 'totius geniturae tributa . . . patiatur occurrere' by specifying the deity's agrarian-related largesse.

Divinely produced agrarian blessings comprise the centrepieces of the theological statements of both Cyprian and Arnobius. With the exception of *tempora* (cf. Tertullian's *temporum*), the terms common to both Cyprian and Arnobius, which are absent from Tertullian, are *pluvias*, *ventos*, and *messium* (Cyprian); and *fruges* (Arnobius). All three agree that the blessings are dependent upon the divine will: Tertullian uses *patiatur occurrere*; Cyprian has *Dei nutu*; and Arnobius gives *subministrat*. Cyprian uses *beneficiis*, with which we should compare Arnobius' *beneficia*, observing again that the term is not found in Tertullian, to emphasize the universal availability of God's blessings. Epicurean teaching rejected the idea both that a deity controlled the natural elements and that he desired thereby to bless mankind. So the doctrines of divine sovereignty and providence most probably came to the rhetor by way of the bishop. Comparing the former's method of literary borrowings from Lucretius, moreover,[59] we may observe the following similarities: Arnobius has typically condensed his source (Cyprian); left him unnamed; and reworked his source's vocabulary in conformity with his argument and literary taste.[60] The exact parallels are quite striking, providing the high esteem with which the martyr-bishop was held in the early fourth century. And its religious significance should not be underestimated both with respect to North African Christian influence on the one hand, and yet more evidence to argue against an Epicurean connection on the other. Finally, both preface their arguments by referring to pagan practices: Cyprian affirms God's patience in tolerating them; Arnobius underscores the discrimination of the gods who favour those practising them. It is quite reasonable to conclude that Cyprian's *De bono patientiae*, 4. 58–68, is the immediate source of *Adv. nat.* 3. 24. 8–17.

---

[58] *Largendi* occurs in *De pat.* 7. 12. 13; and *largendo* in 7. 13. 2: see G. Claesson, *Index Tertullianus*, 3 vols. (Paris, 1974–5), 2. 886.

[59] The main authority for Lucretius' influence (mainly literary) upon Arnobius is H. Hagendahl, *Latin Fathers and the Classics* (SGLG 6; Göteborg, 1958), 12–47; cf. Macrobius' indebtedness to Gellius in the *Sat.*, but the latter is never named: see R. Z. Austin, 'Macrobius', *OCD* 635.

[60] For the conceptual background in other ante-Nicene writers, see Simmons (1985), 215 f.

IV. *The Christian God and Saturn: Conflict and Competition*

During the Diocletianic Age in North Africa, worshippers of Saturn venerated him in the rural plains of Numidia and in the wheat-growing region stretching from Carthage and Nabeul (Neapolis) on the east coast to Orléansville (Castellum Tingitanum) in the west as the dispensator of crops.[61] The first fruits of the crop were offered to this god of the harvest in the area where the *Adv. nat.* was written, Béja-Le Kef, in the proconsular province.[62] Also, in Siliana, central Tunisia, about 48 km. south-east of Le Kef, the famous Boglio stela,[63] which was first published in 1945 by Charles-Picard,[64] was discovered. Its engraver has realistically sculptured three work-scenes of a large farming estate contemporaneous with Arnobius: a man and a yoke of oxen; workers with sickles at harvest time; and transportation of produce and the sacrifice of victims. Saturn is enthroned on the highest of three levels. The religious message is clear: the workers of the estate confide in Saturn as the great lord of the harvest. Representing one of the most significant pagan affirmations of the belief in divine providence derived from Roman North Africa, the monument reveals the perseverance of the Saturn cult well into the period of the Tetrarchy.[65] Other epigraphical data from the same age are the Cherchel mosaic; the inscription from the *fundus Aufidianus*; and the reaper of Mactar's epitaph (*c.*AD 270), found in a Tunisian city only about 61 km. south-east of Le Kef.[66]

Arnobius accentuates the celestial lordship of the Christian God (3. 24. 8 f.: *rex poli*), who provides the winds, harvests, and rain. Originating from Ksar-Toual-Zouameul (Vicus Maracitanus),[67] an inscription similarly conveys Saturn's power over the wind, land, and waters.[68] On another monument from the same site the deity holds a sickle in the first register, accompanied by the sun and moon in the second, and a

---

[61] Cf. C. Poinssot, 'Statues du temple de Saturne (Thugga)', *Kar* 6 (1955), 30–45, for stelae depicting the deity holding the sickle at (e.g.) the region of Siliana (p. 41, no. 30); Mactar (p. 41, no. 31); Constantine (p. 42, no. 41); cf. *CPER* 3. 25; on the wheat map of Roman N. Africa (to the Tetrarchy), see *SAH* 193.

[62] *SAM* 1. 291 f. nos. 1 f., 5 f.; *SAH* 192, n. 1; 194; 195 n. 1.

[63] *SAH* 97 f.; 190 f.

[64] *SAM* 1. 227 f. no. 9, corresponding to Pl. ix fig. 4. Cf. G. C.- Picard, *Les religions de l'Afrique antique* (Paris, 1954), 120 f.

[65] *SAH* 98 f.

[66] C. Lepelley, *Les cités de l'Afrique romaine au bas-empire*, 2 vols (Paris, 1979–81), 1. 34 f.; Peyras (1975), 216; *CIL* 8. 11824.

[67] *SAM* 1. 230 no. 1 (= *ILT* 573).

[68] Ibid.

dedicant offering incense upon an inflamed altar.[69] Arnobius criticizes the latter practice in 3. 24. Saturn was worshipped as the majestic *dominus caeli*, and we can be confident to conclude that he and the Christian God were engaged in an intense conflict during the late third and early fourth centuries. Finally, the term corresponds to the name of Saturn's predecessor, Baal Shamin,[70] it is depicted on hundreds of Saturnian stelae, and it is synonymous with Arnobius' *rex poli*.[71]

Saturn was believed to be the lord of the harvests in Roman North Africa. For example, it was undoubtedly a thank-offering to the god that persons depicted on stelae at Djemila (Cuicul), Algeria, gave to Saturn who had evidently blessed their harvest.[72] Agrarian symbols related to the cult are found in abundance: ears of grain, the cornucopia full of fruits, grapes, the hoe, plough, and the yoke. Saturn was the principal agrarian deity in North Africa[73] who usually dominates the wider group of deities associated with this function and region.[74] His devotees called him *senex*, an epithet employed by Arnobius in 4. 26. 11, and he often is depicted as a very jealous god, even horrifying to those followers who might consider abandoning his cult for the Christian faith.[75] His regal position within the North African pantheon; his obvious Semitic image as a potentially hostile, jealous god; his cruelly demanding the ultimate sacrifice of children; and the fear-evoking characteristics of his nature; undoubtedly all combined to offer an ascendant, often militant, and defiantly intransigent Christianity its most serious competition and conflict on North African soil. And in light of this conflict, the pages of the *Adv. nat.* are quite revealing.

We may begin to analyse exactly how revealing the work is by first recalling that during the time Arnobius was writing, an extensive drought was most probably occurring in his region. Also, there is convincing evidence that the Saturn cult still existed at this time, and Africa Proconsularis (and Bycazena) had a higher concentration of cultic strongholds. An inscription dated 8 November 323, almost a generation after Arnobius, from Béja (Vaga) proves that a priesthood hierarchically ordered was functioning. Although we cannot answer all the questions

---

[69] *SAM* 1. 236 nos. 5 f.; 237 nos. 7 f.

[70] *SAH* 436.

[71] For the historical and religious background see Simmons (1985), 224.

[72] Cf. M. Leglay, 'Les stèles à Saturne de Djemila-Cuicul', *Lib* 1 (1953), 37–88.

[73] *SAH* 153–214.

[74] *SAH* 237.

[75] Cf. Frend (1952), 76–80.

about the final stages of this conflict, we can be safe to conclude that
Saturn and his devotees, his priests, the parents of whose children were
sacrificed to him at birth,[76] the wealthy farmers, slaves, and peasant-
workers who worked the tiny fields of the imperial domains throughout
North Africa, did not surrender to the Christians without a sustained
resistance. If the fields were parched by drought in (at least) the central
region of the proconsular province in 302, a Christian *evangelical
campaign* that offered the divine largesse, as Arnobius put it, 'aequaliter
bonis malis' (3. 24. 13), might have appeared the best way, and perhaps
the only way, to attempt to eradicate the Christians' greatest rival in
North Africa. For it was in the cultic slogan, *bonis bene*, found on a
good number of monuments dedicated to Saturn, that the exclusive
claims of this national god of Roman North Africa, 'well-being for the
good ones' (i.e. as long as they remain faithful to Saturn), found both
their greatest religious expression and their most profound influence to
stay loyal to him.

Arnobius frequently demonstrates that the Christian God is the true
lord of the land, elements, and natural processes. He grants to mankind
the right to keep the produce (*fructum*) of the land.[77] This was one of
the salient religious concepts which expressed the agrarian lordship of
Saturn, symbolized most often by the sickle,[78] and well known to
Arnobius.[79] Beautifully engraved upon a cultic monument is the concept
that Saturn could give as well as receive *fructum*: a huge basket placed
upon an altar is full of all kinds of agricultural produce.[80] We may also
refer to the sacrificial bull found on a stela from Béja-Le Kef facing
ears of grain which grow in a field.[81] Finally, on the farm close to the
Djebel Mansour, a stela depicts Saturn standing with a lunar crescent

---

[76] This actually began as infant, later changed to substitutionary, sacrifice. Excellent
discussion of the literary allusions to the former appear in *SAH* 314–32; cf. M. Muller,
et al., 'Recherches anthropologiques sur les ossements retrouvés dans des urnes puniques',
SAP (1952), 160–73; the latter was the *molchomor* ritual, and at N'gaous (Nicivibus),
Algeria, *c.* mid-3rd cent. AD, evidenced by four inscriptions (*SAM* 2. 68–74 nos. 1–4,
Pl. XXXI figs. 1 ff.) and denoting a 'great nocturnal sacrifice', an infant formerly promised
to Saturn during pregnancy now is sacrificially replaced by a lamb ('agnum pro vicario');
see *SAH* 336–41. One may rightly wonder whether there were any vestiges of this
practice in the Christian baptismal rituals of N. Africa (cf. *SAH* 490 ff.; Frend (1952),
30).

[77] *Adv. nat.* 1. 29. 17 f.

[78] *SAH* 142–6.

[79] *Adv. nat.* 6. 12. 5 ff.; cf. 4. 9. 16 f.; *SAH* 450 ff.

[80] See the basket full of produce on the Saturn altar at Henchir-es-Srira in *SAM* 1,
Pl. X no. 4.

[81] *SAM* 1. 291 no. 1, Pl. VII fig. 1.

appearing above his left elbow.[82] Although the creation myth of the *Timaeus* probably influenced Arnobius' attributing the creation of the sun and moon to God, the remark of 1. 29. 20 ff. appears to have another origin:

Who has established the fires of the sun to warm the vital elements and make things grow lest the elements of life become listless through being held in a stupor of inactivity? Since you believe the sun is a god, are you not interested in his founder and maker? Since with you the moon is a goddess, do you not care to know who begot and fashioned her?

Two important facts surface here. First, Tertullian identifies as pagan the religious belief in the divinity of the sun because it makes produce to ripen.[83] Second, the agrarian connection in Arnobius is quite clear, he is explicit about the lord of the sun and the moon, and he is obviously drawing from a distinct and well-known religious tradition for his sources. The question now remains: what is the identity of this tradition?

To answer this question, we may first observe that the stelae are numerous which portray Saturn situated between his two acolytes, the sun and the moon.[84] One stela found in the Béja-Le Kef area represents the classical concept of Saturn derived from χρόνος or *time*: above the god's head appear *sol*, *luna*, and the other days of the week. It is significant that in book 3, which has the subtheme of criticizing a number of agricultural deities, Arnobius attacks this pagan religious concept:

This very same point can be made similarly in the case of Saturn. For if by this name time is meant, as the Greek philologists declare, making Kronos identical with chronos, then Saturn is no divinity at all. Who is so crazy as to say that time is a god when it is merely the measuring of a certain period included in a continuous perpetual succession? (*Adv. nat.* 3. 29. 24–30)

Another concept which possibly reveals the conflict between Christianity and the Saturn cult occurs in *Adv. nat.* 1. 29. 24 f.: the divine epithet *genitor* is used to describe the High God's creative powers. Unlike that of other Latin writers of antiquity, who normally use it to designate a

---

[82] Cf. N. Ferchiou, 'Temoignages du culte de Saturne dans le Jebel Mansour (Tunisie)' *CahTun* 26 (1978), 23 fig. 1.

[83] Cf. also *Ad nat.* 1. 13; 2. 5.

[84] *SAH* 223 ff.; and *SAM* 1. 38, no. 3, from the proconsular Saturnian stronghold Djebel-Bou-Kourneïn: votive stela, Saturn is veiled, holds the sickle, and appears with a bust of the sun and the moon, very popular in Saturnian iconography.

lesser demiurgic deity,[85] Arnobius' use discloses a conceptual parallel with ideas found in Saturnian theology.[86] Here *genitor* denotes the great creator of the earth and the father of humanity.[87] Note that Arnobius knows the Christian God as both father and lord of the lesser deities, and Saturn is acknowledged to be the creator of the great gods.[88] Frequently *genitor* is employed by Arnobius to describe Saturn's pre-eminent position as creator within the Romano-African pantheon.[89] The religious concept is well attested during the Christian period within the Saturn cult located in Roman North Africa.[90]

Arnobius also uses the epithet *pater* (*Adv. nat.* 1. 28. 40 ff.) to accentuate the High God's pre-eminence over all other deities. He is father of all generally,[91] of the gods,[92] and it is only by his paternal gift that they exist.[93] The modern authority on the Saturn cult has argued that Arnobius' use of this term reveals a familiarity with the religious associations of the great African god.[94] Again it appears that a main part of the polemics of the *Adv. nat.* focuses upon the pagan antagonist Saturn, who was worshipped as the *pater deorum* of Arnobius' homeland.[95]

We must now turn our attention to the most important epithet used by Arnobius which sheds more light upon the religious conflict between Saturn and Christ. The text is *Adv. nat.* 1. 30. 1–8:

Has the idea not entered into your mind of reflecting, of considering, in whose possessions you live; in whose property you are; whose land that is which you wear out; whose is that air which you breathe in and out; whose springs you consume, whose water; who has arranged for the blasts of winds; who has devised the wavy clouds; who has granted to the fruitful powers of seeds their special characteristics?[96]

---

[85] See Simmons (1985), 169 ff.

[86] i.e. pagan religious ideas concerning the nature of Saturn.

[87] *SAH* 114.

[88] *Adv. nat.* 3. 29. 32: 'magnorum esse procreatorem deorum'.

[89] Ibid. 2. 70. 10; 2. 70. 18; 3. 30. 7; 4. 20. 5.

[90] *SAM* 1. 104 no. 1; cf. *SAH* 114.

[91] *Adv. nat.* 1. 28. 4.

[92] Ibid. 1. 28. 25.

[93] Ibid. 1. 28. 40 f.

[94] *SAH* 8.

[95] Cf. Macrobius, *Sat.* 1. 7; *Adv. nat.* 1. 28. 30–4: 'Nam si omnes concedimus unum esse principem solum, quem nulla res alia vetustate temporis antecedat, post illum necesse est cuncta et nata esse et prodita et in sui nominis prosiluisse naturam.'; and *SAH* 8 n. 5.

[96] 'Nonne cogitatio vos subit considerare, disquirere, in cuia possessione versemini, cuia in re sitis, cuius ista sit quam fatigatis terra, cuius aer iste quem vitali reciprocatis

He has received a tradition which maintains that God owns the land, and he is lord of both celestial and terrestrial realms. Epicureanism can be ruled out as a possible source, as can Stoicism and Platonism. Saturn was, however, thought capable of sending the rain to his devotees. Indeed, he was thought to be the supreme lord over heaven and earth.[97] According to Arnobius, the God of the Christians owns the land and is in full control of the natural and (especially) agrarian processes. He is the *summus rex*, the head and pillar of all existent things, and the great lord of the earth.[98]

The reference at the end of the passage concerning God's ability to make seeds *fruitful* is very significant.[99] The whole passage underscores the divine concern to provide for the material needs of humanity, and the Christian God is placed in contradistinction with Apollo, Mercury, Aesculapius, Hercules, and Diana,[100] all of whom were associated with the Saturn cult.[101] Of special importance here are Mercury's association in North Africa with the production of olive oil;[102] the reference to the need of rain in 1. 30. 6 ff.; and to the occurrence of drought throughout the work; the remark about pagan and Christian production of olive oil found in the same text (1. 21) mentioning that gods send the rains to water the fields; the archaeological evidence indicating the existence of olive orchards north of Sicca;[103] and the epigraphical evidence attesting the worship of Mercury[104] and Saturn at Sicca. After weighing all available data, one does *not* necessarily get the impression that this enumeration of deities in *Adv. nat.* 1. 30. 8 ff. is intentionally arbitrary and written to look absurd![105]

We must now analyse the use of the significant term *seminum frugiferas* found in *Adv. nat.* 1. 30. 6 f., its relation to the other Arnobian texts in

---

spiritu, cuius abutamini fontibus, cuius liquore, quid ventorum disposuerit flamina, quis undosas excogitaverit nubes, quis seminum frugiferas potestates rationum proprietate distinxerit?'

[97] *SAH* 138 f.; *SAM* 1. 289 no. 7.

[98] *Adv. nat.* 1. 27. 7; 1. 29. 4 f.; 1. 30. 1–8.

[99] Ibid. 1. 30. 6 ff.

[100] Ibid. 1. 30. 8 ff.

[101] See *SAH* 242–6; Tert. *Ap.* 23; *CIL* 8. 999.

[102] *SAH* 244.

[103] See Ch. 3 §11.

[104] See Ch. 3 §11.

[105] Commenting on *Adv. nat.* 1. 30. 8 f., Le Bonniec (1982) 273, observes: 'Le choix des cinq divinités nommées ici s'explique mal: on attendrait *Iuppiter pluit* . . . Arnobe avait-il une intention précise? On a l'impression que sa liste de dieux est volontaire arbitraire, voir absurde.'

which it appears, and the occurrence and function of *frugifer* as an agrarian-related epithet recurrent within Roman North African religious paganism. First, there are only two other passages in the *Adv. nat.* in which *frugifer* (or the closely-related *frugiferius*) occurs. In 1. 38. 15 f., a text indebted to Lucretius and Quintilian,[106] the rhetor depicts a truly omniscient Christ who has shown, 'quod frugiferum primo atque humano generi salutare', and one qualification of this general remark is 'rationes quas habent semina' (1. 38. 27). Even in Augustine's day Saturn's agrarian lordship was still being related, *inter alia*, to the growth of seeds for agricultural production.[107] The second passage is 6. 10. 23 ff., which refers directly to the Saturn cult: 'Among your gods we see the fierce face of a lion smeared with pure vermilion and named Frugiferius.'[108] This epithet (*frugiferio*) is without doubt describing one of the two most important deities related to the national cult of North Africa.[109] It could refer either to Saturn himself or to his consort, Caelestis.

The interpretation *Frugiferius* = Caelestis is based upon the assumption that Arnobius is describing Saturn's consort because she is often represented with a lion's head and a human body.[110] But he is more concerned to stress the *appearance* of the face itself (*mero oblitam minio*) than to inform his readers whether the image is part lion, part human; or indeed lion *in toto*. The latter is possible since the *stelae* are numerous that depict a lion who represents and sometimes replaces Saturn.[111] The lion-headed statue found at Bir Derbal, Tunisia, situated about 40 km. north-west of Le Kef, which does appear to be Caelestis, supports Leglay's interpretation of the Arnobian passage.[112] Yet examples of cultic sites providing evidence of Saturn's replacement by a lion are Tébessa (Theveste), Algeria, and Béja (Vaga), Tunisia.[113] The best possible conclusion to draw from this is that whether Arnobius, by using the epithet *frugiferius*, is directly referring to Saturn or Caelestis, it is almost

---

[106] See Ch. 6 *ad init.*

[107] *Civ. Dei* 7. 19.

[108] *Adv. nat.* 6. 10. 23 ff.: 'Inter deos videmus vestros leonis torvissimam faciem mero oblitam minio et nomine Frugiferio nuncupari.'

[109] Cf. Leglay (1953), 74; *SAH* 8; A. J. Festugière, 'Arnobiana', *VC* 6 (1952), 250; *COTh* 407 n. 26; Le Bonniec, *BAGB* (1974), 205, and his different view (1982), 81; cf. also *CPER* 3. 29–37.

[110] Cf. Tert. *Ap.* 16. 13 (CChr: Dekkers); *CPER* 3. 31 f.; and *SAH* 8.

[111] *SAH* 139–42.

[112] *SAM* 1. 288.

[113] Ibid. 266 no. 2; 349 no. 45.

200 The Supreme God and Saturn

certain that he has felt the need to attack the Saturn cult. And nevertheless it is equally significant that Leglay interprets the symbol of the Saturnian lion as signifying, *inter alia*, the forces of nature.[114]

The term *frugifer* was a very important epithet of Saturn. Denoting the god's ability to provide his worshippers with the agricultural produce of the land, its use is attested at Hr.-Mest (Mustis), Khamissa (Thubursicu Numidarum), Khenchela (Mascula), Hr.-el-Hammam (Aquae Flavianae), Djemila (Cuicul), Bir-Haddada, Kh.-Guidra (Sertei), Tigzirt, and Ksar Faraoun (Volubilis).[115] One may also add such sites as Aïn Tounga (Thignica),[116] Teboursouk (Thubursicu Bure),[117] Sousse (Hadrumetum),[118] and one worth quoting, Aïn Zana (Diana Veteranorum): 'deo frugum Saturno frugifero Aug[usto]',[119] and more as well.[120] Between Tunis and Le Kef, at Hr.-Mest (Musti), an altar was dedicated *c*.AD 209–11 to the three deities, Nutrix, Saturnus frugifer, and Janus Pater under Septimius Severus.[121] Finally, it was not until *c*.364–7 that the temple of Saturnus frugifer at Cuicul (Djemila) was destroyed.[122] The logical question to ask now is: why does Arnobius restrict the use of *frugifer* to the Christian God (1. 30. 6) in an agrarian-related passage? Also, is there any significance that the only pagan god (or goddess) who receives this apellation is Saturn (or his consort, Caelestis)?[123]

A serious consideration of the fact that the epithet was used to proclaim Saturn as the supreme god of agrarian fertility,[124] compared with its restricted use in the *Adv. nat.*, may provide a glimpse of one of the greatest conflicts in North African religious history during the Roman Empire. And there are various explanations for the reason why Arnobius does not use *frugifer* as a personal epithet for the Christian God. First, he possesses an obvious disdain for any but purely abstract

---

[114] *SAH* 141.
[115] *SAH* 122.
[116] *SAM* 1. 125 = *CIL* 8. 1406: under the double protection of Hercules and Frugifer.
[117] Ibid. 203.
[118] Ibid. 255.
[119] *SAH* 120; *SAM* 2 77 no. 2 = *CIL* 8. 4581.
[120] *SAH* 120–4.
[121] *SAM* 2. 340 no. 3: 1. 221 no. 2; *SAH* 90 and n. 15.
[122] Leglay (1953), 37.
[123] For the association of Caelestis and other deities see: Tamas Gesztelyi, 'The Cult of Tellus Terra Mater in North Africa', *ACUSD* 8 (1972), 75–84; *CIL* 8. 2226; 8. 9195; 8. 8433; *SAH* 243 ff. (Saturn and Mercury); *SAH* 123 (Magna Mater); and the important *Adv. nat.* 1. 30. 6 f.
[124] *CPER* 3. 19; *SAH* 123.

appellations, a practice probably derived from his pre-Christian Neoplatonic theology which in a strict academic sense demanded an apophatic
description of divinity.[125] Second, the concept of God as the lord of
nature, land, and the harvest plays a relatively small but significant part
in his overall perception of deity, strongly indicating Christian (and
specifically Cyprianic) influence. Finally, noteworthy is his insistence
throughout the work, especially in books 5–7, that there is a great
qualitative difference between the High God and the pagan deities of
the myths and contemporary belief.[126]

One of the most frequently used divine epithets of the Saturn cult
was *dominus*. It was the most important of all the sacred names given
to the god,[127] and although this Semitic concept was used to describe
other deities,[128] it usually possessed a limited meaning;[129] and it was
often found alone to designate Saturn's absolute sovereignty and omni-
potence.[130] Indeed, the concept of *Saturnus dominus terrae* who brings
about the fecundity of the crops and blesses the harvests is present on
many stelae, and notably those also inscribed with *dominus* alone.
Deriving from Hr.-es-Srira, an exemplary dedication was inscribed
with the substitutionary title *dominus*.[131] Restricting the analysis to
the proconsular province, the epithet appears frequently on Saturnian
monuments originating from such cultic strongholds as Aïn Tounga
(Thignica)[132] and Djebel bou-Kourneïn,[133] both of which were situated
in fertile areas. If we keep in mind Tertullian's remark that God's
cognomen is *dominus*,[134] and that Lactantius' frequent use of the term
might have served to oppose Saturn's lordship,[135] it would appear that
Arnobius' employment of the epithet provides further evidence of the
conflict and competition which occurred between Christianity and the
Saturn cult in North Africa during Diocletian's reign.

---

[125] See Ch. 4 §1.
[126] See Simmons (1985), 236 ff.
[127] *SAH* 124.
[128] e.g. Ceres, Aesculapius, Mercury, Victoria, Pluto, Silvanus.
[129] *SAH* 124.
[130] *SAM* 1. 22 no. 14 (Carthage).
[131] Ibid. 308 f. no. 2, Pl. x fig. 4 (= *CIL* 8. 23145). Of the few monuments bearing dates, this is one of the latest: 25 June AD 265.
[132] *SAH* 124 n. 2; *SAM* 1. 141 no 44; 142 no. 48; 144 no. 52 (= *CIL* 8. 15132); 188 no. 234 (= *CIL* 8. 15140).
[133] *SAM* 1. 59 no. 92 (= *CIL* 8. 24153); 66 no. 138; 72 no. 208.
[134] *Ap.* 34. 1 (CChr: Dekkers): 'Augustus, imperii formator, ne dominum quidem dici se volebat. Et hoc enim Dei est cognomen.'
[135] Cf. *SAH* 8 n. 5.

The last chapter of the section of the *Adv. nat.* under investigation,
I. 29–34, contains Arnobius' concluding argument that *deus omnipotens*,
a common Christian epithet of the period,[136] transcends any predications
of time and rules the ages and seasons as their sower: 'sator saeculorum
ac temporum' (*Adv. nat.* I. 34. 12).[137] Of *c.*3,000 monuments (or
fragments) related to the Saturn cult, only two depict the deity as the
sovereign lord of the four seasons, and both derive from Béja-Le Kef
(Sicca). One portrays the god enthroned and flanked by the sun and
moon,[138] and the other reveals his association with time (*Kronos*), in the
form of every day of the week, engraved and listed separately upon a
dedicatory stela. The second register of the first monument portrays the
four seasons: a hooded winter holds a duck; spring carries a basket and
a bough; summer possesses an ear of grain; and autumn, a bunch of
grapes and a basket of agricultural produce.[139] On the second, four
females dressed in tunics are bearing the same agrarian symbols, but in
order (left to right) of autumn, summer, spring, and winter.[140] Without
referring to the *Adv. nat.*, Leglay's interpretation of these stelae is worth
quoting: 'Saturne, maître du Temps, est le seigneur des Saisons et des
Jours.'[141]

We may go further concerning *sator*. It appears that the Christian
High God, mentioned in the final chapter of an agrarian-related section
(*Adv. nat.* I. 29–34) which emphasizes the deity's sovereignty over
heaven, earth, the natural elements, and fertile seeds, has conveniently
replaced Jupiter's father (Saturn) in I. 34. According to the chronological
development of the Saturn cult, this replacement makes sense because
the latest dated inscription, 8 November AD 323 from (incidentally)
Béja (Vaga), reveals an acute Jovian influence upon the cult. And it will
be recalled that the famous Boglio monument,[142] dating from the late
third century and originating not far from Sicca, has the Jovian eagle
engraved with wings spread above an enthroned Saturn, who in turn is
flanked by Castor and Pollux.[143] The Saturnian term *sator* also occurs

---

[136] Cf. *ILT* 470b: the martyrs under Diocletian who died for *deus omnipotens*; for later
periods see: Optatus, *De schis. donat.* I. 1 (*CSEL* 26: Ziwsa); *Conc. Carthag. sub Grat. a.*
345–48, *praef.* I. 9 (CChr: Munier).
[137] *Sator* does not appear in Tert. *Ap. 18. 2.*
[138] Cf. e.g. *SAM* 2. 217 no. 13 (Djemila = Cuicul), Pl. XXXIII fig. 5.
[139] *SAM* I. 292 no. 5.
[140] Ibid. no. 6.
[141] *SAM* I. 292 no. 7, Pl. VII fig. 5.
[142] *SAH* Pl. III.
[143] *SAH* 99.

in the Latin literary tradition, specifically recalling the Varronian explanation of *saturnus* being a derivative of *satus*.[144] Arnobius' phrase, 'Saturnum praesidem sationis' (*Adv. nat.* 4. 9. 16 f.), appears to have been inspired by Varro.[145] Yet there are several reasons to adduce that dependence upon the classical literature does not rule out personal existential knowledge of the subject matter.[146] First, the *Adversus nationes* was evidently not intended to address party[147] or regional[148] interests, but the *nationes*. Second, he is a cultured pagan of the intelligentsia and, according to Jerome, a successful rhetorician who has been professionally trained in the art of elocution to speak and write in a literary style commensurate with his cultural milieu. Indeed, a later pagan and probably himself a North African[149] was cognizant of a tradition which described Saturn as 'the author of times and seasons'.[150] Also, Lactantius, who was the student of Arnobius, is familiar with the term as a divine epithet for Saturn.[151] Finally, it should not be interpreted simply as a coincidence that *sator* is employed in the *Adv. nat.* exclusively to describe the Christian High God.[152]

Classical writers reveal that Kronos was the Greek equivalent for Saturn,[153] and Arnobius criticizes this religious concept in book 3:

For if by this name is meant, as the Greek philologists declare, making Kronos identical with chronos, then Saturn is no divinity at all. Who is so crazy as to say that time is a god when it is merely the measuring of a certain period included in a continuous perpetual succession? And so that fellow too, will be removed from the list of the denizens of heaven, one whom hoary antiquity declared and handed down to the later ages as having Caelus for his father, to

---

[144] Varro, *De ling. lat.* 5. 64; cf. Macr. *Sat.* 1. 10. 20. G. Herbig, 'Satre-Saturnus', *Philol* 74 (1917), 446–59, suggests that *saturnus* derives from an Etruscan 'Gentilgott' and is etymologically related to *satrius, satrenus*, etc. cf. *SAH* 459.

[145] Cf. Aug. *Civ. Dei* 7. 13, on the question who is Saturn?: 'unus, inquit [Varro], de principibus deus, penes quem sationum omnium dominatus est.'

[146] Cf. *SAH* 8.

[147] With perhaps the exception of bk. 2, which Arnobius himself acknowledges is a planned digression in 3. 2. 1–4.

[148] Revealed by his attacks upon Porphyry, his polemical horizons were much broader than N. Africa.

[149] See T. D. Barnes, 'Aspects of the Background of the City of God', *RUO* 52 (1982), 64–80.

[150] Macr. *Sat.* 1. 22. 8; On the *tempus* relation see *Civ. Dei* 7. 19; 7. 21; *Sat.* 1. 8. 6 f.; *Div. inst.* 1. 12; Cic. *De nat. deor.* 2. 64. 25.

[151] *Div. inst.* 1. 23.

[152] *Adv. nat.* 1. 34. 12; 2. 45. 3.

[153] Soph. *Androm.* fr. 122; Plut. *Quaest. rom.* 272. 34 E (LCL: Babbit); Sextus Emp. *Pyr.* 3. 208 (LCL: Bury); Porph. *Abst.* 2. 27. 2. 2 (Budé: Bouffartigue–Patillon).

be the progenitor of the 'great gods', planter of the vine, bearer of the pruning hook.[154]

Although he is attacking the traditional Varronian etymology which attempted to explain the meaning of the deity's name, the main significance of this passage is that it appears in book 3, a principal theme of which was the vituperation of several important agrarian deities. For example, as we note below, in 3. 6 Saturn heads what is apparently a syncretistic list of agrarian deities similar to one found at a *pagus* located near Sicca. Also, a number of conceptual similarities between Christianity and the Saturn cult is found in 3. 24. Finally, 3. 29 begins a systematic attack upon various prominent agrarian deities which continues for five chapters (i.e. 3. 29–34). His conclusion is also revealing for two reasons. First, since an allegorical interpretation of Saturn's name is erroneous, he should be removed from the celestial realm.[155] Second, because of his knowledge of the god's pre-eminent position as the Lord of the land and harvests in the North African pantheon, his diatribe is not restricted solely to the literary classical tradition, and this is clearly conveyed in the attack upon Saturn as the progenitor of the great gods (3. 29. 32). The term *procreator* is used elsewhere in the *Adv. nat.* only to describe the High God (1. 31. 2) and Jupiter (4. 23. 21 f.). Because of Saturn's henotheistic position *vis-à-vis* North African religious paganism under the Roman Empire, exemplified by the appellations of both *procreator deorum* and *pater deorum*, and the rise of Christianity during the Tetrarchy, it appears that an aggressive competition was occurring, when Arnobius was writing the *Adv. nat.*, between the two religions especially in the areas of divine providence and sovereignty.

At the end of the same passage (3. 29. 32) Saturn is called the 'planter of the vine' (*vitisatorem*), an epithet which vividly conveys the pagan belief in the deity's agrarian lordship and the reliance of the pious upon the god to provide a productive harvest. It was logical to believe, as many inscriptions dedicated to Saturn prove, that if the deity was somehow supernaturally responsible for planting the seed, he was also able to protect its growth until harvest. This is the characteristic of

---

[154] 'Nam si tempus significatur hoc nomine, Graecorum ut interpretes autumant, ut quod χρόνος est habeatur Κρόνος, nullum est Saturnium numen. Quis est enim tam demens, qui tempus esse dicat deum, quod mensura cuiusdam est spatii in continua serie perpetuitatis inclusi? Atque ita ex ordine tolletur et iste caelestium, quem Caelo esse editum patre, magnorum esse procreatorem deorum, vitisatorem falciferum vetustas edidit prisca et minorum transmisit aetati' (*Adv. nat.* 3. 29. 25–34).

[155] Cf. *Adv. nat.* 3. 29. 30 f.: 'ordine tolletur et iste caelestium'.

Saturn's nature that Arnobius attacks in his reference to the 'protector of sowing' ('Saturnum praesidem sationis') in 4. 9. 16 f. This particular aspect of his argument, therefore, appears to have been inspired more by an existential involvement in (or simply a profound awareness of) the conflict between the Saturn cult and Christianity, rather than a purely intellectual debate based completely upon literary sources. In conjunction with this conclusion, the following data should be carefully considered: the remark in 1. 21. 6 ff., that pagans and Christians cultivate the olive and the grape, compared with Saturn the *vitisator* attacked in 3. 29. 32; the Saturnian stelae derived from Béja–Le Kef which depict an anthropomorphic autumn holding a bunch of grapes, and Arnobius' challenge to let the gods make the pagans' autumn vineyard harvests full;[156] and the archaeological evidence confirming the cultivation of vines, fruit trees, and the olive during the Roman period in the countryside north and east of Sicca,[157] interesting in light of the description of the god in 6. 12. 5 ff.: 'Saturn with his crooked sickle is the guardian of the countryside like some pruner of the too luxurious branches.'[158] It is unreasonable to assume that all of Arnobius' attacks upon Saturn are strictly academic and derived solely from the classical literary tradition. And if he uses a majority of his Saturnian passages to denigrate the anthropopathic depictions of the gods in Graeco-Roman mythology, this comes as no surprise: he does so much in respect of a vast majority of the gods named in his work.[159]

V. *Topography and Chronology*

Beginning with the Mystery Religions at the end of the Roman Republic, and continuing with religious movements such as the imperial cult under the Roman Empire, a strong current of religious syncretism had

---

[156] Ibid. 1. 21. 6 f.: 'Ex olivis vestris atque vinetis plenam faciant autumnitatem fundi'; for the Saturnian evidence see e.g. *SAM* 1. 292 nos. 5 (Pl. VII fig. 4) and 6 (Béja-Le Kef).

[157] Cf. R. Lantier and L. Poinssot, 'Note sur les établissements agricoles d'époque romaine dans le Kef', *SNAF* (May 1928), 211–16; B. H. Warmington, *The North African Provinces from Diocletian to the Vandal Conquest* (Cambridge, 1954), 55; Lassère (1977), 55; J. Heurgon, 'Inscriptions Etrusques de Tunisie', *CRAI* (1969), 526–51; and generally, *IAAN* 4. 1–52.

[158] *Adv. nat.* 6. 12. 5 ff.: 'Saturnus cum obunca falce custos ruris, ut aliquis ramorum luxuriantium tonsor'.

[159] For details of this interpretation see Ch. 8.

first penetrated the old cults and later began to make them more culturally diversified. By the time of Arnobius this process was still exerting an influence upon the religions of the Empire, and according to the available evidence, North Africa's national deity was affected. An important passage occurs in *Adv. nat.* 3. 6. 1–11:

And yet let no one think that we are perversely unwilling to take upon ourselves allegiance to the other divinities, whoever they are. For we raise up devout spirits and our hands in supplication, and we do not refuse to go wherever you invite us, provided only we learn who those 'divine beings' are whom you urge upon us and who may rightly be associated with the Supreme King and Prince in worship. 'Saturn', he says, 'and Janus are such; Minerva, Juno, Apollo, Venus, Triptolemus, Hercules, and the rest to whom antiquity in reverence dedicated magnificent temples in almost all the cities.'[160]

Of primary importance here is that Saturn comes first in the list, quite natural for a North African enumerating the deities who should be worshipped together with the Christian *princeps and summus rex*. Indeed, Saturn is the first god mentioned in book 3, the argument of which develops an attack upon the immoralities of the anthropomorphic gods. Note also the remark about *antiquity*. For the Romans—and this was especially true concerning their religious sentiments—'older' was more trustworthy and therefore better; 'newer' was invariably seen as a threat to the sacred character of the *mos maiorum* which had caused the rise of the greatest empire the world had ever known. Celsus in the second century had only begun to disparage what Porphyry later saw as a great weakness of this new religion from the East, and that was its recent origin. Yet Saturn had been worshipped first by the Phoenicians many years before he became the principal deity of North Africa under the Empire. It is therefore prudent to draw two conclusions from this passage: Arnobius was compelled to defend against the accusation that Christianity was false because it had recently been founded; and the list of gods in 3. 6 and other sections of the *Adv. nat.* appear to relate to the religious syncretism of the late third and early fourth centuries AD

The first conclusion is analysed in the final chapters. Concerning

---

[160] 'Et tamen ne nos quisquam pervicaciter arbitretur sacramenta nolle suscipere ceterorum quaecumque sunt numinum. Devotas etenim mentes et manus protendimus supplices neque aspernamur quocumque invitaveritis accedere, si modo discamus, quinam isti sunt divini quos nobis ingeritis, et quos par sit adiungi summi regis ac principi venerationi. Saturnus, inquit, et Janus est, Minerva Iuno Apollo Venus Tripolemu Hercules atque alii [et] ceteri, quibus magnificas aedes cunctis paene in urbibus religios consecravit antiquitas.'

religious syncretism within the Saturn cult and its relation to the *Adv. nat.*, an inscription found only 16 km. south-east of Sicca, at the small village of Pagus Veneriensis (Koudiat-es-Souda, Tunisia), is highly revealing. Its short distance from the home of Arnobius and its name show that it was under the civil administration of Sicca. We may also assume that a close religious affiliation existed between the two locations, as the common worship of Jupiter, Saturn,[161] Minerva, and of course, Venus,[162] would indicate. The inscription reads:

Iovi, Saturno, Silvano, Caelesti, Plutoni, Minervae, Veneri, Aug[ustis] sacr[um] pagus Veneriensis patrono L[ucio] Antonio Brittano, curatoribus P[ublio] Octavio Marcello sacerd[ote] Saturni . . .[163]

Even though a priest of Saturn appears among the *curatores*, Poinssot[164] and Leglay[165] have noted that it is Jupiter who heads the list of gods. Neither has suggested a date, but an intelligent guess might be the same general period as those inscriptions from Siliana (the Boglio stela) and Béja (dated 8 November 323)[166] because of an obvious Jovian influence. Another piece of evidence is the Saturn stela derived from either Le Kef or Béja which reveals an association of Saturn with Juno, Venus, and Minerva. A similar inscription, commented upon by Frend,[167] contains a dedication by a priest of Saturn to Silvanus, Mercury, and other deities at Aziz ben Tellis (Idicra) near Constantine (Cirta), Algeria. Finally, found in Leglay's dossier and coming from the same site are two inscriptions dedicated to Saturn and a rather large group of deities.[168] Although the latter are not dated but probably derive from the period under consideration, it is clear that the religious syncretism of the later Roman Empire was exerting a strong influence upon the Saturn cult of the early fourth century.

W. H. C. Frend was the first scholar to suggest that the passage cited (*Adv. nat.* 3. 6. 1–11) describes this religious syncretism. Only a few English historians have posed the question—albeit in passing—of the

---

[161] See *SAM* 1. 291 ff.

[162] *CIL* 8. 15881.

[163] *CIL* 8. 27763; *SAM* 1. 294 no. 1: Pagus Veneriensis = Koudiat-es-Souda, Tunisia.

[164] L. Poinssot, 'Note sur une inscription de Koudiat-es-Souda (Tunisie)', *CRAI* (1913), 424–8.

[165] *SAM* 1. 294 no. 1.

[166] Beschaouch, (1968), 253–68.

[167] Frend, (1981, repr.), 456 n. 121: *CIL* 8. 8246.

[168] e.g. Nutrix, Jupiter, Hercules, Venus, Mercury, Testimonius; cf. *CIL* 8. 8264 D; 8. 4477; *SAM* 2. 63 no. 1; *CIL* 8. 8247; *SAM* 2. 63 f. no. 2.

possibility that the Saturn cult was still alive in Arnobius' day.[169] Leglay
has interpreted the passage as betraying a divine hierarchy quite normal
for an African.[170] Also noteworthy is the fact that, with the exception
of two pagan deities, all of the gods found in the Arnobian list also
occur in the section of *SAH* which analyses Saturn and his relation to
other deities.[171]

The significance of the aforementioned concepts depicting the Christian God's relation to the land in the *Adversus nationes*, especially the
deity's sovereign rule over the agrarian life, is explicable in light of what
appears to have been an initial, intense conflict which occurred between
the Saturn cult and the Christian Church in North Africa in the latter
part of the third century.[172] During the same period Christianity was
continuing to spread geographically and organize internally, and as a
consequence of this growth and development Christ and Saturn came
into sharp competition with each other for the religious devotion of the
North Africans. Monceaux proposed the theory of 'conversions en
masses' from Saturn to the rising sun of North African Christianity to
explain how this great religious transition took place.[173] Frend later
researched the problem,[174] discovering that the last datable inscription
related to the cult, from Sillègue (Novar), Algeria, is AD 262 or 272.[175]
After this date, he argued, within a generation only Christian inscriptions
appear. He thus concluded that between 240 and 275 'worship of Saturn
appears to have ceased almost entirely' (i.e. in Numidia), because the
next datable inscriptions are Christian.[176] Leglay's trilogy on the Saturn
cult has produced a different thesis. Accepting the Sillègue inscription
as the last datable of the cult, he (1966) maintained that among the
stelae not dated, which form the majority, it is all but absolutely certain
that such characteristics as their form, decoration, textual style, and the
style of the dedicatee's apparel permit dates ranging from the end of

---

[169] Cf. Nicholson (1984), 106 n. 50: 'Nor need we think that Saturn, the god who
looked after the agricultural interests of the towns, was dead.'

[170] *SAH* 8, commenting upn *Adv. nat.* 3. 6. 1–11, it reveals an 'hiérarchisation bien
normale pour un africain'.

[171] See Merlin (1908), 12 f. (Apollo); on the Apollo–Sol association: *SAM* 1. 292 nos.
5, 7; cf. *Adv. nat.* 3. 33. 10–13; *CIL* 8. 15577 (Nutrix, Frugifer, and Janus); *ILT* 710:
'Saturni Soli Lunae Marti Mercuri Iovi Veneri'.

[172] Monceaux 1. 10 f.

[173] Ibid. 11.

[174] Frend (1952), 76–86.

[175] Ibid. 84: *CIL* 8. 20435.

[176] Frend (1952), 83.

the third century to the beginning of the fourth century.[177] This makes sense, since Augustine knew of worshippers of the deity in his own day.[178] Yet since the publication of *SAH* and *SAM*, a stela consecrated to Saturn on 8 November AD 323, found only *c*.64 km. north of Le Kef (Sicca) in the environs of the Zahret Midiène, *c*.16 km. due west of Béja, has been discovered.[179] Originating in the vicinity of the oued Kasseb and probably associated with an open-air temple,[180] the inscription provides irrevocable evidence that the Saturn cult continued to the end of the first quarter of the fourth century, and undoubtedly beyond this period, because it records the existence of a hierarchically ordered priesthood.

The Saturn cult was therefore still in existence in the north-western part of Africa Proconsularis when Arnobius was writing against the pagans, and there is no reason to believe that the situation was qualitatively different in other regions of the province. And the fact that the monument originates from the environs of Le Kef may elucidate the meaning of the concepts of divine providence, sovereignty, and benevolence, especially as they relate to God's lordship over the land, which appear in the thought of Arnobius. From the same general period, within a generation, come the famous Boglio stela and the *ex-voto* stelae from central Tunisia preserved in the British museum,[181] both having been dated *c*.AD 289–95 at the beginning of the renewal of the rural economy of North Africa.[182] Chronologically, geographically, and theologically this evidence coheres well with the *Adv. nat.*, and we can justifiably suggest that an intensive Christianizing of former Saturn cultic sites had already materialized, and in some areas, particularly in the proconsular province, the battle between Christ and Saturn was

---

[177] *SAH* 96–105; cf. Frend (1952), 83: 'The mass of the population seems to have changed its allegiance with startling suddenness.' At least in respect of the proconsular province, the conversion was much more gradual.

[178] *Enarr. in psalm cxlv* 12: 'In domino deo suo est spes etiam, illius qui colit Saturnum'; just before this he notes: 'multi enim habent multos deos, et dicunt eos dominos suos et deos suos.' If the cult had already been moribund, Augustine would not have written these words; cf. also *De cons. evan.* I. 23. 34; *SAH* 7; 104 n. 1; M. D. Madden, *The Pagan Divinities and Their Worship as Depicted in the Works of Saint Augustine, Exclusive of the City of God* CUAPS 24; (Washington, DC, 1930), 46–53 (Saturn).

[179] See Beschaouch (1968).

[180] Ibid. 255.

[181] *SAM* 1. 255 f. nos. 4 ff., Pl. viii figs. 3 ff.

[182] Leglay (*SAH* 99–104) argues that such temples as those at Cuicul, Abthugni, Thuburbo Maius, Thuburnica, etc., continued to be used for worship throughout the 4th and the beginning of the 5th cents.

fiercely continuing. And because many of these localities were not far from the city of Sicca (Le Kef) where Arnobius was writing the *Adv. nat.*,[183] it is apparent that the latter is a reliable witness to probably the most cataclysmic transference of religious loyalties which occurred during the history of both the Roman Empire and the Christian Church in North Africa.[184]

Eighteen years after the *Adv. nat.* was written and only 64 km. from Sicca, it is certain that the Saturn cult was still alive. And one can assume that it extended geographically beyond the confines of the immediate areas of Vaga (Béja) because one priest named on the monument bears the title of *magister*, denoting a superior rank within a college of priests.[185] Saturn holds the classical Jovian sceptre in his left hand, suggesting a Saturn–Jupiter syncretism with which we should compare what we have observed regarding *Adv. nat.* 1. 34,[186] and various late stelae dated later than AD 295, originating from central Tunisia[187] and during the Tetrarchy. Above the pruning hook (cf. *Adv. nat.* 6. 12. 5 f.) of the deity the sculptor engraved the sun. The other acolyte of Saturn, the moon, however, is absent, a fact that led Beschaouch to conclude that this may indicate an insistence upon the solar association of the god.[188] This is interesting in light of Apollo's appearance in *Adv. nat.* 1. 30. 8[189] and 3. 6. 8 (in fourth place after Saturn); the statue of Saturn which stood in the temple of Apollo at Bulla Regia (Hamman Daradji); and fragments of Saturnian stelae, statuettes, and statues found together with the statues of Apollo (and Jupiter and Mercury)[190] at Tébessa (Theveste), which led Gsell to suggest that they were mutilated by Christians at about the end of the fourth or the beginning of the fifth century.[191] Both Leglay[192] and Beschaouch[193] have argued that the

---

[183] Cf. now also W. H. C. Frend, *The Rise of Christianity* (Philadelphia, 1984), 446: 'In proconsular Africa Saturn's cult lasted longer.' By 'longer' he means than in Numidia and the Mauretanias; and Libeschuetz's critical comment (1979: 231) that epigraphic evidence almost entirely ceased in the second half of the third century, and this 'phenomenon was universal'.

[184] See Simmons (1985), 245–51.

[185] See Beschaouch (1968), 262.

[186] See *SAM* 1. 292 no. 7, Pl. VII fig. 5.

[187] *SAH* 98 f.; cf. *SAM* 1. 255 f. nos. 4 ff., Pl. VIII figs. 3 ff.

[188] Beschaouch (1968), 263.

[189] See pp. 198 ff., above.

[190] *SAH* 102.

[191] Ibid.

[192] *SAH* 96–105.

[193] Beschaouch (1968), 262: 'Il confirme que, malgré la propagation victorieuse du Christianisme, le culte de Saturne africain demeurait vivant et florissant.' Perhaps this is

Saturn cult continued throughout the fourth century, and it would appear from the evidence analysed above that the very fertile areas of north and central Tunisia, including the region Béja-Le Kef, comprised a very significant stronghold for the cult in the proconsular province.

VI. *Conclusions*

The *Adversus nationes* was written during a period of great religious conflict and competition. Two very powerful forces were simultaneously confronting the Christian Church in North Africa, the Roman Empire and the cult of Saturn, and whether one accepts the sudden replacement theory of Frend or the more gradual and time-consuming hypothesis of Leglay, it is logical to suggest that in Arnobius one glimpses a few impacts resulting from the most cataclysmic event in North Africa up to his time. God depicted as the lord of nature and the agrarian processes, who sends the rains, blesses the crops, and has created the sun to make things grow, is a conception of deity which indeed comprises a small but very important part of Arnobius' overall understanding of the manner in which the Christian God providentially relates himself to man and his world. The immediate Christian source underlying this concept is the *De bono patientiae* of Cyprian. Whether Arnobius has carried with him any former pagan religious concepts into his Christian views of the agrarian lordship of the deity is not ascertainable, but certainly possible in light of the conceptual parallels noted above with the Saturn cult.

It would be quite difficult to imagine that Christianity could have succeeded in replacing the Saturn cult as the predominant religious expression in Roman North Africa without experiencing some kind of assimilation by the Christian God of various aspects of Saturn's lordship. Although this study has not been conducted on the basis of an understanding of Saturn as being only an agrarian deity, and although his all-encompassing imperium possessed a jurisdiction in heaven and earth, it is nevertheless clear that Arnobius felt morally obligated to address the concepts of divine providence, sovereignty, and benevolence *vis-à-vis* the agrarian conflict between Saturn and Christ. In an area as

going beyond the evidence provided principally by one stele. The cult appears to have existed longer and over a wider area in the proconsular province, especially in the northern and central regions.

important for agriculture as Sicca Veneria, the proposed assimilation theory makes perfect sense, especially in light of the historical, literary, and archaeological data analysed above: the occurrence of drought in Arnobius' immediate geographical area; the fine points of his critique of North African agrarian deities, but particularly Saturn; the very close conceptual and literary parallels existing between *Adv. nat.* 1. 29–34 and certain epigraphic data pertaining to agricultural ideas and practices frequently related to the Saturn cult; and the evidence pointing to a late third-century renewal of the rural economy in Roman North Africa and the significant role played by Saturn in this event, specifically in central Tunisia.

If it is true that the ecclesiastical hierarchy of Roman North Africa was organized according to the structure of the civil provincial government,[194] it is possible that such *pagi* as *Pagus Veneriensis* (Koudiat-es-Souda); and such *castella* as Nebeur (Hr. Sidi Merzoug) and Ucubi (Hr. Kaoussat) were among the communities dependent upon the *cathedra principalis* of Sicca Veneria.[195] One of the main evangelical priorities of the North African Church in this case might have been an emphasis upon the Christian God's concern for the material well-being of all persons, an idea rather admirably expressed in *Adv. nat.* 3. 24. 1–17. A widespread pagan belief in the failure of the gods to assure prosperity might have been one of the contributing causes of the success of Christianity during this period.[196] But we still must ask what did the pagan find appealing about the Christian concept of divine providence, especially during the occurrence of famine, which he might not have found in the Saturn cult? To pose the question from another perspective, if the pagans were thinking that the gods (especially Saturn) were failing to provide prosperity (*salus*), what will have made them think *differently* about the God of the Christians? The answer may indeed never be satisfactorily retrieved from the many mysteries of North Africa's history, but a solid assumption will be that it is found in the national religious consciousness of the Africans themselves. For it must be remembered that as the Saturn cult gave way to Christianity, and from the perspective of history it occurred rather suddenly, so also did Christianity yield to Islam.

Considering the tension existing between pagans and Christians in

---

[194] See *PCEAfr* 3. 210.
[195] For *pagus* see: G. C.-Picard, 'Le pagus dans l'Afrique romaine', *Kar* 15 (1969–70), 3–12.
[196] See Frend, *CHA* 2. 463.

respect of agrarian concerns found principally in books 1 and 3 of the *Adversus nationes*, and acknowledging the tradition which Arnobius has received about divine providence, it is quite clear that the contemporary conflict between Christianity and the Saturn cult had already begun to make itself felt in the rural communities around Sicca Veneria (cf. *Adv. nat.* 1. 21. 1–8). And it was upon those rural agricultural communities (*rura*), probably stricken by drought, that Saturn 'cum obunca falce custos ruris' (*Adv. nat.* 6. 12. 6), was beginning to encounter sharp opposition from the Christian Church's concerted efforts to win the countryside.

We may give seven conclusions derived from the data analysed in this study. First, it is possible that *pagi* like Pagus Veneriensis (Koudiat-es-Souda) surrounding Sicca were under the direct episcopal supervision of the bishop of their *principalis cathedra*, and an organized evangelization of these rural parishes at this time will have accentuated the Christian God's ability to improve the present agricultural crisis. Second, the Judaeo-Christian concept of the miraculous power of God to bring about temporal benevolence and a reversal in the *status quo*, as it was manifested in the natural order, might have offered a real sense of safety to many who were beginning to have reservations about the old order's ability to provide tangible solutions. Third, since Arnobius is almost totally ignorant of Christian doctrine, scripture, and tradition; and since we have established that he was dependent upon Cyprian for both literary and theological purposes; we can further theorize that the *De bono patientiae* might have been required catechetical reading. The bishop of Sicca might have advised Arnobius to read it before formal instruction began and his pledge of faith was completed, in order to put this former enemy of the faith on the right path. It was therefore his prior experience which influenced him to select and paraphrase *De bono pat.* 4 and incorporate it into his argument in the agriculturally-significant passages of books 1 and 3. Fourth, the concept of the Christian God who indiscriminately blesses the harvests of pagans and Christians might have been perceived to be more intellectually reputable than that of the sectarian favouritism upheld by the devotees of Saturn.

The fifth conclusion concerns the fact that there was a strong propensity towards a monotheistic view of deity within North African religious paganism. Monotheistic tendencies apparently go far back into prehistoric Berber religious culture, and Saturn himself was a sovereign deity and remained in this position until the later phases of his reign when his cult began to be syncretized with other pagan cults. But when Saturn confronted Christ religious syncretism was replaced with theological assimilation. For example, *pater* denoted Saturn's pre-eminent rank within the Roman North African pantheon, and we can with just cause conclude that Arnobius' concept of *pater* does not derive solely from Neoplatonism. Indeed, it was a religious idea that Saturninus of Thugga (Dougga) describes in *Sent. Episcop.* 52: 'Gentiles quamvis idola colant, tamen summum Deum patrem creatorem cognoscunt et confitentur.' The concept of Saturn the great and all-powerful divine father was easily assimilated to the Christian 'High God'. And it would be superfluous to add to this stratum the interrelated agrarian concepts which have already been noted, and which both traditions had in common. It seems that as long as it did not endanger their orthodoxy, the Christians freely borrowed from a rich source of religious concepts already many centuries old and deeply imbedded in the national consciousness of the people of Africa, and this in turn enabled Christianity to protect its uniqueness and to bridge the religious gap between it and paganism. And although we do not know exactly how it happened or precisely how many years were necessary for its completion, we can conclude that this religious assimilation process of the Christians, evidenced in Arnobius, made the national conversion of the North Africans from paganism to Christianity, from the known to the unknown, a little less culturally shocking.

The sixth conclusion concerns the concept of an immanent, accessible, and personalized deity which, contrary to what many have argued is lacking in Arnobius, often characterizes the Christian God of the *Adversus nationes*. His understanding of a personalized God whom the worshipper can experience cannot have been derived from Neoplatonism. We may go further: the concept of an immanent deity found in a number of passages in the *Adv. nat.* most often appears in a description of Christian worship, usually prayer, and this connection predominates throughout most of the Arnobian divine epithets. These facts strongly suggest an existential involvement in Christian worship and the appeal of a Christian deity who was both sovereign and personal. It was the latter characteristic of the divine nature which Saturn did not possess, because his supreme position in the North African pantheon required that he be conceived as being distant from humans. According to Leglay, it was his inaccessibility to humans that probably led to Saturn's downfall.[197] Saturn, in brief, was always thought to be sovereign, but

---

[197] Cf. *SAH* 486.

was never thought to be accessible and personal. The accessibility of God, however, is the most prominent feature of the Christian tradition about God which Arnobius has incorporated into his work. If the individual pagan began to believe that a deity could be both sovereign and accessible, omnipotent and personally experienced, this concept might well have made the existential difference during difficult and unpredictable agricultural conditions, to justify a change in his religious allegiance.

If we add to this personalized concept of deity the belief that God's providence was universal and, as was not the case of the Saturn cult, not restricted to his own followers, but available indiscriminately to all humans, we might reasonably conclude, as Arnobius himself has done in *Adv. nat.* 3. 24, that the equality of all before the great *rex poli* (3. 24. 8 f.) was a concept which was intellectually more reputable. Its tangible, practicable effects were undoubtedly achieved in the Christian concern to see temporal *salus* come to all. We are basing this conclusion upon evidence derived from Arnobius, for the neophyte claims that the members of his new religion are 'sharers of their own substance, and united by the bonds of kinship with all on whom the sun shines' (4. 36).

The final concept concerns eschatology. We have not covered this in our study, but we do analyse its function in Arnobius' soteriology in the following chapters. Suffice it here to observe that his understanding of 'salvation' is predominantly eschatological: Arnobius evinces a clear and strong belief in the *munus immortalitatis* given to humans by the Christian High God. It was a concept that was not so clearly defined nor personalized in the Saturn cult. And an emphasis upon the reality of a better life in the hereafter makes sense in light of the probably unpleasant agrarian situation in Roman North Africa during the writing of the *Adversus nationes*.

8

The Divinity of Christ and the Mortality of the Gods

Arnobius' Response to Porphyry's Hecatean Oracle and Commentary

I. *The State of Research: Porphyry,* Viri Novi, *and Arnobius*

Early this century Bousset suggested that a Hermetic and Neo-pythagorean group were the main adversaries behind the diatribe of *Adversus nationes* 2. 13.[1] One year later Kroll argued that Porphyry was the principal source of book 2.[2] Jerome Carcopino later attempted to identify the *viri novi* of *Adv. nat.* 2. 15. 2 f. as Hermetists who followed both Pythagoras and Plato.[3] A. J. Festugière then postulated that the *viri novi* comprised a heterogeneous Gnostic sect which adhered to Hermetic, Oriental Gnostic, Neopythagorean, and Neoplatonic doctrines.[4] The pendulum again swung towards Porphyry when Pierre Courcelle discovered several literary parallels existing between extant fragments of the Κατὰ Χριστιανῶν and a number of passages in *Adv. nat.* 2. 13–57.[5] And we should not overlook Bidez in respect of the Arnobius–Porphyry connection, who also early this century noticed a

[1] W. Bousset, 'Zur Dämonologie der Spätern Antike', *Afr* 18 (1915) 150 n. 1.
[2] W. Kroll, 'Die Zeit des Cornelius Labeo', *RM* NF 71 (1916) 356.
[3] *Aspects mystiques de la Rome païenne* (Paris, 1941), 293–300.
[4] 'La doctrine des "Uiri noui" sur l'origine et sur le sort des âmes d'après Arnobe, II, 11–16', *ML* (Paris, 1940), 97–132; repr. in *Hermétisme et mystique païenne* (Paris, 1967), 261–312. The latter is used here. Festugière's argument is accepted without critical analysis by McCr, e.g. 309 n. 64.
[5] 'Les sages de Porphyre et les "uiri noui" d'Arnobe', *REL* 31 (1953), 257–71; cf. id., 'La polémique antichrétienne au début du IVᵉ siècle', *RHR* 147 (1955), 122 f.; and 'Anti-Christian Arguments and Christian Platonism: From Arnobius to St. Ambrose', in A. Momigliano (ed.), *The Conflict Between Paganism and Christianity in the Fourth Century* (Oxford, 1963); cf. also W. H. C. Frend, *Martyrdom and Persecution in the Early Church* (Grand Rapids, repr. 1981), 483, who follows Courcelle (1963); and K. Meiser, 'Studien zu Arnobius', *SBAW* (1908), 5; Abhandlung, 3–40, p. 4: on the *vos* of *Adv. nat.* 2. 13. 8, 'er meint damit wohl des Celsus ἀληθὸς λόγος und die 15 Bücher des Porphyrios Κατὰ Χριστιανῶν . . .'. Cf. also the works of Beatrice listed in the Bibliography.

correspondence between *Adv. nat.* 2. 13 and 2. 62, both of which deal
with 'magic', and *Civ. Dei* 10. 9 which relates to Porphyrian theurgy
derived principally from *De regressu animae*.[6] M. Mazza later modified
Festugière's thesis: the *viri novi* were a homogeneous Gnostic sect
heavily indebted to Iranian ideology, and Numenius probably served as
mediator.[7] Fortin's fundamental article is also related to the problem of
identifying the adversaries of Arnobius.[8] Interpreting the *viri novi* of
Adv. nat. 2. 15. 2 chronologically, Fortin argues that it is reasonable to
search for possible literary parallels in the writings of the period
immediately succeeding Arnobius.[9] Such writers as Cassiodorus (*De
an.*) and Nemesius (*De nat. hom.*) provide evidence that Arnobius is
attacking a Neoplatonic group in book 2.[10] This corroborated Courcelle's
thesis by demonstrating the presence of Porphyrian philosophical metaphors (e.g. *clavus*, *gluten*) in the same book.[11] Only five years before the
publication of Fortin's article, P. Hadot had also noticed a good number
of literary parallels in Porphyry, Arnobius, and Marius Victorinus.[12] To
sum up the state of research briefly surveyed, it is noteworthy that the
aforementioned works have the following in common: (1) they are
restricted to *Adv. nat.* 2 and (2) they mainly focus upon the identity of
the *viri novi* named in *Adv. nat.* 2. 15. 2 f.[13]

However, notwithstanding a few beneficial remarks made by O'Meara[14]
and Wilken,[15] the question whether Porphyry might be the principal

[6] J. Bidez, *Vie de Porphyre le philosophe neo-platonicien* (Gand, 1913), 160.
[7] 'Studi Arnobiani I. La dottrina del "Viri Novi" nel Secondo Libro dell'Adversus Nationes di Arnobio', *HEL* 3 (1963), 111–69.
[8] E. L. Fortin, 'The *Viri Novi* of Arnobius and the Conflict Between Faith and Reason in the Early Christian Centuries', in D. Neiman and M. Schatkin (eds.), *The Heritage of the Early Church* (Rome, 1973), 197–226. R. Laurenti, 'Il Platonismo di Arnobio', *SF* 4 (1981) 51, suggests that Arnobius' opponents include early Platonists as well as Neo-platonists; cf. B. Amata, *Problemi di antropologia arnobiana*, *BSR* 64 (Rome, 1984), 40 ff.
[9] Fortin (1973), 204 f.
[10] Ibid. 206–9.
[11] Ibid. 219: 'Since the metaphors of the glue and the nail are both foreign to Plotinus but known to have been employed in combination by Porphyry, one may legitimately infer that Arnobius' source is more directly Porphyrian than Plotinian.'
[12] See his *Marius Victorinus*, 2 vols. (Paris, 1971), 2. 999; cf. id., *Porphyre et Victorinus* (Paris, 1968).
[13] I accept as valid the arguments of Kroll, Bidez, Courcelle, Hadot, and Fortin as they apply to the Porphyry–Arnobius connection. Eusebius also calls Porphyry and his followers 'New Men', on which see Beatrice (1988), 121.
[14] J. J. O'Meara, *Porphyry's Philosophy From Oracles in Augustine* (Paris, 1959), 145 f. He agrees with Courcelle (1953) that Porphyry is the main opponent of *Adv. nat.* 2.
[15] R. L. Wilken, 'Pagan Criticism of Christianity: Greek Religion and Christian Faith', in W. R. Schoedel and R. L. Wilken (eds.), *Early Christian Literature and the Classical Intellectual Tradition* 117–34. *TheolHist* 53 (Paris, 1979), 123: *Adv. nat.* 1. 36 is a response

opponent in *Adv. nat.* 1 has not been investigated.[16] Two important considerations arise. First, if Porphyry is the main enemy who receives the attack upon Neoplatonic anthropocentric soteriology[17] of *Adv. nat.* 1, it is worthwhile investigating the possibility that some of his anti-Christian propaganda might be present in book 1. Also, a logical method of investigating this possibility in respect of any book of the *Adv. nat.* should include an analysis of Eusebius' *PE* and *DE*, the two Christian works which contain more fragments of Porphyry's anti-Christian writings than any other source. If Eusebius and Arnobius, who were contemporaries, both had Porphyry as a common enemy—and considering the fact that the *PE* and *DE* of Eusebius contain the fragments noted—it is reasonable to assume that the Father of Church History may shed further light upon the Arnobius–Porphyrian connection.

II. *Porphyry of Tyre*

It is necessary to give the chronological information related to the contemporaries, Arnobius and Porphyry. Turning to the former, it has been concluded that he was a teacher of rhetoric in Sicca and wrote his work during the period AD 302–5, when the Great Persecution of Diocletian was occurring. Porphyry, also called Malchos,[18] was born at Tyre on 5 October 234,[19] and may have been a Christian in his early

---

to the *Phil. or.*; cf. Simmons (1985), 263 n. 15; and R. L. Wilken, *The Christians as the Romans Saw Them* (New Haven, Conn., 1984), 154.

[16] Cf. McCr. 249 n. 143; J. R. Laurin, 'Orientations maîtresses des apologistes chrétiens de 270 à 361', *AnGreg* 61 (Rome, 1954), 146–85; LeB 196. See now the important work by P. F. Beatrice, 'Un oracle antichrétien chez Arnobe', in Y. de Andia, (ed.), *Memorial Dom Jean Gribomont* (Rome, 1988), 107–29, which came to me just before I finished the present manuscript. Cf. also M. J. Edwards, 'How many Zoroasters? Arnobius, *Adversus Gentes I 52*', VC 42 (1988), 282–9, who argues that Arnobius was 'acquainted with the writings of his great contemporary either at first or at second hand'.

[17] Although Porphyry stressed more than Plotinus man's need of divine aid in the redemptive process (ἡ τῆς ψυχῆς σωτηρία = the goal of philosophy), he yet 'retains an intellectualist and anthropocentric view of human relations with the divine', according to Andrew Smith, *Porphyry's Place in the Neoplatonic Tradition* (The Hague, 1974), 104.

[18] Eun. *Vit. Soph.* 456 (LCL: Wright); *Vit. Plot.* 21 (LCL: Armstrong); see also E. R. Dodds, 'Porphyry', *OCD* 864 f.; F. Copleston, *A History of Philosophy*, 9 vols. (New York, 1962), I. 2, 216 f.; Bidez (1913), 5.

[19] V. J. Bouffartigue and M. Patillon, *Porphyre: De L'Abstinence* (Tome I, Paris, 1977; Budé), p. xi.

life.²⁰ During his studies at Athens Longinus changed his name to
Πορφύριος.²¹ He became a disciple of Plotinus in Rome in the summer
of 263,²² and in August 268, due to suicidal tendencies, his master
advised him to go on holiday. He responded positively and travelled to
Lilybaeum, Sicily, and it was there that he heard of his master's death
in 270.²³ He died *c*.305²⁴ shortly after publishing the *Enneads*.²⁵

Porphyry was apparently a polymath, having written between fifty-
seven and seventy-seven works during his lifetime²⁶ on subjects as
diverse as embryology,²⁷ vegetarianism,²⁸ an allegorical interpretation of
Homer,²⁹ and many other philosophical and religious works.³⁰ And it
may have been due to his insatiable thirst for knowledge both practical
and theoretical that he left Sicily for North Africa, perhaps to do
zoological research in Carthage for his *De abstinentia*.³¹ Concerning his

---

²⁰ There was a similar tradition about Ammonius, denied by Eusebius (*HE* 6. 19. 7–
10). Porphyry's more than ordinary knowledge about Christianity might suggest an early
involvement in the faith. Yet the *Ep. An.* provides evidence that already in his pre-
Plotinian period (before 263) he was intensely interested in comparative religious studies
(cf. *Vit. Plot.* 16). Augustine remarks that Porphyry was involved in the faith in *Civ. Dei*
10. 28, but nowhere else implies this. Socrates maintains (*HE* 3. 23. 37 (*PG* 67. 445))
that he left the Church because certain Christians assaulted him at Caesarea. Bidez (1913),
11, correctly observes that Vincent of Lerin's remark (Commonit. 17: *PL* 50. 663) that
Porphyry and Origen met when they were old is an interpolation of *Eus. HE* 6. 19. 5.
See also R. M. Grant, 'Porphyry among the Early Christians', *RC* (1973), 181–7.
²¹ Eun. *Vit. Soph.* 456.
²² *Vit. Plot.* 4.
²³ Ibid. 11.
²⁴ Cf. Dodds, *OCD* 864; Bouffartigue–Patillon (1977), p. xiii; and Barnes (1981), 175.
²⁵ Armstrong (LCL: *Enn.*), p. ix, suggests between 301 and 305; Bouffartigue–Patillon
(1977), p. xiii, agree with J. Igal, *La cronologia de la vida de Plotino de Porfirio* (Madrid,
1972), 126: *c*.300; I mainly follow T. D. Barnes, 'The Chronology of Plotinus' Life',
GRBS 17 (1976), 65–70, for the above dates, with the exception of his date of birth.
²⁶ Cf. Dodds, OCD 864, who does not disagree with Bidez's no. of 77 for the
Porphyrian corpus of works; R. Beutler, 'Porphyrios', *PW* 22. 1, col. 276, suggests 57
according to Suidas' titles, surviving texts, and ancient writers who mention Porphyry's
writings. Bouffartigue–Patillon (1977), pp. xiii f., agree with Beutler. See the former, pp.
xiv–xvii, for recent editions.
²⁷ I agree with Bouffartigue–Patillon (1977), p. xv, on the Porphyrian authorship of *Ad
Gaurum*. Dodds, OCD 864, believes it was probably Porphyry rather than the 2nd-cent.
physician Galen.
²⁸ *De abstinentia*.
²⁹ *De antro nympharum*. This covers *Od.* 13. 102–12.
³⁰ Eunapius, *Vit. Soph.* 457, informs us that there was no branch of learning that he
neglected. Cf. B. Croke, 'Porphyry's Anti-Christian Chronology', *JTS* 34 (1983), 168–
85.
³¹ The reasons for his trip to North Africa and how long he stayed there are unknown.
He was in Carthage, however, long enough to rear a partridge (*Abst.* 3. 4. 7). Bouffartigue–
Patillon (1977), p. xviii, suggest the date 268–71 for the visit to Carthage.

legacy, this 'chain of Hermes let down to mortals'[32] had a more profound
effect upon Latin philosophical speculation in the West than his master,
and such men as Chalcidius, Marius Victorinus, and Boethius came
under his intellectual influence.[33] He still had very devoted followers in
North Africa in St Augustine's day.[34]

There is still not a consensus about the date of Porphyry's Κατὰ
Χριστιανῶν,[35] but Barnes's theory that it appears to have been written
at the end of the third or the beginning of the fourth century AD has
much to commend it.[36] If this date is correct, the *CC* may very well
have had a close connection with the persecution. Only a few fragments
of the original fifteen books remain, and scholars have for long disagreed
as to whether Harnack's attribution of fifty-one passages of Macarius
Magnes' *Apocriticus* to the *CC* are genuinely Porphyrian.[37] Yet of the
twenty-seven studies that have been made of the *Apocriticus* since the
ninth century, Goulet's thesis (1974) submitted at the University of
Paris and supervised by Hadot, has made it fairly certain that M.
Magnes used the *CC* in the work.[38] The problems of interpreting the
CC with any semblance of accuracy are further compounded by the

[32] Eun. *Vit. Soph.* 457.
[33] See Copleston (1962), 227 f.; Hadot's works (1968, 1971); Fortin's (1973) article; and
Courcelle (1969), 33–46.
[34] *Civ. Dei* 10. 29.
[35] *Adversus* is often favoured by Jerome, e.g. *Comm. in Gal.*, prolog (*PL* 26. 371 f. =
Harnack *CC* fr. no. 21); cf. *Contra* in Aug. *Ep.* 102. 8 = Harnack *CC* fr. no. 81; A. B.
Hulen, *Porphyry's Work Against The Christians: An Interpretation* (YSR 1; Scottdale, Pa.,
1933), 4 ff.; Bouffartigue–Patillon (1977), p. xix, who agree with A. Cameron, 'The Date
of Porphyry's Κατὰ Χριστιανῶν', *CQ* 17 (1967), 382–4: AD 271; also J.-M. Demarolle,
'Un aspect de la polémique païenne à la fin du IIIe siècle: le vocabulaire chrétien de
Porphyre', *VC* 26 (1972), 117–29; cf. also D. Hagedorn and R. Merkelbach, 'Ein neues
Fragment aus Porphyrios *Gegen die Christen*', *VC* 20 (1966), 86–90.
[36] T. D. Barnes, 'Porphyry Against the Christians: Date and Attribution of Fragments',
JTS NS 24 (1973), 424–42. A. Meredith, 'Porphyry and Julian Against the Christians',
ANRW II. 23. 2, 1119–49, favours Barnes's date. Cf. the cogent argument against Barnes
by Brian Croke, 'The Era of Porphyry's Anti-Christian Polemic,' *JRH* 13 (1984), 1–14.
[37] Demarolle (1972), *passim*; A. Smith (1974), 132 n. 18; and Frend (1981 repr.), 524
n. 49, accept the *Apocr.* passages as Porphyrian. I follow the Greek text of A. Harnack,
'Kritik Des Neuen Testaments von Einem Griechischen Philosophen Des 3. Jahrhunderts',
(TU 37; Leipzig, 1911), 1–150; an Eng. tr. with introd. by T. W. Crafer, *The Apocriticus
of Macarius Magnes* (London, 1919). The collection of fragments is found in A. Harnack,
'Porphyrios *Gegen die Christen*. 15 Bücher, Zeugnisse, Fragmente und Referate', *AKPAW*
(1916), 1–115.
[38] R. Goulet, *Makarios Magnès. Monogénès (Apocriticus)*, 2 vols. (Thesis; University of
Paris, 1974), 1. 287. Goulet has identified no less than 23 parallels between the *Apocr.*
and fragments of the *CC* found in other sources. Cf. also C. Evangeliou, 'Porphyry's
Criticism of Christianity and The Problem of Augustine's Platonism,' *Dion* 13 (1989),
51–70, esp. p. 67.

fact that one is entirely dependent upon the Christian opponents of Porphyry as sources of the extant fragments.[39] And because such writers as Eusebius, Apollinaris of Laodicea, Methodius of Olympus, and Philostorgius wrote refutations of the *CC*, we may justifiably assume that it was perceived as posing a great threat to the Christian Church during a very delicate period of its development.[40] Finally, having already been condemned by Constantine,[41] all copies of the work were ordered to be burnt by Theodosius II and Valentinian III.[42]

The chronology of other Porphyrian works classified as anti-Christian has not been established. Concerning the Περὶ τῆς ἐκ λογιῶν φιλοσοφίας (*Phil. or.*), a work which is significant for this and the following chapters, a good number of scholars have suggested a pre-Plotinian (i.e. before 263) date for this defence of Hellenistic religious culture.[43] Others have placed its publication in the post-Plotinian period. Thus O'Meara has suggested that it was written after 268, and *Phil. or.* and *De reg. an.* are one and the same work.[44] Years ago Chadwick theorized that Porphyry's remark about having been called away on business of the Greeks appearing in *Ad Marc.* 4, may have been due to Diocletian's request that he prepare a defence of traditional religion against the Christians.[45] Wilken has maintained that *Phil. or.* resulted from the trip, and the

---

[39] e.g. Eusebius, Jerome, Augustine, Epiphanius, Theodoret, Theophylact, Didymus the Blind; see Hagedorn–Markelbach for the latter's *Comm. in Iob* found in 1941. A. Benoit, 'Le "Contra Christianos" de Porphyre; où est la collection des Fragments?', in *Paganisme, Judaïsme, Christianisme* (Paris, 1978), 271–5, gives an updated list of the fragments. See also P. Nautin, 'Trois autres fragments du livre de Porphyre "Contre les Chrétiens"', *RB* 57 (1950), 409–16.

[40] 'Methodius of Olympus', *ODCC* 910; Jerome, *Comm. in. Matt.* 24. 16 ff. (SC: Bonnard = Harnack *CC* fr. no. 44), says that Eusebius and Apollinaris each wrote three books.

[41] Soc. *HE* 1. 9. 30; *Cod. Theod.* 15. 5. 66 = *CJ* 1. 5. 6.

[42] *CJ* 1. 1. 3.

[43] e.g., Bidez (1913), 15; G. Wolff, *De Philosophia Ex Oraculis Haurienda Librorum Reliquiae* (Hildesheim, 1962; repr. of Berlin, 1856), 38; Lewy, *COTh* 449; and Barnes (1981), 175. It is interesting that Ruth Majercik, in her recent work, *The Chaldaean Oracles* (SGRR 5; Leiden, 1989), 3, refers to the existence of 'Chaldaean notions' in the work of Arnobius. Majercik's work provides an excellent introduction for the interested student, plus text, translation, and commentary.

[44] O'Meara (1959), 35 ff.

[45] H. Chadwick, *The Sentences of Sextus* (TS 5; Cambridge, 1959), 142: 'a strange and cryptic phrase which may perhaps mean that he had been invited to attend the confidential deliberations which preceded the launching of the persecution of the Church under Diocletian in 303. (Porphyry would be a natural person to consult about such a project, as the author of several formidable books against the Christians.)'

'priest of philosophy' who wrote the three books mentioned by Lactantius (*Div. inst.* 5. 2) is Porphyry.[46]

III. *The Argument Related to the Divinity of Christ*

It appears that the *CC*, the *Phil. or.*, and the *De reg. an.* have provided fuel for the Arnobian fire of book 1. As one student of the great anti-Christian writer has put it, 'The Church won by answering Porphyry out of Porphyry, employing his own methods against himself with amazing effectiveness.'[47] And although this was not stated with Arnobius in mind, the present study will demonstrate that Porphyry's Hecatean Oracle derived from *Phil. or.*, which rejects the divinity of Christ and depicts the Christians as foolish infidels, was the religious basis of a large part of the attack upon Christianity to which Arnobius responds in book 1. Also, supplementary passages derived from the *CC* and *De reg. an.* will be analysed when they shed further light upon the identification of the adversaries of the *Adversus nationes*.

We now turn to Eusebius and Augustine who both wrote works in response to the anti-Christian polemics of Porphyry. The two main texts are *DE* 3. 7 and *Civ. Dei* 19. 23.[48] In the former, Eusebius attempts to exonerate Christ from the charge that he was simply a charlatan, and the combined texts (*DE* and *Civ. Dei*) clearly reveal the Porphyrian dirt that he has swept under the rug. He does not, therefore, inform his readers that the Christians are involved in error and they worship the soul of Jesus because they are estranged from the truth. He does state, similar to Augustine's quotation from the same source, that Porphyry claimed the Christians were ignorant for such worship. More importantly, however, Eusebius deletes entirely the Porphyrian commentary which unequivocally discloses the Neoplatonist's true thoughts about the holy man Jesus: he is directly responsible for causing the Christians to be entangled in error and to be cut off completely from acquiring any knowledge of immortal Jupiter. Although Augustine incorporates

---

[46] Wilken (1979), 131; Chadwick (1959), 143 and n. 1.

[47] Hulen (1933), 54, on the *CC*. Most studies of Porphyry's anti-Christian arguments concentrate on the *CC*, and as Wilken (1979: 118 f.) notes, the *Phil. or.* is often ignored. Cf. also H. Chadwick, 'Oracles of the End in the Conflict of Paganism and Christianity in the Fourth Century', in E. Lucchesi and H. Saffrey (eds.), *Memorial A. J. Festugière* (1985), 125–9.

[48] Eus. *DE* 3. 7 (*PG* 22 (Eus. 4), 236 f.); Aug. *Civ. Dei* 19. 23 (LCL: Greene). See Appendix I below.

the remark that the gods hate the Christians because they were prevented by fate from receiving their gifts and therefore acquiring knowledge of God, Eusebius ignores it completely. This remark is undoubtedly a reference to the High God who appears in the fragments of the *Phil. or.* in the *PE*. This man Jesus, so Porphyry interpreted the oracle found in *Civ. Dei* 19. 23, gave the Christians the fatal gift of entanglement in error.

A number of scholars who had studied the oracle and accompanying commentary had already amazed De Labriolle: Geffcken believed that Porphyry did not attack Christ himself; Harnack said that he was a devotee of Christ; Bidez argued that the oracle was a noble conciliation which Christians themselves could accept. And the French scholar posed an important question which has apparently gone unnoticed: 'on doit se demander si cette bienveillance apparente ne prépare une tactique hostile.' And he was apparently the first to observe that Eusebius only gives Porphyry's criticism of the Christians.[49] Yet Wilken has argued that 'Porphyry sought to give Jesus a place within his religious scheme.'[50] Also, Barnes has maintained that 'Many years before he wrote *Against the Christians*, even before he became a pupil of Plotinus, he had composed *On Philosophy from Oracles* in three books, which depicted Jesus in a far more favourable light.'[51] It must be emphasized, however, that both scholars failed to analyse Apollo's oracle which found praise-worthy Jesus' condemnation to the cross as the result of judges whose verdict was just (*Civ. Dei* 19. 23); the fine points of the commentary on the Hecatean oracle given by Porphyry; and the contradictions between Apollo's oracle and that of Hecate; as well as the criticism of Porphyry's real intention given by Augustine. Finally, the best analysis of the Hecatean oracle in the post World War II era has been made by O'Meara, and it is worth quoting:

The burden, however, of the text cited is that Christ in the opinion of the oracle was not God. He was *piissimus*, *pietate praestantissimus*, and again *piissimus* and *pius*; his soul was immortal as were the souls of all *pii*; but his body shared

[49] P. De Labriolle, *La réaction Païenne* (Paris, 1934), 235.
[50] Wilken (1979), 123; also id. (1984), 152 f.
[51] Barnes (1981), 175. It is inaccurate to state that he wrote many years before he became Plotinus' disciple. If one argues that the concepts found in the fragments of *Phil. or.* reflect a pre-Plotinian mentality, one may note (1) that Porphyry had to write an *Apologia pro Nuptiis Suis* (so Chadwick (1959), 143) in the midst of criticism that he deviated from Plotinus' doctrine; and (2) his attempts to bring the *via salutis* to the non-philosopher, already present in *Phil. or.*, nullifies the method of dating a Porphyrian work on the grounds of 'intellectual development' alone.

224 *The Divinity of Christ*

forever the fate of all bodies. So far was he from having any special union with Wisdom, that he merited condemnation for having misled his followers: 'illa uero anima aliis animabus fataliter dedit errore inplicari'. The emphasis at once on Christ's 'piety' and nothing more is remarkable.[52]

Eusebius apparently defended against the accusation that Christ was a magician in *DE* 3. 7 by dissociating himself as far as possible from the argument put forward by Porphyry that Jesus was responsible for his disciples' entanglement in error. He not only critically edited the anti-Christian works of Porphyry, but he also quoted them out of context, and evidently felt justified by doing this because his adversaries had similarly attacked the Christians by misconstruing the literary texts upon which their religious beliefs had been founded. And a principal belief was the deity of Christ, clearly attacked and rejected in both oracle and commentary. The reason that Eusebius deleted the bad stuff from the passage was undoubtedly because of his need to use Porphyry's 'praise' of Christ to defend against the charge that he had been a sorcerer. Is it indeed possible that such a great defender of Christ's divinity simply ignored the Porphyrian rejection of it? The answer is certainly no. In *DE* 3. 6 he introduces Porphyry by emphasizing Christ's holiness, wisdom, and ascension. The Hecatean oracle follows (3. 7). Then he begins a detailed defence of Christ's divinity: he who conceived nothing mortal or human told his disciples to make disciples of all nations.[53] At the end of 4. 10 he affirms that Jesus was born like us and arrayed with mortality, but he was God and not man.[54] Finally, towards the end of the following book he reaches his climax, and the construction of his phrases indicates that the Hecatean rejection of Christ's deity is the object of his attack.[55]

In *De cons. evan.* 1. 7. 11, Augustine refers to pagans who speak of Jesus Christ as having possessed the most distinguished wisdom, but only as a man. His disciples claimed more for their master than he actually was by calling him God:

. . . qui dominum ipsum Iesum Christum culpare aut blasphemare non audent eique tribuunt excellentissimam sapientiam, sed tamen tamquam homini,

[52] O'Meara (1959), 53. Cf. also R. Joseph Hoffmann, *Porphyry's Against the Christians* (Amherst, N.Y., 1994), 169–71.
[53] *DE* 3. 7 (*PG* 22. 240).
[54] *DE* 4. 10 (*PG* 22. 281).
[55] *DE* 5. 22. (*PG* 22. 404), citing Hosea 11: 9: Ἐνταῦθα καὶ διὰ τούτων ὁ θεὸς Λόγος ἐνανθρωπήσας πρὸς τοὺς ἄνθρωπων αὐτὸν ἅγιον, ἀλλ' οὐ θεὸν εἶναι ὁμολογοῦντας · "Θεὸς ἐγώ εἰμι, φησὶ, καὶ οὐκ ἄνθρωπος ἐν σοὶ ἅγιος".

discipulos vero eius dicunt magistro suo amplius tribuisse quam erat, ut eum
filium dei dicerent et verbum dei . . . et ipsum ac deum patrem unum esse,
honorandum enim tamquam sapientissimum virum putant, colendum autem
tamquam deum negant.

The pagans desire evidence that Christ is God, yet acknowledge him to
be the wisest of men.[56] Augustine responds by calling this an unworthy
praise of Christ.[57] Porphyry is described as a vain eulogizer of Christ:
the disciples lied when they said that Christ was God because he was
nothing more than a man of exalted wisdom. His disciples taught
something totally different from what he had taught them.[58] It appears
that the Hecatean oracle and Porphyry's commentary were important
weapons of the anti-Christian propaganda of Porphyry published sometime before the Diocletianic Persecution, and they were still powerfully
influential in Roman North Africa during Augustine's day.

Worthy to mention is a similar oracle given by Lactantius, which is
most probably Porphyrian and uttered by the Milesian Apollo.[59] If this
is correct, it appears that Porphyrian literature written before the
persecution was used quite extensively in the pagan–Christian contemporary debate, and it is logical to conclude from available data, as
we noted in Chapter 1, that this debate focused upon whether Jesus
Christ was God. Indeed, the argument that Jesus was simply a mortal
continued in the *CC*, and one example is Porphyry's attempt to play
off the λόγος προφορικός against the λόγος ἐνδιάθετος. Since Jesus was
neither one, he was not λόγος at all.[60] But the argument began with
Phil. or., a work whose anti-Christian purpose has not been fully
acknowledged by modern scholarship, although the evidence suggests
otherwise, and the list of Porphyrian works found in the *PE* supports

---

[56] *De cons. evan.* 1. 8. 13.
[57] Ibid. 1. 14. 22.
[58] Ibid. 1. 34. 52.
[59] *Div. inst.* 4. 13. 11.
[60] Theophylact, *Enarr. in evan. S. Ioan.* 12 (*PG* 124. 1, col. 1141 = Harnack *CC* fr.
no. 86): Εἰ γὰρ Λόγος, φησὶν, ὁ 'Υιὸς τοῦ θεοῦ, ἤτοι προφορικός ἐστιν ἢ ἐνδιάθετος· ἀλλὰ
μὴν οὔτε τοῦτο, οὔτε ἐκεῖνο· οὐκ ἄρα οὐδὲ λόγος ἐστίν. Nullifying the Johannine Logos in
this way was tantamount to accentuating his mortality. The same motive is found in
Epiphanius, *Adv. haer.* 51. 8 (*PG* 41. 902 = Harnack *CC* fr. no. 12), where Porphyry
analyses the contradictions of the birth narratives of Mt. 2: 3 and Lk. 2: 39; cf. Aug. *Ep.*
102. 28 (= Harnack *CC* fr. no. 85): Solomon said that God did not have a son; and
Jerome, *Ep.* 57. 9 (= Harnack *CC* fr. no. 2): Porphyry maintains that there is a
contradiction between Mt. 1: 22 f. and Is. 7: 14, showing why an intellectual should reject
the doctrine of the Virgin Birth as nonsense.

this interpretation.[61] Of all these, the *CC* is in second place, after *Acr. in philol.*, for the least number of citations (4), suggesting that Porphyry's main method of attack in the *CC* was to criticize Christian beliefs by using scripture against his opponents. It may seem likely, therefore, that Eusebius used Porphyry to attack Porphyry, especially since he sometimes uses the *Abst.* against the *Phil. or.* to attempt to demonstrate that the Neoplatonist often contradicted himself. And it is the same method revealed in the extant *CC* fragments used by Porphyry. Eusebius also uses a text from Plato's works against Porphyry to prove that there was a qualitative difference between the doctrines of master and disciple, the same method which Porphyry uses in order to drive a wedge of credibility between Christ and his followers. The same methods of attacking Porphyry are found in Augustine's anti-Porphyrian works, and in Arnobius' attack upon his opponents. A tentative conclusion can be made from an analysis of the aforementioned Porphyrian fragments (oracle and commentary): the *Phil. or.* appears to have posed a double threat to the Christians. First, it was constructive by offering a twofold soteriology to the pagans (one for the philosopher and another for the common man). Second, it was destructive by striking at the central concept of Christian soteriology in that it rejected the divinity of Christ. And according to Augustine, the main motive of both oracles (i.e. of Apollo and Hecate) was to prevent people from becoming Christians.[62]

We are now prepared to analyse this important anti-Christian literature. The basic thesis of *Phil. or.*, clearly expressed in the introduction, is that the oracles of the gods provide the one certain source for salvation. The Hecatean oracle was found in book 3, which was entitled Περὶ Ἡρώων, and the final two sections covered Christ and the ignorance of Christians, respectively.[63] Porphyry explicitly stated that the gods had now revealed the truth to humans.[64] Although one must remember that it is formulated from an educated pagan's perspective, the soteriological argument of the oracle and the commentary is straightforward. First, on the question as to whether Jesus is God, the answer is absolutely negative. Second, it therefore follows that Christ was simply a good human being. He was human, and therefore mortal, in

---

[61] See Appendix II below.

[62] *Civ. Dei* 19. 23: 'Una est tamen et illius et huius intentio, ut nolint homines esse Christianos, quia, nisi Christiani erunt, ab eorum erui potestate non poterunt.'

[63] See Wolff (1962), 38–43, esp. 43.

[64] *PE* 4. 7.

both *anima* and *corpus*.[65] Yet by describing Christ as a pious human
'sicut et aliorum piorum', and who is subordinate to the fates, he is not
only nullifying the deity of Christ and thus—and this appears to be his
main polemical goal—invalidating any salvific benefits (*dona*) which may
result from worshipping him, he seems also to be tactfully positing that
Christ was himself in need (or had been at one time in need) of
salvation.[66] This is not surprising because the gods themselves were not
exempt from, nor were they thought to be superior to, the power of the
fates, an idea which may well have been derived from Chaldaean
theology. Eusebius mocks Porphyry's subordinating the gods to the fates
in *PE* 6. 1 because they differ in no way from other men and, therefore,
do not reveal any work of a truly divine nature. After quoting an oracle
that enslaves Zeus to the fates, Eusebius advises his opponents to confess
the Lord of fate who can effect a change (6. 3). Porphyry maintains that
the deliverance from the bonds of fate is a gift of the gods (6. 4).
Eusebius concludes: there is nothing divine in this concept (*PE* 6. 6).
According to Porphyry, only the initiated are delivered from the bonds
of destiny (*heimarmene*).[67] The logic of this theology, and this is one of
the subtly destructive attacks upon Christ made by Porphyry in *Phil.
or.* that modern scholarship has not fully recognized, would therefore
have it that Jesus was not only a mortal man, but something like a
second-class human, subject to the fates like the rest of the uninitiated
masses. It makes sense to find that after he has complimented Jesus the
wise man, Porphyry goes on to demonstrate that he did not offer any
new or significant religious truth that the pious pagan could not already
receive from his own gods.[68]

According to such writers as Proclus[69] and Lydus,[70] Chaldaean theology held that the practising theurgist was not subject to the law of
heimarmene, and it seems fairly certain that Arnobius is attacking this
concept in *Adv. nat.* 2. 62. 1–6:

And let not that which is said by some who have a smattering of knowledge
and take a great deal upon themselves, intrigue you or flatter you with vain

[65] Cf. also *PE* 5. 1.
[66] Porphyry also refers to the gift of God in the *Ad Marc.*
[67] See *COTh* 451 f.
[68] *Civ. Dei* 19. 23: after acknowledging that Jesus forbade men to pay heed to the evil
demons, Porphyry adds: 'Hoc autem . . . et dii praecipiunt et in superioribus ostendimus,
quem ad modum animum advertere ad Deum monent et illum colere ubique imperant.'
[69] *Tim.* 3. 266. 18 = *COTh* 212 n. 142.
[70] *Mens.* 2. 10.

hope, that they are born of God and not subject to the laws of fate; and that if they lead a life of fair restraint, His palace lies open to them and that after the death of the body, they are brought back without any hindrance at all to their ancestral seat, as it were . . .[71]

By subordinating Christ and his followers to the fates, Porphyry consequently classified both in the category of the common masses who themselves needed to acquire immortality through theurgical elevation prescribed by Chaldaean theology. Porphyry's statement in the commentary (*Civ. Dei* 19. 23), 'pius et in caelum, sicut pii', makes sense in light of Chaldaean theological influence, according to which the souls of the common masses did not ascend to the highest (*Noetic*) sphere where the highest and supreme deity exists, but rather only to the astral gods.[72] Seen in the light of this pagan religious background, the locating of Jesus' soul by Porphyry 'in caelum' quickly loses its complimentary value that some have forced upon it, and so it should, because it was Porphyry's intention from the beginning of his anti-Christian literary career to attack the fundamental scriptural and theological doctrines and practices that lay at the heart of Christian faith and piety. In other words, he actually never intended to compliment Christ. For by maintaining that all the followers of Christ are fated not to receive *dona deorum* and subsequent knowledge of Zeus, Porphyry is essentially arguing that Christ did *not* provide such benefits during his earthly life. His fatal gift to his followers—to be contrasted with the salvific gifts given by the gods to their worshippers—is therefore entanglement in error,[73] guidance away from the truth,[74] and disaster.[75] Hence Christianity is anti-salvific in propagating the need to worship a dead mortal.[76] According to Augustine, both oracle and commentary had continued to play a significant role in the anti-Christian Neoplatonic propaganda in Roman

---

[71] 'Neque illud obrepat aut spe vobis aeria blandiatur, quod ab sciolis nonnullis et plurimum sibi adrogantibus dicitur, deo esse se gnatos nec fati obnoxios legibus, si vitam restrictius egerint, aulam sibi eius patere, ac post hominis functionem prohibente se nullo tamquam in sedem referri patritam . . .'. O'Meara (1959), 146, was the first to suggest an association between the *Phil. or.* and this passage. The *aulam* has an exact parallel with a number of Chaldaean theological texts: see *COTh* 212 f. and 266, for the soteriological argument related to fate.

[72] *COTh* 452; *Civ. Dei* 10. 9, referring to *De reg. an.*

[73] *Civ. Dei* 19. 23: 'errore implicari'.

[74] Ibid. 'hanc colunt aliena a se veritate'.

[75] Ibid. 'periculum'.

[76] Ibid. 'ex eo in eis facile praecepsque periculum'. The 'faliter dedit' clearly implicates Christ for feigning divinity and being responsible for cutting off his followers from *deorum dona* and *Iovis agnitionem*.

North Africa during his day.[77] And he himself concluded that Porphyry's argument was reminiscent of the Photinian heretic 'qui tantummodo hominem, non etiam Deum noverit Christum.'[78]

IV. *A New Investigation: Porphyry and* Adversus Nationes *I*

In turning to Arnobius, it is important first to note that every premise of the Hecatean Oracle and, more importantly the Porphyrian commentary associated with it, is attacked in *Adv. nat.* 1. 34–47. In this section Arnobius attempts to prove the deity of Christ against the charge that he was only *mortalis* by emphasizing (1) his superhuman, and therefore divine, *munera* (or *dona*) given to humanity; and (2) his superiority over the fates! It will be recalled that these were the two salient features of Porphyry's attack upon the deity of Christ. It comes as no surprise, therefore, that Arnobius prefaces his argument by stressing Jupiter's *mortality*: how can this god demand that humans worship him when in fact he was born like all humans? The pagans should not take pride in their worship of Jupiter because he was 'in utero matris suae formatus'.[79] The divine epithet used by Arnobius to describe the High God of the Christians in this section, *inter alia*, is *fons rerum*, which is definitely Chaldaean, and it is also found in Eusebius' theological terminology.[80] Also, in *Adv. nat.* 1. 34, the Christian High God has conveniently replaced Jupiter's father, Saturn, and has been given some Saturnian epithets.[81] He argues that if the gods are hostile towards the Christians alone, neither they nor the pagans know God.[82] Arnobius continues in the same section by saying the same things about Jupiter that Porphyry said about Christ.[83] And it must be emphasized that book 1 begins by refuting the use of oracles in the pagan attack upon Christianity.[84]

---

[77] Ibid.

[78] Ibid.

[79] *Adv. nat.* 1. 34. 17. Cf. 1. 34. 15–22.

[80] The epithet *fons rerum* is indebted to Chaldaean theology, with which we should compare *DE* 4. 1 (*PG* 22. 252), and *Adv. nat.* 2. 2. 12–15: 'An ulla est religio verior ... quam deum principem nosse ... qui bonorum omnium solus caput et fons est.'

[81] e.g. Sator, Dominus.

[82] *Adv. nat.* 1. 35. 7–11.

[83] Cf. I. Opelt's sagacious remark in 'Schimpwörter bei Arnobius dem Älteren', *WS* N.F. 9 (1975), 163: 'Bei der Kritik an der Konzeption der Einzelgötter nimmt Jupiter eine Sonderstellung ein.' Note that he is subordinated to the fates in *Adv. nat.* 5. 14. 24 f.

[84] Cf. O'Meara (1959), 146, who associates *Adv. nat.* 1. 1 with *Phil. or.*; and Eus. *PE* 5. 1 = Harnack *CC* fr. no. 80.

A principal pagan charge against the Christians which Arnobius retorts throughout books 3–7, appears in *Adv. nat.* 1. 36. 1–6:

'But', they say, 'the gods are not hostile to you because you worship the Omnipotent God but because you maintain that a man, born a human being, and one who suffered the penalty of crucifixion, which even to the lowest of men is disgraceful punishment, was God, and you believe that He still exists and you worship Him in daily prayers.'[85]

Porphyry found no fault in the worship of the Christian God, but the idea that the gods vituperate those who worship a condemned mortal was clearly expressed in his commentary upon the Hecatean oracle.[86]

There follows (*Adv. nat.* 1. 36. 6–32) a long list of deities containing, *inter alia*, Faunus, Aesculapius, Mercury, and Apollo. Quoting from selected texts in *Phil. or.*, Eusebius notes that Porphyry offered hymns to each of these deities, thereby praising the fact that they had been in their mother's womb, born of a mortal mother, and so forth (*PE* 3. 14). He just before gives lengthy citations from *De cult. sim.* (*PE* 3. 11 f.) showing how Porphyry allegorized the names of various Greek deities, and with this one should compare the last half of *Adv. nat.* 3, as well as the list in 1. 36. 6–32. After giving his parody of the births of the deities, Arnobius asks: 'hine ergo Christum coli et a nobis accipi et existimari pro numine vulneratis accipiunt auribus . . . Haec est iustitia caelitum, hoc deorum iudicium sanctum?' (1. 36. 32–7). The remark about wounded ears appears to be a response to Porphyry's statement that the Christians, fated not to receive the god's gifts or a conception of Immortal Jupiter, shut up their ears to the gods.[87] And it is after quoting from the *Phil. or.* himself that Eusebius makes a similar conclusion.[88]

According to Augustine, Porphyry argued through Hecate that Christ was mortal in his soul (*anima*) and body (*corpus*), and the Christians, who were fated not to receive gifts from the gods (*dona deorum*) were entangled in error by Christ. Christians were therefore alienated from the truth. To turn to Arnobius, we may note the fine points of his attack upon the pagans: 'But let us grant, yielding to you for the

---

[85] M. Magnes, *Apocr.* 4. 22, responds to the pagan attack upon the idea that a deity entered a 'place full of blood and gall' (i.e. Mary's womb).

[86] Cf. *Civ. Dei* 19. 23: ' "In Deum vero", inquit, "generatorem et in regem ante omnia, quem tremit et caelum et terra atque mare et infernorum abdita et ipsa numina perhorrescunt; quorum lex est Pater, quem valde sancti honorant Hebraei." '

[87] Ibid.

[88] Cf. *PE* 3. 14.

moment, that Christ was one of us in mind, spirit, body, weakness, and condition of life: is He not deserving of being called God and being felt God by us on account of the favour of so many blessings?'[89] The response reveals even closer parallels with the Porphyrian commentary. If pagans worship gods like Liber and Ceres,[90] even more so should Christians worship Christ 'qui ab erroribus (cf. Porphyry (*Civ. Dei* 19. 23) 'errore implicari') nos magnis insinuata veritate traduxit' (*Adv. nat.* 1. 38. 12 f.; cf. Porphyry: 'aliena a se veritate'). And in the preface to the *Phil. or.* Porphyry made it clear where one could go to receive a revelation of the truth: Ἕξει δὲ παροῦσα συναγωγὴ πολλῶν μὲν τῶν κατὰ φιλοσοφίαν δογμάτων ἀναγραφήν, ὡς οἱ θεοὶ τἀληθὲς ἔχειν ἐθέσπισαν (*PE* 4. 7). Such scholars as Klussmann, Brakman, and more recently, Hagendahl[91] have studied the literary and conceptual parallels between Lucretius' eulogy of Epicurus (*De. rer. nat.* 5) and Arnobius' praise of the great blessings which Christ has bestowed upon his worshippers found in 1. 38.[92] Hagendahl has established how, but not why, the eulogy was used by Arnobius,[93] and this appears to have had the purpose of presenting Christ as the great giver of superhuman *munera* to his followers. And it is the mighty acts of Christ in the form of divine gifts bestowed upon man that actually prove his deity. This is a great contrast with Porphyry's representing the fickle humanity of Jesus in the *CC* by underscoring the contradictions between his words on the one hand, and his deeds on the other.[94]

The fact that Christ is depicted as the revealer of scientific knowledge to his disciples might also have the *CC* in mind because in the fifteenth book Porphyry asserted that the evangelists were ignorant of both secular

---

[89] *Adv. nat.* 1. 38. 1–5.

[90] Every god in this passage except Hercules has an agrarian association which may suggest the use of Porphyrian anti-Christian propaganda by a Neoplatonic group who blamed the crop failures and resultant food shortage in N. Africa on the Christians: see *Adv. nat.* 1. 3; 1. 9 ff.; 1. 13–16; 1. 19 ff.; 1. 29.

[91] E. Klussmann, 'Arnobius und Lucrez oder ein Durchgang durch den Epicuraïsmus zum Christentum', *Philol* 26 (1867), 362–6; C. Brakman, *Miscella altera* (Leiden, 1913); H. Hagendahl, *Latin Fathers and the Classics* (Göteborg, 1959; SGLG 6), esp. ch. 2, 12–47.

[92] Cf. McCr 287 n. 176; Hagendahl (1958), 18 ff., has established that Arnobius used Lucretius as a model for 1. 38, but he was not an Epicurean himself; cf. C. Marchesi, 'Questioni Arnobiane', *ARIV* 88 (1928–9), 1009–32. One must distinguish between Lucretian philosophical influence and literary borrowing for polemical purposes.

[93] Hagendahl did not attempt to identify the opponent(s) behind 1. 38.

[94] Jerome, *Adv. Pelag.* 2. 17 (*PL* 23. 578 f. = Harnack *CC* fr. no. 70). This concerned the contradiction inherent in Jesus' denial to go to Jerusalem and his actual visit there in Jn. 7: 8 ff.

and divine matters.[95] It will be recalled that Porphyry believed that Christ's fatal gift to his followers was the entanglement in error which prevented them from receiving *dona deorum*. In the *Phil. or.* he also affirmed that Jesus had not revealed any new religious truth to humanity (*Civ. Dei* 19. 23). Another purpose for *Adv. nat.* 1. 38, therefore, and following chapters is to show that the disciples were the direct recipients of Christ's teachings, and they taught exactly what their master had taught them. It was a dangerous accusation not taken lightly by the Christians. For example, in *De cons. evan.* 1. 16. 24, we find the Porphyrian argument that Jesus cannot be blamed for the Christians' refusal to worship the gods because the disciples' teaching was different from that of their master. And we may compare Eusebius' panegyric of Christ in *DE* 3. 5, located two chapters before he gives the Hecatean Oracle. Christ's doctrines, he argues, were those of a philosopher, and the disciples carried to others what they had learned from him. Why suspect that those who heard Christ's doctrines invented their account of their teacher's work?

The Hecatean Oracle and the Porphyrian commentary upon it formed the centrepiece of Arnobius' attack in the section under analysis (*Adv. nat.* 1. 34–47), but theological concepts and technical terms derived from Chaldaean theology which Porphyry himself utilized, appear to have been incorporated into Arnobius' polemical argument as well. Note the following similar passages:

Αἰπεινὴ μὲν ὅδος μακάρων τρηχεῖά τε πολλόν . . . ἀτραπιτοὶ δε ἔασιν ἀθέσφατοι ἐγγεγαυῖαι   (Porph. *Phil. or.* 1, in Eus. *PE* 9. 10)

. . . qui velut caecos passim ac sine ullo rectore gradientes ab deruptis, ab deviis locis planioribus reddidit [sc. Christus]   (Arnob. *Adv. nat.* 1. 38. 13 ff.)

According to Porphyry, the way to the gods is steep and rough, and within there are innumerable paths. Arnobius declares that Christ has brought back his followers who did not have a guide from the precipices (*deruptis*) and paths lying away from the high roads to the smoother places. This seems to represent an antithetical argument related to two opposing theories of divine guidance to, and revelation of, the truth. One can go further. The negative sense of *deruptis*, here used in a

---

[95] Id. *Hom.* 75, *De prin. Marc.* (= *Comm. in Matt.* 3. 3 = Harnack *CC* fr. no. 9): 'Locum istum impius ille Porphyrius, qui adversum nos conscripsit, et multis voluminibus rabiem suam evomuit, in quarto decimo volumine disputat, et dicit: "Evangelistae tam inperiti fuerunt homines, non solum saecularibus, sed etiam in scripturis divinis, ut testimonium quod alibi scriptum est, de alio ponerent propheta."'

soteriological context, i.e. concerning that condition from which Christ delivers lost (*caecos*) humanity, suggests a literary retortion upon the Chaldaean theological concept which equated κρημνός[96] with Tartarus: οὐδὲ τὸ τῆς ὕλης σκύβαλον κρημνῷ καταλείψεις.[97] The oracles promised the neophyte deliverance from the *precipice* (κρημνός = Tartarus; cf. Arnobius: *deruptis*) through theurgical elevation. The concept most probably lies behind Porphyry's concluding remark in his commentary on the oracle: 'ex eo [sc. Christo] in eis facile praecepsque periculum.' On the latter word, note that in *Adv. nat.* 2. 2, a passage which has already been identified as betraying Porphyrian influence by Hadot, Arnobius appears to have this insult in mind: 'Et non in cunctos et lumen praetenderit vitae et periculum ignorantionis amoverit?'

To turn to other parallels, in *Phil. or.* Porphyry maintained that the revelatory function of the terrestrial angels was to manifest the truth about the Father by declaring his *height* and *depth*. According to Arnobius, Christ's redemptive mission to earth produced similar results:

. . . alios [sc. angelos] autem, qui in terris ea quae Patris sunt et altitudinem eius profunditatemque, declarent. (Porph. *Phil. or.* (or *De reg. an.*) in Aug. *Civ. Dei* 10. 26)

. . . deus monstravit[98] [sc. Christus] quid sit, quis, quantus et qualis: qui profundas eius atque inenarrabiles altitudines . . .[99] (Arnob. *Adv. nat.* 1. 38. 16 ff.)

Lewy's *Chaldaean Oracles and Theurgy* contains a long mystic hymn discovered by Augustine Steuchus in 1540, which appeared in book 2 of *Phil. or.*,[100] and the second part of which dealt with ministering spirits. Porphyry's attached scholium explains the meaning of these spirits:

Ὅτι τρεῖς τάξεις ἀγγέλων ὁ χρησμὸς οὗτος δηλοῖ τῶν ἀεὶ τῷ θεῷ παρεστώτων,

---

[96] Note that both McCr and LeB give *praecipices* for *deruptis*. Bryce–Campbell give 'precipitous'.

[97] See *COTh* 213; also 298: the Chaldaean term 'deep' is called 'precipitous' because Tartarus is depicted as a chasm.

[98] LeB 306, suggests that 'profundas . . . altitudines' in Arnobius is an echo of Romans 11: 33. Yet the closer literary and conceptual parallels, the opponent's argument attacked in both general (1. 34–47) and immediate (1. 38) contexts, and the similar theological ideas found in both passages, suggest that Porphyry's ideas are being skilfully used against him.

[99] Criticism of Jesus' followers for apostasizing from the true worship of the gods was a cardinal accusation of the *Phil. or.*: cf. Wilken (1979), 123.

[100] See *COTh* 10 n. 26 for the full Greek text which mentions the names of Porphyry and *Phil. or.*

τῶν χωριζομένων αὐτοῦ καὶ εἰς ἀγγελίας καὶ διακονίας τινὰς ἀποστελλομένων
καὶ τῶν φερόντων ἀεὶ τὸν αὐτοῦ θρόνον. Τοῦτο "οἵ σε καθ᾿ ἦμαρ ἄγουσι",
τουτέστι· διηνεκῶς φέρουσι· τὸ δὲ "ἀοιδιάουσιν ἐσῶδε" ἀντὶ τοῦ ἄδουσιν ἕως
νῦν.[101]

Thus one order of angels perpetually stands before the High God,
another is separate from Him and these are sent to earth for certain
messages/ministrations, and another represents those who are forever
around his throne singing hymns to him. Eusebius is most probably
responding to the same Chaldaean concept in *DE* 3. 3 (*PG* 22. 193):

Ἐν τοῖς δογματοῖς τῶν αὐτοῦ λόγων παρειλήφαμεν ἐναί τινας μετὰ τὸν ἀνωτάτω
θεὸν δυνάμεις ἀσωμάτους τὴν φύσιν καὶ νοερὰς κογικάς τε καὶ παναρέτους, τὸν
παμβασιλέα χορευούσας ὧν πλείους καὶ μέχρι ἀνθρώπων νεύματι τοῦ Πατρὸς
διά τινας σωτηρίους οἰκονομίας ἀπεστάλθαι· ἃς δὴ γνωρίζειν καὶ τιμᾶν κατὰ τὸ
μέτρον τῆς ἀξίας ἐδιδάχθημεν, μόνῳ τῷ παμβασιλεῖ θεῷ τὴν σεβάσμιον τιμὴν
ἀπονέμοντες·

He apparently had Porphyry's last two angelic orders in mind, and due
to his knowledge of Judeo-Christian angelology, he was able to separate
these heavenly beings from Christ. Note that although they are sent by
the High God's will on salvific missions, they nevertheless fall short of
receiving worship. Evidently Arnobius did not have this rich tradition
upon which to depend: thus Porphyry's messengers are disqualified as
authentic intermediaries between the High God and humans. Finally,
another important observation is that both Eusebius (*DE* 3. 3) and
Arnobius (1. 38) are praising Christ the Teacher in their response to
the Hecatean Oracle and Porphyrian commentary.

We now turn to the Father's height and depth. Proclus has preserved
a Chaldaean hymn which Lewy suggests was addressed to the planetary
gods, and it contains the invocation: οἵ τὸν ὑπέρκοσμον πατρικὸν βυθὸν
ἴστε νοοῦντες.[102] Knowledge of the hypercosmic Paternal Depth is the
direct result of contemplating upon it. We note similarities between
Arnobius and Porphyry in their understanding of contemplating the
divine, especially observing their use of Pythagorean silence, in the final
chapter below. Now it is important to take note of Lewy's definition of
the phrase above. 'Depth' here is the pleroma of the intelligible world.
All divine intelligences think the Father. Hence the planetary gods are
alone 'able to expound the mystery of his intellectual emanations and

See *COTh* 14 n. 31; Wolff (1962), 145 f., Buresh, 104 no. 28 = Theos. no. 27.
Proclus, *Crat.* 57. 25 (*COTh* 159 n. 351); *OC* fr. 18, p. 70.

the hierarchic order of His supercelestial court'.[103] He goes on to say that only one of these gods could have revealed the mysteries of the High God's existence to the Chaldaeans, and this was brought about mainly by Apollo. The latter plays an important role in *Phil. or.*, and the picture one gets from this is fairly clear, namely that Porphyry attributed to these heavenly intermediaries the ability to reveal the truth about the existence of the High God. 'Height' appears to designate the object of the Platonic–Chaldaean metaphysical cognition. Proclus again informs us that the divine is inaccessible to mortals who think according to the body, and only those who lift themselves up to the heights (i.e. in intellectual contemplation) will find him accessible.[104]

In 1. 39 Arnobius makes two main points. First, Christ, who is described as Teacher, has led him from polytheistic error to the truth,[105] which should be contrasted with the Hecatean scathing proclamation that Christians were estranged from the truth. The remark may have also served the dual anti-Porphyrian purpose of disclosing Christ as the only authentic 'via universalis animae liberandae.'[106] Also, the fact that he begins 1. 39 by stressing the vanity of venerating the *simulacra* may suggest that Arnobius is attacking Porphyry's pagan apology for this practice in his Περὶ ἀγαλμάτων.[107] And book 6 contains a lengthy criticism of the worship of images as well. Eusebius also claims that Christ's teaching has turned all nations away from the delusions of idols to embrace the knowledge and worship of the God who is over all. This, he adds, ratified the oracles of old (Jer. 16. 19).[108] Four chapters before he partially cites from the Hecatean Oracle (*DE* 3. 3), Eusebius argues that Christ was not a deceiver because he taught philosophy in its highest form to his disciples; he taught the truth; he was the author of a divine philosophy, not of a vulgar type, and so forth. And then

---

[103] *COTh* 161.

[104] *OC* fr. 116, p. 95.

[105] *Adv. nat.* 1. 39 is the only passage that describes in detail (cf. 3. 24. 6 ff.) Arnobius' pagan beliefs/practices before his conversion to Christianity.

[106] *De reg. an.* in Aug. *Civ. Dei* 10. 32. Porphyry had researched the moral teachings of the Indians, Chaldaean 'magic', philosophy, and the histories.

[107] Cf. Wolff (1962), 42. The pagan opponent of M. Magnes finds the idea that gods dwell in the images much purer than the doctrine of the incarnation (*Apocr.* 4. 22).

[108] Wilken (1979), 133, has observed that Eusebius uses this Greek term deliberately to oppose the Porphyrian Supreme God. The passage referred to is *PE* 1. 3. I have noticed similar divine epithets used by Arnobius and Porphyry, e.g. Ζεὺς κεφαλή (*caput*); Ζεὺς πρῶτος (*deus primus*); Ζεὺς βασιλεύς (*deus rex*); ἁπάντων ἀρχιγένεθλος (*prima causa*); μέγας ἀρχὸς ἁπάντων (*deus princeps*). For the Arnobian epithets see Ch. 4. Porphyry's epithets come from *PE* 3. 9.

immediately before citing from *Abst.*, he concludes that these were the *gifts* of our Saviour's teachings to his disciples (*DE* 3. 3). Arnobius' similar conclusion (1. 39) is that such *dona Christi* demonstrate that he is *deus*, and such gifts are not restricted to the temporal sphere.[109] It is significant here that Arnobius can speak of Christ's salvific blessings upon man as *dona*, especially since Porphyry in the Hecatean Oracle and commentary insisted that the Christians were fated not to receive *dona deorum*.

The next two chapters (*Adv. nat.* 1. 40 f.) respond to the accusation that Christ died an ignominious death. This coheres with the argument that Christ was *mortal*, and in the Hecatean Oracle Jesus' condemnation to death indicates as much. Yet we recall that Augustine found it contradictory that Apollo could praise the judges who correctly sentenced Jesus to the cross, and Hecate's 'compliments' for his piety and wisdom.[110] There might also be some significance in the fact that Pythagoras heads Arnobius' list of holy men who met a violent death (1. 40. 60), in developing the counter-charge against the pagan mockery of Christ's death, and both Porphyry[111] and Iamblichus[112] wrote biographies extolling his great deeds. The accusation that Christians worship a mortal appears again in *Adv. nat.* 1. 42. Arnobius reminds his readers that Christ is God because of his *dona* which he bestows upon his worshippers.[113] And now a new concept appears which may seem strange in light of what he says elsewhere about corporeal existence:[114] Christ is called 'praesidem nostri corporis' (1. 42. 7). 'The call to separate soul from body seems to be the major ethical injunction which Porphyry lays upon us in his moral treatises.'[115] Indeed, even in his pre-Plotinian

---

[109] *Adv. nat.* 1. 39. 15–19: 'Ita ergo Christus non habeatur a nobis deus neque omni alioquin [qui] vel maximus potest excogitari divinitatis adficiatur cultu, a quo iamdudum tanta et accepimus dona viventes et expectamus, dies cum venerit, ampliora?'

[110] '. . . cur ergo damnatus est? oraculo respondit dea: Corpus quidem debilitantibus tormentis semper oppositum est . . .'.

[111] See the recent edition with translation and introduction by E. Des Places, *Porphyre. Vie de Pythagore. Lettre à Marcella* (Paris, 1982; Budé).

[112] He literally accepts the traditional miracles attributed to Pythagoras. See J. Bidez, 'Le philosophe Jamblique et son école', *REG* 32 (1919), 29–40. Note that Arnobius attacks 'vos appello qui Mercurium, qui Platonem Pythagoramque sectamini' in 2. 13. 8 f.

[113] *Adv. nat.* 1. 42. 1–4: 'Natum hominem colitis. Etiamsi esset id verum, locis ut in superioribus dictum est, tamen pro multis et tam liberalibus donis quae ab eo profecta in nobis sunt deus dici appellarique deberet.'

[114] Earthly life in a body is frequently referred to disparagingly as bondage: cf. 1. 40; 2. 25, 27, 30, 33, 37, 61, 76 f. Most of these appear in book 2 where the exalted anthropology of the Neoplatonists is criticized.

[115] A. Smith (1974), 20.

soteriological views he posited that this was necessary, and we recall his famous dictum cited by Augustine that 'omne corpus esse fugiendum ut anima post beata permaneret cum Deo'.[116] In his refutation of this concept, Arnobius depicts Christ not only as mortal, but also as the divine guardian of that aspect of man's being which lay outside the pale of Neoplatonic soteriology.[117] Yet it may be directly related in a negative sense to the Chaldaean concept of the salvation of the body which later Neoplatonists discuss.[118] Taking *Adv. nat.* 1. 42. 7 out of context, we may perhaps be inclined to translate—as some have already done— *corporis* as 'community', denoting the Church as the Body of Christ, but a close inspection of the evidence provides a different interpretation. First, *Adv. nat.* 1. 45 f. enumerates a long list of *dona Christi*, and most are based upon an understanding of *salus* as meaning physical health. MacMullen's remark that what 'pagans did pray for . . . was health, first', perfectly fits Arnobius' comprehension of the human temporal experience of *salus.*[119] He says so much in *Adv. nat.* 6. 16. 5 f.: good health heads the list of things for which pagans pray to the gods' images. Second, *daemon* (or forms of it) appears only six times, and once (1. 45. 6) it describes those evil beings who cause physical disease. The same belief appears in Chaldaean thought and was quite widespread in the Graeco-Roman world. But the Chaldaeans seem to have been almost fanatical in their use of apotropaic rites to cure physical illnesses. Proclus relates that the Chaldaeans had 'efficacious phylacteries for every limb of the human body'.[120] They used such materials as amulets, stones, and plants in conjunction with conjurations thought capable of exorcizing the demon causing the illness. Hence the importance Arnobius places upon Christ's healings of the body without using any material aids in 1. 44–6, and the criticism of the magicians' use of such aids in 1. 43. Eusebius (*DE* 3. 6) also explicitly divorces the use of amulets, enchantments, and incense made from herbs from the teachings and practices of both Christ and his disciples. And noteworthy is the fact that both Eusebius (*DE* 3. 6: in the chapter preceding his citation from the Hecatean Oracle) and Arnobius (1. 43. 1–5) respond to the accusation

---

[116] *Civ. Dei* 10. 29: a frequent theme of *De reg. an.* in Aug.; cf. Ibid. 13. 20: corporeal resurrection denied; 22. 26: the soul must be free from all bodily contact to be happy; he also rejected metasomatosis (incorrectly called metempsychosis by some) into animal bodies; cf. also 12. 27 and 13. 29; *Vit. Plot.* 1.

[117] Contrast this with LeB 168, on *Adv. nat.* 1. 42. 2.

[118] *COTh* 216.

[119] See R. MacMullen, *Paganism in the Roman Empire* (New Haven, Conn., 1981), 51.

[120] *COTh* 290 f.

that Christ was a magician who became acquainted with esoteric Egyptian knowledge.[121]

Is Christ God? is the next question to which he responds (*Adv. nat.* 1. 42. 8 f.), and again it appears that he had the Hecatean Oracle and commentary in mind.[122] Arnobius continues in 1. 42 by wondering whether his opponent, becoming more insane, will demand proof of his statements about Christ. This demand to prove the credibility of a particular religious idea appears in most books of the *Adv. nat.* and is one of the main themes inherent in Arnobius' method of literary retortion. We can make the same observation concerning the *PE*, the *DE*, and *De cons. evan.*, all of which have Porphyry as the principal antagonist. The main Porphyrian accusation which set off fireworks right across the Roman world was that Christians cannot offer any evidence to prove the truthfulness of their religious beliefs. They only assent to an intellectually unverified 'faith'. The 'proof' offered by Arnobius is significant:

No greater proof exists than the credibility of His acts, than the unusual quality of His miracles; than all those ordinances of fate broken and dissolved, which the peoples and tribes saw brought to pass in broad daylight with not a single disagreeing voice; nor will those whose ancient and ancestral laws He showed to be full of vanity and the most empty superstition dare to charge Him with falsity.[123]

There are four main proofs given. First, there was something about his works and new powers that prove Christ's divinity. We recall that in *Civ. Dei* 19. 23 Porphyry argued that Christ offered nothing new in respect of teaching, and he undoubtedly is the enemy behind *Adv. nat.* 1. 42 and *DE* 3. 5 ff. who called Christ a deceiver. (He had to explain the miracles in some way.) Note that Eusebius refutes the charge that Christ worked miracles by magic by showing that it was a strange and divine being who was incarnated (*DE* 3. 6). Second, Christ has broken the laws of fate. This is an apparent response to Porphyry's remark that Christ's fatal gift to the Christians was entanglement in error: they were fated not to receive *dona deorum*. And we have already noticed that

[121] Eusebius also insists (*DE* 3. 6) that neither Jesus, nor his teaching, nor his followers have had anything to do with performing miracles by using libations or incense, i.e material aids.

[122] Hagendahl (1958), 18, has concluded that these words derive from the Lucretian eulogy of *De rer. nat.* 5. 8. It might have been that the eulogy furnished him with what appeared to be the best literary response to Porphyry.

[123] *Adv. nat.* 1. 42. 14–21.

Eusebius attacked Porphyry's subordinating the gods to fate and challenged him to confess the Lord of fate, namely Jesus Christ.

The third proof given is the unanimous and united witness that people have given about Christ's powers. Hence the harmony and uniformity existing between the words and deeds of Christ and his disciples. The reference to eye-witnesses may be related to statements made elsewhere about the miracles being publicly performed, which in turn may be a retortion of *PE* 5. 1 (= Harn. *CC* fr. 80), where we hear Porphyry's grumbling that since Jesus appeared humanity has not received any public assistance from the gods. The attempt of Porphyry to drive a wedge of credibility between Christ and his disciples was taken very seriously by Eusebius and Arnobius.[124] Both ask why did the disciples witness to Christ unto death, when they were able to live in harmony with the pagans?[125] Both acknowledge that they bore witness with one mind or faith.[126] Both wonder how educated men could have deceived the entire world.[127] And Eusebius stresses the credibility of an eyewitness account as well.[128] Comparison should also be made between *DE* 3. 7, appearing immediately after quoting from the Hecatean Oracle, and *Adv. nat.* 1. 50, both emphasizing that Christ sent fishermen, farmers, and the uneducated throughout all nations. The fourth proof is the teaching of Christ which has caused many pagans to abandon their ancestral traditions. Again, both Arnobius (2. 12) and Eusebius (*DE* 3. 7) elaborate upon this point with precision. And they apparently took to heart Porphyry's (*PE* 1. 1) finding the faith of the Christians intellectually inferior. Observe the following examples given by Eusebius (*PE* 1. 5) and Arnobius (2. 8 f.) of situations in the lives of pagans in which they also use faith: voyages; journeys; sowing the earth; getting married; raising children;[129] depending upon physicians; warfare; and accepting a philosophy, both giving examples of Plato, Aristotle, Epicurus, and Stoicism. Again, since it is certain that Eusebius is attacking Porphyry, these close parallels between Arnobius and Eusebius shed further light upon the present argument that the *Adv. nat.* was written mainly as a response to the anti-Christian propaganda of Porphyry.

---

[124] Also Aug. in *De cons. evan.*

[125] *DE* 3. 5; *Adv. nat.* 1. 54.

[126] *DE* 3. 5; *Adv. nat.* 2. 12.

[127] *DE* 3. 5; *Adv. nat.* 1. 55; cf. 1. 52.

[128] *DE* 3. 6.

[129] Sailing, sowing, marrying, and begetting children appear in C. Cels. 1. 11. Chadwick noted the similarities between Arnobius and Origen. Closer parallels exist between the former and Eusebius.

In *Adv. nat.* 1. 43 f., Arnobius responds to the charge that Christ was a deceiver/magician, and that it was by magic that he performed his miracles. Eusebius responds to an identical accusation, and this is almost certainly Porphyrian.[130] For it does appear certain that the latter is on record for arguing that Christ performed no authentic miracle,[131] and he did assert that the disciples used magic in their evangelistic missions.[132] From information found in this section and other passages in the *Adv. nat.*, 'magic' would appear to denote the theurgical practices which characterize post-Plotinian Neoplatonism. The accusation that Christ was a magician would therefore represent an interpolation by a Neo-platonic group of practising theurgists, indebted to Chaldaean theology and anti-Christian propaganda via Porphyry, into the Hecatean Oracle and commentary. 'Magic' used thus poses no problem for this interpretation, for Augustine similarly equates magic with theurgical practices.[133] Indeed, the appearance of a philosophical group in Roman North Africa at this period who called themselves followers of Plato and practised theurgy, will have given Arnobius ample reasons to designate them *viri novi*.[134]

Chapters 45–7 comprise the climax of the argument begun in 1. 34. The goal is to prove that Christ was not a mortal—and therefore he was and still is divine—by enumerating the many *munera* which have intermittently appeared throughout the argument since 1. 36. After the initial question, 'Ergo ille mortalis aut unus fuit e nobis?', the refrain, 'unus fuit e nobis?' appears eleven times in 1. 45 f. The fact that Arnobius used his very limited knowledge of the NT in this section may imply that his opponents were using the scripture of the Christians in their attack upon Christianity.[135] And this is exactly what we should expect to find, since it was Porphyry, who evidently concluded that the method of Celsus' attacking Christianity predominantly from within his own Graeco-Roman cultural milieu was no longer effective, who revolutionized and undoubtedly revived

---

[130] Cf. Barnes (1981), 177 n. 101.

[131] *DE* 3. 5. 95 f. = Harnack *CC* fr. 7.

[132] *De cons. evan.* 1. 15. 23. Cf. *DE* 3. 5 and *Adv. nat.* 1. 54: both respond to the charge that the disciples were liars. The text in Arnobius begins his defence of scripture.

[133] *Civ. Dei* 10. 9. Cf. *Apocr.* 3. 1, which compares Christ's being spat upon with the disappearance of Apollonius from the imperial court.

[134] Cf. *Adv. nat.* 2. 11. 4; 2. 13. 9; 2. 14. 3 f.; 2. 62.

[135] Cf. *Apocr.* 3. 3 for an example of a similar method of attacking Christianity. If the extant fragments give us an accurate picture, it served as the centre-piece of Porphyry's method in *CC*.

the anti-Christian movement by using the main weapon of the Christians, scripture, against them. Also, we may note in this connection the long series of impassioned refrains, based upon a method of literary retortion, found in *Adv. nat.* 4. 24–7, climaxing in 4. 28. The latter forms the second of six résumés found in the work (analysed below) of the argument that the anthropomorphic and anthropopathic depictions of the gods in the myths prove they are *mortalis*. And, again, it should not be surprising to discover that Arnobius is much more effective in his attack upon paganism than his 'defence' of Christianity, because the method he used to attack paganism, literary retortion, thereby enabling him to use the pagans' weapons against them, was the same weapon that Porphyry used in attacking Christianity.[136] Between each refrain Arnobius lists the *munera Christi* to prove his divinity. In his conclusions in 1. 47 he notes that it is not the miracles alone that prove his greatness, nor did he do these for self-aggrandisement, but that unbelievers might know what a true God is.[137] Finally, as Porphyry repeated himself in the commentary about Christ being a mortal subordinated to the fates, Arnobius repeats himself likewise by making the opposite point.[138] Note that the plural corresponds to *fata* of the commentary, and the way the sentence is constructed emphasizes Christ's power over the fates. Finally, the healings of Jesus have made it 'clearer than the sun itself that He was more powerful than the fates' (1. 47).

One major conclusion that can be deduced from the aforementioned data is that the Hecatean Oracle and Porphyry's commentary upon it served a useful purpose in the anti-Christian propaganda disseminated in Roman North Africa during the period immediately preceding the outbreak of the Diocletianic Persecution. Although scholarship has traditionally focused upon the *Contra Christianos* as the most important work representative of the pagan intelligentsia during this period, the *Phil. or.* should now be considered as a serious piece of anti-Christian propaganda in its own right. Indeed, echoes of the Hecatean/Porphyrian argument reverberated more than a century later in Arnobius' homeland: 'Porphyrius . . . Dominum Christum . . . quippe in ipsa carne contempsit quam propter sacrificium nostrae purgationis adsumpsit.'[139] We may be

---

[136] i.e. in the *CC*.

[137] *PE* 1. 2 = Harnack *CC* fr. no. 1, which should be compared with *Adv. nat.* 2. 4. 5–9.

[138] *Adv. nat.* 1. 42.

[139] *De reg. an.* in *Civ. Dei* 10. 24.

almost certain that the gauntlet had been picked up many years before by the professor of Sicca Veneria. And such a response to the subtle but vicious[140] attack upon the deity of Christ that Porphyry developed in the *Phil. or.*, accentuating above all his *mortality*, to which two great doctors of the Church, Eusebius and Augustine, responded with sharp counter-attacks, would perhaps help to explain the absence of any reference to the birth narratives and the name *Jesus* in the *Adversus nationes.*[141]

---

[140] Porphyry's introductory remarks, therefore, should be read in light of his comm. on the Hecatean Oracle and the present interpretation: 'Praeter opinionem, inquit, profecto quibusdam videatur esse, quod dicturi sumus. Christum enim dii piissimum pronuntiaverunt et immortalem factum et cum bona praedicatione eius meminerunt' (*Civ. Dei* 19. 23). Note the *immortalem factum*.

[141] In general see H. D. McDonald, 'The Doctrine of God in Arnobius, *Aduersus Gentes*', *Stud Patr* 9 (1966), 75–81, but 'doctrine' may indeed be going too far.

9

The Mortality of the Gods
A Predominantly Literary Retortion of Porphyry's Rejection of Christ's Divinity

A predominantly literary method of retortion functions as the primary medium through which Arnobius develops his counter-attack upon Porphyry according to the main theme permeating the *Adversus nationes*: the pagan deities are mortal because of their anthropomorphic and anthropopathic depictions in the Graeco-Roman myths. This argument is found throughout books 1, 3–7, and is indirectly used in book 2. Arnobius turns Porphyry's main premiss against him by arguing that the gods of the myths are mortal because of their human forms and emotions. He also frequently attempts to prove that the sub-human emotional disturbances caused by the immoral acts of the gods classifies them with brute beasts. Although he may perhaps legitimately be called heterodox in his understanding of creation, and is apparently ignorant of all the Old Testament and most of the New Testament, he is emphatic upon one basic point: Christ is *deus* in his being, great deeds, and gifts, and, therefore, worthy of mankind's worship. Through him alone comes the immortalization of the soul. Finally, the rejection of the deity of Christ was strongly present in the pagan attack upon Christianity in the East and West, represented by Eusebius in the former, and Arnobius in the latter. The doctrine of the deity of Christ appears to have been at the heart of the argument between the pagan and Christian intelligentsia in the period before the outbreak of the Great Persecution. This might indicate an organized dissemination of Porphyrian anti-Christian propaganda throughout a much wider geographical area of the Roman Empire than has been formerly thought.[1] And Arnobius' familiarity with this propaganda may suggest his personal use of it when he was an outspoken critic of Christianity.[2]

---

[1] This would cohere with the theories of Chadwick and Wilken, yet having a wider geographical significance.

[2] Thus, as we have already seen, many passages in books 1–2 can be interpreted as recantations (*retractationes*) of his former position as an opponent of the Church.

There has not been a meticulous analysis of the function of this apologetical method (literary retortion), specifically in books 3–7, and how it is organically related to the pagan attack in books 1–2. The main premise of his argument, found in *Adv. nat.* 4. 18, is that the origin of the pagans' concepts of deity derive totally from their own religious literature. It is almost certain that Arnobius, similar to his contemporary Eusebius, used Porphyry's method against him, for if the extant fragments of the *Contra Christianos* give us an accurate account of his main method of attacking Christian beliefs, Porphyry vilified Christianity basically from within its own literary tradition. Arnobius devotes six chapters to the pagan attack upon scripture (1. 54–9). A principal complaint is that it was written by liars (1. 54 ff.). Eusebius responds to the same charge, and Augustine spends much time proving that this was simply not true.[3] Augustine also responds to the accusation that the authors of scripture were unlearned and common men, an insult taken seriously by Arnobius and Eusebius.[4] In *Adv. nat.* 1. 56 we find the accusation that certain insertions, additions, modifications, and omissions of words, syllables, and even letters have occurred in the writing of scripture. And Augustine often deals with the charge that omissions and interpolations apparent in a biblical text discredit its credibility.[5] We undoubtedly see in both cases the sharp mind of Porphyry, striving always for grammatical exactness and clarity, and conciseness in the written composition, and this was obviously due to his philological training under Longinus in Athens. For example, in the preface of the *Phil. or.*, he vows that he has added nothing to, nor taken away anything from, the oracles with the exception of correcting an erroneous phrase; changing it for greater clarity; completing a defective metre; and striking out anything not conducive to the purpose.[6] We can imagine that he found much to criticize in the Bible! Eusebius himself admitted that the oracles of Porphyry were adorned with fine poetry and inflated by the grandeur of language.[7]

As noted in Chapter 1 (§11), the description of the biblical writers as uneducated appears to have been a frequent theme in the *CC*.[8] Also,

---

[3] Cf. *De cons. evan.* 2. 3. 7; 2. 12. 29.

[4] *Adv. nat.* 1. 50, 52, 58.

[5] *De cons. evan.* 2. 5. 15 f.; and indeed book 2 *passim*.

[6] *PE* 4. 7.   [7] *PE* 4. 1.

[8] All derived from Jerome: *Hom.* 11 *in Psalm.* 77 (Harnack *CC* fr. no. 10): Matthew was ignorant for putting Isaiah instead of Asaph in Mt. 13: 35; *Comm. in Ioel* 2. 28 (CChr: Adriaen = *CC* fr. no. 5); cf. *Hom.* 75, *De prin. Marc.* (= *Comm. in Matt.* 3. 3 and *CC* fr. no. 9).

Porphyry explained the disciples' ability to perform miracles as being due to having knowledge of and practising magical arts. Arnobius attacks a similar accusation in book 1:

Hoc enim dicit Porphyrius: Homines rusticani et pauperes, quoniam nihil habebant, magicis artibus operati sunt quaedam signa. Nam fecerunt signa et in Aegypto magi contra Moysen. Fecit et Apollonius, fecit et Apuleius: et infinita signa fecerunt.[9] Porph. *CC* in Jerome, *Hom.* 14 *in Psalm.* 81 (CChr: Morin = Harnack *CC* fr. no. 4).

... ex immensa illa populi multitudine, quae suam gratiam sectabatur admirans, piscatores opifices rusticanos atque id genus delegit imperitorum, qui per varias gentes missi cuncta illa miracula sine ullis fucis atque adminiculis perpetrarent.   Arnob. *Adv. nat.* 1. 50. 8–13.

Another passage very similar to these is found in Augustine, where he defends the charge that magic was used to perform miracles.[10] And immediately after giving his partial citation from the Hecatean Oracle, Eusebius (*DE* 3. 7) proves the divine nature of Christ's teaching, in response to the charge that he and his disciples were sorcerers, because men of the fishermen's class, rustics, and the uneducated were able to teach it to people all over the world. Arnobius follows the text cited above by mentioning that the miracles of Christ and his disciples were brought about by either a command or a physical touch. His conclusion denotes a concern to concede the social background of the disciples, but again he totally rejects the charge that magic was used.[11] In the passage cited above Porphyry gives Apollonius and Apuleius as examples of pagan miracle workers. In 1. 52 Arnobius enumerates a long list of magicians. Among these are Apollonius—Apuleius does not appear— and Julian. The latter was the elder Julian who edited, along with his son Julian, the Chaldaean Oracles during the reign of Marcus Aurelius.[12] It was from the younger that Porphyry drew some of his materials in

---

[9] Cf. Eus. *C. Hier.* 4 (*PG* 22. 304): Christians were called βεβουκολημένοι = *rustici*. Hierocles also compared Apollonius to Christ. The pagan in *Apocr.* 4. 5 on Matt. 24: 4 f. (false Christs will come) observes: 300 yrs. have passed and no one has appeared unless one adduces Apollonius.

[10] Cf. *De cons. evan.* 1. XI. 17, appearing between references to Porphyry: 'Illud quoque attendant, qui magicis artibus tanta potuisse et nomen suam ad populos in se convertendos arte ipsa consecrasse delirant.'

[11] *Adv. nat.* 1. 50. 34–7: 'Neque quicquam est ab illo gestum per admirationem stupentibus cunctis, quod non omne donaverit faciendum parvolis illis et rusticis et eorum subiecerit potestati.'

[12] Cf. E. R. Dodds, 'Chaldaean Oracles', *OCD* 226; *COTh* 3 ff.

writing the *Phil. or.*[13] and *De reg. an.* 'The Chaldaean Oracles were brought to the notice of the Neoplatonists (to whom we owe all the information we possess upon this subject) by Porphyry.'[14] Arnobius' challenge to the magicians is that they perform the same kind of healing miracles by (theurgical) incantations as uneducated Christians have done many times with bare commands.[15]

In turning to the pagan attack upon scripture (*Adv. nat.* 1. 54–9), four chapters are given to refuting the charge that the biblical writers were liars who fabricated falsehoods about Christ.[16] This accusation is found in the *CC*,[17] Hierocles,[18] and the pagan opponent of Macarius Magnes.[19] In book 14 of the *CC* Porphyry asserted that Paul's censure of Peter for not straightway going on his evangelistic mission was a falsehood (*mendacium*). His main point was that these leaders were not acting in one accord.[20] A similar pagan argument lies behind Arnobius'

---

[13] *COTh* 15.

[14] *COTh* 7.

[15] *Adv. nat.* 1. 52. 19 ff.: 'experiri libet et recognoscere an cum suis efficere diis possint quod ab rusticis Christianis iussionibus factitatum est nudis.'

[16] Eus. *HE* 6. 19. 2 ff. = *CC* fr. no. 39. In Sicily Porphyry wrote treatises against the Christians attempting to slander their scriptures. He mentioned those who had interpreted them.

[17] Jerome, *Ep.* 57. 9 (*Ad Pammachium*: CSEL 54: Hilberg) = *CC* fr. no. 2: 'non ut evangelistas arguam falsitatis—hoc quippe imperiorum est, Celsi, Porphyrii, Iuliani . . .'; cf. *Adv. nat.* 1. 57. 13 f.: 'Falsitatis arguitis res nostras: et res vestras arguimus falsitatis'; Jerome, *Comm. in Matt.* 9. 9 (SC: Bonnand) = *CC* fr. no. 6: 'Arguit in hoc loco Porphyrius et Iulianus Augustus vel inperitiam historici mentientis vel stultitiam eorum sui statim secuti sunt Salvatorem, quasi inrationaliter quemlibet vocantem hominem sint secuti, cum tantae virtutes tantaque signa praecesserint quae Apostolos ante quam crederent vidisse non dubium est.' Cf. *Adv. nat.* 1. 54. 10 f.: 'At numquid dicemus illius temporis homines usque adeo fuisse vanos mendaces stolidos brutos'; and 1. 55. 1; 1. 56. 1 f.; 1. 57. 1; Jerome, *Comm. in Gal. prolog.* (*PL* 26. 371 f.) = *CC* fr. no. 21; cf. the new fragment in Hagedorn and Merkelbach (1966), 86, Did. the Blind, *Comm. in Iob* 10. 13; and Jerome, *Comm. in Dan.* 1. 1 (CChr: Glorie) = *CC* fr. no. 11.

[18] Eus. *C. Hier.* 2. (*PG* 22. 300): Peter and Paul were liars, unlearned, and unskilled.

[19] A well-worn theme in the *Apocr.* 5. 2. 12: the evangelists invented the events about Jesus; 2. 15 (on Jn. 12: 31): judgement is a fairy tale and the Gospels are obscure; 3. 2: Mt. 26: 36 is unclear; 3. 4: the swine story (Mt. 8: 31 f.) is myth, humbug, mockery, and flat laughter convicting Christ of baseness; 3. 5: Mt. 19: 24 are the words of a man in distress; 3. 6: Mt. 14: 25 (Jesus walks on water) is childish; cf. *Adv. nat.* 1. 54. 14: 'puerili adsertione'; *Apocr.* 3. 19: Peter is especially criticized; 3. 21: Peter was unforgiving in Acts 5: 1–11; 3. 22: he was impious and involved in base things; he (Jesus) was crucified despite having keys to the kingdom; scripture is inconsistent; and Paul is attacked in e.g. 3. 2, 3. 30, 4. 4. The reference to Peter in *Adv. nat.* 2. 12. 23 makes sense in light of the pagan attack upon him, especially if he was the patron of Sicca in Arnobius' time (see Ch. 3). Peter also received special criticism from Porphyry, analysed in the next chapter.

[20] Jerome, *Comm. in Gal. prolog.* (*PL* 26. 371 f.) = *CC* fr. no. 21: 'et sceleratus ille Porphyrius, in primo operis sui adversum nos libro, Petrum a Paulo obiecit esse

response to the charge that Christian writers are liars. The success of the world-wide evangelization is explained as being due to the harmonious agreement of disparate nations which have agreed on the truth of the Christian religion. It must be emphasized that this is a recurrent theme of the *PE*, *DE*, the *Civ. Dei* where Augustine attacks (bk. 10) Porphyry's views about the *via universalis animae liberandae*, and also *De cons. evan.* For Arnobius (and the others mentioned) the purpose of making such a comment appears to have been in response to the universal salvation theme, and to the charge that there was a great disparity between the teachings of Christ and those of his disciples.[21]

It is necessary now to demonstrate the specific manner in which the response to Porphyry's rejection of Christ's deity is developed in the *Adversus nationes*. There is one *grand thème littéraire* in the work related to the pagan gods of the myths: in respect of their anthropomorphic depictions and anthropopathic behaviour, all pagan religious literature accentuates the humanness, and therefore the mortality, of the deities. The discussion of divine anger serves as a sub-theme under the anthropopathic motif and is *not* the main theme of the work.[22] In developing the anthropopathic motif, Arnobius indeed argues that the expression of *ira* among the deities proves their humanness, mortality, and therefore perishability. Yet he also makes the same point concerning such emotions as *adfectio, adfectus, aegritudo, cupiditas, gaudium, libido, passio, perturbatio, sensus, tristitia*, and *voluptas*.[23] The main purpose of his argument is to demonstrate that Porphyry's rejection of Christ's deity, while simultaneously classifying him as a good and wise mortal, could easily be turned against him.

I. *The Anthropopathic Deities of the Pagans*

It is first very important to observe that there are six résumés of the anthropopathic motif in the *Adversus nationes*. In each instance he

reprehensum, quod non recto pede incederet ad evangelizandum: volens et illi maculam erroris invere, et huic procacitatis, et in commune ficti dogmatis accusare mendacium, dum inter se Ecclesiarum principes discrepent.'

[21] *Adv. nat.* I. 55. 1–5: 'Quodsi falsi ut dicitis historia illa rerum est, unde tam brevi tempore totus mundus ista religione completus est, aut in unam coire qui potuerunt mentem gentes regionibus dissitae, ventis caeli convexionibusque dimotae?'

[22] This is in opposition to the thesis of Micka.

[23] I am giving here only a representative list of examples to demonstrate Arnobius' main argument.

emphasizes his main point with precision: if the deities emotionally behave in this manner, they are of an earthly, and therefore *mortal*, race. Résumé one[24] comprises all of 1. 18:

> But if this is true and it has been examined and proven certain that the gods boil with anger and are shaken by emotion and disturbance of this sort, they are not immortal and eternal nor should they be thought to possess any of the quality of divinity. For where there is any disturbance, there, of necessity, as the philosophers think, must be passion; and where passion exists, there emotional excitement is a logical consequence. Where emotional excitement is, there grief and sorrow are; where grief and sorrow are, there is room for lessening of powers and for decay, and if these two cause trouble, dissolution is near at hand—death which ends all and takes away life from every sentient being.

Like a chain reaction, therefore, *adfectus* leads to *passio, perturbatio, dolor et aegritudo, imminutio et corruptio*, which finally culminates in *interitus* and *mors*. The term *ira* introduces the chapter, and it will be observed that here and elsewhere in the *Adv. nat.* it is one anthropopathic term amongst many which serves Arnobius' overall polemical purpose. His conclusion is quite clear: gods that display emotions of this kind are not immortal (*immortalis*), eternal (*perpetuus*), nor do they possess any divinity (*divinitas*).

The second résumé is found in 3. 12. 13–22.[25] He has ended eleven chapters in which the anthropomorphic gods of the myths are attacked. Against the following definition he puts the individual deities whom he criticizes in the remaining chapters of the book, and again his object is to prove that they are mortal:

> Our opinion on this matter is as follows: all divine essence, which neither at any time began to be nor at any time will come to an end of life, is without features of body and possesses nothing like the forms by which the external delimitation of members usually defines and bounds the body's frame. For whatever is like this, we think is mortal and subject to perishing, and we do not believe anything can attain to life eternal which an unavoidable end hems in, however remote the terms of its existence.

With this we should contrast Arnobius' understanding (e.g. 1. 31; 3. 19) that the Christian High God absolutely does not possess any form. By attempting to prove that deities who possess corporeal forms cannot

---

[24] Henceforth = R1.
[25] Henceforth = R2.

attain eternal life, Arnobius has begun to touch upon the natural conclusion evolving from his mortality theme: a mortal cannot grant immortality to another mortal.

The third résumé[26] occurs in 4. 28. He has already completed a sustained attack upon the anthropomorphic representations of the gods.[27] His argument is that corporeality denotes mortality, which in turn leads to perishableness (3. 1–19, esp. 12).[28] Then there follows a section (3. 20–4. 27) which includes the anthropopathic motif. Note also that in 4. 27. 24 he has concluded that the sexual lust of the gods proves they are *generis humani*. His main summary appears in 4. 28. 1–8:

Plainly, where there are weddings, marriages, childbirths, nurses, arts, debilities; where there is liberty and slavery; where there are wounds, slaughter, bloodshed; where loves, desires, passions; where there is every frame of mind coming from restless emotions—there you have nothing divine . . .

His selection of terms like *debilitates, condicio servitutis*, and *generis et terrenae fragilitatis* in the context of an argument against the anthropopathic nature of the gods, strongly suggests a retortion of Porphyry's Hecatean Oracle and commentary. For in the Oracle Hecate stressed the weakness of Christ's body in that it suffered debilitating torments like any mortal (*Civ. Dei* 19. 23: 'Corpus quidem debilitantibus tormentis semper oppositum est'). And we noted that Arnobius responds to the accusation that Christ was mortal like other mortals in his mind, soul, and body (*Adv. nat.* 1. 38. 1–4), and there also we find the phrase 'fragilitatis et condicionis unius'. It is 'divine' behaviour of this kind enumerated in 4. 28. 1–8 that causes Arnobius again to conclude:

Therefore, you either must search for other gods in whom all these things do not occur—for those in whom they do occur are of a human and earthly race—or if these whose names and character you have declared are the only ones who exist, you erase them by your beliefs. For all the things you relate are mortal.

In the pericopae noted above from *Adv. nat.* 4. 28, the key phrases are 'generis et terrenae fragilitatis', 'humani sunt generis atque terreni', and now, the *coup de grâce*: 'mortalia sunt'. This is exactly the same charge

---

[26] Henceforth = R3.

[27] This is a complementary sub-theme to the anthropopathic motif and both can be classified under the main argument, turned against Porphyry, that the pagan gods/goddesses are mortal.

[28] The best work to date on this section of the *Adv. nat.* is J. M. P. B. van der Putten, *Arnobi Aduersus Nationes, 3, 1–19, uitgegeven met inleiding en commentar* (Thesis; Leiden, 1970).

brought against Christ by Porphyry in the Philosophy of Oracles!

The fourth résumé occurs in 6. 2,[29] which immediately precedes a chapter that might have been written as a response to Porphyry's criticism, in the *CC*,[30] of the Christians for not offering sacrifice and incense to the gods. After enumerating the ideal characteristics of the gods, negatively underscoring anthropopathic terms,[31] he gives his typical conclusion:

For it is characteristic of a transitory race and of human weakness to act by contraries. Besides, the maxims and pronouncements of the wise declare that those who are touched by passion, are subject to suffering, grief, deterioration, and that those who are given to any emotions cannot but be subject to the laws of mortality.

Again affirming the form and emotional behaviour of the deities, Arnobius has placed his fifth résumé in 7. 4–5.[32] In 7. 4 he disproves the pagan concept that the sacrifices give the gods pleasure. Just before this he develops the corporeal/incorporeal antithesis which is also found in Porphyry: 'But if a god, as is said, has no body and cannot be touched at all, how is it possible that what is bodiless should be nourished on corporeal things; that what is mortal should sustain what is immortal and contribute to the well-being of something with which it cannot come in contact and to which it cannot give vitality?' (7. 3. 27–31). He then argues that the deities should not be moved by pleasure (*voluptas*), not overcome by passion (*libido*), nor be affected by sensations (*sensus*) like animals. A being so affected must be mortal:

For what is overcome by pleasure, must be subject to its opposite, sadness, nor is that which trembles with joy and is exalted by trivial gladness capable of existing free from the anxiety of grief. The gods, however, ought to be free from either emotion, if we want them to be eternal and without the frailty of mortals. (*Adv. nat.* 7. 4. 7–13 = R5a).

As we observe in the final chapter, we can be almost certain that in this text, and in several others in book 7, Arnobius is using Porphyry's

[29] Henceforth = R4.

[30] Aug. *Ep.* 102. 16 = *CC* fr. no. 79 (from book 7): 'Accusant, inquit, ritus sacrorum, hostias, thura, et cetera, quae templorum cultus exercuit; cum idem cultus ab ipsis, inquit, vel a Deo quem colunt exorsus est temporibus priscis, cum inducitur Deus primitiis eguisse.' Cf. *Adv. nat.* 6. 1. 5–12; and 6. 3. 1–3: 'Sed templa illis extruimus nulla nec eorum effigies adoramus, non mactamus hostias, non tura ac vina libamus'; and cf. 6. 27. 1–6.

[31] e.g. *adfectus, cupiditas, ira, perturbatio*, and *voluptas*.

[32] Henceforth = R5a (7. 4) and R5b (7. 5), respectively.

sacrificial theory derived from *Abst.* against a contradictory theory derived from *Phil. or.* and the same method is used by Eusebius in *PE* 4. 7–12. For now we move on to 7. 5. 5–22 (= R5*b*):

> But if we hold to that definition which we should persistently and always remember, namely, that all agitation of spirit is unknown to the gods, the consequence is a conviction that the gods are never angry; indeed, rather, no passion is farther from them than that which, being most like to savage and wild beasts, agitates those who suffer it with stormy feelings and brings them to the danger of destruction. Whatever is harassed by any emotion is evidently capable of suffering and frail. What is subject to suffering and frailty, must necessarily be mortal. But anger harasses and destroys those who suffer from it. Therefore what is subject to the passion of anger must be called mortal. Now, we know that the gods must be perpetual and possessed of an immortal nature; and if this is certain and clear, anger is far removed from them and from their state of existence. The conclusion is that by no consideration is it proper to wish to appease the gods above that which you see cannot be reconciled with their blessed state.

Divine anger is the specific emotion upon which he concentrates because he is refuting the sacrificial theory related to the appeasement of the deities with animal victims. There is no reason to insist that he is indebted to Epicurean philosophy in this text, and indeed R5*a* demonstrates the opposite: Epicureans believed that the blessed and happy immortals expressed *voluptas* in the *intermundia*. Note his use of *definitionem* implying a planned attack according to a definite philosophical doctrine. *All* agitation, not just anger, must be unknown to a being in order that it be classified 'divine': otherwise it is mortal.

Arnobius has inserted his final résumé in 7. 35–6.[33] These chapters appear at the climax of the attack upon pagan sacrifices, which is the pagan practice that receives the longest refutation of any in the work. If book 7 was written before the end of 305, when Christians had already been forced to sacrifice or burn incense to the gods, the length and the impetuosity of the attack are understandable, especially since there would appear to be a good possibility that the State Persecution was given prominent intellectual support and justification by Porphyry's anti-Christian propaganda. He asserts in 7. 34. 1–6 that the pagans do not know what a god is, his nature, substance, character, and whether he has bodily form. We recall that in 1. 38. 16 ff., Arnobius attributes to Christ alone the revelation of what a true God is, his greatness,

---

[33] Henceforth = R6.

character, depths, and indescribable profundity, and this statement appears to be anti-Porphyrian. Ignorance of these characteristics of a *deus verus* has caused the pagans to fall into these concepts of deity (3. 34. 10 f.). After making a detailed comparison of pagan and Christian concepts of deity in 3. 35 f., he again gives the same conclusion as he did in 1. 18, 3. 12. 13–22, 4. 28. 26–31, 6. 2. 22–7, 7. 4. 7–13, and 7. 5. 5–22, concerning the anthropopathic behaviour of the gods:

> In your appraisal of them the divinities grow angry and perturbed and are given over and subject to the other mental states. We think that such emotions are foreign to them, for they belong to savage beings and those who run the course of mortality.

A similar argument is found in 7. 4. 1–13, where *ira* is not mentioned, and he is attacking the pagan idea that sacrifices give the gods pleasure (*voluptas*). This is an erroneous notion of deity because whatever experiences pleasure must also experience its opposite, sadness (*tristitia*). A true god cannot display either emotion, if he is to be free from the frailty of mortality.[34] Some scholars have argued that this passage betrays a distinct Epicurean influence, but this is an inaccurate interpretation:[35] Epicurus,[36] Philodemus,[37] Torquatus,[38] Velleius,[39] and Lucretius,[40]—in short, a vast majority of Epicureans of any repute—believed that the gods enjoyed (katastematic and kinetic) 'pleasure in every part of their being'.[41]

II. *Arnobius' Attack upon the Anthropopathic Behaviour of the Pagan Deities*

In book 3 of Cicero's *De finibus*, where an exposition of Stoic ethics given by Cato is found, there appears a definition of human emotions which apparently not only has informed Arnobius' polemical argument

[34] *Adv. nat.* 7. 4. 11 ff.: 'Utroque autem affectu debent esse dii liberi, si eos esse perpetuos et mortalium volumus fragilitate privatos.'
[35] e.g. McCr 605 n. 9, simply states, 'The Epicurean View'.
[36] Diog. Laer. 10. 128.
[37] In Diels, *AKPAW* 7 (1915): *De dis* fr. 85, 5 ff., p. 17; fr. 77, p. 67.
[38] Cic. *De fin.* 1. 9. 31.
[39] Cic. *De nat. deor.* 1. 19. 51.
[40] *De rer. nat.* 1. 1: Venus = *voluptas* = the personification of the Epicurean *summum bonum*; 2. 172: 'dea voluptas'; 3. 28: 'divina voluptas'; 6. 26: 'bonum summum' = *voluptas*; 6. 94; 4. 1085.
[41] Rist (1972), 154.

related to the anthropopathic behaviour of the pagan deities, but also was significant in Augustine's anti-Porphyrian criticism. It is necessary to give the Latin text:

Nec vero perturbationes animorum, quae vitam insipientium miseram acerbamque reddunt (quas Graeci πάθη appellant, poteram ego verbum ipsum interpretans morbos appellare, sed non conveniret ad omnia; quis enim misericordiam aut ipsam iracundiam morbum solet dicere? at illi dicunt πάθος; sit igitur perturbatio, quae nomine ipso vitiosa declarari videtur; nec eae perturbationes vi aliqua naturali moventur; omnesque eae sunt genere quattuor, partibus plures, aegritudo, formido, libido, quamque Stoici communi nomine coporis et animi ἡδόνην appellant, ego malo laetitiam appellare, quasi gestientis animi elationem voluptariam:) perturbationes autem nulla naturae vi commoventur, omniaque ea sunt opiniones ac iudicia levitatis; itaque his sapiens semper vacabit. (*De fin.* 3. 10. 35, LCL: Rackham)

In book 8 of *De Civitate Dei*, Augustine demonstrates the vanity of Apuleius' demonology which followed the Platonic tradition by affirming that the demons were intermediaries between the gods and man. His primary goal is to show that Christ is the only genuine mediator between man and God. In 8. 17 he follows closely the text above quoted from Cicero. The Greeks believe that *perturbatio* = πάθος = 'passio diceretur motus animi contra rationem'. Augustine wonders why the demons' minds (*animis daemonum*) can be affected by these emotions, but they are not found in the beasts. He continues his argument, and again it is necessary to give the Latin text:

In hominibus autem ut sint istae perturbationes, facit hoc stultitia vel miseria; nondum enim sumus in illa perfectione sapientiae beati quae nobis ab hac mortalitate liberatis in fine promittitur. Deos vero ideo dicunt istas perturbationes non perpeti, quia non solum aeterni, verum etiam beati sunt.

He is here attacking *De deo Socratis*, but who are the Greeks who form the subject of *dicunt*? In *Civ. Dei* 9. 3 he quotes *De deo Soc.* 12: Apuleius asserts that the demons, who were gods according to the poets, express every kind of human emotion. Any such expression is alien to the celestial divinities.[42] In 9. 4 he identifies the Greeks of 8. 17 as either the Platonists and the Peripatetics, or the Stoics. Apuleius' gods were located 'in alta aeteria sede . . . procul a conversatione mortalium' (9. 7). Demons are 'animo passiva', but not gods (9. 8): from the latter he

---

[42] 'Quae omnes turbelae tempestatesque procul a deorum caelestium tranquillitate exultant.'

separated entirely all the passions (*passionibus*) to which the former are subject. According to the Platonists, the gods exist in *aetheria* to avoid being contaminated by contact with men.[43] He continues by using the Platonic concept of being like God (*similem Deo fieri*) to show that Christ is the one true mediator because his divinity makes him equal with the father, and his humanity made him like humans (9. 17). We realize the main target at whom he has aimed for two books (8–9) when we come to his diatribe against Porphyry's mixed up theology in book 10. After giving a story from *De reg. an.* about the binding and loosing of the divine powers, Augustine remarks:

Quo indicio dixit apparere theurgian esse tam boni conficiendi quam mali et apud deos et apud homines disciplinam; pati etiam deos et ad illas perturbationes passionesque deduci quas communiter daemonibus et hominibus Apuleius adtribuit, deos tamen ab eis aetheriae sedis altitudine separans et Platonis asserens in illa discretione sententiam.   (*Civ. Dei* 10. 9).

Finally, he again compares the concepts of deity espoused by the Platonists, Apuleius and Porphyry, in *Civ. Dei* 10. 27, and his observations are very significant for Arnobiana:

Quanto humanius et tolerabilius consectaneus tuus Platonicus Apuleius erravit, qui tantummodo daemones a luna et infra ordinatos agitari morbis passionum mentisque turbelis honorans eos quidem, sed volens nolensque confessus est; deos tamen caeli superiores ad aetheria spatia pertinentes, sive visibiles quos conspicuos lucere cernebat, solem ac lunam et cetera ibidem lumina, sive invisibiles quos putabat, ab omni labe istarum perturbationum quanta potuit disputatione secrevit! Tu [sc. Porphyrius] autem hoc didicisti non a Platone, sed a Chaldaeis magistris, ut in aetherias vel empyrias mundi sublimitates et firmamenta caelestia extolleres vitia humana, ut possent dii vestri theurgis pronuntiare divina . . .

The main battle lines drawn in these passages are clear. First, he demonstrates how far Porphyry had fallen from the true Platonic tradition by claiming that he had learned some of his doctrines from Chaldaean teachers. Apuleius was a purer Platonist because at least he did not attribute human emotions to the celestial deities, but only to the demons. Porphyry elevated human weakness to the etherial heights. He evidently had the objective of turning against Porphyry the latter's insult that there was a great disparity between the teachings of Christ and his disciples. Second, Augustine refers to the celestial gods to

---

[43] *Civ. Dei* 9. 16, referring to *Symp.* 203 A.

whom Porphyry attributed human emotions. Demons do not enter the discussion. It must be emphasized here that Arnobius frequently informs his readers that it is the *caelites* or *dii caelestes*[44] who are the principal objects of his attack upon the anthropopathic conceptions of the gods, and unlike all the ante-Nicene apologists who preceded him, he never calls them demons. This latter fact has puzzled scholars attempting to account for the rhetor's silence on the subject. Yet if he is indeed turning the Hecatean Oracle and commentary against Porphyry, it would be logical to expect that Arnobius might directly attack the Neoplatonist's celestial gods, who were capable of suffering human passions and mental agitations, rather than the demons. And as it has been the case so often, we also find Eusebius condemning the same concept of deity immediately before quoting from the *Abstinentia*.[45] He admonishes the pagans to worship the High God beyond the universe with befitting thoughts, and to regard him not in a fleshly sense in awe of the elements of the cosmos, but as one Divine Power, impossible to describe or conceive, who pervades all things in an incorporeal manner.[46]

In the Christians' response to Porphyry we clearly see a polemical method which is more complex than a simple literal interpretation of the Graeco-Roman myths. On the one hand Porphyry contaminated the true Platonic conception of deity which rigorously separated any contact between the gods and humans, by attributing to the gods the ability to experience passions and mental agitations; on the other hand, he made it evident that they could not be of any salvific benefit to mortals because the gods existed on the same frail emotional level of existence as they did. Arnobius (and others) took full advantage of the weaknesses of the Porphyrian position by again doing to the great Neoplatonist what he had done to the Christians: they turned his argument concerning the nature of the gods against him by using his own Platonic tradition, strongly reinforced by Stoic psychological concepts,[47] to prove that Porphyry was inconsistent, contradictory, and most important for the contemporary conflict between Graeco-Roman paganism and Christianity, not loyal to his master, Plato.

The general vituperation of the gods continues beyond the sixth résumé, however, and in the final section of the work, 7. 38–51, his

---

[44] *Adv. nat.* 1. 1. 6 and 7. 3. 8.
[45] *PE* 3. 3.
[46] Ibid. 3. 6.
[47] The reader is referred to the analysis of these Stoic concepts in Simmons (1985), 306–12.

object is to disprove the divinity of the three great deities, Jupiter, Aesculapius, and the Great Mother. The details of his commentary upon Jupiter—his stupidity, his vile and destructive vengeance, his criminal personality, his childishness and inconsistencies, and above all his mortality—provide evidence that he is not *deus*. His argument may represent a retortion of Porphyry's Hecatean Oracle and commentary, but some elements are reminiscent of the attack upon Christian 'salvation-history' which characterized the *CC* as well. As he develops his assault upon the character of the great god of the Romans—and we may add, the other two deities also—he has two main objectives. First, he disproves the belief that the gods actually intervened in human history. Second, these so-called theophanies of the past cannot be used to give 'spiritual' meaning in the present. The appeal to those ancient religious traditions that preceded the advent of Christianity by hundreds of years was an important fact used by Porphyry often in his anti-Christian propaganda. And it was because of their abandonment of these ancestral traditions that he argued for the execution of Christians.[48]

If we ask how these concepts might have taken upon themselves some political meanings, the answer would undoubtedly be that the deities were thought to have worked within and throughout history to make the great and glorious Roman Empire an unprecedented world power, an idea that began to effloresce into something approaching a political theology in the later Roman Empire. It is clearly present in a number of the persecuting edicts, as well as Diocletian's *Edictum de pretiis rerum venalium* and *Edictum de incestis nuptiis*; and we do not have any good reason to think that it was not found in the *Edictum de Christianis*, for in the preface to the Edict Against the Manichees we hear that 'it is the height of criminality to re-examine doctrines once and for all settled and fixed by the ancients, doctrines which hold and possess their recognized place and course.'[49] Porphyry had the same high respect for ancestral religious customs. One of his objections to the Christians was their insistence upon the fact that their God had uniquely revealed himself, from Moses and the prophets to the incarnation and the Apostles, for the redemption of mankind. Hence the need in his mind to set right the falsehoods of prophecy as in the case of Daniel; and to make it perfectly clear that Jesus was simply a man, the disciples were lying magicians, the Bible was inconsistent, and the credibility gap

[48] *PE* 1. 2. 2.
[49] *RCS* 2. 580 f.

between the teachings of Christ and his disciples was too great to believe in either. Besides, Christians could not offer any proof which might convince the intellectual that the tenets of their religion were true. They were fated not to receive gifts from the gods, according to Porphyry, and they were therefore unable to acquire *agnitionem Iovis*. It is understandable, in light of these accusations, that Arnobius rather zealously attempted to disprove Jupiter's divinity (7. 38–7. 44. 48), and emphasized the great and divine gifts given by Christ not only to his disciples, but also to the world.

It will be recalled that Porphyry emphasized the ignorance of Christ's disciples. The gist of this criticism appears to have been that a god would not reveal himself to the simple-minded from the working classes that the Bible records. Arnobius may have selected the T. Latinius myth intentionally to retort these specific accusations back upon Porphyry. For example, Jupiter chooses a backward man from the country to be his messenger, both unknown and obscure, unacquainted with city life, who probably did not know what a dancer is. It is obvious that he is stressing the ignorance of Jupiter's spokesman. If the *rusticus senior* delayed in responding to Jupiter's revelation due to his ignorance, why did the 'god' kill his children? Finally, three more times he offers evidence that Jupiter was not *deus* by demonstrating his sub-human mortality.

Aesculapius is his next victim. He seeks to prove that he was not divine, but one born in the womb of a woman, and according to pagan literature, a bolt of lightning killed him.[50] This is undoubtedly a retortion of Porphyry's rejection of Christ's deity because he was born a human being and died an ignominious death.[51] It will be recalled that Porphyry specifically named Aesculapius and 'other gods' in the *CC* who had vacated Rome since the Christians began to exist, and they had not revealed any public blessings since them.[52] Arnobius then begins to analyse the ludicrous theophany of Aesculapius: a snake was imported to Rome from Epidaurus.[53] This pretentious theophany was of a creature that crawls like worms born in the mud.[54] Quite vividly the biological and physical features of the snake are described,[55] facts which prove

---

[50] *Adv. nat.* 7. 44. 57–61.
[51] Ibid. 1. 36. 1–6.
[52] *PE* 5. 1 = *CC* fr. no. 80.
[53] *Adv. nat.* 7. 44. 64 f.
[54] Ibid. 7. 44. 65–75.
[55] Ibid. 7. 45 f.

that it was of a terrestrial species.[56] Inconsistencies of the myth are analysed.[57] An appearance in the form of a repulsive animal causes doubts as to whether Aesculapius was a *verus deus*,[58] an apparent retortion of Porphyry's rejection of the form of Christ's theophany.[59] The fact that the veracity of this myth is based upon eyewitnesses[60] should be contrasted with the miracles (*dona*) of Christ's earthly theophany 'quae populi gentesque suo geri sub lumine nullo dissentiente viderunt', and which therefore offer proof that he was God.[61] We have already observed that both Eusebius and Arnobius prove Christ's deity by referring to eyewitness accounts of his divine powers.[62] Arnobius uses the same kind of evidence to disprove the deity of Aesculapius: the theme of the entire chapter (7) is developed around the beginning question: 'Sed si deus [sc. Aesculapius], inquit, non erat?' It would appear certain that this question is a retortion of *Adv. nat.* 1. 42. 8 f., which we have concluded is a response to the Hecatean Oracle: 'Ergone, inquiet aliquis furens iratus et percitus, deus ille est Christus?' His answer to the former question is that if it had such features as those enumerated in 7. 45 f., it could not have been a god.[63] It was simply a snake and nothing more.

Generally, Arnobius does appear to be turning the tables against the Hecatean Oracle and Porphyry's commentary upon it, which was apparently being used by a Porphyrian Neoplatonic group in North Africa. In what follows fragment 80 of the *CC* appears to be in mind, and it has already appeared as a possible connection with the beginning of the *Adversus nationes*.[64] (This evidences the skilful intertwining of counter-attacks upon Porphyrian arguments from more than one work.) In the *CC* fragment Porphyry asserted that since Jesus began to be worshipped, there had been no public aid given to humanity by the gods. One should not marvel at the persistence of the plague in Rome because Aesculapius and the other deities have left. Note that Arnobius appears to be responding to this remark in his comment that if the deity had been summoned to drive out the plague many years ago, Rome

---

[56] *Adv. nat.* 7. 46.
[57] Ibid. 7. 45. 21–30.
[58] Ibid. 7. 45. 34.
[59] Cf. *PE* 1. 1 and *Adv. nat.* 1. 42. 14–21.
[60] *Adv. nat.* 7. 46. 15.
[61] Ibid. 1. 42. 17 f.
[62] Cf. *Civ. Dei* 19. 23, *DE* 3. 5 ff., and *PE* 5. 1.
[63] *Adv. nat.* 7. 46. 45–9.
[64] *PE* 5. 1 = *CC* fr. no. 80.

should have been made forever immune to 'any injurious breeze'.[65] He refers in 7. 47. 20, as he had done in 1. 1. 3, to the authority of the oracles, and in both cases *CC* fragment 80 appears to have been the accusation which he attacks. He continues by acknowledging that from the time the snake was imported to the present, Rome has often been broken by diseases. Where was the god at these periods, why has he not protected Rome since then, and why did he not prevent any dreadful thing from entering it?[66] Either the snake arrived at Rome when the plague had already dissipated, and therefore Aesculapius is a pseudo-saviour, or the hymns of the fates do not provide any true predictions because the prescribed remedy in them proves the ineffectiveness of the god's *auxilium* (7. 48. 28) to Rome after his arrival. Thus all periods since that time have not benefited from his so-called assistance.

Arnobius closes the work with the same objective in mind: he offers proof that the Great Mother is not divine. He had already argued in 5. 8. 22 f., that the goddess was not divine but human, and this appears to have been written in response to the pagan (Porphyrian) rejection of Christ's deity in 1. 42. 1: 'Natum hominem colitis.' Four passages elucidate his position.[67] He begins by referring to the histories relating that King Attalus sent a small stone and nothing else from Phrygian Pessinus.[68] And it may indeed be in the form of personal retractations that his vilification of these three pagan gods, who progressively degenerate into an idiot fond of horse racing, a snake, and a stone, has been made. He thus closes seven admirable books written during a very difficult period in the history of the North African Church under the Roman Empire, by noting that such imbecilities have caused the perdition of mankind under the auspices of the great powers responsible for Rome's imperium. Perhaps there could not have been a better way for a North African Christian to end his work: he was writing when the Tetrarchy, probably in collaboration with Porphyry, the most formidable enemy of the Church in antiquity, was attempting to eradicate the Christian faith. Considering the evidence brought forth up to this point in the study—and there is more given below—Arnobius' work was a

[65] *Adv. nat.* 7. 47. 12–16.
[66] Ibid. 7. 47. 19–25.
[67] Ibid. 7. 49. 11–19; 7. 50. 13 ff.; 7. 51. 1–5; 7. 51. 15 f. The Great Mother was worshipped at Sicca: see the epitaph of a priest of the goddess, Q. Valerius Severus Platienses, in *CIL* 8. 1649.
[68] This is an example of Arnobius' acceptance of the historicity of the myths when it will cohere with his polemical purpose. Again, the direct attack upon the sacred history of Roman religious paganism recalls Porphyry's method in the *CC*.

refined, meticulously-planned, and brilliant counter-attack against the Porphyrian camp!

We must make a final observation about the last two deities mentioned by Arnobius in book 7, Aesculapius and the Great Mother. Augustine's main opponent in book 10 of *De Civitate Dei* is Porphyry. The principal literary source criticized by him is the Neoplatonist's *De reg. an.*, and some of the details of his argument shed further light upon the Arnobius–Porphyry connection in *Adv. nat.* generally, but especially concerning book 7. In 10. 1–8, Augustine demonstrates that the miracles recorded in the Bible confirm God's promises and show that the Christian religion therefore offers proof that it alone can show the way of true worship and sacrifice to man. He then finds repugnant Porphyry's illicit Chaldaean arts (= theurgy) which led him to the disastrous belief that gods are subject to emotional agitation (10. 9 f.), and he uses Porphyry's *Ep. An.* (10. 11) to demonstrate how the Neoplatonist could contradict himself in his own words. Miracles are the centrepiece of his argument for seven chapters (12–18). He then refers (10. 12) to the Platonists who offer miracles as proof of their beliefs. The word used for proof here, *testantibus*, corresponds to Arnobius' assertion that Christian belief derived from scripture is based upon witnesses (1. 57. 22: *testibus*), while pagans only have opinions (*opinionibus*). Three chapters deal with Christian miracles (*Civ. Dei* 13–16) in this way. He then turns to the subject of sacrifice in 10. 16, specifically to the Platonists who practise theurgy. Two of the miracles used by these pagans to prove that their deities deserve sacrificial worship are: the accompaniment of the god Aesculapius with the serpent on the voyage to Rome, and the importation of the statue of the Great Mother from Phrygia into Rome. Both are given in the same order as they appear in Arnobius. Note that Arnobius and Augustine are both attacking notions of sacrifice, and we observe below that there are a good many parallels between Arnobius and Porphyry in *Adv. nat.* 7, the theme of which is sacrifice. Also, Augustine names Porphyry as the principal advocate of the sacrificial beliefs which he has been attacking (10. 26) in the section preceding his second detailed account of the Neoplatonist's belief that the gods are subject to passions and mental agitations (10. 27).

III. *Conclusions*

Taking all the evidence into consideration, we may be pretty certain that three of Porphyry's anti-Christian works were current in Roman North Africa during the period immediately preceding the outbreak of the Diocletianic Persecution in February 303. These were the *Contra Christianos*, the *De regressu animi*, and the *Philosophia ex oraculis*. In the next two chapters we show that Arnobius was also familiar with *De abstinentia*. These were undoubtedly used as pagan propaganda and understood as giving intellectual justification to the official state programme against the Christians. Yet as in the case of both Augustine's and Eusebius' response to Porphyry's anti-Christian propaganda (Eusebius more than Augustine), Arnobius appears to have paid most of his attention to the *Phil. or.*, due to its rejection of the deity of Christ, as being possibly detrimental to one of the basic tenets of his new religion. And because it is certain that Porphyry was in North Africa (*Abst.* 3. 4. 7) during the period in which Arnobius, according to Jerome, was attacking the Christian faith, it is quite logical to suggest that Arnobius had access to these works of the Neoplatonist, if not to the man himself. We can further suggest that he might well have been a follower of Porphyry before his conversion to Christ, and it was Porphyry's anti-Christian propaganda that he used in attacking the faith. If this is true, the pledge of faith requested by the Bishop of Sicca, according to Jerome, was presented in the form of the *Adv. nat.* as a personal recantation of formerly-held Porphyrian (anti-Christian) beliefs.

The *CC* appears to have exerted its influence upon the rhetor's polemical argument principally in the general response which he gives to the pagan attacks upon the inconsistencies of the Bible; its very poor quality as a piece of literature, namely that its authors were semi-literate and untrustworthy men of the working classes, and were liars, and the assertion made by Porphyry that Christians could not prove what they believed was true. *Faith* was intellectually disreputable. The *CC* may also have inspired Arnobius in respect of the development of his method of attacking the pagans primarily from within their own religious traditions. He bases his attack upon the beliefs and practices of the pagans, as Porphyry had done in the *CC* firmly and almost exclusively upon Christian religious literature. Also, both the selection of the work's title and the organization of his books may have been in response to the *CC*. If Porphyry was as merciless in his attack upon Christianity as Arnobius is in his criticism of the pagans, we can now have a better

understanding of the *Adv. nat.* as an historical document. Not only is
it one of the last ante-Nicene works written by a Christian, but it may
also give us an indirect indication as to why so many Church Fathers
responded to Porphyry's anti-Christian works, and with so much
hostility. Finally, the *CC* may help to explain a chronological problem
related to the references to the persecutions of Christians in the *Adversus
nationes*. In Chapter 2 we concluded that all references which precede
Arnobius' allusion to the First Edict (4. 36) do not provide convincing
evidence that they describe the persecution of Christians under Diocletian. Porphyry argued that Christians should be executed for their
abandonment of religious ancestral customs (*PE* 1. 2. 2). We may
perhaps best explain the discrepancy as follows: all references before 4.
36 are made in response to Porphyry; those that come after (including
4. 36) are made in response to Diocletian's Edicts.

Scholarship from henceforth should acknowledge the *Phil. or.* of
Porphyry as a much more dangerous threat to the Church than has
hitherto been claimed. Eusebius, Augustine, and Arnobius reveal its
threat to their religion because of Porphyry's subtle but vicious attack
upon the deity of Christ. Christ was indeed very wise and pious, but
only as a mortal. Hence Arnobius', and to a certain extent also Eusebius',
emphasis upon the *superhuman* knowledge and exploits of Christ in *Adv.
nat.* 1; and their insistence upon the divinity of Christ in his being,
teaching, and miracles. Concerning the latter, the fact that Arnobius
and Eusebius make it clear that Christ (and his disciples) performed
miracles without using any material aids strongly suggests that the target
of both authors is Chaldaean soteriological practices related to physical
health. Both Eusebius and Arnobius show evidence also that they have
responded to Porphyry's angelology which is indebted to Chaldaean
theology. Although the response of each is quite different,[69] they are in
agreement that Christ alone is the mediator and revealer of any knowledge of the divine world. Finally, considering Arnobius' penchant for
technical Chaldaean theological language, we may conclude that it is a
Chaldaean-Neoplatonic group that he attacks in books 1–2, which is
exactly what we should expect from the suggested date of the *Adv.
nat.* and the Porphyrian connection with Arnobius' overall polemical
argument.

We may also conclude that there is a close relationship between the

[69] As we noted, Eusebius was able to draw from his knowledge of Judeo-Christian
angelology: therefore his similarity with Porphyry's angelology is more striking.

pagan attack upon Christian concepts of deity in books 1–2, and Arnobius' counter-attack upon pagan notions of deity in books 3–7. A significant fact that must be kept in mind for future research in Arnobiana is that there is a grave danger inherent in interpreting an Arnobian text out of its natural context and, therefore, not understanding the relationship between individual concepts and the general literary (thematic) context in which they are found. Thus it is prudent to dispense with an approach to a particular text which has the main objective of ascertaining the extent to which Arnobius can be defined as orthodox, non-orthodox, or heterodox. It is the pagan polemical argument which addressed the basic tenets of the Christian Church for the main purpose of seeing the whole complex fall to pieces, that has been the principal determining factor in the development of Arnobius' *theological* statements about Christ, and in his criticism of Graeco-Roman concepts of deity. And both in respect of its general tone and specific details, as the last three chapters of this study reveal, that polemical argument is predominantly Porphyrian–Chaldaean.

The Stoic list of emotions (in four main classifications) found in Cicero's *De fin.* 3. 10. 35 and commented upon by Cato, has certainly informed Augustine's polemical argument concerning Porphyry's attributing to the celestial deities (and not to the demons as Apuleius did in *De deo Socratis*) an ability to be subject to emotional disturbances/mental agitations. In respect of technical language employed,[70] the principal opponents attacked in the work, and his insistence that *any* emotional expression proves irrefutably the mortality of a being, we may conclude that the same philosophical tradition is the immediate source of Arnobius' polemical argument. This is made directly in response to Porphyry's rejection of the divinity of Christ in *Phil. or.*, that the anthropopathic behaviour of the Graeco-Roman deities establishes that they are mortal. Finally, the definition of a *verus deus*, and the fact that Christ alone has revealed knowledge of what a true God is, especially delineating the divine remoteness from man which too many have misinterpreted as Epicurean, has evidently served the same purpose in Arnobius as it served in Augustine (*Civ. Dei* 9. 16: depending upon *Symp.* 203 A): to prove how very far from the pure doctrines of his master (Plato) Porphyry had fallen.

[70] e.g. *voluptas, aegritudo, perturbatio*, etc.

10

The Soteriological Argument
Christus the 'Via Universalis Animae Liberandae'

I. *The Philosophical Approach: Classical Platonism and Porphyry*

A consistent theme in classical Platonic philosophy was that two basic aspects of human existence were viewed as antagonistic to each other: on one hand there was the spiritual life, nurtured and informed by contemplation of the world of Being; on the other, there was the corporeal life from which the contemplator had to separate himself in order to be pure. Plato emphasized the necessity of separating soul from body to attain pure knowledge. This could not be realized through the bodily senses, but only by thought. The avoidance of contact with the body was rigorously affirmed as the principal method by which this contemplation occurs.[1] Mind must be divorced from the body to behold the actual realities in the world of Being with the eye of the soul.[2] Purification (κάθαρσις) thus entailed the separation, as far as possible, of the soul from the body, by training the soul to avoid having intercourse with the body and to live truly liberated from the latter's fetters.[3] One must practise self-restraint (σωφροσύνη) which controlled the passions,[4] so that the soul which is most like the divine, immortal, and intellectual realm can live by gathering itself to itself alone, and not associate itself with the body.[5] If the philosopher remains in this state of being, controlling his passions, when death occurs his purified soul goes to live with the gods happily ever after.[6] Salvation (σωτηρία), therefore, is brought about by the release of the soul from its corporeal prison by

[1] *Phaedo* 65 B–C.
[2] Ibid. 66 D–E.
[3] Ibid. 67 C–D.
[4] Ibid. 68 C.
[5] Ibid. 80 B–81A.
[6] Ibid. 81 A.

contemplation upon the world of Being and self-development in the virtues. The soul which leaves the body still defiled by its close association with the physical realm is weighed and dragged down to the world of Becoming. Those who purified themselves by philosophy henceforth live without bodies.[7] They find the gods as companions because they now possess kindred natures.[8] Thus in the temporal realm of Becoming it is of utmost necessity to acquire, and be nourished by, virtue and wisdom (ἀρετῆς καὶ φρονήσεως).[9]

Turning to Porphyry, whether it was directly related to his attempt to disqualify the Christian religion as a 'via universalis animae liberandae', he sought for a way to offer the non-philosopher a way of salvation, while at the same time attempting to be true on most points to the Platonic system. Yet it was only a natural result of his formulation of a soteriological programme for the common man, made during the general period when he was attempting to prove that Christ was not divine and could not offer any salvific benefits to humanity, that both his opponents in the Church and his supporters in the pagan religious world would infer that Porphyry's critical *and* constructive approach to the Christian problem might precipitate the Church's destruction. Responding to the Hecatean Oracle and commentary, Augustine recognizes the main objective of Porphyry's 'praise' of Christ through the goddess, and his condemnation of him through Apollo.[10] Although we are totally dependent upon Porphyry's enemies for our information regarding the contents of *Phil. or.*, we can be fairly certain that a primary objective of the work was to prove that Christ was mortal and could not give any *dona deorum* to man. And in the preface of the work (*PE* 4. 7) it is clear that Porphyry was offering not only doctrines to the philosopher, but also giving a proof of the excellence of the deities; an encouragement to practise theosophy, which is put in contradistinction with philosophy (*PE* 4. 6 and 7); a *via salutis universalis*, affirming the *Phil. or.* to be the one sure source of salvation; and truth revealed directly by the gods (*PE* 4. 7). As it would appear from the available sources, the work was evidently constructed to serve as a kind of pagan religious manual pointing the way of salvation to the common man,

---

[7] Ibid. 114 C; See C. Evangeliou, 'Porphyry's Criticism of Christianity and the Problem of Augustine's Platonism', *Dion* 13 (1989), 51–70.

[8] *Phaedo* 108 C.

[9] Ibid. 114 C.

[10] *Civ. Dei* 19. 23: 'Una est tamen et illius et huius intentio, ut nolint homines esse Christianos, quia, nisi Christiani erunt, ab eorum erui potestate non poterunt.'

supported by traditional piety and the divine revelations of the gods. It looks as though Porphyry was attempting to offer to the pagans what the Christians had been using for nearly three centuries—a scripture based upon the authority of divine revelation in full support of the Roman religious *mos maiorum*. It would have not only reinforced the political wing of the persecution, but also made Diocletian quite satisfied to find literary propaganda of a positive and constructive nature which supported his own traditional religious proclivities.

It is important now to give an overview of Porphyry's philosophy. First, he places more emphasis upon the flight from the body than Plato and Plotinus. One must separate oneself from the flesh and the attraction of the passions. Otherwise one remains nailed to them.[11] Porphyry's method of accomplishing this is by turning to thought (τὰ νοητά) in a permanent inactivity (ἀμελετησίαν) away from sensations that awake the passions; man nails himself to god and detaches himself from the body and sensitivity. Salvation is obtained by such acts and not by understanding discourses (*Abst.* 1. 57. 1). The philosopher must die to the things of this world (*Abst.* 2. 61. 8). His real being is that aspect most estranged from the body which hands cannot touch and only thought can know (*Ad Marc.* 8). Man must cut himself off from sensible things (τῶν αἰσθητῶν) and passions (τῶν παθῶν) and be elevated to the intellectual life (πρὸς νοερόν).[12] Everything of a mortal nature (τῆς θνητῆς φύσεως) in the world of Becoming must be indeed entirely abandoned.[13] The gist is that the soul is in an alien state of existence when it is in a mortal body. In his Epistle to Boethius he used the Platonic argument from similarity: the soul is like the divine (ὁμοία τῷ θείῳ), and immortal (ἀθανάτῳ), invisible (ἀειδεῖ), inseparable (ἀσκεδάστῳ), indissoluble (ἀδιαλύτῳ), essential (οὐσιωμένῳ), and firmly established in incorruption (συνεστῶτι ἐν ἀφθαρσίᾳ).[14] In order to return to the Being to whom man is essentially related, two things must be done: flee everything mortal and corporeal and contemplate the truly intellectual life.[15] As Augustine informs us, it was a recurrent theme in Porphyrian soteriology.[16]

---

[11] This latter concept receives sharp criticism in *Adv. nat.* 2. 13. 32, as Fortin has noted; cf. *Abst.* 1. 31. 5; See the excellent introduction in R. Majercik, *The Chaldaean Oracles* (SGRR 5; Leiden, 1989); and the analysis of Porphyry's religious philosophy in P. Hadot, 'Neoplatonist Spirituality: Plotinus and Porphyry', *CMS* 230–49.

[12] *Abst.* 1. 30. 1.   [13] Ibid. 1. 30. 4.

[14] *PE* 11. 28.

[15] *Abst.* 1. 30. 5.

[16] *Civ. Dei* 10. 29.

Another feature of Porphyry's philosophical method of saving the human soul is his stress upon the Platonic concept of being like God. Let the *nous*, so he informs his wife, follow God by reflecting him in its effort to resemble him. Otherwise it will become spotted by passions.[17] To become like God one must be liberated from the slavery of the body and service to passions.[18] Suppressing the bodily pleasures is conducive to obtaining the good, and this is done by maintaining an impassibility in the soul and an assimilation to God.[19] For it is only in the impassibility of the soul that this assimilation can take place,[20] and one must extirpate the passions to accomplish this. Porphyry can also speak of the importance of honouring the 'gods' in a rather traditional sense. One gives them reverence in virtue and wisdom.[21] Smith is correct to say that 'Porphyry retains an intellectualist and anthropocentric view of human relations with the divine.'[22] The reason for this appears to have been that Porphyry, more than Plato and Plotinus, associated himself closely with his Greek religious tradition.[23] It is a concept clearly found in each of his anti-Christian works. Finally, another important theme in Porphyry which relates to the Platonic doctrine of being like God, and which is analysed below, is his insistence upon the individual's having the right notions of the gods.[24]

There also exists a Supreme Deity in the intellectual realm according to the Porphyrian system.[25] He is often called the First God (ὁ πρῶτος θεός)[26] who is incorporeal (τὴν ἀσώματον φύσιν)[27] without shape (μήτε μορφὴν)[28] or intelligible form (ἰδέαν ἔχων),[29] enthroned above intellect and intelligible form.[30] He is immobile (ἀκίνητος), indivisible (ἀμέριστος), not contained in anything, and is in need of nothing external to himself.[31] He is the Father of all beings (πάντων πατὴρ),

---

[17] *Ad Marc.* 13.
[18] *Abst.* 3. 27. 11.
[19] *Abst.* 1. 54. 6.
[20] *Abst.* 2. 43. 3.
[21] *Ad Marc.* 22 f.
[22] A. Smith (1974), 104.
[23] *Ad Marc.* 18.
[24] *PE* 4. 22; *Abst.* 2. 34; 2. 38.
[25] *Abst.* 1. 57. 2; 2. 34. 2; 3. 5. 4.
[26] Ibid. 2. 37. 1; *Vit. Plot.* 23.
[27] *Abst.* 2. 37. 1; 1. 57. 3.
[28] *Vit. Plot.* 23.
[29] Ibid.
[30] Ibid.
[31] *Abst.* 2. 37. 1.

simple (ἁπλούστερος), pure (καταρώτερος), and entirely self-sufficient (αὐταρκέστατος).[32] One who approaches him must be really and ritually pure.[33] This purity is brought about when man has extirpated his passions, begins to be nourished by knowledge of divine things, and these in turn make him divine because of his correct notions of the divine. Man is therefore sanctified by an intellectual sacrifice.[34]

To be mortal means to exist in a body. Already in *Phil. or.*—if indeed it was written before *De reg. an.*—Christ is disqualified as a deity. As we have seen, he was a good and wise mortal (*Civ. Dei* 19. 23). In *De reg. an.* we find that Porphyry hated the concept of the incarnation,[35] and his reasons are clear in light of the above. Thus he could easily dispense with Christ as the *via universalis animae liberandae*, although he searched for such a universal way in *philosophia verissima*, the moral practices of the Indians, and the Chaldaean initiations, and finally concluded that it exists but simply had never come to his attention.[36] His own solution appears to have been achieved in the development of a twofold soteriological system: the Platonic way of salvation delineated above was retained with some modifications (he rejected the concept of the transmigration of the soul into the bodies of animals) for the philosopher; and the theurgical purifications strongly indebted to Chaldaean theology for the non-philosopher. The latter did not enable the soul to return to God. These rites purify only the spiritual part of the soul which receives images of corporeal things, but they do not lead to immortality.[37] Finally, most probably because of his philological training and his personal interests in comparative religious studies, Porphyry paid far more attention to the religious traditions of his culture than both Plato and Plotinus. For example, we find a refined exegesis of the myths using the allegorical method of interpretation in his works.[38] He appears to have maintained fairly consistently that the myths contain

[32] *Abst.* 1. 57. 3.
[33] Ibid.
[34] Ibid. 2. 45. 4.
[35] *Civ. Dei* 10. 28 f.
[36] Ibid. 10. 32; See J. J. O'Meara, 'Indian Wisdom and Porphyry's Search for a Universal Way', in R. Harris (ed.), *Neoplatonism and Indian Thought* (1982), 5–25.
[37] Ibid. 10. 9. See E. des Places, 'Éléments de sotériologie orientale dans le Platonisme à la fin de l'antiquité', in U. Bianchi and M. Vermaseren (eds.), *La soteriologia dei culti orientali nell'Impero Romano* (1982), 243–53.
[38] *PE* 3–4; On the allegorical interpretation see P. Sellew, 'Ancilles or Christ? Porphyry and Didymus in Debate over Allegorical Interpretation', *HTR* 82: 1 (1989), 79–100.

and convey, albeit obscurely, the reality of the divine realm.[39] Whether related to his philosophy or to his religious treatises, this great respect for τὴν παλαιὰν σοφίαν represents a constant theme in his writings. We may give six principal features of his system which are important for the present enquiry:

1. An emphasis upon human need of the divine in the salvific process.
2. The necessity to flee all contact with the body.
3. A respect for the religious traditions of the past which includes the Greek religious literature.
4. An attempt to provide a *via salutis animae universalis* to all people.
5. A total rejection of Christ as divine and therefore as the saviour of man.
6. The importance of having the correct concepts of deity.

II. *The Response of Eusebius and Augustine to Porphyry: General Observations*

As we have already noted in the preceding chapter, a principal opponent of Eusebius in *PE* and *DE* is Porphyry. It is important briefly to outline the principal themes inherent in Porphyry's anti-Christian position in *PE* 1–5, and Eusebius' response to it. In *PE* 1. 2 the pagan accusation appears that the Christians are atheists and impious for apostatizing from the ancestral gods revered by every nation. Eusebius then observes, after quoting from the *CC* text that praised Sanchuniathon's history of the Jews, that the latter writer did not treat God or the heavenly powers as divine, but as mortals who were also wicked.[40] After citing from Philo's *History of the Jews* covering the history and names of the Phoenician gods (*PE* 1. 10), and taking information from Diodorus (*PE* 2. 1) and Clement of Alexandria (2. 3) to criticize Egyptian concepts of deity, he turns to Greek theology. He first affirms that Christians have been rescued from such delusions as if from a disease by the grace of Almighty God, the ineffable power of the Saviour's teaching, and sound reasoning. The latter is a response to Porphyry's remark that Christians

---

[39] *De ant. nymph.* 18: 'but when we consider the great wisdom of antiquity, and how much Homer excelled in an accurate knowledge of every virtue, it must not be denied that he has obscurely indicated the images of things of a more divine nature in the fiction of a fable.'

[40] *PE* 1. 9. See M. Smith, 'A Hidden Use of Porphyry's History of Philosophy in Eusebius' *Preparatio Evangelica*', *JTS* 39 (1988), 494–504.

only have an unreasoning faith.[41] The purpose of this divine deliverance is to prevent the adorable and divine name of God being honoured with dead mortals who were not only unscrupulous, but also incontinent, wanton, cruel, and even insane. It is impious to degrade God's name to male and female parts of the human body, to the nature of brute beasts, and to honour as divine inhuman crimes which result in severe penalties if they are committed by humans (*PE* 2. 4). An announcement that he will consider the Greek interpretations of the gods to ascertain whether they carry anything worthy of the gods ends book 2. Before citing a Porphyrian text and after he has criticized the physical explanations of the gods given mainly by Plutarch (3. 1–3), he concludes that the names of the elements are those of dead mortals. He again introduces into this theme the immoralities of the deities and wonders why the Greeks have given to the elements the immoral practices of mortals, 'acts which bear upon their very face mortality and human passion'.[42]

It is obvious that Eusebius is offering to his pagan opponents evidence as to why the Christians do not worship their deities, resting his case upon their mortality and anthropopathic behaviour. In *PE* 3. 5, after citing *Abst.* 4. 9, he argues against Porphyry's position in this work that men and animals have a share in reason. This is important to note for Arnobius responds to the same concept. Porphyry's allegorization of an Orphic hymn to Zeus, which enumerates the god's bodily parts, receives criticism in 3. 10. What rational man would address god in this way, especially since god is incorporeal. In *PE* 3. 10 divine incorporeality is put in contradistinction to the human body. The soul is both rational and immortal and preserves an image of God. It is also immaterial, incorporeal, and capable of virtue and wisdom. This stress upon the incorporeal nature of God is a direct response to Porphyry who saw a likeness between man's body and God's mind. The complete separation of the nature of God from all perishable matter and the necessity to contemplate him in thought and silence, make it clear that Eusebius is employing Porphyrian concepts against Porphyry to establish that the Christians have the right concept of God, and they therefore correctly worship him. We analyse below similar concepts in Arnobius, especially his use of Porphyry's Pythagorean silence as a means of contemplating the divine. Note that Eusebius has made the same assertion in *PE* 3. 6: Jesus has taught mankind to worship God with the right notions: his

[41] *PE* 1. 2; 1. 3.
[42] *PE* 3. 3.

nature is incorporeal and intelligent. He began the passage by affirming that the Greeks did not know anything about the truly divine, incorporeal, and intelligent natures. After giving lengthy quotes from Porphyry's *On Images* (*PE* 3. 11), he again stresses the divine incorporeality, Porphyry's attempt to allegorize the myths, and wonders why his opponents do not reject the myths if they claim that they correctly worship God (3. 13). He again concludes that right worship of God manifests itself in purified thoughts, correct doctrines, the impassibility of the soul, and by growing as far as possible like God. The gist is that the fundamental concepts inherent in the myths are incompatible with the correct concept of deity, and are therefore not conducive to growing like God in contemplation. Using Porphyry's oracles enumerating the births of various deities derived from *Phil. or.*, he accentuates their births from human women (*PE* 3. 14) and their human passions (*PE* 3. 15). He contrasts these ideas with the true sacrifices that men everywhere now offer to God: holy prayers, purified thoughts, and a soul free from passions (4. 4).

He now begins to show how inconsistent Porphyry was on the subject of sacrifice. Porphyry specifically used the oracles of the gods in *Phil. or.* to defend this practice (*PE* 4. 7–9), but he argued against it in *Abst.* (*PE* 4. 10–12). The basic elements of this (Porphyrian) definition of correct worship are:[43] nothing related to the senses can be offered to the High God; an apophatic understanding of the divine (cf. *Adv. nat.* 3. 19); and the importance of worshipping God in the impassibility of the soul with pure thoughts and silence. In what follows in *PE* 4. 12–15, Eusebius contrasts Porphyry's defence of the anthropomorphic and anthropopathic deities in *Phil. or.* There is nothing worthy of the divine, he argues, in the concept of deities who can be dragged down by mortals; who are capable of compulsion by humans (*PE* 5. 9); who, Porphyry proves, are enslaved to passions (*PE* 5. 15). If they were real deities, they would only enter the thought in the human soul, and that thought should be purified from every filth and stain.

We now turn to *De Civitate Dei* 8–10 to observe the main features of Porphyry's attack and Augustine's response. Platonists believe in the divine immutability (8. 6). The corporeal–spiritual antithesis is then analysed. Plato thus defined the good as living in conformity with virtue, to know God and imitate him whose nature is incorporeal (8. 8). In 8. 12 the purpose for writing is given: should one worship one God or

---

[43] He quotes *Abst.* 2. 34 in *PE* 4. 11.

many? After giving Plato's conception of the gods as good beings, honourable and allied with the wise in the fellowship of virtue (8. 13), Augustine further defines them, following the classic Platonic doctrine, as not being subject to human emotions and as being far removed from them.[44] Thus all passions are alien to the nature of a divine being, an argument which we have already seen clearly developed by Arnobius in *Adv. nat.* 1 and 3–7 (i.e. R1–6). Relying upon the demonology of Apuleius, Augustine maintains that demons are *animae passivae* and therefore experience all kinds of passions and mental agitations; gods are not of this nature, being wise and virtuous.[45] In 9. 6 he begins to prove why such demons cannot be accepted as genuine intermediaries between gods and men.[46] Why turn to these disturbed beings when they obviously cannot help man to improve his moral conduct? (We observe below that Arnobius similarly argues in respect of the gods.) The main problem with Apuleian demonology is that, although he got the incorporeal and corporeal antithesis right, he nevertheless showed that demons were unable to offer moral assistance to humans due to their anthropopathic behaviour.[47] Thus Apuleius' demonology, in so far as it applies to soteriology, is actually incompatible with the Platonic doctrine of being like God.

We have already noticed that *Civ. Dei* 10 principally attacks Porphyry's soteriological concepts, and true sacrifice is a central theme. For the non-philosopher Porphyry envisaged a way of salvation that employed the practice of theurgy which won the favour of the gods, angels, and demons. Arnobius gives the same three in *Adv. nat.* 2. 35. 17 f., and Festugière has already suggested the connection between this text and *Civ. Dei* 10. 19. Augustine then finds objectionable Porphyry's attributing to the gods the ability to be subject to *perturbationes passionesque* (10. 9). He then compares Porphyry's doctrine with that of Apuleius to prove

---

[44] *Civ. Dei* 8. 14: 'Habent [sc. daemones] enim cum diis communem inmortalitatem corporum, animorum autem hominibus passiones.'

[45] Ibid. 8. 17: 'Deos vero ideo dicunt istas perturbationes non perpeti, quia non solum aeterni, verum etiam beati sunt.'

[46] Ibid. 9. 6: 'Subiecta est ergo mens daemonum passionibus libidinum formidinum irarum atque huiusmodi ceteris. Quae igitur pars in eis libera est composque sapientiae qua placeant diis et ad bonorum morum similitudinem hominibus consulant, cum eorum mens passionum vitiis subiugata et oppressa, quidquid rationis naturaliter habet, ad fallendum et decipiendum tanto acrius intendat, quanto eam magis possidet nocendi cupiditas?'

[47] Ibid. 9. 17.

how far from the true Platonic tradition the former had deviated.[48] It is interesting in light of the present enquiry that Bidez noted years ago that Arnobius is the only writer who has revealed a vestige of doctrines derived from Porphyry's *De reg. an.*, independent of Augustine. Other scholars such as (in chronological order) Courcelle, O'Meara, Fortin, Frend, and Beatrice have agreed, the former two offering convincing evidence that Porphyry is the principal adversary behind *Adv. nat.* 2, and Beatrice makes the same connection with book 1.[49] The texts given by Bidez which appear to be criticizing the kinds of theurgical practices mentioned in *Civ. Dei* are:

Adv. nat. 2. 62. 6–9: . . . neque quod magi spondent, commendaticias habere se preces quibus emollitae nescio quae potestates vias faciles praebeant ad caelum contendentibus subvolare . . .

Adv. nat. 2. 13. 33–6: Quid illi sibi volunt secretarum artium ritus, quibus adfamini nescio quas potestates, ut sint vobis placidae neque ad sedes remeantibus patrias obstacula impeditionis opponant?

Adv. nat. 2. 62. 1–6: Neque illud obrepat aut spe vobis aeria blandiatur, quod ab sciolis nonnullis et plurimum sibi adrogantibus dicitur, deo esse se gnatos nec fati obnoxios legibus, si vitam restrictius egerint, aulum sibi eius patere, ac post hominis functionem prohibente se nullo tamquam in sedem referri patritam.

As we have already noted, the use of *aulam* in the third text has a number of parallels with Chaldaean texts. Also, the fact that Arnobius appears to be attacking Chaldaean–Neoplatonic theurgical practices sheds further light upon his argument that a divine being *ipso facto* cannot experience any passion or mental agitations. Thus also Augustine in *Civ. Dei* 10. 11, and Eusebius in *PE* 5. 10, after both have attacked Porphyry's conception in *Phil. or.* that gods are capable of suffering such passions, can use the same author's *Ep. An.* to show that he held the opinion that an incorporeal divine being cannot be enticed by mortals, or that it is by nature impassible. And according to Methodius, who is responding to the *CC*,[50] Porphyry used the concept of divine impassibility in the *CC* to argue against the doctrine of the incarnation: Jesus was not impassible; he therefore was not divine. As we have seen in Eusebius, Augustine, and Arnobius, the argument could easily

[48] Ibid. 10. 10. Cf. P. F. Beatrice, 'Quosdam Platonicorum Libros', *VC* 43 (1989), 248–81; and G. Luck, 'Theurgy and Forms of Worship in Neoplatonism', *RSM* (1989), 185–225.

[49] Courcelle (1954), 257 ff.; Fortin (1973); O'Meara (1959), 8 f.

[50] Methodius, *Contra Porphyrium*, Harnack *CC* fr. no. 84, in *GCS* 27. 503: Bonwetsch.

be turned against the Neoplatonist by using his own works against him.

Porphyry thought that he had good reasons to reject the incarnation of Christ. His soteriological system demanded one to flee the body, to overcome the passions, to involve oneself in pure thought of the divine.[51] But the Christians claimed that their saviour was born with a human body. Augustine responds by showing that God's love provided a way, by means of the incarnation, for men to come to him who was far from the mortal.[52] And his response to Porphyry's search for the *via universalis animae liberandae* is to demonstrate that (1) Christ is the one way of salvation for the whole person, soul, mind, and body;[53] and (2) Christ is the only way of salvation granted to all nations universally by God's compassion.[54]

III. *The Importance of Evidence: A Critical Examination of Religious Concepts*

According to Eusebius and Augustine, a basic method of Porphyry in combating Christian ideas was the use of his opponents' religious texts against them to prove the falsity of their claim to the truth. We have seen that Arnobius uses the same method against the pagans. Furthermore, Porphyry's basic premiss in the *CC* appears to have been that Christians were unable to offer any clear evidence of the certainty of their beliefs.[55] This attitude coheres with his remark about Ammonius Saccas: he was a Christian and had been brought up among the faithful by his parents, but he gave this teaching up as soon as he began to be a thinking man and study philosophy.[56] He argued that there is no rational proof to support the Christian faith. Christians too simplistically assent to it without any examination. Faith is unreasonable because it is not supported by a clear demonstration of the evidence of the things it promises. As noted in Chapter 1 Porphyry was therefore essentially

[51] *Civ. Dei* 10. 29: 'omne corpus esse fugiendum ut anima possit beata permanere cum Deo.'
[52] Ibid.
[53] Ibid. 10. 32.
[54] Ibid.: 'Haec est igitur animae liberandae universalis via, id est universis gentibus divina miseratione concessa.'
[55] *PE* 1. 1 = Harnack *CC* fr. no. 1, which may have come from *Phil. or.* as well: see Wilken (1979), 127. Appendices III and IV are to be read in conjunction with this section.
[56] Eus. *HE* 6. 19. 5–7.

calling upon his enemies to offer rational proof that the tenets of their faith were true. This seemed only fair because he and later Neoplatonists in North Africa were able to offer many proofs to demonstrate that their Graeco-Roman religious traditions were firmly established in the truth.[57] And these proofs included the miracles of the deities recorded in the annals and other authoritative sources.

It would be unnecessary to cite all the passages of the *PE* and *DE* where it appears that Eusebius is responding to Porphyry's accusation that Christians cannot prove their beliefs. There is ample evidence in both works to establish this position.[58] Indeed, we may give one example, the evidence of the universal extension of the Christian religion, which is found in Eusebius, Augustine, and Arnobius. Note the following which are paraphrases of the texts:

DE 3. 5: Before he cites the Hecatean Oracle in 3. 7, and responding to the charge that Christ did not work the miracles which his disciples relate, he states that the ignorant disciples worked no deception (i.e. they did not use magic) by teaching his deeds in country, town, the queen of cities (Rome), the Persian, Armenian, Parthian, and Scythian races, some reaching the ends of the world, going to the Indians, crossing the ocean, going to the British Isles: this was not the work of magicians.

Adv. nat. 2. 12: Arnobius refers to the public miracles performed by Christ and his disciples, united in the most disparate nations to agree to the same faith: in India, among the Seres, Persians, Medes, in Arabia, Egypt, Asia, Syria, among the Galatians, Parthians, in Achaea, Macedonia, Epirus, in all the islands and provinces, and in Rome too. Peter's encounter with Simon Magus follows, and he stresses that Peter vanquished his power only by the words spoken from his mouth.

De cons. evan. 1. 32. 49: Augustine has referred to the applauders of Christ in 1. 7, specifically naming Porphyry and noting his 'praise' of Christ in the Hecatean Oracle. In this passage he now asks what those perverse applauders of Christ and slanderers of Christians have to say to the facts about the biblical predictions of the Lord's advent: did Christ cause these to be fulfilled by magic? The Church has extended to all nations, enlarged her tent beyond Rome and its empire, to the territories of the Persians, Indians, and other barbarian nations.

It is necessary to give a few examples of Augustine's response to Porphyry's criticism found in *De cons. evan.* He first acknowledges that his opponents attack Christian scripture with a more than ordinary

---

[57] *Civ. Dei* 10. 17.
[58] e.g. *PE* 4. 1; 4. 4; 4. 10; 9. 1–2; 10. 4; *DE* 1. 1; 1. 5; 2. 2; 3. 1; 3. 2; 3. 5.

and careful investigation. The purpose is to show that the Bible is contradictory.[59] As Eusebius had done in the *DE*, Augustine pays acute attention to the need to provide evidence from scripture to show that this is not true. Hence we often read that he wishes to demonstrate the credibility of a particular text;[60] or he uses a phrase like, 'it has been acutely observed' in providing his proof;[61] or that a certain text requires the greatest attention and carefulness, or careful inquiry.[62] We recall that Porphyry argued that Christians were unable by *clear demonstration* to provide evidence of the truth of the things *promised* in their faith. In *De cons. evan.* 1. 30. 46, Augustine uses Psalm 19: 6 to *prove* that the things *promised* therein about the name of Christ spreading to all nations are now set forth as accomplished facts in the *clearest light.*

Not a single biblical text is used in Arnobius' attack upon pagan religious practices and ideas in *Adv. nat.* 3–7. This may very well prove to be a great asset in our attempts to understand Porphyry the polemicist, especially his critical methods employed in the *CC*. For it is probably in Arnobius' attack in 3–7 that we see a reflection of the same kinds of arguments used and methods of literary criticism developed by Porphyry in his anti-Christian work. Both kept the interpretation of their opponents' scriptures at none other than a literal level: Porphyry attacked the Alexandrian allegorical interpretation of the Bible,[63] and Arnobius refutes the same kind of method used by his opponents.[64] Both demonstrate the inconsistencies, falsehoods, stupidity, contradictions, and ridiculous ideas inherent in the literature of their enemies. And both were acutely aware of the importance of offering proof of the truth of their own religious literature and the falsity of the myths/scripture of their opponents. Finally, two significant observations are necessary. First, the *Adversus nationes* possesses a plethora of passages in which Arnobius offers a clear demonstration of evidence to establish the truth of the Christian religion, and the reader is referred to Appendix III below for a representative list. After carefully analysing these data, it should be fairly clear that Arnobius is responding to the same Porphyrian

[59] Aug. *De cons. evan.*, *Praef.* 2. 1: See esp. now R. B. Harris, 'Faith and Reason in the Early Neoplatonists', *DA* 1 (1987), 6–17.

[60] *De cons. evan.* 2. 2. 4.

[61] Ibid. 2. 4. 8.

[62] Ibid. Cf. 1. 32. 49 f.; see the excellent analysis in M. J. Hollerich, 'Myth and History in Eusebius' *De Vita Constantini*', *HTR* 82: 4 (1989), 421–45.

[63] Eus. *HE* 6. 19. 4.

[64] *Adv. nat.* 3. 29–35; 5. 32–45. See B. Amata, 'Mito e paideia in Arnobio di Sicca', in S. Felici (ed.), *CUNC* 35–50. See Appendix III below.

criticism of Christian faith as one finds in Eusebius and Augustine. But Arnobius does not stop by simply providing evidence for the truth of Christianity, in books 3–7 he also mounts an offensive by demanding clearly established proof from the pagans that their concepts of the gods are based upon facts. Again the number of passages that can be given is very large, and the reader is referred to Appendix IV for a representative list.

We may conclude that Arnobius has responded to Porphyry's criticism of Christian faith by using the same basic argument against him, namely that it is the pagans who accept the myths about the gods without reason and examination; a careful analysis of these stories proves that the pagans are confused, uncertain, and entirely inconsistent as to the right concept of deity; and the proof of the premises of his argument is derived directly from the myths themselves. As Porphyry used the miracles of the gods to prove their divinity, Arnobius used the miracles of Christ which are superior to those of the gods, to prove that he was divine. As the Neoplatonist meticulously studied Christian scripture to disprove its sacred origin, Arnobius also paid acute attention to the details of the myths to demonstrate that nothing divine appears in them. Like Porphyry before him, he was not able to allow his opponents the freedom to explain away any piece of evidence from their religious literature which might support his argument. And the fact that Arnobius was able to demonstrate the inconsistencies about a particular story appearing in several different sources, supports his contention that there is no agreement in the myths, one does not know what to believe, and one cannot find any truth in them about the gods. We may recall that Porphyry's criticism of the Synoptic Gospels employed the same kind of argumentation, and it would not be unreasonable to suggest that Arnobius has responded to this specific attack of the Neoplatonist.

There are a good number of general similarities between Eusebius and Arnobius. Like Eusebius, the rhetor attempts to demonstrate that Christians have had good reasons, and have used right judgement, in abandoning the religious *mos maiorum*. Both exonerate the Christians from the charge of atheism and provide evidence that the pagans should be accused in this manner. Like Eusebius, who we know was definitely attacking Porphyry, Arnobius attacked the allegorical method. Both also show the great disparity between the Christian conception of the High God who is incorporeal and impassible, and the pagan notions of the gods who are both corporeal and subject to passions, which we have seen are Porphyrian concepts. Finally, both Eusebius and Arnobius attempt to demonstrate that the Christians have the truly spiritual worship of God.

The same can be said about Augustine and Arnobius. Both argue that since the gods are subject to emotions, they cannot help man in his morality. They also stress the proof of the divine origin of Christianity on the basis of its universal extension. Yet it is in Augustine's response to Porphyry's criticism of the Bible that we find a good number of significant parallels between the methods used by both Arnobius and the Neoplatonist in the attempts to destroy the credibility of each other's sacred literature. Augustine notes that his opponents attack scripture with an extraordinary investigation, and Arnobius uses the same method in attacking paganism. Porphyry tried to show the contradictions of scripture; that the stories were silly, false, and incredible; that the concept of Jesus as divine was philosophically disreputable; that an individual text within a Gospel, as well as similar stories found in the synoptics, disclosed too many contradictions and inconsistencies for the Bible to be accepted as truth. As we have seen, Arnobius made the same points in his attack upon pagan religious literature. The main objective of both arguments—to prove to their opponents that they must seek the *via salutis animae universalis* in a source other than their own sacred literature—is the same.

IV. 'Christus Via Salutis Universalis Animae': The Geographical Argument

A basic theme common to the polemics of Eusebius, Augustine, and Arnobius is the universal extension of Christianity. The first accusation to which Arnobius responds by referring to the geographical expansion of the faith appears in *Adv. nat.* 1. 6. 1–5:

Actually, regarding the wars which you say were begun on account of hatred of our religion, it would not be difficult to prove that after Christ was heard on earth, not only did they not increase but in great measure were reduced as a result of the repression of fierce passions.

Eusebius (*PE* 1. 4) also argues that after the advent of Christ, prepared by the *Pax Romana*, wars have decreased. Arnobius stresses the ability of Christ's teachings to help humans overcome their violent passions. Here only six chapters into his work he begins to develop one line of argumentation inherent in his soteriology: Christ can help humankind to extirpate such passions; the gods cannot because they are capable of suffering them and therefore are mortal. He continues (1. 6. 14 f.) by affirming that if men would lend an ear to 'His wholesome and peaceful commandments' the world would live in 'most placid tranquility' and come together in 'wholesome harmony'. Eusebius also asserts that people of all sexes, ages, and classes lend ears to Christ's words which enable them to overcome vices of all kinds.[65] The central idea in both is that Christianity benefits people everywhere in the world. And note Augustine's case against Porphyry: 'Haec est igitur animae liberandae universalis via, id est universis gentibus divina miseratione concessa.'[66] It appears that one of the nuances of *via universalis animae liberandae*, according to Porphyry's quest to find it, was strictly geographical. That is to say, he appears to have searched for a way of salvation which might be applicable to all nations and races in the world.

In *Adv. nat.* 1. 42, which we have argued was written as a direct response to the Hecatean Oracle and Porphyry's commentary upon it, Arnobius again offers proof of Christ's divinity on the basis of the unanimity among those who saw him perform miracles in daylight. He refers to the eyewitness account as being superior to mere opinions.[67] Eusebius, immediately before giving the same Porphyrian accusation ridiculing Christian faith in *DE* 1 as he gives in *PE* 1. 1, challenges his opponents to see with their eyes the miracles of Christ attested in the Gospels. And both writers refer to the existence of Christians among the Persians and Scythians; to the pagan accusation that Christians have apostatized from worshipping the gods, both mentioning the Greek mysteries, the cities, and the country where the gods are worshipped;[68] and that Christians deserve severe punishment for not worshipping them.[69] Porphyry in *Phil. or.* evidently argued that traditional polytheism was the true way of salvation because it was to the gods that 'whole peoples, both rulers and ruled, in cities and in country districts, offer animal sacrifices'.[70] Much like Arnobius in 5. 29, Eusebius again refers to the polytheistic worship of the gods in temples, in the form of mysteries, and both in city and country regions, before attacking

---

[65] *PE* 1. 4; see Evangeliou (1989), 64 ff.

[66] *Civ. Dei* 10. 32.

[67] *Adv. nat.* 1. 57.

[68] *DE* 3. 6; *Adv. nat.* 1. 16; 5. 29. 5 f., which should be compared with *PE* 1. 2.

[69] Eusebius also refers to the presence of the Christian religion in cities and towns in *PE* 4. 4 and *DE* 3. 7.

[70] *PE* 4. 10.

Porphyry in *PE* 14. 10. We note that Arnobius offers similar evidence in *Adv. nat.* 2. 5. 7–14.[71]

According to Arnobius, all nations have been evangelized in a brief period of time. Not even barbaric nations have been neglected. The result of this evangelization has been the abandonment of harsh behaviour and the adoption of peace brought about by the love of Christ. These are the main points of Arnobius' argument here.[72] Note that in *Phil. or.*, Porphyry asserted through an oracle of Apollo that the Greeks were in error in finding the salvation of the soul, but the Barbarians found many paths to the gods.[73] Two groups were the Egyptians and Phoenicians, and perhaps this gives us a clue as to why Eusebius[74] states that these races started evil polytheistic delusions; and that Greeks *and* Barbarians together adhere to the word of Jesus Christ.[75] He later in the same passage says that the Greeks and the most savage Barbarians 'and those who dwell in the utmost parts of the earth' have overcome their 'irrational brutality' and live now according to a 'wise philosophy'.[76] The spreading of Christianity throughout the world in a brief amount of time is emphasized in the *DE* as well.[77]

In the list of miracles performed by Christ given in *Adv. nat.* 1. 46, Arnobius attempts to prove the divinity of Christ on the basis of his teaching the disciples the true religion, who immediately filled the entire world. We have noted in Chapter 1 that a major argument developed by the pagans of this period against Christianity was the reasonableness of rejecting the Christians' claim to superior truth on the basis of Christ's and his disciples' ability to perform miracles. The disciples were given the authority to perform miracles without the use of any material aids or magic arts.[78] We have already noted that Porphyry in the *CC* attributed the miracles of the *rusticanos* to the practice of magic, an accusation which he had already made in *Phil. or.* The main points of Arnobius' argument in 1. 50 are: (1) Christ not only performed

---

[71] 'Nonne vel haec saltem fidem vobis faciunt argumenta credendi, quod iam per omnes terras in tam brevi temporis spatio inmensi nominis huius sacramenta diffusa sunt; quod nulla iam natio est tam barbari moris et mansuetudinem nesciens, quae non eius amore versa molliverit asperitatem suam et in placidos sensus adsumpta tranquillitate migraverit.'
[72] *Adv. nat.* 2. 5.
[73] *PE* 14. 10: a quotation from *Phil. or.*
[74] *PE* 1. 6.
[75] *PE* 1. 4.
[76] Ibid.
[77] *DE* 1. 6: *bis*; 3. 2; cf. 1. 2; 2. 2.
[78] *Adv. nat.* 1. 50.

miracles himself, but he also gave this power to his disciples; (2) the disciples have been empowered to do this in Christ's name; (3) both Christ and his followers are exonerated from the charge of practising magic; (4) he specifically chose fishermen, workers, farmers, and uneducated persons; (5) these were sent through various nations of the world to perform miracles; (6) they did not use any material aids, only Christ's name. If we turn to Eusebius, in the section of the *DE* which immediately follows his citing of the Hecatean Oracle (3. 7), we find the same points being made: Jesus was no sorcerer; proof of the divine power shown by Christ's selection of fishermen, rustic, common, and uneducated men; the disciples were empowered to work miracles in Jesus' name; they went to all nations and rapidly made many disciples in his name;[79] and Christ and his disciples healed by a word or the name of Jesus. Finally, Arnobius ends his text by referring to the amazement of those present when Christ and his followers performed their miracles, and Eusebius accentuates the astonishment of the spectators of the disciples' miracles in the name of Jesus.

A final observation needs to be made concerning the anti-Christian propaganda which focused upon Peter. We can be fairly certain as to why Eusebius and Arnobius rather frequently emphasize the short time it has taken for Christianity to extend throughout the world.[80] First, note the general remark in *Civ. Dei* 10. 32, attributed to Porphyry, that the persecution would soon destroy the faith. Also, in *Civ. Dei* we find that Porphyry asserted that Peter ensured by practising magic that Christianity would exist for exactly 365 years.[81] Augustine acknowledges the many pagans who believed in this oracular prediction[82] in North Africa. (We analyse the charge that Peter was a magician below.) In *Adv. nat.* 2. 6, Arnobius also refers to those who unite in *credulitas* throughout the world, and this appears in the book where he attacks the philosophical *via salutis* and two chapters before a text possessing many elements in common with Eusebius' list of examples of pagan faith. There follows a defence of Christian *credulitas* in 2. 11: the pagans

---

[79] Eusebius here, and Arnobius in 4. 13, where the latter is undoubtedly referring to Chaldaean invocations (cf. Lewy's *rulers* in *COTh* 202), both give Egyptians, Persians, Armenians, Chaldaeans, and Indians in reference to worship of the One God.

[80] Cf. *DE* 3. 5 and *Adv. nat.* 2. 12.

[81] *Civ. Dei* 18. 53. See H. Chadwick, 'Oracles of the End in the Conflict of Paganism and Christianity in the Fourth Century', in E. Lucchesi and H. Saffrey (eds.), *Memorial A. J. Festugière* (1985), 125–9; and M. V. Anastos, 'Porphyry's Attack on the Bible', in L. Wallach (ed.), *The Classical Tradition* (Ithaca, NY, 1966), 421–50.

[82] *Civ. Dei* 18. 54.

addressed believed in Plato, Cronius, and Numenius, which is an apparent allusion to Porphyry or a Porphyrian sect; and so Christians believe in and assent to Christ. This is undoubtedly a response to *CC* fragment 1.[83]

We recall that Arnobius mentions one Christian predecessor by name in the *Adv. nat.*, Peter, and that he might well have been the patron saint of Sicca during Arnobius' life. The text is 2. 12, and we analyse first lines 7–13:

Virtutes [sc. Christi] sub oculis positae et inaudita illa vis rerum, vel quae ab ipso fiebant palam vel ab eius praeconibus celebrabantur in orbe toto, ea subdidit adpetitionum flammas et ad unius credulitatis adsensum mente una concurrere gentes et populos fecit et moribus dissimillimas nationes.

Observe his remark that Christ could not be thought to make any clear promises if he were to surmise like the philosophers,[84] which appears to be a direct response to Porphyry's assertion that Christians cannot offer a clear demonstration that the promises of the faith are true. In the passage above, we again find an emphasis upon the public (*palam*) manifestation of both the miracles of Christ and those of his disciples, *in orbe toto*, which is a recurrent theme in books 1–2. Eusebius makes the same point in vivid detail. In response to those who claim that the disciples did not carry on their ministry in public,[85] he says that they stood in the middle of the city in the Agora and preached to passers-by with a loud voice. He then makes use of the universal redemption theme and emphasizes the disciples' miracles.[86] Arnobius above argues that Christ's power has enabled man to vanquish his passions, the same point made by Eusebius.[87]

Arnobius then enumerates the many nations to which the miracle-working power of Christ and his disciples has spread, and similar passages are found in *DE* 3. 5 and *De cons. evan.* 1. 32. 49. The confrontation between Peter and Simon Magus follows.[88] Peter conquered his adversary by his mouth when he uttered the name of Christ.[89] The description of an injured and disgraced Simon, who eventually

---

[83] On Porphyry, Numenius, *et al.*, see M. J. Edwards, 'Porphyry and the Intelligible Triad', *JHS* 110 (1990), 14–25.
[84] *Adv. nat.* 2. 12. 4 f.
[85] οὐ κατὰ πλῆθος: *PG* 22. 241.
[86] *DE* 3. 7.
[87] Ibid. 3. 5.
[88] *Adv. nat.* 2. 12.
[89] Ibid. 2. 12. 24.

commits suicide, ends the story. Two questions arise here: why did he insert the story here, and what is its central message?

Augustine may help to solve the problem. In *Civ. Dei* 18. 53 f., he responds to Porphyry's special hatred for Peter. O'Meara's suggestion that his source is *Phil. or.* is undoubtedly correct.[90] Thus the oracles of the gods did not accuse Christ of sacrilege, but 'Petrum autem maleficia fecisse subiungunt, ut coeretur Christi nomen per trecentos sexaginta quinque annos, deinde conpleto memorato numero annorum, sine mora sumeret finem.'[91] The specific charge is that Peter ensured that Christ's name would be worshipped, and he did this by practising magic.[92] We recall that Arnobius insists upon Peter's performance of his miracle in his encounter with Simon by speaking the name of Christ. In *Civ. Dei* 18. 54, Augustine informs his opponents that the faith first ignited Jerusalem with extraordinary success, thousands being converted to the name of Christ with bewildering promptness. He then adds: 'Hoc si nullis magicis artibus factum est, quor credere dubitant eadem virtute divina per totum mundum id fieri potuisse, qua hoc factum est?' Remember Arnobius' 'vel quae ab ipso fiebant palam vel ab eius praeconibus celebrabantur in orbe toto.' And Eusebius may be responding to the same Porphyrian argument: these words were said in a corner (after mentioning that the disciples will triumph through the name of Christ!), he supposes, so how was it possible that his disciples left their own country and converted people of every race in the world?[93] This he says after citing the Hecatean Oracle. Porphyry's difficulty was what to do with *per totum mundum*, or how to explain the universal diffusion of Christianity. It is quite clear from Augustine that he did not accept the idea that the same divine power which had worked in Jerusalem, which he easily explained away as being due to Peter's use of magic, could have manifested itself throughout the whole world.[94] We again see the Porphyrian wedge working its way between Christ and his disciples to show the great credibility gap. And again it is an argument derived from *Phil. or.* with which we are confronted. Augustine, like Arnobius, apparently felt the need to give a story, albeit from the Bible, depicting Peter who healed only through the *name* of Jesus.[95] And he,

---

[90] O'Meara (1959), 67–72.
[91] *Civ. Dei* 18. 53.
[92] Ibid.
[93] *DE* 3. 7.
[94] *Civ. Dei* 18. 54.
[95] Ibid.

like Arnobius in 1. 50, shows that the same miracles performed by Christ were performed by his disciples without the use of magic.[96] We conclude that Arnobius and Augustine are responding to the same accusation derived from *Phil. or.*, which attributed Peter's ability to perform miracles to the use of magic.

By using the charge of magic against the disciples, by arguing that persecutions would bring about the end of Christianity, or that the religion was predicted to live 365 years, Porphyry could provide 'scientific evidence' to establish that it was not the *via universalis animae liberandae*. He appears to have been particularly committed to proving that its vast geographical extension throughout the Roman Empire did not have any divine connection or explanation. Conversely, Arnobius offers proof of Christ's deity to a great extent on the basis of his miracles performed without the use of magic; that the disciples were dependent upon the same power as he, and they did these works throughout the world in the name of Christ; and that therefore the Christian religion provided the only way of salvation to all people everywhere.

V. *'Christus Via Salutis Universalis Animae': The Philosophical Argument*

In *Civ. Dei* 10. 32 Augustine responds to Porphyry's attempts to discover a *via universalis animae liberandae* by showing how Christianity offers such a way. First, he affirms that it is the universal way for all nations, and we have analysed this concept in the preceding section. Second, he argues that the way of Christ purifies the whole person,[97] an interesting statement because Porphyry mentions purificatory sacrifices for soul and body in *Phil. or.*, and from the *Civ. Dei* we can deduce that he added to these the *via salutis* for the human intellect.[98] The latter provided a way for the philosopher, whereas through theurgical practices the non-philosopher could experience a purification of the soul.[99] It is possible that *Civ. Dei* 10. 32 and *PE* 14. 10 reveal that Porphyry also incorporated the human body in his soteriological system, but we need not go that far. First, we have already noted that his principal concern was to flee the body and escape through pure thought and silence to the intellectual

---

[96] *Civ. Dei* 18. 54.

[97] 'Haec via totum hominem mundat et inmortalitati mortalem ex omnibus quibus constat partibus praeparat.'

[98] *PE* 14. 10.

[99] *Civ. Dei* 10. 9.

realm. Second, by corporeal purifications in *Phil. or.*[100] he probably is referring to the Chaldaean concept of the 'salvation of the body', which Lewy has convincingly interpreted as 'a medical, not an eschatological term', which applies 'to the immunity against demonic infection with disease'.[101] Certain apotropaic rites, one being a kind of purificatory sacrifice, neutralized these demons.[102]

The principal soteriological text in the *Adv. nat.* is 2. 65. After affirming that it is Christ's power alone to grant salvation to human souls, he continues to develop the theme that Christ is the only *via salutis animae*:

> then you must also accept this necessarily from us, that from no one can the souls receive the power of life and of safety from harm except from Him whom the Most High King has placed over this duty and office. The Almighty Ruler has willed this to be the way of salvation, this, as it were, to be the door of life, through which alone is entrance to the light; and there is no other possibility, either of creeping in or walking in: everything else has been closed off and secured by an impregnable bulwark.[103]

In 2. 13 he lays the foundation of his attack upon the philosophical way of salvation. He addresses the followers of Mercury, Plato, and Pythagoras. The Platonic concept of the flight of the soul from the world of becoming to occupy itself in contemplating upon the divine is then attacked.[104] He notes the corporeal–incorporeal antithesis, that his opponents extirpate all passions from their souls, and the esoteric rites which enable the soul to make its journey back to its ancestral home. The latter very probably describes Chaldaean theurgical practices.[105] Noteworthy in the same passage is the remark that his philosophical opponents nail themselves to their bodies, which has already been established as a Porphyrian influence.[106]

---

[100] *PE* 14. 10.
[101] *COTh* 216.
[102] Ibid. 290.
[103] *Adv. nat.* 2. 65. 33–40: 'et hoc necesse a nobis est ut debeatis accipere, ab nullo animas posse vim vitae atque incolumitatis accipere nisi ab eo quam rex summus huic muneri officioque praefecit. Hanc omnipotens imperator esse voluit salutis viam, hanc vitae ut ita dixerim ianuam, per hanc solum est ingressus ad lucem neque alias datum est vel inrepere vel invadere ceteris omnibus clausis atque inexpugnabili arce munitis.'
[104] Ibid. 2. 13. 14–17.
[105] See R. M. Berchman, 'Arcana Mundi Between Balaam and Hecate: Prophecy, Divination, and Magic in Later Platonism', in D. Lull (ed.), SBL Seminar Papers (1989), 107–85.
[106] Fortin (1973), 218 ff.

He quickly comes to a major objective of book 2, which is to disprove the immortality of the soul. He develops this around the main theme of Christ the *via salutis animae*. In a rare moment when Arnobius actually criticizes Plato, he rejects the idea that an immortal being cannot suffer pain.[107] Put in contradistinction to this is his own belief in the *media qualitas animae* which he attributes to Plato.[108] Although souls are of an indeterminate nature, knowledge of the *Summus Rex* immortalizes them, otherwise they shall suffer for an indefinite period in a burning Gehenna after which time they shall perish.[109] This concept, described in *Adv. nat.* 2. 14, appears to have a Porphyrian–Chaldaean correspondence as well: according to Lewy, the Chaldaeans apparently believed in vicious demons 'who cast the soul after death into the abyss of Tartarus',[110] a concept he ties in with Porphyry's remark in *Ep. An.* 3, that the Chaldaeans invoked terrestrial subterranean deities.[111]

In 2. 25 he uses the ambiguous term *viri novi* to identify his opponents, and we can offer the following interpretation: this group refers to a Porphyrian–Chaldaean Neoplatonic movement in the process of establishing itself in North Africa probably during the last two decades of the third century AD. The word *novi* would therefore convey a chronological[112] and functional meaning. The latter relates to the mixture of Platonic philosophy and Chaldaean theology which might have appeared 'new' in the sense of 'strange' to Arnobius and his readers, and this also might explain why he frequently uses Plato against Porphyry. We see the same method being used in Eusebius and Augustine. This employment of Plato undoubtedly was successful in retorting Porphyry's 'credibility gap' which he tried to construct between Jesus and his disciples; and again Eusebius and Augustine also seem to enjoy not only disclosing to the world certain inconsistencies in the works of Porphyry, but also those found in Plato on the one hand and his so-called follower on the other.

---

[107] *Adv. nat.* 2. 14. 12–15.

[108] Ibid. 2. 36.

[109] Ibid. 1. 38; 1. 39; 2. 12; 2. 14; 2. 29; 2. 33 f.; 2. 36; 2. 46; 2. 53; 2. 54; 2. 61 f.; 2. 78.

[110] *COTh* 308.

[111] *COTh* 289 n. 112.

[112] As Fortin correctly argues in his article (1973). It is interesting that Eusebius also refers to Porphyry and his followers as the 'new men' (*neoi*), on which see P. F. Beatrice, 'Un oracle antichrétien chez Arnobe', in Y. de Andia (ed.), *Memorial Dom Jean Gribomont* (Rome, 1988), 107–29.

The basic concepts of the *viri novi* on the soul appear in 2. 15. 1–7, and it is important to give the Latin text:

Quare nihil est quod nos fallat, nihil quod nobis polliceatur spes causas, id quod a novis quibusdam dicitur viris er inmoderata sui opinione sublatis, animas immortales esse, domino rerum ac principi gradu proximas dignitatis, genitore illo ac patre prolatas, divinas sapientes doctas neque ulla iam corporis attrectatione continguas.

The emphasis to flee the body is, as already noted, a prominent feature of Porphyrian soteriology. The importance of maintaining one's moral integrity by controlling the passions is another aspect of this teaching, and note that the terms used (*cupiditas* and *libido*) also appear in his attack upon the anthropopathic behaviour of the gods of the myths.

Further evidence to establish that Porphyrian–Neoplatonic philo-sophical concepts are refuted in *Adv. nat.* 2 appears in 2. 16. He refutes the view that the human soul is immortal by asking his opponents to investigate who they are, which has already been interpreted as a direct response to *CC* fragment 1. Observe his next question: 'Are you willing, having laid aside partiality, to reach the conclusion in your silent thought that we are animate beings either in all respects like the rest or separated from them by no great difference?' This is a clear attack upon Porphyry's psychological concepts (i.e. the soul is immortal, divine, etc.) by using his argument, found in the *De Abstinentia*, that humans *and* animals possess reason, against him. Compare also Arnobius' 'animate beings' (*animantia*) and Porphyry's ἔμψυχος which are used to describe both humans and animals possessed with rational faculties.[113] The rhetor's 'silent thought' (*cogitationibus tacitis*) corresponds to Porphyry's use of the Pythagorean concept of silence as an inherent feature in his contemplation of the divine.[114] Note that he ends his argument by tactfully using a Platonic concept against Porphyry: the doctrine of the transmigration of human souls into the bodies of animals clearly demonstrates that men and animals do not share any appreciable difference in their natures. But a remark in *Civ. Dei* 10. 30 further qualifies Porphyry's position:

Si post Platonem aliquid emendare existimatur indignum, cur ipse Porphyrius nonnulla et non parva emendavit? Nam Platonem animas hominum post mortem

---

[113] Cf. *Abst.* 2. 33.
[114] Ibid. 2. 34. 2. See M. J. Edwards, 'Two Episodes in Porphyry's Life of Plotinus', *His* 40 (1991), 456–64.

revolvi usque ad corpora bestiarum scripsisse certissimum est. Hanc sententiam Porphyrii doctor tenuit et Plotinus; Pophyrio tamen iure displicuit. In hominum sane non sua quae dimiserant, sed alia nova corpora redire humanas animas arbitratus est.

The *alia nova corpora* coheres with the Porphyrian 'omne corpus esse fugiendum ut anima possit beata permanere cum Deo'.[115] Arnobius' diatribe continues through 2. 17–18, and as we have pointed out, the psychological experiment of *Adv. nat.* 2. 20–8, which attempts to disprove the Platonic doctrine of ἀνάμνησις, was probably written as a response to concepts found in Plotinus and Porphyry.

In *Adv. nat.* 2. 27 Arnobius specifically explains why the Platonic doctrines of recollection and the immortality of the soul are mutually and logically contradictory.[116] When the soul descends to take on corporeal existence and forgets the things of its former existence, the natural mutability of the soul proves that it is capable of suffering *passio* and is therefore not immortal. The main reason that they are not immortal is because they are not the direct creations of the High God who alone can immortalize *any* being, including the gods. The latter concept is brought out clearly in *Adv. nat.* 2. 36. 1–12, which is dependent upon *Timaeus* 41 AD. He continues by disparaging the morality of his enemies: there is no fear of divine judgement and no need to keep one's soul free from passions, for those whose souls are immortal and therefore not subject to the laws of the fates.[117] We recall that Porphyry distinctly maintained that deliverance from the bonds of fate is a gift of the gods,[118] and in the Hecatean Oracle and commentary he argued that Christians were fated not to receive such *dona deorum*.[119] And we have observed that the Chaldaeans claimed that the practising theurgist was not subject to the laws of fate. If this cardinal doctrine is kept in mind, we can understand why Porphyry's subjecting Christ and his followers to fate was taken so seriously by the Christians.

Porphyry's concept of the purpose of the soul's descent to the world of Becoming is given by Augustine and is probably derived from *De reg. an.*: 'Dicit etiam ad hoc Deum animam mundo dedisse, ut materiae cognoscens mala ad Patrem recurreret nec aliquando iam talium polluta

---

[115] *Civ. Dei* 10. 29.
[116] *Adv. nat.* 2. 27. 7–17.
[117] Ibid. 2. 29. 16 f.
[118] *PE* 6. 4.
[119] *Civ. Dei* 19. 23: *DE* 3. 7.

contagione teneretur.'[120] Arnobius devotes five chapters (2. 39–43) to refuting this concept. It is significant for the present study to observe that in 2. 41 he asks whether God sent the souls, who were strangers to 'savage passions',[121] in order to build amphitheatres and butcher's shops: in one humans are killed; in the other poor animals are slain. The latter's flesh is chewed up with the teeth and given to the cruel belly. The language used here suggests that Porphyry's *Abstinentia*, especially his argument that one should not eat the flesh of animals, might have been in Arnobius' mind when he wrote this section. This particular diatribe comes to an end in 2. 43:

Quid dicitis, o suboles ac primi progenies numinis? Ergone sapientes illae atque ex causis principalibus proditae genera haec animae turpitudinum criminum malitiarumque noverunt atque ut exercerent, ut gererent, ut percelebrarent haec mala, abire atque habitare iussae sunt has partes et humani corporis circumiectione vestiri?[122]

With Augustine's 'ut materiae cognoscens mala' compare Arnobius' 'noverunt . . . haec mala', and the fact that both attack the belief that God sends the souls[123] to earth for the purpose of recognizing evils in the world. Finally, notice the pagan comment placed immediately after his attack upon the aforementioned Porphyrian concept: 'Sed sua, inquitis, voluntate, non regis missione venerunt.' This very probably expresses the Plotinian view of the descent of the soul being precipitated by an audacity and its 'desire to be self-centred'.[124] The two views together would indicate a debate between the Porphyrian and Plotinian views of the soul's descent carried on within the sect of the North African *viri novi*.[125]

Finally, in *Adv. nat.* 2. 62, Arnobius rejects the pagan notions of salvation which was the purpose of the *digressio* of book 2.[126] We have agreed with Bidez and Courcelle that the reference to the magicians' prayers presupposes Chaldaean theurgical practices.[127] We may add only

---

[120] *Civ. Dei* 10. 30.

[121] *Adv. nat.* 2. 41. 1 f.

[122] Ibid. 2. 43. 1–7.

[123] Compare Augustine's 'ad hoc Deum animam mundo dedisse', and Arnobius' 'Idcirco animas misit' in *Adv. nat.* 2. 39–42 (i.e. a recurrent refrain).

[124] See Rist (1967), 116, on *Enn.* 5. 1. 1.

[125] See also O'Meara (1959), 146, who first suggested a connection with Porphyry and *Adv. nat.* 2. 43.

[126] As Bidez, Festugière, and Courcelle have observed.

[127] Cf. also O'Meara (1959), 8; Kroll, *RM* (1916), 309–57.

that in 2. 62. 3 f.[128] Arnobius makes the same point as he does in 2. 29. 16 f.: his opponents claim exemption from the laws of the fates, which is definitely Chaldaean. Also, compare the *aulam dominicam* of 2. 33. 18 and the *aulam* of 2. 62. 4, both designating the eschatological habitation of his opponents' souls. We showed in Chapter 4 that Synesius and Damascius use αὐλή to describe the specific place to which the disembodied souls were thought to ascend according to Chaldaean theology. This also seems to be the use of *aulam* in *Adv. nat.* 2. 37. 5. We can be certain he is not using his own designation and can completely agree with Amata: 'In nessun luogo dell'*Adversus Nationes* si accenna "dove" i salvati vivranno la loro felicità.'[129]

If we return to the main soteriological text in *Adv. nat.* (2. 65), we recall Arnobius' insistence upon Christ being the only way of the soul's salvation.[130] In 2. 5 he acknowledges that people of various social classes (slaves, commoners, children) and outstanding intellectual ability (orators, grammarians, rhetors) now are coming to Christ, and 'even those who explore the profundities of philosophy.' He later responds to Porphyry's question about what has happened to those who died before the advent of Christ[131] by affirming that God's mercy has been granted also to them.[132] Note 2. 64. 1–3: 'Sed si generis Christus humani, ut inquitis, conservator advenit, quor omnino non omnes aequali munificentia liberat?' And the answer: 'non aequaliter liberat qui aequaliter omnes vocat?' Christ the *via salutis animae* is available to all persons regardless of age, sex, social status, and intellectual ability; to those who died before his advent; and this *via salutis animae universalis* equally liberates all who come to him (2. 64. 3). Geographically, socially, intellectually, chronologically, and in terms of all being liberated alike, Christ is the universal way of the soul's salvation. This indeed is the main soteriological message of book 2, and it appears to have been directed towards Porphyry's rejection of Christ as the *via universalis animae liberandae* and his soteriological system which offered one *via*

---

[128] *Adv. nat.* 2. 62. 3 f.

[129] B. Amata, 'Destino finale dell'uomo nell'opera di Arnobio di Sicca (III–IV sec. d. C.)', in S. Felici (ed.), *Morte E Immortalità Nella Catechesi Dei Padri Del III–IV Secolo* (BSR 66; Rome, 1985), 47–62. See also I. P. Culianu, 'Le vol magique dans l'antiquité tardive', *RHR* 198 (1981), 57–66.

[130] 'ab nullo animas posse vim vitae atque incolumitatis accipere nisi ab eo quam rex summus huic muneri officioque praefecit. Hanc omnipotens imperator esse voluit salutis viam'.

[131] Cf. *Adv. nat.* 2. 63.

[132] Cf. *Civ. Dei* 10. 32.

salutis animae to the philosopher and another to the common man.

VI. *Notions of Deity and Contemplation of the Divine*

Arnobius' principal objective in attacking the anthropomorphic and anthropopathic depictions of the deities in the myths is to offer evidence that pagan notions of deity are wrong, they do not contain a particle of truth in them, they do not benefit those who believe in them, and therefore are anti-soteriological. We note three important factors related to this attack: (1) an exegesis of the names of the gods; (2) a method of literary retortion that he argues is free from prejudicial interpretations, i.e. his evidence is derived from the myths, the histories, the annals, and the mysteries themselves; and (3) an exclusive analysis of the deities *qua* deities, and not demons, whether good or bad. The basic premiss of Arnobius' argument is that any concept of deity the pagan forms in his mind will ultimately be influenced by, and derived from the notions of deity found in the myths.[133] Hence by using the stories about the deities as the basis of his attack upon their credibility, and by keeping the interpretation at a literal level, he can demonstrate clearly that the pagan concepts of deity are false. The literary motif of book 3 is that the anthropomorphic deities are not truly divine. We may give a few examples as to how Arnobius shows the falsity of these notions. Christians are confused about which gods to worship: they will not, however, worship those whose characters have been befouled by the stories fabricated about them (3. 6). The stories prove their non-existence (3. 6). Pagan ideas of divinity are full of impious fictions.[134] There is absolutely no agreement about the specific identity of the gods (3. 35), and the difference of opinion on this subject is too great for anybody to be able to ascertain the truth. If the myths were truthful, all would be in agreement about the identities, natures, names, and functions of the gods.[135]

This is the same charge to which Arnobius responds in his apologetical section (books 1–2), and we have seen that he frequently proves the credibility of the Christian religion on the basis of disparate nations, peoples, and races, even barbarians, who have united on one and the

[133] *Adv. nat.* 4. 18. 10–30.
[134] Ibid. 3. 29. 2.
[135] Ibid. 3. 37. 10–14.

same conclusion that this faith is the true way of salvation. Arnobius is responding to Porphyry in these passages, and we particularly recall that one basic method of biblical criticism employed by him[136] was the demonstration of the inconsistencies and contradictions occurring in the Bible. It therefore could not be relied upon as the truth. Porphyry especially concentrated upon the Synoptic Gospels.[137] In turning to Arnobius, we find the same method of argument used: conflicting opinions about the names of the gods causes uncertainty about their real identities, and this produces doubt as to whether they exist at all.[138] There is no unanimous and therefore trustworthy verdict about the gods, but only a great diversity of opinions about them, and there is no method available to enable one to ascertain which concept contains the truth.[139]

The argument intensifies in books 4–5. Greek and Roman scholars of outstanding intellectual abilities have proved that only one name can correspond to one being. Yet the myths give five different Jupiters, five Suns, five Mercuries, four Vulcans, three Dianas, and so forth.[140] Hence pagan religion is both confusing and erroneous, and the worshipper knows not what to think about the deities.[141] We see here Arnobius the rhetor using his critical exegetical skills against the pagans, and we can say the same about the *suasoria* of the five Minervas in 4. 16. How can one correctly perform one's religious duties without knowing which of the five goddesses to worship? He again expounds the meaning of the names and powers of the deities, basing his argument upon the principle of one name to one being, to prove that pagans derive their religious beliefs from misconceived notions of the gods found in the myths. Such stories slander the gods' majesties,[142] and they should have been erased from humanity rather than learned by heart.[143] He concludes his argument in book 4 by asserting that it is indeed the pagans' notions of the deities that have caused all the miseries in the world.[144]

These notions are not conducive to receiving *salus deorum*: there is no benefit to be had in worshipping these gods. Arnobius frequently

---

[136] Cf. Eus. *HE* 6. 19. 4.
[137] Cf. *De cons. evan.*
[138] *Adv. nat.* 3. 26–34.
[139] Ibid. 3. 40. 22–8.
[140] Ibid. 4. 14 f.
[141] Ibid. 4. 15.
[142] Ibid. 4. 32.
[143] Ibid. 4. 33.
[144] Ibid. 4. 37. 10; cf. also 1. 19–21.

accentuates the fact that there is nothing worthy of the name and power of *deus* found in the religious literature of the pagans. He affirms that it is not hard to influence him to worship the gods, but he demands that the pagans show him something worthy of the name of deity.[145] There is no reason why one should pray to the gods because they are responsible for the occurrence of evil in the world.[146] He is not expressing belief in the existence of the mythical deities, but only showing that the totality of Graeco-Roman religious culture is firmly established upon the misconceptions of deity. The pagans have not been able to find the truth in their religious literature because Christ alone has revealed the nature of a *deus verus*. The direct relationship between correct worship and true concept of deity is quite conspicuous in the *Adversus nationes*,[147] and we may add that Porphyry argued the same way in the *Abstinentia*. A truly inward or 'spiritual' worship of the deity which did not involve the practice of animal sacrifice is a salient feature of his philosophical argument in that work.[148]

Arnobius also rather consistently emphasizes not only that there is no truth in pagan concepts of deity, but also where religious truth can be found. One very good example of this critical and constructive approach to the problem appears in *Adv. nat.* 4. 24. 1–7:

If you will but open the mind's eye and look at the real truth without clinging to any pet idea of your own, you will find that the causes of all the miseries with which, as you say, the human race has long been afflicted, flow from this kind of notions about your gods which you have held from ancient times, and which you have refused to change for the better though the truth has been set before your eyes.

Again, it is clear that he is referring to the apologetical section where he shows that Christ has shown the truth about polytheism and has revealed *deus verus*. Christians, he argues, are threatened with their lives to worship ludicrous blocks of wood in the form of human beings. This only provides *evidence* that pagans irrationally force their religious beliefs upon the Christians rather 'than to give in and consent to acknowledged truth'.[149] He further maintains that he can inform his adversaries about the One God with *evidence* derived from 'truthful authors'.[150] Even

---

[145] Ibid. 4. 17.
[146] Ibid. 3. 28.
[147] Ibid. 4. 30. 16–21.
[148] *Abst.* 2. 34.
[149] *Adv. nat.* 6. 11. 27 f.
[150] Ibid. 1. 7 and 3. 1. 1–4.

common sense possessed by all mortals will acknowledge that pagan deities are the products of false opinions.[151] All of these assertions represent counter-charges brought against the pagans in response to Porphyry's accusation that Christians assent only to *faith* without first examining the *evidence* of the things promised therein.

If Christians espouse the correct conception of deity, it follows that only they are involved in the right worship of God. We may give 1. 31 as a representative passage which also betrays Porphyrian theological designations. In the text a prayer, pregnant with philosophical concepts characterized by a strong apophatic understanding of the divine,[152] is offered to the High God. There is a Christianized formula added to the end which begs for God's mercy to be given to those persecuting the Christians. It is important to note that the form of the prayer corresponds to a hymn to the Chaldaean High God, which in turn was modelled on the fixed scheme of ancient religious hymnology, and it appeared in book 2 of Porphyry's *Philosophia ex oraculis*.[153] This hymn and Arnobius' invocation have the following elements in common: (1) an invocation of the High God; (2) a reference to the deity's abode; (3) a petition that the one who prays may be heard; (4) a reference to the specific aptitude of the invoked power to fulfil the prayer; and (5) an exposition of the power of the invoked deity.[154] Note especially the reference to silence in *Adv. nat.* 1. 31. 14, which should be compared with Porphyry's remark in *Abst.* 2. 34. 2. Chaldaean soteriology also stressed the importance of remaining silent before the deity.[155] We have a correspondence with Eusebius, who employs the same Porphyrian–Pythagorean–Chaldaean concept in *PE* 3. 10: God is to be worshipped separate from all perishable matter by contemplating him in silence. Eusebius even quotes *Abst.* 2. 34 in *PE* 4. 11 and *DE* 3. 3! Porphyry goes further than simply emphasizing the use of pure thoughts of the divine in order to worship him, however: "οὕτως ἡμεῖς ἀπαρξόμεθα αὐτοῖς ἐννοιῶν τῶν περὶ αὐτῶν καλῶν εὐχαριστοῦντες ὧν ἡμῖν δεδώκασι τὴν θεωρίαν, καὶ ὅτι ἡμᾶς διὰ τῆς αὐτῶν θέας ἀληθινῶς τρέφουσι, συνόντες τε καὶ

---

[151] *Adv. nat.* 4. 9. 1–4.

[152] Ibid. 1. 31.

[153] Theos. no. 27, *COTh* 10 and n. 26. We have another hymn of Porphyry preserved in *PE* 3. 9, addressed to Zeus, in which he allegorizes the anthropomorphic depictions of the god found therein.

[154] Cf. Lewy, *COTh* 10 and n. 26.

[155] *Adv. nat.* 1. 31. 14: 'qui ut intellegaris tacendum est', and Porphyry's remark in *Abst.* 2. 34. 2, which may have influenced Arnobius: διὰ δὲ σιγῆς καθαρὰς καὶ τῶν περὶ αὐτοῦ καθαρῶν ἐννοιῶν θρησκεύομεν αὐτόν.

φαινόμενοι καὶ τῇ ἡμετέρᾳ σωτηρίᾳ ἐπιλάμποντες." It must have been
the idea of consecrating oneself to the gods by offering good thoughts
about them in contemplation that Arnobius found so offensive. Hence
his attempt to prove that (1) pagans cannot form any concept of deity
unless it derives from the myths which, in turn, offer nothing but false
conceptions of the gods;[156] and (2) such notions are not beneficial in
man's worship of God.

In a section of book 1 which responds to Porphyry's rejection of
Christ's divinity, Arnobius attributes to Christ the ability to see clearly
into the hearts of individuals.[157] Christ allows himself to be comprehended in the individual's thoughts so that he may pray to him.[158]
The term used for 'comprehended' is *concipere*, which is frequently used
in the *Adv. nat.* to describe the mental process whereby the pagans form
a concept of deity, and which is naturally misconceived because it is
impossible to think upon the divine without the notions of deity derived
from the myths at once coming into one's mind. In attacking Porphyry
in *Civ. Dei*, Augustine distinguishes between the former's angelic beings
who browbeat mortals into sacrificing to them and worshipping them,
and the Christian God upon whom it is blissful to contemplate.[159]
Eusebius, who attacks the same practices in *PE* 4. 21, makes the same
point, adding that the Word of God dwells in the hearts of his
believers.[160] In 2. 13. 15 ff. he specifically mentions Plato and the
Theaetetus and the doctrine found therein that the soul must flee the
earth and involve itself in thought and contemplation of the divine.[161]
He also addresses in the same chapter those who follow Mercury, Plato,
and Pythagoras. In 2. 16. 16 he refers to the *cogitationibus tacitis* of his
opponents, using the concept related to animal psychology developed
in the *Abstinentia* (analysed in the final chapter below). True contemplation of the divine, emphasizing the necessity to flee the world of
Becoming by elevating oneself in thought which is both a mental and a
spiritual process, is the noetic experience in which salvific knowledge
takes place.[162] Porphyry also emphasized the need to unite with God in
contemplation by elevating oneself to him.[163] Arnobius appears to be

[156] *Adv. nat.* 4. 18.
[157] Ibid. 1. 46. 16 f.
[158] Ibid. 1. 27. 18.
[159] *Civ. Dei* 10. 16.
[160] Cf. *Adv. nat.* 4. 30. 16–21 and *Abst.* 2. 34.
[161] *Adv. nat.* 2. 13. 15 ff.
[162] Ibid. 2. 60. 21–32.
[163] *Abst.* 2. 34. 3.

claiming that true contemplation and the right concept of the Divine
belong only to his new religious ideas of deity. And 4. 18 establishes
the fact that no mental concept of deity can be developed without being
derived from the religious literature of the pagans. We note that
Porphyry explicitly argued in the *Abstinentia* that contemplation of the
Divine could be done to one's advantage in conjunction with worshipping
the images in the temples. It is good, he says, 'to dwell with the statues
of the gods . . . by which the soul tends to the contemplation of their
divinities.'[164] Arnobius' response to such concepts in 6. 4. 9–14, is
significant: 'And yet we think that every single god, if by virtue of his
name he stands for anything, ought to hear, as if he were present,
whatever anyone in any part of the world says. Indeed, he ought to
grasp in anticipation whatever anyone conceives in the silent twilight of
his thoughts.' The reference to silent thoughts (*tacitis sensibus*) here
seems to be a direct attack upon the Porphyrian–Chaldaean theology of
the *viri novi*.

A text that should be compared with *Adv. nat.* 2. 60. 21–32, cited
above, is 3. 19. 11–18, especially the remark about conceiving the deity
in the silence of one's mind:

Whatever you say about God, whatever you conceive in the silence of your
mind, passes over and is corrupted into human applications nor can it have the
mark of a meaning of its own because it is expressed in our own words and
words designed for human affairs. There is only one thing most certainly
understood by man concerning the nature of God: your realization and conviction
that mortal man's speech is powerless to set forth anything about Him.

He affirms here, like Porphyry in *Abst.* 2. 34. 2, that the Λόγος
Προφορικός cannot be appropriated to human expression of the Divine.
Contemplation also played a significant thematic role in *Phil. or.* (*PE*
4. 7), which is interesting in light of what we have observed concerning
Arnobius' argument *vis-à-vis* pagan notions of deity, namely that Porphyry selected oracles which would prove the excellence of the deities
(*PE* 4. 6). It appears also that in *Phil. or.* he defined the contemplation
of the gods' excellence on the basis of the inseparability of correct
concepts of the gods and true worship of them. And he specifically
stated that *Phil. or.* would offer the only source of salvation, and by
that he meant, of course, for the common man (non-philosopher).
F. Maternus' remark concerning Porphyrian soteriology is noteworthy:

[164] *Abst.* 4. 6.

'Pythagoras etiam et noster Porphyrius religioso putant animum nostrum silentio consecrari.'[165]

The manner in which Eusebius certainly, and Arnobius most probably, have responded to this concept, to the extent of incorporating it into their own soteriological understanding of the deity, suggests that Porphyry might have used the concept in his anti-Christian propaganda. And although *silence* does not appear in *Civ. Dei* 19.23, which includes a quote from *Phil. or.*, it is important to analyse it in detail.[166] First, Porphyry argued that Jesus strictly taught that men should not worship the *minoribus spiritibus*, and with this we should compare *Adv. nat.* 2. 3. 9 f., tactfully put on the lips of a pagan who finds fault with Christ's doctrine.[167] Second, Jesus taught men to worship the *caelestes deos*, which is the term frequently used by Arnobius, in addition to *caeles/caelites*, to designate the objects of his attack upon the pagan notions of deity.[168] Third, Christians are fated not to receive *dona deorum*, and this includes even a concept of immortal Jupiter.[169] We recall that a principal diatribe against the pagans developed by Arnobius is that their misconceptions of deity have caused them erroneously to establish the entirety of their religious culture upon false concepts of the gods. Fourth, Christians have rejected the gods and only pretend to worship the High God. They actually worship demons. This helps to explain why Arnobius

---

[165] *Math.* 7. 1. 1: Bouffartigue–Patillon (1977), 10; cf. also Chadwick (1959), 180, for sources on *silence* in ancient thought.

[166] *Civ. Dei* 19. 23: ' "Sunt", inquit, "spiritus terreni minimi loco quodam malorum daemonum potestati subiecti. Ab his sapientes Hebraeorum (quorum unus iste etiam Iesus fuit, sicut audisti divina Apollinis, quae superius dicta sunt), ab his ergo Hebraei daemonibus pessimis et minoribus spiritibus vetabant religiosos et ipsis vacare prohibebant; venerari autem magis caelestes deos, amplius autem venerari Deum Patrem. Hoc autem," inquit, "et dii praecipiunt et in superioribus ostendimus, quem ad modum animum advertere ad Deum monent et illum colere ubique imperant. Verum indocti et impiae naturae, quibus vere fatum non concessit ab diis dona obtinere neque habere Iovis inmortalis notionem, non audientes et deos et divinos viros, deos quidem omnes recusaverunt, prohibitos autem daemones et hos non odisse, sed reverei. Deum autem simulantes colere, ea sola per quae Deus adoratur non agunt. Nam Deus quidem, utpote omnium Pater, nullius indiget; sed nobis est bene, cum eum per iustitiam et castitatem aliasque virtutes adoramus, ipsam vitam precem ad ipsum facientes per imitationem et inquisitionem de ipso. Inquisitio enim purgat," inquit, "imitatio deificat affectionem ad ipsum operando." '

[167] 'Sed minoribus supplicare diis homines vetuit.'

[168] For *caelestes deos* see *Adv. nat.* 1. 35. 8; 3. 4. 20; 3. 14. 1; 3. 29. 31; 4. 26. 2; 4. 33. 1; 5. 12. 6; 6. 15. 17; 7. 3. 8; 7. 12. 13; 7. 13. 9; 7. 16. 24; 7. 44. 64; and for *caeles/caelites*: 1. 1. 6; 1. 26. 2; 1. 36. 36; 3. 42. 13; 4. 34. 12; 4. 37. 23; 5. 30. 17; 5. 35. 18; 6. 2. 31; 6. 15. 20; 6. 20. 3; 7. 12. 1; 7. 26. 28; 7. 34. 26; 7. 36. 16; 7. 38. 29.

[169] *Civ. Dei* 19. 23: 'neque habere Iovis inmortalis notionem.'

demonstrates that in worshipping their High God, the Christians are involved in the truly spiritual worship of God. Fifth, Porphyry saw a correlation between worshipping the High God and seeking knowledge of him, a concept which is expressed in *Adv. nat.* 2. 60. 21–32. Sixth, Porphyry clearly maintained that the Christians paid a great moral price for pretending to worship the High God: they do not do those things by which alone the deity is adored. Hence they do not practise justice, chastity, and the other virtues. The arguments of the earlier apologists, from Justin Martyr onward, which accused the pagans of immorality because they had immoral deities to imitate, had now come full circle, and Porphyry could modify it somewhat and turn it against his enemies.

VII. *'Christus Via Salutis Universalis Animae': The Moral Argument*

In beginning this section we may make a few observations about Eusebius' references to the names and notions of the gods which appear in *PE*. After citing a number of ancient sources related to explaining the names of the gods, he affirms that it is unholy to honour the adorable name of God with mortals who have long been dead (*PE* 2. 4). He then analyses the concept that the elements received the names of deities (2. 6), and later examines the exegesis of the names of the gods found in Plutarch (3. 1) and Diodorus (3. 3). The *Ep. An.* is attacked because of the reference to the Egyptian practice of giving divine names to the celestial elements (3. 4). After giving a lengthy passage from *Abst.*[170] dealing with Egyptian theology, he concludes that Christ's gospel is admirable in that it teaches men to worship with correct thoughts the God of the elements (3. 6). In 3. 11 he criticizes Porphyry's exegesis of the gods' names in *Cult. sim.*, where he used the allegorical method. Eusebius' strategy, like that of Arnobius, is to demonstrate that there is nothing worthy of the name and power of deity in Greek theology (*PE* 3. 2). Clearly referring to the same concept of deity which Augustine found so disgusting (*Civ. Dei* 10. 9), Eusebius says that his opponents degraded 'the venerable and adorable name of God to the level of their own passions' (*PE* 5. 3). He uses *Ep. An.* to prove that the ancients have not passed down any worthy notion of God (14. 9). It is not right to blame the Christians because they have forsaken the conjectures of Greek theology (14. 10), and he adds that they despise such teachings

---

[170] *PE* 3. 6. See M. Smith (1988), 494–504.

with well-proved judgement, undoubtedly a response to *CC* fragment
1. After devoting nine chapters to surveying Greek theology, he turns
to the physical philosophers to learn whether any worthy notion of God
has come down to modern times (*PE* 14. 9). Again, the general form
of the polemical argument of both Eusebius and Arnobius related to the
names and power of the gods, and the correlation that both make
between right notion of deity and true worship, strongly suggests that
both have Porphyry as a common enemy.

Arnobius' main strategy in discussing morality in books 1–2 is to
prove that those humans who follow Christ and worship the High God
are empowered to overcome passions and thus live a truly virtuous life.
In *Adv. nat.* 1. 63. 23–30 he vividly portrays a Christ who enabled man
to live such a life during his earthly ministry:

For when, thinking much about the dangers of souls, and also on the other
hand, about their evil tendency to vice, the Introducer, Master, and Founder
directed His laws and ordinances to the end of fitting duties, did He not destroy
the haughtiness of pride? Did He not quench the flames of passion? Did He
not twist the weapons from their hands and cut them off from the hotbeds of
every vice?

It is the direct result of Christ's laws that 'flames of passion' were
extinguished. He elsewhere asserts that Christ's teachings and laws have
enabled humans to overcome violent passions, and they have decreased
the number of wars occurring since Christ's advent. A correlation
between worshipping the High God and experiencing an amelioration
of one's moral conduct is also clearly made in *Adv. nat.* 1. 27. 16–22.[171]
Here he uses some of the same terms as he does in the attack upon the
anthropopathic behaviour of the gods to prove their mortality (*libidinis
adpetitus*). Also, the divine 'gifts' (*munera*) which, we recall, Porphyry
argued were not available to the Christians because of their false worship
of Christ, are the results of the individual's contemplation of God. His
reference to cleansing the spot (*labe*) concerns that process whereby the
soul is kept impassible: passions are extirpated, otherwise the soul may
become soiled. We may compare *Abst.* 2. 34, where Porphyry maintains
that the interior language of the soul is inappropriate for honouring the
divine when it is soiled by the soul's passions: one's sacrifice to God is

---

[171] 'Nam cuia proni ad culpas et ad libidinis varios adpetitus vitio sumus infirmitatis
ingenitae, patitur se semper nostris cogitationibus concipi ut, dum illum oramus et mereri
eius contendimus munera, accipiamus innocentiae voluntatem et ab omni nos labe
delictorum omnium amputatione purgemus.'

accomplished by the impassibility of the soul. The close connection
between morality and worship of the Christian God suggests again that
Porphyry's sixth premiss (above) on the immorality of the Christians is
being refuted. Note also that in *Adv. nat.* 2. 12, in responding to
Porphyry's assertion that Peter was a magician and in the development
of the theme of the universal diffusion of Christianity, he asserts that it
was Christ's 'unheard-of power over nature' that quenched the fires of
passions and united the world in one faith.

   Man is completely dependent upon God to experience both temporal
and eschatological salvation. All of 2. 33 is devoted to demonstrating
that humans cannot bring about their *salus animarum* on their own
efforts, unlike the doctrine of the *viri novi*; nor can they reach the world
beyond on their own power; nor arrive at the Lord's palace unless the
rerum dominus himself grants this to man. Thus the philosophers who
fight to extirpate passions from their souls prove that the goal of such
struggles is unattainable.[172] Only Christ is the guardian of the soul, and
his guardianship is not restricted to granting immortality to the soul,[173]
but also concerns giving aid to man to overcome the passions.[174]
Christians fight against the passions because of the *media qualitas animae.*
If they thus acquire knowledge of God they will experience the
immortalization of their souls; if not, they will be thrown into a burning
hell by wild and vicious monsters where they will suffer for an indefinite
period and then perish. Yet the pagan philosophical concept of the
immortality of the soul nullifies the whole purpose of living in accordance
with a strict moral code,[175] and even if one were to become pure and
cleansed from all vices, one would still have to receive the 'gift' of
Christ in order to experience an immortalization of one's soul.[176]

   One final observation is necessary in relation to Arnobius' understanding of the interrelationship between worship and morality, which
is a concept formulated apparently with Porphyry's sixth premiss in
mind: Christians only pretend to worship the High God and do not do
those things by which God is adored. These are justice, chastity, and
'the other virtues'.[177] There may be some significance, in light of this,
in the claim put forward in *Adv. nat.* 4. 36, that in the Christians'

[172] *Adv. nat.* 2. 50. 18–22.
[173] Ibid. 2. 65.
[174] Ibid. 2. 13.
[175] Ibid. 2. 29.
[176] Ibid. 2. 66. 1–7.
[177] *Civ. Dei* 19. 23.

conventicula the High God is worshipped[178] and there nothing else is uttered 'but what makes men kind, what makes men gentle, modest, virtuous, chaste'.[179] This interpretation does not necessarily contradict what we concluded in Chapter 2, that it is an apparent allusion to the First Edict of Diocletian's Great Persecution, because there is good reason to believe that Porphyry's anti-Christian propaganda was disseminated throughout the eastern and western provinces of the Roman Empire during the period immediately preceding the official state persecution of the Christian Church.

VIII. *Conclusions*

We have analysed various salient features of the Porphyrian–Chaldaean soteriological propaganda which formed the centrepiece of the great literary campaign against the Christians before and during the emperor Diocletian's persecution. Porphyry, who was writing as probably the most erudite philosophical and religious authority of the period, and was probably supported officially by the Roman government, developed a twofold system of argumentation which resulted in making him the most formidable antagonist of Christianity in antiquity. The main strategy of this system was (1) the eradication of Christianity, and (2) the offer of salvation not only to the philosopher but also to the common man. It appears that *The Philosophy of the Oracles* played a highly significant role in the development of this strategy, and we can make this assumption on the basis of the analysis of the data common to the polemics of Augustine, Eusebius, and Arnobius.

Porphyry was the most dangerous enemy of Christianity in antiquity for several reasons. First, he had evidently decided to abandon the method of attacking the faith developed by Celsus in the second century, which used the prominent authors of Graeco-Roman literary culture against the doctrines and practices of the Christians. The argument had apparently lost its steam by the end of the third century, and pagan intellectuals intent upon annihilating the Church were in search of a new programme. Therefore Porphyry devised a plan to attack Christianity from within its own tradition by using scripture as his main weapon. And according to extant sources which cite him, the strategy

[178] *Adv. nat.* 1. 24: 'summus oratur deus'.
[179] Ibid. 1. 24. 27 f.

was quite effective because of its aggressiveness in mounting an offensive against the Church against which it was not immediately prepared to defend itself. The brilliance of it all was in the element of surprise, and it threw the Church, stunned and alarmed, nervously on the defensive. But Porphyry evidently felt compelled to go further than the development of a strong attack upon his enemies in order to destroy them, and this constructive component in his methodology presupposes a meticulously planned soteriology produced in the form of *The Philosophy of the Oracles*. The great threat which this treatise posed for the Church was found in the offer of salvation to the common man, and this meant essentially anyone, based on the authority of divine revelation (the Oracles) and in full support of the Roman religious *mos maiorum*. If we add one more factor to this—a highly superstitious and traditionally religious emperor (Diocletian) who despised the Christian religion and probably gave imperial support to the dissemination of Porphyry's anti-Christian literature throughout the Roman Empire before the persecution began—it is little wonder why so many Christians both saw in him the arch-enemy of the faith and why so many wrote refutations of him.

How did the Christians succeed in responding to Porphyry? They argued that he himself was inconsistent on the subject of animal sacrifice. He also was thought to have deviated from pure Platonism. Because of the contradictory nature of the myths, the Christians turned his own method of literary criticism against him. The doctrine of divine impassibility, moreover, was strongly debated, and the practice of theurgy was caricatured as magic, which was an admirable defence of the Porphyrian accusation that the disciples performed miracles by the use of magical arts. Both groups demanded clear and irrefutable evidence of the truth of their religious beliefs. Also, the attempt to provide mankind with a universal way of salvation was a very important facet of the contemporary soteriological debate. Both Christians and Porphyrians tried to make a credibility gap between the leader of the movements attacked and his disciples: Porphyry argued that the disciples were not true followers of Jesus; and the Christians accuse Porphyry of deviating from the teachings of Plato and combining Platonism with Chaldaean religious practices. Not only was Plato used against Porphyry in order to make him appear disreputable as a Platonist, but the Christians also used Porphyry against Porphyry by analysing the contradictions and inconsistencies found in his many works with as much zeal, we can imagine, as he expressed in his studies of biblical criticism.

When we analyse those passages of Augustine and Eusebius where it is known that Porphyry is being refuted, and compare them, as we have done, with a good number from the *Adversus nationes* where Arnobius is refuting pagan charges, the similarities are both too much alike and too numerous simply to conclude that it is a matter of coincidence in the case of Arnobius, who does not mention Porphyry by name in his work.

Finally, we have only touched the tip of the iceberg in relation to the connection between Eusebius and Arnobius, a subject within Arnobiana, patristic theology, and Church history which has hitherto been no more than virgin territory. And we may expect that intensive research in this area of Christian apologetics, especially the relationship between and common data within the anti-Christian works of Augustine and Eusebius, made in conjunction with the *Adversus nationes et alia*, will produce an even clearer picture of the great conflict and controversy which occurred during the Age of Diocletian between Christianity and paganism.

I I

The Argument Concerning Animal Sacrifice

As far as I know no one has analysed *Adv. nat.* 7 to see if there is any connection between Arnobius' argument concerning animal sacrifice and Porphyry's philosophical doctrines on the same subject found in his *Abstinentia*. This is the objective of the present enquiry. Porphyry's basic argument in *Abst.* is that animals should not be sacrificed to the gods because they possess both the λόγος προφορικός and the λόγος ἐνδιάθετος. He begins to develop his argument in book 1 against the Stoic and Peripatetic view that humans do not owe any justice to animals because justice is practised only within a community which possesses reason. In book 3 Porphyry argues against the Stoics mainly by using their own philosophical concepts against them and attempting to prove that animals possess both the inner reasoning of thought and the external reasoning of the word. We may note that this debate probably goes back to the Middle Academy, and it is found at the end of book 4 of the *Contra Celsum* where Origen takes up the Stoic position that the irrational animal exists for the sake of the rational.[1] In any case, the Christians were not the only enemies to be attacked by Porphyry with their own doctrines, and it appears that Arnobius had used some of the main lines of argumentation found in *Abst.*, with perhaps some dependence upon Aelian, Pliny, Plutarch, and others, in developing his criticism of (1) in *Adv. nat.* 2, the concept of the immortality and the divinity of the soul which his opponents espouse; and (2) comprising the whole of book 7, the soteriological importance of sacrificing animals, which is the pagan religious practice that receives the most lengthy refutation in the *Adversus nationes*.

In *Adv. nat.* 2. 16 ff. Arnobius develops the position that man should

---

[1] My doctoral thesis (Edinburgh, 1985) contains a study of the possible similarities between the *Adv. nat.* and the *Abst.* Three years after my thesis P. F. Beatrice, 'Un oracle antichrétien chez Arnobe', in Y. de Andia (ed.), *Memorial Dom Jean Gribomont* (Rome, 1988), 107–29, esp. p. 119, argued also that such similarities exist. On the Stoic position in the *C. Cels.* see H. Chadwick, 'Origen, Celsus, and the Stoa', *JTS* 48 (1947), 34–49.

not be considered superior to the animals. We recall that in 2. 16 he asks his opponents to search out and investigate who they are, which has been interpreted as a direct response to *CC* fragment 1. In the same chapter we also noted a reference to his opponents' *cogitationibus tacitis* (1. 16) which is a concept found also in *Abst.* 2. 34. 2. Finally, the latter is a Pythagorean and Chaldaean concept, and Arnobius identifies his enemies in 2. 13 as followers of Mercury, Plato, and Pythagoras. It would be superfluous to enumerate the many other texts in book 2 alone which evince Porphyrian influence.

Arnobius begins to prove that men and animals should be enrolled in the same class because of the similarities between the constitutions of their bodies. Note the conceptual similarities between *Adv. nat.* 2. 16. 16–20: 'Vultis favore deposito cogitationibus tacitis pervidere animantia nos esse aut consimilia ceteris aut non plurima differitate distantia? Quid est enim, quod nos ab eorum indicet similitudine discrepare?'; and *Abst.* 3. 7. 1: φαίνεται δὲ ἡ παραλλαγή, ὥς φησί που καὶ Ἀριστοτέλης, οὐκ οὐσίᾳ διαλλάττουσα, ἀλλ' ἐν τῷ μᾶλλον καὶ ἧττον θεωρουμένῃ· There is no qualitative or essential difference between man and animal. Porphyry continues by observing that all the world is generally agreed that the dispositions of animals and humans are similar at least in respect of sensation and general organization of the sense organs and those of the body.[2] Arnobius concurs, giving the specific examples of the common possession of skeletal systems and connecting sinews.[3] We may now compare *Adv. nat.* 2. 16. 19 f. (cf. 7. 4; 7. 9); 'Vel quae in nobis eminentia tanta est, ut animantium numero dedignemur adscribi?'; with *Abst.* 3. 25. 3: Οὕτω δὲ καὶ τοὺς πάντας ἀνθρώπους ἀλλήλοις τίθεμεν [καὶ] συγγενεῖς, καὶ μὴν [καὶ] πᾶσι τοῖς ζῴοις. Depending upon Pythagorean doctrine, Porphyry adds to the concept of man and animal being in the same race the fact that both have the same kind of soul.[4] Both Arnobius and Porphyry refer to the separation into male and female sexes to support their arguments that man and animal both possess common physical characteristics.[5] Both note that animals have sexual intercourse in order to have young.[6] The specific example of

[2] *Abst.* 3. 7. 2.
[3] Cf. Pliny, *HN* 11. 87. 215: bones (asses and dolphins) and 11. 88. 217: sinews.
[4] *Abst.* 3. 26. 1.
[5] *Adv. nat.* 2. 16. 27 ff. and *Abst.* 3. 22. 7.
[6] *Adv. nat.* 2. 16. 29–32; *Abst.* 3. 22. 7, adding that they use their sexual organs with pleasure; cf. *Abst.* 3. 10. 5: sexual continence in animals is more admirable than in man; see also Plutarch, *Brut. anim. rat.* 990 C–D; Ael. *De nat. anim.* 1. 24; 1. 50; 6. 39.

breathing through the nostrils may have come from Pliny,[7] and *Abst.* 3. 7. 3 gives the ass's lung as as example. Both observe that animals eat, drink, urinate, and defecate.[8] Arnobius and Porphyry note that animals repel hunger and watch for food, the latter being more specific, which is what we might expect.[9] Both polemicists state that animals feel diseases.[10] But finally, Arnobius uses the Platonic doctrine of the transmigration of souls into bodies of animals against Porphyry because, as we have already noticed, Porphyry did not accept this concept.

Keeping in mind that the cutting edge of Arnobius' argument is the use of the Stoic doctrine of the λόγος ἐνδιάθετος in animals to disprove man's superiority to the beasts, the principal objective being to destroy the premisses of the doctrine of the soul's divinity and immortality, we note the important statement in *Adv. nat.* 2. 17. 1 f.: 'Sed rationales nos sumus et intellegentia vincimus genus omne mutorum.' In *Abst.* Porphyry affirms that animals possess reason and intelligence (λογισμοῦ καὶ φρονήσεως). Plutarch could argue in a similar way by referring to animals that specialize in medicine, providing food, warfare, hunting, self-defence, and even music.[11] But a closer parallel with the Arnobian passage is *Abst.* 3. 15. 3, where Porphyry argues that animals manifest a rational intelligence (συνέσεως λογικῆς) in the acquisition of human arts: Ὅταν δὲ καὶ τέχνας ἀναλαμβάνῃ καὶ ταύτας ἀνθρωπίνας.[12] Arnobius responds to the question which begins 2. 17 by saying that he would believe that man was superior to animals if all men lived rationally and wisely, refrained from forbidden things, and none 'through his depraved intellect and blindness of ignorance asked for what was alien and even hostile to himself'. His words for 'depraved intellect' are *pravitate consilii*. A similar position is taken by Porphyry in *Abst.* 3. 19. 3: Πῶς δὲ οὐκ ἄλογον πολλοὺς τῶν ἀνθρώπων ἐπ' αἰσθήσει μόνον ζῶντας ὁρῶντας, νοῦν δὲ καὶ λόγον οὐκ ἔχοντας, continuing his argument by showing how men have surpassed animals in ferocity and their criminal acts. Arnobius gives a list of technical skills employed by animals in 2. 17. 16 f., and he may have used *De sollertia animalium* to argue against

---

[7] *Adv. nat.* 2. 16. 25 ff.; Pliny, *HN* 11. 72. 188; cf. 11. 100. 246: 'Nam simiarum genera perfectam hominis imitationem continent facie, naribus, auribus.'

[8] *Adv. nat.* 2. 16. 32–5; *Abst.* 3. 12. 4; 3. 14. 1; 3. 23. 5; the latter comes from Plutarch, *Brut. anim. rat.* 992 D: lynxes excrete; the swallows turn their tails upward, their backsides outward, and then they defecate.

[9] *Adv. nat.* 2. 16. 35–40 and *Abst.* 3. 14. 1.

[10] *Adv. nat.* 2. 16. 40–3 and *Abst.* 3. 7. 3.

[11] *Brut. anim. rat.* 961 B.

[12] *Abst.* 3. 15. 1.

Porphyry: animals make nests;[13] they make dwellings in rocks and crags"[14] they burrow in soil;[15] their construction of homes shows intelligence.[16] He ends 2. 17 by observing that if animals only had hands, they would create new works of art. Yet *parens natura* did not give them hands with which to work. Plotinus makes a similar point: nature has no hands or feet with which to work, and he compares the craftsmen who practise their arts with their hands, noting also that nature is a forming principle in plants and animals.[17] We may note in passing that beaks and claws were commonly found in the ancient texts which dealt with animal physiology and psychology.[18] A closer parallel to Arnobius can be found in the Stoic Balbus: 'Quam vero aptas quamque multarum artium ministras manus natura homini dedit.'[19] And the examples given in *Adv. nat.* 2. 18 should also be compared with Balbus' list of arts and crafts made by man's hands in *De nat. deor.* 2. 60. 150 ff. It is quite clear that Arnobius is using the Stoic concept of the λόγος ἐνδιάθετος possessed by animals to argue against the doctrine, espoused by his enemies, which held that the soul was immortal, rational, all-wise, and divine. Porphyry indeed appears to be the principal opponent underlying this diatribe, and a main source who has furnished Arnobius with many of his specific examples, observations, and philosophical concepts.

Arnobius similarly uses the same kind of Porphyrian source and method of argumentation in several passages in the seventh book where he develops a lengthy criticism of the practice of animal sacrifice. First, we must get a clear picture of Porphyry's position related to animal sacrifice. Eusebius explicitly informs us that Porphyry enjoined through the oracles of Apollo the performance of animal sacrifice, specifically pointing out that animals were to be offered to the etherial and heavenly powers (ταῖς αἰθερίοις καὶ οὐρανίοις ζωοθυτεῖν; *PE* 4. 8), the latter corresponding to Augustine's *caelestes deos* in *Civ. Dei* 19. 23, both of which appeared in *Phil. or.* And we should not overlook Arnobius' *caelestes* (also *caeles/caelites*) who are found frequently in his attack in book 7. In *Civ. Dei* 10. 10 we are told that Porphyry, in the *De reg. an.*,

---

[13] *Adv. nat.* 2. 17. 12 ff.; *De soll. anim.* 983 B–E; cf. Ael. *De nat. anim.* 4. 38.
[14] Cf. *De soll. anim.* 966 F: the spider that makes its web is producing a work of art; and *Adv. nat.* 2. 17. 25.
[15] *Adv. nat.* 2. 17. 26 f.; *De soll. anim.* 968 A–B: the complex passages of anthills; 972 A: the hedgehog's lair.
[16] *Adv. nat.* 2. 17. 28–35; *De soll. anim.* 974 A.
[17] *Enn.* 3. 8. 1.
[18] Plut. *De soll. anim.* 983 B–E; Ael. *De nat. anim.* 1. 31; Pliny, *HN* 11. 98. 243.
[19] *De nat. deor.* 1. 60. 150.

encouraged purificatory sacrifices to gods who could be bound by *passionibus et perturbationibus*, and later we are told that he learned this practice from Chaldaean schoolmasters (10. 27). Augustine also relates that he elevated human frailty to 'aetherias vel empyrias mundi sublimitates et firmamenta caelestia' (10. 27). We should not forget that a principal theme of *Civ. Dei* is the nature of true sacrifice. In *PE* 4. 9 a lengthy passage from *Phil. or.* is given to show that Porphyry *encouraged* the offering of animal sacrifices; but this is followed by a long introduction (*PE* 4. 10) to *Abst.* 2. 34, which takes up two chapters (4. 11–12), and these are in turn followed by a long quote from Apollonius of Tyana in Philostratus, and three more chapters which quote from the *Abstinentia*,[20] all of which argued *against* offering sacrifices to the gods. In *Abst.* 2. 34 (quoted above) Porphyry states that one must not sacrifice any of the things of sense to the High God, nor the outward speech, nor inner speech when it is defiled by passion in the soul, but only a 'pure silence' and pure thoughts concerning him. Sacrifice, he continues, is perfected in the impassibility of the soul and contemplation of the divine. Eusebius quotes *Abst.* 2. 43 in *PE* 4. 19, where Porphyry states that the wise man will not offer sacrifices (i.e. to demons), but will try to make, by every endeavour in the impassibility of his soul, a clearly formed conception of that which truly exists, to grow like God and those beings about him, and to grow unlike wicked men, demons, and everything which delights in what is both mortal and material.[21] It is obvious that Eusebius devotes a good part of book 4 to demonstrating that Porphyry contradicted himself on the subject of animal sacrifices: in *Phil. or.* he encouraged it, and in *Abst.* he rejected it, except to demons which a wise man would not do anyway. On the one hand, there was the practice which was so earthly, corporeal, bloody, and material; on the other, the true sacrifice in silence and pure thought, contemplation of the divine in clearly formed conceptions of the world of Being, and the necessity to flee mortal and material things. One was centred in an understanding of deity which viewed the gods as capable of suffering passions, and the other stressed being like the High God and those about him, a concept important for the present analysis, by means of extirpating the passions from the soul. These Porphyrian texts

[20] *PE* 4. 14–16.

[21] ἀλλ᾽ ἔκ τε ψυχῆς ἔκ τε τῶν ἐκτὸς πᾶσαν σπουδὴν ποιούμεθα θεῷ μὲν καὶ τοῖς ἀμφ᾽ αὐτὸν ὁμοιοῦσθαι, ὃ γίγνεται δι᾽ ἀπαθείας καὶ τῆς περὶ τῶν ὄντως ὄντων διηρθρωμένης διαλήψεως καὶ τῆς πρὸς αὐτὰ καὶ κατ᾽ αὐτὰ ζωῆς, πονηροῖς δὲ ἀνθρώποις καὶ δαίμοσι καὶ ὅλως παντὶ τῷ χαίροντι τῷ θνητῷ τε καὶ ὑλικῷ ἀνομοιοῦσθαι.

revealing such particular contradictions appear to have influenced the development of Arnobius' argument in *Adv. nat.* 7. Finally, in *DE* 1. 10 and 3. 3—the latter quotes *Abst.* 2. 34 as does *PE* 4. 11 f.—Eusebius uses Porphyry's rejection of sacrifice discussed in the *Abstinentia* to justify the Christians' rejection of it. Men of Old Testament times did not consider sacrifice to be sinful because they had not been taught that the souls of men and beasts are alike, that is to say, rational and intelligent (*DE* 1. 10).

We are now prepared to analyse the seventh book of the *Adversus nationes*. Arnobius begins book 7 by using Varro to support his argument that sacrifices should not be offered to the gods because they do not possess sensation: 'Quis est enim pectoris tam optunsi, qui aut rebus nullum habentibus sensum hostias caedat et victimas aut eis existimet dandas qui sunt ab his longe natura et beatitudine disiugati?'[22] Nothing sensible should be offered to the divine, so argued Porphyry, whether in sacrifice or in word.[23] Before we analyse our main text, let us note *Adv. nat.* 7. 5. 12–15 (R5*b*): 'Quicquid enim vexatur rei alicuius e motu, passibile esse constat et fragile: quod passioni fragilitatique subiectum est, id necesse est esse mortale,' placed in the context of criticizing the concept of appeasing the divine wrath with sacrifice. That is the same concept that Eusebius and Augustine find so disgusting in the theology of Porphyry.

McCracken's heading of *Adv. nat.* 7. 9 is quite accurate: *Why should innocent animals be sacrificed for guilty humans?* A *suasoria* featuring a talking ox rather pitifully pleading for his life in the name of justice takes up most of the chapter. The specific idea of a speaking animal might have been inspired by Plutarch, *Brut. anim. rat.* 986 F–987 A, where Gryllus becomes a pig and explains his experiences in the animal world with human speech. By using the talking ox who expresses himself articulately to defend his right to live, Arnobius not only drives home his argument with conviction and eloquence, he is also (again) using in 7. 9 the same basic Stoic concepts, with a few additions, as he does in 2. 16 ff. We now turn to the important text of *Adv. nat.* 7. 9. 1–8:

Ecce si bos aliquis aut quodlibet ex his animal, quod ad placandas caeditur mitigandasque ad numinum furias, vocem hominis sumat eloquaturque his verbis 'ergone o Iuppiter, aut quis[quis] alius deus es, humanum est istud et

[22] *Adv. nat.* 7. 1. 10–14.
[23] *Abst.* 2. 34.

rectum aut aequitatis alicuius in aestimatione ponendum, ut cum alius peccaverit, ego occidar et de meo sanguine fieri tibi patiaris satis . . .'[24]

Citing Plutarch, De soll. anim. 2, Porphyry, in Abst. 3. 20. 7, gives the Pythagorean attitude towards animals as being humane and pious, and Arnobius' 'humanum . . . rectum . . . aequitatis' suggests that this has influenced his choice of words. The ox continues his speech by defending his innocence: he is only a 'dumb animal' who has never wronged the deity by neglecting to celebrate his games, swearing by him, and so forth.[25] The ox now asks why should he be killed: 'An quod animal vile sum nec rationis nec consilii particeps, quemadmodum pronuntiant isti qui se homines nominant et ferocitate transiliunt beluas?' With this we should compare Abst. 3. 19. 3: Πῶς δὲ οὐκ ἄλογον πολλοὺς τῶν ἀνθρώπων ἐπ᾽ αἰσθήσει μόνον ζῶντας ὁρῶντας, νοῦν δὲ καὶ λόγον οὐκ ἔχοντας, πολλοὺς δὲ πάλιν ὠμότητι καὶ θυμῷ καὶ πλεονεξίᾳ τὰ φοβερώτατα τῶν θηρίων ὑπερβεβληκότας, παιδοφόνους καὶ πατροκτόνους, and Arnobius' reference to the killing of parents et alia in 7. 9. 41–3. Special penalties awaited the soul of those who committed violent crimes against their parents, according to the Platonic tradition.[26] Plutarch, in De esu. carn. 994 A–B, also said that man outdoes the beasts in cruelty by his own slaughters. According to Bouffartigue and Patillon, Sandbach's fragment 193 of a Plutarchian work is Porphyry's source in Abst. 3. 19. 3.[27]

In Adv. nat. 7. 9. 25 f., the ox asks: 'nonne spiritus unus est qui et illos et me regit?', which may be related to the remark in 2. 16, already analysed, that man and beast should be classified in the same number, or that they are of the same race. If this is what Arnobius intended to communicate, then Theophrastus' remark that men and animals are of the same race because the principles of their bodies are by nature the same, which also appears in Abst. 3. 25. 3, may be the immediate source of the passage. The enumeration of the bodily senses and organs which follows this statement, given by the ox to prove that man and animal are alike, certainly supports this interpretation. Arnobius is clearly using

[24] The English is: 'Suppose an ox, or whatever animal you please, slain to appease and soothe the fury of the deities, were to take the voice of a man and speak out in these words: "O Jupiter, or whatever other god thou art, is this, then, humane or right, or is it to be regarded as fair at all, that when someone else has sinned, I should be killed and from my blood thou shouldest allow satisfaction to be given thee?"'

[25] Adv. nat. 7. 9. 9–20.

[26] Phaedo 113 E–114 A.

[27] Cf. Bouffartigue–Patillon (1977), 138.

the kind of 'scientific method' which Porphyry demanded from the
Christians to prove the credibility of their faith, in order to disprove
the pagan concept that animal sacrifice spiritually benefits man.

In turning to the enumeration mentioned, Arnobius first refers to the
fact that the bodies of both man and animal are affected by the same
kinds of senses.[28] The same concept is expressed by Porphyry, who
quotes a rather lengthy passage from *De sollertia animalium*, in *Abst.* 3.
21. 9.[29] The possession of sensation denotes *ipso facto* the possession of
intellection: Arnobius introduces the latter a few lines below, 7. 9. 26 f.
A closer parallel also comes from *Abst.* (7. 7. 1–7. 8. 1), and Porphyry's
source is the παλαιοί, which may refer to the tradition of the Old or
Middle Academy.[30] In this passage Porphyry argues that the sensations
which affect man and animal are the same. His list includes taste, sight,
smell, and hearing. Both Arnobius and Porphyry base their arguments
upon the belief that animals possess the λόγος ἐνδιάθετος (cf. *Abst.* 3.
7. 1). Porphyry even continued his argument by giving examples of
animals that are superior to man in respect of the possession and use of
various senses.[31] Both polemicists are maintaining that just because the
internal organs of man and animal are the same in number and
arrangement, as well as in function, it is necessary to conclude that
animals are rational beings. And rational beings should not be offered
to the gods in bloody sacrifices; hence the logic of Arnobius' mentioning
that animals possess such internal organs as livers, hearts, intestines,
with which we should compare Porphyry's line of argumentation in
Abst. 3. 7 f. In *Adv. nat.* 2. 16. 29–32, we observed that Arnobius
mentioned the begetting of young among the animals as the result of
sexual intercourse. In 7. 9. 29–32, the emphasis is upon love of the
young and the delight felt by the parents when offspring are born. Again
depending upon *De sollertia animalium*, Porphyry develops the same
kind of argument in *Abst.* 3. 22. 7,[32] where the idea appears that the
principle of social life and justice that manifests itself in the affection

[28] *Adv. nat.* 7. 9. 26 f.: 'non consimili ratione respiro et video ceteris adficior sensibus?'
[29] *Abst.* 3. 21. 9: ὅθεν ἀνάγκη πᾶσιν οἷς τὸ αἰσθάνεσθαι, καὶ τὸ νοεῖν ὑπάρχειν.
[30] Οὕτω σχεδὸν ἁπάντων τὰ σώματα ὁμοίως τοῖς ἡμετέροις κατὰ τὰ πάθη. Τά γε μὴν τῆς
ψυχῆς πάθη ὅρα εἰ μὴ πάντα ὅμοια· καὶ πρῶτά γε τὴν αἴσθησιν. Οὐ γὰρ δὴ ἀνθρώπου μὲν ἡ
γεῦσις χυμῶν, ἡ δὲ ὄψις χροιῶν, ἢ ὀσμῶν ἢ ὄσφρησις ἀντιλαμβάνεται, ἢ ψόφων ἡ ἀκοή,
ἢ θερμῶν ἢ ψυχρῶν ἢ ἁφὴ ἢ τῶν ἄλλων ἁπτῶν, οὐχὶ δὲ καὶ τῶν ζῴων ἁπάντων ὁμοίως.
[31] *Abst.* 3. 8. 3–9.
[32] Τὴν γοῦν πρὸς τὰ ἔγγονα φιλοστοργίαν ἀρχὴν μὲν ἡμῖν κοινωνίας καὶ δικαιοσύνης
τιθέμενοι, πολλὴν δὲ τοῖς ζῴοις καὶ ἰσχυρὰν ὁρῶντες παροῦσαν, οὔ φασιν αὐτοῖς οὐδ'
ἀξιοῦσι μετεῖναι δικαιοσύνης·

which humans have for their young, and that although the Stoics
acknowledged the expression of such affection among animals, they
denied the latter any participation in justice. We recall that Porphyry's
argument in *Abst.* is that animals possess both kinds of reason, and he
defends the concept that humans owe animals justice, against the Stoics
and Peripatetics, because they practise it within a community possessed
of reason. He uses the Pythagorean concept of the necessity of maintaining a relationship between man and animal based upon justice; and
one manifestation of this virtue was, of course, to abstain from eating
the meat of animals. This necessitated the killing of an innocent creature—and here we must compare Arnobius—which was
in turn tantamount to committing an injustice. Both Arnobius and
Porphyry use the common scientific observation of the ancient world
that animals show intelligence in caring for their young,[33] base it upon
Stoic concepts and Pythagorean justice, and use this as evidence as
to why animals should not be sacrificed to the gods because they
possess reason.

A new concept is now introduced into the ox's speech in 7. 9. 32–6:
'Of course, they are possessed of reason and use articulate speech. But
how do they know whether I, too, do what I do by a reasoning of my
own and whether the sound which I utter is not my own method of
language and one understood by us alone?'[34] Although Juba II's work
on animal behaviour, now unfortunately lost, dealt with the ability of
various animals to mimic human speech,[35] it is doubtful that he explained
this on the basis of Stoic philosophy. Besides, Arnobius makes it clear
that animals possess the ability to speak in an intelligible language to
each other, and here we are met with the Stoic doctrine of the λόγος
προφορικός. A similar concept is found in *Abst.* 3. 3. 3: λόγου γε ὄντος
μέτοχα τὰ ζῷα τὰ φωνητικά, τῶν μὲν ἀνθρώπων κατὰ νόμους τοὺς
ἀνθρωπείους φθεγγομένων, τῶν δὲ ζῴων κατὰ νόμους οὓς παρὰ τῶν
θεῶν καὶ τῆς φύσεως εἴληχεν ἕκαστον. His source is the ambiguous
'ancients' which again probably refers to a tradition dependent either
upon the Old or Middle Academy. The same source argued that it was
egotistical for man to deprive animals of the possession of both kinds

---

[33] Cf. Ael. *De nat. anim.*, prolog.; 1. 4; 1. 18; 2. 19; 2. 40; 3. 8; 3. 10; 3. 16; 10. 8; Plut.
De soll. anim. 966 B; 970 E; 983 B; 962 A; Pliny, *HN* 8. 80. 215.
[34] *Adv. nat.* 7. 9. 32–6: 'Sed rationes illi sunt et articulatas exprimunt voces. Et unde
illis notum est an et ego facio meis rationibus faciam et vox ista quam promo mei generis
verba sint et solis intellegantur a nobis?'
[35] Cf. Pliny, *HN* 8. 45. 107.

of reason.[36] Also, just as the Greeks cannot understand the language of
the Scythians who speak to themselves distinctly and articulately, so it
is with the animals: they speak in a language known to themselves.[37]
Although the animals make sounds that are unintelligible to humans, it
would be impudent to conclude that they therefore do not possess
reason under the pretext that they themselves do not understand what
they are saying.[38]

We now come to the very important conclusion to the ox's speech:

Ask Piety whether it is more just that I be slain, done away with, or that man
should be pardoned and be free from punishment for what he has done. Who
formed iron into a sword? Was it not man? Who brought disaster upon races,
slavery upon nations? Was it not man? Who mixed deadly poisons and offered
them to parents, brothers, to wives, to friends? Was it not man? Who conceived
or devised so many misdeeds that they can scarcely be set forth in ten thousand
annals or days? Was it not man? Is not this, then, bestial, monstrous, savage,
does it seem to thee, O Jupiter, unjust and barbarous for me to be killed, for
me to be slain, that thou mightest be appeased and that acquittal rest on the
guilty?[39]

The gist is that it is not pious (cf. *pietatem*) or just (*aequius*; *iniustum*)
to slaughter an innocent animal while the real criminal is pardoned. He
now introduces into his argument the Pythagorean concept of justice
between man and beast. According to Plutarch, it was the Stoics who
said that humans have no compact of justice with the animals.[40] In *De
soll. anim.* 964 E, he informs us that Pythagoras reintroduced the concept
of justice towards animals, that is, he abstained from eating them,
refused to sacrifice them to any deity, and practised kindness towards
them.[41] We recall that immediately after citing *Abst.* 2. 34, Eusebius
gives a text from Philostratus containing the very 'spiritual' theology of
Apollonius of Tyana, both of whom rejected animal sacrifice.[42]

Porphyry's principal source for *Abst.* 2. 5–32 was Theophrastus' Περὶ
Εὐσεβείας, and for the present investigation we are particularly interested
in 2. 22–4, adequately summed up by Bouffartigue–Patillon: 'Il est
impossible de sacrifier des animaux sans injustice ou sans impiété:

[36] *Abst.* 3. 2. 4.
[37] Ibid. 3. 3. 4 ff.
[38] Ibid. 3. 4. 4.
[39] *Adv. nat.* 7. 9. 36–49.
[40] *De esu. carn.* 999 A–B; cf. 994 E: animals seek justice.
[41] Cf. also *De soll. anim.* 959 F.
[42] *PE* 4. 10; *Abst.* 2. 34. 2.

injustice si l'on tue des animaux inoffensifs, impiété si l'on sacrifie les autres, qui sont indignes d'être offerts.'⁴³ Similar to the statement made by Arnobius' ox, Theophrastus *apud* Porphyry asserts: Ἐν τῷ δέ γε θύειν ἀναιροῦντες τὰ μηθὲν ἀδικοῦντα τῶν ζῴων, ἀδικήσειν ὁμολογοῦμεν.⁴⁴ Porphyry follows *De soll. anim.* here, but he adds that those who practise this are preferred to those (i.e. the Stoics) who say that this practice destroys habitual justice. Referring again to the 'ancients' in 3. 18. 1, Porphyry skilfully uses the Stoics' argument against them: τῆς δὲ δικαιοσύνης πρὸς τὰ λογικὰ οὔσης, καθάπερ φασὶν οἱ ἀντιλέγοντες, πῶς οὐχὶ καὶ πρὸς ταῦτα εἴη ἂν ἡμῖν τὸ δίκαιον;. He begins book 3 with the affirmation that the best expression of justice in piety towards the gods is above all to abstain from the eating of animal flesh.⁴⁶ In 3. 1. 4 he acknowledges that the doctrine of justice towards animals, which has its basis in the belief that animals are rational and possess both sensation and memory, derives from Pythagoras. According to this doctrine, so argues Porphyry, humans should extend justice to every animal. Finally, the theme of justice and piety towards animals, derived from Pythagoras (who is named), specifically in the form of abstinence, takes up the concluding chapters of book 3.⁴⁷

We end by observing a number of other parallels between Arnobius (book 7) and Porphyry (*Abst.* and *Phil. or.*). In 7. 3 Arnobius argues that the divine has no body: the incorporeal cannot be nourished by the corporeal. Porphyry gives the similar idea that one must not sacrifice to the God who is over all anything that is sensible, either in holocaust or in word; there is nothing material which does not immediately become impure for an immaterial being. In the same text Porphyry maintains that the best sacrifice to the High God is pure thoughts and pure silence cultivated in the impassibility of the soul. Yet we have noticed above in the works of Eusebius and Augustine, that the same philosopher held that the 'heavenly powers' (*caelestes deos*) were capable of suffering disturbing passions or mental agitations, and we have concluded that it is this specific doctrine, espoused by Porphyry in *Phil. or.* and *De reg. an.* under Chaldaean influence, which Arnobius criticizes in the development of his attack upon the anthropopathic behaviour of the deities throughout *Adv. nat.* 1, and 3–7. In light of this, we observe now that book 7 is pregnant with such anti-anthropopathic texts, its

⁴³ Bouffartigue–Patillon (1977), 5.
⁴⁴ *Abst.* 2. 24. 2.
⁴⁶ Ibid. 3. 1. 2.
⁴⁷ Ibid. 3. 26 f.

principal theme is animal sacrifice, and both Eusebius and Augustine use similar arguments against Porphyry in the same context. For example, note that in *Adv. nat.* 7. 4 the rhetor attacks the concept that the sacrifices give the deities pleasure (*voluptas*), which he exclaims is a passion which causes them to behave like a base animal. Hence if they feel this, they must have the five senses, and therefore they are mortal (R5*a*) because whatever has sensation must also have a body. He vacillates from Stoic concepts of the passions detrimental to the human soul, to the Pythagorean doctrine of justice towards all animals (against the Stoics), and returns again to Stoicism. This does not mean that he was syncretistic, confused, or pessimistic—because in *Adv. nat.* 2. 26 ff., he argues that man should not be considered superior to the animals— as perhaps too many Arnobius scholars have erroneously argued. He can use a philosophical concept to attack one of an opposite position in one section of his work, and later reverse the process, all for polemical purposes, and we should not think badly about him. The Christians of his time were fighting for their lives against a number of formidable foes. (Origen employs the same method of argumentation at the end of *C. Cels.* 4.) In such vacillation he is simply doing to Porphyry what Porphyry himself had done to many of his enemies: he is taking his enemy's ideas and using them against him.

We conclude that Arnobius in book 7, like Eusebius in *PE* 4 and Augustine in *Civ. Dei* 10, has carefully analysed the contradictions inherent in Porphyry's works which dealt with the subject of animal sacrifice, and has exploited these to ensure that his great contemporary enemy was presented with a strong counter-attack: he uses Stoic concepts about the passions harmful to the soul to criticize Porphyry's theology delineated in *Phil. or.* and *De reg. an.*, which encouraged sacrificing to deities which are capable of suffering passions; and Stoic doctrines of the λόγος ἐνδιάθετος and λόγος προφορικός, in addition to the Pythagorean doctrine of justice and piety towards the gods, the same concepts used by Porphyry in *Abst.*, to provide evidence that such sacrifices were both impious and unjust. He can also use the same two Stoic concepts to argue against the views of the human soul, espoused by his Neoplatonic– Chaldaean adversary, and his view that the gods are capable of suffering passions. The gist of Arnobius' argument is quite clear: Porphyry has turned the normal theological understanding of the God–man relation- ship upside down by divinizing man and humanizing the gods.

In *Abst.* 2. 24. 1 Porphyry gives three reasons why men sacrifice to the gods: to honour them, to give them thanks, and to ask for their favours; Arnobius attacks the first and the last of these in 7. 10 ff. and 7. 13, respectively. The latter refers to men who are savages because they eat the flesh of animals, thus breaking the law of humanity that united both men and beast (7. 4), which appears to be Pythagorean. In criticizing the concept of sacrificing to the gods for favours, he remarks: 'Cum enim ordinem vertere et fatalia nequeant constituta mutare, quid rei, quid causae est fatigare et obtundere eorum aures velle quorum auxiliis nequeas supremis in necessitatibus fidere?' (7. 10. 25–9); and with this we should compare *PE* 6. 1–6, where Porphyry, in the *Phil. or.*, explicitly subjected the gods to the power of fate. In *Adv. nat.* 7. 19, the sacrificial laws maintain that white victims should be sacrificed to the gods above, and black victims to the infernal gods below. We may offer a parallel in *PE* 4. 9, where Eusebius gives a passage from *Phil. or.* containing an oracle of Apollo and a Porphyrian commentary, and the correspondence is rather striking. In 7. 16, Arnobius says that birds are among the victims offered to the gods above; with which we should compare *PE* 4. 9, again taken from *Phil. or.*, which prescribes that birds be sacrificed to the gods of the air. Both *Adv. nat.* 7. 10 ff. and Porphyry (*Phil. or.* in *PE* 4. 9) contain the concept that the gods above—Porphyry adds those of the ether—receive sacrifices in order that they might give good things to humankind and thus avert evils. Both also attack the belief that gods receive pleasure from the sacrifices (*Adv. nat.* 7. 4; *Abst.* 2. 60. 3). Both argue that sacrifices encourage one to commit sin due to the belief that one can buy off transgressions committed against the deity.[48] Both apparently follow the same story, taken from book 26 of Theopompus' *Philippica*,[49] about the rich man who sacrificed a great quantity of his cattle to the gods, and the poor man who lived in a modest home and only burnt incense in their honour.[50]

---

[48] *Adv. nat.* 7. 8; *Abst.* 2. 60. 3.

[49] Bouffartigue–Patillon (1977), 204 n. 1.

[50] *Adv. nat.* 7. 12; *Abst.* 2. 16. 1–5: the difference being that the former makes the rich man the good man to argue against the belief that gods favour those who can bribe them with many gifts; and the latter, arguing against animal sacrifice, obviously favours the incense-burner.

Conclusions

Porphyry's disqualification of Christ as the *via universalis animae liberandae*, and his attempt to offer such a way to the non-philosopher, appears to have been a principal reason why Arnobius has attempted to prove that Christ is the only *via salutis animae universalis*. The latter has also apparently taken Porphyry's criticism of the faith just as seriously as Eusebius did in the *PE* and *DE*. And like Eusebius, he can use the same argument not only to 'prove' that Christianity is the only way of universal salvation for the soul, but also to provide evidence clearly demonstrating the fact that everything about Graeco-Roman religious culture is a lie.

It was in exposing the inconsistencies, contradictions, and therefore falsehoods in Porphyry's works themselves that Eusebius, Arnobius, and (later) Augustine apparently concluded that they could easily refute the criticism of the Christian religion. This was especially the case in respect of his *via salutis* for the common man, which encouraged the use of sacrifices to the gods who were thought capable of suffering passions. Arnobius, Eusebius, and Augustine have taken issue with him on this subject. A major inconsistency was the great difference in the two soteriological ways, one emphasizing the necessity to flee everything related to the body, mortality, and the passions; the other so clearly associated with the corporeal, the mortal, and the passions. This is not to say that the Christians ignored the fine points of each way, and that they did not give Porphyry credit for something that must have been much more admirable than they will allow. It simply appears to be a valid assumption that they were not in a position to give many compliments. Hence another clear issue in the Christian–pagan debate was the impassibility of the divine nature. Arnobius and Eusebius both argue that their faith offers the correct notion of deity; and therefore the Christians are involved in the truly spiritual worship of the High God, whom they worship in contemplation, right concepts, and in silence. Pagans have nothing more than misconceptions of deity and therefore do not benefit from their false worship.

Arnobius and Eusebius have noticed also the inconsistencies of Porphyry on the subject of sacrifice in the *Philosophy on the Oracles* and the *Abstinentia*. Arnobius uses the philosophical concepts of Porphyry's *Abst.* to do to him the same thing that he did to the Stoics, namely, to use Porphyry's arguments against him. So he uses the two kinds of reason of Stoicism and the concept of justice and piety towards the

animals of Pythagoreanism, derived from the *Abstinentia*, to develop his
argument, against the kind of animal sacrifice encouraged in *Phil. or.*
He also uses Stoic concepts about the passions to attack Porphyry's
sacrificial-theurgical theories which held that the heavenly gods were
able to experience these emotions. It was worship of this kind that
proved the misconceptions of deity espoused by the pagans. On a
philosophical level, Arnobius also uses the Stoic concept of the λόγος
ἐνδιάθετος to prove that man and animal are of the same race, both are
rational beings, and therefore man should not be considered superior to
the animals: he is not divine, immortal, and ready to 'fly to the Lord's
palace'. We have noted in earlier chapters and here that Arnobius attacks
a Chaldaean–Neoplatonic group, and chronologically, religiously, and
polemically this interpretation makes perfect sense. Their theurgical
practices mentioned in *Adv. nat.* 2. 13, 2. 33, and 2. 62, and the higher
way of salvation realized in the daily struggles to extirpate the passions,
come to nought: it is only Christ's gift which enables man to experience
true *salus*. Only Christ can help humans to overcome the passions that
would otherwise destroy them. And only Christ has revealed to humanity
the knowledge of *deus verus*: He is the genuine *via salutis animae
liberandae*. Porphyry's philosophical way divinized man, and his religious
way humanized the gods. Both failed to offer man any true way to
God.[51]

---

[51] Cf. Beatrice (1988), 128: 'Arnobe entre donc de plein droit parmi les témoins
chrétiens de l'œuvre antichrétienne de Porphyre: il témoigne de sa diffusion parmi les
païens d'Afrique à une date très haute, et surtout il témoigne que cette œuvre devrait être
identifiée avec la *Philosophie des oracles*.'

12

Epilogue

Arnobius was a professor of Latin rhetoric who taught in the North African city of Sicca Veneria during the reign of Diocletian. These two conclusions to the present study are significant for several reasons. First, they are significant for the history of Christianity in Roman North Africa specifically, and in the Roman Empire in general. Second, the work of Arnobius, the *Adversus nationes*, is to be understood as an important document resulting from the great religious conflict and competition that occurred during the Age of Diocletian. We have seen a regional aspect to this struggle in the form of the acute kind of competition going on in the North African Provinces between Christianity and the Saturn cult. Yet there was also a universal conflict happening within the Roman Empire, and the *Adversus nationes* played an important role in providing a sustained and enlightened response to the anti-Christian propaganda which was published before the beginning of the Great Persecution in February 303. The suggestion that Arnobius wrote his work between the period 302 and before the Persecution had ended in 305, is very significant in light of several events related to the history of Christianity in the Roman Empire and in North Africa.

In respect of the history of the Church in North Africa, we have concluded that in the *Adv. nat.* the reader may discover a few glimpses of what was already beginning to be the greatest upheaval in the religious history of North Africa: the conflict and competition between Christianity and the cult of Saturn. The latter was the national cult of North Africa, and the god Saturn was conceived as the great lord of all in both a cosmological and a terrestrial sense. He was the true lord of heaven and earth, who controlled the elements, who blessed the crops, and who made the seeds fruitful. He was thought to be the undisputed *deus frugifer* and the agrarian deity *par excellence* in Roman North Africa, but in all other provinces of the empire his identity and many of his functions as a deity were quite differently conceived. Hence the importance of analysing the biographical information concerning Arnobius given by Jerome, and we have concluded that the latter has given information about Arnobius on which we may reasonably rely. We do not know whether he was born or even died in North Africa, but we can be almost certain that he was living there when he wrote his work. It is not surprising, in light of these data, to find a conception of the Christian God that has come under the influence of the great god of the North Africans. We have analysed the principal text which depicts a providential deity who blesses *aequaliter* the crops of pagans and Christians alike (*Adv. nat.* 3. 24), who makes the sun to shine, sends the rains, and provides for the material needs of man, as one such Saturnian text. A number of passages in book 1 also reveal a concept of God as controller of the natural elements, and we have concluded that his use of *frugifer* to describe the High God's specific way that he blesses the seeds to make them fruitful, was probably written during a period in North Africa when the agrarian situation was characterized by drought and subsequent crop failure. The immediate source of his Christian theology which informed his concept of divine providence and supplied him with a precise theological vocabulary and a highly revered authority was the *De bono patientiae* of Cyprian. Thus the Christian–pagan debate in North Africa concerning concepts of deity centred around the doctrine of providence in the context of this contemporary agrarian crisis; the belief in an all-powerful deity who controlled the natural elements, and the competition between Saturn and the Christian God over who was the legitimate Lord of the harvest. Arnobius' contribution to the debate appears to have been his emphasis upon the Christian God's bestowing blessings upon all regardless of their religious affiliation, and combining with this concept the practice of sharing one's possessions with all persons both Christian and pagan (cf. *Adv. nat.* 4. 36); and a strong affirmation of a clear and unambiguous eschatology, neither of which was as clearly conceived or taught in the Saturn cult. It is quite clear from this that the Christians were better organized institutionally and better equipped theologically to take their message of divine providence, in time of need, to those who were outside the camps of both Christian Church and Saturn cult.

Yet overwhelmingly the evidence related to the contemporary Christian–pagan debate on the subject of concepts of deity has forced us to re-examine the arguments of Kroll, Bidez, Courcelle, O'Meara, Hadot, Fortin, Frend, and Wilken who have to varying degrees associated the polemics of Arnobius in book 2 with a good number of Porphyry's philosophical ideas. O'Meara and Wilken inspired the present writer to investigate the possibility that Arnobius may be responding to Porphyry in book 1 as well. Yet immediately the realization occurred that Eusebius, who has hitherto been an unknown entity in the Arnobius–Porphyrian theory, might also shed some light on the problem, and we have seen that he has been immensely helpful. Neither have we ignored Augustine, who was instrumental in Bidez's suggestion at the turn of the century, and in Courcelle's in 1954, that Arnobius is clearly responding to the *De reg. an.* and the *CC* in book 2. One significance of the present study is that Porphyry's polemical arguments cannot be restricted to book 2 of the *Adversus nationes*, and one example is the response of Arnobius in book 1 to the Hecatean Oracle which formed an important part of Porphyry's anti-Christian propaganda before the Great Persecution began. Arnobius has also taken Porphyry's rejection of Christ's deity, thereby concluding that he was mortal in soul, mind, and body, and turned it against him by using the Stoic concepts of the passions that can harm the human soul (*De fin.* 3. 10. 35), to argue that it is the pagan deities who are mortal. The principal object of his criticism of the athropopathic depictions of the deities in the myths was Porphyry's conception of the deities in heaven, discussed in *Phil. or.* and *De reg. an.*, who are capable of suffering passions or mental agitations. Especially in respect of this subject, but indeed in relation to many others, Arnobius, Eusebius, and Augustine have attempted to do to Porphyry what Porphyry himself did to the Christians: they have fought their enemy not only on his own intellectual ground, but they have also used his methods of argumentation, his own religious and philosophical concepts, and the inconsistencies and contradictions clearly present in his own writings, and turned them against him.

Arnobius, Eusebius, and Augustine have all attempted to show in their own way how far Porphyry has fallen from the true Platonic tradition. Arnobius and Eusebius can take over Porphyry's terminology related to the right concepts of deity conducive to the right kind of worship; the importance of overcoming the passions; the flight to the divine in contemplation; and the specific use of the Pythagorean and Chaldaean concept of silence before the deity; all of which clearly prove that it is the Christians who have the correct conception of deity, who have the truth, and therefore they possess in Christ the true way of salvation. Arnobius and Eusebius have taken very seriously Porphyry's contention that Christian faith does not have any 'scientific evidence' which might clearly demonstrate that the promises contained therein are true. They respond throughout their works (*Adv. nat.*, *PE*, and

DE) by (1) using the literature of their opponents as evidence to prove that there is no truth in polytheism, and (2) providing evidence from their own religious tradition which clearly demonstrates the truth of their beliefs. Hence Arnobius and Eusebius develop the latter around miracles seen by persons from all over the world; the universal diffusion of Christianity which has occurred as the result of divine support; the same power that was in Christ operated in his disciples; and that Christ is the saviour of all persons, everywhere, and for all time. Porphyry was mixed up with Platonism on the one hand, and Chaldaean theology and practices on the other.

Arnobius is clearly as much determined to prove the divinity of Christ and that He alone has revealed to humanity the conception of *deus verus* and thus the only way of salvation, as he is to prove the mortality of the gods and that the myths do not reveal any clear conception of *deus verus*; therefore they do not benefit their worshippers in any way, much less provide them a way of salvation. Christ as the *via universalis salutis* is concerned in a geographical sense, and in an ontological sense as well, by soteriologically blessing the whole of an individual's being, soul, mind, and body. And the fact that Arnobius incorporates the human body into his soteriological understanding of Christ presupposes that he is both faithful to the biblical picture of Christ as the Great Physician, thereby providing a way of experiencing physical *salus* through him, and it is highly suggestive that he is responding to Porphyry, who in the *Phil. or.* and undoubtedly under Chaldaean influence, encouraged purificatory sacrifices for the body. The fact that Arnobius mounts a counter-attack upon the Hecatean Oracle partly by showing that Christ was divine because he healed physical diseases, thus overcoming the laws of fate, supports this interpretation: Porphyry's conception of deities who are subjected to the fates and therefore cannot heal physical diseases (*PE* 6. 1–6) is undoubtedly the object of this emphasis upon Christ as the healer of the body.

The significance of the contemporary Christian–pagan debate, at least to the degree that Arnobius' work sheds light on that debate, reveals itself especially in the specific work which not only received serious attention from Arnobius, but also Eusebius and Augustine. That work was Porphyry's *On the Philosophy of Oracles*, and it would appear from the evidence that has been pieced together in the present work that Porphyry's Hecatean Oracle and his commentary upon it, both of which totally rejected the deity of Christ, was perhaps one of the most dangerous pieces of anti-Christian literature, in addition to the *Contra Christianos*, during the ante-Nicene period. It was dangerous because it offered both a critical and a constructive approach to the Christian problem as Porphyry perceived it. On the critical side, Christ was a mortal, supposedly good and pious, who was nevertheless condemned by right-minded judges; who got his followers entangled in error; who practised Egyptian sorcery; who taught one doctrine and his disciples another; and the disciples were fated never to receive any blessings from the gods, and never to be able to form a conception of Jupiter the immortal; who only pretended to worship the High God; and who did not worship God by those things which such worship demands, namely the virtues, the gist being that the Christians were immoral because of their false worship, and this was due to not having the right conception of God; and we may add the criticism of Peter who was accused of being a magician, derived from *Phil. or.*, to which Arnobius responds in 2. 13. On the constructive side, Porphyry claimed that *Phil. or.* could be accepted now as the sure source of salvation; he used the oracles of the gods to prove, after critical examination of the evidence, the excellent natures of the deities, thereby showing to his readers that his discussion provided the right concept of deity; he supported the traditional practices of polytheism which had lived in the Graeco-Roman world throughout the centuries, and especially the use of animal sacrifice as a way of worshipping the deities; and he even included much philosophical discussion, and it is because of this double approach (philosophical and religious) in the *Phil. or.* (and also in the *De reg. an.*) that we have concluded that Porphyry offered one way of salvation to the philosophers and another to the non-philosophers. If we add to this work the fact that Porphyry apparently approached the Christian problem critically and constructively also in the *De reg. an.*, and Arnobius' response to Porphyry's attempt to prove the credibility of polytheism by referring to the miracles of the Magna Mater and Aesculapius at the end of *Adv. nat.* 7 reveals that he did, the two works together undoubtedly posed unprecedented problems for the Christian religion. Yet the fifteen-volume work *Contra Christianos*, which appears to have gone totally over to the offensive by critically examining the Bible to prove its inconsistencies, must have been the crowning event to Porphyry's career as an anti-Christian polemicist, and the pagan world now had an anti-Christian trilogy that it understood to be authoritative, 'scientific', highly respectful, spiritually and intellectually beneficial, and encyclopaedic in its scope. And there is evidence that Arnobius is aware of some of the very dangerous arguments directed towards Christianity, as well as those which supported religious and philosophical paganism, derived from all three works.

This now brings us to the most important question of all: what significance does the Arnobius–Porphyry connection have for helping us to understand both Arnobius the pagan and the Christian, and what significance does this have for the history of the Church under the Roman Empire, specifically under Diocletian's reign?

Perhaps if we go back to Jerome's biographical information concerning Arnobius we may get a clearer picture of the rhetor. We recall that according to Jerome, Arnobius always used to fight against the Christian religion, and it was this that made the bishop hesitant when he sought admission into his Church. We have assumed that if Arnobius was as vicious and skilful in his attack upon the Church as he was in his criticism of pagan practices and beliefs, the bishop will have had every good reason for being suspicious of him.

We have seen that Arnobius is responding to Porphyry in many more passages of his work than has hitherto been thought. In book 1 he defends against the Hecatean Oracle and Porphyry's commentary upon it. In book 2 we have argued that Porphyry is the principal opponent of Arnobius. In books 3–7, where Arnobius criticizes the anthropo-morphic and anthropopathic gods of the myths to prove that they are mortal because they suffer emotions and mental agitations, the rhetor is responding to the Neoplatonist's assertion that Christ was mortal. We have argued that a major source for his argumentation is the Stoic doctrine of the passions which harm the soul found in *De fin.* 3. 10. 35. Finally, the brilliant way that Arnobius uses the Stoic doctrine of the λόγος ἐνδιάθετος and the λόγος προφορικός in book 7, as well as the Pythagorean concept of justice and piety towards the animals, and the Pythagorean–Chaldaean doctrine concerning silence before God, again betrays a clear and undeniable Porphyrian connection. And in response to the accusation that Christian scripture was inconsistent and con-tradictory, which was developed by Porphyry in several of his works, Arnobius was able, like Eusebius and Augustine, to take Porphyrian ideas found in one work (e.g. piety and justice towards animals) and use them against ideas he upholds in another work. For example, in the *Abst.* he argued against animal sacrifices, and in the *Phil. or.* he encouraged them. And because Diocletian's fourth edict demanded universal sacrifice, the seventh book of the *Adversus nationes* is extremely important as an historical document because it reveals the developing conflict between the Christian and pagan intelligentsia about animal sacrifice during the early fourth century.

A new conclusion has been drawn, and a new theory proposed, in the often complex, confusing, and controversial subject of Arnobiana. We have already suggested that Arnobius' apology (*Adv. nat.* 1–2) might best be considered not as an *apology* in the classical sense, but rather a written testimony, in the form of personal retractions of his public criticisms of Christianity (cf. Jerome), to prove the sincerity of his desire to become a member of the Church at Sicca. He indeed appears to be familiar with much of the anti-Christian propaganda of his contemporary Porphyry, and it makes very good sense to theorize that he is probably retracting the Porphyrian criticism of the faith which he himself had been using in his own attack upon Christianity. For what newly converted Christian, most probably not yet under catechetical instruction, who is ignorant of the OT and apparently much of the NT, and who has been called by various scholars 'confused', 'heterodox', 'unorthodox', 'heretical', and 'half-pagan', would seriously think that he could write an apology of the Christian faith? He was certainly not writing merely a rhetorical exercise, and he is sincere in his Christian beliefs. The possibility that he did use Porphyry's arguments against Christianity as a pagan would help us better to understand Jerome's remark that he always used to attack the faith, and the bishop's reluctance immediately to admit him into the membership of his Church. For we may rightly ask what bishop would not have been apprehensive when the professional rhetor in the college at Sicca—at the forum where such instruction was usually given—who had been breathing Porphyrian fire upon every basic tenet of the faith of which he was the guardian, approached him to be accepted into his Church? This interpretation exonerates Arnobius from the above charges, but it does so without reading into the pages of the *Adversus nationes* something that is not there. The evidence is quite convincing that the principal adversary of the work of Arnobius is Porphyry.

The other part of our question is: what significance does the Arnobius–Porphyry connection have for the history of the Christian Church under the Roman Empire, specifically during the Tetrarchy? Because the history of the early Church is *inseparable* from the history of the Roman Empire, the *Adversus nationes* is an important historical document not only because it gives the reader a good picture of the state of the paganism of the period and of the relations between Church and State, but perhaps more importantly because it is the last *apologetic* work written by a Christian during the last Great Persecution and immediately before the sanctioning of the Church by Rome. The period between Diocletian and Constantine was critical for the history of the Church, and we have noticed that Arnobius, supported by evidence derived from Augustine and Eusebius, is responding to many of the anti-Christian statements of Porphyry: the correct concept of deity; the nature of a *verus deus*; the temporal and eschatological benefits of worship; and the precise definition of religious sacrifice. Based on the foregoing analyses of Porphyrian propaganda, we can certainly conclude that the *Philosophia ex oraculis* must have been a brilliant piece of anti-Christian literature. This much is clear, but it was also an excellent apology for Graeco-Roman religious concepts and practices which gave full support to traditional polytheism. The way that Porphyry claims that the work could be viewed as the only sure source of salvation strongly suggests that he incorporated everything in this work which might help all pagans in their search for salvation in the context of their own religious culture. He also appears to have paid particular attention to encouraging animal sacrifice, and we have noted Arnobius' response to his anthropopathic conception of the deities to whom such sacrifices should be made, and how he uses Porphyry against Porphyry to argue for the mortality of the deities who are believed to receive these sacrifices. We recall that Arnobius' attack upon the sacrifices corresponds chronologically, religiously, and thematically to the Fourth Edict of the Diocletianic Persecution. The legal records of Crispina's trial on 5 December 304 at Theveste support the interpretation that book 7 of the *Adversus nationes* is understandable in light of the Empire's attempt to force the Christians to sacrifice to the gods. Arnobius is responding to actual historical events which took place sometime before the end of AD 305. He is attacking the sacrificial concepts of Porphyry found in *Phil. or.* with philosophical concepts derived mainly from the *De abstinentia*. Could there possibly be any relation between the official state enforcement of sacrifice and the attack upon the sacrificial concepts of the *Philosophia ex oraculis*?

The reader may recall that Chadwick years ago (1959: 142 f.) suggested that Porphyry's statement, found in *Ad Marc.* and written *c.*AD 300, that he had been called away on business of the Greeks, 'may perhaps mean that he had been invited to attend the confidential deliberations which preceded the launching of the persecution of the Church under Diocletian in 303. (Porphyry would be a natural person to consult about such a project, as the author of several formidable books against the

Christians.)' The *Phil. or.* will have undoubtedly been viewed by Diocletian as the kind of propaganda capable of strengthening the traditional polytheism that he apparently always zealously and super-stitiously respected. Its anti-Christian character will have been viewed as providing invaluable support to the state persecution of the Christians. And Porphyry's encouraging his fellow pagans to sacrifice to their deities in *Phil. or.* will certainly have given strong support to the enforcement of the Fourth Edict. We may now offer this hypothesis: *Phil. or.* had already been written before the aforementioned deliberations took place. By the time Porphyry attended them, the work was already well known in the East. It is a good possibility that at the meeting Diocletian might have made the decision to disseminate the *Phil. or.* to at least some if not all of the western provinces.

But as we have noted, according to Arnobius (and Eusebius and Augustine), Porphyry's conception of deity failed just as much as his conception of man: he turned the normal understanding of the God–man relationship upside down by divinizing man and humanizing the gods. This might not have given either an accurate or fair picture of his opponent's views, but neither does Eusebius nor Augustine; and we may add, neither did Porphyry.

APPENDIX I

The two main texts of the anti-Porphyrian polemics of Eusebius and Augustine are given below.

'Praeter opinionem,' inquit, 'profecto quibusdam videatur esse quod dicturi sumus. Christum enim dii piissimum pronuntiaverunt et inmortalem factum et cum bona praedicatione eius meminerunt; Christianos vero pollutos, inquit, et contaminatos et errore implicatos esse dicunt et multis talibus adversus eos blasphemiis utuntur.' Deinde subicit velut oracula deorum blasphemantium Christianos et post haec: 'De Christo autem,' inquit, 'interrogantibus si est Deus, ait Hecate: 'Quoniam quidem inmortalis anima post corpus incedit, nosti; a sapientia eutem abscisa semper errat. Viri pietate praestantissimi est illa anima; hanc colunt aliena a se veritate.' Deinde post verba huius quasi oraculi sua ipse contexens: 'Piissimum igitur virum,' inquit, 'eum dixit et eius animam, sicut et aliorum piorum, post obitum inmortalitate dignatam et hanc colere Christianos ignorantes. Interrogantibus autem,' inquit: 'Cur ergo damnatus est?' oraculo respondit dea: 'Corpus quidem debilitantibus tormentis semper oppositum est; anima autem piorum caelesti sedi insidet. Illa vero anima aliis animabus fataliter dedit, quibus fata non adnuerunt deorum dona obtinere neque habere Iovis inmortalis agnitionem, errore implicari. Propterea ergo diis exosi, quia, quibus fato non fuit nosse Deum nec dona ab diis accipere, his fataliter dedit iste errore implicari. Ipse vero pius et in caelum, sicut pii, concessit. Itaque hunc quidem non blasphemabis, misereberis autem hominum dementiam; ex eo in eis facile praecepsque periculum.' (Aug. *Civ. Dei* 19, 23; LCL: Greene)

"Παράδοξον ἴσως δόξειεν ἂν τισιν εἶναι τὸ μέλλον λέγεσθαι ὑφ' ἡμῶν· Τὸν γὰρ Χριστὸν οἱ θεοὶ εὐσεβέστατον ἀπεφήναντο καὶ ἀθανατον γεγονότα, εὐφήμως τε αὐτοῦ μνημονεύουσι." Καὶ ὑποβὰς ἐπιλέγει· "Περὶ γοῦν τοῦ Χριστοῦ ἐρωτησάντων εἰ ἔστι θεὸς φησίν·" Ὅτι μὲν ἀθανάτη ψυχὴ μετὰ σῶμα προβαίνει, Γιγνώσκει σοφίη τετιμημένος· ἀλλά γε ψυχὴ Ἀνέρος εὐσεβίη προφερεστάτη ἐστὶν ἐκείνου. "Εὐσεβέστατον ἄρα ἔφη αὐτὸν, καὶ τὴν ψυχὴν αὐτοῦ, καθάπερ καὶ τῶν ἄλλων, μετὰ θάνατον ἀπαθανατισθῆναι, ἣν σέβειν ἀγνοοῦντας τοὺς Χριστιανούς. Ἐπερωτησάντων δὲ διὰ τί ἐκολάσθη ἔχρησεν· Σῶμα μὲν ἀδρανέσιν βασάνοις αἰεὶ προβέβληται· Ψυχὴ δ' εὐσεβέων εἰς οὐράνιον πέδον ἵζει. Καὶ ἐπιλέγει μετὰ τὸν χρησμὸν ἐξῆς· "Αὐτὸς οὖν εὐσεβὴς, καὶ εἰς οὐρανοὺς ὥσπερ οἱ εὐσεβεῖς χωρήσας. Ὥστε τοῦτον μὲν οὐ βλασφημήσεις, ἐλεήσεις δὲ τῶν ἀνθρώπων τὴν ἄγνοιαν." Ταῦτα καὶ νῦν ὁ Πορφύριος. (Eus. *DE* 3. 7 (*PG* 22 (Eus. 4) 236 f.)

APPENDIX II

A list of Porphyry's works found in the *PE* is given below. A table of citations appears at the end, and the reader is referred to Chapter 8, pp. 225 ff., above.

1. *PE* 1.2.1–4 (SC): *CC* fr. 1 Harn.
2. *PE* 1.4.7 (SC) = *Abst.* 4.21.
3. *PE* 1.9.7–10 (SC) = *Abst.* 2.5.
4. *PE* 1.9.11 (SC) = *Abst.* 2.7.
5. *PE* 1.9.21 (SC): *CC* fr. 41 Harn. (bk. 4 of *CC*).
6. *PE* 3.4.1 f. (SC) = *Ep. An.* (fr.).
7. *PE* 3.4.12 (SC) = *Abst.* 4.9.
8. *PE* 3.4.13 f. (SC) = *Abst.* 4.9.
9. *PE* 3.7.1. (SC) = *De cult. sim.* = Fr. 1, Bidez (p. 1*1.1–10).
10. *PE* 3.7.2 ff. (SC) = *De cult. sim.* = Fr. 2, Bidez (2*1–3*6).
11. *PE* 3.9.1–5 (SC) = *De cult. sim.* = Fr. 3, Bidez (3*7–7*4).
12. *PE* 3.11.1 (SC) = *De cult. sim.* = Fr. 4, Bidez (7*5–7).
13. *PE* 3.11.4–10 (SC) = *De cult. sim.* = Fr. 5, Bidez (7*8–8*2).
14. *PE* 3.11.7 (SC) = *De cult. sim.* = Fr. 6, Bidez (8*3–13).
15. *PE* 3.11.9–16 = *De cult. sim.* = Fr. 7, Bidez (9*1–11*13).
16. *PE* 3.11.22–44 (SC) = *De cult. sim.* = Fr. 8, Bidez (11*14–18*9).
17. *PE* 3.11.45–3.13.2 (SC) = *De cult. sim.* = Fr. 10, Bidez (18*10–23*14).
18. *PE* 3.14.4 (SC) = *Phil. or.* (fr.: Wolff, 125 f.).
19. *PE* 3.14.5 (SC) = *Phil. or.* (fr.: Wolff, 125 ff.).
20. *PE* 3.14.6 (SC) = *Phil. or.* (fr.: Wolff, 125 ff.).
21. *PE* 3.14.7 (SC) = *Phil. or.* (fr.: Wolff, 132).
22. *PE* 3.15.3 (SC) = *Phil. or.* (fr.: Wolff, 127 f.).
23. *PE* 4.7.1 (SC) = *Phil. or.* (fr.: Wolff, 109 f.).
24. *PE* 4.8.1 (SC) = *Phil. or.* (fr.: Wolff, 110).
25. *PE* 4.8.2 (SC) = *Phil. or.* (fr.: Wolff, 110).
26. *PE* 4.9.1 f. (SC) = *Phil. or.* (fr.: Wolff, 111–17).
27. *PE* 4.9.3–7 (SC) = *Phil. or.* (fr.: Wolff, 118–21).
28. *PE* 4.11.1 (SC) = *Abst.* 2.34.
29. *PE* 4.12.1 (SC) = *Abst.* 2.34.
30. *PE* 4.14.1 (SC) = *Abst.* 2.7.
31. *PE* 4.14.2 (SC) = *Abst.* 2.11.
32. *PE* 4.14.3 (SC) = *Abst.* 2.12.
33. *PE* 4.14.4 (SC) = *Abst.* 2.13.
34. *PE* 4.14.5 f. (SC) = *Abst.* 2.24.
35. *PE* 4.14.7 (SC) = *Abst.* 2.27.

36. *PE* 4.14.8 f. (SC) = *Abst.* 2.60 f.
37. *PE* 4.15.1 (SC) = *Abst.* 2.36.
38. *PE* 4.15.2 (SC) = *Abst.* 2.58.
39. *PE* 4.16.1–9 (SC) = *Abst.* 2.54 ff.
40. *PE* 4.16.10 (SC) = *Abst.* 2.27.
41. *PE* 4.18.1 (SC) = *Abst.* 2.43.
42. *PE* 4.19.1 f. (SC) = *Abst.* 2.43 and 2.52.
43. *PE* 4.20.1 (SC) = *Phil. or.* (fr.: Wolff, 152 ff.).
44. *PE* 4.22.1–4 (SC) = *Abst.* 2.38 f.
45. *PE* 4.22.5–9 (SC) = *Abst.* 2.40 f.
46. *PE* 4.22.10 ff. (SC) = *Abst.* 2.41 f.
47. *PE* 4.23.1–5 (SC) = *Phil. or.* (fr.: Wolff, 147–50).
48. *PE* 5.1.10 (SC) = *CC* fr. 80 Harn.
49. *PE* 5.6.1 (SC) = *Phil. or.* (fr.: Wolff, 128 f.).
50. *PE* 5.7.1 (SC) = *Phil. or.* (fr.: Wolff, 122 f.).
51. *PE* 5.7.3 f. (SC) = *Ep. An.*
52. *PE* 5.7.4 f. (SC) = *Phil. or.* (fr.: Wolff, 123 f.).
53. *PE* 5.7.6 (SC) = *Phil. or.* (fr.: Wolff, 122 f.).
54. *PE* 5.8.1–7 (SC) = *Phil. or.* (fr.: Wolff, 154–8).
55. *PE* 5.8.8–11 (SC) = *Phil. or.* (fr.: Wolff, 159 f.).
56. *PE* 5.8.12 (SC) = *Phil. or.* (fr.: Wolff, 160).
57. *PE* 5.9.1–8 (SC) = *Phil. or.* (fr.: Wolff, 162).
58. *PE* 5.9.9 (SC) = *Phil. or.* (fr.: Wolff, 162).
59. *PE* 5.10.1–9 (SC) = *Ep. An.*
60. *PE* 5.10.10 (SC) = *Ep. An.*
61. *PE* 5.10.11 (SC) = *Ep. An.*
62. *PE* 5.11.1 (SC) = *Phil. or.* (fr.: Wolff, 129 f.).
63. *PE* 5.12.1 f. (SC) = *Phil. or.* (fr.: Wolff, 130 f.).
64. *PE* 5.13.1 f. (SC) = *Phil. or.* (fr.: Wolff, 131 f.).
65. *PE* 5.13.3 f. (SC) = *Phil. or.* (fr.: Wolff, 133 f.).
66. *PE* 5.14.1 (SC) = *Phil. or.* (fr.: Wolff, 138 f.).
67. *PE* 5.14.2 (SC) = *Phil. or.* (fr.: Wolff, 134–7).
68. *PE* 5.15.1 f. (SC) = *Phil. or.* (fr.: Wolff, 137).
69. *PE* 5.16.1 (SC) = *Phil. or.* (fr.: Wolff, 172 ff.).
70. *PE* 6.1 (Gifford) = *Phil. or.* (fr.: Wolff, 166).
71. *PE* 6.1 (Gifford) = *Phil. or.* (fr.: Wolff, 166 ff.).
72. *PE* 6.2 (Gifford) = *Phil. or.* (fr.: Wolff, 168 f.).
73. *PE* 6.3 (Gifford) = *Phil. or.* (fr.: Wolff, 170 ff.).
74. *PE* 6.4 (Gifford) = *Phil. or.* (fr.: Wolff, 165).
75. *PE* 6.5 (Gifford) = *Phil. or.* (fr.: Wolff, 169).
76. *PE* 6.5 (Gifford) = *Phil. or.* (fr.: Wolff, 175 f.).
77. *PE* 9.2 (Gifford) = *Abst.* 2.26.
78. *PE* 9.3 (Gifford) = *Abst.* 4.11.

79. *PE* 9.10 (Gifford) = *Phil. or.*
80. *PE* 9.10 (Gifford) = *Phil. or.*
81. *PE* 9.10 (Gifford) = *Phil. or.*
82. *PE* 10.3 (Gifford) = *Acr. in philol.*
83. *PE* 10.3 (Gifford) = *Acr. in philol.*
84. *PE* 10.3 (Gifford) = *Acr. in philol.*
85. *PE* 10.9 (Gifford) = *CC* fr.
86. *PE* 11.28 (Gifford) = *Ep. ad Boeth. de an.*
87. *PE* 14.10 (Gifford) = *Ep. An.*
88. *PE* 14.10 (Gifford) = *Ep. An.*
89. *PE* 14.10 (Gifford) = *Ep. ad Boeth. de an.*
90. *PE* 14.10 (Gifford) = *Phil. or.*
91. *PE* 15.11 (Gifford) = *Ep. ad Boeth. de an.*
92. *PE* 15.11 (Gifford) = *Ep. ad Boeth. de an.*
93. *PE* 15.11 (Gifford) = *Ep. ad Boeth. de an.*
94. *PE* 15.16 (Gifford) = *Ep. ad Boeth. de an.*

The number of citations from each work appearing in the list above can be given as follows:

Acr. in philol.	3
CC	4
Ep. ad Boeth. de an.	6
Ep. An.	7
Cult. sim.	9
Abst.	25
Phil. or.	40
Total	94

APPENDIX III

The data given below are to be analysed in conjunction with Chapter 10 § 3.

Adv. nat. 1. 2. 1: 'Let us therefore examine the precise significance of the belief they hold' (all translations are from McCr) 'Inspiciamus igitur opinionis istius mentem'; 1. 22. 9 f.: pagan accusations are 'not clearly proven by examining any witness': 'non cognitionis alicuius testimonio comprobatae', 1. 42: someone will ask whether one can prove Christ = God: no greater proof than in his miracles, esp. overcoming fate, that people saw in daylight without any disagreement: this is in his response to the Hecatean Oracle and commentary (v. Ch. 8); 1. 47: Christ's miracles performed so that unbelievers might know that what was promised was not false: 1. 47. 8 f.: 'sed ut homines duri atque increduli scirent non esse quod spondebatur falsum': apparently a direct response to Porphyry's remark that Christians cannot offer proof of the credibility of such promises noted above (p. 274); Arn. adds to this that this proof makes it 'clearer than the sun' (11. 18 f.: 'sole ipso est clarius') that Christ was more powerful than the fates (responding to the Hecatean Oracle: v. Ch. 8): cf. Porphyry's μηδένα ... δύνασθαι δι' ἀποδείξεως ἐναργοῦς (etc.): 1. 48. 27 f.: asking the pagans to give his evidence 'attentive examination' ('si volueritis attendere': found in a passage where a comparison between the gods' healings with those of Christ is made, and revealing possible Chaldaean healing practices, v. pp. 236 f. supra); 1. 54: proof from eyewitness accounts, 'clearer than the day itself' (11. 7 f.: 'luce . . . clarior'): DE parallel noted on p. 238 supra; Ib.: proof from universal extension of Christianity: cf. Eus. and Aug. pp. 275 f. supra; and cf. esp. Adv. nat. 1. 55: nations once separated have united on one conclusion and risk capital punishment: cf. DE p. 238; 1. 57: Christian eyewitness evidence compared with mere pagan opinions; 1. 61: pagans refuse to let Christians explain incarnation; 1. 64: Christ promised unfounded hopes (1. 36: 'spes etiam vanissimas polliceri'); 1. 65. 25: Christ promises 'air castles': 'fatua dona promittit'; 2. 4: 'But all these things will be demonstrated more plainly and more clearly when we shall proceed further.'; 2. 4. 1 f.: 'Verum haec omnia inlustrius commemorabuntur et planius,'; 2. 6: 'But perhaps those who now throughout the world are acting in concert and uniting in agreement of 'credulity' seem to you stupid and silly.'; 2. 6. 1 ff.: 'Nisi forte obtunsi et fatui videntur hi vobis, qui per orbem iam totum conspirant et coeunt in istius credulitatis adsensum.'; 2. 10: Christians and pagans share 'credulitas': pagans are not in agreement with theirs; 2. 11: Christians believe in and assent to Christ, whereas pagans believe Plato, Cronius, and Numenius: v. p. 160 supra for the probable Porphyrian connection with this passage: 2. 11. 4 f.: 'Vos Platoni, vos Cronio, vos Numenio vel cui libuerit

creditis: nos credimus et adquiescimus Christo.'; 2. 11: mighty miracles brought
out publicly: these can bring anyone to belief (cf. *DE* 3. 7: disciples did not
speak in public; cf. *CC* cf. no. 80 = *PE* 6.1: since Christ appeared there have
not been any public blessings from the gods; cf. *Adv. nat.* 1. 1: gods have
abandoned the world due to Christians, and pagans who say this speak 'ex
oraculo', probably referring to *Phil. or.*; 2. 12: if Christ spoke like a philosopher,
who would say that he makes any 'clear promises'?; 2. 12: text noted *supra* p.
239, and note that pagan accusations rob them of faith; 2. 16: 'Are you willing
to inquire, to search out, to investigate what you yourselves are?': 'Vultis
quaerere pervestigare rimari, quid sitis vos ipsi?'; 2. 20: 'And that we may show
you more clearly and more patently of what worth is man whom you believe to
be very like the Higher Power,'; 1. 1: 'Et ut vobis clarius manifestiusque
monstremus': pp. 160 f. *supra* for probable Porphyrian connection; 2. 34: why
does Christian *credulitas* seem stupid to those who criticize it? why ridicule
them for the promise of immortality, and note esp. 2. 34. 9–30: 'Si nobis haec
gaudia, hoc est fugiendae mortis, Plato [in] Phaedro promisisset aliusve ex hoc
choro possetque eam praestare atque ad [in] finem pollicitationes adducere,
consentaneum fuerat eius suscipere nos cultus a quo tantum doni expectaremus
et muneris. Nunc cum eam Christus non tantum promiserit verum etiam
virtutibus tantis manifestaverit posse compleri, quid alienum facimus aut stul-
titiae crimen quibus rationibus sustinemus, si eius nomini maiestatique sub-
sternimur, a quo speramus utrumque, et mortem cruciabilem fugere et vitae
aeternitate donari?' A demonstration of the rationality of faith based upon
evidence of miracles which prove that Christ's promises can be believed, and
using Plato against Porphyry's criticism of Christian faith/*credulitas*; 2. 39: lack
of agreement in pagan beliefs; 2. 50: clear proof that the soul is not
immortal; 2. 51: if pagans (Neoplatonists) gave their beliefs a searching
examination, they similarly would criticize in themselves what they do in
Christians; the concept of descent of the soul is not anything 'examined and
placed in the light of clearest truth': 11. 14 f.: 'exploratum aliquid dicitis et
in luce positum manifestissimae veritatis'; 2. 54. 2 f.: 'Considerandum est
nobis sollicite et cura inspiciendum non parva' (a pagan speaks); cf. 2. 56;
2. 57; 2. 58; 2. 59; 2. 60: Christians do not investigate what cannot be
known, as philosophers do (cf. 2. 59); 2. 61: pagan examination/investigation
of various questions not to be preferred to salvific knowledge of God; 2.
67: one should look at the reason and not the fact why Christians abandon
ancient institutions; and not to set forth against them what they abandoned,
but examine what in particular they follow; 2. 68: Christians have acted
against common sense and judgement in forsaking ancestral religious customs;
cf. 2. 71; 2. 74: Porphyrian investigation as to why Christ came so late and
cf. *Civ. Dei* 10. 32; 2. 76: Porphyrian disqualification of Christianity as way
of truth due to persecutions and cf. *Civ. Dei* 10. 32; 2. 78: pagans are asked
to stop obstructing their hopes by 'senseless investigations' (1. 1: 'quaestionibus

vacuis'); and not to insist on the reason for the gift of salvation being offered; antithesis of belief and unbelief.

It should be fairly clear that Arnobius is responding in the above texts to the same Porphyrian criticism of Christian faith (*CC* fr. 1: p. 274 *supra*) as one finds in Eusebius and Augustine.

APPENDIX IV

The data given below are examples of Arnobius' apparent response to Porphyry's accusation that the tenets of the Christian faith cannot be proved on the basis of tangible evidence. They demonstrate how Arnobius, in addition to Eusebius and Augustine, has turned Porphyry's argument against him. See Chapter 10 esp. §III.

Adv. nat. 3. 6: due to foul myths about the gods the pagans demonstrate that they do not exist; 3. 7: Cicero should be refuted, rebutted, and proved to be speaking impiously; if pagans wish to show by examination that the stories about the gods are true, they fear the evidence of the truth: 3. 7. 14: 'veritatis testificationem'; 3. 23: concept of tutelary deities is not based on certified truth: 1. 12: 'non explorata veritas comprehendit'; 3. 32: he maintains 'on sure grounds' (1. 15: 'si ratione profertur et adseveratur certa') that certain deities do not exist; 3. 34: he ascertains, establishes, and shows the truth of the matter that Diana, Ceres, and Luna cannot be the same goddess; again like Porphyry's criticism of the Christians, Arnobius in 3. 37 argues that diversity of opinion as to the exact identity of the muses proves that (i.e. this is a sign) it is the pagans who know nothing about the truth; if the fact were 'clearly known, the voice of all would be one and the agreement of all would tend towards and reach the conclusion of the same belief'; cf. 3. 38. 1–4: 'Quonam modo igitur religionis potestis integrare vim plenam, cum circa ipsos erretis deos, aut ad venerabiles invitare nos cultus, cum nihil nos certi de ipsorum numinum comprehensione doceatis?'; 3. 39 f.: no agreement about the identity of the deities; 3. 42: uncertain and conflicting notions of deities; a thousand different views; it is manifestly clear that it is the pagans who cannot say anything certain about the deities; he begins by pointing out that it is evident from the pagans' books that they are confused about the deities; how can they ask a god for help if it cannot be ascertained and established which to invoke?; 3. 44: a demand that the pagans stand upon one harmonious opinion about the gods, otherwise they destroy by conflicting notions the confidence in the whole system; 4. 3: Christians cannot determine whether the pagans have discovered the truth; 4. 5: they must clarify the meaning of 'gods on the left' for the understanding; 4. 7: the facts of their beliefs bring pagans to understand the truth, i.e. their concepts of deity are imagined falsities; 4. 15: it is true, certain, and 'demonstrated from the testimony of acknowledged fact' that pagan concepts of deity are confused; 4. 17: we can demonstrate the same regarding the Mercuries, etc.; 4. 18: concepts of deities are taken directly from the pagans' writings; 4. 27: if checked and proven beyond doubt, his argument reveals that the deities are of a human race (before

R3); 4. 30: Christians clearly demonstrate that pagans shamefully treat their deities; 5. 8: he uses the 'careful computations' of Varro, that 'investigator of antiquity', to show that the Great Mother was recently born; 5. 15: it would be stupid to demand proofs of these silly myths; 5. 16: rites of the Great Mother, have they 'been verified and found worthy of credence?'; 5. 20: he makes clear to pagans how they insult the deities; 5. 30: if a true examination is made, it is the pagans who are the real atheists; 5. 31: it is clear they provoke divine anger; 5. 33: the need to examine (1. 16: 'inspicere' cf. 1. 2. 1) the allegorical method; 5. 39: it is established that the mysteries refer to actual historical events, thus one cannot allegorize the immoral/illogical elements found therein; 6. 14. 4 ff.: 'Quidnam est istud, homines, quod ipsi vos ultro in tam promptis ac perspicuis rebus voluntaria fallitis et circumscribitis caecitate?'; 6. 26: it is proven and established that fear of the images is nothing; 7. 4: a sacrificial theory examined and thoroughly investigated; cf. 7. 5; 7. 19: the proof and discovery of an inquiry about sexual distinctions among the gods: these concepts are 'most foolish delusions'; 7. 26: proof that antiquity did not find incense necessary; without reason, 'sine ullis . . . rationibus' this practice has been introduced in modern times; 7. 30: pagans know in their hearts that Christians speak the truth about the sacrifices; 'and the reason is, with you a custom having no basis in reason takes precedence rather than the reality of things looked into and appraised in a search for the truth': 11. 18–21: 'primum quia apud vos valet nullam habens consuetudo rationem quam rerum inspecta natura veritatis examinatione ponderata'; 7. 39: he now comes to his central thesis: a close inspection ('inspicere') must be made to ascertain whether the pagan deities of the myths actually exist; 7. 41: these stories are believed to have the character of the miraculous (11. 1 ff.: 'miraculi speciem . . . habere creduntur'), which is the basis of Porphyry's attempts to prove the credibility of the myths: the reader is asked to review pp. 274 ff. *supra* for the Porphyrian connection; yet the stories only have a 'resemblance to truth' (1. 6: 'veritatis similitudine'); he then adds (11. 7 ff.): 'Ceterum si penitus intueri res factas, personas et personarum volueris voluntates, nihil esse repperies diis dignum . . .'; 7. 43: 'if you weigh the circumstances thoroughly'; 7. 44: after investigating the facts of the story of Jupiter and the dancer, he concludes (11. 44–8): 'Quae si penitus cuncta et sine ulla partium gratificatione pendantur, non tantum longe longeque ab diis esse repperiuntur aliena, verum (a) quovis homine sentiente communia nec ad studium veri rationum cognitionibus erudito.'; 7. 44: on the importation of Aesculapius: Arnobius states that a close analysis of the pagans' statements, as the result of demonstrating from their own authorities, reveals the fact that he was not a deity; 7. 44: the 'tested truth' of the annals shows that only a snake was sent to Rome (11. 64–7): 'Ex Epidauro tamen quid est aliud adlatum nisi magni agminis coluber? Fidem si annalium sequimur et exploratam eis adtribuimus veritatem, nihil'; and finally 7. 45. 16 f.: 'Non arbitramur evincere atque obtinere vos posse, Aesculapium illum fuisse serpentem,', which is again interesting because (1) Porphyry demanded the same kind of rational proof, and not just a foolish belief, from the Christians to show that their beliefs were true, and he used the same kind of rational arguments; (2) Porphyry (and later Neoplatonists in North Africa) used this same story of Aesculapius' importation from Epidaurus (v. Ch. 9, pp. 259 f. *supra*, for the evidence appearing in *Civ. Dei*) to offer proof of the credibility of pagan religious concepts of the deities; (3) the basis of this proof was the miracles recorded in the annals (cf. Arnobius' reference to pagans' belief that the stories have a miraculous character in 7. 41, and the 'tested truth' of the annals concerning the Aesculapius myth in 7. 44.

BIBLIOGRAPHY

1. Editions of the Latin Text of the *Adversus Nationes*

Sabaeus, Faustus, *Arnobii Disputationum Adversus Gentes Libri 8* (Rome, 1543).

Gelenius, Sigismundus, *Arnobii Disputationum Adversus Gentes Libri 8* (Basle, 1546).

La Barre, Renatus Laurentius de, *Arnobii Afri Opera omnia quae extant* (Paris, 1580).

Canterus, Theodorus, *Arnobii Disputationum Adversus Gentes Libri 7* (Antwerp, 1582).

Ursinus, Fulvius, *Arnobii Disputationum Adversus Gentes Libri 7* (Rome, 1583).

Elmenhorst, Geverhardus, *Arnobii Disputationum Adversus Gentes Libri 7* (Hannover, 1603).

Stewechius, Godescalcus, *Arnobii Disputationum Adversus Gentes Libri 7* (Antwerp, 1604).

Heraldus, Desiderius, *Arnobii Disputationum Adversus Gentes Libri 7* (Paris, 1605).

Elmenhorst, Geverhardus, *Arnobii Disputationum Adversus Gentes Libri 7* (Hamburg, 1610).

Canterus, Theodorus, *Arnobii Disputationum Adversus Gentes Libri 7* (Cologne, 1618).

Stewechius, Godescalcus, *Arnobii Disputationum Adversus Gentes Libri 7* (Douai, 1634).

Rigault, Nicolas, *Arnobii Disputationum Adversus Gentes Libri 7* (Paris, 1643).

Salmasius, Claudius, and Thysius, A., *Arnobii Adversus Gentes Libri 7, cum recensione viri celeberrimi et integris omnium commentaris* (Leiden, 1651).

Canterus, Theodorus, *Arnobii Disputationum Adversus Gentes Libri 7* (Paris, 1654).

Priorius, Philippus, *Sancti Caecilii Cypriani Opera. Accedunt Marci Minucii Felicis Octavius, De Idolorum Vanitate, Arnobii Adversus Gentes Libri 7* (Paris, 1666).

Canterus, Theodorus, *Arnobii Disputationum Adversus Gentes Libri 7* (Leiden, 1680).

Le Nourry, Nicola, *Arnobii Adversus Gentes Libri 7* (Paris, 1715).

GALLANDIUS, A., *Arnobii Adversus Gentes Libri 7* (Venice, 1768).
OBERTHÜR, C., *Opera Omnia Sanctorum Patrum Latinorum 5* (Würzburg, 1783).
ORELLI, JOSEPH CONRAD, *Arnobii Afri Disputationum Adversus Gentes Libri 7* (Leipzig, 1816).
CAILLAU, A. B., *Collectio Selecta SS. Ecclesiae Patrum*, 15, (Paris, 1829), 237–490.
HILDEBRAND, G. F., *Arnobii Adversus Gentes Libri 7* (Halle, 1844).
MIGNE, J. P., *PL* 5 (Paris, 1844), 349–1372.
OEHLER, FRANCISCUS, *Arnobii oratoris Adversus Nationes Libri Septem* (Bibliotheca Patrum Ecclesiasticorum Selecta; Leipzig, 1846), vol. 12.
REIFFERSCHEID, AUGUST, *Arnobii Adversus Nationes Libri 7* (Vienna, 1875), CSEL 4.
MARCHESI, CONCETTO, *Arnobii Adversus Nationes Libri 7* (CSLP 62; Turin, 1934).
LE BONNIEC, HENRI, *Arnobe, Contre les Gentils, Livre I* (Paris 1982).

II. TRANSLATIONS OF THE *ADVERSUS NATIONES*

OUDAAN, JOACHIM, *Arnobius d'Afrikaner tegen de Heydenen verat in zeven boeken. Uyt het Latijn vertaalt* (Harlingen, 1677).
ROESSLER, C. F., *Bibliothek der Kirchen-Vater.* (Leipzig, 1777).
BESNARD, F. A., *Des Afrikaner's Arnobius sieben Bücher wider die Heiden* (Landshut, 1842).
ALLEKER, J., *Arnobius Sieben Bücher gegen die Heiden* (Trier, 1858).
BRYCE, H., and CAMPBELL, H., *The Seven Books of Arnobius Adversus Gentes* (ANCL 19; Edinburgh, 1871 (= ANF 6; Buffalo, 1886)).
MCCRACKEN, G. E., *Arnobius of Sicca: The Case Against the Pagans* (ACW 7–8; New York, 1949).
LAURENTI, R., *Arnobio, I sette libri contro i pagani* (Turin, 1962).
LE BONNIEC, H., *Arnobe, Contre les Gentils, Livre I* (Paris, 1982).

III. GENERAL BIBLIOGRAPHY

Works below preceded by an asterisk (*) are related to Arnobius. Those preceded by a dagger (†) are related to Porphyry.
†ABRAMOWSKI, L.,'Marius Victorinus, Porphyrius und die römischen Gnostiken', *ZNTW* 74 (1983), 108–28.
*ALTANER, B., and STUIBER, A., *Patrologie* (Freiburg, 1978).
*AMATA, B., 'Testimonianze di Arnobio Afro sulle assemblee liturgiche agli inizi del sec. IV', *EphLit* 98 (1984), 513–25.

*Amata, B., *Problemi di antropologia arnobiana* (BSR 64; Rome, 1984).

*—— 'Destino finale dell'uomo nell'opera di Arnobio di Sicca (III–IV sec. d. C.)', in S. Felici (ed.), *Morte e immortalità nella catechesi dei Padri del III–IV secolo* (BSR 66; Rome, 1985), 47–62.

*—— 'La cristologia di Arnobio il vecchio', *Academia Bessarionis* (1986).

*—— 'Mito e paideia in Arnobio di Sicca', in S. Felici (ed.), *CUNC* (Rome, 1988), 35–50.

*Amatucci, A. G., *Storia della letteratura latina cristiana* (Turin, 1955).

†Anastos, M. V., 'Porphyry's Attack on the Bible', in L. Wallach (ed.), *The Classical Tradition* (Ithaca, NY, 1966), 421–50.

Armstrong, A., 'Salvation, Plotinian and Christian', *DR* 75 no. 240 (1957), 126–39.

—— 'The Self-Definition of Christianity in Relation to Later Platonism', In E. P. Sanders (ed.), *Jewish and Christian Self-Definition* (London, 1980), 74–99.

†Attridge, H. W., and Hata, G. (eds.), *Eusebius, Christianity, and Judaism* (Detroit, 1992).

†Atzberger, L., *Geschichte der christlichen Eschatologie innerhalb der vornicänischen Zeit* (Freiburg, 1896).

Austin, R., 'Macrobius', *OCD* 635.

*Axelson, B., 'Zur Emendation alterer Kirchenschriftsteller', *Eranos* 39 (1941), 74–81.

*—— 'Randbemerkungen zu Arnobius', *Eranos* 40 (1942), 182–3.

*—— 'Textkritisches zu Florus, Minucius Felix und Arnobius', *Kungl. Humanistiska Vetenskapssamfundets i Lund Årsberättelse* 1 (1944–5), 40–62.

Baaziz, S., 'Le culte de Neptune dans l'Afrique romaine' (unpub. Master's thesis; Bordeaux III, 1973).

*Badham, C., 'Arnobius and the Gospel of Peter', *Academy* 1243 (1896), 177.

*Baehrens, W., 'Arnobiana', *BPW* 37 (1917), 1291–8.

*—— 'Randbemerkungen zu Arnobius', *BPW* 42 (1923), 352–4.

Bandinelli, R., *Rome: La fin de l'art antique* (Paris, 1970).

Barbel, J., 'Christos Angelos', *Theoph.* 3 (Bonn, 1941).

*Bardenhewer, O., *Patrology* (Freiburg, 1908), tr. T. J. Shahan.

*Bardy, G., 'Arnobius', *RAC* 1 (Stuttgart, 1950), 710 f.

Barnes, J., and Chadwick, H., 'A Letter Ascribed to Peter of Alexandria', *JTS* NS 24 (1973), 443–55.

Barnes, T. D., *Tertullian* (Oxford, 1971).

—— 'Lactantius and Constantine', *JRS* 63 (1973), 29–46.

†—— 'Porphyry Against the Christians: Date and Attribution of Fragments', *JTS* NS 24 (1973), 424–42.

—— 'Imperial Campaigns, AD 285–311', *Phnx* 30 (1976), 174–93.

—— 'The Chronology of Plotinus' Life', *GRBS* 17 (1976), 65–70.

—— *Constantine and Eusebius* (Cambridge, Mass., 1981).

—— 'Aspects of the Background of the City of God', *RUO* 52 (1982), 64–80.

—— *The New Empire of Diocletian and Constantine* (London, 1982).

—— 'The Constantinian Settlement', in Attridge and Hata (1992), 635–57.

*BASTGEN, M., *Quaestiones de locis ex Arnobii Adversus Nationes opere selectis* (Münster I.W., 1887).

BAYNES, N. H., 'The Great Persecution', in S. A. Cook, *et al.* (eds.), *CAH* 12 (Cambridge, 1981), 646–77.

*BEATRICE, P. F., 'Un oracle antichrétien chez Arnobe', in Y. de Andia, *et al.* (eds.), *Memorial Dom Jean Gribomont* (Rome, 1988), 107–29.

†—— 'Quosdam Platonicorum Libros', *VC* 43 (1989), 248–81.

BEAUJEAU, J., Le Paganisme romaine sous le Haut Empire', *ANRW* II. 16. 1, 3–26.

BECHTEL, F., *Die Historischen Personennamen des Griechischen bis zur Kaiserzeit* (Halle, 1917).

BENKO, S., *Pagan Rome and the Early Christians* (London, 1984).

†BENOIT, A., 'Le *Contra Christianos* de Porphyre: où en est la collection des fragments?', in *Paganisme, Judaïsme, Christianisme* (Paris, 1978), 261–75.

†BERCHMAN, R., 'Arcana Mundi between Balaam and Hecate: Prophecy, Divination, and Magic in Later Platonism', in D. Lull (ed.), SBL Seminar Papers (Atlanta, 1989), 107–85.

*BERKOWITZ, L., *Index Arnobianus* (Hildesheim, 1967).

BERTHIER, A., CHARLIER, R., and JUILLET, J., 'Le *Bellum Jurgurthinum* de Salluste et le problème de Cirta', *RecConst* 64 (1950–1), 3–145.

—— 'Note sur l'épigraphie du Kef', *RecConst* 68 (1953), 177–98.

—— 'Colonia Cirta Sittianorum', *RecConst* 70 (1957–9), 91–118.

*BERTHOLD. A., 'La Statue animée et la conjecture d'Arnobe', *AR* 18 (1915), 134.

BESCHAOUCH, A., 'Mustitana. Recueil des nouvelles inscriptions de Mustis, cité Romaine de Tunisie. Tome I', *Kar* 14 (1967–8), 123–223.

—— 'Une stèle consacrée à Saturne le 8 Novembre 323', *BACTH* NS 4 (1968), 253–68.

—— 'Le Territoire de Sicca Veneria (El-Kef), nouvelle Cirta, en Numidia Proconsulaire (Tunisie)', *CRAI* (1981), 105–22.

†BIDEZ, J., *Vie de Porphyre* (Gand, 1913; repr. Hildesheim, 1964).

—— 'Le Philosophe Jamblique et son école', *REG* 32 (1919), 29–40.

BIRLEY, A. R., 'A Persecuting Praeses of Numidia under Valerian', *JTS* NS 42 (1991), 598–610.

BLAISE, A., *Dictionnaire Latine–Français des auteurs chrétiens* (Paris, 1954).

†BOER, V. DEN, 'A Pagan Historian and His Enemies: Porphyry Against the Christians', *CP* 69 (1974), 198–208.

*BOISSIER, G., *La Fin du paganisme* (Paris, 1903).

BONAMENTE, G., and NESTORI, A., *I Cristiani e L'Impero Nel IV Secolo* (Macerata, 1988).

BONNER, S. F., *Education in Ancient Rome from the Elder Cato to the Younger Pliny* (London, 1977).

*BORTOLUCCI, G., *Arnobii Adversus Nationes II,6 ed una Ipotesi di Pietro Giordani* (Ghent, 1926).

BOUFFARTIGUE, J., and PATILLON, M., *Porphyre De L'Abstinence Tome I Livre I* (Paris, 1977); *Tome II Livres II–III* (Paris, 1979), Budé.

BOURGEOIS, C., 'Neptune et le dauphin à Mactar', *BACTH* NS 9 (1973), 17–23.

—— 'Les Eaux de Mactar (Tunisie), *Kar* 17 (1973–4), 185–93.

BOUSSET, W., 'Zur Dämonologie des späteren Antike', *Afr* 18 (1915), 134–72.

*BRAKMAN, C., *Miscella* (Leiden, 1912).

*—— *Miscella altera* (Leiden, 1913).

*—— *Miscella tertia* (Leiden, 1917).

*—— *Arnobiana* (Leiden, 1917).

BRAUN, R., *Deus Christianorum: Recherches sur le vocabulaire doctrinal de Tertullien* (FLA; Paris, 1962).

†BRISSON, L., 'L'oracle d'Apollon dans la Vie de Plotin par Porphyre', *Ker* 3 (1990), 77–88.

BROUGHTON, T. R. S., *The Romanization of Africa Proconsularis* (2nd repr., Westport, Conn., 1972).

BROWN, P., 'Religious Dissent in the Later Roman Empire: The Case of North Africa', *Hist* 46 (1961), 83–101.

—— *Augustine of Hippo: A Biography* (Berkeley, Calif., 1967).

*BRUNNER, G., 'Arnobius ein Zeuge gegen das Weihnachtsfest?' *JfLW* 13 (1933), 172–81.

*BULHART, V., 'Arnobiana', *WS* 71 (1958), 168–9.

*BUONAIUTI, E., *Il cristianesimo nell'Africa romana* (Bari, 1928).

*BURGER, C., *Die Theologische Position des Älteren Arnobius* (Diss., Heidelberg, 1970).

CADOUX, T. J., 'Names, Personal', *OCD*, 720–1.

CAGNAT, R., '14 Novembre 1905. Séance de la Commission de l'Afrique du Nord', *BACTH* (1905), cxcix–ccii.

—— '13 Novembre 1923: Séance de la Commission de l'Afrique du Nord', *BACTH* (1923), 188–97.

—— '9 Décembre 1924. Séance de la Commission de l'Afrique du Nord', *BACTH* (1924), 211–23.

—— and GAUCKLER, P., *Les monuments historiques de la Tunisie. Première Partie: Les monuments antiques* (Paris, 1898).

—— CHATELAIN, L., and MERLIN, A., *Inscriptions Latines d'Afrique. Tripolitaine, Tunisie, Maroc* (Paris, 1923).

CALDERONE, S., 'Il pensiero politico di Eusebio di Cesarea', in Bonamente and Nestori (1988), 45–54.

†CAMERON, A., 'The Date of the Kata Christianon', *CQ* NS 17 (1967), 382–4.

CAMPS, G., 'L'Inscription de Béja et le problème des Dii Mauri', *RAfr* 98 (1954), 233–60.

——*Aux Origines de la Berbérie: Monuments et rites funéraires protohistoriques* (Paris, 1961).

CAPUTO, G., and GOODCHILD, R., 'Diocletian's Price-Edict at Ptolemais (Cyrenaica)' *JRS* 54 (1955), 106–15.

CARCOPINO, J., *Aspects mystiques de la Rome païenne* (Paris, 1941).

†CASEY, M., 'Porphyry and Syrian Exegesis of the Book of Daniel', *ZNTW* 81 (1990), 139–42.

†CASEY, P. M., 'Porphyry and the Origin of the Book of Daniel', *JTS* 27 (1976), 15–33.

CAVALIERI, P. F. DE', *Nuove note agiografiche* (Rome, 1902), ST 9.

——*Note agiografiche fasicolo 8°* (ST 65; Rome, 1935).

*CAYRÉ, F., *Manual of Patrology* (Paris, 1935).

CHADWICK, H., 'Origen, Celsus, and the Stoa', *JTS* 48 (1947), 34–49.

——*Origen: Contra Celsum* (Cambridge, 1953).

——*The Sentences of Sextus* (Cambridge, 1959).

——'Justin Martyr's Defence of Christianity', *BJRL* 47 (1965), 275–97.

——*Early Christian Thought and the Classical Tradition* (Oxford, 1966).

——'The Relativity of Moral Codes: Rome and Persia in Late Antiquity', in W. R. Schoedel and R. L. Wilson (eds.), *Early Christian Literature and the Classical Tradition in Honorem Robert M. Grant* (Theol Hist; Paris, 1979), 135–53.

——'Oracles of the End in the Conflict of Paganism and Christianity in the Fourth Century', in E. Lucchesi and H. Saffrey (eds.), *Memorial A. J. Festugière* (Geneva, 1985), 125–9.

CHARLES-PICARD, G., 'Les Sacredotes de Saturne et les sacrifices humains dans l'Afrique romaine', *RecConst* 66 (1948), 117–123.

*——*Les Religions de l'Afrique antique* (Paris, 1954).

——'Le Pagus dans l'Afrique romaine', *Kar* 15 (1969–70), 3–12.

——'Les Fouilles de Mactar Tunisie, 1970–1973', *CRAI* (1974), 9–33.

CHARLIER, R., 'La Nouvelle série de stèles puniques de Constantine et la question des sacrifices dits "Molchomor" en relation avec l'expression BSRM BTM', *Kar* 4 (1953), 1–48.

†CHEJNE, A. G., 'Ibn Hazm of Cordova on Logic', *JAOS* 104, no. 1 (1984), 57–72.

CLAESSON, G., *Index Tertullianus*, 3 vols. (Paris, 1974–5).

CLARK, D. L., *Rhetoric in Greco-Roman Education* (New York, 1957).

†CLARK, M. T., 'Marius Victorinus Afer, Porphyry, and the History of Philosophy', in R. B. Harris (ed.), *The Significance of Neoplatonism* (Norfolk, 1976), 265–73.

*CLOSA, F. J., 'Lectura critica de los autores latinos por los humanistas del siglo de oro', *AFFB* 11 (1985), 7–17.

*COLOMBO, S., 'Arnobio Afro e i suoi sette libri *Adversus Nationes*', *Didask* 9 (1930), 1–124.

—— (A Review of Marchesi's Edition), *RFIC* NS 13 (1935), 390–2.

*CONTRERAS, C. A., 'Christian Views of Paganism', *ANRW* II. 23. 2, 974–1022.

CONYBEARE, F. C., *Philostratus, The Life of Apollonius of Tyana and The Treatise of Eusebius against Hierocles* (Cambridge, Mass., 1912; LCL, 2 vols.).

*COPLESTON, F., *A History of Philosophy*, 9 vols. (New York, 1962).

*CORSSEN, P., 'Zu Arnobius V, 12 and VI', *BPW* 30 (1910), 382–3.

*†COURCELLE, P., 'Les Sages de Porphyre et les "uiri noui" d'Arnobe', *REL* 31 (1953), 257–71.

*—— 'La Polémique antichrétienne au début du IVe siècle. Qui sont les adversaires païens d'Arnobe?' *RHR* 147 (1955), 122–3.

*—— 'Anti-Christian Arguments and Christian Platonism: from Arnobius to St. Ambrose', in A. Momigliano (ed.), *The Conflict Between Paganism and Christianity in the Fourth Century* (Oxford, 1963), 151–92.

*—— *Late Latin Writers and their Greek Sources* (Cambridge, Mass., 1969), tr. H. E. Wedeck.

CREED, J. L., *Lactantius* De Mortibus Persecutorum (Oxford, 1984), OECT.

†CROKE, B., 'Porphyry's Anti-Christian Chronology', *JTS* 34 (1983), 168–85.

†—— 'The Era of Porphyry's Anti-Christian Polemic', *JRH* 13, no. 1 (1984) 1–14.

*CROSS, F. L., *The Early Christian Fathers* (London, 1960).

*—— and LIVINGSTONE, E. A. (eds.), *The Oxford Dictionary of the Christian Church* (Oxford, 1978).

*CRUTTWELL, C. T., *A Literary History of Early Christianity* 2 vols. (London, 1893), 2. 630–42.

†CULIANU, I. P., 'Le Vol magique dans l'antiquité tardive', *RHR* 198 (1981), 57–66.

CUMONT, F., *Les religions orientales dans le paganisme romain*, 4th edn. (Paris, 1929).

*DALPANE, F., 'Sopra la fonte di un passo di Arnobio (V, 18)', *SIFC* 9 (1901), 30.

*—— *De Lucretii Imitatione apud Arnobium* (Florence, 1901).

*—— 'Se Arnobio sia stato un Epicureo', *RSA* 10 (1905), 403–35.

*DAMSTÉ, P. H., 'Emendatur Arnobius (*Adv. nat.* I, 62)', *Mnem* 45 (1917), 165.

DAREMBERG, C., and SAGLIO, E., *Dictionnaire des antiquités Greques et Romaines* 5 vols. (Paris, 1877–1917).

DAVIES, J. K., 'Lexicon of Greek Proper Names: a Progress Report', in N. Duval and H. Pflaum, *L'Onomastique Latine* (CNRS 564; Paris, 1977), 465–71.

Bibliography 345

DAVIES, P. S., 'The Origin and Purpose of the Persecution of A.D. 303', *JTS* 40 (1989), 66–94.

DECRET, F., *L'Afrique Manichéenne. (IVe–Ve Siècles)*, 2 vols. (Paris, 1978).

—— and FANTAR, M., *L'Afrique du nord dans l'antiquité: Histoire et civilisation (des origins au Ve siècle)* (Paris, 1981).

DELEHAYE, H., 'Contributions récents a l'hagiographie de Rome et d'Afrique', *AB* 54 (1900), 265–315.

†DEMAROLLE, J. M., 'Un aspect de la polémique païenne à la fin du IIIe siècle: le vocabulaire chrétien de Porphyre', *VC* 26 (1972), 117–29.

DENIS, C., 'Note sur une basilique chrétienne du Kef', *BACTH* (1893), 144–5.

—— 'Fouilles d'une Nécropole Romaine, au Kef (Tunisie)', *BACTH* (1894), 374–8.

DEONNA, W., 'Mercure et le scorpion', *Lat* 17 (1958), 641–58.

DESANGES, J., *Catalogue des tribus Africaines de l'antiquité classique à l'ouest du Nil* (Dakar, 1962).

—— *Pline l'Ancien. Histoire Naturelle. Livre V, 1–46. 1ère partie. (L'Afrique du Nord)* (Budé; Paris, 1980).

†DES PLACES, É., *Oracles Chaldaïques* (Budé; Paris, 1971).

—— 'Les Oracles chaldaïques dans la tradition patristique africaine', in F. L. Cross (ed.), *StudPatr* 11, part 2 (1972), 27–41 (= TU 108).

*—— 'Les Oracles chaldaïques', *ANRW* II. 17. 4, 2299–335.

†—— 'Éléments de sotériologie orientale dans le Platonisme à la fin de l'antiquité', in U. Bianchi and M. Vermaseren (eds.), *La soteriologia dei culti orientali nell'Impero Romano* (EPRO; Leiden, 1982), 243–53.

—— *Porphyre. Vie de Pythagore. Lettre à Marcella.* (Budé; Paris, 1982).

DESSAU, H., 'Gaetuli', PW 7, cols. 461–5.

DIELS, H., 'Philodemus über die Götter. Drittes Buch I. Griechischer Text', *AKPAW* (1916), Nr. 4, 1–69, fr. 77, 67.

DILLON, J., *The Middle Platonists* (Ithaca, NY, 1977).

DÖBSCHÜTZ, E. VON, *Das Decretum Gelasianum de libris recipiendis et non recipiendis* (TU 38; Leipzig, 1912).

DODDS, E. R., 'New Light on the Chaldaean Oracles', *HTR* 54 (1961), 263–73.

—— *Pagan and Christian in an Age of Anxiety* (Cambridge, 1965).

†—— 'Porphyry', *OCD*, 864–5.

—— 'Iamblichus', *OCD*, 538.

DODGEON, M. H., and LIEU, S. N. C. (eds.), *The Roman Eastern Frontier and the Persian Wars A.D. 226–363* (London, 1991).

*DÖLGER, F. J., 'Das Garantiewerk der Bekehrung als Bedingung und Sicherung bei der Annahme zur Taufe', *AChr* 3 (Münster, 1932), 260–72.

DOUBLET, M. G., 'Note sur deux monuments antiques de Tunisie', *BACTH* (1892), 129–35.

*DOUGLAS, J. D. (ed.), *The New International Dictionary of the Christian Church* (Exeter, 1974).

*DREYER, O., 'Schellings bisher unbeachtete Konyecturen zu Arnobius und anderen antiken Autoren', *Philol* 113 (1969), 111–28.

*DUCHESNE, L., *Early History of the Christian Church* (London, 1912).

DUNCAN-JONES, R. P., 'City Population in Roman Africa', *JRS* 53 (1963), 85–90.

DUVAL, N., 'Études d'archéologie chrétienne nord-africaines VII', *MEFRA* 91 (1979), 1015–19.

——and DUVAL, Y., 'Fausses basiliques (et faux martyrs): quelques 'bâtiments à auges' d'Afrique', *MEFRA* 84 (1972), 675–719.

——and PFLAUM, H. G., *L'Onomastique Latine* (Paris, 1977), CNRS 564.

——BARATTE, F., and GOLVIN, J.-C., 'Les Églises d'Haidra, VI: La basilique des martyrs de la persécution de Dioclétien. Bilan de la campagne 1983', *CRAI* (1989), 129–73.

DUVAL, Y., *Loca Sanctorum Africae. Le culte des martyrs en Afrique du IVe au VIIe siècle*, 2 vols. (Rome, 1982).

*——'Sur la biographie et les manuscrits d'Arnobe de Sicca', *Lat* 45 (1986), 69–99.

*EDWARDS, M. J., 'How Many Zoroasters? Arnobius, *Adversus Gentes I52*', *VC* 42 (1988), 282–9.

†—— 'Numenius, Phercydes, and the Cave of the Nymphs', *CQ* 40 (1990), 258–62.

†——'Porphyry and the Intelligible Triad', *JHS* 110 (1990), 14–25.

†——'A Late Use of Empedocles: The Oracle on Plotinus', *Mnem* 43 (1990), 151–5.

†——'Two Episodes in Porphyry's Life of Plotinus', *His* 40 (1991), 456–64.

EDWARDS, P., *The Encyclopedia of Philosophy*, 8 vols. (New York, 1967).

*EHRHARD, L., *Études de la critique de la civilisation chez Arnobe* (Strasbourg, 1936).

*EHWALD, R., 'Zu Arnobius und Cicero', *Philol* 51 (1892), 747.

*ELLSPERMANN, G. L., *The Attitude of the Early Christian Writers toward Pagan Literature and Learning* (CUAPS 82; Washington, DC, 1949).

ENNABLI, A., 'Sicca Veneria', *PECS* 834.

——'Simithu (Chemtou)', *PECS* 841.

*ENSLIN, M. S., Review of McCracken's translation, *Crozer Quarterly* 26, no. 4 (1949), 363–5.

ENSSLIN, W., 'The Reforms of Diocletian', *CAH* 12: *The Imperial Crisis and Recovery A.D. 193–324*, 383–408.

ERIM, K., and REYNOLDS, J., 'The Copy of Diocletian's Edict on Maximum Prices from Aphrodisias in Caria', *JRS* 60 (1970), 120–41.

ERIM, K. T., and CRAWFORD, M., 'Diocletian's Currency Reform: A New Inscription', *JRS* 61 (1971), 171–7.

ESPÉRANDIEU, É., 'Quelques notes sur plusieurs basiliques de la subdivision du Kef (Tunisie)', *Bulletin de la Société des Sciences Lettres et Beaux-Arts de Cholet* 1 (1881–6), 99–104.

—— *Épigraphie des environs du Kef: inscriptions recueillies en 1882–1883* (Paris, 1884).

—— *Épigraphie des environs du Kef. Zanfour-Djebel Haneche-Henchir Touit Khanguet-El-Kdim-Henchir Meded Henchir-Madjouba.* (Paris, 1885).

—— *Épigraphie des environs du Kef (Tunisie). Medeina & Ksour Abd-El-Melek (Althiburos-Uzappa)* (Paris, 1884).

—— 'Note sur quelques basiliques chrétiennes de Tunisie', *BACTH* (1884), 158–60.

—— 'Note sur des fouilles executées aux citernes du Kef (Tunisie)', *BACTH* (1885), 568–71.

—— *Étude sur Le Kef* (Paris, 1889).

—— 'Inscriptions inédits recueillies en Tunisie par M. Denis et communiqués par M. Espérandieu', *BACTH* (1892), 154–69.

EUZENNAT, M., and MARION, J., *Inscriptions antiques du Maroc. 2: Inscriptions Latines* (Paris, 1982).

†EVANGELIOU, C., 'Porphyry's Criticism of Christianity and the Problem of Augustine's Platonism', *Dion* 13 (1989), 51–70.

*FASCE, S., 'Paganesimo africano in Arnobio', *Vic* 9 (1980), 173–80.

†FERCH, A. J., 'Porphyry: an Heir to Christian Exegesis?', *ZNTW* 73, nos. 1–2 (1982), 141–7.

FERCHIOU, N., 'Témoignages du culte de Saturne dans le Jebel Mansour (Tunisie)', *CahTun* 26 (1978), 9–25.

—— 'Remarques sur la colonisation en Proconsulaire, au cours du premier siècle après J. C.', *CahTun* 28 (1980), 9–55.

FERRERO, I. M., 'La figura de Diocleciano en la *Historia Augusta*', *SHHA* 2–3 (1984–5), 225–37.

*FERRINI, C., 'Die juristischen Kenntnisse des Arnobius und Lactantius', *ZSSR* 15 (1894), 343–6.

*FESTUGIÈRE, A. J., 'Arnobiana', *VC* 6 (1952), 208–54.

*—— *La Révélation d'Hermès Trismégiste* (Paris, 1944–54), 4 vols. 3: (1953) *Les Doctrines de l'âme, suivi de Jamblique: Traité de L'âme; et de Porphyre: De l'animation de l'embryon.* 4: (1954) *Le dieu inconnu et la gnose.*

—— *Epicurus and His Gods* (Oxford, 1955), tr. C. W. Chilton.

*—— *Hermétisme et mystique païenne* (Paris, 1967), 261–312: 'La Doctrine des "uiri noui" sur l'origine et le sort des âmes'.

FÉVRIER, J. C., 'La Ville antique de Mactar en Tunisie', *Kar* 8 (1958), 1–166.

FÉVRIER, P. A., 'Martyrs, polemique et politique en Afrique (IVᵉ–Vᵉ siècles)', *RHCM* 1 (1966), 8–18.

—— 'Urbanisation et urbanisme de l'Afrique Romaine', *ANRW* II. 10. 2.

FINLEY, M. I. (ed.), *Studies in Ancient Society* (London, 1974).

FISHWICK, D., and SHAW, B., 'The Formation of Africa Proconsularis', *H* 105 (1977), 369–80.

*FOAKES-JACKSON, F., *Studies in the Life of the Early Church* (London, 1924).

*FONTAINE, J., Review of Le Bonniec, *REL* 60 (1982), 362–5.

FORRAT, M., and DES PLACES, É., *Eusèbe. Contre Hiéroclès* (Paris, 1987), SC 333.

*FORTI, G., 'Sulla Pedagogia di Arnobio', *RSF* 15 (1962), 200–15.

*FORTIN, E. L., 'The "Viri Novi" of Arnobius and the Conflict Between Faith and Reason in the Early Christian Centuries', in D. Neiman and M. Schatkin (eds.), *The Heritage of the Early Church* (CCA 195; Rome, 1973), 197–226.

FOUCHER, L., 'À propos d'images dionysiaques', *BACTH* NS 10–11 (1974–5), 3–8.

†FOX, R. LANE, *Pagans and Christians* (New York, 1987).

*FRANCKE, K. B., *Die Psychologie und Erkenntnisslehre des Arnobius* (Diss., Leipzig, 1883).

FREND, W. H. C., 'The *Memoriae Apostolorum* in Roman North Africa', *JRS* 30 (1940), 32–49.

*—— *The Donatist Church* (Oxford, 1952).

—— 'The Gnostic-Manichaean Tradition in Roman North Africa', *JEH* 4 (1953), 13–26.

—— 'The "Seniores Laici" and the Origin of the Church in North Africa', *JTS* 12 (1961), 280–4.

—— 'A Note on the Great Persecution in the West', in G. J. Cuming (ed.), *Studies in Church History* (London, 1965), 2. 141–8.

*—— 'The Christian Period in Mediterranean Africa, *c.* A.D. 200–700', *CHA* 2. 410–89.

*—— A review of Kraft's book, *CR* 17 NS (1967), 389 f.

*—— 'Arnobius', *OCD* (1970), 122.

—— 'The Failure of the Persecutions in the Roman Empire', *SAS* (1974) 263–87.

*—— *Martyrdom and Persecution in the Early Church* (Grand Rapids, 1981).

—— 'Fussala: Augustine's Crisis of Credibility (Ep. 20*)', in C. Lepelley (ed.), *Les lettres de Saint Augustine Découvertes par Johannes Divjak* (Paris, 1982), 251–65.

—— 'The Divjak Letters: New Light on St. Augustine's Problems, 416–428', *JEH* 34 (1983), 497–512.

—— 'A Note on Religion and Life in a Numidian Village in the Later Roman Empire', *BACTH* (1984), 261–71.

*—— *The Rise of Christianity* (Philadelphia, 1984).

*—— 'Prelude to the Great Persecution: The Propaganda War', *JEH* 38 (1987), 1–18.

*FREPPEL, M., *Commodien, Arnobe, Lactance et autres fragments inédits* (Paris, 1893).

*FRIEDRIKSEN, P., 'Apocalypse and Redemption in Early Christianity', *VC* 45 (1991), 105–22.

FRIER, B. W., *Libri annales pontificum maximorum. The Origins of the Annalistic Tradition* (AAR 27; Rome, 1979).

Bibliography 349

*Gabarrou, F., *Arnobe, son œuvre* (Paris, 1921).
*—— *Le Latin d'Arnobe* (Paris, 1921).
*Gaiser, K., *Il paragone della caverna* (Naples, 1985).
*Gareau, E., 'Le Fondement de la vraie religion d'après Arnobe', *CahEA* 11 (1980), 12–23.
Gascou, J., 'Le Cognomen 'Gaetulus, Gaetulicus' en Afrique Romaine', *MEFR* 82 (1970), 723–36.
Gauckler, M., 'Rapport épigraphique sur les decouvertes faites en Tunisie par le service des antiquités dans le cours des cinq dernières années', *BACTH* (1897). 362–471.
*Geffcken, J., *Zwei Griechische Apologeten* (Leipzig, 1907).
†—— *The Last Days of Greco-Roman Paganism* (Amsterdam, 1978), tr. S. Mac-Cormack.
*Gessinger, J., and Rahden, W. von, *Theorien vom Ursprung der Sprache* (Berlin, 1989).
Gesztelyi, T., 'The Cult of Tellus Terra Mater in North Africa', *ACUSD* 8 (1972), 75–84.
*Gierlich, G., *Arnobius von Sicca. Kommentar zu den ersten beiden Büchern seines Werkes Adversus nationes* (Diss. Mainz, 1985).
*Gigon, O., 'Arnobio: cristianesimo e mondo romano', (Rome, 1982), *MCC* 87–100.
Glare, P. G. W., *The Oxford Latin Dictionary* (Oxford, 1968–82), 8 fascicles.
Glover, T. R., *The Conflict of Religions in the Early Roman Empire* (London, 1909).
Gobert, E. G., 'Essai sur la litholatrie', *RAfr* 92 (1948), 24–110.
*Godet, P., 'Arnobe l'Ancien', *DTC* i. 1985–6, A. Vacant and E. Mangenot, eds. (Paris, 1903).
*Gomperz, H., 'Zu Arnobius', *RM* 64 (1909), 153–5.
Goodchild, R., 'Diocletian's Price-Edict at Ptolemais (Cyrenaica)', *JRS* 45 (1955), 106–15.
Goodspeed, E. J., *A History of Early Christian Literature* (Chicago, 1942).
Gordon, A. E., *Illustrated Introduction to Latin Epigraphy* (London, 1983).
Goulet, R., *Makarios Magnes Monogénès (Apocriticus)*, 2 vols. (Thesis; University of Paris, 1974).
†—— 'Porphyre et Macaire de Magnésie', *StudPatr* 15, part 1 (TU 128; Berlin, 1984), 448–52.
Grandjean, Y., *Une nouvelle arètalogie d'Isis àMaronée* (Leiden, 1975).
*Grant, M., *Greek and Latin Authors* (New York, 1980).
*Grant, R. M., 'Studies in the Apologists', *HTR* 51, no. 3 (1958), 123–34.
†—— 'Porphyry among the Early Christians', *RC*, Studia I. H. Wazink Oblata (Amsterdam and London, 1973), 181–7.
—— 'Eusebius and Imperial Propaganda', in Attridge and Hata (1992), 658–83.
Griffiths, J. G., *The Isis-Book (Metamorphoses, Book XI)* (Leiden, 1975).

350   *Bibliography*

*GSELL, S., *Histoire ancienne de l'Afrique du Nord*, 8 vols. (Paris, 1914–28).
—— *Inscriptions Latines d'Algérie*. 1: *Inscriptions de la Proconsulaire* (Paris, 1922).
*GUAGLIONE, A., 'Arnobio, *Adversus Nationes* IV, 31', *RSC* 14 (1966), 109–10.
*GUERARD, C., 'La Théologique negative dans l'apophatisme grec', *RSPT* 68 (1984), 183–200.
*GUGLIELMINO, C., 'La dottrina di Arnobio', *ND* 1 (1947), 99.
*GUINAGH, K., 'Justifying the Newer Edition of Arnobius', *TPAPA* 38 (1936), 37.
*—— 'Arnobiana', *CW* 29 (1936), 69–70.
GWYNN, A., *Roman Education from Cicero to Quintilian* (Oxford, 1926).
†HADOT, P., *Porphyre et Victorinus* (Paris, 1968).
—— 'Bilan et perspectives sur les Oracles Chaldaïques', in *COTh* 703–20 s.v. 'Lewy'.
*—— *Marius Victorinus: Recherches sur sa vie et ses œuvres*, 2 vols. (Paris, 1971).
†—— 'Neoplatonist Spirituality: Plotinus and Porphyry', in A. Armstrong (ed.), *CMS* (New York, 1986), 230–49.
*HADZSITS, G. D., *Lucretius and his Influence* (London, 1936).
HAERTEL, G., 'Die Religionspolitik der Römischen Kaiser von Diokletian bis Justinian', *ACUSD* 22 (1986), 69–86.
†HAGEDORN, D., and MERKELBACH, R., 'Ein neues Fragment aus Porphyrios "Gegen die Christen" ', *VC* 20 (1966), 86–90.
*HAGENDAHL, H., 'La Prose métrique d'Arnobe. Contributions à la connaissance de la prose littéraire de l'Empire', *Göteborgs Högskolas Årsskrift* 42 (1936), 1–265.
*—— 'En Ovidiusreminiscens hos Arnobius', *Eranos* 35 (1937), 36–40.
*—— Review of Marchesi's *Arnobii Adversus Nationes Libri 7*, *Gnomon* 16 (1940), 21–5.
*—— *Latin Fathers and the Classics* (SGLG 6; Göteborg, 1958).
*—— *Von Tertullian zu Cassiodor* (SGLG 44; Göteborg, 1983).
*HALLMAN, J. R., 'The Mutability of God: Tertullian to Lactantius', *TS* 42, no. 3 (1981), 373–93.
HAMMOND, N. G. L., *A History of Greece to 322 BC* (Oxford, 1967).
*—— and SCULLARD, H. H., *The Oxford Classical Dictionary* (Oxford, 1970).
HANDS, A. R., *Charities and Social Aid in Greece and Rome* (London, 1968).
*HANSLIK, R., 'Arnobius', *RGG*, ed. K. Galling (Tübingen, 1957), i. 631–2.
*HARNACK, A., *Geschichte der Altchristlichen Litteratur bis Eusebius* (Leipzig, 1893–1904).
—— 'Porphyrius, "Gegen die Christen", 15 Bücher: Zeugnisse, Fragmente und Referate', *AKPAW* (1916).
HARRIES, J., 'The Rise of Christianity', in J. Wacher (ed.), *The Roman World* (London, 1987), 796–811.
†HARRIS, R. B., 'Faith and Reason in the Early Neoplatonists', *DA* 1 (1987), 6–17.

†HATHAWAY, R. F., 'The Neoplatonist Interpretation of Plato: Remarks on its Decisive Characteristics', *JHP* 7 (1969), 19–26.

HELM, R., *Eusebius Werke* (Berlin, 1956; vol. 7, GCS 47).

HERBIG, G., 'Satre-Saturnus', *Philol* 74 (1917), 446–59.

HEURGON, J., 'Inscriptions Étrusques de Tunisie', *CRAI* (1969), 526–51.

*HIDÉN, K. J., *De Arnobii Adversus nationes Libris 7 commentationes I–III* (Helsinki, 1921).

*——— *De casuum syntaxi Arnobii in De Arnobii Adversus nationes libris VII commentationes*, 3 (Helsinki, 1921).

HILAIRE, LT., 'Étude sur les gisements mégalithiques des régions du Kef et du Ksour-Thala', *BACTH* (1898), 314–30.

*HOFFMAN, A., 'Coniectanea in Arnobium', *Jahns Archiv* 13 (1847), 140–58.

†HOLLERICH, M. J., 'Myth and History in Eusebius' *De vita Constantini*', *HTR* 82: 4 (1989), 421–45.

——— 'Religion and Politics in the Writings of Eusebius: Reassessing the First Court Theologian', *CH* 59 (1990), 309–25.

*HUG, T., *Beitrage zur Kritik lateinischer Prosaiker* (Basel, 1864).

†HULEN, A. B., *Porphyry's Work Against the Christians: An Interpretation* (Scottdale, Pa., 1933), YSR 1.

*HURST, G. L., *An Outline of the History of Christian Literature* (London, 1911).

IKURITE, G., 'Notes on Mortality in Roman Africa', *MusAfr* (1973), 59–68.

†JERPHAGNON, L., 'Les sous-entendus anti-chrétiens de la *Vita Plotini* ou l'évangile de Plotin selon Porphyre', *MH* 47 (1990), 41–52.

*JESSEN, J., *Über Lucrez und sein Verhältnis zu Catull und Spätern* (Kiel, 1872).

*JIRANI, O., 'Mythologické Prameny Arnobiova Spisu', *Lysty Philologicke* 35 (1908), 1–11; 83–97; 163–88; 323–39; 403–23.

JOCELYN, H. D., 'Varro's *Antiquitates rerum diuinarum* and Religious Affairs in the Late Roman Republic', *BJRLM* 65, no. 1 (1982), 148–205.

*JOHNSON, H., 'Adversus Nationes VII, 18', *CR* 23 (1909), 81–2.

†JOLIVET, J., 'Abelard et Guillaume d'Ockham, lectures de Porphyre', *CRTP* 6 (1981), 31–57.

JONES, A. H. M., *The Later Roman Empire 284–602* (Oxford, 1964), 3 vols.

——— MARTINDALE, J. R., and MORRIS, J. (eds.), *The Prosopography of the Later Roman Empire*. 1, *A.D. 260–395* (Cambridge, 1971).

JONES, D. L., 'Christianity and the Roman Imperial Cult', *ANRW* II. 23. 2, 1023–54.

*JORDAN, H., *Geschichte der altchristlichen Literatur* (Leipzig, 1911).

*JUFRESA, M., 'La divinidad y lo divino en Arnobio', *BIEJ* 7 (1973), 61–4.

*JÜLICHER, A., 'Arnobius', *RCA* (Stuttgart, 1896).

KAJANTO, I., *Onomastic Studies in the Early Christian Inscriptions of Rome and Carthage* (Helsinki, 1963), AIRF 2. 1.

——— 'The Latin Cognomina', *SSFCHL* 36: 2 (1965), 1–418.

——— 'The Emergence of the Late Single Name System', in Duval–Pflaum (CNRS 564; 1977).

352 *Bibliography*

*KARPP, H., *Probleme altchristlichen anthropologie* (Gütersloh, 1950).

KEE, H. C., *Miracle in the Early Christian World* (New Haven, Conn., 1983).

KELLY, J. N. D., *Jerome: His Life, Writings and Controversies* (London, 1975).

*KETTNER, G., *Cornelius Labeo: Ein Beitrag sur Quellenkritik des Arnobius* (Naumburg, 1877).

*KIDD, B. J., *A History of the Church to A.D. 461* (Oxford, 1922).

*KIHN, H., *Patrologie* (Paderborn, 1904).

*KIRSCHWING, O., *Qua ratione in Arnobii libris ars critica exercenda sit* (Diss., Leipzig, 1911).

*KISTNER, K., *Arnobiana* (Progr., St Ingbert, 1912).

KLEVE, K., *Gnosis Theon* (Oslo, 1963), SO suppl. 19.

*KLUSSMANN, E., *Quaestiones Arnobianae criticae* (Leipzig, 1863).

*—— 'Emendationes Arnobianae', *Philol* 26 (1867), 623–41.

*—— 'Arnobius und Lucrez, oder ein Durchgang durch den Epicuraismus zum Christentum', *Philol* 26 (1867), 362–6.

*KNAPP, C., 'A "Correctio" and "Addendum" to Professor Guinagh's "Arnobiana"', *CW* 29 (1936), 152.

*KOCH, H., 'Zu Arnobius und Lactantius', *Philol* 80 (1925), 467–72.

—— *Cyprianische Untersuchungen* (Bonn, 1926).

*—— 'Arnobius', *RGG* 1 (1927), 560–1.

*—— 'Zum Ablativgebrauch bei Cyprian von Karthago und anderen Schriftstellern', *RM* 87 (1929), 427–32.

KOENIG, I., 'Lactanz und das "System" der Tetrarchie', *Lab* 32 (1986), 180–93.

KOLB, F., *Diocletian und die Erste Tetrarchie* (Berlin, 1987), UALG Band 27.

—— 'L'ideologia tetrarchica e la politica religiosa di Diocleziano', in Bonamente and Nestori (1988), 17–44.

KOTULA, T., '*Utraque lingua eruditi*. Une page relative a l'histoire de l'éducation dans l'Afrique romaine', *CollLat* 102 (1969), 386–92.

*KRAFT, P., *Beitrage zur Wirkungsgeschichte des alteren Arnobius. Klassisch-Philologischen Studien* (Wiesbaden, 1966), Heft 32.

*KRAUZE, W., *Die Stellung der frühchristlichen Autoren zur heidnischen Literatur* (Vienna, 1958).

†KROLL, W., *De Oraculis Chaldaicis* (Breslau, 1894).

*—— 'Die Zeit des Cornelius Labeo', *RM* 71 (1916), 309–57.

*—— 'Arnobiusstudien', *RM* 72 (1917), 62–112.

*—— Review of G. Wiman, 'Textkritiska Studier', *BPW* 52 (1932), 630–1.

*—— Review of C. Marchesi's *Arnobii Adversus Nationes Libri 7*, *BPW* 55 (1935), 1082–4.

*KRÜGER, G., *Geschichte der Altchristlichen Literatur in den ersten drei Jahrhunderten* (Freiburg and Leipzig, 1895).

*—— 'Arnobius', *RPTK* 2 (Leipzig, 1897), 117 f.

*—— 'Arnobius', *NSH* (London, 1908).

*KURTZ, J. H., *Church History*, 3 vols. (London, 1888), tr. J. MacPherson.

*LABRIOLLE, P. DE, *Histoire de la littérature latine chrétienne* (Paris, 1920).

*—— 'Arnobe', *DHGR* 4. 544.

—— *La Réaction païenne* (Paris, 1934).

LAISTNER, M. L. W., *Christianity and Pagan Culture in the Later Roman Empire* (New York, 1951).

LAKS, A., and MILLOT, C., 'Réexamen de quelques fragments de Diogène d'Œnoanda sur l'âme, la connaissance et la fortune', in J. Bollack and A. Laks (eds.), *Études sur l'Épicurisme antique* (Lille, 1976), 319–57.

LANCEL, S., *Acts de la conférence de Carthage en 411* (Paris, 1972), SC 194.

—— 'À propos des nouvelles lettres de S. Augustin et de la Conférence de Carthage en 411', *RHE* 77, nos. 3–4 (1982), 446–54.

LANTIER, R., and POINSSOT, L., 'Note sur les établissements agricoles d'époque romaine dans Le Kef', *SNAF* (May 1928), 211–16.

LASSÈRE, J. M., *VBIQUE POPVLVS: Peuplement et mouvements de population dans l'Afrique romaine de la chute de Carthage à la fin de la dynastie des Sévères (146 a.c.–235 p.c.)* (Paris, 1977).

*LAURIN, J. R., 'Orientations maitresses des apologistes chrétiens de 270 à 361', *AnGreg* 61 (Rome, 1954), 146–85.

*LAURENTI, R., *Arnobius Maior I Setto Libri Contro I Pagani* (Turin, 1962).

—— 'Il Platonismo di Arnobio', *SF* 4 (1981), 3–54.

*—— 'Sangue e sacrificio in Arnobio', in F. Vattioni (ed.), *Sangue e Antropologia Biblica nella Patristica* (Rome, 1982), 455–79.

*—— 'Spunti di teologia arnobiana', Orph 6 (1985), 270–303.

LAW, R. C. C., 'North Africa in the Period of Phoenician and Greek Colonization, c.800 to 323 B.C.', *CHA* 2. 87–140.

*LE BONNIEC, H., 'Quelques passages litigieux du texte d'Arnobe', *REL* 29 (1961), 52–4.

*—— 'Arnobiana', *Lat* 70 (1964), 365–73.

*—— 'De quelques corrections abusives au texte d'Arnobe', *Revue de Philologie* 45 (1970), 41–7.

*—— Review of Van der Putten's 1970 thesis, *REL* 31 (1972), 274.

*—— 'Arnobe témoin et juge des cultes païens', *BAGB* (1974), 201–22.

*—— 'Une faute rituelle dans la pompe des jeux', *Mélanges P. Boyancé* (Rome, 1974), 501–11.

*—— 'Le témoignage d'Arnobe sur deux rites archaïques du Mariage Romain', *REL* 54 (1976), 110–29.

*—— *Arnobe. Contre Les Gentils. Livre I* (Paris, 1982), Budé.

*—— 'L'exploitation apologétique par Arnobe de *De natura deorum* de Cicéron', *Caes* 19 (1984), 89–101.

*LEBRETON, J., and ZEILLER, J., *The History of the Primitive Church* (London, 1947), tr. E. Messenger, 4: *The Church in the Third Century*.

*Leckelt, E., *Über das Arnobius Schrift Adversus Nationes* (Neisse, 1884).

Leclercq, H., 'Kef (El)', *DACL* 8. 1, 689–701.

Leglay, M., 'Les Stèles à Saturne de Djemila-Cuicul', *Lib* 1 (1953), 37–76.

——'Junon et les Cereres d'après la stèle d'Aelia Leporia trouvée à Tebessa', *Lib* 4 (1956), 33–53.

——*Saturne Africain Histoire* (Paris, 1966) (= SAH).

——*Saturne Africain Monuments* (Paris, 1966), 2 vols., 1: *Afrique Proconsulaire*; 2: *Numidie-Maurétanies*.

——'La Vie religieuse a Lambèse d'après de nouveaux documents', *AntAfr* 5 (1971), 125–53.

*Leigh, M., 'A Christian Sceptic of the Fourth Century: Some Parallels Between Arnobius and Paschal', *HJ* (1920–1), 319–25.

Lemke, D., *Die Theologie Epikurs: Versuch einer Rekonstruktion* (ZMKA 57: Munich, 1973).

*Le Nourry, N., 'Dissertatio Praevia in Septem Arnobii disputationum Adversus Gentes Libros', *PL* 5. 365–714.

Lepelley, C., *Les Cités de l'Afrique romaine au bas-empire*, 2 vols. (Paris, 1979–81).

——'Chrétiens et païens au temps de la persécution de Dioclétien: le cas d'Abtungni', *StudPatr* 15, part 1 (TU 128; Berlin, 1984), 226–32.

Leschi, L., 'Le Centenarium d'Aqua Viva', *RAfr* 87 (1943), 5–22.

Leveau, P., 'L'Agricola de Biha Bilta. À propos d'une inscription recemment découverte dans la région de Mateur', *CahTun* 26 (1978), 7–13.

*†Lewy, H., *Chaldaean Oracles and Theurgy: Mysticism, Magic and Platonism in the Later Roman Empire* (Paris, 1978).

Lézine, A., 'Sur la population des villes africaines', *AntAfr* 3 (1969), 69–82.

*Liebeschuetz, J. H. W. G., *Continuity and Change in Roman Religion* (Oxford, 1979).

†Lloyd, A. C., 'Porphyry and Iamblichus', in A. H. Armstrong (ed.), *The Cambridge History of Later Greek and Early Medieval Philosophy* (Cambridge, 1967), 283–301.

†——'Porphyry', *EP* 6. 411 f.

*Löfstedt, E., *Beiträge zur Kenntnisse der späteren Latinität* (Diss., Stockholm, 1907).

——'Patristische Beiträge', *Eranos* 10 (1910), 6–24.

——*Arnobiana* (Lund-Leipzig, 1917).

Lordkipanidze, G. A., Kiguradze, N. S., and Todua, T. T., 'An Early Christian Stele From Picunda', *VDI* 194 (1990), 63–7.

*Lorenz, T., *De Clausulis Arnobianis* (Diss., Breslau, 1910).

Louth, A., 'The Date of Eusebius' *Historia Ecclesiastica*', *JTS* NS 41, pt. 1 (1990), 111–23.

†Luck, G., 'Theurgy and Forms of Worship in Neoplatonism', in J. Neusner (ed.), *RSM* (Oxford, 1989), 185–225.

*MACKAIL, J. W., *Latin Literature* (London, 1895).

MACKENDRICK, P., *The North African Stones Speak* (London, 1980).

*McCRACKEN, G. E., 'Arnobii Adversus Gentes', *CJ* 42 (1947), 474–76.

*—— 'Critical Notes to Arnobius' *Adversus Nationes*', *VC* 3 (1949), 39–49.

*—— 'Arnobius', in L. A. Loetscher (ed.), *The Twentieth Century Encyclopedia of Religious Knowledge* (Grand Rapids, 1955).

*McDONALD, H. D., 'The Doctrine of God in Arnobius, Adversus Gentes', *StudPatr* 9, part 3 (TU 94; Berlin, 1966), 75–81.

*McGIFFERT, A. C., *A History of Christian Thought*, 2 vols. (London, 1933), 2: *The West from Tertullian to Erasmus*.

*McHUGH, M. P., 'Arnobius', in E. Ferguson (ed.), *EEC* (New York, 1990), 96 f.

MACMULLEN, R., *Paganism in the Roman Empire* (New Haven, Conn., 1981).

—— 'Two Types of Conversion to Early Christianity', *VC* 37, no. 2 (1983), 174–92.

—— *Christianizing the Roman Empire. A.D. 100–400* (New Haven, Conn., 1984).

*MADDEN, J. D., 'Jesus as Epicurus. Arnobius of Sicca's Borrowings from Lucretius', *CCC* 2 (1981), 215–22.

MADDEN, M. D., *The Pagan Divinities and Their Worship Depicted in the Works of Saint Augustine, Exclusive of the City of God* (CUAPS 24; Washington, DC, 1930).

MAHJOUBI, A., 'Découvertes archéologiques dans la région de Béja', *CahTun* 7 (1959), 481–7.

—— 'Stèles à Saturne d'el-Afareg', *CahTun* 15 (1967), 147–56.

—— *Les Cités romaines de la Tunisie* (Tunis, 1969).

—— 'Découvertes archéologiques dans la région de Béja. Pierres funéraires et stèles votives à Saturne trouvées à Kef Rechga et aux environs de Béja', *RTSS* 12 (1975), 15–44.

*†MAJERCIK, R., *The Chaldaean Oracles: Text, Translation, and Commentary* (SGRR 5; Leiden, 1989).

MANDOUZE, A., *Prosopographie chrétienne du Bas-Empire.* 1: *Afrique (303–533)* (CNRS; Paris, 1982).

*MARCHESI, C., 'Questioni Arnobiane', *ARIV* 88 (1929), 1009–32.

*—— 'Il Pessimismo di un Apologista Cristiano', *Peg* 2 (1930), 536–50.

*—— 'Per una nuova edizione di Arnobio', *RFIC* NS 10 (1932), 485–96.

*—— *Storia della Letteratura Latina* 2 (Milan, 1965), 433–43.

*—— 'Questioni Arnobiane', in P. Ferrarini (ed.), *Scritti Minori di Filologia e Letteratura I–III* (Florence, 1978), *Opuscoli Academici* 13.

*MARCOVICH, M., 'Demeter, Baubo, Iacchus, and a Redactor', *VC* 40 (1986), 294–301.

MARROU, H. I., *Saint Augustin et la fin de la culture antique* (Paris, 1938).

—— *Histoire de l'éducation dans l'antiquité* (Paris, 1948).

*MARTIN, J., 'Arnobius der Ältere', *LTK* 1 (Freiburg, 1957), 891.

MASON, K. (ed.), *Tunisia. February 1945. Naval Intelligence Division BR 523 (Restricted) Geographical Handbook Series for Official Use Only* (Oxford/Cambridge, 1945).

*MASTANDREA, P., *Lettori cristiani di Seneca filosofo* (Brescia, 1988).

MATTINGLY, H., 'The Imperial Recovery', *CAH* 12 (Cambridge, 1939), 297–351.

——and SYDENHAM, E. A., *The Roman Imperial Coinage* (London, 1923).

*MAYER, E., *De refutationis formis quae inveniuntur in Arnobii libris 7 Adversus Nationes* (Graz, 1939).

*MAZZA, M., 'Studi Arnobiana I. La Dottrina dei "viri novi" nel secondo libro dell' "Adversus nationes" di Arnobio', *Hel* 3 (1963), 111–69.

*MEISER, K., 'Studien zu Arnobius', *Sitzungsberichte der Bayerischen Akademie der Wissenschaften*, Philos.-Philol.-Hist. Klasse 5 (1908), 19–40.

*MELLILLO, G., 'Arnobio e l'ultima vicenda della *Lex Cincia*' *Labeo* 8 (1962), 62–72.

†MEREDITH, A., 'Porphyry and Julian Against the Christians', *ANRW* II. 23. 2, 1119–49.

MERLIN, A., *Le temple d'Apollon à Bulla Regia* (Paris, 1908).

——and POINSSOT, L., 'Les inscriptions d'Uchi Majus', *TDAA* 2 (1908), 9–22.

——*Inscriptions Latines de la Tunisie* (Paris, 1944).

MESNAGE, P., *Le Christianisme en Afrique* (Paris, 1912).

MEURSIUS, I., *Criticus Arnobianus* (Leiden, 1598).

*MICKA, E. R., *The Problem of Divine Anger in Arnobius and Lactantius* (Washington, DC, 1943), CUASCA 4.

MILLAR, F., *The Emperor in the Roman World (31 BC–AD 337)* (Ithaca, NY, 1977).

——*The Roman Near East 31 BC–AD 337* (Cambridge, Mass., 1993).

MILLER, P. C., 'A Dubious Twilight: Reflections on Dreams in Patristic Literature', *CH* 55, no. 2 (1986), 153–64.

*MOEHLER, J. A., *La Patrologie* (Louvain, 1844).

MOHRMANN, C., 'Les Emprunts grecs dans la latinité chrétienne', *VC* 4 (1950), 193–211.

MOMIGLIANO, A., 'Some Observations on the *Origo Gentis Romanae*', *JRS* 48 (1958), 56–73.

MOMMSEN, T., *Monumenta Germaniae Historica. 3: Chronica Minora Saec. IV. V. VI. VII* (Berlin, 1898).

——*Gesammelte Schriften*, 7 vols. (Berlin, 1909), 7: *Philologische Schriften.*

*MONCEAUX, P., *Histoire littéraire de l'Afrique chrétienne depuis les origines jusqu'à l'invasion arabe*, 7 vols. (Paris, 1901–23), 2: *Saint Cyprien et son temps* (1902); 3: *Le IVᵉ siècle, d'Arnobe à Victorin* (1905), esp. 241–86.

MONTAUT, M., '3° inscriptions du Kef', *BACTH* (1934–5), 34 ff.

MOREAU, J. L., *De la Mort des Persécuteurs*, 2 vols. (Paris, 1954), SC 39.

MOREL, C., 'Nomen (onoma)', Daremberg–Saglio, 4. 1, 88–96.

*MORICCA, U., *Storia della letteratura latina cristiana*, 2 vols. (Turin, 1923), 1: *Dalle origini fino al tempo di Constantino*.

MOSSHAMMER, A. A., *The Chronicle of Eusebius and the Greek Chronographic Tradition* (Cranbury, NJ, 1979).

MOULE, H. C. G., 'Arnobius', in W. Smith and H. Wace (eds.), *A Dictionary of Christian Biography*, 4 vols. (London, 1877), 1. 167 ff.

MÜLLER, D. H., 'Alba Longa', PW 1. 1301 f.

MULLER, M., DEPREUX, R., MULLER, P., and FONTAINE, M., 'Recherches anthropologiques sur les ossements retrouvés dans des urnes puniques', *SAP* (1952), 160–73.

*MULLINGER, J. B., *The Ancient African Church: Its Rise, Influence and Decline* (Cambridge, 1869).

*MULVEY, T. J., 'The Seven Books of Arnobius Adversus Nationes' (Ph.D. thesis, NY University, 1908).

MUSURILLO, H., *The Acts of the Christian Martyrs* (Oxford, 1972).

†NAUTIN, P., 'Trois autres fragments du livre de Porphyre "Contre les Chrétiens"', *RB* 57 (1950), 409–16.

*NEANDER, A., *A General History of the Christian Religion and Church*, 2 vols. (London, 1872), tr. J. Torrey.

NESTORI, A., 'Eusebio e il luogo di culto cristiano', in Bonamente and Nestori (1988), 55–62.

*NEWTON, A. W., 'The *Adversus Gentes* of Arnobius. A Study in Christian Apologetics', *LPSL* 52 (1897–8), 155–79.

*NICCOLI, M., 'Arnobio', *EncItal* (Milan, 1929), 551.

*NICHOLSON, O. P., 'Lactantius: Prophecy and Politics in the Age of Constantine the Great' (D.Phil. thesis, Oxford University, 1981).

*—— 'The Date of Arnobius' Adversus gentes', *StudPatr* 15, part 1 (TU 128; Berlin, 1984), 100–7.

—— 'Flight from Persecution as Imitation of Christ: Lactantius' *Divine Institutes* IV, 18, 1–2', *JTS* NS 40, pt. 1 (1989), 48–65.

NILSSON, M., 'The New Conception of the Universe in Late Greek Paganism', *Eranos* 44 (1946), 20–7.

—— 'The High God and the Mediator', *HTR* 56 (1963), 101–20.

*NIRSCHL, J., *Lehrbuch der Patrologie und Patristik* (Mainz, 1881).

NOBBS, A. E., 'Revolt in the Time of Diocletian. The Evidence of the Paniskos Papyri', *AH* 16 (1986), 132–36.

*NOCK, A. D., *Conversion* (Oxford, 1933).

—— 'A Vision of Mandulis Aion', *HTR* 27 (1934), 53–104.

*NORDEN, E., *Die Antike Kunstprosa* 2 (Leipzig and Berlin, 1909), 946–7.

OGILVIE, R. M., *The Library of Lactantius* (Oxford, 1978).

O'MEARA, J. J., *The Young Augustine* (Dublin, 1954).

*†—— *Porphyry's Philosophy from Oracles in Augustine* (Paris, 1959).

†O'MEARA, J. J., 'Indian Wisdom and Porphyry's Search for a Universal Way', in R. Harris (ed.), *Neoplatonism and Indian Thought* (Norfolk, 1982), 5–25.

OPELT, I., 'Schimpwörter bei Arnobius dem Älteren', *WS* NF 9 (1975), 161–73.

*ORR, J., *The History and Literature of the Early Church* (London, 1913).

*ORSAVAL, F., *Mysterium ok Arnobiusnal* (Budapest, 1914).

*PARATORE, E., 'Arnobio', *RR* 18 (1947), 263–72.

†PARKE, H. W., *The Oracles of Zeus. Dodona-Olympia-Ammon* (Oxford, 1967).

†—— *The Oracles of Apollo in Asia Minor* (London, 1985).

*PASCAL, C., 'Emendationes Arnobianae', *RFIC* 32 (1904), 1–9.

*PASCHOUD, F., 'L'Intolérance chrétienne et les païens', *CNS* 11 (Oct. 1990), 545–78.

PAVAN, M., 'Cristianesimo e impero romano nel IV Secolo d.c.', in Bonamente and Nestori (1988), 1–16.

*PELIKAN, J., *The Christian Tradition: A History of the Development of Doctrine*, 5 vols. (Chicago 1971–89). 1: *The Emergence of the Catholic Tradition (100–600)* (1971).

PÉPIN, J., *Théologie cosmique et théologie chrétienne (Ambrose, Exam. I 1, 1–4)* (Paris, 1964).

*—— *Mythe et allégorie* (Paris, 1976).

*PERRIN, M., 'Lactance lecteur d'Arnobe dans l'Epitome des Institutions?', *REAug* 30 (1984), 36–41.

PETERS, F. E., *The Harvest of Hellenism* (New York, 1970).

*PETIT-MENGIN, P., 'Inscriptions de la région de Milev', *MEFR* 79 (1967), 165–205.

*—— 'La Survie d'Arnobe', *REL* 45 (1967), 168–72.

PEYRAS, J., 'Le fundus aufidianus: étude d'un grand domaine romain de la région de Mateur', *AntAfr* 9 (1975), 181–222.

PFLAUM, H. G., *Inscriptions Latines de l'Algérie*, 2 vols. (Paris, 1957), 2: *Inscriptions de la confédération Cirtéenne de Cuicul et de la Tribu des suburbres*.

*PHILLIMORE, J. S., 'Arnobiana', *Mnem* 48 (1920), 388–91.

*PINTUS, G. M., 'Arnobio e il pari di Pascal', *San* 10–11 (1987–8), 145–51.

†PIRIONI, P., 'Il soggiorno siciliano di Porfirio e la composizione del Κατὰ Χριστιανῶν' *RSCI* 39 (1985), 502–8.

PISTORIUS, P. V., *Plotinus and Neoplatonism* (Cambridge, 1952).

*PLUMPE, J. C., 'Some Critical Annotations to Arnobius', *VC* 3 (1949), 230–6.

*POETZEL, R. K., 'Arnobius the Elder', *NCE* 1, ed. W. J. McDonald (London, 1967).

POINSSOT, C., 'Statues du temple de Saturne (Thugga)', *Kar* 6 (1955), 30–45.

POINSSOT, L., 'Quelques inscriptions de Tunisie', *BACTH* (1911), 302–10.

—— 'Note sur une inscription de Koudiet-Es-Souda (Tunisie)', *CRAI* (1913), 424–8.

POINSSOT, L., and QUONIAM, P., 'Bêtes d'amphithéâtre sur trois mosaïques du Bardo', *Kar* 3 (1952), 127–65.

PORTMANN, W., 'Zu den motiven der diokletianischen Christenverfolgung' *His* 39 (1990), 212–48.

PRÉCHEUR-CANONGE, V. T., *La Vie rurale en Afrique d'après les mosaïques* (Tunis, 1962; PUT 6).

*PUTTEN, J. M. P. B. VAN DER, 'Arnobii Adversus Nationes, 3, 1–19, uitgegeven met inleiding en commentar' (Thesis, Leiden, 1970).

*——'Arnobiana', *VC* 25 (1971), 40–50.

*——'L'Emploi de nec et neque dans Arnobe', *VC* 25 (1971), 51.

*——'Arnobe croyait-il à l'existence des dieux païens?', *VC* 25 (1971), 52–5.

*QUACQUARELLI, A., 'La parentesi negli apologeti retori latini da Tertulliano a Firmico Materno', *Orph* 4 (1957), 63–75.

*QUASTEN, J., *Patrology*, 3 vols. (Utrecht and Antwerp, 1953), 2: *The Ante-Nicene Literature After Irenaeus*, 383–92.

*QUISPEL, G., Review of Rapisarda, *VC* 2 (1948), 123.

*RAINY, R., *The Ancient Catholic Church* (Edinburgh, 1902).

*RAND, E. K., *Founders of the Middle Ages* (Cambridge, 1928).

*——'The Latin Literature of the West from the Antonines to Constantine', *CAH* 12: *The Imperial Crisis and Recovery. A.D. 193–324*, 571–610.

*RAPISARDA, E., *Clemente Fonte di Arnobio* (Turin, 1939).

*——*Arnobio* (Catania, 1946).

RAYNAL, D., 'Culte des martyrs et propagande Donatiste à Uppena', *CahTun* 81–2 (1973), 33–72.

REHM, A., 'Kaiser Diokletian und das Heiligtum von Didyma', *Philol* 93 (1938), 74–84.

REINACH, M. S., 'Monuments chrétiens de Tipasa', *BACTH* (1893), 129, Pl. XIII.

REYNOLDS, J. M., and WARD PERKINS, J. B., *The Inscriptions of Roman Tripolitania* (London, 1952).

RICCOBONO, S., BAVIERA, J., FERRINI, C., FURLANI, J., and ARANGIO-RUIZ, V., *Fontes Iuris Romani Antejustiniani*, 3 vols. (Florence, 1941–3).

RIST, J. M., *Plotinus: The Road to Reality* (Cambridge, 1967).

——*Stoic Philosophy* (Cambridge, 1969).

——*Epicurus: An Introduction* (Cambridge, 1972).

ROBERT, L., *Les fouilles de Claros* (Limoges, 1954).

ROGER, M., *L'Enseignement des lettres classiques d'Ausone à Aucuin* (Hildesheim, 1968).

*RÖHRICHT, A., *Die Seelenlehre des Arnobius nach ihren Quellen und ihrer Entstehung untersucht* (Hamburg, 1893).

*——*De Clemente Alexandrino Arnobii in irridendo Gentilium Cultu Deorum Auctore* (Hamburg, 1893).

ROLL, I., 'A Latin Imperial Inscription from the Time of Diocletian Found at Yotvata', *IEJ* 39 (1989), 239–60.

ROMANELLI, P., *Storia delle province romane dell'Africa* (SII 14; Rome, 1959).

*ROSE, H. J., 'Arnobius, Adversus Nationes VI, 12', *CR* NS 5 (1955), 20–1.

*RYBA, B., 'Sigismundus Gelenius a jeho vydani Arnobia a Minucia', *Listy Filologické* 52 (Prague, 1925).

ST-JEAN, M., 'Le Kef', *BACTH* (1923), 188–97.

—— 'Le Kef', *BACTH* (1924), 211–13.

STE CROIX, G. E. M. DE, 'Aspects of the "Great" Persecution', *HTR* 47 (1954), 75–113.

—— 'Why Were the Early Christians Persecuted?', *SAS* 210–49.

SALADIN, H., 'Rapport sur la mission accomplie en Tunisie (Le Kef)', *NAM* 2 (1892), 556–9.

SALAMA, P., *Les Voies romaines de l'Afrique du Nord* (Algiers, 1951).

—— 'Le Militaire archaïque de Lorbeus', *MelCarth* (Paris, 1964–5), 97–115.

*SALVATORELLI, L., *Storia della letteratura latina cristiana dalle origini alla metà del VI secolo* (Milan, 1946).

SAMUEL, A. E., *Greek and Roman Chronology: Calendars and Years in Classical Antiquity* (Munich, 1972).

SANDBACH, F. H., '*Ennoia* and *Prolepsis* in the Stoic Theory of Knowledge', *CQ* 24 (1930), 44–51.

*SANTINI, C., 'Il lessico della spartizione nel sacrificio romano', *L'Uomo* 9. 1–2 (1985), 63–73.

*SANTORELLI, P., 'Parodia virgiliana in Arnobio', *Maia* 41 (1989), 241–50.

SCHAFF, P., *The Oldest Church Manual* (Edinburgh, 1885).

*—— *History of the Christian Church*, 2 vols. (Edinburgh, 1892).

**SCHARNAGL, J., *De Arnobii Maioris Latinitate* (Progr., Görz, 1895).

*—— 'Zur Textgestaltung des Arnobius Conflictus', *WS* (1916), 382–4.

*SCHEIDWEILER, F., 'Arnobius und der Marcionitismus', *ZNTW* 45 (1954), 42–67.

*SCHMALZ, J. H., 'Zu Arnobius Adversus Nationes IV, 13', *WKP* (1913), 1245–6.

*SCHMID, W., 'Christus als Naturphilosoph bei Arnobius: Erkenntnis und Verantwortung', *Festschrift Theodor Litt* (Dusseldorf, 1960), 264–84.

SCHNEEMELCHER, W., and WILSON, R. M. (eds.), *New Testament Apocrypha*, 2 vols. (London, 1965).

*SCHOEDEL, W., and WILKEN, R. (eds.), *Early Christian Literature and the Classical Intellectual Tradition* (TheolHist 53; Paris, 1979).

*SCHULZE, E. F., *Das Übel in der Welt nach der Lehre des Arnobius* (Diss., Jena, 1896).

SCHWARTZ, E., 'Zum *Decretum Gelasianum*', *ZNTW* 29 (1930), 161–8.

*SCHWENTNER, E., 'Arnobius über das Grammatische Geschlecht', *Wörter und Sachen* (1939), 92–3.

SCULLARD, H. H., *From the Gracchi to Nero: A History of Rome 133 B.C. to A.D. 68* (London, 1982, 5th edn.).

†SELLEW, P., 'Ancilles or Christ? Porphyry and Didymus in Debate over Allegorical Interpretation', *HTR* 82: 1 (1989), 79–100.

SESTON, W., *Dioclétien et la Tétrarchie* 1: *Guerres et Réformes (284–300)* (Bibliothèque des Études Françaises d'Athènes et de Rome, 162; Paris, 1946).

*SHACKLETON BAILEY, D. R., 'Arnobiana', *RFIC* 116 (1988), 198–202.

*SIHLER, E. G., *From Augustus to Augustine* (Cambridge, 1923).

SIMON, M., 'Un document du syncrétisme religieuse dans l'Afrique romaine', *CRAI* (1978), 500–24.

SIMMONS, M. B., 'A Study of Graeco-Roman Pagan and Christian Soteriologies of the Second Century' (STM Thesis (unpub.): Yale Divinity School, New Haven, Conn., 1982).

*——'Concepts of Deity in Arnobius of Sicca in the Context of the Contemporary Pagan–Christian Debate' (Thesis, Edinburgh, 1985).

*SINISCALCO, P., 'Arnobio', in A. Di Berardino (ed.), *DPAC* (Marietti, 1983), 1. 377–9.

*——'Arnobius of Sicca', in Angelo Di Berardino (ed.), EECh (Oxford, 1992), tr. Adrian Walford, 2 vols., I. 82.

*SIRNA, F. G., 'Arnobio e l'eresia marcionita di Patrizio', *VC* 18 (1964), 37–50.

SIRONEN, E., 'The Edict of Diocletian and a Theodosian Regulation at Corinth (Plate 52)', *Hesp* 61 (1992), 223–6.

*SITTE, A., *Mythologische Quellen des Arnobius* (Vienna, 1970).

SKEAT, T. C., *Papyri From Panopolis in the Chester Beatty Library Dublin* (Dublin, 1964), CBM no. 10.

SMAIL, W. M., *Quintilian on Education* (Oxford, 1938).

SMEDT, C. DE, 'Passiones tres martyrum africorum SS. Maximae, Donatillae et Secundae', *AB* 9 (1890), 107–10.

†SMITH, A., *Porphyry's Place in the Neoplatonic Tradition* (The Hague, 1974).

†SMITH, M., 'A Hidden Use of Porphyry's History of Philosophy in Eusebius' *Preparatio Evangelica*', *JTS* 39 (1988), 494–504.

SMITH, M. F., 'Fragments of Diogenes of Oenoanda Discovered and Rediscovered', *AJA* 74 (1970), 51–62.

——'New Fragments of Diogenes of Oenoanda', *AJA* 75 (1971), 357–89.

——'Seven New Fragments of Diogenes of Oenoanda', *Hermathena* 118 (1974), 110–29.

——'More New Fragments of Diogenes of Oenoanda', in J. Bollack and A. Laks (eds.), *Études sur l'Épicurisme antique* (Lille, 1976).

*SORENSEN, J. P., 'The Myth of Attis: Structure and Mysteriosophy', in id. (ed.), *Rethinking Religion: Studies in the Hellenistic Process* (Copenhagen, 1989), OP 30. 23–30.

*SOUTER, A., Review of Marchesi's *Arnobii Adversus Nationes Libri* 7, *CR* 49 (1935), 209.

362 *Bibliography*

*SPANNEUT, M., *Tertullien et les premiers moralistes africains* (Gembloux and Paris, 1969).

SPEIDEL, M. P., and PAVKOVIC, M. F., 'Legio II Flavia Constantia at Luxor', *AJPh* 110 (1989), 151–4.

SPINDLER, P., *De Arnobii genere dicendi* (Diss., Strasbourg, 1901).

*STANGE, C., *De Arnobii Oratione I–II* (Saargemünd, 1893).

*STANGL, T., 'Arnobiana', *BPW* 30 (1910), 125–8, 157–60.

*—— 'Bobiensia', *RM* 65 (1910), 93.

STADE, K., *Der Politiker Diocletian und die letzte große Christenverfolgung* (Diss. Frankfurt, 1936).

STILLWELL, R., MacDONALD, W. L., and McALLISTER, M. H. (eds.), *Princeton Encyclopedia of Classical Sites* (Princeton, NJ, 1976).

*STRACHY, M., *The Fathers Without Theology* (London, 1957).

SWIFT, L. J., 'Arnobius and Lactantius: Two Views of the Pagan Poets', *TPAPA* 96 (1965), 439–48.

*TABARAUND, M. M., *Arnobe* (BUAM 2; Paris, 1811).

TEUTSCH, L., *Das Städtewesen in Nordafrika in der Zeit von C. Gracchus bis zum Tode des Kaisers Augustus* (Berlin, 1962).

*THOMAS, P., 'Observationes ad scriptores latinos: ad Arnobium', *Mnem* 49 (1921), 63–4.

*THÖRNELL, A., *Arnobius, Adversus Nationes VII, 21* (= *Strena Philologica Upsaliensis: Festskrift Per Persson*) (Uppsala, 1922).

TIBILETTI, C., 'Politica e religione nelle persecuzioni cristiane', in Bonamente and Nestori (1988), 195–204.

TILLEY, M. A., 'Scripture as an Element of Social Control: Two Martyr Stories of Christian North Africa', *HTR* 83, pt. 4 (1990), 383–97.

*TIMPANARO, S., 'Carm. epigr. 881 e Arnobio I, 16', *FRIC* 108 (1980), 422–30.

*TIXERONT, J., 'Arnobe', *DPCR* 1 (Paris, 1925).

—— 'Réflexions sur l'implantation ancienne de l'agriculture en Tunisie', *Kar* 10 (1959), 1–50.

TOUSSAINT, P., 'Note sur la région reconnue en 1897 par le 2ᵉ brigade topographique de Tunisie', *BACTH* (1898), 196–225.

TOUTAIN, J., *Les Cités romaines de la Tunisie* (Paris, 1896).

—— 'Notes sur quelques stèles votives des environs de Medeina (Tunisie)', *BACTH* (1919), 101–5.

—— *Les Cultes païens dans l'Empire Romain*, 3 vols. (Paris, 1920), 3: *Les Cultes indigènes nationaux et locaux: Afrique du Nord, Péninsule Ibérique, Gaule.*

TREVES, P., 'Philodemus', *OCD*, 818 f.

TROUILLARD, J., *La Purification Plotinienne* (Paris, 1955).

*TSCHIERSCH, W., *De Arnobii Studiis Latinis* (Jena, 1905).

*TULLIUS, F., *Die Quellen des Arnobius im 4., 5., und 6. Buch seiner Schrift Adversus Nationes* (Bottrop, 1934).

TURNER, C. H., 'Arles and Rome: The First Developments of Canon Law in Gaul', *JTS* 17 (1966), 236–47.

†TURNER, J. D., 'The Figure of Hecate and Dynamic Emanationism in the Chaldaean Oracles, Sethian Gnosticism, and Neoplatonism', *SCent* 7 (Winter, 1989–90), 221–32.

*TZSCHIRNER, H. G., *Geschichte der Apologetik I* (Leipzig, 1805).

*VALDITARA, G., 'A proposito di un presunto ottavo re di Roma' *SDHI* 54 (1988), 276–84.

*VOGT, J., 'Toleranz und Intoleranz im constantinischen Zeitalter: Der Weg der Lateinischen Apologetik', *Saec* 19 (1969), 344–61.

WALDHERR, G., *Kaiserliche Baupolitik in Nordafrika* (Frankfurt, 1989).

*WARFIELD, B. B., 'Africa and the Beginnings of Christian Latin Literature', *AJT* 11 (1907), 95–110.

*WARMINGTON, B. H., *The North African Provinces from Diocletian to the Vandal Conquest* (Cambridge, 1954).

*—— 'Sicca Veneria', *OCD*, 984 f.

*WASSENBERG, F., *Quaestiones Arnobianae Criticae* (Diss., Münster, 1877).

*WASZINK, J. H., Review of McCracken, *VC* 4 (1950), 117 f.

*WEYMANN, C., *Textkritische Bemerkungen zu Arnobius Adversus Nationes: Festschrift Sebastian Merkle* (Düsseldorf, 1922), 386–95.

*—— 'Arnobius über das Steinbild der Magna Mater', *Historisches Jahrbuch der Görresgesellschaft* (1916), 75 f.

WHITTAKER, C. R., 'Land and Labour in North Africa', *Klio* 60 (1978), 331–62.

†WHITTAKER, T., *The Neo-Platonists: A Study in the History of Hellenism* (Cambridge, 1918).

*WILKEN, R. L., 'Pagan Criticism of Christianity: Greek Religion and Christian Faith', in Schoedel and Wilken, 117–34.

*—— *The Christians as the Romans Saw Them* (New Haven, Conn., 1984).

WILKES, J. J., *Diocletian's Palace, Split* (Sheffield, 1986).

WILLIAMS, S., *Diocletian and the Roman Recovery* (New York, 1985).

*WILLMANN, M., 'Les Procédés et la valeur de la critique des cultes païens dans l'Adversus Nationes d'Arnobe', *REL* (1943–4), 182.

WILMANNS, G., *Corpus Inscriptionum Latinarum* (Berlin, 1881: vol. 8 = North Africa). Suppl. vols. 1–5, 1891–1942.

*WIMAN, G., 'Nagra Arnobiusställen', *Eranos* 25 (1927), 278–80.

*—— 'Textkritiska Studier till Arnobius', *Svenskt Arkiv för hum. Avhandl.* 4 (Göteborg, 1931).

*—— 'Ad Arnobium', *Eranos* 45 (1947), 129–52.

WITT, R. E., *Isis in the Graeco-Roman World* (London, 1971).

*WLOSOK, A., *Laktanz und die Philosophische Gnosis* (Heidelberg, 1960).

*—— 'Zur Einheit der Metamorphosen des Apuleius', *Philol* 113 (1969), 68–84.

*WLOSOK, A., 'Zur lateinischen Apologetik der Constantinischen Zeit (Arnobius, Lactantius, Firmicus Maternus)', *Gymn* 96 (1989), 133–48.

†WOLFF, G., *Porphyrii de Philosophia ex oraculis haurienda librorum reliquiae* (Hildesheim, 1962).

WOODS, D., 'Two Notes on the Great Persecution', *JTS* NS 43, pt. 1 (1992), 128–34.

*WÖRTER, F., *Die christliche Lehre über das Verhältnis von Gnade und Freiheit von den Apostolischen Zeiten bis auf Augustinus* (Freiburg, 1856).

*WRIGHT, D. F., 'War in a Church-Historical Perspective', *EQ* 57 (1985), 133–61.

*WRIGHT, F. A., *Fathers of the Church* (London, 1928).

XERES, S., 'La riabilitazione di Valeriano e la politica anticristiana nell'epoca diocleziana', *RIL* 118 (1984), 69–76.

YACOUB, M., 'La Christianisation des thèmes païens d'après des monuments Tunisiens', *CARB* 19 (1972), 331–50.

ZIEGLER, K., 'Zeugitana regio', PW 10a. 251.

*ZINK, M., 'Kritisches zu Arnobius', *Blätter f.d. Bayer. Gymn* 7 (1871), 295–312; 8 (1872), 292–316.

*—— *Zur Kritik und Erklarung des Arnobius* (Bamberg, 1873).

INDEX OF PASSAGES CITED

GENERAL INDEX

religious and philosophical thought (*cont.*):
soul 160 f., 266 f.; doctrine of
silence 270 f., 287, 294, 296 f., 305; gods
subject to passions 260, 401; philosophy
of 266–9; psychology of 287, 299 f.;
soteriology of 31, 218, 226 f., 265–9,
284 f., 287, 302; Supreme God of 235
267; universal way of salvation 23, 247,
279
see also Arnobius; Augustine; Chaldaean
theology; Diocletian; Eusebius; oracles;
Neoplatonism; *and individual works*
prayer: in Arnobius 127 ff.; for the
dead 128, 142; the Lord's 129
Proclus 13, 139, 168, 170, 227, 235; and
Chaldaean theology 234 f
van der Putten, J. M. P. B. 136, 173, 174,
249
Pythagoras 161, 285, 314; doctrine of
justice 313; doctrine of silence 270 f
Pythagoreanism 13, 73, 294 f., 305, 313,
324

Quasten, J. 1, 113, 120, 124, 132

rhetoric: Arnobius a teacher of 7; in North
Africa 113–17
Rist, J. M. 133, 135, 150, 151, 152, 161,
252, 289

salvation: *Phil. or.* as a source of 24; *via
universalis* of Porphyry 23
Saturn, cult of 229, 319 f.; and the *Adv.
Nat.* 15 f., 190 f.; African agrarian
deity 8; in Africa Proconsularis 186,
212; agrarian symbols of 8, 15, 186,
194; agricultural sites of 200; ambiguous
eschatology of 215; and Arnobius 197,
208; at Béja (Vaga) 15; and Béja-Le Kef
(Sicca) 195 f., 202, 207; and Boglio
stela 15, 209; in 4th cent. North
Africa 194 f., 210 f.; and child
sacrifice 194 f.; and Christian
evangelical campaign 195, 213; conflict
with Christianity 194 f., 196, 200, 201,
205, 208 f., 210, 211 f., 213 ff.;
connection with agriculture 185 ff.; as
creator 197; cultic sites of 199 f.; as *deus
frugifer* 15, 186 f., 198 ff.; in Diocletian's
age 188; and divine providence 190; as
dominus 15, 186, 194, 201; and the *falx
arboraria* 187; on farms 186; as
father 197; genealogy of 57; as

genitor 196; 'gradual change'
theory 208, 211; on imperial
estates 186; jealousy of 194; Jovian
influence upon 202; latest inscription
of 202; lion as symbol of 200; literary
evidence for 186; lord of the
harvest 193, 204; 'mass conversions'
theory 208, 211; monotheistic
tendencies 213 f.; mother of 62;
mythological reign in Italy 58; in
Numidia 188; as 'Old Man' (*Senex*) 16,
194; at *Pagus Veneriensis* 207; as *Pater
deorum* 197; and personal religion 214;
Phoenician associations 206; priesthood
of 207; principal god of Roman North
Africa 15; as *procreator* 204; provider of
fructum 195; 'religious assimilation'
theory 211 f.; and religious
syncretism 198, 206 f.; revelation
through dreams 119; as *Rex poli* 193; as
Sator 202 f.; Semitic nature of 194; and
the Severan Dynasty 187; at Sicca 15; at
Siliana 15; and the Sun and Moon 193,
196, 202; surviving monuments 15; in
Tunisia 186; at *Vicus Maracitanus* 193;
as *Vitisator* 204
Scheidweiler, F. 2, 19, 163
Schoedel, W. R. 11, 24, 72, 217
scripture 77–81; argument against in the
Contra Christianos 27; pagan attacks
upon 28–9; *see also* Arnobius;
Augustine; Eusebius; Hierocles;
Porphyry
Seston, W. 36, 37, 40, 107
Sicca (Le Kef) city of Roman North
Africa 209 f.; Ager Siccensis 99;
aqueduct at 102; aristocrats at 100;
Arnobius' residence 6; an Augustan
colony 97; baths at 102; bishop of 6,
122–5, 213, 261; buildings at 100 ff.;
Byzantine period 112; Christian
basilicas at: Ksar-el-Ghoul and Dar-el-
Kous 102; Christian necropolis at 102;
cisterns at 102; cult of St Peter at 111–
3; deities worshipped at: Cereres 103,
dedications to *deis parentibus* 103, *di
superi* and *inferi* 103; Fortuna
Redux 103, Hercules 103, Honos and
Virtus 103; Jupiter 103, Mercury 103,
Neptune 103, Pietas Augusta 103,
Roma 103, Saturn 15, Sol 103,
Venus 103, 104, Virtus Augusta 103;

DATE DUE

			Printed in USA